Due Return Date Date	Due Return Date Date

HISTORY OF THE
GERMAN NOVEL

HISTORY OF THE GERMAN NOVEL

HILDEGARD EMMEL

English-language edition prepared by
Ellen Summerfield

WAYNE STATE UNIVERSITY PRESS
DETROIT · 1984

Library of Congress Cataloging in Publication Data

Emmel, Hildegard, 1907–
  History of the German novel.

  Abridged translation with revisions of: Geschichte des deutschen Romans.
  Bibliography: p.
  "German novels in English translation"-p.
  Includes index.
  1. German fiction—History and criticism.
I. Summerfield, Ellen, 1949–   . II. Title.
PT741.E5413   1984   833'.009   84-15164
ISBN 0-8143-1770-7

Contents

Preface

It was not until late in my career as a Germanist, in fact its last stage, that I traveled to the United States to accept a professorship in German literature at the University of Connecticut. Having had no prior experience with American students, I was uncertain as to what topics to choose for my graduate-level seminars. At the time I was deeply absorbed in research on the German novel in preparation for writing a complete history of the genre. I hoped to include the students in my research and to share my own excitement and problems with them. At the same time I wondered if my expectations were not unreasonable. After all, I had grown up with German literature and had been reading German novels all my life. As a European, I was familiar with the cultural heritage from which they derived. And I was, of course, reading them in my own language. Would this generation of young Americans, I wondered, find the novels to be of any interest at all? Would they wish to spend their time and effort reading and rereading, studying and analyzing works as complex, lengthy, and demanding as Robert Musil's *Man without Qualities* and Hermann Broch's *Death of Virgil*?

The response I received to the novels introduced in my first seminars quelled any doubts I might have had. The American students became intensely involved with the novels. Some of them told me it was the intellectual challenge that drew them to the novels. Most of the students were intrigued by the novels' themes and showed appreciation for their artistic quality. It seemed not to matter from which century the novels were chosen. The twentieth century was always highly popular, but one of my most successful seminars dealt with the novels of Goethe's contemporaries. It was gratifying for me to see how seminar discussions and term papers inevitably led to doctoral theses. During my fourteen years at the university, most of my students wrote theses about German novels, including interpretations of Gottfried Keller's *Green Henry*, Günter Grass's *Dog Years*, Hermann Broch's *The Sleepwalkers*, Uwe Johnson's *Anniversaries*, Martin Walser's *Half Time*, Rainer Maria Rilke's *The Notebooks of Malte Laurids Brigge*, and others. A significant number of these theses have been published in book form and many of their authors now hold professorships in German literature in American universities.

Needless to say, I owe a debt of gratitude to all my former students who helped to make my experience in the United States so rewarding. Perhaps I might use this preface as a forum to acknowledge their integrity in the learning process and their commitment to the difficult task of exploring a foreign literature. I also wish to thank them for what they taught me about the German novel. Through their eyes I came to appreciate more fully the depth and richness of a genre whose appeal transcends borders of time, language, and nationality. It became apparent to me that there are countless authors—beyond the handful of universally known names such as Franz Kafka, Thomas Mann, and Günter Grass—who have the potential to captivate the foreign reader.

It is this conviction that the German novel has something of value to offer to a wide audience that leads me to support wholeheartedly the publication of my history of the German novel in English. Just as the German original is not intended merely for the specialist but is written for a more general public as well, the English version addresses itself to all students and teachers of literature who wish to learn more about the German novel but are not sufficiently versed in German to read the original. Students of comparative literature should find the book particularly useful.

Though several years have elapsed since the third volume was published in 1978, it did not seem advisable to update the information in the final chapter for the English version. The advantage of being current seemed to me to be outweighed by the risks inherent in making judgments from a perspective too close to the material. Thus I prefer to forgo a discussion of the latest novels by authors such as Max Frisch, Günter Grass, and Martin Walser. Nor will I attempt at the present time to find a place in the history for such leading contemporary novelists as Peter Handke and Thomas Bernhard. Perhaps the occasion to analyze the novels of the past decade will present itself at a later date.

I have read the English version in its entirety, reviewed it carefully, and approved all the changes. I am in complete agreement with all the cuts and deletions and feel that the deletions have in no way damaged the essence of the history. Quite to the contrary, the shortened version is probably much more serviceable to the foreign reader than a thousand-page, unabridged translation would be. The reader who compares the English version with the original will find that some sections have been changed entirely. In several cases Ellen Summerfield asked me to rewrite sections which seemed too technical for the English-speaking reader, as with Friedrich Hölderlin's *Hyperion* and Alfred Döblin's *Berlin Alexanderplatz*. Other sections had to be expanded to provide additional information or explanations. For example, one can assume a German audience's basic familiarity with the plots of Thomas Mann's *Buddenbrooks* and Theodor Fontane's *Effi Briest*, whereas this is not true of the English-speaking reader. Both of these interpretations were rewritten for the English version. Even apart from these more radical changes, the reader should not expect the English version to follow the original as closely as would a translation. While there can be no dispute that the English version is true to the original in all essential elements, many small changes have been made to make the work more suitable for the English speaker. I deeply appreciate the fine work done by Ellen Summerfield and join her in the hope that this volume will serve to bring interested English-speaking readers closer to the outstanding works of German fiction.

Hildegard Emmel

Translator's Preface

When almost twenty years ago, at the request of the Francke publishing house in Berne, Switzerland, Professor Hildegard Emmel embarked on a venture to write a complete history of the German novel, she expressed serious reservations whether the task could be accomplished. Though much valuable work had been done on specific periods, authors, and themes, and several partial histories had been written, no attempt at a comprehensive history had been made in decades. The sheer mass of literature to be considered was no doubt the greatest obstacle. How could a single researcher possibly read all of those novels? How could Emmel be sure of not forgetting something important? How could she ever become familiar with all the pertinent secondary literature? Furthermore, it was not at all clear how the material should be organized and what literary methods should be applied. As with all undertakings of this magnitude, she was faced with many unknowns and had little idea at the beginning as to what shape the project would eventually take.

What emerged during a thirteen-year period of research and writing was the three-volume *Geschichte des deutschen Romans* (1972, 1975, 1978). Professor Emmel had written a definitive work, the only complete history of the German novel in existence. It traces the history from the late Middle Ages through the Age of Goethe to the present time, including novels of the 1970s. The work has been exceptionally well received by reviewers and readers alike and is universally praised as a highly readable introduction to the genre. This readability is due in large part to Professor Emmel's in-depth interpretations. While never actually summarizing the plots of novels, she always combines sufficient background and plot information into her interpretations to enable those unfamiliar with the novels to follow the discussion easily. Thus the reader is provided with detailed analyses of the major works of German fiction rather than with what would amount to thousands of brief descriptions of novels. The reader is not overwhelmed by facts, names, and titles, but is able to acquaint himself with the styles and themes of individual novels and novelists, while at the same time achieving an understanding of the genre's historical development.

Not long after Professor Emmel's third and final volume appeared, she asked me if I might be interested in writing a revised version of the history for the English-speaking reader. My association with Professor Emmel has always been a rewarding one, both professionally and personally, and I felt that I was sufficiently familiar with her ideas and research to undertake the English version. We had first met when I was a graduate student in German at the University of Connecticut, where she held a chair in Germanic languages and literatures. I wrote my doctoral thesis on Ingeborg Bachmann's *Malina* under her supervision and served as her research assistant from 1972 to 1975, during the time she was working on her second volume. I agreed to write the English version of the history because it seemed highly desirable that a work as important as this be made available to the English-speaking public.

The English-speaking reader will most certainly find the section on the twentieth century particularly attractive, since many of these authors—Thomas Mann, Franz Kafka, Günter Grass, Max Frisch, Elias Canetti—have achieved international recognition and are widely read in translation. The discussion of their works takes into consideration the social conditions of the times, breakthroughs in psychological and scientific thought, and the political situation in twentieth-century Germany. Professor Emmel's personal experiences during the National Socialist era and her ten-year professorship in East Germany allow her a rare perspective on modern political developments and their importance to the novel. In order to respect the reader's interests, the emphasis of the English version has been shifted to give somewhat more weight to the modern period. But the real value of the work lies in its historical perspective; the twentieth century cannot be properly understood without the historical background and development. Moreover, the earlier novelists are, though usually less well known to the foreign reader, in every respect as outstanding and significant as today's writers. The value of introducing them to the English-speaking reader is indisputable.

It should be noted that some of the authors treated are relatively unknown to German readers as well. One may at first glance ask why such lengthy passages have been dedicated to authors such as Johann Michael von Loën, Christoph Martin Wieland, Charles Sealsfield, Karl Leberecht Immermann, and Wolfgang Koeppen. In my estimation these very passages can be counted among the most engaging and worthwhile in the book. They are excellent examples of the author's original research and reflect her spirited, fresh approach to literary scholarship. In contrast, Professor Emmel has taken the liberty of treating a number of popular authors—Heinrich Böll, Hermann Hesse, Christa Wolf, Heinrich Mann—with somewhat more dispatch than the reader might expect. In the preface to her first volume, Professor Emmel admits that such decisions on literary canon are often subjective, but she defends this subjectivity as legitimate. She explains that a literary historian is also a reader, and as a reader he must rely on his own judgment and personal tastes in questions of literary quality.

The reader may be surprised to find that works from other literatures are often mentioned and occasionally discussed at length. The history of the German novel is in fact so closely tied to the development of the novel in other countries that it is often difficult or inappropriate to isolate it from them. It is one of the strengths of this history that the author possesses an overview of world literature and can show the relationships and interdependence, as in the section on the British novelists Henry Fielding, Laurence Sterne, and Samuel Richardson in the eighteenth century and on the Russian writer Maxim Gorky in the twentieth. James Joyce, Marcel Proust, and John Dos Passos all play a role in the history of the German novel. The German novel has its own tradition but also has a place within the larger context of European and world literature.

To my mind one of the treats for the English-speaking reader is that authors he may already know as lyricists, dramatists, or essayists—Heinrich Heine, Bertolt Brecht, and Rainer Maria Rilke—are now introduced as novelists. These three authors gained their fame in other genres and are widely read in translation as practitioners of other forms. Yet, as the author shows, they wrote masterful novels which deserve renewed attention. This applies to Johann Wolfgang von Goethe as well, whose drama *Faust* is known all over the world and generally overshadows his other works, including his four novels. As a lifelong Goethe scholar and author of two books on Goethe, Hildegard Emmel is able to give us new insights into Goethe, illuminating his unique contribution to the novel as well as defining his place in its history.

Perhaps the most important, and the boldest, statement of the book lies in its organization. Professor Emmel realized at an early stage in her research that the categories traditionally used in literary classification (Classicism, Romanticism, Realism, Biedermeier, Naturalism, Expressionism) were of little value in structuring the history of the German novel. Rather than trying to make the novels fit into predetermined categories, she discarded the categories altogether. She pronounced them "worn out" (*verschlissen*) and proceeded to arrange the material according to categories suggested by the novels themselves; that is, the novels serve as orientation points and provide the categories necessary for classification. Thus chapter headings such as "The Era of Goethe's *Wilhelm Meister*" and "A New Start—Grimmelshausen" evolved. These headings are not meant to be definitive descriptions of a period, but simply serve as a neutral, flexible framework for ordering elements so unique and so different from each other as to defy any attempt at systematic, permanent classification.

Just as the author prefers not to be bound to a system of literary classification, she does not adhere to a particular critical orientation, such as formalism, psychoanalytical criticism, sociological criticism, or the like. Her approach to methodology is eclectic, the methods of interpretation varying from one work to another. The more important the work, the more methods it may require. The best method of interpretation, the author believes, is to use a variety of methods well.

With regard to my own method of procedure, I have translated many sections of the book directly, but I have made changes and revisions where necessary and have condensed the book to about two-thirds the original length. The book as a whole is actually more an English *version* or *adaptation* of the original than a faithful translation. It is addressed to the informed reader, who may be familiar with other languages and literatures but most likely knows little or no German and has little prior knowledge of German literature. In general I found it unnecessary to eliminate an author altogether in the name of abridgment. Instead, it was usually possible simply to favor an author's major works over minor ones that do not influence the history to the same extent and are primarily of interest to the specialist. For example, the later works of Christoph Martin Wieland are mentioned by title but not discussed, as is the case with various novels by Jeremias Gotthelf, Wilhelm Raabe, Theodor Fontane, and others. Though the completeness of the original had to be sacrificed, the English-speaking reader has at least gained a familiarity with each of these author's major works and can pursue further studies if so inclined. Although the general purpose was to reduce the text sufficiently to make one English volume from the original three, in a few cases it was necessary to lengthen sections to provide supplementary information. Whenever material was substantially changed or added, Professor Emmel rewrote the section specifically for the English version. At times I was able to draw on her other books and articles for additional information, as from *Das Gericht in der deutschen Literatur des 20. Jahrhunderts* (Berne: 1963) in the section on Hermann Broch's *The Sleepwalkers* and from *Was Goethe vom Roman der Zeitgenossen nahm* (Berne: 1972) for the interpretation of Christoph Martin Wieland's *Don Sylvio*.

All the English translations of quotations from German novels are my own. Because, as I have often heard Professor Emmel say, quotations in works of literary history serve the same purpose as illustrations in works of art history, I have tried to preserve as many of the quotations as possible. They give the reader a direct impression of the author's style and language. I have not included page numbers with quotations, since these would only refer the reader to pages in the original German novels. Likewise, I have avoided the use of footnotes whenever possible, since they usually refer to works of secondary literature written in German. Should the reader nonetheless wish to locate page numbers or secondary sources, he can find the appropriate information in the original *Geschichte des deutschen Romans*.

Since it is assumed that the reader may wish to locate English translations of the novels mentioned throughout the work, an appendix provides a listing of such translations. In compiling the list, it was astonishing to see how many works had actually been translated, though some translations are no longer in print and may be difficult to obtain. In most cases the titles I have used to refer to the novels within the text of the history correspond to the titles in the list. However, I did at times prefer to use a more literal translation than the one chosen by the translator. For example, I used *The Blinding* rather than *Auto-da-fé* for Elias Canetti's *Die Blendung* and *Call Me Gantenbein* instead of *A Wilderness of Mirrors* for Max Frisch's *Mein Name sei Gantenbein.* Where no translation exists, I simply translated the title myself.

I would like to acknowledge several colleagues and friends who have read and criticized all or part of the manuscript and whose corrections, advice, and encouragement were invaluable to me: Dr. Joe Fugate (Kalamazoo College), Dr. John Nirenberg (San Francisco State University), Kathryn Quigley, Dr. George Reinhardt (University of Connecticut), and Dr. Pardon Tillinghast (Middlebury College). I would also like to thank Claire Clemens, Jerrolyn Hurlbutt, and Elizabeth Thornton for their indefatigable assistance in typing and preparing the manuscript and Dr. Phillip Pirages (Kalamazoo College) for his thorough job of proofreading. For help in compiling the appendix I would like to thank Deborah Galef, a former student at Middlebury College, and Robert Vrecenak of the Wilbur Cross Library at the University of Connecticut, who showed me how to use the computer to search for translations. For his advice and moral support I am grateful to Dr. Hugh Clark of the University of Connecticut Research Foundation. I express sincere appreciation to Dr. C. L. Lang of the Francke Verlag in Berne for his gracious and unqualified cooperation in making this project a reality. I also extend a special word of thanks to Doreen Broder of the Wayne State University Press for her sensitive, skillful editing and excellent suggestions. For their constant support and encouragement I thank my parents, Helene and Powell Summerfield.

I am especially indebted to the author herself, Hildegard Emmel, who has been an inspiration, mentor, and friend for so many years. She has contributed in many ways to this volume, both in terms of overall concept and individual passages. The work of translation and adaptation is a joy and a pleasure when the original is as lucid, fascinating, and superbly written as Hildegard Emmel's *Geschichte des deutschen Romans.* I am very glad to have had the opportunity to collaborate with her on this project and now to see her work available in English.

Ellen Summerfield

PART ONE

HISTORICAL
DEVELOPMENT

1 / Two Beginnings

Definition and Background

A history of the German novel must begin with the admission that it is difficult to determine exactly when the novel made its first appearance. The need for a starting point is self-evident, yet a decision on the question of origins depends on how the novel is defined. This itself is problematic; any single definition proves to be simplistic and inadequate. To understand what the novel is, it is necessary to view its history. Through the centuries the genre has undergone profound changes and assumed numerous forms. Works of very different structure, style, and content have all been categorized as novels. Indeed, one should not think in terms of "the" German novel, but rather of many German novels. Together they constitute a historical phenomenon of wide variability, which can only be understood and described as such.

The Frenchman Pierre Daniel Huet, who made the first attempt in Europe to define the genre *Romans* (the German word for novel is also *Roman*), recognized as early as 1670 that the meaning of the term changed with historical changes in the art form. Huet wrote that in the past the word *Romans* had primarily been used to designate works written in verse. In the usage of his day, however, it had taken on the opposite meaning, referring to love stories written in prose (*Traité de l'Origine des Romans*, 1670).

The definition is problematic in other languages as well. Difficulties arise when one tries to distinguish between the novel and shorter prose forms or when the style approaches that of another genre. In order to provide a working definition for his lectures on *Aspects of the Novel* (1927), E. M. Forster stated that "any fictitious prose work over fifty thousand words will be a novel for the purposes of these lectures."

Since we generally agree today that the novel is written in prose, it seems appropriate to begin the history of the German novel with the first appearance of narrative prose in the late Middle Ages. Thus the verse epics of the Middle Ages are excluded. It should be noted, however, that not all literary historians would agree with this decision. Walther Rehm begins his *History of the German Novel* (*Geschichte des deutschen Romans*, 1927) with the statement, "The form of the novel in the Middle Ages is the epic," and proceeds to discuss the medieval courtly epic in his first chapter.[1] This standpoint is defensible in light of the unquestionable similarities between the medieval epic and the modern novel—both are lengthy narrations which express a Weltanschauung, take place in a broad setting, present many char-

3

acters, and have subplots. These common attributes led German medievalists to adopt the term *Roman* in reference to works of the Middle Ages, such
as the *Artusroman* (Arthurian "novel"), the *höfischer Roman* (courtly "novel"),
and the *Gralroman* ("novel" of the Holy Grail). But medievalists fully recognize the differences between the two, and their use of the term serves
primarily to distinguish the epic from other works of the same period, rather
than to link it with the modern novel. In fact, there is little to be gained by
blurring or denying the differences, as Rehm has done, for they are decisive
and outweigh the similarities. Not only was the language of the epic strictly
regulated by the laws of verse, but its content and themes were governed by
the predetermined and absolute medieval world order. Moreover, the medieval author claimed to be telling true stories that he could document, and
usually this was indeed the case. Narration was essentially a retelling based
on sources that offered proof to both author and audience of the tale's truth,
of its historical authenticity. When an author occasionally changed his source
material, elaborated upon it, or expressed personal opinions, he did so for
didactic reasons—to interpret the story for his particular audience and to
demonstrate the exemplary moral behavior of his characters within the fixed
system of values. This subordination to tradition and authority began to change
in modern times as man assumed more responsibility for his role in life and
came to express personal, subjective views in his writings. But the process
was slow. Most of the great seventeenth-century novels, though written in
prose, were still more closely related to the ideology of the Middle Ages than
to that of the modern novel. The development of the modern novel did not
begin until the eighteenth century. The genre then acquired its essential
function: to serve the need of the individual to express himself and his own
world view and thereby to realize his special and unique nature.

   The first popular fiction appeared in Germany relatively late, about 1400.
Translations and adaptations based on French originals found favor with
German readers, and a rich narrative literature began to flourish. The demand for colorful reading matter rapidly increased among both aristocrats
and burghers, and the invention of movable type made a large distribution
possible. Countess Elisabeth von Nassau-Saarbrücken (1379–1456), who
translated French *chansons-de-geste* into German prose during the decade
1430–40, is credited with introducing the French prose romance of chivalry
to the German reader (*Herpin, Sibylle, Loher and Maller, Hug Schapeler*).
Soon other writers were producing German prose versions of French prose
and verse romances, novellas from the Italian Renaissance, and occasionally
material from Latin sources. In the midfifteenth century Eleonore von
Österreich (1433–1480) translated the French prose romance *Pontus and
Sidonia*, and a decade later the mayor of Berne, Thüring von Ringoltingen
(1415–1483), translated *Beautiful Melusine*. Many of the works which the

German Romanticists later designated "German *Volksbücher*" (folk books, chapbooks) were actually translations from foreign literatures which came into the hands of the German public during the sixteenth century. They were so appealing to German tastes that they continued to be printed in the eighteenth and nineteenth centuries. The Romanticists, unaware of their foreign origins, saw them as charming examples of native folk literature. Along with the works derived from foreign originals, narratives with material indigenous to Germany, such as *Herzog Ernst, Wigalois, Parzival,* and Eilhart von Oberge's version of *Tristan,* were widely read. Also popular were collections of humorous anecdotes (*Schwanksammlungen*), such as *Till Eulenspiegel* and *Schildbürger.* Especially noteworthy are the original German creations *Fortunatus* (1509) and *Dr. Faust* (1587); both are anonymous.

The First Novelist—Jörg Wickram

Proceeding from the above discussion on the definition of the novel, we may regard Jörg Wickram (1500–1560) as the first German novelist. A versatile Alsatian burgher, Wickram was active in the arts as a playwright and as founder of the *Meistersinger* school in Colmar. His first two novels, *Galmy* (1539) and *Gabriotto* (1551), were echoes of the romance of chivalry and, as such, of little artistic value. The theme of *Galmy,* the love of a simple knight for a married duchess, had already been treated many times in European literature. Wickram's novel ends with the marriage of the lovers after the duke's death. Having no firsthand knowledge of court life, the author was not equal to his great theme. The world he creates is artificial, with rhetoric taking the place of expressions of passion. *Gabriotto,* even weaker than *Galmy,* is again a tale of forbidden love between members of different social classes. By varying the traditional theme to conform to his own moral views—the two pairs deny themselves the fulfillment of their love—Wickram was left with a lifeless construction; the plot's impetus was entirely lost.

Not until Wickram brought his own problems and ideas to the novel did he succeed in creating original, genuinely appealing works. He is recognized for two novels, *A Lesson for Boys* (*Der Knabenspiegel,* 1554) and *The Gold Thread* (*Der Goldfaden,* 1557). They are simply structured narrations in which Wickram used character and plot to express his views on prevailing social conditions. Both works revolve around the social advancement of a person of humble birth. In *A Lesson for Boys* a poor peasant's son achieves success after success—in his early school years as well as at the university— through his own ability, diligence, and exemplary behavior. He finally attains the position of chancellor. By contrast, Wilbaldo, the spoiled son of a knight, neglects all responsibilities, disobeys his father and teacher, and leads a life of increasing slovenliness and disorder. Having squandered all the money secretly sent to him by his mother, he is forced to become a swineherd. But poverty serves to bring about reform: Wilbaldo gains insight into his own situation and, like the prodigal son, returns home to give his life a new direction. Wickram's character scheme—an individual's worth in society is inversely related to his station at birth—demonstrates the injustice of a social system that favors the nobility and disdains the lower classes. The stereotyped characterization is a consequence of the author's didactic intent.

In *The Gold Thread* this didacticism is masked by the poetic luster of the work, its fairy-tale atmosphere, its appealing characters, and the artistic motifs. Nevertheless, the plot structure corresponds to that of *A Lesson for Boys*. A poor shepherd's son, Lewfried, proves himself worthy of knighthood, marries a count's daughter, and inherits the count's estate. Although *The Gold Thread*, like Wickram's first two novels, is once again a romance of chivalry, the author's attitude toward the aristocracy has changed. He no longer portrays the nobility as living in a distant, self-contained world where behavior is questionable and foreign to the burgher's way of thought, but shows how similar values unite his own class with the nobility. Nevertheless, Wickram was not a revolutionary and did not think in terms of the dissolution of class structure. His only concern was that a man's state within the existing order be determined by his ability and moral conduct. Correspondingly, he considered the mode of life and political power of the nobility to be goals worthy of pursuit.

Within this context Wickram demonstrated his concept of an ideal social structure. Class distinctions were not meant to be fixed, insurmountable barriers. Instead, friendly relations existed among social groups, even if the differences were, on occasion, sharply underlined. As in *A Lesson for Boys*, children of different social classes grow up together: Lewfried is raised in the home of a wealthy merchant and thus is able to attend school. Wickram may have had his own childhood in mind here. He is thought to have been the illegitimate son of an eminent patrician and may well have grown up with the same privileges as his legitimate brothers and sisters, not feeling the distance separating him from them by reason of birth until later. In any case we note that in the childhood battles described in the third and fourth chapters, the social standing of the pupils plays an important role. Lewfried's victory as the leader of his classmates in a battle against youths from another school is a vindication of his honor. The boys from the second school, many of noble birth, had looked down upon Lewfried and his companions because their leader was only a shepherd's son. When the twelve year old finds himself immersed in new conflicts which challenge his honor, he feels forced to flee and leaves his foster-parents' home with great sadness. He must now travel a long, obstacle-filled path before he can be ennobled. On the basis of his unquestionable merit and numerous heroic deeds, he is finally dubbed a knight by the king. The need for this ceremony as a precondition to the marriage between Lewfried and the count's daughter exemplifies the conservative attitudes underlying Wickram's writings. Lewfried's achievements are recognized and rewarded within the existing class structure, which remains intact.

Among the many elements that Wickram has borrowed from romances of chivalry, the use of the lion motif lends the work a special charm. The lion first appears among his father's flocks before Lewfried's birth and behaves like a tame domestic animal. It later becomes Lewfried's faithful companion (the name Lewfried means "peaceful lion") and aids him when his life is endangered. The inexplicable conduct of the lion distinguishes Lewfried as a special person graced by God. Possible sources for the motif are *Herpin* or *Iwein*, the knight with the lion, but there are no direct points of comparison.[2]

In his use of songs in the plot Wickram was probably influenced by literary models in a similar way. It seems likely that he was inspired by *Pontus and Sidonia*. But Lewfried's songs, and previously a song of Wilbaldo, have the special function of promoting the plot. At the court where Lewfried works as a kitchen boy following his flight from home, he attracts the count's attention by his singing. He also communicates his feelings of love to Angliana, the count's daughter, by means of song. It is noteworthy that Wilbaldo's song and two songs of Lewfried are included in their entirety within the prose text, a practice later adopted by Johann Wolfgang von Goethe in *Wilhelm Meister* and by the Romanticists. The songs serve to reveal what is secret and to air those thoughts which the singer cannot express directly because of his inner constraints or social position. He is dependent on the perceptive listener for an interpretation of their content.

The unique motif of the gold thread, which gives the novel its title, was most likely Wickram's own invention. It is closely related to Lewfried's artistry in song and plays a central role in the love story. Angliana introduces the motif when she decides to make Lewfried unhappy so that his sadness might inspire him to song. Instead of presenting him with the usual New Year's present which all the other servants receive, she mockingly gives him a gold thread from her embroidery and demands that he preserve it so well that he be able to show it to her the following year. Lewfried secretly cuts open his chest above the heart, places the thread in the wound, and then sews it together again. The power of his love enables him to disregard the pain. In a song printed in the text he tells Angliana that he has closed the thread in his heart and one would have to split his chest to obtain it. Unable to understand what this means, she demands the thread back. Before her eyes Lewfried cuts open his chest and hands her the undamaged thread, thereby winning her love. In competition with chivalric poetry, Wickram has thus created an unusual test for his young hero. All the elements that characterize courtly love are present here. The perfection of a character who at the end is deemed worthy of knighthood should manifest itself in his ability to love, to suffer, and to master the art of song.

With this novel Wickram reached his highest achievement. The German Romanticist Clemens Brentano reacted favorably to *The Gold Thread* and published a new edition in 1809. Other Romantic authors also received the work warmly. It seems that Wickram expended himself in the writing of *The Gold Thread*, for his last novel, *Of Good and Bad Neighbors* (*Von guten und bösen Nachbarn*, 1556), which was published before *The Gold Thread* in 1556, is of considerably less artistic quality than the two preceding works. It is a family story which spans three generations and is set entirely in a burgher milieu. The value of the novel lies in the attempt to give this setting its own themes. The idea of depicting differences in neighbors' attitudes and thus making city life the subject of a novel was potentially fruitful, but Wickram did not possess the artistic means to give significance and charm to the commonplace. His first romances of chivalry were outdated and his last effort, *Of Good and Bad Neighbors*, was evidently premature.

Jörg Wickram had no successors. Not until the midseventeenth century did innovative forms of the German novel reappear. In the meantime, literary styles and tastes underwent fundamental changes. The narrative literature of the late Middle Ages lost its decisive impact, though new works did appear sporadically and those already published continued to be read. As evidence of the widespread demand for this literature, in 1578 the Frankfurt publisher Siegmund Feyerabend brought out a large folio volume, the *Book of Love* (*Buch der Liebe*), containing thirteen of the most well-known narrations of the day—*Pontus and Sidonia*, *Tristan*, *Wigalois*, and Wickram's *Galmy* and *Gabriotto*, to name a few—and as early as 1587 found it necessary to print a second edition.

Symptomatic of the new tastes and indicative of future developments in the genre was the novel *Amadis*, a fantastic creation that was enormously popular throughout Europe in the sixteenth century. A Spanish romance of impressive language and style, it was written in 1508 by Garci Ordóñez de Montalvo (c. 1440–c. 1500), who incorporated an earlier model, probably from the late Middle Ages. Montalvo later added a fifth book to his original four, and in the next decades *Amadis* continued to grow. Beginning in 1540 it was adapted into French and by 1556 already comprised sixteen books. The first German edition was published in 1569 and by 1593 the novel had swollen to twenty-four books (approximately twenty-five thousand pages in quarto format). The continual expansion of the work was a result of its popularity as well as of the unlimited variations possible in the world of fantasy.

The public was apparently insatiable in its desire to read ever more of the countless adventures that were arbitrarily continued, repeated, or varied. This was probably due in large part to the fact that the world of fairies, giants, sorcerers, and monsters did not correspond to any concrete political or social realities. The primary motive behind the knight-errant's deeds is love, and he remains faithful to his lady through all trials. Heroism is united with feeling, and an element of sentimental refinement points to the courtly-historical novel of the seventeenth century.

But we are still a long way from new, original creations, and translations and adaptations again formed the basis of literary effort. These translations were not faithful reproductions. In general, the contents were freely paraphrased and the material adapted to one's own environment. Thus the Munich town clerk Simon Schaidenreisser (c. 1500–c. 1573) usurped Homeric stories to write his *Odyssea* (1537), an adventure novel with local color. Johann Fischart (1546–1590) brought his own language and style to his adaptation of François Rabelais's *Gargantua et Pantagruel* (1575). By expanding it to three times its original length he was able to exhibit his overflowing talent. Fischart had previously translated the sixth book of *Amadis* (1572). A German adaptation by Johann Tschorn of the late Greek Heliodorus's (?3rd century) work *Aethiopica* had a great, sustained literary impact; from 1559 to 1641 it was reprinted ten times.

A New Start—Grimmelshausen

When original novels again appeared in Germany, Wickram's works belonged to a long-forgotten era. The novelists of the seventeenth century did not look back to Wickram; instead, they modified forms of the novel which had evolved in other European literatures and had been introduced to German readers in translation. These forms are: the pastoral novel (*Schäferroman*), the courtly-historical novel (*höfisch-historischer Roman*), and the picaresque novel (*Schelmenroman*).

In Germany the pastoral novel was short-lived, and no noteworthy examples of the genre were written. Martin Opitz's (1597–1639) *The Idyll of the Nymph Hercinie* (*Schäferei der Nymphe Hercinie*, 1630) deserves mention only because of its famous author and because it serves as an example of the pastoral form in Germany. Otherwise, the pastoral element is important as a motif integrated into the courtly-historical novel.

This applies in particular to Philipp von Zesen's (1619–1689) *The Adriatic Rosemund* (*Die adriatische Rosemund*, 1645). It is the first original German novel since Wickram. Prior to *Rosemund*, Zesen had translated novels from the French, including Madeleine de Scudéry's *Ibrahim Bassa* and

François du Soucy Gerzan's *African Sophonisba,* a task which undoubtedly helped refine his literary abilities. Indeed, *The Adriatic Rosemund* is a work of unique artistry. The title character, sorrowful because she doubts her beloved's loyalty, retreats to the countryside and dedicates herself to the life of a shepherdess. The idyllic setting outside Amsterdam serves as therapy for her sufferings; in "such quiet and such peace" she was able to "disentangle her confused thoughts again, to set her troubled mind to rest." Zesen emphasizes that the state of extreme inner discontent demands isolation, for amidst other people the soul is unable to release its burden. This viewpoint attributes a special function to pastoral solitude, similar to the role of isolation in Pietism and Sentimentalism *(Empfindsamkeit).* Once solitude came to be seen within a social context, it was no longer possible to use an idyll as the sole setting of a novel. The pastoral scene is productive only insofar as it is regarded as a spiritual island distinct from other settings. The revival of pastoral themes in the eighteenth century is founded on this concept.

Although the scene of action is limited in comparison to other seventeenth-century novels including Zesen's later works, his characters are not provincial. Nor do they fail to travel. The title alludes to Rosemund's foreign heritage; she was born in Venice and is living with her parents and sister in Amsterdam when she meets Markhold, a German on his way to Paris. The continuation of his journey, and thus their separation, results in Rosemund's anguish and her retreat to a pastoral existence. Markhold's experiences in France occupy entire sections of the novel, and conditions in the Republic of Venice as well as in Germany, now and in the past, are the subject of their conversations following his return to Amsterdam. But the emotional interaction between the lovers, which Zesen declared to be the decisive element of the work, evolves in the same setting where it began and also ends there with Rosemund's grief and lingering illness. She slowly wastes away after realizing that she and Markhold can never marry because of confessional differences. Rosemund's father demands not only that she remain a Catholic but that she raise any daughters she may later have in this faith. Since Markhold, a Protestant, cannot consent, the situation of the pair is hopeless.

Zesen has portrayed a conflict which, at the time of the Thirty Years' War and only one hundred years after the Reformation, must have been regarded as highly modern and which provides a credible motivation for Rosemund's misery and despair. The conflict gives the work, as a family novel, a genuine tension which Wickram could not yet achieve in *Of Good and Bad Neighbors.* Nevertheless it lacks uniformity. Instead of concentrating on the convincing plot, Zesen glorifies the incomparable main character: in the preface he speaks of "celestial Rosemund," who is more "angelic than human." This and many other things in the novel may seem curious to the modern reader. Despite all the novel's peculiarities it is apparent that the author wishes to write of serious emotional matters and that the theme which captivates him is the spectrum of human feelings. Nor can one disregard the fact that the elevation of Rosemund is an expression of the demand of that age for spiritualized, grandiosely heroic figures. Zesen's contemporaries also created stylized characters in their courtly-historical novels.

The courtly-historical novel is well described by its name: though usually set in the historical past, it is an idealized representation of seventeenth-century European court life. Its authors, many of noble birth, were all learned men, knowledgeable in history, literature, and theology. They chose ancient Roman, Egyptian, Indic, Germanic, or biblical times as their setting and included full historical and cultural background information as an essential element. The extreme length of many of these works is related to their historical detail. Despite the historical context, however, the characters behave as exemplary members of the seventeenth-century courtly world, displaying virtue, dignity, integrity, and constancy at all times. The plot brings them into difficulties and hardships from which they emerge as heroes. The structural scheme of unification, separation, and reunification is inherited from Heliodorus. The hero and heroine fall in love at the beginning of the novel but are then separated by cruel and difficult circumstances leading to complicated plot developments. Always faithful to each other, they must undergo many trials and travel long distances before they are finally reunited. The courtly-historical novel is characterized by its simple and conciliatory ending: the hero and heroine, together with other pairs whose stories parallel that of the main couple, are finally married in splendid celebrations. This ending, often following an intricate, entangled, long, and confusing plot, is an expression of the author's belief in an eternal order. Emphasis is placed on spirituality and the hereafter; the characters' morality and courage in the face of death derive from their religious faith.

The "high" style and idealism of the courtly-historical novel are best expressed in the writings of Duke Anton Ulrich von Braunschweig-Wolfenbüttel (1633–1714). His voluminous works, *The Illustrious Syrian Aramena (Die durchleuchtete Syrerin Aramena,* 1669–73) and *The Roman Octavia (Die römische Octavia,* 1677–1707), are outstanding literary accomplishments, but they pose difficulties for the modern reader because of their extreme length. *Aramena* comprises five volumes and *Octavia* six. Critic Richard Alewyn observes that an energetic reader would have to devote "twelve hours a day to it for six weeks" in order to complete the seven thousand pages (in quarto format) of *Octavia.*[3] In addition to length, the overwhelmingly complex structure of both novels makes them unappealing to many readers. The ingeniously woven, seemingly labryinthine plot structure demands particular patience and attentiveness from the reader. Hundreds of characters appear in each of the novels. The main characters, over forty in each work, have their own individual plots which are intertwined or overlapping. In addition, the majority of these characters change their identity, in some cases more than once. For political reasons, infant princes and princesses are kidnapped or abandoned and are surprised in later years to learn of their mistaken identity. Other characters evade enemies or unwanted suitors by disguising themselves. Thus confusing situations arise. Because each person must contend with deception on the part of others, all feel uncertain. Everyone deceives and is deceived, and the characters as well as the reader are forced to grope in the dark. But Anton Ulrich masterfully commands a complete overview of the connections and relationships; he alone decides when and where clarification is desirable. For long stretches, circumstances surrounding situations or persons are left unexplained. In the end, however, deceptions and misunderstandings are clarified, apparent contradictions resolved, and, after long separations and hardships, many couples are united.

Both novels take place in historical settings, *Aramena* in the Orient during the Age of the Patriarchs and *Octavia* in Rome and Dacia from 68 to 70 A.D. But the historical background either plays a minor role or has been altered by the author. Almost all of his main characters are purely fictitious and behave like noblemen from the world of Duke Anton Ulrich. Though the time span of the action is relatively short—in *Aramena* approximately one and one half years and in *Octavia* two years—the novels actually encompass a much longer time period as a result of the author's particular method of narration: all of the main characters' background stories are narrated at some point. These stories usually aid in clarifying relationships which hitherto had been uncertain, but they can also promote further confusion by introducing new persons and raising more unanswered questions. Whereas the background stories are narrated linearly with an emphasis placed on important occurrences, the events set in the present are related almost on a day-to-day basis. The many scenes from court life, including conversations and deliberations often taking place simultaneously, result in an epic picture of overwhelming breadth and richness. The fullness did not, however, prevent Anton Ulrich from developing a careful logic, even if it is not always apparent to the reader, and a certain epic atmosphere pervades the works. It derives from the author's emphasis on a universal, binding ethic and his attention to the art of social living. What matters is not superiority in the bloody battles, though personal courage is expected, but steadfast endurance of incomprehensible cruelties and composed suffering in the face of the unknown.

Philipp von Zesen's later works, *Asenath* (*Assenat*, 1670) and *Simson* (1679), are taken from biblical history. Of the two, *Asenath*, the story of Joseph and his wife, is the more skillfully written. It was probably inspired by *Joseph the Chaste*, a novel by Zesen's contemporary Hans Jakob Christoffel von Grimmelshausen; in any case, Zesen quotes from the work. As a scholarly author he was much better acquainted with source material than Grimmelshausen and added an enormous appendix of scholarly notes. He also differs from Grimmelshausen in that he emphasized Joseph's statesmanship, his insurpassable diligence, and his importance as a patriarchal leader. As in *Rosemund*, he was concerned with raising the main characters to the heroic ideal of the times. Joseph and Asenath are an exemplary pair: they are grand and dignified, each destined to assume an extraordinary role in the state hierarchy while simultaneously endowed with an individual fate and capable of emotional sensitivity. In many respects, Asenath is an intensification of the qualities depicted earlier in Rosemund. She embodies spirituality within the political context of the novel.

Another exemplary couple is portrayed in Heinrich Anselm von Zigler und Kliphausen's (1663–1699) work *The Asiatic Banise* (*Die asiatische Banise*, 1689). Events from India's history provide Zigler with the bloodstained background for the story of the virtuous pair, Prince Balacin and Princess Banise, who remain loyal to each other through atrocities and exotic cruelties and are united in the end. The novel gives a special place to rhetorical utterances conveyed in a grand style. When Banise, who is to be sacrificed to the war god, stands before the sacrificial block ready for execution, she delivers a long, powerful, well-planned oration on the nature of death. The norm of conduct for heroes of the courtly-historical novel is illustrated in this scene, in the princess's unshakeable composure and in her supreme mastery of the situation. But Zigler does not always conform strictly to this norm in *The Asiatic Banise*, becoming on occasion more personally involved with his characters than the "high" style of the genre would allow. *The Asiatic Banise* is actually a later and somewhat relaxed form of the courtly-historical novel. It was well received far into the eighteenth century, and one of its characters, the tyrant Chaumigrem, is mentioned in Goethe's *Theatrical Mission*.

Goethe also makes reference to Andreas Heinrich Buchholtz's (1607–1671) *Hercules and Valisca* (1659) in the sixth chapter of *Wilhelm Meister's Apprenticeship*. With *Hercules* and its sequel *Herculiscus and Herculadisla* (1665) Buchholtz hoped to take the place of the popular *Amadis*, which he considered shameful. But his very emphasis on religious values and his tendency to moralize were detrimental to the novels. A fixed system of good and evil inhibits the free development of the action. Buchholtz did achieve considerable popularity in his time and was still read in the eighteenth century. Pietistic readers, including Goethe's "Beautiful Soul" in the *Apprenticeship*, undoubtedly found the novels especially appealing.

Also highly praised in the seventeenth century was Daniel Caspar von Lohenstein's (1635–1683) *Arminius* (1689). A heroic figure who defeated the Romans in the Teutoburg Forest (A.D. 9), Arminius represents the virtuousness of the Germanic peoples as contrasted with the immorality of the Romans. Filled with information on political, philosophical, and religious matters, *Arminius* is actually less a novel than an attempt at a historical account.

A special place among seventeenth-century novelists is occupied by Hans Jakob Christoffel von Grimmelshausen (1621?–1676). His most famous book, *The Adventurous Simplicissimus (Das abenteuerliche Simplicissimus Teutsch,* 1669), has fascinated readers to the present day. If the continued popularity of a work beyond its own time were to be used as a criterion, then the history of the German novel could begin with *Simplicissimus.* Its style of narration is fascinating, its wisdom inexhaustible, the vitality of its main character astounding. The narrator Simplicius Simplicissimus, who tells his own story, is neither a significant personality nor a noble and dignified character like the heroes in other novels of the same period. He is merely a common person, an Everyman. A product and victim of his time, he appears to learn from his experiences but is led to folly again and again. Despite repeated resolutions to improve himself on life's journey, he is no further ahead at the end than at the beginning. The closeness the reader feels for this character combined with the ironical distance Simplicius maintains toward himself and his world serves to engage the reader's attention throughout.

The overwhelming success of the novel in its time was equalled by few other works in world literature. Soon after publication of the original work comprised of five books, Grimmelshausen added a *Continuatio* as a sixth book. A revised, expanded edition entitled *Baroque-Simplicissimus (Barock-Simplicissimus)* quickly followed. Grimmelshausen then published an abundance of sequels called "Simplician Writings," including the four short novels *Courage, the Adventuress (Die Landstörzerin Courasche,* 1670), *The Singular Life Story of Heedless Hopalong (Der seltsame Springinsfeld,* 1670), and *The Enchanted Bird's Nest I & II (Das wunderbare Vogelnest I & II,* 1672, 1673). One of these, *Courage, the Adventuress,* inspired Bertolt Brecht in the conception of his famous play *Mother Courage and Her Children (Mutter Courage und ihre Kinder,* 1941). Grimmelshausen's other novels, written before and after *Simplicissimus,* were not nearly as popular. His *Joseph the Chaste (Der keusche Joseph,* 1667) is, in contrast to Philipp von Zesen's *Asenath,* narrated in a direct and lively fashion; its style has much in common with *Simplicissimus.*

The story of Simplicius takes place during the Thirty Years' War (1618–48). Unaware of his real background, the nameless youth is raised in the Spessart Mountains by a peasant he assumes is his father. While tending his flocks and playing a song on his bagpipe in praise of peasant life, he is taken by surprise by soldiers on horseback. He is forced to see his presumed parents tortured and their home plundered; the boy escapes and watches from a distance as the house is destroyed by flames. He wanders frightened and exhausted through the woods and is given shelter by a hermit, who names him Simplicius because of the child's apparent ignorance and simplicity. He does not know his own name—as he explains, his mother called him "boy" or "rascal"—nor does he know the meaning of common words such as "people" and "village." Over the next two years the hermit teaches him to read and write and instructs him in the Christian faith. After the old man's death Simplicius remains in the woods for another half year, but, after marauding soldiers steal his household goods and modest provisions for the winter, he is forced to leave his isolation.

In the world he now enters, the knowledge he acquired from the hermit is of little use. Upon his arrival at the fortress of Hanau, he is arrested as a spy because the governor mistakes his strange appearance and naiveté for a disguise. When it is learned that he lived with the hermit, who was the governor's brother-in-law, he is released and becomes a page. Realizing that the boy resembles his missing sister, the governor gives him privileged treatment. But Simplicius does not adapt well to his new life. At every step he is aware of the discrepancies between the behavior of those around him and the teachings of the hermit. The godlessness and openly displayed sinfulness of society astonish him. In addition, he is not suited to his duties. He performs poorly, and his inexperience results in many slips for which he is severely punished. In a garrison muster the governor has him entered in the roll as Simplicius Simplicissimus, "thus making me, like a bastard child, the first of my lineage, though, as he says himself, I look like his own sister." Simplicius's difficulties culminate in a dreadful ordeal, an attempt by the governor to confuse him and derange his mind in order to convert him into the court fool. This does not succeed, however, since Simplicius, warned of what is to come, endures the torment and then plays the fool with such skill and wit as to mock the governor and his entire court.

After he is suddenly captured from the governor's court by Croatian troops, his life is totally engulfed by the ragings of war. His fortunes rise and fall as he passes from one group of soldiers to another. He experiences destitution, degradation, imprisonment with the imminent danger of torture, and unexpected rescue. He wins a true and loyal friend, Herzbruder, and Olivier is a dangerous companion who tempts him to evil. He becomes a daring, elegant dragoon who gains fame and riches as the "Huntsman of Soest." During six months in the hands of the Swedes he pursues studies and has many amorous adventures. Forced to marry, he leaves for Cologne to retrieve his possessions, but he meets with difficulties and therefore takes the opportunity to travel to Paris. There he performs in the opera at the Louvre before the king, wins the admiration of all by his song and appearance, and receives the name "Beau Alman." The ladies of highest society extend secret invitations to him. When the excitement becomes too much for him, he flees Paris. On his journey he becomes very ill, loses his money, is ultimately disfigured by the illness, and must make his way as a quack doctor.

Back on German soil, he becomes a simple solider as before and meets both Herzbruder and Olivier again. With Olivier he plunders and accumulates great wealth; with Herzbruder he makes a pilgrimage to Maria Einsiedeln and becomes a Catholic. After the death of his wife in Lippstadt, he marries a peasant girl from the Black Forest and buys a farm, but the marriage proves to be a bad mistake. At the same time he is reunited with his presumed father from the Spessart and learns for the first time of his noble heritage. His mother had given birth during flight from the Battle of Höchst (1622) and had left him with the peasant couple shortly before her death. The hermit was his true father and the governor of Hanau his uncle; he had been christened Melchior Sternfels von Fuchsheim. When his second wife dies, Simplicius gives his property to his foster parents, devotes himself to many studies, descends into the depths of the Mummelsee, sets out once again on a long journey, reaches Russia and Asia, and becomes a Turkish galley slave. Freed by the Venetians, he makes a pilgrimage to Rome and then returns to the Black Forest, where he lives as a hermit.

In the *Continuatio* Simplicius embarks on new adventures which end with a shipwreck on a desert island. This island offers the disillusioned hero a refuge which he decides never to leave again. The question of whether the *Continuatio* is a meaningful supplement to the novel or is injurious to its artistic integrity remains open. Indisputably, the original five books in themselves form a remarkably close-knit, unified whole; a continuation does not seem necessary. On the other hand, the faraway, fantastic quality of the aging man's island existence does offer a new perspective. The fertile island reveals itself to be an "earthly paradise," a contrast to the world of men from which Simplicius declares he has received "more bad than good" and "more vexation from enemies than pleasure from friends." Regardless of whether Europe is at war or at peace, there is "disquiet, perpetual misery," and "worst of all . . . no hope for improvement." Although the island sanctuary anticipates Johann Gottfried Schnabel's *The Isle of Felsenburg*, the two are very different in that Simplicius's rejection and abandonment of the world cannot be overcome by changes in modes of life; they are final. This finality is expressed in both the original work and in the *Continuatio*.

Simplicius's thoughts about his own life and his insight into the transience of the world are the subject of an extended lament in the final chapters of the fifth book. Shortly before his death, the hermit had spoken to Simplicius about the importance of self-knowledge, and Simplicius, having returned to the Black Forest, comes upon the maxim "Know thyself" ("Nosce te ipsum") in his books. In an attempt to follow the dictate he reflects on his existence:

> My life has not been life, but death, my days a heavy shadow, my years a heavy dream, my lusts heavy sins. . . . My heart is burdened with sorrows, for all good deeds I am lazy, sluggish, and ruined; worst of all, my conscience is fearful and grieved. . . . My body is weary, my mind confused, my innocence lost, my best years wasted, the noble times gone; nothing gives me joy, and, moreover, I have come to despise myself. When I entered this world after my blessed father's death, I was simple and pure, upright and honest, truthful, humble, retiring, modest, chaste, shy, pious, and devout, but I soon became malicious, false, deceitful, haughty, restless, and entirely godless—vices which I learned without a teacher. . . . I looked only to the present and to my immediate gain, without once giving thought to the future or to the account I would one day have to give of myself before God!

Simplicius's lament on his wasted life is followed in the next chapter by a lament on the world: "Adieu world, for no trust can be placed in you, there is nothing more to hope of you. . . ." These deliberations lead him to resume his life as a hermit. The narrator is fully conscious of the unity of a work which leads back to the hermitage, saying explicitly, "and began my Spessart life again." But he slyly adds, "whether I will stay there to the end of my days, like my father of blessed memory, remains to be seen." This uncertainty allows for the possibility of a continuation.

Self-reflection and self-knowledge, as well as the insight into the transience of all earthly things, are also found in other passages of the novel. They are certainly to be seen in connection with the author's personal experiences. Yet at the same time they place *Simplicissimus* in the tradition of the European picaresque novel, which originated in Spain. The first example of the genre is the anonymous work *Lazarillo de Tormes* (1554). Written in the first person, it consists of a series of episodes in which the servant boy Lazarillo, cast out among strangers at an early age, passes into the service of various masters, gains knowledge about the world, and, disillusioned by his experiences, becomes a pícaro (rogue, adventurer). By means of cunning and cleverness, he is able to turn situations to his own advantage and eventually obtain an official position, a wife (an archpriest's mistress), and modest prosperity. Many similar narrations, such as the famous *Guzmán de Alfarache* (1599) by Mateo Alemán, followed Lazarillo, and translations and imitations soon appeared in German. The perspective of the pícaro reverses the idealism characteristic of heroes in novels of chivalry as well as seventeenth-century courtly-historical novels. These heroes embodied the virtues which society demanded of them and devoted their lives to the realization of their ideals. The pícaro, on the other hand, has no commitments. Under his various masters he is forced into contact with young swindlers whom he must outwit and whose trickery he must outdo if he is to survive. It is typical that the pícaro meditates on life and the world in general. Between adventures he reflects on the inconstancy and perishability of human life.

Just as Grimmelshausen borrowed elements from the picaresque novel, he also utilized scholarly and literary writings as resource material. The long-held belief that he was a natural talent who created on his own, having had no formal exposure to classical education, has been found incorrect. Today it is assumed that the author, as opposed to his hero Simplicius, attended school in his native city of Gelnhausen for a number of years. His literary images and metaphors are evidence of vast knowledge, including a familiarity with works from classical antiquity. The similarities between *Simplicissimus* and Wolfram von Eschenbach's *Parzival* (1200–1210) are so striking that Grimmelshausen may well have known and used it, and his "Adieu, world" at the end of the novel is probably based on Aegidius Albertinus's German rendition of a similar passage by Antonio de Guevara. Particularly important to the overall composition of *Simplicissimus* is the astrological knowledge which Grimmelshausen possessed as a compiler of almanacs.

Even more difficult than the question of literary dependence is that of concrete realities portrayed in the novel. There is no doubt that Grimmelshausen drew on personal experiences in creating his story and main character, even though specific examples are difficult to prove. But rather than attempt to identify those aspects which Grimmelshausen owed to existing literature or his own experiences and those which he created independently—this question has been the source of much controversy among literary scholars—it seems more fruitful to concentrate on that which defines Grimmelshausen's contribution to the novel: his gift of narration. Filled with an infinite joy in narration, Grimmelshausen treats his subject with playful skill and imagination and, at the same time, with extreme precision and deliberation. The secret of his narrative style is the perspective: Grimmelshausen focuses on the standpoint of the fictitious narrator Simplicius, through whom events are presented. Whatever Simplicius considers worthy of narration is expressed as he sees it. Thus the satire is also determined by Simplicius: that which surprises him, which he ridicules, which seems wrong to him, is the focus of attention. It is important that he can also regard himself satirically. The absolute consistency in the narrative perspective lends unity to the character and story of Simplicius.

Grimmelshausen, like Wickram, was to find no true successors or imitators. The considerably younger Johann Beer (1655–1700) was an adept narrator, but his works, rediscovered in the late 1920s by Richard Alewyn, have unquestionably been overestimated. It is indeed possible to open one of his novels at any point and to be struck immediately by the amusing, fresh, and lively nature of the narration. Unfortunately the excitement does not last; Beer is incapable of constructing an extended epic narration. He tells a thousand stories, often very charming, but sometimes silly and unnecessarily coarse. Among the approximately twenty novels Alewyn has credited to him, a difficult task in view of Beer's many pseudonyms, the best example of his talents is the double novel *German Winter Nights* (*Teutsche Winternächte*, 1682) and *The Amusing Summer Days* (*Die kurzweiligen Sommertäge*, 1683).

Unlike Grimmelshausen and Beer, Christian Weise (1648–1708) pursued specifically nonliterary goals in his works. They were quite popular in his time, especially *The Three Worst Archfools in the Whole World* (*Die drei ärgsten Erznarren in der ganzen Welt*, 1672). The book was considered both entertaining and instructive, as was intended by the author. A young nobleman with his tutor and other companions sets out on a journey to find the three greatest fools in the world. The journey actually serves the purpose of educating the young man toward a worldly, practical, or, in seventeenth-century terms, "political" (*politisch*) form of life. From an artistic point of view, the novel has little value. Awkwardly and tediously narrated, it is made up of banal details strung together. Its importance, as with Weise's other works, lies in its reception. Not only did the public enjoy the novels, but other authors, in particular the talented Johann Riemer (1648–1714), were stimulated by them. They laid the foundation for the so-called political novel.

None of the seventeenth-century novel types can be applied to Christian Reuter's (1665–1712) *Schelmuffsky* (1696–97). "Whoever reads this book without becoming enraptured in some way is a Philistine and can certainly be found among the characters," Clemens Brentano wrote. Brentano, along with the other Romanticists Achim von Arnim, Joseph Görres, and the Brothers Grimm, thought highly of the book. The narrator and hero is a braggart and liar who comically exaggerates and distorts reality, all the while caricaturing and criticizing society. But the work cannot compare to Grimmelshausen's *Simplicissimus*. The tradition of the novel broke off once again, and many decades elapsed before a work of similar quality reappeared in Germany.

2 / Goethe and His Contemporaries

The Novel Depicts Man's Inner Story

The Age of Goethe, a period of exceptional achievement in the history of the German novel, began with Christoph Martin Wieland in the mid-1760s, soon found its foremost representative in Johann Wolfgang von Goethe, and was still alive in the late 1790s with Jean Paul, Friedrich Hölderlin, and Novalis. The works of Goethe and his contemporaries cannot be seen in connection with the German novel of the seventeenth century but are related to changing social conditions in eighteenth-century Europe and are expressions of the new spirit and ideals of the time. To be sure, the novels of the past century were still read into the mid-1700s, but they had no influence on future artistic developments. The novels of the Age of Goethe were products of the modern spirit and thought.

Those scholars who emphasize literary continuity and development through the centuries have shown considerable concern about the period between the great seventeenth-century novels and the Age of Goethe, that is, from approximately Lohenstein's *Arminius* (1689) to Wieland's *Don Sylvio* (1764). In *The Gallant Novel* (*Der galante Roman*, 1961) the critic Herbert Singer is disturbed by the existence of a "gaping hole" between these works. In his estimation literary historians have either tried to cover up the gap by means of "clever chapter divisions" or have bridged it in a makeshift fashion by referring to Johann Gottfried Schnabel's *The Isle of Felsenburg* and Christian Fürchtegott Gellert's *The Life of the Swedish Countess G.* But despite an exhaustive search through the popular fiction of the era, Singer was not able to discover a single important work or author. In his introduction to *The German Novel between Baroque and Rococo* (*Der deutsche Roman zwischen Barock und Rokoko*, 1963), he is forced to admit that it proved to be "impossible . . . to establish that hypothetical straight line" by means of which he had hoped to "connect the seventeenth-century novel with that of the Goethe era."

The researcher Marianne Speigel's (*Der Roman und sein Publikum im früheren achtzehnten Jahrhundert, 1700–1767*, 1967) proud claim to have closed the gap by applying sociological criticism is bewildering. Proceeding from the known fact that we have no novels other than popular fiction—so-called *Trivialromane* or *Unterhaltungsromane*—from the early eighteenth century, Spiegel argues that since this genre is "primarily determined by the wishes, favorite themes, and values of the reading public, . . . the reader becomes the focus of interest." But even if her demand that the "development of the novel must be determined according to reader reception" were to be met, the question as to how the gap would be closed remains unanswered. Popular fiction does not become original merely because a different method of study is applied. Literary historians can occupy themselves at most tangentially with light fiction, even if the same material is of great consequence to the literary sociologist. Singer's conclusion, which Spiegel tried to avoid by use of a different method, is indeed correct: "We must be content to register a gap, a 'missing link,' in the tradition of the German novel." Another scholar, Wolfgang Kayser, describes the situation accurately when he states that "for many decades the novel sinks . . . to the level of light entertainment" (*Entstehung und Krise des modernen Romans*, 1954).

But why must a continuous development from one literary phase to another be established at all? In their search for continuity, literary historians have often overlooked or forgotten the relationship between German literature and European developments. It is no coincidence that the new era begins with a man as well read and versed in foreign languages as Wieland. Important stimuli from other countries, particularly from England, preceded the rise of the eighteenth-century German novel. Furthermore, the missing link is hardly surprising if one takes the entire history of the German novel into account. Its beginnings cannot even be determined with certainty, and after Jörg Wickram the tradition is abruptly discontinued. Almost ninety years separate Wickram's *The Gold Thread* (1557) from Philipp von Zesen's *The Adriatic Rosemund* (1645). Thus the seven and one-half decades which seem so strangely barren to Singer had already been exceeded once before.

The popular fiction which flourished in the late seventeenth and early eighteenth centuries is difficult to classify, but certain types of novels reflective of the general interests and inclinations of the readers can be identified. At first, fiction was dominated by the so-called gallant novel (*galanter Roman*); these were love stories, but with neither the heroic adventures and poetic qualities nor the emphasis on constancy and loyalty typical of the earlier courtly-historical novel. Instead, the gallant novels concentrated on amusing confusions and mix-ups and exploited opportunities for frivolities. Among the prominent authors were August Bohse (1661–1742), who wrote over twenty novels, Christian Friedrich Hunold (1681–1721), whose four novels appeared in many editions, and Leonhard Rost (1688–1727), with at least nine novels to his credit. The titles illustrate the themes: *The Lovers' Jealousy* (*Die Eifersucht der Verliebten*, Bohse 1689), *The Labyrinth of Love* (*Der Liebe Irrgarten*, Bohse 1696), and *The Hermit in Love* (*Der verliebte Eremit*, Rost 1711).

The adventure novel soon became as widely circulated as the gallant novel. In 1719, Daniel Defoe's *Robinson Crusoe*, the most successful work of the century, was published in English. By the following year, several German translations had already appeared, and countless imitations quickly followed. But that which characterized the genuine *Robinson Crusoe*, the combination of adventure and morality, was almost universally lost. In order to increase sales, travelogues were often falsely advertised as "Robinsonades." The travel novel (*Reiseroman*) had long been popular, ever since the age of exploration had widened the horizons of many Europeans and daring seamen had taken the place of wandering craftsmen and itinerant scholars. Readers liked stories about those who had gone to sea, seen foreign lands, and become acquainted with exotic peoples. Such adventurers could acquire fantastic treasures on their journeys and return to their homeland with great wealth, but they could just as easily meet with accidents, be shipwrecked, taken prisoner, plundered, or murdered.

Defoe's famous story of a shipwrecked man is a re-creation of man's ascent from homeless wanderer to superior master of a relatively secure domestic existence. The author's main concern is the psychological development of his hero. The island upon which Robinson Crusoe is cast remains to the end a place of exile, an isle of banishment, and to the end Crusoe continues to hope for rescue and a return to civilized society. Yet he succeeds in overcoming his initial desperation and in accepting his situation as a reality which places certain tasks before him. He adopts an ideal of the time: to be content with little and to bear misfortune with grace. At the same time he becomes a pious man, which gave the book particular value in the eyes of Defoe's readers. Defoe's gift for psychological characterization is revealed in the depiction of Robinson Crusoe's emotional vacillations and the gradual strengthening of his will. Furthermore, the novel exemplifies the new eighteenth-century world view: a trust in man's powers of reason and in his practical abilities, qualities which enable him to be self-sufficient and distinguish him as the master of creation. In the many imitations and adaptations of *Robinson Crusoe*, these vital elements were forgotten.

The only German work among the mass of "Robinsonades" which further develops the problems presented by Defoe and also stands out as a noteworthy accomplishment with regard to artistic form is Johann Gottfried Schnabel's (1692–ca. 1752) *The Isle of Felsenburg* (*Die Insel Felsenburg*, 1731–43). The work appeared in four parts, the first of which is the most valuable and complete in itself; in the twentieth century it has generally been published alone. In its time the novel had great relevance; Goethe read it in his youth and it was known to all of Schnabel's contemporaries. Although Schnabel like Defoe bases his novel on a shipwreck, he writes not of one man's island existence but of an entire island community. More than three hundred descendants of an original shipwrecked pair, together with others who join them later from Europe, live in isolation on the Isle of Felsenburg. Within the course of the novel each person who originally came from Europe relates his own life story, which always begins in Europe and ends on the island. By intertwining the events narrated, that is, by interrupting them at critical points and continuing them later, the impression is created that the life stories are connected in intricate ways. Events far removed from one another in time and space are juxtaposed to create a unified picture of the tensions between the continent and the island, thereby reflecting a contrast in ideas as well.

The Isle of Felsenburg begins with the story of Eberhard Julius, the narrator of the novel. After giving the particulars of his childhood, youth, and education, he introduces the main plot by explaining the importance of a letter he received in Leipzig, dated May 1, 1725. On the basis of this letter, which promises that a secret will be divulged, Eberhard Julius hurriedly leaves for Amsterdam, where a ship waits to take him across the equator and past St. Helena to the Isle of Felsenburg. This is the "promised land" to which Eberhard has been summoned by his great-granduncle, Albertus Julius, who reigns there as sovereign prince. Its secret is gradually revealed to Eberhard: it is the location of an ideal society.

Beginning with Eberhard's landing, the novel functions on three levels: it presents his direct impressions, often accompanied by personal opinions; objective descriptions of the conditions on Felsenburg; and accounts of the history of the island community and of the lives of its inhabitants. Albertus Julius, the patriarch and last survivor of the shipwreck in 1646, is the primary witness to the development of the Felsenburg community. The recounted story of his youth and the background stories of others who later came to Felsenburg illuminate the miserable and oppressive conditions in Europe: persecution, intrigues, dangers, and suffering. Because the unethical practices of the corrupt and sinful are allowed to flourish in Europe, the honest, upright people of Felsenburg had difficulty establishing themselves there. After overcoming hardships at the outset, they have no other wish but to spend their lives on the island in "peace and tranquillity." They live in freedom, equality, and brotherhood; neither class distinctions nor a monetary economy exist. They are filled with a spirit of love, are committed to their marriage partners and to God, and fully respect the special status of Albertus Julius. Unlike Robinson Crusoe, they do not wish to return to Europe and carefully protect their island from outside intrusion. When Albertus's sons sight passing ships, their mother warns, "Let them go, my children, since we do not know whether they are good or bad people." Albertus later succinctly states, "It is my wish that none of my children ever set foot on European soil." Contact with the outside world is only established when necessary—

when islanders need to find a spouse or when craftsmen are brought from Europe. To those stranded there as well as to those who voluntarily joined the community, Felsenburg is a blessed asylum. "To the end of my days I will thank God for bringing me to such a place" ends one of the typical life stories.

Literary research has long pointed out thematic similarities between the *Continuatio* of Grimmelshausen's *Simplicissimus* and *The Isle of Felsenburg*, but the influence which the earlier work may have had on Schnabel has not been determined. Though it is possible that the *Continuatio* may have provided the decisive stimulus for Schnabel's island refuge, it is more likely that it was only one of a number of models, including Defoe's *Robinson Crusoe* and other contemporary writings. In any case, the island existence of the aging Simplicius was a literary prototype which proved to be productive throughout European literature. The question as to whether an island should be a place of exile (as in *Robinson Crusoe*) or of refuge raises problems which allow for different solutions. Interestingly, both Grimmelshausen and Schnabel condemned Europe and declared the island to be a refuge, but their times were far too different to justifiably speak of similar philosophies, and their island sanctuaries served entirely different purposes.

Just as the possible thematic influence of Grimmelshausen on Schnabel must be considered, one cannot overlook the structural similarities between *The Isle of Felsenburg* and the seventeenth-century novel. The use of life histories in the construction of a complex narration is reminiscent of courtly-historical novels; the short time period of the main plot can be considerably expanded by this method. Despite Schnabel's seventeenth-century structuring and his strikingly outdated language, *The Isle of Felsenburg* is a modern work and belongs to the new age. The theme is part of the eighteenth century, the century of the French Revolution and the American Constitution. Schnabel gives shape to the progressive ideas of the time in an imaginary society and at an imaginary location; his remote Isle of Felsenburg serves not as an escape from the world, as in Grimmelshausen's work, but exists for the purpose of a new and better life. The broadening of the narrative time through the inclusion of the characters' past histories suggests the historical development of a new society and reflects the conflict between the old and new eras.

The new era could not have been more than a dream to the author himself. Schnabel spent his entire life under oppressive conditions. At the age of two he lost his parents. He may well have experienced much of what his fictional characters relate, including a childhood spent with irresponsible relatives as well as insurmountable difficulties in finding a secure and satisfying means of existence. During the writing of *The Isle of Felsenburg* he was employed as a court barber and valet in Stolberg. His whereabouts in his later years (after 1743) as well as the year of his death remain unknown.

Utopian principles also underlie Johann Michael von Loën's (1694–1776) long-neglected novel *The Upright Man at Court (Der redliche Mann am Hofe*, 1740). Goethe, who was Loën's grandnephew, described the work as a "didactic novel" which was "well-received because it demanded morality from courts where cleverness alone prevailed (*Dichtung und Wahrheit*, Book Two). The structure and style of the novel are basically conservative; as in the seventeenth-century courtly-historical novel, the story of separated lovers is a central structural element and inserted life histories interrupt and retard the action. Only five such discourses are included, however, and the novel is basically uncomplicated and easy to read, in keeping with the "didactic" intentions of the author. The main plot develops without the intervention of a narrator, as if it were a true story, and there is only one subplot.

In contrast to the traditional structure, Loën's theme is political and progressive: an individual of honest conviction can bring reform to a "thoroughly corrupt world." This challenge far surpasses the ideas presented by Schnabel in *The Isle of Felsenburg*. Whereas the honest people on Felsenburg escape the dangers of European society by isolating themselves in a place which they carefully close off to outsiders, Loën's "upright man" is active and successful amid the evils of society. The political philosophy expressed reflects the optimism of the early Enlightenment, the belief in the power of reason and in man's ability to shape his world.

According to Loën, one man—entirely on his own—has the capacity to assert himself as a moral force in a world whose values he rejects. This man is the Count of Rivera, an exemplary eighteenth-century personality in appearance, character, and education, as well as in his influence on others. When the King of Aquitania summons him to the court and appoints him chamberlain, he has been living on his country estate "in sweetest peace." The invitation to the court is not welcomed, but is "completely contrary to his wishes. He loved his freedom, his books, and country life. . . . What should I do at court, he asked himself, where one mocks the simplicity that I love, and where one considers no traits to be more despicable than honesty and virtue? Oh no! My beloved soil, you give me more joy than all the luxury of the court and all the false superiority of its blind worshippers." He embodies the apolitical and unambitious man who has no desire to possess or wield power. But a respected friend helps to convince him that he can find contentment by "helping others to become content," by courageously arming himself "against evil and tyranny and fighting for the rights of man." Also, he realizes that his own character does not have to change or suffer as a result of service at court. This is of primary significance to the design of the novel. The hero neither develops, nor adapts, nor changes; in the end he is the same "upright man" he was in the beginning.

As opposed to the count's extreme steadfastness, the people he encounters at court are characterized by their instability and educability; this is the prerequisite for the count's success in reforming the state. Because the King of Aquitania is "not entirely of a bad nature" and his minister is weak but not evil, the count can find room for change, even if his success is at first limited. Eventually, as a result of his virtue and wise advice, the land "blooms with prosperity," the effect of "vices which had previously poisoned the court" is lessened, and the monarch becomes a "paragon of justice, goodness, and order." At the end of the novel the count is the land's most powerful minister; he is granted the title, coat of arms, and privileges of a duke.

The central figure in the novel's love story, the Countess of Monteras, is also a model of integrity. She and Rivera, in accordance with the traditional pattern, fall in love at first sight, but the relationship is interrupted, and they must endure suffering and separation before the final joyous reunion. The disruptive element here is the king, who wishes to marry the countess. Although Rivera, as a loyal subject of the king, suppresses his own feelings and yields to the king, his life is nevertheless endangered for a long period of time by the king as well as by others at the court. Throughout the ordeal, the countess displays exemplary behavior; she rejects the king and withdraws from the court. Loën writes of her, "the Countess of Monteras is a young lady of an honorable and delicate disposition, who disdained the throne in order to save her favors for a count whom, on account of his virtues, she considered to be more worthy." In the end the king is prepared to consent to marry a princess of equally high birth. The conduct of the Countess of Monteras has a decisive influence on both the king and the count toward a resolution of their conflict. The king learns to understand that his will is subject to the countess's feelings which he must respect, and the count in turn learns that he cannot sacrifice his love for the sake of allegiance to the king. Nor can he disregard his own emotions.

By depicting the virtuous count and the steadfast, self-assured countess, Loën demonstrates a positive concept of man which he sees as the basis for social reform. In addition to this concept of man and human relations, he expresses in detail other ideas which he considers central to the reorganization of the state. They are presented to the reader in two forms: through the description of a social utopia within the novel and by means of an appendix entitled "Free Thoughts—on the Improvement of the State." The essence of the utopia is revealed by its name—Christianopolis. It is a small colony, located within the domain of the fictitious King of Argilia. This location within the borders of a political state distinguishes it from all other European social utopias which—from Thomas More to Schnabel's *The Isle of Felsenburg*—were conceived on remote islands. By virtue of its proximity to the rest of society, Christianopolis not only provides a refuge to outcasts and the world-weary but also serves as a stimulus for reform and as a model for the entire state. Christianopolis is integrated into the plot by the count's visit there; he hopes to imitate the utopia in his own state of Aquitania. Loën dedicates almost all of chapter 11 to the founding of the community and the lifestyle of its inhabitants. The practicalities—clearing the woods, building houses and roads, and supplying water—are as important to Loën as the spiritual bonds within the society. He is particularly concerned that the community be open to all nationalities and religions: "One saw all types of men and sects living quietly together."

In "Free Thoughts," the appendix, Loën outlines in detail his criticism of contemporary conditions. All classes and institutions are denounced, with criticism always accompanied by concrete examples. In the first section on royal courts, Loën deplores the excessive expenditures of courts which support a nobility living in leisure and luxury. He also regrets the surplus of idle state officials and servants who are a source of disturbance and confusion. In other sections he discusses the corruption of the system of justice, the failures of the police, the neglected state of the military, and the foolishness of the scholars. He depicts so many problems, some having such deep roots, that the novel's contention that one man can bring about change on a grand scale hardly seems defensible. But Loën insists on the possibility of improvement, as evidenced by the title of his appendix and by his practical suggestions. He claims that the "improvement of the state is by no means as difficult as one might think." Although Loën wrote "Free Thoughts" as an appendix and had it published separately, he did consider it part of the novel and integrated it in a unique fashion. According to the fictional plot, the count is the author of "Free Thoughts," and the essay is mentioned twice within the novel.

A remarkable aspect of *The Upright Man at Court* is that Loën includes skeptical views which would seem at first glance to undermine or contradict the work's idealistic statement. As a prime example, the King of Argilia, who supports and protects Christianopolis, regards the count's "Free Thoughts" with skepticism. He explains that "the suggestions would be valid," if it were not for an insurmountable obstacle, namely, "man himself." Man "opposes . . . his own well-being and hurls himself deliberately, as it seems, to destruction." Thus the utopian theme of the novel is placed in doubt. Such doubts and reservations are not isolated aberrations but an integral part of the work; by no means does optimism alone reign in *The Upright Man at Court*. It is true that the novel ends harmoniously—this was mandated by literary tradition—but the awareness of the corrupt nature of the world forms a necessary counterpart to the idealistic theme. Accordingly, the count finds himself subject to the greatest perils, uncertainties, and difficulties throughout the novel. He is persecuted for his ideas, and his virtues bring him into danger. Even at the end of the novel, after he has achieved extraordinary successes, he is forced to flee the kingdom, and a long period of time elapses before he can finally return to realize his goals in Aquitania. This demonstrates that the state to which Rivera dedicates himself is a terrifying institution. His undertaking is always accompanied by danger and risks, and the problem of survival is a continuous one. Loën's novel focuses on the question of how the dangerous state can be improved. It is not simply a matter of the hero's survival but, above all, of his success in changing the state. For the modern reader, *The Upright Man at Court* and its appendix is a work of incontestable merit.

However, the eighteenth-century public was more attracted to the novels of Samuel Richardson (1689–1761): *Pamela* (1740), *Clarissa* (1747), and *Grandison* (1753). The subject matter, particularly in the first novel, *Pamela, or Virtue Rewarded*, was largely responsible for the impact. The perseverance of the servant girl Pamela in resisting seduction by her master made for suspenseful reading, and her reward was a satisfying confirmation of middle-class morality. Also, Pamela's social rise through marriage created a sensation. But Richardson's literary contribution and his influence on his successors is primarily due to the new form of epistolary novel which he created in *Pamela* and developed further in *Clarissa*. Letters do not simply serve as communication between correspondents, but, as a means of self-expression, they reflect the nature and course of an individual's emotions which become more heightened and refined by the very act of writing. Pamela becomes more aware of the nuances of her own feelings as she attempts to describe them in letters. Furthermore, by having the heroine speak for herself, Richardson lends credibility to the expressed sentiments. As the author he seems to step back completely, thereby letting the reader form his own comprehensive picture from the various subjective statements. Events in the outside world are visible only as reflected in the letters; the author concentrates not on the occurrences themselves but on how they affect the individual. The method of narration in *Clarissa* has been called "polyperspective,"[1] because Richardson distributes the narrative perspective among several different letter-writers. *Clarissa* is considered to be his best novel.

Richardson's influence on German literature resulted not only in the adoption of the epistolary novel but also in the expansion and intensification of an atmosphere of sentimentality. The origins of this atmosphere cannot be precisely determined; many influences from outside of Germany came together to promote its growth and development. Within Germany, pietistic thought and its gradual secularization had long since laid ground for the influx of sentimentality. There is no doubt that Richardson contributed to promoting the sentimental atmosphere; at the same time, the fact that this atmosphere already existed in Germany can be seen as one reason for his overwhelming popularity. The German reader was already familiar with sentimental literature by French authors. Novels such as *La Princesse de Clèves*

(1678) by Marie-Madeleine de La Fayette, *Manon Lescaut* (1731) and *Histoire de M. Cleveland* (1731–39) by Antoine-François Prévost, and *La Vie de Marianne* (1731) by Pierre Marivaux had prepared the way for Richardson.

In England the appearance of *Pamela* evoked a direct reaction which was also to be of the utmost literary significance in Germany: approximately a half-year later Henry Fielding (1707–1754) published a parody entitled *An Apology for the Life of Mrs. Shamela Andrews*, and shortly thereafter, his first novel, *The History of the Adventures of Joseph Andrews and of His Friend Mr. Abraham Adams* (1742) appeared. Fielding, who had previously written only comedies, including many successful farces, was repulsed by the questionable virtue of Pamela. The entire style of her unbelievable and, as he saw it, calculating self-analysis provoked him. By his mocking rejection of Richardson's book he achieved a major breakthrough in narrative style.

Fielding begins *Joseph Andrews* as a parody on Richardson. The hero Joseph, a servant boy who is introduced as Pamela's brother, informs her in two letters that he has withstood attempts at seduction by the lady of the house, choosing instead to preserve his chastity. For his virtue Joseph is dismissed from service. But the novel soon frees itself from its original satirical purpose and develops a life of its own. When Joseph Andrews sets out on extended travels after his dismissal, the author becomes overwhelmed by the world to be explored and by the vitality of his fictional characters. Indeed, the book is "Written in Imitation of the Manner of Cervantes, Author of Don Quixote," as Fielding tells us on the title page. His knowledge of Cervantes seems to have influenced the parodistic beginning. It has also influenced the transition to a broad epic form and to a style of narration determined by a narrator who is fully aware of his own position as narrator. *Joseph Andrews* marks the beginning of a totally new form of the novel, which reaches its pinnacle with Fielding's most famous novel *The History of Tom Jones, a Foundling* (1749).

In the introductory chapters to the eighteen books into which he divides *Tom Jones*, Fielding has the narrator discuss his principles of narration in the form of a gay, witty debate with future readers and critics. These chapters are of incomparable importance to the history of the novel. They demonstrate Fielding's discovery of the fictitious narrator. This discovery is intimately bound to the historical era in which it originated. The eighteenth century recognized the worth of the individual and learned to view the feeling, thinking "I" as a determining power. As Käthe Friedemann explains in her book *The Role of the Narrator in the Epic* (*Die Rolle des Erzählers in der Epik*, 1910), the personal narrator—evaluating, feeling, and observing—symbolizes "the theory of cognition recognized since Kant, namely, that we do not know the world as it is, but as it is filtered through the medium of an observer."

By recognizing that the author was not simultaneously the narrator but rather invented a narrator through whom he could speak, Fielding won new freedom and independence. The narrator of *Tom Jones* is involved in a playful game with everyone: the reader, the critics, the fictional characters, and, above all, his own position. As he sees it, his position as narrator justifies his playfulness as well as his independence from any critical authority: "for as I am, in reality, the founder of a new province of writing, so I am at liberty to make what laws I please therein. And these laws, my readers, whom I consider as my subjects, are bound to believe in and to obey." In order to persuade the readers to accept the role forced upon them, the narrator assures them that "I am, indeed, set over them for their own good only, and was created for their use, and not they for mine. Nor do I doubt, while I make their interest the great rule of my writings, they will unanimously concur in supporting my dignity, and in rendering me all the honour I shall deserve or desire" (II, 1). The fictitious narrator requires a fictitious reader, who is also the author's creation. Whereas Richardson, by means of his tone, directed his writing towards a definite group of readers—the Puritan family—Fielding gives the impression that the narrator shapes his reader by giving him information and explanations, always being careful to keep the reader's spirits high. Occasionally the narrator appeals to the reader's cleverness, and under special circumstances he prepares him by means of obvious hints. The reader, even if he is regarded as a "subject"—this attitude is derived from Cervantes—receives friendly and obliging care, and there is no question that narrator and reader are on good terms with each other.

By contrast, the narrator's relationship with his critics is most strained. His irritability cannot be overheard, as when he labels the critics "reptiles." For a "little reptile of a critic," he says, to "presume to find fault" with any of the novel's parts "without knowing the manner in which the whole is connected and before he comes to the final catastrophe, is a most presumptuous absurdity." He admits that he has used strong language to describe the critics, but claims that there is no other word which is "at all adequate to express the difference between an author of the first rate, and a critic of the lowest" (X, 1). As proudly and arrogantly as the author proclaims his superiority, he is nevertheless acutely aware that it is endangered. He is wary of the ignorant and hasty critics, whom he opposes from the beginning by taking the offensive. What worries him is that they will make judgments without possessing an overview of the work—Fielding knew that his novel was skillfully designed—and that they will display a lack of understanding in their assessment of the characters.

Since Fielding wants to portray "Human Nature" (I, 1) in his work, his characters are not perfect; their very lack of perfection is an expression of his main artistic objective. Therefore, the narrator warns critics "not to condemn a character as a bad one, because it is not perfectly a good one" (X, 1). The imperfections in the character of Tom Jones are often underscored in the novel as "wantonness, wildness, and want of caution" (III, 7), and towards the end he is even labeled a "rogue" (XVII, 1). Not only Tom Jones is vulnerable to criticism, but the esteemed Squire Allworthy also has his weaknesses, and they are explicitly pointed out. Fielding's new form of the novel, which began as a parody of Richardson's novel of virtue, derives its vitality from a view of man which includes human mistakes and weaknesses and from a philosophy which denies the precept that virtue leads to rewards and sin to ruin. With these considerations, Fielding opened a new, wide horizon, an opportunity for the novel to become a serious, respected genre. The form of the modern novel is unthinkable without this horizon.

Fielding had a strong influence on the rise of the novel in the Age of Goethe, particularly on Wieland. Yet the effect of Laurence Sterne (1713–1768) was even more sustained. Whereas Fielding narrates in an epic sequence, Sterne is no longer concerned with linear events but with intervening thoughts and feelings. In his novel *The Life and Opinions of Tristram Shandy, Gentleman* (1760–67) Tristram tells his own story; this, however, does not constitute the plot. In any event, the book gives very little of his life, no more than his procreation, birth, and first years. The uniqueness of Sterne's narrative method lies in the very interruption of the narrative. Digressions are the essence of the narration; they carry the plot forward. As Sterne explains, "In a word, my work is digressive, and it is progressive too, — and at the same time" (I, 22). This results in Tristram's story concluding with an event that took place five years before his birth, that is, the novel ends four years before it begins. Neither plot nor time proceeds in a linear fashion toward a goal or conclusion. This unique style is best described by Sterne when he refers to it as "conversation":

> Writing, when properly managed (as you may be sure I think mine is) is but a different name for conversation: As no one, who knows what he is about in good company, would venture to talk all;—so no author, who understands the just boundaries of decorum and good breeding, would presume to think all: The truest respect which you can pay to the reader's understanding, is to halve this matter amicably, and leave him something to imagine, in his turn, as well as yourself (II, 11).

The narrator's partner in discussion is the reader, who is called upon to participate. As in a real conversation, the subject under discussion is less important than the conversants themselves. How long a topic stays alive depends on the conversants; if they give the conversation a different turn, then the previous topic is simply lost.

Soon after *Tristram Shandy*, Sterne's *Sentimental Journey through France and Italy* (1768) appeared. The richness of sensory impressions is a captivating aspect of the work, but its essence lies in the personal involvement with which Sterne narrates. He used the word "sentimental" to describe it. Sentimental refers to the predominance of feeling in the encounter between the traveler and the world. The narrator introduces a new way of experiencing the world: "Sentimental Journey," a journey of the heart. The sentimental traveler is so sensitive to stimuli and reacts with such intensity that he gives new contours to the world around him.

Oliver Goldsmith's (1728–1774) novel *The Vicar of Wakefield* (1766) also aroused fascination in Germany. Readers were impressed by the vicar's unshakeable faith through all of life's trials and by his untiring efforts to realize his ideals in his direct surroundings.

The influence of English authors on the development of the novel in Germany was substantial. Ironically, it was Richardson, the least respected today, who had the greatest effect. Among the first of the many works influenced by Richardson was Christian Fürchtegott Gellert's (1715–1769) *The Life of the Swedish Countess G. (Das Leben der schwedischen Gräfin von G.*, 1747–48). The novel was highly esteemed by Gellert's contemporaries in Germany as well as in England and France; later, however, its literary quality became the subject of controversy. It has been much discussed by literary historians, but the many opinions expressed have neither improved nor clarified the work. It makes a disunified impression because of conflicts in the author's own mind as well as in the historical situation.

The countess's story begins at a Swedish court, where, in the absence of the count, she is pursued by an unscrupulous, powerful prince. Because she refuses him and maintains her virtue, the count is persecuted. He is banned from the court, sent on a dangerous mission, accused unjustly of having neglected his duties, and finally sentenced to death. Only imprisonment in Russia saves him from execution by his countrymen. The countess, who believes him to be dead, flees to Amsterdam with his best friend, Herr R., whom she eventually marries. The return of the count many years later brings about an irreconcilable conflict which the countess describes: "I was reunited with a man whom I loved extraordinarily, but had to leave a man whom I loved no less." A professor of poetry, rhetoric, and ethics, Gellert seems to have designed the entire background story with its outdated conventions in order to demonstrate the exemplary moral conduct of his characters. He spares the countess from having to make the impossible choice. It is the admirable Herr R. who resolves the conflict by returning his wife to the count: "I hereby entrust my wife to you, and from this moment on I will transform my love into reverence." Because the count is also magnanimous, a complicated arrangement resembling a double marriage is the end result.

Although the countess resumes her marriage with her first husband, her love for her second husband continues; she attributes the propriety of their relationship entirely to him. She would have reestablished her marriage with him following the death of the count, had he not also died shortly thereafter.

The Life of the Swedish Countess G. is in many respects a compendium of the trends and aspirations of the times. It also testifies to the helplessness of its author who was confronted with a Weltanschauung—that of the Enlightenment—which did not allow for the contradictions of life. Gellert does not evade situations that show the shortcomings of the prevailing world view, which called for self-possession at all times (*Gelassenheitsideal*). When the imprisoned count contemplates the possibility of never returning home, he writes, "I saw no more reason for composure but cause enough to despair." Such a statement casts doubt on the validity of the world view underlying the countess's story. The obvious discrepancy between content and world view gives the work the character of an experiment; Gellert may have thought of the novel as an art form in which Weltanschauung as well as human behavior could be examined through experiment and discussion.

Of the many other novels written under Richardson's influence only a few are noteworthy accomplishments. Sophie von La Roche's (1730–1807) *The Story of Fräulein von Sternheim* (*Geschichte des Fräuleins von Sternheim*, 1771) was enormously popular in the 1770s. It is a skillfully arranged epistolary novel in which different letter-writers portray the events from different perspectives. The Storm and Stress generation was particularly fascinated by its "total individualization of character," which is how Wieland, a friend of Sophie von La Roche, describes the book in the preface. The breakthrough of man's true, individual "nature," which the decade of Storm and Stress writers demanded, was acclaimed in La Roche's novel. An excellent example is provided by a ballroom scene in which the heroine, a victim of intrigues, openly displays her defiance for her relatives' plan; they want her to become the mistress of the ruling prince. In front of everyone she quickly leaves the ballroom, tearing off her mask and jewelry and expressing her contempt for the plan to her relatives and the prince. This scene exemplifies an elemental rebellion against customs of the court which are demeaning to the individual.

The new and unique contribution of the novel is its depiction of how the young woman, who is disgraced, persecuted, and finally abducted, resists her misfortune. She reacts actively by involving herself in social work. "I am still able to do good," she states and finds opportunities for social action everywhere—at a school for young girls, helping with family care, or tutoring. "She was not satisfied with good thoughts; all of her convictions had to become action." Her social activity brings benefit to others, but at the same time—and this defines its value within the context of the novel—it also means self-discovery. Her self-image, which is based on the knowledge that she possesses the strength to do meaningful work, allows her to survive and find her own way.

Sophie von La Roche's novel is the first German *Frauenroman* of consequence.[2] Although readers had long been accustomed to women as the title characters in novels, they were surprised to find such an active and independent heroine. All of the previous female title characters had possessed praiseworthy qualities, but there were none like Fräulein von Sternheim. The historical importance and impact of this novel cannot be overlooked. Nevertheless, in general, its style is intolerable to the modern reader. The tastes of the "age of sentiment" influenced every sentence in a way that is often embarrassing. This may be the reason why the themes are not entirely convincing.

The works of Johann Timotheus Hermes (1738–1821) were also widely read. His *Story of Fanny Wilkes* (*Geschichte der Fanny Wilkes*, 1766) was not only modeled after English authors but was also set in England. Hermes's *Sophie's Journey from Memel to Saxony* (*Sophiens Reise von Memel nach Sachsen*, 1770–72) is an epistolary novel in five volumes which depicts burgher life in Germany.

The depths to which the novelistic literature inspired by Richardson declined is demonstrated by Johann Martin Miller's (1750–1814) *Siegwart, a Cloister Story* (*Siegwart, eine Klostergeschichte*, 1776). This flat, lachrymose book brought world fame to its author, was translated into many languages, and rivaled Goethe's *Werther* (1774) in popularity. Anyone who has read it and knows how successful it was in the eighteenth century can place little faith in the general public's taste. Those theories such as Marianne Spiegel's (*Der Roman und sein Publikum*) which claim that literary history should be determined according to reader reception seem absurd when one considers what would have become of the German novel if it had been dependent on such a readership: Goethe's novels would not exist.

At a time when the novels being written did not reflect positively on the tastes of readers, Christoph Martin Wieland (1733–1813) came onto the scene. In his first novel, *Nature's Victory over Schwärmerei or The Adventures of Don Sylvio de Rosalva* (*Der Sieg der Natur über die Schwärmerei oder die Abenteuer des Don Sylvio von Rosalva*, 1764), the narrator speaks in a fashion totally new to German literature. His ironic style, at once playful and witty, wise and insightful, free and independent, is the prerequisite for the presentation of the theme summarized in the novel's title. Though formulated in eighteenth-century language, it is a modern theme, one which is concerned with disillusionment; with the question of appearance vs. reality; with error, delusion, and truth; and with man's freeing himself from deception, whether it be of a personal or general nature. In the entire body of

German literature of that time, no comparable work existed which could have served as Wieland's stimulus or model. His extraordinary accomplishment, long unappreciated and even today seldom fully recognized, becomes evident when one looks at German literature preceding and contemporary to Wieland and realizes his talent could not have developed if he had been dependent on German literary tradition alone.

Like Fielding, whose works he knew well, Wieland was indebted to Cervantes. His narrator as well as his fictional characters makes reference to Don Quixote, thereby indicating to the reader that the story of Don Sylvio should be seen as part of the tradition begun by the most imposing of all European novels. The comparison between Don Sylvio and the Knight of La Mancha illustrates the cultural level to which Wieland laid claim. At the same time, it becomes evident that Wieland did not wish to divorce himself from European literary tradition to assume an independent position, but saw himself in relation to the great works of European literature. They served as his framework and were ever-present as his standard. He incessantly quoted other authors and works, not as a scholar whose references are exact repetitions of the original, but as a playful, imaginative artist whose prose is filled with allusions and hints, with variations, glimmerings, and inferences. Readers well-versed in European literature are thus provided with unending entertainment. Many references can be precisely identified, but others can only be sensed and are difficult to place. From the many allusions to Laurence Sterne, it seems likely that Wieland had read the parts of *Tristram Shandy* that were published at the time. As for his relationship to Alain-René Lesage's famous *Gil Blas*, Wieland left no doubt. He not only used the Spanish backdrop but took names of persons and places (Donna Mencia, Hyacinthe, Dorothea von Jutella, Lirias), plot elements, and character portraits from Lesage's novel.

Don Sylvio begins in a dilapidated castle in a remote Spanish province, where the seventeen-year-old Don Sylvio has been raised by an eccentric aunt. As the narrator comments, the young hero is "only a few steps away from adventures such as had not entered a whirling brain since the days of his countryman, the Knight of La Mancha." We learn more about the young boy's mental state in a chapter entitled "Psychological Considerations." Among the "talents" which nature granted in abundance to Don Sylvio were "an extraordinary sensitivity" and a "strong disposition to tenderness." The narrator explains that "young people of this nature love all ideas which make a lively impression on their heart and awaken passions which, lying in a light slumber, are ready to respond to the slightest sound." If in addition the young people are living "far from the world, in the solitude and simplicity of the countryside," then the effect of fantasy on their spirit is much stronger, for they are forced to "fill in the emptiness," mingling "imagination with feeling, the wondrous with the natural, and falsehood with truth." Don Sylvio, true to this description, does not know how to distinguish between the imaginary world of literature and sensory impressions of the "natural" world. He does not doubt the veracity of the "most unbelievable things"; to him, the "poetic and enchanted world" had displaced the world of reality.

In this frame of mind, Don Sylvio discovers books of fairy stories stored away in the castle. He reads them secretly, since his aunt does not approve of them, and soon his thoughts and feelings are totally immersed in a magical world he considers to be real. He imagines encounters with fairies, nymphs, and dwarfs, believing himself to be the recipient of their messages, promises, and requests. One morning, while chasing after a blue butterfly, he finds a precious medallion in the grass with a portrait inside of a young woman of incomparable beauty. He immediately falls in love with her, concluding that she is a princess who has been transformed into a butterfly; he must set her free and win her for himself. He sets off from the castle with his loyal servant Pedrillo, who is modeled after Cervantes's Sancho Panza, to find the butterfly and break the spell. In one of the reflections accompanying the plot, the narrator interprets Don Sylvio's behavior by referring to two types of reality which exist: "things . . . which really do exist outside of us" and "others which exist only in our minds." The second have the same effect as the first; indeed, they provide the "motivation for most actions of the human race." For example, when Alexander marched on India, he was following an "illusion just as insignificant" as Don Sylvio when he sets out to break the spell of the blue butterfly. At least Don Sylvio "has the advantage that his illusion did no harm, while the illusion of the conqueror of Asia brought misfortune to half the world."

The princess is actually a young, wealthy widow, Dona Felicia, who had lost the medallion containing a picture of her grandmother. After a series of adventures Don Sylvio and his companion reach the nearby estate where she lives with her brother Don Eugenio. Though Don Sylvio is enraptured by Dona Felicia and realizes that the portrait closely resembles her, he feels an obligation to remain loyal to his fairy princess. Felicia, who has fallen in love with Don Sylvio, tries to free him from his illusions and is supported by all those present at the estate. Displaying no mockery, scorn, or contempt but only patience and understanding, they bring the young hero to reason. The philosopher and scientist Don Gabriel assumes a particularly productive and active role in convincing Don Sylvio of the truth. The transforming power of love and a two-year journey through Europe, which serves to fill with real ideas the empty space left in Don Sylvio's mind after the "banishment of the fairies," bring his talents to full fruition. It is reminiscent of the courtly-historical novel that *Don Sylvio* ends with several marriages, including of course that of Don Sylvio and Felicia.

The plot itself is only moderately impressive, but Wieland used it to elucidate what was important to him: the mental process. It is suspenseful at every stage because of the manner in which it is narrated; the narrator conveys a sense of urgency and excitement, giving us the impression that highly significant psychological truths are being revealed. Indeed, Wieland's use of fairy-tale motifs is a gracious, charmingly rococo means of disguising a serious theme which affected him personally: the healing of the *Schwärmer*. The complex concept of *Schwärmerei* (dreaming, fantasizing, exultation) was of utmost existential importance in that era. It refers to a capability for fascination which results in deceptions. The reasons for *Schwärmerei* as well as the psychology behind overcoming it are presented in *Don Sylvio* as fascinating themes. Wieland's hope, expressed in the title, that the *Schwärmer* could be cured by a "victory of nature" remains unclear or at least open to discussion. The novel does not provide an explanation for the title. A possible interpretation would be to substitute the word "reality" for "nature" in the phrase "victory of nature," but even that is not satisfactory. It seems that the title phrase "victory of nature" should be seen as a poetic expression and not as a formula to be further analyzed.

Influenced as Wieland was by the great novels of the past, his *Don Sylvio* in turn served as a model for German novels which followed. That Wieland had a decisive influence on Goethe has to date been little recognized or appreciated by literary historians. Yet the similarities in plot as well as overall design between *Don Sylvio* and Goethe's *Wilhelm Meister's Apprenticeship* cannot be overlooked. An investigation of those elements which Goethe borrowed from Wieland's first novel reveals surprising insights into Goethe's creative process. Even more far-reaching and difficult to determine is Wieland's importance to the generation of young Romanticists. Whether one wishes to see Novalis's "blue flower" (*blaue Blume*) as reminiscent of the blue butterfly; or finds similarities between *Don Sylvio* and Ludwig Tieck's *Franz Sternbald's Wanderings* (1798), Friedrich Schlegel's *Lucinde* (1800), and E. T. A. Hoffmann's *The Golden Pot* (*Der goldene Topf*, 1814); or simply compares the "romantic youths who roam all over the world searching for an ideal" with Wieland's young heroes, Wieland had an undeniably important effect on future authors.[3]

However, none of the later authors could match the free, cheerful mood, the light, refreshing quality of *Don Sylvio*. It was intended to be an amusing book and to stimulate laughter or else it would have, according to Wieland, "failed its purpose." Within the novel specific mention is made of medications which "split the sides" and of the wish for an "investigation into the diverse physical, moral, and political advantages . . . which human society could derive from writings . . . which bring about laughter." But Wieland's own life at that time was full of painful episodes. He was fully aware of the contrast between his personal situation and his literary product and wrote that "one would be astonished at how I was able to write such a humorous book while in such emotional anguish."[4] *Don Sylvio* did not originate from biographical conditions which were integrated into or reflected in the work but was created in opposition to such conditions, in resistance to life's oppression.

Wieland had already begun his most famous novel, the *Story of Agathon (Geschichte des Agathon*, 1766–67, 1773, 1794), in the early 1760s, but he interrupted work on it during the creation of *Don Sylvio*, probably because he did not yet feel equal to its demands. Of course, at that time he could hardly have realized the magnitude of these demands, particularly since the novel was still so little respected as a literary form in Germany that its use, in general, meant a willingness to sacrifice rather than strive for high quality. What motivated Wieland to avail himself of this inferior genre, which had sunk to an extraordinarily low level since the decline of baroque culture, is difficult to explain. It is certain that he wanted to reach a broad public, and he knew that the demand for fiction was growing. But can we assume that he really knew so little about the public's tastes and expectations, intellect and education? In any case, his disappointment over the reception of *Agathon* does indicate that he misjudged the public.

A highly qualified authority, the contemporary dramatist and critic Gotthold Ephraim Lessing (1729–1781), confirms the fact that it was *Agathon's* new and unique nature which prevented it from being noticed or understood. In his *Hamburg Dramaturgy* (section 69, 29 December 1767), Lessing quotes a long passage from *Agathon* and remarks that this work, "unquestionably among the most excellent of our century, seems to have been written much too early for the German public. In France or England it would have caused a sensation; the name of the author would be on everyone's lips. But we Germans? We have it, and we leave it at that." Lessing expresses his own admiration for the novel and condemns the critics who responded to it with "deep silence" or a "cold and indifferent tone." Calling *Agathon* "the first and only novel for the thinking person with classical taste," he continues, "A novel? We'll give it this title only so that it may attract a few more readers." The few who might be turned away by the term are "not important anyway."

It is characteristic of that period in the history of the German novel that Lessing is not entirely certain whether or not to call *Agathon* a novel; he saw the work as so new and unprecedented that the term did not seem appropriate. The extent to which *Agathon* could be regarded as the first realization of the genre's true potential is expressed in Friedrich Blanckenburg's (1744–1796) *Attempt on the Novel (Versuch über den Roman*, 1774), the first theoretical treatise on the novel in Germany. The only novel other than *Agathon* which Blanckenburg singles out as exemplary is Fielding's *Tom Jones*, but he emphasizes that "Wieland has indisputably taken a further step towards perfection." He saw *Agathon* as the ideal novel, fulfilling every expectation; all novels should be similar to it. Blanckenburg's statements reveal the boldness of Wieland's choice of the novel in the 1760s. The contempt for the genre among Wieland's contemporaries corresponded in fact to the realities of the times; the novels being published were indeed not for the "thinking person with classical taste." Blanckenburg proclaims his "honest" belief that "a novel can provide a very pleasant and very informative pastime, . . . not only for the lady of leisure, but also for the thinking person." Here and elsewhere, Blanckenburg's theories were very much shaped by Lessing. His assessment, for example, that "we probably have no more than two or three such novels, perhaps only one" is almost identical to Lessing's.

Although Blanckenburg's general theories on the novel were not original—he knew that himself—his contribution should not be underestimated. He possessed a decided sensitivity for literary quality and uniqueness and was able to recognize in Wieland's novel the possibilities inherent in a genre long considered inferior. What Blanckenburg stressed as the essence of the novel is the "nature of man, his inner state." He believed that the novel should give emphasis to emotions, thoughts, and feelings and that the plot should be based on the "changes in the mental state" of the characters so the reader can recognize the "effect" of occurrences and events and comprehend "the inner story of man" (*die innere Geschichte des Menschen*). With this description Blanckenburg captured the essence and originality of *Agathon*; the inner story of man as presented in *Agathon* was new to the German novel.

Of course, Wieland made extensive use of literary models; he was quite familiar with European as well as classical literature. Even more important to Wieland than *Tom Jones*—in which Fielding also tells the story of a young man who is deserving of the reader's involvement but without placing emphasis on his inner story—may have been the understanding of human psychology achieved by French novelists. Claude-Prosper Jolyot de Crébillon, with his *Les égarements du coeur et de l'esprit ou mémoires de M. de Meilcour* (1736), could have inspired Wieland, the literary scholar Friedrich Sengle claims, in portraying the psychology of eroticism. The French travel novel, such as François Fénelon's *Les aventures de Télémaque, fils d'Ulysse* (1699), André Michel Ramsay's *Voyages de Cyrus* (1727), and Jean Jacques Barthélemy's *Voyage du jeune Anacharsis en Grèce* (1757–88), may have stimulated Wieland as well, since these travel novels were also *Bildungsromane* and used the backdrop of antiquity. That the Romanticists later accused Wieland of plagiarism was unjust. Wieland did not copy from anyone; nor did he imitate any other authors. Cultural acquisitions became inseparably fused with his own style and were used for his own purposes. His vast knowledge was a source from which he could draw freely, even wastefully, to the benefit and delight of his readers. Neither in German nor in other European literatures had a novel like *Agathon* yet appeared. Both Lessing and Blanckenburg knew this.

As in *Don Sylvio*, the central theme of *Agathon* is the problem of *Schwärmerei*. But *Agathon* is less concerned with overcoming *Schwärmerei* and ending a half-crazed state than with illustrating how the enthusiasm and exultation that accompany *Schwärmerei* serve to liberate one's strengths and illuminate one's existence. Unlike Don Sylvio, Agathon is not simply to be freed from mistaken fancies; he is not merely supposed to forget delusions which originated in remote isolation and to abandon his dreams. Instead, his inclination towards *Schwärmerei* is part of his nature and the prerequisite for his most valuable traits. Life leads him through broad, often questionable realms of experience in which he can grow and develop only because he is a *Schwärmer*; otherwise, these realms would have little meaning for him, and he would react with indifference.

The reader learns that Agathon was raised in Delphi—the novel is set in ancient Greece—and fled at the age of eighteen after a jealous priestess separated him from his beloved Psyche. During flight he found his father, whom he had never known. As the son of this wealthy and respected Athenian citizen, he went to Athens, received citizenship there, and became a pupil and friend of Plato. He quickly achieved a reputation, public offices, and success; he dedicated himself to the good of the republic and was revered by the people, but envious competitors caused his banishment from the city.

The story opens at this point. Forced to leave Greece, Agathon is captured in Thrace by pirates, who take him to Smyrna and sell him as a slave to the rich sophist Hippias. Agathon has few duties in his master's house, a "temple of the most elaborate sensuality." He is welcome to partake in all the refined pleasures of luxury and desire, but prefers to sit alone in the splendid gardens, lost in memories of his youth and in dreams of an ideal future. Since he had intended from the beginning to educate Agathon as his successor, Hippias does not wish to leave him to his own thoughts. He attempts to convince Agathon of his own philosophy. The materialist and skeptic does not, however, succeed in dissuading the idealist from his platonic beliefs; Agathon remains true to his ideals and true to himself. This is the outcome of the first major section of the novel.

The debate between Hippias and Agathon revolves around the question of whether Agathon can live his life in his own way and whether he will achieve happiness. The problem of happiness or well-being (*eudemonia*), in addition to that of *Schwärmerei*, is a theme of the novel. Hippias formulates his assessment of Agathon in their first long discussion:

O young man, I have listened to your digressions long enough. What kind of web of fantasies has the liveliness of your imagination spun? Your soul is suspended in continual enchantment, alternating between tormenting and delightful dreams, and the true state of things remains as hidden from you as the visible world from a blind man. I pity you. . . . Your bearing, your talents entitle you to strive for all the happiness possible in human life. But your way of thinking alone will make you unhappy. Accustomed to seeing nothing but ideal people around you, you will never learn the art of using others to your own advantage. In a world which will know you as little as you know it, you will wander about like an inhabitant of the moon and will never be in the right place other than in the wilderness or in Diogenes' tub.

Agathon reacts to Hippias's lecture with a smile which turns into a laugh after Hippias leaves. He says to himself:

You believe you are telling me something new when you call my way of thinking *Schwärmerei* and proclaim the fate it will bring upon me with the certainty of a prophet. . . . O Hippias, what is it that you call happiness? You will never be capable of knowing what happiness is. . . . Let me always be a *Schwärmer*. . . . Nature has denied you this sensitivity, these inner faculties which define the difference between us. . . . Indeed, men of the world cannot be blamed for thinking of us as somewhat moon-struck; for who would expect them to believe that they lack something that is part of the complete person?

What distinguishes Agathon is his pride, his self-confidence, and his self-knowledge, as well as the certainty of his convictions. In the confrontation of ideas, Wieland has not merely described differing philosophies but has succeeded in creating a conflict between individuals who totally embody these philosophies, who radiate these schools of thought by their very existence, in every word and deed. Debate, reflection, and essay are essential elements of this philosophical novel. Its epic development is not retarded by intellectual discussion and reflection but, on the contrary, is realized therein.

Since Agathon cannot be convinced by means of oratory, Hippias believes himself forced to try other means. He attacks Agathon's virtue in a more direct way by alluring him with an experienced courtesan, the beautiful Danae, whose past remains unknown to Agathon. She succeeds in enchanting the youth; he believes he has found the highest spiritual perfection in her beauty and yields to his feelings and to the fulfillment she offers him. Not only is Agathon transformed by love, but Danae, at first motivated only by vanity and the opportunity to test her charms, is also stirred by a deep affection for Agathon. In the story of their love, Wieland shows himself to be a master of his art. He displays a profound understanding of sensual and spiritual processes as he leads the reader from stage to stage, alternating between reflection and action. Structurally and contextually the love between Agathon and Danae counterbalances the previous discord between Agathon and Hippias. Agathon ends the relationship after Hippias reveals Danae's true occupation and past to him, but his euphoria had already begun to diminish.

Agathon's decision to leave Smyrna and never to see Danae again is strengthened by a favorable opportunity to sail for Syracuse that very day. There, he is told, Plato is highly respected and exercises great influence over the tyrant ruler Dionysius. Agathon immediately fancies himself helping his revered teacher to accomplish the "glorious deed" of "transforming the unrestrained tyrant into a benevolent ruler and bringing happiness to the entire nation." But upon his arrival in Syracuse he finds that Plato has gone again, since Dionysius was receptive to his philosophy for only a short time. The thought that he could have more success than Plato leads Agathon to take advantage of the chance to win Dionysius's favor and to accept his offer to remain at the court as his confidant and advisor.

This situation shows Agathon in a new light; his behavior does not seem to correspond to his previous character traits. He now works carefully, with worldly "restraint and finesse" and "artificial shrewdness." Although this behavior may seem questionable, the danger in condemning it is expressed in a detailed and forceful exposition which focuses on the question of maintaining a consistent personality under changing conditions: "It is impossible . . . that we alone should remain unchanged while everything around us changes." To be sure, in "moral novels" the heroes remain the same—at the age of twenty they are already as perfect as is hardly conceivable for wise men at the age of sixty—but "in life it is different." It is further explained that "we have already seen our hero in different situations, and in each one, due to the influence of circumstances, he was a little different from what he really is." In Delphi he appeared to be a "mere speculative enthusiast," and in the course of time he showed himself to be "a devout *Schwärmer*, a Platonist, a republican, a hero, a Stoic, a sensualist," although he was in fact "none of these." However, of his true character, that part of him which remains constant and will endure the many different changes, "we cannot yet speak."

Agathon's attempt to take action and promote the welfare of the country by means of accommodation and compromise can only succeed for a short time. No matter how much he tries to disregard his own principles and to tolerate lesser evils in order to prevent greater ones, no compromise is sufficient. Certain limits are placed on him anyhow because of the nature of his undertaking: the overall reform of conditions in the land. It is inevitable that he make mistakes in such a situation, particularly since self-love and self-deception play an appreciable role in his decisions from the beginning of his Syracuse endeavor. Eventually he loses Dionysius's favor and is imprisoned. Through the intervention and threats of his friend Archytas in Taranto, he is set free and can leave Sicily.

As was the case when Agathon left Smyrna, a detailed exposition again follows his departure. Discussion revolves around the question of how the failure of Agathon's undertaking in Syracuse affects his character. It is postulated that his knowledge of the world must have led him to lose faith in man and to allow for the possibility that Hippias, whose views are confirmed by experience, may have been correct. But since Agathon's virtue needs "no other advocate" than "his own heart," since his moral values are fused with his entire being, the disenchantment which inevitably will result from his failure in Syracuse can indeed lessen his moral enthusiasm, but it cannot change his character. Wieland does not favor the complete healing of Agathon's *Schwärmerei*. Of course he admits that it is better to be "healthy and without raptures" than to suffer from a "fiery fever." But in the same breath he speaks of the disadvantages of a cure. Just as he previously asked "To the delicate soul, what is love without *Schwärmerei?*" he now emphasizes that virtue without fascination is "a very unattractive thing, lacking luster" and of little use. Wieland is fully aware that he has not developed a logical argument, but rather has done precisely what he defends in the case of his hero: he has made a decision of the heart, which can always be attacked on a rational basis. Therefore, he continually reformulates his position and never finds a convincing ending.

The harmonious conclusion of *Agathon* is clearly unsatisfactory to its author. Wieland brings Agathon to the republic of Taranto, the perfect surroundings for him. Here he is a welcome guest of the wise statesman Archytas, in whose home he again meets his first love Psyche after many years separation. He discovers that she is his sister and the wife of Archytas's son. He is also reunited with Danae. The question as to whether their renewed friendship will again become love is left unanswered. Wieland expresses his discontent with the ending by means of a fictional editor who, from the beginning of the novel, presents the story of Agathon to his readers in the form of an old Greek manuscript. This enables Wieland to provide a critical perspective on and discussion of the narration at many different points in the novel. At the beginning of the last book the editor criticizes the author of the original manuscript. While the story until that point had conformed to the "strictest laws of probability," the last chapter seems improbable and utopian, the result of the Greek author's wish to supply a satisfactory ending and happy future for his hero. The editor declares that his own intentions had already been fulfilled without this last part and that Agathon's further experiences are of no interest to him. Thus the novel would not need a conventional ending but could justifiably remain open. Wieland's fictional editor rejects the concept of teleological narration in the style of Heliodorus which "ends to everyone's satisfaction . . . with joyous rediscovery of lost friends and several marriages." This is a description of the traditional ending in the seventeenth-century courtly-historical novel. Such an ending, which corresponds to a pious view of the world, was no longer convincing to Wieland. But he had no other solution to offer and evidently did not want to risk openly stating that the inner story of his hero could not and did not visibly lead to anything, that it is life itself and thus has no conclusion.

Wieland's *Agathon* testifies to strengths and possibilities in man which are equal to, if not more important than, reason. His fear that the hero might experience a decline in such strengths is stronger than his fear that they could be overabundant. Wieland was evidently convinced that a man of Agathon's nature brings more into the world than the world can return to him. This means an inevitable disparity in his relationship to the world, stemming from the fullness and superiority of his potential which can never be realized.

In his *Attempt on the Novel* (1774), the theorist Blanckenburg, convinced that only a few worthwhile novels existed, outlined the requirements future novels would have to incorporate to satisfy his wishes. In the same year twenty-four-year-old Johann Wolfgang von Goethe (1749–1832) published a "small book" (*Büchlein*)—so-called in the Preface—titled *The Sufferings of Young Werther* (*Die Leiden des jungen Werthers*, revised edition, 1787). *Werther* became one of the most famous novels in the German language. Immediately translated into many languages, it became the most widely read book of the era and fulfilled Blanckenburg's demands. Blanckenburg said that man's inner story consisted of "a series of changing and different mental states." This is precisely the case in "the story of poor Werther." The story is Werther's inner story, and it unfolds before the reader as Werther suffers through a "series of changing and different mental states" while simultaneously describing the process. The theme, language, and style, the characters and their situations as well as the setting are all concentrated on a depiction of inner states which, carefully linked with each other and tightly connected with external occurrences, press toward the ending: Werther's suicide.

The attention the novel received is due in large part to this ending. Suicide had been a much-discussed theme since the Renaissance. Opinions were sharply divided on the question. There were great examples from classical antiquity, and some liberal views were expressed in modern times. But among Christians, suicide was forbidden and punishable. In Jean-Jacques Rousseau's (1712–1778) novel of great passion, *La Nouvelle Héloïse* (1761),

St. Preux, prevented from marrying Julie because of class differences, defended suicide in a long letter but did not actually take his own life. The novel *Werther*, on the other hand, is designed towards self-destruction from the outset. Since Werther's feelings alone are decisive, the consequences are inevitable; his suicide is a result of the absolute nature of his feelings. In his noteworthy review of the novel, Blanckenburg spoke of Werther's "ever-increasing and ever-developing sentimentality." Werther's "heart" (*das Herz*) cannot abandon the object of its love and cannot draw back. By nature Werther is not inclined to exercise restraint, for he considers his heart to be his great treasure to which nothing else can compare.

The epistolary form of the novel corresponds exactly to this content. The only letter-writer is Werther, who communicates his innermost thoughts and feelings to a friend. Toward the end, as his excitement becomes despair, the fictitious editor of Werther's letters takes over. In its narrative objectivity, this report provides an artistic balance to Werther's last, disjointed expressions of passion.

Goethe's readers thought that *Werther* must have some relation to events in the author's life, and Goethe was often asked about possible parallels. An examination of the autobiographical elements which contributed to the conception of the novel is most valuable since, for the first time in the history of the German novel, contemporary life entered directly and recognizably into a novel. It is known that from the end of May to September 11, 1772, Goethe lived in Wetzlar, where, in compliance with his father's wishes, he was to become familiar with the legal profession at the *Reichskammergericht* (Imperial Supreme Court). He was little concerned with this dusty institution of law and instead spent time with a number of young lawyer friends, enjoying the nearby countryside during the pleasant summer months. When he met Lotte Buff (b. 1753) and her fiancé Johann Christian Kestner (b. 1741) at a ball on June 9, he was at first unaware of their engagement. A warm relationship developed between Goethe and the couple. Goethe felt a sincere, unsettling affection for Lotte and made use of every opportunity to be with her. However, his friendship with Kestner was equally sincere. A man of outstanding character, Kestner showed a great deal of understanding for the gifted poet whose nature was so radically different from his own. The fact that Goethe did not damage the relationship of the engaged pair can be credited to the conduct of all three parties. On September 11 Goethe departed without a farewell. A lively correspondence followed, which gradually diminished after the appearance of *Werther*. The letters reveal how devoted Goethe was to both Kestners (they married on Easter Sunday, 1773) and how attached he remained to Lotte long after his departure from Wetzlar.

Of further significance for the novel are the circumstances surrounding the suicide of C. W. Jerusalem (b. 1747), secretary to the Brunswick Embassy, on October 30, 1772, in Wetzlar. The death had a sensational and widespread impact. Goethe had known Jerusalem from their student days in Leipzig and had seen him occasionally in Wetzlar. In fact, Jerusalem was also at the ball on June 9, 1772. Goethe asked Kestner for a detailed account of the incident and learned that prior to his suicide Jerusalem was dissatisfied both professionally and socially and was in love with a married woman. He withdrew, took long walks, and abandoned himself to his ill humor. Details of his death from Kestner's report appear word for word in *Werther*. What is particularly striking is that Jerusalem borrowed the pistols for his last deed from Kestner; in the novel Werther borrows them from Lotte's fiancé Albert.

Goethe began writing *Werther* in February, 1774, and finished it in a few weeks. It was published in the fall and was an immediate success. In general, even where it was received with the utmost enthusiasm, readers were more interested in the veracity of its contents than in its poetic unity. They failed to understand that *Werther* is a work of art complete in itself, not an image of reality but a created world. This was extremely vexing to Goethe. For decades he felt himself bothered by inappropriate questions: "But did Werther really live? Is it all really true? What town can claim as its own the lovely Lotte? Oh, how oft I have cursed the foolish pages which made my youthful suffering public property."[5] In *Poetry and Truth* (*Dichtung und Wahrheit*, 1814), Goethe's anger can still be detected when he speaks of his attempts to avoid being recognized as the "author of *Werther*." He could not even escape the inquisitive public, which pursued him throughout his life, by traveling incognito. He was forced to realize that "author and public are divided by an enormous chasm" (book 13).

Goethe's own statements about the novel clearly indicate that he saw Werther as a character who possessed an independent life. Werther contained a part of Jerusalem as well as of himself; the author was no longer capable of separating the completely fused elements. In a letter to the Swiss poet Johann Kaspar Lavater on April 26, 1774, Goethe wrote, "And now I have loaned my emotions to his story, and thus it makes a wonderful whole." Kestner, who was quite upset that much in the novel resembled actual occurrences and yet had been so totally changed, received a letter from Goethe on November 21, 1774, which said, "Even at the risk of my life I would not want to rescind Werther. . . .—Werther must—must be! You both are not feeling *him*, you just feel *me* and *yourselves*. . . . That I am still alive, I owe to you—therefore you are not Albert."

In his "young Werther," Goethe created a character who epitomizes the sentimental nature. Werther possesses no qualities which could counteract or balance his highly perfected sentimentality. His ability to react to stimuli, to perceive the world as an endless realm of possibilities for emotional arousal and excitement, is extraordinary. At every step his passions and feelings rule.

In addition to his extreme sensitivity, Werther also has the ability to verbalize his emotions. *The Sufferings of Young Werther* gives the inner story of a character in a special way: Werther creates his own inner story by translating his feelings into words. As he expresses his feelings, he also describes the world around him that stimulates these feelings, thus allowing the reader to visualize his surroundings. Of course, only those people and things that arouse his emotions and affect his heart are described. Similarly, the importance of the different settings to the novel's plot is dependent on their relationship to the heart. In the idyllic pastoral landscape at the beginning of the novel, the heart comes to life. It enjoys the countryside, children and simple common people. The breakthrough of feeling is only possible in a natural setting such as this. In the society at court the heart has no place. "Worldly men" are its enemies, and relationships established in this environment cannot last. This division into conflicting settings from the standpoint of the heart corresponded to eighteenth-century thought, but Goethe was not merely concerned with demonstrating the validity of eighteenth-century concepts. He showed that the sentimental person is brought to ruin by his own nature. Because he is totally subject to his feelings, his passion destroys the very idyll which arouses it. The sufferings of the sentimentalist annihilate "the feeling heart."

From the beginning, this suffering is the most important theme of Werther's letters. He suffers because the fullness of his fervent heart is not matched by a reciprocating world. Contact with nature and with simple people can occupy his spirits for a time, even providing him with moments of bliss and security. But the pain, which had only temporarily ceased, soon returns. Werther uses the word *"Einschränkung"* (limitations, confinement, restriction) to describe his suffering (I, May 22, 1771). The thought of his unused potential, which is wasting away, makes him aware of the inadequacy of his situation. "Oh how all this presses upon my heart" (I, May 17, 1771). In his judgment, the sufferer can find little comfort in the world. Yet he does have one source of strength which lies within himself: "As confined as he is, he still preserves a sweet feeling of freedom in his heart in the knowledge that he can leave this prison whenever he wishes" (I, May 22, 1771). This passage, found in Werther's letters two-and-one-half weeks after he began writing on May 4, 1771, alludes to his death before his meeting with Lotte and long before his conflict at court. Artistically, the passage could be seen as a means of foreshadowing his suicide. With regard to the character Werther, it shows that he was predisposed to commit his deed even before the world offered him cause or motivation. The idea that the world is a prison also appears in many of the young author's other works in relation to man's compelling need for freedom.[6]

Specific forms of Werther's general, existential suffering are his sufferings in love and in his profession. His misery is embodied in these two areas, and this provides the framework for the novel. The love story seems to receive more emphasis, but actually Werther's professional despair is part of his inner story from the beginning and is intertwined with the love story. The two books into which the novel is divided show Werther's relationship to the different realms of his world in rhythmical alternation. The books are constructed in a parallel fashion with motifs, places, and persons from the first book recurring in the second. Corresponding to Werther's changed situation, they appear in a different light in the second book. Werther's belief that "the active and inquisitive powers of man are restricted" within narrow limits (I, May 22, 1771) leads him to search for peace and healing in a pastoral landscape. He finds them for a time in the illusion of living in harmony with the idyllic world. His meeting with Lotte and the rapid surge of his affection form the middle section of the first book. Here he is already so overcome by feeling that he believes that Lotte returns his love. The relationship among all three characters, which begins with Albert's arrival and ends with Werther's decision to depart, takes up the last part of the first book.

An agitated discussion on suicide between Werther and Albert further develops the theme alluded to previously in the work and prepares the reader for the ending. Werther's last act is explained and justified in this discussion. He speaks of a sickness, which is reminiscent of Wieland's comparison of *Schwärmerei* to a "fiery fever." But Werther speaks, and here the difference from Wieland is immediately apparent, of a "fatal disease." Nature is "so attacked by it that her powers are partly consumed, partly so incapacitated that she cannot rise again" (I, August 12, 1771). This is not a mere comparison with a sickness; Werther has actually been afflicted, and he realizes it. In later letters he tries to describe the change which has occurred: his feelings now behave differently, and, as a result, nature and existence as a whole appear differently to him. Where full life once rushed to meet him, he now sees a world which slips away from him and consumes him. It is as if something "like a curtain has been drawn back from my soul, and the scene of unending life is transformed before my eyes into the abyss of the eternally open grave. . . . Heaven and earth and their weaving forces surrounding me: I see nothing but an eternally devouring, eternally ruminating monster" (I, August 18, 1771).

With the passing wish for ordered activity amid despair and passion, the connection with the second book of the novel is established. At the beginning of this part Werther is shown to be equal to the demands of his duties at court. But he cannot bear the stresses of the human interaction associated with his professional activity. After causing a scandal at court for failing to observe proper decorum in his relation to the aristocrats, Werther requests dismissal. A few weeks later he is with Lotte again.

Lotte's marriage to Albert during Werther's absence intensifies his passionate desire and leads him to thoughts such as: "She would have been happier with me than with him" (II, July 29, 1772), and "What if Albert should die?" (II, August 21, 1772). A parallel plot concerning a peasant lad, which Goethe first introduced in the new edition of 1787, shows how pure love leads to criminality; the peasant boy murders his rival. "No one shall have her, and she shall have no one," he explains with composure. Prior to the murder, Werther had already declared the story of the unhappy youth to be his own; later he considers himself as irretrievably lost as the murderer. But unlike him, Werther wishes to die alone, perhaps as punishment for the sin of desiring another man's wife or as a sacrifice for Lotte. Such reasons are mentioned in the last letters but are either reinterpreted or dropped altogether. Directly before his death, he once again expresses regret that he is unable to die for her.

The allusions to the Gospel of St. John in Werther's last letters are striking. They were discovered by Herbert Schöffler, who saw them as being "in the most intimate agreement with the title" of the book which proclaims it "an account of suffering and death, . . . a passion-story."[7] No matter how one wishes to judge these biblical allusions, they are indeed present and are meant neither as blasphemy nor as a profaning of the gospel. Rather, they testify to the seriousness of Werther's suffering, to the young Goethe's sensitivity to the language and spirit of the Fourth Gospel, and to the power of his artistry. Different spiritual worlds are inseparably united in an expression of passion such as that in Werther's letter to Lotte on the morning of the last day: "I'll go ahead to my Father, to your Father. I shall bring my lament to Him and He will comfort me until you arrive, and I shall fly towards you and clasp you and remain with you in eternal embraces beholding the face of the Eternal." At this point the quiet voice of the editor allows Goethe to bring the reader back to the physical world. Rather than counteracting the extreme emotionality of Werther's letters, the neutral statements about his death actually serve as a final intensification.

The Era of Goethe's Wilhelm Meister

The decades between Goethe's *The Sufferings of Young Werther* (1774) and his *Wilhelm Meister's Apprenticeship* (1795–96) were years of experimentation with the novel. During the same time authors continued to imitate and modify known forms. The abundance and variety of literary efforts during these years are astonishing and incomparable. Most novels of the period influenced Goethe to some degree; many which do not seem particularly significant in their own right were still part of the literary development leading to *Wilhelm Meister's Apprenticeship* and prepared the way for this work. Even those works which Goethe rejected may well have influenced him, if only by their negative effect. Though it would hardly be possible to record all of the influences to which Goethe was subjected during this time, nonetheless the general panorama can be illuminated.

In the 1770s the flood of Sterne imitations reached its highest level. Joachim Christoph Bode's (1720–1793) translation of *Tristram Shandy* was published in 1774, the same year as *Werther*. Sterne had previously been read in Germany in the 1760s, and his works were recognized and valued in leading literary circles. Before Bode, J. F. Zückert had published a translation of *Tristram Shandy* in eight volumes (1763–65). But the fascination with Sterne first began with Bode's adaptation of *Sentimental Journey* in 1768. Readers during the "age of sentiment" strongly identified with this book and then eagerly seized upon Bode's *Tristram Shandy* as well. Ironically, the very weaknesses of this translation smoothed the way for the reception of Sterne's difficult work and intensified its impact. Bode altered the original English style so that it was pleasing to his German readers. Whereas Sterne is cleverly elegant, detached, and attentive to the charm of conversation, Bode uses familiar speech, slang, and dialect, and does not shy away from blunt and uncouth language. His style is often darker and heavier than Sterne's, but that is exactly what appealed to the public. Modeled after the spirit and tastes of the Storm and Stress period, the style was perfectly suited to the readers' expectations. Bode's translation as well as the many Sterne imitations of the era all deviated from the essence of the English model.

Sterne's imitators generally wanted their work's origin to be immediately evident. The first Sterne imitation, Johann Georg Jacobi's *The Winter Journey* (*Die Winterreise*, 1769), alludes to its model in the title as did many subsequent works, such as Johann Gottlieb Schummel's *Sentimental Journeys through Germany* (*Empfindsame Reisen durch Deutschland*, 1771–72), Moritz August von Thümmel's *Journey of Sentimental Travels in the Southern Provinces of France* (*Reise in die mittäglichen Provincen von Frankreich*, 1791–1805), and Friedrich Nicolai's (1733–1811) *The Life and Opinions of Sebaldus Nothanker* (*Das Leben und die Meinungen des Herrn Magister Sebaldus Nothanker*, 1773–76). Whereas Nicolai's novel is a clearly constructed work, many of the other imitations are formless, diffuse, and chaotic. This applies to Theodor von Hippel's (1741–1796) *Life Histories on an Ascending Line* (*Lebensläufe nach aufsteigender Linie*, 1778–81) and Johann Carl Wezel's (1747–1819) *Life Story of Tobias Knaut, the Wise, Otherwise Called the Stammerer* (*Lebensgeschichte Tobias Knauts, des Weisen, sonst Stammler genannt*, 1773–76), which the well-informed scholar Michelsen considered, despite the work's "serious weaknesses," to be "undoubtedly the best among German Sterne-imitations."[8] All these attempts at assimilation and imitation are based on misunderstandings. Because the German authors were incapable of seeing Sterne's subtle artistic form, they believed they were following his example through their formlessness. Insufficient structure and lack of unity were the result.

The extent to which the epoch of sentimentality raised questions about human nature and the character of the sentimentalist is seen in the novels of Friedrich Heinrich Jacobi (1743–1819). His work *Eduard Allwill's Papers* (*Eduard Allwills Papiere*, 1775–76) directly reflects his personal relationship with Goethe and his painful disappointment at failing to win Goethe's permanent friendship. Jacobi was a sentimentalist who felt an irrepressible need for emotional outpourings. His concept of togetherness, derived from the friendship cult of his time, resulted in expectations of the relationship with Goethe which, due to Goethe's different nature, could not possibly be realized. In the novel Jacobi expresses his criticism of the genius who fails others in love by having the female characters reject Allwill, the title figure. Given Jacobi's emotionality and his capacity for devotion and self-sacrifice, it seems fitting that he developed his theme from the perspective of women suffering in love and that the decisive opinions and judgments are spoken by women. The character Sylli von Wallburg describes Allwill as "a horrible man . . . powerless to love." She also discusses the "unspeakable humiliation" felt by those whose efforts in love fail; they have "fled from themselves" in order to live for the other, and now they have "no existence left, none within themselves, none in the other." Luzia, the young woman whose fate is thus described, has the last word, again a condemnation of Allwill: "Always a powerful genius . . . marked by the hand of God so that no man dares to touch you." Jacobi's indictment of Goethe is extreme and can be explained by the bitterness of one who believed he had no existence left after he saw himself rejected as a friend. The novel is less an artistic effort than a direct confession of the author's own experience and suffering. It is also a penetratingly sharp criticism of his times. His analysis touches on the tragedy inherent in genius as well as on the danger of an overabundance of feeling, a theme evidenced in *Werther* as well.

Goethe and Jacobi both recognized and described this danger. One should note that Jacobi had already planned and partially written the first letters of *Eduard Allwill's Papers* before reading *Werther*. His work is not an imitation of Goethe's novel, not even in the parts which prove to be similar. These similarities only demonstrate that the immediate understanding reached between Goethe and Jacobi on their first meeting in the summer of 1774 was founded on common ties which neither one fully recognized at the time. They did not yet know of each other's novels: *Werther* had not yet appeared and *Allwill* was still in the process of conception. The extent of their affinity, despite all their differences, is seen in the character Amalia in *Eduard All-*

will's Papers. She seems to be a literary sister of Natalie in *Wilhelm Meister's Apprenticeship.* In addition, the thought that Allwill could be saved by love alone, expressed by Luzia at the end of the novel, is an indication of the spiritual kinship between Jacobi and Goethe.

By the time Jacobi wrote his second novel *Woldemar* (1777–79), he was no longer as deeply hurt by the loss of Goethe's affection, but the problems connected with the "age of sentiment" still oppressed him. *Woldemar* is the story of a "soul-friendship," its origination, its fulfillment, and its crisis. The crisis in a seemingly perfect friendship between Woldemar and a cultured, intelligent woman stems from Woldemar's sentimental nature and from his excessive demands on friendship and love.

In the same year that the first part of *Woldemar* appeared, Johann Heinrich Jung (1740–1817), called Stilling, published the first book of his autobiography, *Henrich Stilling's Youth* (*Heinrich Stillings Jugend*, 1777). He had written the short book in 1772 soon after leaving Strasbourg. As a medical student there, he had come into contact with Goethe and the entire Storm and Stress circle. Jung's manner of expressing himself "properly and agreeably" was very appealing to Goethe. As Goethe wrote in *Poetry and Truth* (book 9), "Stilling told his life story with particular charm and knew how to make all the past events come alive for the listener." Goethe further stated, "I urged him to write it down and he promised to do so." Goethe himself made some editorial changes and sent the manuscript for publication. The book was a great success. The ability to make the past "come alive" also characterizes Jung's style from a modern standpoint and explains the work's significance as a forerunner of a realistic form of narration which first evolved in the nineteenth century.

The ambiguous and controversial term "Realism" can already be applied to Jung's autobiography as well as to works such as Ulrich Bräker's (1735–1798) *The Life Story and Real Adventures of the Poor Man of Toggenburg* (*Lebensgeschichte und natürliche Abenteuer des armen Mannes im Tockenburg*, 1789). The difference between autobiography and novel should not be confused. On the title page of Jung's life story are found the words "A true story," but Jung was actually using his own story to show the rule of divine providence. In order to make visible the workings of providence in critical situations, he carefully constructed these situations using many details. His "realistic" presentation serves the purpose of confession. The "basis of his energy was an indestructible belief in God and in help flowing directly from Him," said Goethe (*Poetry and Truth*, book 9).

Jakob Michael Reinhold Lenz's (1751–1792) short novel fragment *The Forest Dweller* (*Der Waldbruder*, 1797) is also indebted to Goethe. The distorted, Werther-like traits of Herz, the main character of the novel, provide the motivation for grotesque happenings. Herz falls in love with a countess whom he has never seen on the basis of letters she has written to others. At a ball he is charmed by a woman he mistakenly believes is the countess. Because he has no more money—he claims to have been robbed—he goes into the forest and lives as a hermit. The story begins at this point and is told in the form of letters. The work, which seems to parody a Werther imitation, reveals the hand of a talented writer of comedies. As in *Woldemar*, the sentimentalist, overpowered by his own exuberance, fails to perceive the true situation; the ideas originating in his own inner world hide reality from him.

Criticism of the sentimentalist was expressed several decades earlier in Wieland's first novel *Don Sylvio* and recurred in the works of many novelists who illuminated specific traits of their sentimental heroes. Since these heroes—Don Sylvio, Agathon, Werther, Woldemar, Herz, Belphegor, Anton Reiser, Wilhelm Meister—all contain autobiographical elements, they are expressions of the authors' self-knowledge, and, simultaneously, of their self-criticism. At that time the element of self-criticism was much stronger than social criticism. This can be seen most clearly in satirical treatments of the conflict between the sentimentalist and his society. In its own way, *Don Sylvio* was already a satire, "a type of satirical novel," Wieland himself said (August 5, 1763, letter to Salomon Gessner). It does not concentrate on society, but rather on the young boy whose mind becomes confused by literature. This motif, which often recurs in the German novel, serves to focus the reader's attention on the strange behavior of the youth.[9] Social conditions are significant only insofar as they provide the background for his story. Only gradually do conditions as such become more important to Wieland and other contemporary novelists and begin to develop a life of their own.

The sorrowful adventures of a sentimentalist in a thoroughly evil world form the basis of Johann Wezel's *Belphegor* (1776). Wezel was a gifted author whose talents Wieland highly respected. In a letter to him, Wieland wrote that he has "all the essentials" to be "our Fielding," but that he must "just obtain some good spirits" (July 22, 1776). He felt that *Belphegor*, a novel reminiscent of Voltaire's *Candide*, was too misanthropic. But Wezel was seldom in good spirits. His life was unhappy, and at an early age he began to show signs of a mental illness from which he suffered for thirty-four years. Wezel never found a light style for his satire; without this, any extended representation of foolishness and wickedness becomes difficult to endure. Because of his apparent inability to laugh freely, the world he describes produces uneasiness and anxiety in the reader. This also applies to many parts of his best novel *Herrmann and Ulrike* (1780), a work constructed with impressive deliberation. The several main themes are almost all traditional: the social rise of the main character, Herrmann, from low status to a high official position; his marriage to the Baroness Ulrike; the couple's loyalty to each other throughout difficulties, separations, and intrigues; the seduction of Ulrike by her lover, Herrmann; and the purification which results from renunciation and from the performance of one's duties (these last two are the more modern themes). In the end, the oppressed are victorious and the oppressors defeated. Like Belphegor, Herrmann is not perfect. Passionate and seducible, he is subject to his moods and commits hasty actions. Nevertheless, he is a man of great character. Both he and Ulrike are incapable of intentional wrongdoing. Since the story takes place in the author's own time, his satire often has the effect of social criticism and may have been so intended. The satire is not limited to one class; it is aimed equally at aristocrat, burgher, and servant.

Wieland's *Story of the Abderites* (*Geschichte der Abderiten*, 1781, appeared 1774–80 in *Teutscher Merkur*), which represents the climax of his second artistic period and is regarded by many as his best novel, is entirely satirical in design. The notable exception to this is that the three important Greek historical figures who appear in the novel, Democritus, Hippocrates, and Euripides, are not satirized at all. On the contrary, they are spoken of so seriously throughout that their superiority and appropriate behavior are always impressively visible. But it is precisely the perfection and illustriousness of these characters which contribute to Wieland's unique form of satire. His seriousness is not set apart from satire, as is the case with Wezel; rather it increases the satirical effect. The foolishness and stupidity of the Abderites become evident in their behavior towards the irreproachable historical figures.

The novel is divided into five books. Each of the three books which comprise part 1 of the novel presents the encounter of the people of Abdera with one of the historical figures. The first book focuses on Democritus, a native of Abdera, who returns home after extensive travels only to experience disagreements and conflicts with his fellow Abderites. In the second book the senate invites Hippocrates to come and examine Democritus and to report to them on his sanity. While Euripides is traveling through Abdera (in book 3), he attends a performance of his *Andromeda* and afterwards enters into a conversation with the theatergoers. At first they do not believe that he is Euripides; then they request that he perform the play with his own company, and Abdera experiences a genuine Euripidean performance. The last two books (part 2) present the Abderites among themselves. "The trial for the sake of a donkey's shadow" in the fourth book and the problems with an increasing plague of frogs in the final book show that the foolishness, in combination with the struggles for power by different groups and the destructive role played by the priests, endangers the existence of the entire city-state. At the end the Abderites must evacuate their city because, in addition to the proliferation of frogs, which they had protected as holy animals, they have been stricken by a plague of rats and mice.

The foolishness of the Abderites is described as follows: "Their fantasy won such a great lead over their reason that it was never again possible for their reason to catch up. At no time were they at a loss for new ideas, but their ideas were seldom appropriate to the situation at hand." With this statement ideas are touched upon which were already of importance in *Don Sylvio* and *Agathon*. The foolishness of the Abderites is a variation of *Schwärmerei*; like the youths in the earlier works, the Abderites also see reality in terms of their own imagination. In their case we see that superstition, a topic that was to preoccupy Wieland in later years, is one of many things that confuse the mind. Whatever the reasons, the foolishness of the Abderites cannot be eliminated; nor does it undergo any type of change or development. However, it can express itself in different ways. At times, the Abderites seem good-natured and friendly. It is important that they can occasionally laugh at themselves and can quickly forget or at least overlook unpleasantries. Their inappropriate behavior is often merely comical and condemns itself. The two examples which the narrator introduces at the beginning are typical. At great expense, the Abderites had a famous sculptor build a fountain with many statues for their marketplace, only to determine in the end "that there was hardly enough water to moisten the nose of a single dolphin"; or they proudly placed a masterpiece, a small, ivory Venus by Praxiteles, on such a high obelisk that it could no longer be recognized.

It is not only a question of harmless pranks and mistakes. Abderite foolishness can take on threatening forms and make it impossible for anyone of a different nature to live in the city. This is demonstrated by Democritus's situation. The origin and progression of Democritus's conflict with the Abderites are carefully traced. Basically, the problem is that the Abderites do not think highly of the famous Democritus. They consider him to be a conceited, overly clever, faultfinding, yet actually very entertaining, oddity. The reason he is not respected has nothing to do with jealousy; quite simply and honestly, his fellow citizens do not see him as a great man. They cannot see him as a great man because he is their antithesis and constantly opposes them in discussions. By introducing the well-traveled scholar, Wieland places a strong and convincing adversary in opposition to the foolishness. Democritus is such a superior character that he is able to play satirical games with his opponents through several chapters. After realizing that he cannot converse on a rational and logical basis with the Abderites, he tells them incredibly wild farces and thus can communicate with them on their own level. Eventually, however, he begins to withdraw from them. It has become evident to him that the Abderites are not at all capable of recognizing him for what he is, and he realizes that he cannot be "useful" to his fatherland; rather, he should take care to "at least insure his own safety." The soundness of Democritus's position is confirmed within the novel by Hippocrates. He too finds it necessary to defend himself against the Abderites, using mockery as his weapon. After recommending to the people that they should go to Democritus for treatment, Hippocrates departs.

Wieland's satire becomes most biting when the Senate charges that Democritus is a fool and, according to law, should be put into a "dark little chamber." That instead Hippocrates is summoned shows that the Abderites can occasionally act decently and properly. But their reasons for this decision as well as their method of carrying out the undertaking are entirely "Abderitish," and the affair itself remains a bitter game. This duplicity is essential, for danger and ridiculousness are kept in an even balance and the possibility for laughter is not damaged. In the first book the author had already indicated that a philosopher in Athens was in much greater danger than in Abdera.

> The Abderites were, despite all their human weaknesses, . . . not a very malicious people. In their midst Socrates would have been able to grow as old as Nestor. They would have regarded him as a strange fool and made fun of his seeming silliness, but the matter of the poison cup was not in their character. Democritus treated them so sharply that a less jovial people would have lost its patience.

This indicates that the foolishness of the Abderites can only be judged correctly if their behavior is compared to that of other peoples, and in many respects they do not fare badly by such a comparison. It must be conceded that they did turn to the right man, for whatever reasons, when they called upon Hippocrates.

The Abderites appear likeable in the third book, when they are captivated by the Euripidean performance. It seems surprising that they should so appreciate the theatrical production, but in fact their fascination is a direct result of their "Abderiteness." They are so "deceived" by the decorations and the music, the delivery and the voices that they experience the happenings on stage as reality and are completely involved emotionally—hoping and praying, loving and hating, crying and laughing. "Euripides himself confessed that the play had never been experienced with such total feeling." Wieland adds the comment that "the great disposition of the Abderites to let themselves be deceived by the arts of fantasy and imitation" is one of their most likeable traits.

The encounters with the three famous Greeks, which end with the third book, have shown three entirely different reactions to the Abderites. Democritus struggles and argues with them until he finally withdraws; Hippocrates is bored and does not take the trouble to hide it; Euripides is in the best mood of his life and plays the role of Abderite.

The last two books show the consequences of the Abderites' character traits when public questions—politics and religion—are concerned. The Abderites are hopeless victims of the power struggles of party leaders and priests. "The trial for the sake of a donkey's shadow"—the point of dispute is whether the dentist, who rented a donkey, has the right to sit in its shadow or must pay the owner an additional fee for its use—brings the "unfortunate city," as Abdera is now called, into total confusion and disorder. There are bloody street riots, the ambitious priests misuse the people's faith, the citizenry splits into two unyielding groups which continuously fight each other with new arguments and tricks, and the judges are perplexed and helpless. Not until the people have torn the donkey to pieces in a moment of utter fury is the problem solved by compensating both parties from the state treasury. As is typical of the Abderites, their mood immediately changes to a spirit of gaiety that unites all. Democritus, who disappears from Abdera after the trial episode, no longer experiences the quarrels among priests, politicians, and scientists about combating the proliferation of frogs; nor is he present when his fellow citizens are forced to flee from the frogs and mice.

The extent to which the novel expresses criticism of the times has been a point of debate in Germany ever since its appearance. Literary scholars have usually seen in the Abderites a representation of the German Philistine. However, any interpretation which attempts to equate the Abderites with a specific group is one-sided and contrary to the essence of the work. Wieland himself always stressed the general applicability of the story. He argued passionately and eloquently with contemporaries, some of whom felt hurt by the work, explaining that he wanted to be understood as a poet. To those who demanded specifics, he tried to describe the subtle interplay between experience and fantasy. He writes that "One cannot say, Abdera is here, or Abdera is there! Abdera is everywhere, and to a certain extent we are all at home there. Where is the son of man who has not said or done something Abderitish in his life?" (*Merkur*, September 1778). The question of social criticism becomes meaningful within this context. Wieland admits that there "are regions on earth . . . where Abderitism flourishes more than in others"; nevertheless, he does not want to say that it cannot be found everywhere.

On February 16, 1777, three years after writing *Werther*, Goethe made an entry in his diary: "Dictating *Wilhelm Meister*." This is the first mention of a work which was to have an extraordinary impact on an entire generation. But the novel did not appear until almost two decades later (1795–96), when a second, revised version, begun by Goethe in 1794, was published under the title *Wilhelm Meister's Apprenticeship* (*Wilhelm Meisters Lehrjahre*).

The first unfinished version, titled *Wilhelm Meister's Theatrical Mission* (*Wilhelm Meisters Theatralische Sendung*), was never published by its author. There would be no record of it today if a copy had not come to light in 1910.

Unknown to Goethe, Barbara Schulthess, a friend from Zurich, made a handwritten copy of the original manuscript he had sent for her to read and return. The value of this version is inestimable because it allows us to see the entire process of development of Goethe's famous novel. The first version remained a fragment and Goethe made no statements about how it would end. Nonetheless, the underlying concept can be recognized from the existing chapters and is referred to in the title. Throughout its six books, the central questions of the novel fragment are: What is Wilhelm's theatrical mission? Does he really have a mission? Or is he deceiving himself, led astray by his personal situation and the general conditions of the times? However one answers these questions, it is evident that Wilhelm's theatrical mission cannot be regarded as a simple fact; it is a problem which remains open and is closely linked to Wilhelm's inner story. The story of Wilhelm Meister is, like that of Don Sylvio, a variation on the Don Quixote theme. Wilhelm is yet another youth whose mind is confused by literature.

But unlike Cervantes and Wieland, Goethe confronts his hero with the theater, a literary institution which actually existed and was of utmost significance at that time. Wherever Wilhelm goes, he finds theater. Not only do traveling actors earn their living by performing, but tradesmen and workers also act. In all circles and classes people are concerned with the stage and with plays. From the time he was a child, Wilhelm was exposed to and lived with the theater. The puppet theater which his grandmother gave the children for Christmas and the young boy's varied reading matter provided the stimulus for countless productions in which Wilhelm acted or directed a group of young companions. Later he had the opportunity to attend regular performances of a company visiting his town. His association with actors and love for an actress brought him closer to the world of the stage.

While Wilhelm is learning about theater and concentrating his hopes on the stage, his family and career tie him to a realm of life which has no contact with the world of art. Why Goethe chose a milieu so different from his own patrician background has often been asked. By placing Wilhelm in the middle-class, merchant environment, the author creates the necessary tension between Wilhelm's wishes and his surroundings. His departure from home and the decision, however hesitating, not to return is an attempt to escape a daily life which affects him as an "oppressive burden on the soul." It does not allow for the development of a dynamic nature. The setting amid small-time shopkeepers is comparable to the unsophisticated country milieu of Don Quixote. A pathway to a full, meaningful life does not seem possible from either location.

Goethe was not the only author of his day to treat the theme of the *Theatrical Mission*, but he gave it persuasive power by means of a new artistic style. An essential element of this style is his exactness in depicting the milieu, the character from this milieu—in his amiability, seriousness, credibility, and personal integrity—and the theater of the period. What Wieland set up as a model under Cervantes's influence seems to be presented by Goethe as a realistic picture of the times. But it should not be overlooked that the model is visible behind the realistic picture: for Wilhelm, the theater is a place of fulfillment, a place of escape from the narrowness and monotony of his own world. If Goethe, who came from a well-to-do patrician family in Frankfurt, had used his own youth as material, he would not have succeeded in creating this impression, since all the opportunities for education and growth that he needed were indeed available to him, and he always knew how to take complete advantage of them. Wilhelm's youth takes a completely different course from Goethe's, and Goethe tells his character's story as if it were that of a stranger. Naturally he incorporated his own experiences, but he transferred them onto a framework removed from his own person, so that he could report with objective distance. He thus achieved an epic tone new to his writings. As narrator he could judge and lead his hero from a superior position, viewing him with occasional smiles or with ironical skepticism.

The uncertainty as to whether Wilhelm has a theatrical mission is rooted in this narrative style. That he enjoys the theater and has talent as an actor and playwright seems to be apparent at an early age. Yet this combination of interest and talent is not the only or decisive reason that "he, like so many others, was captivated by theater." In the first book, the narrator discusses Wilhelm's motivation: his feelings and imagination were "immovably fixed on the theater, and no wonder. Confined in a city, captive in bourgeois life, oppressed in domesticity, without a view of nature, without freedom of the heart . . . and with the fullness of love, of friendship, of presentiments of great deeds, where should he go? Did not the stage necessarily become a place of healing for him," since there he could "comfortably gaze" at his "emotions and future deeds in all storms from under a secure roof. In short, it will surprise no one that he, like so many others, was captivated by the theater, once one understands how all unnatural feelings for nature were fixed on this focal point." Here the narrator unmistakably expresses his opinion of Wilhelm's fascination for the theater. In the theater Wilhelm found a world that corresponded to the fullness of his heart, a world that Werther searched for in vain. The stage could become the "place of healing" for his sufferings, since his feelings and hopes emerged from the stage in the shape of life. When the narrator speaks of "comfortably gazing" and of "unnatural feelings for nature," he is using sharp phrases. They attest to Goethe's intention, as narrator, to distance himself from the theatrical enthusiasm of his young hero and also to characterize the theater itself with the most sober judgment. He shows that Wilhelm sees his only salvation in the theater because he knows of no place for himself in real life. The theater gives support to his most questionable trait: his lack of a genuine relation to nature.

The irony in the narrator's attitude towards Wilhelm's mission is corroborated by the fact that it is Wilhelm's love for the actress Mariane which induces him to leave his parents' home and dedicate himself totally to the theater. "His destiny . . . was now clear, the lofty goal he saw before him seemed closer as he strived for it at Mariane's side. And for blissful moments he could not help seeing himself as becoming the most perfect actor and creator of a national theater." The assumption underlying this love, as with Agathon's love for Danae, is that the beloved is as inexperienced in love and as ready for devotion as the lover, that she is virtuous and unselfish, and, like him, can only wish for a lasting relationship. His ignorance of her true situation results in constant misinterpretations of her behavior. Believing at first that her reserve is proof of her love, he then falsely concludes that she is disloyal upon discovering that there is another man in her life. Like Agathon, he abandons his beloved immediately after he believes himself betrayed, and his ensuing breakdown needs no further explanation within the novel.

After the emotional ending of the first book, the second book begins calmly. Wilhelm's serious illness and gradual recovery are only reported in retrospect. The main theme progresses as one learns of the hero's continued preoccupation with the theater. His friend and brother-in-law Werner, who would like to convince him of the worldwide importance of trade and win him for the practical affairs of the firm, suggests that he take a business trip, and Wilhelm sets out on travels in order to collect debts and see the world. But he meets performers and actors everywhere. He exclaims, "Must fate . . . always lead me to these people whose company I neither should nor want to keep!" Despite his good intentions, his inclinations prevail, and he is detained by a theater troupe. He enjoys the exchanges of opinion on his "favorite subject" and is delighted by the "great theatrical insights" of the troupe's leader, Madame de Retti. He becomes a financial adviser and supporter, directs and trains actors, corrects verses and translations, and reads aloud to the actors from his own works. His *Belshazzar* is performed to great applause, with the author himself successfully playing the role of Darius in the first production. But he is deeply disappointed by the selfish, base thinking of the actors, for whom he spends almost all his money in the course of a few months. Although he repeatedly resolves to resume his original trip, he remains with the troupe and accompanies it to an engagement in a count's castle. He is further disappointed to learn that even at the court he cannot look for or demand from theater the things he considers essential, though those at court are well disposed toward the actors, care about their performances, and grant privileged treatment to Wilhelm as a playwright. The world he has entered remains full of enigmas for him, and he is forced to see its shortcomings; nonetheless, he cannot withdraw from it. He is troubled by his conflicting emotions and by the uncertainty of his situation, yet knows of no solution. Rapidly he loses touch with the realm of his past and devotes himself conscientiously to all tasks related to the theater.

The novel offers constant alternation between visible, colorful life and Wilhelm's mental states, which are often difficult to grasp. The progression of the plot takes place in this alternation, concentrating on Wilhelm but also showing the activities of a circle of clearly profiled secondary characters. The fact that these characters are a source of endless entertainment to the reader serves to convince the reader that Wilhelm is justified in refusing to leave them. Philine, the Melinas, Mignon, and the Harpist are unforgettable. The frivolous and appealing Philine is carefree and spontaneous, but always seizes her own advantage with certainty. She is responsible for the words, "And if I love you, what concern is it of yours?" Philine and the Melinas occupy a place in the center of theatrical life, which, as Wilhelm learns, is very superficial, revolving around visible success and its benefits. But Mignon and the Harpist come from a different sphere and have little to do with the world of actors. What they offer comes from the heart and is an expression of truth. Both are particularly close to Wilhelm and embody a part of his nature. When, at the end of the last book, he reflects on whether to accept Serlo's offer to join his company, we read: "That he could keep his Mignon with him and would now not need to turn the Harpist away seemed to be important factors in his decision." Thus we become aware that his disassociation from his past has to do with Mignon and the Harpist.

Like an analysis of Wilhelm's mission, a closer look at these two characters leads to the heart of the novel. It is possible that by means of the character Mignon, Goethe has given an indication of his deepest concerns in the *Theatrical Mission*. She does not appear until the third book, and the Harpist not until the fourth. In both cases Wilhelm is profoundly affected, and the narrator describes his reaction in a style entirely free of irony. Later the narrator's tone is also serious and moved whenever he speaks of Mignon and the Harpist. Mignon captures Wilhelm's attention from the first moment, but his special relationship to her develops only gradually. At first it is her unusual, mysterious appearance and behavior which attract him, and he entertains "a thousand thoughts" about her. When she becomes emotionally closer to him, her solemn, reverential manner stirs him "in the depths of his soul," and it is not long before the narrator reports that if Wilhelm "had followed his inclinations, he would have treated her as his daughter and completely claimed her as his own." At first Mignon regards Wilhelm with indifference. When he comes to her aid and protects her from a stranger's molestations, she gives in little by little until she opens herself to him in verse and song and, as the supreme indication of her affection, performs the intricate egg dance for him.

By contrast, Wilhelm and the Harpist establish a relationship immediately. Once again completely disheartened by his unpleasant situation among the moneyless and ill-behaved actors, Wilhelm feels himself "reborn" after hearing the first songs of the Harpist. For Wilhelm the Harpist's songs possess the high reality of art, next to which all details in the foreground of reality disappear.

In Mignon and the Harpist Wilhelm finds an affirmation of himself without which he cannot live. The world of actors is as oppressive to him as that of merchants. By forming a family with the forsaken child and the lonely old man, he gains the resoluteness and stability necessary for continuing on his uncertain path, and, by accepting the two destitute persons with kindheartedness and affection, he achieves the highest human qualities. Humanitarianism and sentimentality are united; a community of kindred souls is formed which the outsider cannot appreciate. This is why the worldly character Jarno condemns Wilhelm's relationships.

Just as Wilhelm finds Mignon and the Harpist within the depressing realm of the actors, two other uplifting encounters occur in times of great discouragement or distress. In the disappointing world of the court Jarno introduces Wilhelm to Shakespeare's plays, marking the beginning of a new life for Wilhelm. In Shakespeare he finds the inspiration denied to him in his immediate surroundings. The second encounter takes place as he is lying wounded in the woods after his company has been ambushed. Suddenly a woman identified as the "beautiful Amazon" appears before him. Visibly sympathetic to his plight, she secures medical help, arranges for further care, and covers him with a cloak which he retains. The "beautiful Amazon" will never leave his thoughts again; she is referred to as a saint who gave his "spirit a new direction." In all the above situations Wilhelm is enriched in a profound way. His capacity for fascination, his ability to respond with enthusiasm afford him spiritual experiences that lift him far beyond the misery of the hour.

When Wilhelm travels to H. to join the talented actor and director Serlo, he has an important task before him, the production of *Hamlet*. The conscientiousness and intensity with which he pursues his *Hamlet* studies earn him not only Serlo's esteem but also that of Serlo's sister Aurelie, a great actress. The novel ends with Wilhelm's acceptance of Serlo's very favorable offer to join his company. On this occasion he reflects on the problem of his "mission," just as the reader does, yet has nothing more to add than is already known. What surprises him is that everything has come about the way he envisioned. This seems to him to be proof that "a calling, a mission" has emerged. Nevertheless, his decision is a source of conflict for him. While his friends are rejoicing at his acceptance into the company, he is again preoccupied with the scene in the woods: The "lovely Amazon . . . came closer, dismounted, human kindness brought her to him, she stood before him, the cloak fell from her shoulders and covered him, her face, her image shone radiantly once again and disappeared." The fragment breaks off here.

It seems likely that Goethe intended to lead Wilhelm away from the theater again. With the "lovely Amazon" and her "human kindness" the author appears to be indicating the sphere into which he wished to bring Wilhelm. Even without a knowledge of *Wilhelm Meister's Apprenticeship*, we would have to presume, judging from the sixth book of the *Theatrical Mission*, that the appearance of the Amazon has a poetic meaning as a counterbalance to the theater. The forest scene marks the beginning of a spiritual plot which competes with the continuing action revolving around the theater. The problem cannot be pursued further, since the text allows for no more than speculation and Goethe made no statements about it. Therefore, the question concerning Wilhelm's mission must also remain open.

The problem of the theater and its potential for the seduction of young people was a theme relevant to authors of that decade. Karl Philipp Moritz's (1756–1793) *Anton Reiser. A Psychological Novel* (*Anton Reiser. Ein psychologischer Roman*, 1785–90) evolved during the same time period as the *Theatrical Mission*. A comparison of the two works reveals surprising similarities in overall design and individual passages. With regard to content as well as vocabulary, style, and the construction of certain paragraphs, it seems almost unbelievable that the authors knew nothing of one another and really did not copy from each other. They met for the first time in November 1786, after both had suddenly departed, unknown to the other, from Germany for Italy. Moritz had left his position as a teacher in a Berlin *Gymnasium*, and Goethe had fled from the court at Weimar. Moritz, seven years younger than Goethe, had already published the first three parts of *Anton Reiser* by 1786 and had never seen Goethe's unpublished novel fragment. He wrote *Anton Reiser* entirely independently of it. This applies also to the fourth part, published in 1790, even if some of the ideas which the authors discussed in Italy may have been incorporated into it. If the effect *Anton Reiser* and its author had on Goethe's revision of the *Theatrical Mission* is any indication, then these discussions may well have influenced Goethe more than Moritz.

In Italy, Goethe felt a common bond with Moritz. "He is like a younger brother of mine," he wrote to Frau von Stein, "of the same cast, but neglected and injured by fate where I have been favored and preferred" (September 13, 1786). This statement is likewise applicable to the authors' two main fictional characters. Anton Reiser comes from a background of poverty and his childhood is unusually unhappy. Moritz designated his work a psychological novel, and in the introduction to the first part he called it a biography, since "for the most part the observations have been taken from real life." As literary research has confirmed, the novel is basically autobiographical, even if many details have been tailored to the main plot. The book is a highly interesting document, a story of youth as it should not be, of a boy's development under adverse conditions.

The young Anton feels neglected and despised by his parents, who are constantly at odds, and is ashamed to be seen by his peers in torn and dirty clothing. His early boyhood years are spent in loneliness and humiliation. When he learns to read, a means of escape presents itself. "Reading suddenly opened a whole new world to him and gave him pleasure that could somewhat compensate for all the disagreeableness in his real world. . . . Thus at an early age he was already driven from his natural world of childhood into an unnatural, ideal world, where his spirit was ruined for a thousand of life's joys which others could experience to the fullest." This passage contains the outline for all further episodes. Because reality is desolate and repulsive, Anton searches for a substitute in an unreal sphere created by his readings and his own imagination.

Moritz thus provides the psychological motivation for Anton's unhealthy sensitivity, his illusions, instability, striving for power, need for recognition, and the many extravagances of his imagination. It is the young boy's environment which, the novel contends, makes a positive human development impossible. In all schools and at the university, Anton feels the same degradation that he had felt earlier in his parents' home and during his apprenticeship. Although he is able again and again to achieve success in his studies and to win the respect of his teachers and fellow students, his poverty—the shabby clothing and the shame of having to accept meals on charity—is a serious spiritual impediment which limits his ability to assert himself and create a place for himself.

The result is that at the end of the book he is no further ahead than he was at the beginning. He has of course become older, and much has happened, but there has been no overall development which could take the form of a progressive plot. Everything Anton does is portrayed in a series of similarly constructed episodes. In other words, he experiences the same thing again and again. This is the structural principle of the novel.

The fact that Moritz remains true to this fundamental principle throughout his hero's story is particularly upsetting in view of the fact that Anton, by following his inclinations over a period of years, acquires a vast knowledge of and familiarity with all the literature of his day. His special passion is the theater. The passion was kindled by classroom recitations, his own readings, and school productions, as well as by unforgettable evenings at the theater during his school years in Hanover, where the most prominent actors of the time appeared in famous plays. But this love of theater is assessed by the author in the same way as he judges Anton's absorption in reading. The wish to be an actor stems from Reiser's need to attain at least once what was always denied him in life:

> He wished for an impressive role, where he could speak with the greatest pathos and project himself into a host of different emotions which he was so fond of but could not have in his real world, where everything was so barren, so miserable. This wish was very natural for Reiser; he had the potential for friendship, for gratitude, for generosity and noble decisiveness, which however slumbered in him untapped, since his external situation caused his heart to shrivel up. No wonder he sought to expand himself again in an ideal world and to indulge in natural feelings! In drama it was as if he found himself again after he had nearly lost himself in his real world. . . . When he went through the scenes of a play he had either read or sketched out in his mind, he then became all of that which he imagined, now generous, now grateful, now hurt and suffering, now vigorous and bravely resisting any attack.

Goethe may have been quite taken aback by this passage, which was printed in 1786, since he had already described Wilhelm's situation in the same way nine years earlier in the first book of the *Theatrical Mission*. At that time, Goethe too had wanted to grasp objectively the phenomenon of a life of deception and to characterize it from a distance. The problem of how to exist between fantasy and reality troubled him for years and finally drove him from Germany. In Italy, he and Moritz were both able to free themselves from their unhappy situations. Therefore, their meeting at this particular time was most fortuitous.

The last part of *Anton Reiser*, written in the same style as the three previous parts, does not offer a remedy or a solution. What will happen to Anton remains an open question. He experiences a serious setback when, after leaving Hanover for Gotha, he is rejected by Eckhoff as an actor. After desperate wanderings he is admitted to the university in Erfurt, but he soon attempts to join a theater troupe again, this time in Leipzig. With his arrival there and his discovery that the company has disbanded, the novel ends.

The narrator often comments on the reasons for the hero's failure in theater. Reiser falsely presumed that "nothing could go wrong, because he felt every role deeply and knew how to present and play it out in his own soul perfectly. He could not see that all this was only taking place *in his mind* and that he lacked the power of projecting outwardly." Therefore, "it was not a genuine profession, not a pure drive to act, which attracted him: for he was more concerned with imagining the scenes in his own mind than with acting them. *He wanted to keep for himself all those things that art demands as a sacrifice."* The author recognized that whoever misuses art by allowing it to be a substitute for life and a means of self-satisfaction has no place in art or in life. His fictional character Reiser does not come to this realization. To that extent the open ending—it remains uncertain whether the novel has been completed—corresponds to the contents: what will and should happen to Reiser cannot be said.

Parallel to *Anton Reiser*, Moritz wrote a second novel which he also published in successive parts: *Andreas Hartknopf, an Allegory* (*Andreas Hartknopf, Eine Allegorie*, 1786) and *Andreas Hartknopf's Years as a Preacher* (*Andreas Hartknopfs Predigerjahre*, 1790). In form and style the work is very different from the autobiographical *Anton Reiser*. Moritz no longer relates the story of his hero chronologically, but presents episodes in which symbolic relationships are of primary importance. It is most remarkable that *Anton Reiser* and *Andreas Hartknopf* were written at the same time—in the field of literary research they are referred to as "parallel novels" (*Parallelromane*)— for seldom does an author create two such different forms of prose expression simultaneously.

Friedrich Schiller's (1759–1805) novel fragment, *The Ghostseer* (*Der Geisterseher*, 1787–89), is a significant work and the beginning of a great composition. The author regarded it as a mere journalistic achievement by means of which he fulfilled his objective: to improve the reputation of his periodical, *Thalia*, and win more readers for it. He was amused and some-times even annoyed by the enthusiasm with which the first parts were received. In a letter to his life-long friend Christian Gottfried Körner, he wrote that he could "acquire no interest" in the "cursed *Seer*" (March 6, 1788). Seldom was he "so aware of spending time sinfully" as with "this scribbling" (March 17, 1788, letter to Körner). It was only the certainty of being able to benefit financially and pay debts from the "public taste" which gradually appeased him to some degree. Nonetheless, when the original 1789 book edition was to be reprinted, he did not use this as an opportunity to continue the novel, but merely made corrections in the previous parts.

Notwithstanding the author's attitude toward his own work, a contem-porary critic was justified in asserting that "we hardly know of anything in the German language, and even in foreign languages there is little which could compare to most scenes of the *Seer* in their lively, thrilling presentation which so strongly arouses and captures the attention of readers of all kinds" (Friedrich Nicolai's *Allgemeine Deutsche Bibliothek*, 1792). In fact, there was nothing comparable in Germany at that time, and none of Schiller's other works, with the exception of *The Robbers* (*Die Räuber*), had such a strong public appeal. The intellectual energy and intensity of the *Seer's* style are still impressive today, especially since its theme, which was of burning interest to Schiller's contemporaries, is not as foreign to modern thinking as it might at first seem. A closer look shows that Schiller's treatment of subjects relevant to the 1770s and 1780s and fascinating to those readers—the conjuration of ghosts and spirits, seances, secret societies, the guidance of one's life by unknown persons—serves as a means of subtle psychological analysis and uncovers central problems of human existence in a stimulating fashion.

Schiller did not invent the motifs on which the plot is based. They were known to everyone. At that time those who claimed to see and conjure up spirits were active in many different locations and derived financial profit from people's superstitions. They used new discoveries in physics and chemistry, which long remained unknown to the general public, as well as simple light and sound effects to amaze groups anxious for marvels. Existing secret societies provided a favorable atmosphere for the meetings. The Freemasons were receptive to occult ideas, and new secret orders and mysterious societies were formed. Under such circumstances, swindlers like Count Alessandro di Cagliostro (1743–1795), the Italian adventurer and magician, could have unimaginable success. The writings on seers and seances also interested those who gave no credence to the sham supernatural demonstrations. They were enticed by the challenge of figuring out and exposing the complicated trickery practiced by charlatans who were able to entrance so many others. The authors of *Trivialromane* knew how to take advantage of the situation by continuously reworking the motifs in new plot variations. A special genre developed, comparable to today's mystery or detective novel.

But Schiller did not make mere superficial use of this popular material. He actually pursued studies on the subject. The impostor Cagliostro had long intrigued him and aroused his interest in critically analyzing supernatural phenomena. To portray the seance scene in the first book, he carefully researched pertinent literature of the day and integrated many details from his readings. In addition, while studying historical sources for his drama *Don Carlos*, he had come across information concerning the questionable role of Jesuits in the sixteenth century. This information coincided with the general opinion of his day, which held that the Jesuits had infiltrated secret societies in order to influence weak or irresolute members and bring about conversions. The world of Catholicism was foreign to Schiller, and he must have regarded a conversion to Catholicism—such as takes place in the novel— with suspicion. By developing the political and psychological aspects of his subject, Schiller not only wrote the story of a fraudulent seer but created a novel of state affairs (*Staatsroman*) which was critical of the times while relating a person's inner story.

In summary, *The Ghostseer* is the story of a prince who, due to a superficial and misguided education, especially in religion, is susceptible to believing in seers' claims and ultimately converts from Protestantism to Catholicism. The internal plot of the fragment is concerned with the prince's psychology. He becomes increasingly involved with and encircled by certain characters until he is completely isolated from his court, which means that he no longer has a source of money. With his conversion to Catholicism, the first part—and the novel as a whole—comes to an end. As the fragment ends, the prince's debts have been paid. There is no doubt that the prince was forced into debt so that whoever paid his debts could gain control over him. The prince comes under the complete control of a mysterious character from the realm of the demagogical seers. The role of this character, known only as the "Armenian," is unclear, but he appears to have been responsible for the entanglements and confusion in the plot. The reader has evidence that the Armenian is the one who was behind the prince's love affair with a beautiful Greek woman. We can assume that the prince's dissension with the court and with his relatives has been deliberately induced so that, in a state of rejection and helplessness, he could be more easily won over.

The finished novel—regardless of whether Schiller ever actually had a complete plan in mind—would no doubt have included much more than the conversion at the end of the fragment. That the novel was planned as a *Staatsroman* of a very special kind can be deduced from various remarks made by the narrator. At the close of the first book he says: "He was a noble man and would certainly have been a credit to the throne had he not been deceived into wanting to ascend to it by means of a crime." This fits with the narrator's statement in the preface that the novel could "perhaps be important as a contribution to the history of deception and aberrations of the human spirit." From the parts of the fragment that we have, we do not learn what the crime was or how the prince was deceived. Schiller gives us no indication of this elsewhere. Apparently his primary concern was the problem of the prince's delusion, the question of how this aberration of a human spirit could have come about, making a noble man the victim of deceit and evil.

In a letter to Körner, Schiller wrote that it would be wrong to think that the prince's behavior was a result of his philosophy. Rather, it derived from his "*uncertain* position between this philosophy [of reason] and his . . . former favorite feelings [for the world of spirits]"; his actions stemmed from the "inadequacy" of reason and the resulting feeling of abandonment. Not reason itself but the "dissatisfaction" with the philosophy of reason provided the psychological motivation (March 9, 1789). This interpretation helps illuminate the central theme. The prince originally believed that the happenings at the seance were genuine. He was eager for the demonstration; as we are told, it was always his "favorite passion" to "come into contact with the world of spirits." But after the swindler is exposed, he is unmerciful and ingeniously perceptive in solving and rationally explaining all the details of the deception. The narrator, who sees this as proof of the prince's enlightened nature, clarity of thought, and logical mind, overlooks the decisive fact that the prince does not defend rationality until the fraud has already been established by none other than the Armenian, who exposes the impostor in order to gain the prince's confidence. This means that the Armenian comprehends the prince's weaknesses and his "uncertain position" better than the narrator. An unmasked impostor is obviously no longer credible to the prince, but he will allow himself to be deceived again and again if his "favorite passion" is addressed and the deception is clever enough, for his powers of reason are not sufficient to constitute the basis for his intellectual life.

The narrator realizes this only gradually. In the beginning of the second book he recognizes that changes have taken place in the prince's thinking. What he says about the prince's childhood is comparable to the childhood of Anton Reiser and, more remotely and in a different way, to that of Wilhelm Meister (*Theatrical Mission*). The prince also felt confined and oppressed in his early years. Religion hindered his development, stood in the way of his inclinations, meant only fear and pressure. "No wonder," comments the narrator, that "he grasped at the first opportunity to flee from such a strict yoke." One is struck by the similarity in language and content of this statement to related passages in *Anton Reiser* and the *Theatrical Mission*. The prince also searches for liberation, but he cannot find it in the same way as the youths who see literature as a substitute for a disappointing reality. Compared to them, he is much more endangered, for he does not succeed in actually breaking away from his previous world. He is afraid of looking too hard at religious questions. "The source of this fear was a bigoted, subjugating education. It had impressed on his delicate soul frightful images which, for the rest of his life, he was never fully able to obliterate." The narrator describes the situation in figurative language: "The prince ran away from his hard master like a slave who, even in the midst of freedom, still carries a sense of bondage with him. He had escaped with his chain and for that reason could become the prey of any swindler who discovered it and knew how to use it." In other words, the prince is the victim of his own inner bondage.

Wilhelm Heinse's (1749–1803) *Ardinghello* (1787) has a place on the periphery of the novelistic tradition which, beginning with Wieland's *Don Sylvio* and continued by Goethe, Moritz, Jacobi, Lenz, and others, is characterized by youthful heroes searching for a new reality. *Ardinghello* was sharply criticized by both Goethe and Schiller; Goethe said that he "detested" it. The novel had an influence on the succeeding era as well as on later generations, including such important figures as Jacob Burckhardt and Friedrich Nietzsche. Heinse united the ideals of the Storm and Stress period with vivid impressions from his three and one-half year sojourn in Italy (1780–83). A decisive element in the novel was undoubtedly his concept of Rousseau, whom he interpreted in his own way; he saw nature and sensuality as inseparable. He sets the novel in sixteenth-century Italy and endows his hero with an energetic and adventuresome spirit and a lust for life, rather than with the lyrical and sentimental traits which predominated at the time.

As productive as novelists were in the decades following *Werther,* almost all of their works, with the exception of Wieland's masterpiece *The Abderites,* can be seen as a prelude to Goethe's *Wilhelm Meister's Apprenticeship* (*Wilhelm Meisters Lehrjahre,* 1795–96). The *Apprenticeship* quickly became the focus of literary attention, which until then had been diffused over a broad artistic landscape. Respected authorities such as Schiller, Wilhelm von Humboldt, Körner, and Friedrich Schlegel were extraordinarily impressed by the work and realized that its uniqueness lay in its original poetic style. For many it became the standard. Naturally, one did not have to conform to it, but authors were nevertheless greatly affected by it for a long time to come. Even esteemed novelists in both the nineteenth and twentieth centuries looked back to *Wilhelm Meister* and saw it as a model for, or a contrast to, their own ideas.

If one compares the indifference with which Wieland's *Agathon* was received with the positive reaction to the *Apprenticeship,* one can see the change in literary attitudes which had taken place in thirty years. To be sure, in his essay *On Naive and Sentimental Poetry* (*Über naive und sentimentalische Dichtung,* 1795), Schiller still echoed the traditional bias by commenting that the novelist is "only" the "half-brother" of the poet. Yet Schiller himself had just followed the evolution of the *Apprenticeship* with intense interest for a period of two years and had voiced his utmost admiration for the work again and again. The extent to which a novel could now be considered a valid expression of the times is evidenced in Friedrich Schlegel's statement that "the French Revolution, Fichte's *Theory of Knowledge,* and Goethe's *Meister* are the greatest tendencies of the age. Whoever takes offense at this combination, for whom no revolution can seem important if it is not loud and material, has not yet elevated himself to a lofty overview of mankind" (*Fragmente,* 1797–98).

The novel creates the impression of complete harmony. Its smooth, unified flow was not impaired by the process of reworking the earlier manuscript; this could not even be detected by its readers. Modern readers may enjoy comparing the versions and will undoubtedly agree that the earlier text has been fused into the *Apprenticeship* so as to conform totally to its design. All the plot lines have been interwoven and led to a conclusion within the new framework. Many parts, including the last books, are completely new; those taken from the *Theatrical Mission* have been changed and rearranged. Some elements of the original version were not used at all, such as the theater director Madame de Retti and the plot events around her. Basically, the six books of the *Theatrical Mission* have been worked into the first four books of the *Apprenticeship,* and four more books have been added.

The difference in narrative style is striking. Goethe's earlier version begins in a cumbersome and heavy manner. Opening with the circumstances of Wilhelm's childhood, it unfolds the story of his youth and only gradually leads to the conflict with his environment and to his relationship with Mariane. In the new version Wilhelm is presented to the reader not as a child but as a vibrant young man in love, enthusiastic about theater, filled with illusions about himself and the world. Even before Wilhelm appears, we are introduced to his charming partner Mariane. As far as their relationship is concerned, there is no need for background information. From the first page, the narrator builds on the immediate present. This does not prevent him from including Wilhelm's childhood experiences with the puppet theater, but, unlike the *Theatrical Mission,* they are now presented as unforgettable and enlivening memories. The reader is caught up in the occurrences and must follow them with alertness and care, for the narrative proceeds briskly and essential points could be almost unnoticed.

Like the narrator, the young pair introduced at the beginning is concerned with fulfillment in the present. Wilhelm's father thinks in terms of his son's secure financial future. But Wilhelm disregards practical considerations, just as Mariane, absorbed with her love for Wilhelm, refuses to think about the imminent return of her rich suitor Norberg, whom she does not love. In the first scene, when the old servant woman Barbara displays gifts from Norberg in order to remind Mariane of her obligation to him, Mariane refuses to listen. She exclaims, "Not a word of all this tonight. . . . When Norberg returns I am his again, I am yours, do with me as you wish. . . . But until then I am mine. . . . All that is mine I will give to him who loves me, whom I love. I will abandon myself to this passion as if it were to last forever." Mariane's "tragic novel" has begun.[10] Her absolute passion clashes with the limitations of her situation: her need for financial security and the impossibility of preventing the suitors from finding out about each other. Distraught after seeing a letter from Norberg, Wilhelm believes himself deceived by Mariane and immediately abandons her, an error that makes him responsible for her death. He soon suspects that he may have been unjust, but neither he nor the reader is enlightened as to the true circumstances until close to the end of the novel. Here Barbara explains how Mariane rejected Norberg and then waited in vain for Wilhelm. She wanted to "reveal everything" and then let him decide whether he should "keep or reject" her. Significantly, Wilhelm recognizes the truth about Mariane at the same time as he is leaving the world of the theater. With Felix, the son she left him when she died, a new period in his life begins. Felix has long been a part of the plot, but his origins were unknown. The actress Philine first points him out:

"A boy is running around, about three years old, as beautiful as the sun; his papa must be most charming."

This example shows how carefully Goethe joined and intertwined the plots. The intricate weaving of endless relationships which are in continuous interplay throughout the novel is characteristic of his style in the *Apprenticeship*. There is no doubt that he already had the entire plan in mind, with its broad range of characters and multiplicity of relationships, when he began to write. The fact that he released the first parts for publication before having finished the work, whereas he had retained the manuscript of the *Theatrical Mission* for years, indicates that he now knew how the novel would develop. It appeared in four small volumes, each containing two books, in January, May, and November 1795 and October 1796. Schiller saw the proofs of the first volume, and thereafter Goethe sent him a copy of each book before publication and received intensive commentary in return, some of which he could still apply to the work before its final printing. Schiller's letters contain some of the most important statements made about the novel—this was also Goethe's opinion—and even today they are a valuable aid in the interpretation of the *Apprenticeship*.

About ten days after receiving the eighth book, Schiller wrote that Goethe had not made a sufficient effort to express clearly and directly the basic idea of the work.

> If I still could find any fault with the whole, then it would be that in such great and deep seriousness, . . . the imagination seems to play too freely with the entirety. . . . In the eighth book you have thrown out different hints as to how you wish Wilhelm's apprenticeship and mastery to be understood. . . . These hints are very nice, but they do not seem to me to be enough [July 8, 1796].

Goethe acknowledged Schiller's objection. "There is no question that the results I seemed to express are much more limited than the contents of the work," he answered immediately, conceding that "the flaw you have correctly noticed comes from my innermost nature, from a certain realistic idiosyncrasy by which I find it comfortable to remove my existence, my actions, my writings from the eyes of men" (July 9, 1796). From this statement it is evident that a "clearer pronunciation of the main idea," as Schiller wished, would be contrary to Goethe's intentions (October 19, 1796). Schiller understood this and stressed that Goethe must unquestionably remain within the "limits" of his "poetic individuality"; "all beauty in the work must be *your* beauty" (July 9, 1796).

These statements by the two authors on the question of formulating the novel's main idea are important to any modern interpretation. An attempt to reduce its contents to a formula would be inappropriate. The world of the *Apprenticeship* cannot be limited and defined. An encounter with the work can be fruitful only if one constantly keeps in mind its rich, diverse life and therein sees the novel's essence.

A question central to the interpretation of the work is again: does Wilhelm have a theatrical mission? Despite the difference in narrative style, the *Apprenticeship* begins with the same theme as the earlier version: Wilhelm is filled with the dream of becoming an actor and creating a national theater. His fascination with the stage seems to develop even more naturally here than in the *Theatrical Mission*. Although he is still destined to enter the merchant class, his milieu is not the narrow, oppressive environment from which literature is the only escape. Goethe no longer needed to place his hero in a confining world in order to motivate his love for theater. Even Wilhelm is of the opinion that his contempt for business life was subjective and developed only as a consequence of his affection for the stage. In general, his story proceeds as it did in the *Theatrical Mission*, and his path leads, as it did then, to the actor-manager Serlo's stage (book 4). In the following book, the performance of *Hamlet*, which was not included in the earlier version, takes place. It is the highlight of Wilhelm's theatrical career. As dramatic adviser, director, and actor in the role of Hamlet, Wilhelm is the enlivening member of the troupe and the others regard him as their "most outstanding actor."

An abundance of literary inspirations makes the fifth book of the *Apprenticeship* an artistic masterpiece. Schiller wrote that he read "the fifth book . . . with downright drunkenness" (June 15, 1795). In it Goethe produced plot elements of overpowering forcefulness and imagination. The appearance of an unknown person to play the ghost in *Hamlet* is one of the most remarkable ideas in German literature. In a mysterious letter which Wilhelm receives before the production, he is assured that a ghost will appear. Since he has not yet cast the part, he decides to leave it unassigned and simply trust in the letter. The actors are not disappointed, for a ghost does appear at the proper moment during the performance. Its dramatic entrance and dignified presence perceptively intensify the play's effect: "The entire audience shuddered," as does Wilhelm as Hamlet, thereby lending authenticity to his acting. Disappearing, still unidentified, the ghost leaves behind a veil on the hem of which Wilhelm finds an embroidered message: "For the first and last time! Flee! Youth, flee!"

It is not disclosed until later that this is the first time the Society of the Tower, a secret society, has actively intervened in Wilhelm's life. Its members had observed Wilhelm for a long time, and he had occasionally spoken with one of its representatives. In the last book, Wilhelm realizes that it was the Abbé, the central figure in the society, who helped him in *Hamlet* "by providing a ghost."

The fascinating ingenuity of the entire Hamlet scene and the fifth book in general can only be fully appreciated if one takes into account the era in which the novel was written, an age in which lodges, secret confederations, and mysterious orders flourished. Suspicious, often masked, emissaries played an important role for prospective and lower-ranking members. The mysterious stranger was a standard element in popular novels dealing with secret societies. Schiller also worked with this figure in *The Seer*. But Schiller used the motifs within the context of seances and seers, whereas in the *Apprenticeship* the motifs have been transformed so as to become unrecognizable. They have been disassociated from the world of their origins and brought into a new context. Nonetheless, the discerning reader will recognize Goethe's irony in using the cult of seers and secret lodges for his own purposes throughout the novel.

Before *Hamlet* was staged, a letter from his brother-in-law Werner had accelerated Wilhelm's decision to give up his neglected business duties and openly acknowledge his commitment to the theater. Werner's picture of bourgeois happiness provoked Wilhelm to counter with a statement of his own dreams, thereby justifying his joining the theater. In the letter Werner summarized his philosophy: "to transact your business, to earn money, to be merry with your own family, and not to trouble yourself with the rest of the world except to the extent that you can make use of it." In reply to Werner's suggestions concerning Wilhelm's possible business activity, Wilhelm asked, "How does it help me to manufacture good iron while my own inner being is full of dross? and how can I put an estate in order if I am at odds with myself? In a word, to cultivate myself, just as I am, has been my deepest impulse and purpose ever since my youth."

Although Wilhelm's need for cultivation is not associated with religion, historically the striving for self-purification and inner peace was tied to religious concepts. The particular way of life which can result from the cultivation of inner experiences in combination with the fostering of an intense belief in God is given expression in the sixth book of the novel, "Confessions of a Beautiful Soul." The "Confessions" are tied to the main plot in that Wilhelm reads aloud from them to the dying Aurelie at the end of the fifth book. Then in the sixth book Goethe interrupts the chronological flow and presents this manuscript to the reader in its entirety. It is the autobiography of a woman who devotes her life to God with tranquillity and contentment. The fact that Goethe devotes so much space to the religious sphere, although it is irrelevant to Wilhelm, indicates that the novel is meant to transcend the immediate involvement of the main character. The world presented in the novel is larger than he can grasp. Because the realm of the "Beautiful Soul" was of such great importance to the eighteenth century and emphasized qualities fundamental to humanitarian thought, it receives a well-defined place in the sixth book. Wilhelm's letter to Werner shows that he possesses an important prerequisite for the type of life described in the "Confessions," the impulse to cultivate harmoniously his own nature. At the same time it also becomes clear that for Wilhelm personally there is no world of cultivation and spirituality outside of the theater. Religion is meaningless to him and he does not feel the power of a cultivating influence from any other realm. Werner's letter arouses his resistance, but he has nothing to oppose it with other than that "impulse" and the love of theater from his childhood. Serlo's timely offer provides him with a favorable opportunity to pursue his longstanding desire for a stage career, and since he has no other alternative, he grasps it.

Wilhelm's decisions are generally not based on practicalities or knowledge. He has blurred ideas about life and often expresses unsubstantiated opinions based on his uniquely personal view of the world. The actress Aurelie has only known him for a short time when she realizes that he can judge poetry much better than he can judge the people around him. "I have hardly ever seen a person who knows so little about and so completely misunderstands the people with whom he lives as you," she says to him after expressing her admiration for his insight into poetry. The problem of the sentimentalist recurs; Goethe had also dealt with it in the *Theatrical Mission*, from which Aurelie's statements are reproduced nearly identically.

Just as Wilhelm's ideas about his future are unclear when he enters the world of the theater, they are just as vague when he leaves it. He originally leaves the company intending to be absent only for a short time in order to fulfill Aurelie's last wish that he deliver a letter to her beloved Jarno. This task brings him into contact with the Society of the Tower, which will continue to be of importance to him. By introducing the society, Goethe gave the novel the new direction, both contextually and structurally, which distinguishes it from the *Theatrical Mission*.

With regard to content, this means that Wilhelm does not have a theatrical mission after all. His stage career is based on a misconception which he must learn to recognize. Since he is not in a position to achieve this insight alone, there is a need for the society to intervene, with each member helping Wilhelm in a different way. They are able to guide him because they possess worldly knowledge and are sustained by values which unite them. The role the society plays demanded a restructuring of the original manuscript. Goethe did not simply add new parts to the *Theatrical Mission*; that is, he did not merely continue the story and lead Wilhelm to the Society of the Tower. Instead, he introduces the members of this group from the beginning of the novel. As the plot proceeds, they become more visible and take an increasingly strong and decisive stand toward Wilhelm. By the time he enters their circle and comes completely and directly under their influence, he already knows a majority of them. An intricate texture of artistically woven threads has been formed.

An unknown stranger speaks with Wilhelm in the last chapter of the first book; in the second book an unknown person takes part in an impromptu performance of the troupe during a boat trip. As Wilhelm later learns, this was the Abbé, the main spiritual figure in the society. Another important figure is Jarno, who meets Wilhelm in the third book; he has the same function as in the fifth book of the _Theatrical Mission_, that of introducing Wilhelm to Shakespeare's works. Somewhat later Jarno tries to help Wilhelm enter into "an active life," but arouses his mistrust by making derogatory comments about Mignon and the Harpist.

Like Jarno, the "beautiful Amazon" is now associated with the Society of the Tower. As in the _Theatrical Mission_, she has an effect upon Wilhelm which extends far beyond their brief meeting in the forest. Significantly, she occupies his thoughts as he signs the theater contract. The Amazon's connection with the society as well as with the "Beautiful Soul," who was her aunt, does not become clear until late in the novel.

In the last two books all the plot lines come together. The problems which have been presented are not solved, but possible solutions are approached. The decision on the question of Wilhelm's theatrical mission has long been in the making, so that now it can be carried through with seeming ease. After Wilhelm has been under the influence of the society for some time, Jarno bluntly tells him to renounce the theater since he has no talent. "Shocked . . . his ego not a little hurt," Wilhelm does not understand Jarno. He sets out nonetheless to fetch Felix and Mignon, whom he had left behind with Frau Melina in the world of the theater. At this point he meets the old servant woman Barbara for the first time in many years and learns the truth about Mariane and her son Felix. Though Wilhelm had planned to take his leave formally from the theater, he soon comes to feel that this departure has already taken place. Even the experience as a spectator is different; the stage no longer produces "an illusion" for him. He writes to Werner, "I am leaving the theater and will unite myself with men whose association, in every sense, must lead me to pure and certain activity." His ensuing initiation into the society, described by the author with light irony, resembles the rites of Freemasons and shows that he is already a changed person. Not until much later does Jarno explain why Wilhelm lacks talent for the stage: "Whoever can only play himself is not an actor. Whoever cannot . . . transform himself . . . into many shapes does not deserve the name." Wilhelm had certainly played many roles quite well, including _Hamlet_, but only because he had been aided by his own temperament and the momentary mood. This, however, is not enough.

The reason the society members do not intervene more vigorously at an earlier time has to do with their concept of education. In a conversation with the Abbé at the beginning of the seventh book, Wilhelm expresses concern that he has spent too much time in the theater to no advantage. But the Abbé rejects this notion, explaining to Wilhelm that everything contributes to one's education. The Abbé believes that error is a means of leading the searching person to clarity and insight. He later claims that "error can only be cured by erring." Wilhelm was allowed to exhaust his error so that the society could be even more sure of eventually winning him over. It is difficult to say what has actually been achieved in the end. Wilhelm has been accepted into a circle of active people. The role he will assume is unknown, but there are many possibilities, as demonstrated by the varied activities of the other members.

To the same extent that his new acquaintances define Wilhelm's new world, those in his previous life diminish in importance but do not completely disappear from sight. Philine, who left the theater even before Wilhelm, is mentioned again at the end of the novel. Lothario, the society member who is hosting Wilhelm, occasionally speaks of Aurelie, as does Felix. Wilhelm continues to feel responsible for Mignon and the Harpist. Since he can no longer sustain the family unit, he gives them into the best possible care. However, they do not survive his transition to the sphere of activity; they both die, as if they were a part of him.

Goethe gives a special poetic luster to the last part of Mignon's life. She has become seriously ill while staying with Lothario's sister, Natalie. The doctor calls for Wilhelm in the hope that her grief and longing can be soothed by Wilhelm's presence. Wilhelm is completely surprised to discover that Natalie is the beautiful Amazon from the woods. While discussing a portrait in her house which resembles her, he also learns that the picture is of the "Beautiful Soul" and that Natalie is her niece. Natalie and the doctor tell Wilhelm of Mignon's transformation. Whereas before she had never wanted to part from her boy's clothing, she now wears a long white dress. A spiritualized being, she is knowingly awaiting her end. The story of Mignon's past is not revealed until after her death. She was born from a marriage between siblings; her father was the Harpist, who, after discovering the truth, is horrified and takes his own life. In the end, Wilhelm and Natalie are united and Wilhelm is informed by the society that he must set out on a journey. This provides the transition for Goethe's last novel, *Wilhelm Meister's Travels*.

A comparison of the work with Wieland's *Don Sylvio* shows striking similarities. The basic outline of the two novels is the same: a group of well-meaning men helps an appealing youth to extricate himself from his errors. By including a cultivated society in their novels, the authors have made a new story from the familiar tale of *Don Quixote*. The individual members of the societies can be compared, as can the ways in which they reach a solution. Further parallels can be seen in settings, in the use of portraits, and in the endings. Many of the similarities can no doubt be attributed to the common experiences of the authors as contemporaries. What cannot be so explained, however, is the fact that the central theme of the *Apprenticeship* is exactly the same as that of *Don Sylvio*.

Goethe was evidently influenced by Wieland to a much greater degree than literary historians have previously realized. Like Wieland, Goethe also wrote a novel in which the entire plot is based on the idea of a mistaken path which leads to a good end. Because the error is instructive, it may not be regretted or deplored. Pleased at how splendidly things have worked out, Don Sylvio's friend Pedrillo wonders what would have become of the youth had it not been for his error: "if we had not been fools and searched for the blue butterfly?" Whatever the case may be, it was unavoidable that the heroes submit to some type of illusion. The discussion on the nature of error in the last parts of the *Apprenticeship* corresponds to the narrator's reflections on foolishness and *Schwärmerei* in *Don Sylvio*.

Literary historians commonly refer to *Wilhelm Meister's Apprenticeship* as a *Bildungsroman*. This definition can certainly be used as long as one is aware that such literary categories are not inherently valid, but merely a matter of convention. The term was first used by Karl Morgenstern (1770–1852) in lectures held between 1810 and 1820 at the University of Dorpat. He originally applied the word to novels written by Friedrich Maximilian Klinger (1752–1831), the curator of the university, but later, under the influence of Blanckenburg's *Attempt on the Novel*, he broadened and modified his concept so that Wieland's *Agathon* and Goethe's *Wilhelm Meister* seemed to fit the description. Morgenstern was not a man of subtle analysis. He was concerned solely with the plot of a novel and with its effect on the reader. The definition which best illustrates his concept states that

> it will be called a *Bildungsroman* first and primarily on account of its contents, because it depicts the hero's *Bildung* [personal growth and education] as it begins and proceeds to a certain level of perfection, but also secondarily because, precisely by means of this depiction, it promotes the *Bildung* of the reader to a greater extent than any other type of novel.[11]

This category could be useful in classifying novels strictly on the basis of plot, but it does not aid in their interpretation. Insofar as the *Apprenticeship* is concerned, the problem of *Bildung* is approached from many sides and could not be treated with greater seriousness. Yet one has an uneasy feeling about the attempt to draw conclusions. The outcome of Wilhelm's *Bildung*, that is, the person he becomes, defies definition in concrete terms.

Variety of Forms at the Turn of the Century

The last decade of the eighteenth and beginning of the nineteenth centuries was a period when varied forms of the novel were colorfully juxtaposed to an even greater extent than during the preceding era. While Wieland was producing his last novels, *Peregrinus Proteus* (1791), *Agathodämon* (1799), and *Aristipp* (1801), Jean Paul emerged as a new author, and his novels, appearing rapidly one after the other, were widely read and admired. Soon after *Wilhelm Meister's Apprenticeship*, the first part of Friedrich Hölderlin's *Hyperion* (1797) was published; two years later the last part followed. Almost simultaneously Novalis began *Heinrich von Ofterdingen*, which he continued writing until shortly before his death in 1801. Ludwig Tieck's first novel, *William Lovell* (1795–96), was succeeded by a completely different work, *The Wanderings of Franz Sternbald* (*Franz Sternbalds Wanderungen*, 1798). Not long afterward, Friedrich Schlegel's *Lucinde* (1799), Clemens Brentano's *Godwi* (1801), and Bonaventura's *The Night Watches* (*Nachtwachen*, 1805) were published. Not only did the new generation of the 1790s manifest differing aspirations and directions from author to author, but individual novelists also took diverse paths within the framework of their own writings.

The great narrative works of Jean Paul (Jean Paul Friedrich Richter, 1763–1825) demonstrate that plot was no longer the vital element of a novel. Consequently, the action did not have to lead to a conclusion. In Jean Paul's works, the plot often slips away from the reader because the author uses it only in order to present his inner world. The style is discursive and whimsical; sudden fancies or inspirations carry the plot forward. Jean Paul delights in the game of metaphors, which he began to play at a young age under Laurence Sterne's influence and later developed with increasing artistry. It is evident that he is not so much concerned with presenting a subject or a situation or with making a statement as with the interplay of narrator and material. The narrator, inexhaustibly imaginative, continuously asserts his presence by interruptions and digressions. Jean Paul uses and discards more plot motifs than any other author. Because they have no special meaning, they can replace each other in rapid succession.

Jean Paul's first novels brought him from obscurity to fame almost overnight. *The Invisible Lodge* (*Die unsichtbare Loge*, 1793) was highly praised by contemporary authors—Karl Philipp Moritz was "delighted" with it and

Novalis is said to have found it "extraordinary"—and *Hesperus* (1795) made him the most popular author of his time. In *The Invisible Lodge*, the main character, Gustav, spends the first eight years of his life below the earth. This was a condition imposed by Gustav's grandmother before his parents were allowed to marry; she wanted their first child to "grow up . . . for heaven." After Gustav has spent the required number of years underground in the company of a poodle and a tutor, he experiences a resurrection. This is one of the most famous scenes in Jean Paul's work. Gustav's teacher has long prepared him for the important day, telling him that if he is very good he will be permitted to die and then enter "heaven," which he describes like the surface of the earth. When the moment finally arrives, the tutor "pushes the gate open behind which the world lay and raises his child up to the earth and beneath the sky." Gustav, filled with emotion, is overcome by the earth's splendors. To him the earth seems to be a paradisical heavenly meadow, and his parents approach him like blessed spirits. The chapter describing Gustav's "Rising from the Death" ends with a reflection on man's real death and what may follow it. "Veiled fate! will our death be like Gustav's?"

In Jean Paul's third novel, *Siebenkäs* (1796–97), resurrection is again a central motif. The plot centers on the lawyer named Siebenkäs, who escapes from his unhappy marriage to Lenette by pretending to die and having his empty coffin buried. He does this on the suggestion of his best friend, Leibgeber. The fake death seems macabre from the standpoint of a conventional plot. Similarly, the resolution of all Siebenkäs's problems in the end seems contrived and unconvincing to the reader. Under a different name, Siebenkäs finds a new profession and is reunited with his true love, Natalie. He had met her during his previous life, but they had parted, and he had never expected to see her again. They are married in the ceremony referred to in the complete title: *Flower, Fruit, and Thorn Pieces; or, The Married Life, Death, and Wedding of the Advocate of the Poor, Firmian Siebenkäs*.

The novel's external plot merely provides the motifs for a presentation of what is actually essential to the work: the resurrection. Many readers may laugh at the fake death, but the humor does not mask its meaning, and even as a game it is not entirely funny. Through the staged death, life becomes recognizable. The death becomes a reality for everyone; all undergo a transformation. Even Leibgeber, who is manipulating the game, cannot escape from it. He needs all his strength to endure the event which has become quite serious for him and Siebenkäs as well. Though Siebenakäs was heavily oppressed by his world, the final farewell tempts him to revoke his decision. He sheds "last tears" before secretly leaving his home and his wife. Siebenkäs's new life begins on an August morning freshened by a storm; he is a transformed person. When we learn at the end that "the sufferings of our friend were over," it is evident that a resurrection has taken place. The fulfillment of Siebenkäs's love through his reunion with Natalie is the type of blissful experience which can only be expected after death.

An examination of the friendship between Siebenkäs and Leibgeber is important to an understanding of the novel and of Jean Paul's characters in general. The two exchange names twice, which seems at first to be a whimsical game: Siebenkäs's original name was Leibgeber, which is what he is called again at the end, and Leibgeber, whose name was Siebenkäs, is nameless at the end, since his friend died with his name. The friends, whose outward appearance is almost identical, are so different in character that the question of the other self arises. These characters as well as other pairs in Jean Paul's works (Albano and Roquairol in *Titan*, Walt and Vult in *The Twins*) seem to lend themselves to an interpretation as doubles, as opposing parts of one personality, as manifestations of the author himself.

The structure of *Titan* (1800–1803) is very different. The work is often referred to as Jean Paul's classical novel. In fact, one cannot fail to recognize the influence of Weimar—that is, of Goethe and Schiller—on its entire design, or at least to recognize Jean Paul's attempt to receive the influence of classical Weimar. It has always been a matter of dispute as to whether this brought about an intensification or diminution of his artistry. The author himself saw *Titan* as his major work and as the best of which he was capable. Whereas he had written his earlier novels in a relatively short time, *Titan* was preceded by years of preparation, and the final writing phase was repeatedly interrupted. Jean Paul exerted himself extraordinarily in order to surpass his previous achievements. He wanted to carry out a deliberate plan and to express an ideal concept in a form which would be appropriate to and harmonious with this plan.

Though not a classical novel, *Titan* does reveal the author's understanding of what a classical novel should be. It is designed towards a conciliatory ending. Albano, the main character, is an idealistic youth, fascinating in appearance and possessing great warmth. He is filled with the desire for beauty, love, friendship, and great deeds. But the fact that he becomes prince of a small German state at the end of the novel is not due to his outstanding personal qualities or his well-planned education. Rather, his rise is attributable solely to his aristocratic heritage. Since neither he nor the reader learns of this heritage until late in the novel, certain plot elements remain mysteriously unexplained until then, giving the work as a whole an elusive quality.

Jean Paul is concerned not only with the cultivation of the future ruler through education and travels, but with his experiences in love as well. The stories of Albano's love for three different women are an intrinsic part of the novel. For reasons incomprehensible to him, Albano is unable to win his beloved Liane as his bride. After her death his guilt feelings nearly result in his loss of sanity. He finds a new spiritual relationship when he meets Linda.

In spite of mutual fascination and many happily shared hours, the independent Linda wishes to evade the bond of marriage. "She could not even accompany a friend to the marriage altar," which she calls the "execution place of feminine freedom, the funeral pyre of the most beautiful, freest love." Nonetheless, she is ready to acquiesce and become engaged if Albano will promise not to participate in any war. She tells him, "Whoever feels that love alone is not enough has not been fulfilled in love." Albano, however, wants to combine "love and freedom" and perceives Linda's demand as a "theft of his freedom and free development." However, the marriage question is not decided on this basis but by an unfortunate incident. One night Linda is seduced by Liane's brother, Roquairol, who takes advantage of her night blindness and the similarity of his voice and handwriting to Albano's, and pretends to be Albano. The next day, during a performance in a tragic play he wrote, Roquairol shoots himself, whereupon Linda declares herself to be his widow. Albano eventually marries Idoine, a ruler's daughter from a small neighboring state who had always impressed Albano by her resemblance to Liane.

The character Roquairol is the Mephistophelian counterpart to Albano, the negative side of his being. Early in the second volume, Jean Paul gives an extensive description of Roquairol, explaining that he is "a child and victim of the century." Roquairol experiences "all the splendidness of mankind, all the emotions of love and friendship and nature which elevate the heart," but he experiences them in poems earlier than he has known them in life, "as an actor and playwright earlier than as a person, on the sunny side of fantasy earlier than on the weather-side of reality." He belongs to those "devastated by life," for whom there is "no new joy and no new truth" and who have "no old one" that is "whole and fresh." They have only a "dried-up future filled with arrogance, disgust, disbelief, and contradictions." Therefore Roquairol plunged into "good and bad diversions and love affairs, and afterwards recreated everything on paper and in the theater, . . . and every depiction hollowed him out deeper, just as cavities remain in the sun from the worlds it once disgorged."

Jean Paul continues the criticism of sentimentality which the older generation had expressed in their novels again and again. The previous generation was aware that literary ideals hindered one's view of reality. Wieland and Goethe struggled all their lives to find a path for their heroes into a world independent of literary and philosophical ideals. Lenz, Jacobi, Wezel, and Moritz also participated in this struggle in their own way. In their novels disillusionment and failure prevail, whereas both Wieland and Goethe at least allude to possible solutions. These solutions are all predicated on an abandonment of former ideals. Just as Don Quixote admits on his death bed that he has been a fool, the youths in Goethe's and Wieland's novels also realize that they will become fools if they do not recognize the windmills for what they are.

Roquairol succumbs to the danger faced by his older literary brothers in a way previously unimaginable: he becomes evil. The development of his relationship to Albano shows this to be a gradual process, but one of which he is fully aware. Through Roquairol's self-analysis and the accompanying expositions, Jean Paul advanced psychological thought into areas which first became more comprehensible in the course of the nineteenth century. It is a telling fact that while Jean Paul was enough ahead of his time to be able to sharply profile a self-destructive character like Roquairol, he nonetheless gave the central role to Albano.

While writing *Titan* Jean Paul was also occupied with a second novel, *Walt and Vult; or, The Twins* (*Die Flegeljahre*, 1804–5). At times he worked on both novels simultaneously in order to "refresh and strengthen himself by such 'alternate writing.'"[12] He even considered linking them together, despite the fact that (or perhaps because) they are complete opposites. The remarkable phenomenon of "parallel novels," so surprising in the case of Karl Philipp Moritz, is repeated here. Like Moritz, Jean Paul was also able to maintain two different styles simultaneously over a period of years. *The Twins* also took ten years to complete (it was begun somewhat later and consequently appeared later than *Titan*). It was, as had been the case with *Titan*, much less successful among contemporaries than Jean Paul's earlier novels, but today it is regarded as his most mature work. As Jean Paul said, his "talent took hold of him," and the two complementary characters, Walt and Vult, are just two "opposite and yet related persons" who together give a picture of the author himself. It is obvious from the book that Jean Paul's portrayal of the brothers is self-interpretation.

The rich interplay between these two characters determines the structure of the novel. As in the earlier novels, the plot is not a strong element. Basically, the events center on Walt's attempts to fulfill a series of stipulations prescribed in a will opened at the beginning of the novel. He has to be a pianist for one day, a head gardener for a month, and a notary for a quarter year. He must shoot a rabbit, correctly edit twelve pages of proofs, teach for a week in the country, and become a pastor—if he is to inherit a large fortune. A young poet and law student, Walt is "childlike, without falseness, pure, naive, and tender." His twin brother Vult is not the opposite of his brother in all respects. A complex character, he describes himself as "good-hearted and full of love, but just too enraged at all men." Like Walt, he is also an artist; as a musician he stands together with his poetic brother against "bourgeois life." Yet the relationship between the two brothers is problematic. Walt often does not understand Vult; he does not notice when he hurts him. Meanwhile, Vult painfully recognizes that he can never mean as much to

Walt as he would like. Jealous and deeply troubled, he quarrels with Walt rather than helping him as he would prefer. When Vult goes away and leaves Walt alone, the novel is over.

In spite of Jean Paul's enormous popularity with readers of his day, particularly with his earlier novels, there were some contemporaries who had reservations about him or rejected him altogether. Goethe, who is said to have called him "the personified nightmare of our time," felt that Jean Paul's works lacked clarity. Jean Paul remained controversial throughout the nineteenth century, although the Austrian author Adalbert Stifter and the Swiss Gottfried Keller saw him as their inspiration. Emphatic praise by the poet Stefan George and his followers resulted in a more widespread recognition of the author. Whether this has contributed to a better understanding of Jean Paul or to misinterpretations remains open; the zig-zag path of available literary research does not provide a basis for judgment. But his uniqueness is indisputable. Because he was an artist unlike any other, literary historians have generally been reluctant to identify him with a specific literary tradition. The concepts of Classicism and Romanticism have long been found inapplicable to Jean Paul. The same is also true of Friedrich Hölderlin.

The originality of Friedrich Hölderlin's (1770–1843) only novel, *Hyperion or the Hermit in Greece* (*Hyperion oder Der Eremit in Griechenland,* 1797–99), overwhelms the reader immediately. The work's essence and uniqueness lie in *Hyperion's* distinctive narrative tone, a penetrating lyrical tone which gives expression to the main character's intense suffering as well as to his strength in overcoming this suffering. The fictional premise of the novel is that Hyperion returns to his homeland after having experienced profound losses, relates his story, and in the telling experiences it anew. The first sentence of the novel embraces the entire story: "My beloved native soil gives me joy and sorrow again." Greece was both his hope and his disappointment. He had fought for the revival of his country—Greek revolutionaries allied with the Russians were defeated in 1770 in their struggle against their Turkish oppressors—and failed. In reminiscing he relives the excitement and enthusiasm with which he took up the struggle as well as the hopelessness and sorrow of defeat. His dreams for his country are equalled by his idealism in love. His beloved Diotima is to him the embodiment of beauty, the "name" for the "highest and best" that men seek. Diotima knew that he was destined for great deeds. She warned him of the dangers of war and violence and died after Hyperion, in his despair over the defeat, no longer considered himself worthy of her. The significance of the novel lies in the verbal expression of spiritual processes; *Hyperion* once again depicts man's inner story. It is not a linear story designed towards an ending, but through the cyclical structuring of the novel and the corresponding theme of the cycle of nature—there is "reconciliation in the midst of strife" and what is lost will return—the "eternal recurrence" of all human possibilities is suggested.

The years during which Hölderlin was working on *Hyperion*—from the first mention of his plan in 1792 to the appearance of the second volume in the fall of 1799—were a time of fundamental change in the literary landscape in Germany. When Novalis (pseudonym of Friedrich von Hardenberg, 1772–1801) began writing *Heinrich von Ofterdingen* (1802) toward the end of 1799, he found himself in a completely different situation from Hölderlin who, not even a decade earlier, had attempted several versions, including a metric text, in his search for an appropriate form. *Heinrich von Ofterdingen* is unthinkable without *Wilhelm Meister's Apprenticeship*. Novalis was set aflame by Goethe's new novel, as was his entire generation. By 1798 an article by Friedrich Schlegel, "On Goethe's *Meister*" ("Über Goethe's *Meister*"), had already appeared. Ludwig Tieck's *The Wanderings of Franz Sternbald*, which begins the series of novels in the tradition of *Wilhelm Meister*, had also been published.

Novalis's preoccupation with the *Apprenticeship* probably began as early as the end of 1796, soon after publication of the last volume, and continued for many years. At different times the novel took on different meanings for Novalis. He could be admiring or critical, reflective, astonished, or polemical. His encounter with the novel made him aware of his own individual path; he recognized that it had to be different from Goethe's. Even before beginning *Ofterdingen*, he had started developing his own theory of the novel. This corresponded to his philosophical leanings and, moreover, he probably would not have been able to assert himself against Goethe's dominance without the support of a theoretical position. The many thoughts on Goethe's art and scientific method which Novalis periodically wrote down reflect an uneasiness that lasted for years. He believed that Goethe's "great style of presentation" was "justifiably . . . so admired." The "true representative of the poetic spirit on earth," he said of Goethe in *Pollen*, a collection of prose fragments (*Blütenstaub*, 1798). But not long afterwards he noted, "Goethe will and must be surpassed," with the qualification that he could only be surpassed like the ancient masters, in "substance and power, in variety and depth—but not as an artist."[13]

Novalis could not find material for his novel in his own age. Instead, he found it in a poeticized Middle Ages. In his essay *Christendom or Europe* (*Die Christenheit oder Europa*, 1799), he drew a utopian picture of history which he carried over to the novel. The essay begins with the description of an illustrious past, then discusses its decline, and ends with the assurance that Christianity will arise again. The dangers of the present are contrasted with the security of the Middle Ages. The essay begins:

> Those were beautiful, splendid times when Europe was a Chris-
> tian land, when *One* Christianity resided in this . . . part of the
> world; *One* great common interest joined the most remote prov-
> inces of this wide spiritual region. . . . Every member of this so-
> ciety was honored everywhere. . . . How cheerfully each person
> could accomplish his earthly day's work.

Novalis sets his novel in such an imaginary world. The central character,
Heinrich von Ofterdingen, is not a historical figure, but his name does appear in the Middle Ages as that of a poet in an anonymous work of fiction,
The Contest of Singers at the Wartburg (*Der Sängerkrieg auf der Wartburg,*
1260). Novalis came across the character while studying chronicles of the
late Middle Ages.

Novalis completed only the first part of the novel, which he wrote from
the end of 1799 to April 1800, and the beginning of the second part. He left
notes containing references to further plans. These notes and his letters to
Tieck and Friedrich Schlegel show the extent to which he actually structured
his novel to differ from Goethe's *Apprenticeship*. To Tieck he wrote that the
"entire work should be an apotheosis of poetry. In the first part, Heinrich von
Ofterdingen will mature as a poet—and in the second part he will be trans-
figured." To Schlegel he explained that "novel and fairy tale should be no-
ticeable in a pleasant mixture" which would become "an even more intimate
mixture" in the second part. The novel "should gradually become a fairy
tale." Considering that Goethe had Wilhelm Meister renounce all his plans
to lead the life of an actor and playwright, then these few sentences from
Novalis's letters suffice to characterize his rebellion. The sharpness of his
polemics against the *Apprenticeship* during the early stage of writing can be
explained by his enthusiasm for his own conception. Quite understandably,
as the creator of *Heinrich von Ofterdingen*, he was so absorbed by it that he
thought of the *Apprenticeship* as "basically a disagreeable and foolish book
. . . unpoetic to the greatest degree with regard to spirit—notwithstanding
the poetic nature of the presentation" (February 1800).

The plot of the first part of *Heinrich von Ofterdingen* reverses the story
of Wilhelm Meister: Heinrich is awakened to the recognition that he has a
calling as a poet. This awakening begins in the first chapter when he dreams
of his beloved, whose face is poised on the petals of the "blue flower." At first
he knows only that his dream has a special meaning. Not until later, when
Heinrich has matured as a poet, does he realize how his beloved and his
profession form a unity. A comparison with Wilhelm's relationship to Mariane in the introductory chapters of the *Apprenticeship*—his "passion for the
stage" was connected with his first love for a woman—makes it evident how
consciously Novalis designed his work as a contrast to Goethe's. As in

Goethe's novel, the worlds of father and son are in opposition. But the son does not consider breaking away from home; instead, the mother leads him away. *She* makes the decision to take a long-desired trip which she expects will "expel the gloomy mood" she had observed in her son for some time. Heinrich rejoices "beyond measure," but when it is time to depart his feelings change: "Heinrich left his father and his birthplace in a melancholy mood. He now realized for the first time what separation is." Again the importance of the mother is emphasized; her closeness "was a great comfort to the boy. The old world did not yet seem completely lost and he embraced it with twice the fervor." Finally on his way, leaving the familiar surroundings, he looks back from a hill with "the most unusual presentiment, as if he were returning to his fatherland from their present destination after long wanderings, and as if he were therefore actually traveling towards it now."

The journey leads from Eisenach, where Heinrich grew up in modest surroundings as the son of a craftsman, to his maternal grandfather in Augsburg. While it is true that Heinrich has undertaken a specific journey and geographical locations are clearly designated, the geographical setting serves only to define the contours of the spiritual landscape more distinctly. By traveling to his mother's birthplace Heinrich has set out on a journey to self-discovery. As he leaves the place of his youth he suspects that he has not left it forever, even if "long wanderings" lie before him. Novalis obviously did not intend his homecoming to be a reintegration into the narrow world of Eisenach, for his journey and return are to be seen in connection with a "glorification," a "poeticization of the world," a "creation of a fairy tale world," phrases which Novalis used in his notes. For this reason there is no real break from the sphere of his father and no departure for distant places. The entire world is a unified whole; eternal homecoming is a central concept. Structurally, the novel is better understood as a circular movement than as a movement forward. This idea is expressed in the profound conversation between the "pilgrim" and the poor girl who knowingly replies to his question "Where are we going?" with "Always home."

Because the maturation of a young poet is the novel's theme and is to be understood as a return home, the actual journey from Eisenach to Augsburg is meaningless. The novel should not be referred to as a "travel novel" (*Reiseroman*). No specific places are described, nor do individuals emerge from among the group of merchants who accompany the mother and son. Rather, the journey takes place in conversations, narrations, and occasional songs. The fact that conversations play such a privileged role and comprise extensive parts of the novel is consistent with the purpose: the spiritual plot can only be expressed in conversation or in metaphorical narrations. Novalis's conversations are special in that they are either based on mutual agreement or quickly lead to agreement. The characters understand each other in conversation and are united through the theme of their discussions.

At the beginning of their journey the topic of conversation between Heinrich and the merchants is poetry. Thus the central theme of the work is presented at the outset. The conversation starts with a mention of their destination: Heinrich is told of the appealing characteristics of his mother's countrymen and advised that he will probably lose his "serious shyness" in the "clear warm air of southern Germany." When talk then turns to the possibilities of his future profession, Heinrich becomes so lively in his replies that the merchants tell him, "It appears to us that you have the gift of a poet. You speak so fluently of your soul's visions, and you are not lacking in well-chosen expressions and appropriate comparisons." They then enlighten him further on the essence of poetry and contrast it with painting and music. As opposed to those arts, poetry is "completely inward." The poet fills "the inner shrine of the spirit with new, wonderful, and pleasing thoughts." He knows how to "arouse those secret powers in us at will" and lets us hear "of an unknown, splendid world through his words." What he stirs in us tears "us from the known present." One can understand foreign words; "the sayings of a poet exercise a magical power."

It may seem remarkable that the merchants should know all of this. Heinrich, his curiosity becoming "hot impatience," believes he has heard it somewhere in his "deepest youth," without having an exact recollection: "But what you say is so clear to me, so familiar, and you are giving me such extraordinary pleasure with your beautiful descriptions." These words reveal that Heinrich's awakening, which began with the dream of the blue flower, is in process. Whereas his mother noticed that after his dream Heinrich was "far quieter and more introspective than usual," he now appears lively, open, and eloquent. The merchants, by recognizing his poetic talent, become inspired themselves. They speak of the power of poets in times past and tell stories in which poets are the main characters. Their second narration fills an entire chapter and tells how a poet wins the daughter of a king. The explanation for the astonishing, at first somewhat unbelievable, behavior of the merchants is later offered by the character Klingsohr, who becomes Heinrich's teacher in Augsburg: "The story of your journey . . . provided me with pleasant entertainment last evening. I noticed that the spirit of poetry is your friendly companion. Your comrades unwittingly became its voice. In the vicinity of an artist poetry bursts out everywhere."

After completing further stages of his journey, Heinrich finally achieves full liberation of his poetic nature at a large social gathering in Augsburg. Mathilde, the beloved of his dreams, appears before him in real life. His grandfather, who leads her to him, and her father, the poet Klingsohr, immediately recognize Heinrich's special nature. His grandfather says that he was "born to be a poet," repeating exactly what the narrator had said of him earlier in the chapter. There is no doubt that this repetition is consciously directed against Goethe, whose Wilhelm had erred in believing himself to be a poet. Just as Wilhelm finds a circle of men who help him to accomplish his departure from the theater, Heinrich also finds a group of men in Augsburg. Their function, however, is quite different; they help Heinrich to "mature as a poet." Whereas Goethe's society is aristocratic, Novalis's is bourgeois. Numerous additional comparisons exist; they can be found at every step throughout the works.

What is striking about Klingsohr's teachings is that he ascribes such importance to reason in addition to emotions. "Enthusiasm without understanding is useless and dangerous." The "cool, enlivening warmth of a poetic spirit" is not the same as "that wild heat of a sickly heart." The young poet "cannot be cool, cannot be sober enough. . . . Poetry wishes to be practiced . . . as a strict art." Heinrich must expand his knowledge and gain useful insights. Klingsohr explains that the "goal of art is not the subject matter itself, but how it is treated." It is important to an understanding of Novalis's concept of the poet that Klingsohr's viewpoint differs greatly from that of the merchants.

Immediately following the pedagogical dialogue between Heinrich and Klingsohr, Heinrich and Mathilde engage in a love dialogue. The previous night Heinrich dreamed that he saw Mathilde drowning, after which they met again and she promised to stay with him forever. Their love dialogue is a continuation of their exchange in the dream. Heinrich and Mathilde assure each other of their inseparability and of the timelessness of their love.

The end of the first part is formed by a fairy tale, as Novalis had written to Schlegel and Tieck. The fairy tale cannot be rationally explained; it is a great myth created by Novalis and inspired by Goethe's fairy tale from the novella *Conversations of German Emigrants (Unterhaltungen deutscher Ausgewanderten,* 1795) and by the tales of other eighteenth-century authors. At the beginning of the second part, Mathilde's death has occurred. As a spiritual being, she is now close to the searching "pilgrim," just as she was united with Heinrich in life through a higher ideal.

In February 1800, Novalis wrote to Ludwig Tieck (1773–1853) that *Heinrich von Ofterdingen* would have many similarities with *The Wanderings of Franz Sternbald (Franz Sternbalds Wanderungen,* 1798), but not its "lightness." Yet, as he stated, "perhaps this shortcoming will not be unfavorable to its content." Though there is no doubt that the friendship with Tieck was "of the greatest importance" to Novalis's literary activity, to today's reader the two novels would seem very different, almost opposites. They are dissimilar in design, in style, and in the traits of the main characters. In comparison to the clear, quiet, certain language of *Heinrich von Ofterdingen,* Tieck speaks in a more casual tone, and not everything said is important. Nonetheless, this does not suggest that his text could simply be condensed; it is part of his style to be more relaxed and expansive.

Franz Sternbald is a painter who, although a favorite pupil of Albrecht Dürer, leaves Nuremberg "in order to expand his knowledge in distant places and then to return after weary travels as a master in the art of painting." His travels lead first to the Netherlands and then to Italy. He is a seeker and a questioner, filled with the anticipation of Italy and homesickness for Nuremberg. Several times along his journey possibilities other than art are suggested to him. Although these would seem to hold more promise for a practical and secure life, he always rejects them without hesitation. He is certain that he is an artist and that he would be unfit for any other activity. Nevertheless Franz Sternbald is not a harmonious character. He is disheartened by his own actions. Self-doubt and an awareness of his instability on one hand and his enthusiasm for art, dedication to it, and loyalty to his revered teacher Dürer on the other result in the picture of a torn, even contradictory figure. His character traits emerge with particular clarity in a conversation with his antithesis, Lukas von Leiden. "You are a very fortunate man," says Sternbald. "That artist is blessed who knows his own worth, who can approach his work with confidence. . . . You can perhaps hardly conceive of the passion I feel for our noble art, . . . but the higher my enthusiasm rises, the deeper my courage sinks at the thought of actually sitting down to paint. I can feel the nobility in the works of other masters, but my mind is so confused at present that I dare not begin work myself." Lukas can only confirm that Sternbald's "trepidation," his "overadmiration of the subject," is "something inartistic." He advises against the journey to Italy: "In your volatile state every new object you glimpse will distract you." But such considerations do not influence the course of events. Franz Sternbald continues his travels, has many colorful experiences, and occasionally paints a picture. He finally arrives in Italy, is deeply impressed, and finds the beloved woman of his dreams.

In an afterword written in 1843, Tieck said that in the planned continuation Sternbald, who did not know his parents, would have found his father as well. The story was supposed to end in Nuremberg. The novel is important as a *Künstlerroman* (novel about an artist), but it remains open as to whether Sternbald is a genuine artist.

Tieck was strongly influenced by Wilhelm Heinrich Wackenroder's (1773–1798) concept of art, and he collaborated with Wackenroder on his *Outpourings of an Art-Loving Friar* (*Herzensergiessungen eines kunstliebenden Klosterbruders*, 1797). For the friar, who can only think of great works of art with a "quiet, holy shudder," the distinction between religion and art is blurred. Such pious reverence for art precludes the possibility of exercising one's own creativity. If Sternbald was meant to assume this or a similar attitude, which is not entirely clear, then he could hardly have developed as a creative artist. But Tieck is actually more concerned with a general human problem. This can occasionally be detected in Sternbald's words, as when he writes from Florence to his friend in Nuremberg, "Continue to paint with eagerness, Sebastian, so that your name will be mentioned one day among the respected artists. You will certainly succeed sooner and better than I. My spirit is too unsteady, too irresolute, too quickly moved by every new thing. I would like to accomplish everything, and for that reason I will not be able to do anything in the end." With this self-interpretation Sternbald is describing a human type which is in no way bound to the circle of artists. There is a great difference between Franz Sternbald and the harmonious character Heinrich von Ofterdingen, who is the "realization of an idea" in accordance with Novalis's theory of the novel.

The main character in Tieck's first novel *William Lovell* (1795–96) was also a problematic personality. The hero, who at first seems to be a good-natured, "lively, cheerful youth, . . . an outstanding young man," submits entirely to evil and no longer shies away from any type of crime. The world, which he had already thought of as a "transitory shadow-game," becomes more and more detestable to him. Through this plot Tieck advanced into areas of thought and emotion new to his time. The experiences and dangers known to the young generation of Romanticists were presented here even before Romanticism had begun. William Lovell is a person who destroys his own strengths by self-reflection to the extent that he is no longer capable of actual experiences, sees himself as a stranger, and becomes an actor playing his own role. This brings to mind the character Roquairol in *Titan*; Jean Paul may, in fact, have been influenced by Tieck.

Friedrich Schlegel's (1772–1829) *Lucinde* (1799) also has a place among the novels of the period. The book can only be designated a novel if the author's own theory of the novel is taken into consideration. According to Schlegel, it is not the narrative element as such which is decisive to the novelistic form: "The only question is this: is the spirit poetic?" As important as Schlegel's theoretical writings are, the reader of *Lucinde* soon realizes that the author could not combine his intellectual brilliance with the gift of artistic productivity. There is no question that the theme expressed in the novel was of concern to the most sensitive minds of the time, but Schlegel was unable to create a convincing novel form.

Julius, the narrator and main character, praises the happiness found in his love for one special woman after a long search and many unsuccessful relationships. His awareness of her uniqueness and the emotional experience of forming a unity with her—a marriage without official sanction—is the theme of the work. Schlegel offers thoughts on a love realized in marriage, reflections on the togetherness of two persons in spirit and body, in memory and desire. The relationship is not to be misunderstood as free love or as an everyday bourgeois marriage. It is meant as a marriage in its most essential sense: through the togetherness of two equal individuals a perfect earthly existence can be realized.

Lucinde can be Julius's partner only because as a painter she is a free, independent person, who, like him, "passionately reveres" beauty, has a "definite predisposition to romanticism," and does not live "in the common world" but in a world she creates and shapes herself. "Only what she loved and honored with her entire heart was actually real to her; everything else was nothing." Neither naive nor innocent when she gives herself to Julius, she is "already the mother of a beautiful, strong boy whom death soon tore away from her."

Julius is also experienced in life. His story prior to meeting with Lucinde is told in the middle section of the book ("Apprenticeship for Manhood") in a manner approximating epic narration. Here Julius appears as one of the unstable, aimless youths whose descent from William Lovell cannot be overlooked. Feeling discontent and empty after many disappointing attempts to find a partner, he finally loses the standard by which to judge his own feelings. Not until he is fully united with Lucinde does he realize what the relationship means for her as well as for himself: that they are mutually enhanced and strengthened and that their union could never be dissolved.

The transformation created by their love is not restricted to them alone; it extends to their surroundings, bringing about harmony so that a "free society" can develop. Notwithstanding everything said about the main theme of love throughout the book, its essence should be seen in its inexpressibility. The infinite transformation experienced in the process of love cannot be grasped as a memory or as a present reality. Such a concept almost justifies the novel's blurred form. This form will first be ripe for discussion in connection with the novelistic experiments of the twentieth century.

Clemens Brentano (1778–1842) created an unusual novel with his *Godwi* (1801). On a first reading its unity is difficult to recognize. The artful game with plot segments takes priority over biographical and chronological succession. On the whole a picture of great confusion results. Novella-like narrations are joined together in a knotted ball, like "a novel run wild," Brentano said, thereby defining the form quite well.

The idea underlying the work is ingenious. Its first volume—an epistolary novel with several letter-writers and insertions of diary entries, documents, poems, and songs—contains the material which the poet Maria was commissioned to revise and organize into a novel. In the opinion of his employer he has ruined the novel. Since Maria feels obligated to continue but receives no more material from his angry employer, he seeks out the hero of his novel, Herr Godwi, in order to write the second volume with his help. He is received with friendliness. Godwi gives him further papers and relates his own life story to Maria in serial form. From this point on the narration has two strands: one formed by Maria and Godwi's companionship in Godwi's castle and the other by Godwi's novel as it develops from written documents and oral reports. During the writing Maria falls ill and finishes the book on his deathbed. After he dies, Godwi furnishes the last information to the reader.

The short book *The Night Watches* (*Nachtwachen*, 1804) by Bonaventura (pseudonym) has been a problem to the literary researcher. Today it is frankly admitted that its author is unknown, but until recently scholars thought they knew his identity. At different times different persons were named: Friedrich Wilhelm Joseph von Schelling, Clemens Brentano, E. T. A. Hoffmann, and Friedrich Gottlob Wetzel. The work is the statement of a very unhappy man who experiences intense existential suffering. Sixteen separate nocturnal vigils are described by the narrator and nightwatchman, Kreuzgang. What he observes is not part of a unified, cohesive world. A deceitful priest, an adulteress, insane and lost people, and poets haunt the dark setting like shadows. It is not surprising that for a long time scholars did not know how to identify the author, let alone how to determine the genre of *The Night Watches*.

At first glance it might seem that the decade at the turn of the century was a period of literary crisis or uncertainty, a time when novels tended toward formlessness. A more careful examination reveals that any such generalization is misleading. If certain authors loosened the traditional forms and were left with a dissolute form themselves, this is not evidence of a general crisis. It indicates the perpetual search for new means of expression during a productive period. How one evaluates formlessness—whether it is seen as a form in itself or as a breakdown in one stage of the search—is dependent upon the standpoint of the observer. It would be just as valid to regard the shattering of form as a genuine and final end in itself as it would be to see it as a transition to a new form. Our opinion of Jean Paul, Friedrich Schlegel, and Clemens Brentano is contingent on how we feel about this question. Furthermore, an understanding of the novel during this period is not based on these authors alone. The most important novelists of the epoch constructed clear, unequivocal, and original forms which differ in all essential elements from the novels of their contemporaries. Of course, the "novel run wild" also has its place in the history, and some may even prefer it. But no matter how one feels about Goethe's *Wilhelm Meister* and Hölderlin's *Hyperion*, it is not possible to speak of them as "wild," nor can this characterization apply in any way to Novalis's *Ofterdingen*.

Demonstration of a Theme in the Novel

At the end of the first decade of the nineteenth century, authors began to use the novel to present specific themes. By that time the novel had established itself as an art form, and many of its possibilities had already been explored; it had served for years as a means of developing the story of an individual. The age eventually had to tire of this, especially since the focus on a central character had always been problematic with regard to plot uniformity—one never really knew how the novel should end. In addition, objective interest in the events narrated had come to replace emotional empathizing with the main character's subjective experiences. The "age of sentiment" had finally passed, and questions of more comprehensive importance took priority. Novelists began to search for interesting themes and mastered them with a certainty acquired from a rich tradition and their own personal abilities.

A work by Goethe is again in the forefront: *Elective Affinities* (*Die Wahlverwandtschaften*, 1809). In this novel strict form is fused with the theme in perfect unity. Goethe supposedly said, as his friend Friedrich Riemer reported in his diary on August 28, 1808, that his intention in the work was "to depict social conditions and their conflicts symbolically." That the social conditions were portrayed with astonishing accuracy was often confirmed by Goethe's contemporaries. The theorist Karl Solger (1780–1819) stated that in a few centuries one would be able to "sketch a perfect picture of our present daily life" from this book, and Romanticist Achim von Arnim wrote to his future wife Bettina Brentano on November 5, 1809, that Goethe observantly chose the "home of an educated, landed nobleman of our time" in order to show the "monotony of idle, inactive happiness." Arnim said he had come to know many people of the kind Goethe describes and "all suffer from a very unusual hypochondria. Separated by education from the real country people, . . . they usually let their domestic soup boil over until no more is in the pot. Nowhere are there more divorces than in these classes. Everything new that enters into their lives must of necessity disturb them in their state of mutual boredom." With a similarity to Solger, Arnim states, that "we wish to give thanks to our Lord God and his servant Goethe that a part of time past has again been stored for the future in a true, detailed representation."

It is interesting that such opinions were expressed about a German novel from the early nineteenth century. These statements are documents of foremost importance in literary history. Whatever one might understand by the term "realistic novel"—this will be discussed below in the section "*Gesellschaftsroman*—Theodor Fontane"—it is evident that Goethe's *Elective Affinities* as well as his other novels could well fall into this category. But the "social conditions" are only a prerequisite for what excited Goethe himself: a symbolic depiction of conflicts. Arnim recognized that Goethe chose particular conditions—the "home of an educated, landed nobleman" of his time—in order to give the conflicts he wished to present the most appropriate social setting.

At the beginning of the novel Charlotte and Eduard are occupied with domestic affairs on their large country estate. Both had first been compelled to agree to other marriages, but, years later, after their respective partners had died, they were finally able to marry and fulfill the dream of their youth. In Charlotte's words they now want nothing but to "live for themselves" and "enjoy undisturbed the happiness found late." Because Eduard's suggestion to extend an invitation to his friend, the Captain, is incompatible with her feelings and gives her a premonition of "nothing good," she originally rejects the idea. But eventually she gives in and also writes to invite her niece, Ottilie, who is living at a boarding school. What then takes place among the four characters causing bonds to be formed between Eduard and Ottilie and between the Captain and Charlotte is described in advance, apparently unintentionally, when the Captain and Eduard explain the chemical concept of elective affinities to Charlotte one evening before Ottilie has arrived.

Goethe introduces the scientific phenomenon of elective affinities exactly as the concept developed historically. The idea originated in the field of chemistry. Albertus Magnus was the first to speak of *affinitas* with regard to chemical bodies, and later Galileo did the same. The term elective affinities appears in 1775 in the title of a work by the Swede Tobern Bergmann: *De attractionibus electivis*. This was translated by the German, Hein Tabor, as *Wahlverwandtschaften* (elective affinities) in 1782. Even before Tabor's translation, the same German word had already been used by Christian Ehrenfried Weigel for the phenomenon, which Bergmann described as follows: "When two substances are joined together and a third, which comes later, separates one from its bond and takes it itself, then this is called a simple elective affinity (*enkel frändskap*), attractio electiva simplex." We know that Goethe had been interested in the phenomenon of elective affinities since 1796, initially from the standpoint of natural science and very soon in a wider sense, although at first he did not use the term itself. In writing of mineral bodies he said, "They have certain stronger or weaker relationships according to their basic properties . . . which appear to be a kind of preference." This is why "chemists also attribute to them the honor of choice in such affinities" (1796).

In the novel, the chemical model is applied to the human world throughout that evening discussion. Notwithstanding the great care and detail with which the processes of inorganic nature are described, parallels with human life are always at hand. Each of the three partners in the conversation makes his own contribution toward shaping the model. The Captain describes the chemical process; Charlotte underscores and evaluates the analogies to society. Eduard, oscillating between the two, jokingly relates the model to the present situation of the three partners, making the point that it would not be "fair" to keep Ottilie away any longer—that is, upon Ottilie's arrival Charlotte would also have company, since the Captain has drawn Eduard away from her for a time.

The reader would be mistaken to assume that the chemical model provides an explanation for the happenings in the novel. It does not offer a rational analysis but, on the contrary, suggests that at their core the events are enigmatic and inexplicable. In the discussion Charlotte, who originally protested against the Captain's visit, now emphasizes in the same vein that "an intimate bond between two persons, seemingly inseverable," can be "dissolved by the incidental introduction of a third person, and one of the partners, once so happily united, is driven out into uncertain space." This experience with human affairs is confirmed by events in the chemical world, where the changes are further advanced by the introduction of yet a fourth substance. As the Captain explains,

> The most important and most remarkable cases are where the attraction, rejection, and realigning take place as if crosswise, where four elements previously joined in pairs are brought into contact and leave their previous bond to enter into new ones. One actually believes that there is some higher purpose in this releasing and seizing, in this fleeing and searching; one credits such elements with some sort of willpower and choice and feels completely justified in using the term "elective affinities."

"Important" and "remarkable," a "higher purpose," "some sort of willpower and choice," one "believes" and "credits"—these are the words used to describe the natural phenomenon. There is no explanation, neither for the chemical process itself nor for the occurrences in the novel. What takes place among the four persons on Eduard's estate can develop freely under the given social and psychological conditions, but in its essence it is a primordial process—important and remarkable—and often observable in the inorganic world.

Just as the social conditions are accurate and were specifically chosen for the case at hand, the characters also seem credible as people of that time. Not entirely unjustifiably, readers have frequently wondered about possible resemblances to persons in real life, particularly with regard to Ottilie. We hear about Ottilie even before her arrival through letters she has written to Charlotte from boarding school. The school is not a favorable environment for her. Overshadowed by Charlotte's successful and ambitious daughter Luciane, she usually does not perform as well as the others. In Charlotte's domestic sphere, however, her own best qualities quickly develop, and she provides a fluidity which has a transforming effect on the group. While Charlotte and the Captain are drawn together through their common interest in designing the new parks surrounding the estate, Eduard's affection for Ottilie's constant, obliging nature grows.

The crosswise process described by the Captain leads to the so-called "shocking event" (*unerhörte Begebenheit*) which, according to Goethe's own definition, is fundamental to any novella.[14] During a night Eduard and Charlotte spend together, "inner inclination and the power of imagination asserted their rights over reality: Eduard held only Ottilie in his arms, Charlotte saw the Captain's image suspended—now closer, now further—before her soul." The next morning Eduard quietly steals away from his wife, and it seems to him that the "sun shone upon a crime." At breakfast, Charlotte and Eduard behave "as if ashamed and repentant" towards the Captain and Ottilie. The child born from this union has features which show a "striking resemblance" to the Captain, and its eyes are Ottilie's. It was "begotten from a double adultery," Eduard later admits to Ottilie. "It divides me from my wife and my wife from me, whereas it should have united us." An "unholy hour" gave this child its life.

After this night it is no longer possible to turn back. Nonetheless, Charlotte would still like to renounce her love for the Captain. The theme of renunciation, which is central to *Wilhelm Meister's Travels*, is touched upon here, but it cannot prevail. Charlotte's idea that "one could return to an earlier, simpler state" and that "what has been released forcibly can be brought under control again" is designated by the narrator as her delusion. Meanwhile Eduard's love for Ottilie intensifies to the extent that, when Charlotte attempts to find a new place for Ottilie to live after the Captain has departed, Eduard leaves the estate. The first part of the novel ends with Eduard's decision to seek his death in war.

The second part of the novel is designed more broadly than the first. Conversations on general topics and entries from Ottilie's diary create a serene atmosphere. A number of characters appear who are not involved with the main plot but function as counterbalancing forces. The sudden entrance of Luciane, for example, causes a passing disturbance; it serves as a foil for Ottilie's self-composure. The insertion of a novella, *The Wondrous Neighbors* (*Die wunderlichen Nachbarskinder*), loosens the form and adds a new aspect to the main theme. Yet Ottilie remains at the center of everything. In the quiet world of mansion and park she realizes "that her love, in order to perfect itself, must become fully selfless." However, when Eduard unexpectedly appears before her at the lake in the park, she once again, but only for a moment, allows herself to hope for a union with him. This scene in the park ends in tragedy. On the return across the lake, Eduard and Charlotte's child slips from Ottilie's arms and drowns. That night Charlotte agrees to a divorce; at the same time Ottilie decides to renounce forever all wishes for a fulfillment of her love.

Goethe wrote the last part of the novel with great emotion. His tone when speaking of Ottilie, or when she herself speaks, as well as his later statements about her is evidence that she affected him more and more as a living person. He referred to her as the "splendid child," even as the "heavenly child." Above all, he wished to emphasize that she makes an independent decision when she opposes the demonic affinity to Eduard and chooses a new path without him. But her attempt to break away from Eduard's sphere of influence fails. She has hardly left the estate on her way to the boarding school, where she hopes to begin her life anew, when Eduard again appears before her. His stubborn insistence, a coincidence, and fateful details contribute to her feeling of entrapment. Her will defeated, she lets herself be taken back the next day. Silent, eating less and less, yet almost giving the outward appearance that she has resumed her old life, she finally dies. To the end, an "indescribable, almost magical attraction" exists between her and Eduard. The delight in being near each other unites them as if they were one person. After her death, Ottilie is regarded by the local population as a saint at whose grave wonders come to pass. Eduard dies soon afterward and is buried next to her.

The following year, under the direct influence of Goethe's *Elective Affinities*, Achim von Arnim (1781–1831) published *Poverty, Riches, Guilt, and Repentance of Countess Dolores (Armut, Reichtum, Schuld und Busse der Gräfin Dolores*, 1810). Its unique form was touched upon by Clemens Brentano when he referred to it as a novel "interwoven with lovely novellas and songs," an "uncommonly rich, beautiful book." No other novel of the period has such an abundance of insertions and corresponds so fully to Friedrich Schlegel's definition in his "Letter on the Novel" ("Brief über den Roman"): "I can hardly think of a novel in any other way than as a mixture of narrative, song, and other forms. Cervantes never composed any differently." For his insertions Arnim used available material from earlier literature, such as folk books, as well as from his own published and unpublished writings. Narrations, recitations, songs, and poems accompany the plot from beginning to end. Arnim even appended a musical score to the second volume, the "Musical Supplement to the Story of Countess Dolores."

Even among Arnim's contemporaries there were objections to the loose structure caused by the profusion of insertions. The impression that the work is formless results primarily from the apparent arbitrariness in arranging the insertions. But a closer look shows that Arnim generally has not been as careless with his insertions as it might seem and that the order in a series corresponds to his Weltanschauung. For him the world is not a comprehensible system; man is not presented with clear-cut options from which he can choose rationally. The hastiness with which he arranged parts of his novel may be explained by the fact that he did not think it so important whether a detail be placed here or there. In a letter to Jacob Grimm he said that the book was "written down hastily," but not "thought hastily" (October 1810).

The novel is a *Zeitroman* (novel about the times)—Brentano used this term in a letter to the jurist Friedrich Karl von Savigny in 1809—with a theme of interest to readers at that time: the adultery of Countess Dolores. Her adultery is the work's central incident. It is the "shocking event" which determines the course of action throughout.

What Arnim stressed in the case of Goethe's novel, that the milieu was chosen precisely to fit the theme, also applies to his own novel. From the social conditions he develops the situation which leads to adultery, having chosen these conditions specifically because they could give rise to the plot events.

The two very young, aristocratic sisters, Klelia and Dolores, are living together in poverty in a ruinous castle. Their father left after having squandered his entire fortune, and their mother is dead. The war aggravates the girls' already difficult situation. Only advantageous marriages can help them, and they follow. Dolores marries the young, well-to-do Count Karl, who displays tender feelings for her and makes every attempt to fulfill her wishes. But the coquettish and frivolous Dolores reveals qualities which are not entirely pleasing to the narrator or to his representative, Count Karl. The narrator shows the reader the extent of Dolores's superficiality in her reaction to the news that the more serious and diligent Klelia has married a Spanish duke in Sicily. Dolores is distressed at the thought that if she had only carried out her desire to travel to Sicily with her sister while she was still engaged to Karl, then the Spanish duke "would have preferred me; the whole wide world would then have been open to me." She pictures in her mind the "splendor of an immeasurably rich ducal palace" and imagines the prestige a duke enjoys at the court. In comparison the "decent but mediocre lot of a wealthy count" fares badly. When a Marquis D. appears on the scene, Dolores falls completely under his control and deceives her husband. But she repents after a long and difficult inner crisis and, transformed by her guilt and repentance, is able to begin a new life with Karl.

Arnim is concerned with showing the great value of Dolores's repentance. It is this idea which, in spite of the many insertions, determines the novel's structure. The arabesques do not conceal the basic plot line, but bring it out even more emphatically: Dolores is supposed to evolve as a new person and be free of her previous flaws. Of great importance is her development as a "good mother," who now personally cares for her children instead of leaving them in the care of others. This is clearly a criticism of the aristocratic women of the day. Arnim's criticism of the times has been artistically integrated into the plot. He pictures his own time as a concrete reality and then lets the possibilities for change, for a better society, become visible. In his opinion this progress presupposes an inner transformation. By means of Dolores's repentance he shows what he considered to be a cure for the times. Even if the contents seem limited and the segment of society dealt with is small, Arnim's narrative energy is nonetheless significant.

Arnim began one other novel which he never completed, the historical novel *The Crown Guards* (*Die Kronenwächter*, 1817). As his background he chose the Age of the Reformation. In order to accurately depict conditions during that time he pursued extensive studies of source materials for years, which was quite unusual for a novelist of his day. The Crown Guards is a secret society which protects the descendants of the Hohenstaufen dynasty, awaiting the time when one of them will revive the former splendor and greatness of the empire. Neither of the two claimants whose stories are told in the novel is able to attain this goal.

The themes demonstrated in *Elective Affinities* and *Countess Dolores* are related to the characters' position within and towards society. Regardless of their fate, they are unmistakably members of their era and of their class. In Ernst Theodor Amadeus Hoffmann's (1776–1822) novels, however, the figures are characterized by a somewhat improbable lack of social ties and concepts. The monastery is the only community where the two main characters, Medardus in *The Devil's Elixirs* (*Die Elixiere des Teufels*, 1815) and Kriesler in *The Life and Opinions of Kater Murr* (*Lebensansichten des Katers Murr*, 1820), can exist under acceptable conditions. The monastery is not only a refuge, but a place where the manner of living is pleasant and harmonious. As a result of their rootlessness, the characters waver between various spheres, are able to exchange one role for another, and remain uncertain of themselves.

In *The Devil's Elixirs*, the monk Medardus, who narrates his own story, decides at a young age to enter a monastery. But he feels the urge to leave, and the old wine he drinks—the "elixirs" entrusted to him along with the monastery's other relics and supposedly brought by the devil—intensifies his agitated state. Because his overexcited behavior is noticed, the prior offers him the chance to travel to Rome in order that, once outside the monastery, he might free himself from his distress and find peace. Medardus has hardly left the monastery when he begins to commit atrocious crimes. He flees, continues his journey in lay clothes, is recognized and brought to trial, but is soon exonerated when a mysterious double (doppelgänger) turns up who claims his name and responsibility for the crimes. Medardus is even able to become engaged to Aurelie, whose brother he murdered. On the morning of their wedding he reveals his identity to her and raises a knife against her when he sees that his double is being led to execution. He frees the double, flees again, and awakens in an Italian sanitarium after having been in a coma for three months. In a monastery near Rome he confesses his crimes and subjects himself to hard penance.

Reports inserted by a fictitious editor gradually reveal that Medardus belongs to a family which has been involved in many types of crimes for several generations. Murder, incest, adultery, and seduction were committed incessantly, placing a burden on the descendants, who in turn committed new offenses. In the end Medardus returns to his monastery in Germany. He attends the ceremony at which Aurelie takes her vows as a nun. She is murdered before the altar by the double, who turns out to be Medardus's half brother.

Hoffmann took many elements from the English novel *Ambrosio or the Monk* (1795) by Matthew Gregory Lewis. In addition, he used motifs from contemporary horror novels. Since he was concerned with the psychological motivation of events, he made exhaustive studies of medical literature, drew from studies of the mentally ill, and consulted psychiatric authorities.

The theme of the novel is a theological as well as a moral and psychiatric problem. How can one deal with the drive to criminality in an educated monk who is aware of all the implications and consequences of his actions and augments his desire for evil by drinking the "devil's elixirs"? The problem is often discussed within the novel and, in the particular case of Medardus, is solved. The solution—theologically and practically—depends on consciously resisting the obsession. Whether this obsession is criminality or insanity cannot be determined. Hoffmann no doubt intentionally left the question open, thus giving an intellectual dimension to what at first seems to be a refined sensationalist novel.

Much in the work remains inexplicable and unsolvable. This is especially true with regard to Medardus's double. He always appears when least expected and is at times seized by insanity. His striking resemblance to his half brother Medardus, his willingness to assume responsibility for his crimes, not only outwardly, but actually to accept the crimes inwardly as his own, and finally his murder of Aurelie directly after Medardus had brought himself to desist from the murder suggest that he is the main character's other self. Nonetheless, he is a separate character. His mysterious appearances at the most varied places and his equally mysterious disappearances give him the aura of abandonment and loneliness, a contrast to the security of the monastic institution to which Medardus can always return, even as a criminal. It is noteworthy that the representatives of the monasteries behave in a superior, insightful, just, and kind manner, as do the sanitarium officials.

As a whole, the novel is an accumulation of horrors. Ghosts, the irrational, and the fantastic give it a quality new to the German novel. The modern
reader might be provoked to thought—if not to mockery—by the frequency
of Medardus's "shudders" or even "ice-cold shudders." Heinrich Heine, who
believed the novel contained "the most frightful and horrifying things imaginable," recognized the importance of the theme, a theme which also concerned Dostoevski, Kafka, and Thomas Mann and has remained a stimulating topic to the present day. As important and relevant as its theme may be
from a modern standpoint, the novel is questionable with regard to artistic
merit. Indisputably, its tight form and equal distribution of plot centers demonstrate Hoffmann's novelistic talent, and he maintained the narrative perspective of the monk extremely well. But many sections of the novel are
difficult to bear and exemplify *Trivialliteratur*.

This is not true of Hoffmann's second novel, the fragment *Kater Murr*.
Although motifs used for a sensationalist effect are not lacking here either, it
is an ingenious book. The full title is *The Life and Opinions of Kater Murr
with the Fragmentary Biography of the Kapellmeister Johannes Kreisler on
Random Sheets of Scrap Paper. Edited by E. T. A. Hoffmann* (*Lebensansichten des Katers Murr nebst fragmentarischer Biographie des Kapellmeisters Johannes Kreislers in zufälligen Makulaturblättern. Herausgegeben von E. T. A.
Hoffmann*). The fictional premise is that "when Tomcat Murr wrote his views
on life he simply tore up a printed book which belonged to his master and
harmlessly used the sheets, partly as a prop and partly as blotting paper.
These sheets remained in the manuscript and were unintentionally printed,
as if they were part of the text!" The editor had failed to look over the manuscript and, as he admits himself, "jumbled-up confusion" resulted. But the
mixed texts—Murr's story and the *Biography of the Kapellmeister Kreisler*—
are easy to separate, since each section is accompanied by a "parenthetical
note," s.p. (scrap paper) or M.c. (Murr continues), to let the reader know
which of the two life stories they come from. Despite this fictional pretense,
it is quite apparent that the two stories belong together. This seemingly curious form of the double novel is an urgent statement. It testifies to the incompatibility of two forms of existence and two spheres of life.

The main narrator is a tomcat: a self-righteous, arrogant Philistine who
is well adapted to society and satisfied with his life of herring and sweet milk.
He is a man of letters, boastful about the culture he has acquired through
contact with his owner, Master Abraham. The four sections of his story imitate the *Bildungsroman*. Each section has two headings: (I) Existential Feelings: Boyhood Months; (II) The Life and Experiences of the Youth: I Too
Was in Arcady; (III) My Months of Apprenticeship: The Caprices of Fortune;
(IV) The Salutary Effects of Higher Culture: The Maturer Months of Man-

hood. Hoffmann is parodying the form of *Wilhelm Meister* as well as Sterne's title *The Life and Opinions of Tristram Shandy*. His tomcat's comments on life can be emotional or learned, reflective or didactic. Murr not only philosophizes, but gives concrete descriptions of his surroundings and adventures. With skill and suspense he tells of the goings-on among the cats and dogs, of events in the cellar and on the roof, in front of the door and in Master Abraham's study. His realm is daily life. As limited as it is and despite its function as a satire on human society, Murr's world presents itself as friendly and charming. The jovial laugh with which the well-meaning and empathetic Master Abraham cares for his beautiful, scholarly tomcat sets the tone for the story.

The animal fable soon proves to be a foil, and Conductor Kreisler emerges as the novel's main character. Kreisler was known to Hoffmann's readers from earlier essays entitled *Kreisleriana* (1814–15). In these essays Hoffmann transferred his own sufferings and ideas to this fictitious character without drawing a self-portrait. Actually Kreisler was more like a partner or friend by means of whom the author attempted to understand himself and his position in the world. In his first *Kreisleriana* essay ("The Musical Agonies of the Conductor Johannes Kreisler"), which appeared anonymously in 1810, Hoffmann depicted the unhappiness of the musician forced to perform in salons and thus compelled to dedicate his talent, strength, and time to the distractions and self-importance of a society with no "sense for art." The conflict between artist and society was part of Kreisler's characterization from the outset. But the *Kreisleriana* are merely a prelude. They do not yet contain the artistic personality who, emanating ecstasy, gaiety, and sharp irony, first comes alive in the novel. Hoffmann needed the large framework and many contrasting characters in order to bring out the surprising, unique, and overwhelming elements of a personality which is only recognizable when set off by other characters.

Kreisler's story is complex and difficult to follow. In the various sections the reader is thrown into the middle of situations and astonishing events which unfold in unforeseeable succession. The only certainty is that they are revolving around a mysterious center. Early in the novel the reader receives an impression of the petty court Sieghartshof, where the deposed Prince Irenäus pretends to rule as if he were still in power. Kreisler comes into contact with this make-believe society when he appears in the court park one summer evening occupied with a precious old guitar. The sixteen-year-old Princess Hedwiga and her friend Julia look on unnoticed as he sings and plays the guitar, becomes dissatisfied with the instrument, tunes it repeatedly and plays again, then addresses it in an outraged speech, and finally flings it into the bushes and departs. The two girls react differently to this scene. Hedwiga finds the stranger frightening, whereas Julia feels attracted to him. Without hesitation she retrieves the guitar, plays it superbly and begins to "sing involuntarily." When Kreisler meets the young girls shortly thereafter, a lively dispute ensues. Hedwiga considers the musician mad and later calls him an "uncomfortable fool"; Julia's judgment, on the other hand, is that he is only "an ironical jester" who affects her "in a strange and not at all unpleasant way."

Further events at the court do not constitute a progressive plot. Instead, there are only partial plots which provide glimpses of a whole but are not cohesively joined. The Princess Hedwiga, who is supposed to marry the sinister Prince Hektor, is drawn to Kreisler. Hektor, meanwhile, is lustfully pursuing Julia, whose mother plans to wed her to the imbecilic Prince Ignaz. The reader soon learns that Kreisler had grown weary of his conductor's position at the Grand Duke's court, and, just before appearing in the park at the Sieghartshof, he had left it. Now he must flee from the court because he has mortally wounded Prince Hektor's aide-de-camp in self-defense. He finds refuge in a nearby monastery. The absurd elements of the external plot are actually only the motivation for the shadow dance of characters around Kreisler, a dance which allows for a clear view of Kreisler again and again and follows paths that are never entirely removed from him. Scenes which at first seemed to serve the purpose of comedy later reveal a connection with the bitterness of Kreisler's existence.

That Kreisler (the German word "*Kreis*" means circle) is using his real name is doubtful from the beginning of the work; even he does not deny that there is some uncertainty about it. Referring to the meaning of his name, he says that one should think of the word circle, "of the wonderful circles . . . in which our entire existence moves, and from which we cannot escape. . . . In these circles the circler [*Kreisler*] circles."

The conductor touches upon the reason for the incompatibility of his existence with that of society, that is, of Murr's world. Kreisler "belongs to a higher existence and considers the demands of this higher existence to be a condition of life." Only in music can he experience the actualization of this "higher existence" and even then only when the moment is favorable. Since he is enclosed within his own "circles," he has no choice but to behave as he does. How could he move in circles of life which possess no reality for him? Thus Kreisler is the name for a person of a certain mold. The fragments of his biography have also been arranged in the form of a circle; there is no plot development when compared with Murr's *Bildungsroman*. This means that a conversation between Master Abraham and Kreisler can take place in the first segment of Kreisler's biography, even though it belongs at the end chronologically. The reader can only understand its significance after a second reading or by carefully leafing back and forth. It is a curious aspect of the novel that Master Abraham is a friend and helper to Kreisler as well as Tom-cat Murr's owner and friend.

Owing to the work's richness, critics have evaluated it from many differ-ent points of view and have offered opposing opinions. It has been called Realistic and also Romantic. Its international appeal has frequently been pointed out; in the nineteenth century it was read in French, English, Rus-sian, and Danish. Its importance to authors such as Heinrich Heine, Karl Leberecht Immermann, Gottfried Keller, and Theodor Storm is often men-tioned. The work has remained unique and inimitable.

The same is true of Goethe's last novel, *Wilhelm Meister's Travels or the Renunciants* (*Wilhelm Meisters Wanderjahre oder die Entsagenden*, 1821, expanded 1829). Its form was little understood until the middle of the twen-tieth century, yet when seen against the background of the literature of the period, the form is hardly as unusual or alienating as literary historians until just a few decades ago had thought. The work is a continuation of the *Ap-prenticeship* with regard to content as well as artistry. Even in its earliest version, the *Theatrical Mission*, the story of Wilhelm Meister was designed as a *Zeitroman*, and Goethe was involved with it as such for over fifty years. Because it remained a *Zeitroman*, it acquired new themes with the changing times. These could no longer be expressed in the novelistic form of the eigh-teenth century, which Goethe himself had been instrumental in developing. Like his contemporaries, who had produced a variety of forms at the turn of the century, Goethe was not simply searching for a different style but was much more concerned with giving shape to his new ideas by means of orig-inal narrative and structural techniques. Although it is true that he contin-ued the story of Wilhelm Meister, Wilhelm is no longer the main character. Other figures are just as important and sometimes take precedence. There is no central plot and chronology plays but a minor role. The work spreads out before the reader as a simultaneity of events in space. It is distinguished by its cosmopolitan character.

This cosmopolitanism is closely linked with the conditions of the times as depicted by Goethe. Essential parts of the novel are determined by his concern about changing conditions and his feeling of responsibility for the many people threatened by the Industrial Revolution. "The rampant growth of technology torments and frightens me," says Nachodine, one of the novel's exemplary characters. "There are only two choices, one as sad as the other: either to grasp at the new and accelerate the destruction, or to break away, take the best and most worthy persons along and search for a more favorable fate on the other side of the ocean." The problem is illustrated by objective accounts of working conditions among the threatened sectors of the popula-tion. In this way Goethe incorporates the emigration wave of the nineteenth century and its causes into the novel. Wilhelm and the representatives of the

Society of the Tower are in close association with the leaders of the emigrants' alliance; they want to join the wanderers and begin anew in America. Before a large group of craftsmen, the character Lenardo discusses the ethos of utility and describes concrete opportunities for practicing it in the world. Like Nachodine, Lenardo embodies the modern, practical, sober-minded person with accurate judgment and technical skill. He distinguishes sharply between the new aspirations of his time and the vague undertakings of the past: "The time has passed when one ran adventurously into the wide world." Instead, the wanderer can say to himself, "Where I am useful, that is my homeland."

Goethe presents the questions of the day as great social problems. They are problems that affect the entire society and can only be combated by universal participation. Therefore, the individual's story is seen under the aspect of "renunciation." Man is no longer regarded as a being who, like Wilhelm in the *Apprenticeship*, can follow the wish to "cultivate himself"; instead, the basis of the *Travels* is the recognition that "every man always finds himself limited, restricted in his situation . . . from the earliest moments of his life." Only by an awareness and acceptance of the situation is it possible to become active and useful as an "organ" of the whole. This thought is repeated throughout the entire book in many variations. The double title, *Wilhelm Meister's Travels or The Renunciants*, indicates that the renunciants are the main characters of the work. Its utopian content is related to the role they play; they are the people who give society new ideals.

Goethe could only present the comprehensive theme of his last novel in a comprehensive manner. Novellas, fairy tales, anecdotes, letters, diary entries, conversations, maxims, verses, and even a drawing of a key are enclosed within the major framework. Most of the insertions are tied to the plot of the frame; that is, they are logically motivated as insertions. Sometimes a story begins as a separate narration and then flows into the frame story; others are complete within themselves. All in all, a distinct separation of frame and insertions would be out of place, for the frame itself also consists of parts, some of which are complete entities.

With regard to the central theme of renunciation, the work is structured so as to divide the characters into groups. The great emigration, which constitutes the frame story, is undertaken by the renunciants, who must adapt their lives to thought and action and have had to learn self-denial. At one time they were all still incapable of renunciation and resembled those persons whose stories are narrated in the inserted novellas. Whereas the frame story deals with the general problems related to the limits on action, the interwoven novellas are concerned with personal, private, and intimate matters. Almost all of the individual stories focus on renunciation of love. The characters experience varying degrees of difficulty and strain in their struggle to relinquish love. The only character who remains true to love is Wilhelm's son, Felix. He provides a counterbalance to the entire renunciation theme by appearing first as an appealing, knowledge-thirsty lad and later as a stormy young man in love.

Felix's nature is completely different from his father's. The question of his education is part of the novel's general theme and also a separate theme in itself. In the "pedagogic province," an educational community founded on utopian principles, Felix is finally promoted after unproductive activity in agriculture to "more lively horsemanship." As an elder poet Goethe created a landscape for youth where each can find "what is suitable to him." Careful attention is paid to each youth in order to determine "what his nature is actually striving towards." The balance created by the "wise men" of the community is demonstrated in Felix's study of horse breeding and Italian. We are told that his plan of studies combines horse breeding, "this seemingly violent and raw" occupation, with "the most tender in the world . . . language practice and development."

An emphasis on practicality prevails in the many passages expressing educational concepts. Similarly, all of the characters apply themselves to practical activities. Wilhelm becomes a surgeon. Jarno, who is now called Montan, takes up the study of rocks and minerals. Philine is a skilled seamstress. As Jarno-Montan explains to Wilhelm, "Your general education and all of its institutions are . . . buffoonery. A thorough understanding, a superior mastery, such as no other in the near vicinity can easily match . . . that is what matters."

Rationality reigns in all parts of the novel which deal with the problem of practical living in the face of changing times, but the work does not totally conform to a rational world view. Just as Felix is not subject to the teachings of renunciation and takes his own course, there is an entire realm where rationality is not the highest goal: the realm of the character Makarie. In the first version of the *Travels*, published in 1821, Makarie was not present. Her inclusion in the final version gives the portrayal of man a new dimension and is essential to the novel's equilibrium. Makarie is a clairvoyant, a woman with an apparently innate relationship to the solar system. The reports about her are given with an unmistakable reserve, and the witness whose testimony is decisive is a mathematician. Possessing "a lucid mind and thus unbelieving," he resisted for a long time before concluding from his calculations that Makarie "not only carries the entire solar system within herself, but moreover she moves spiritually as an integrating part in it." In other words, Makarie's visions withstand a scientific test, but they cannot be rationally explained.

The novel does not end with Makarie but with a few scenes which center on Felix. They are idealized pictures of life, endowed with a certain immediacy by the particular temperament of the young man. They do not mark the end of a plot but would sooner qualify as the beginning of a new plot if what mattered here were a linear progression.

3 / From Heinrich Heine to Thomas Mann

Historical Novel and Zeitroman

The year of the July Revolution of 1830 is not a turning point in the history of the German novel. If a new chapter begins here, it is for practical reasons and does not imply a new beginning. Nor is Goethe's *Wilhelm Meister's Travels* to be seen as the end of a literary era, notwithstanding Heinrich Heine's remark about the "end of a literary period which began with Goethe's cradle and ceased with his coffin."[1] It would, in fact, be more accurate to regard Goethe's last novel as the start of a new direction. Over one hundred years after its appearance, Hermann Broch still referred to it as the "cornerstone of a new literature, a new novel."[2] In the nineteenth century it was also regarded as the "book of the future."[3] While Broch saw its historical importance in its comprehensiveness, readers in the decades after Goethe's death were still primarily affected by the pedagogical, social theme and were impressed with Goethe's "positive picture of new conditions."[4] Its modern theme and depiction of the dynamics of society were consistent with the ideas of progressive nineteenth-century readers for many years to come.

The influence of the *Travels* as well as Goethe's other novels extended into the twentieth century. We now find a continuous novel tradition such as failed to materialize subsequent to Jörg Wickram's writings or the great novels of the seventeenth century. In the decade following Goethe's death a large number of authors used the novel for the specific purpose of analyzing their own times. The *Zeitroman* became a novel genre characteristic of the nineteenth century. The novels of Charles Sealsfield, Karl Immermann, Karl Gutzkow, Gustav Freytag, Friedrich Spielhagen, and Theodor Fontane can be designated *Zeitromane*, as can single works by Heinrich Laube, Jeremias Gotthelf, Gottfried Keller, and Paul Heyse. Yet it is important to realize that, contrary to the widespread belief among literary scholars, the *Zeitroman* did not first come into being subsequent to the July Revolution. Rather, it had already existed for decades when the Young Germans discovered and adopted it as their primary form of expression.[5]

That *Werther* and *Wilhelm Meister* were forms of *Zeitromane* was recognized in the nineteenth century. Ludolf Wienbarg refers specifically to *Wilhelm Meister* when he speaks out against the historical novel in the tradition of Sir Walter Scott and instead recommends to young poets, "Reach into your own time, take hold of life! I know what you will ask. . . . Where to find material for a novel about current times? But I ask in return, where did Goethe find material for *Wilhelm Meister?* Yet understand me correctly. By no means do we want another Wilhelm! He is finished, he was of Goethe and his age. Who and what is of *yours?*"[6] In his theoretical statements Wienbarg accurately describes the relationship between modernity and tradition in the *Zeitroman* of the nineteenth century. The novelistic structure of the previous century could be used and varied in the nineteenth-century *Zeitroman*. Authors saw themselves confronted with the task of writing the *Wilhelm Meister* of their own time, which of course had to differ from Goethe's.

In addition to Goethe's novels, others which can be designated *Zeitromane* also appeared in the decades preceding the French Revolution of 1830. Clemens Brentano used the term *Zeitroman* in 1809 in reference to Arnim's *Countess Dolores*. Arnim had developed a theme of contemporary interest— the adultery of a countess—from the prevailing political and social conditions, and he saw in her repentance and atonement a means of healing for the entire age. Joseph von Eichendorff's (1788–1857) *Presentiment and Actuality (Ahnung und Gegenwart,* 1815) is also a *Zeitroman;* the problem of taking political action during a time which does not allow for such action is the burning issue faced by the main characters.

The *Zeitromane* of the 1830s differ from those of the early nineteenth century, not only because different conditions were incorporated into the works but also because the later authors benefited greatly from the newly developed historical novel. It was primarily Sir Walter Scott (1771–1832), the founder of the historical novel in Europe, who had a lasting effect on German authors. Wilhelm Hauff and Willibald Alexis, who were already writing historical novels in the 1820s, learned from Scott, as did Sealsfield, Laube, Fontane, Gutzkow, Stifter, and Conrad Ferdinand Meyer. The *Zeitroman* of the 1830s was highly influenced by Scott's structuring of dramatic scenes, characterization, use of details, and depiction of events from the perspective of the participants. A new style of writing developed, based on a belief in the intrinsic value of narrated events and not in a meaning beyond the happenings. The historical novel was the prelude and model for the *Zeitroman;* one could study the depiction of historical events to learn how to portray contemporary events. Whether the events took place sixty years before—like the coup d'etat of Charles Stuart in *Waverley* (1814),[7] Scott's first and immediately successful novel—or in the present—like the Polish Revolution in Heinrich Laube's *The Warriors* (1837)—did not significantly affect the style.

Even Heinrich Heine (1797–1856) chose a historical theme for his first novel, *The Rabbi of Bacharach (Der Rabbi von Bacherach,* 1840). As a student in Göttingen Heine delved into the study of Jewish history, an interest first aroused when young Jewish friends in Berlin introduced him to the spiritual world of Judaism. Until then he had known little about Jewish heritage and customs. He also studied the conditions in Frankfurt am Main during the late Middle Ages with the same thoroughness. The first chapter of his novel is set in Bacharach (Heine used the older form Bacherach instead of Bacharach) on the evening of Passover, 1489, and the following two chapters take place in Frankfurt the next day. Heine took the motif which sets his plot into motion from Jacques Basnage (*Histoire des Juifs depuis Jésus-Christi jusqu'à présent*, The Hague 1716), who reported that in the Middle Ages anti-Semites incited persecution of Jews by smuggling corpses of children into Jewish homes and then accusing the Jews of ritual murder. In order to portray his characters, Heine carefully excerpted and compiled information from scholarly works. He was evidently interested in two different types of Jewish character from the late Middle Ages: the pious Jew who was deeply rooted in his religious community and adhered faithfully to the customs and the worldly, widely traveled Jew who was shaped by his contact with many cultures and with Humanism and who, in many cases, was baptized. The main character, the fictitious Rabbi Abraham from Bacharach, has characteristics of both types, but those of the God-fearing scholar and responsible congregation leader predominate.

In his dedication to Heinrich Laube, Heine called the novel "The Legend of the Rabbi of Bacharach," which may give an indication of the significance of Rabbi Abraham's story. It is part of the story of the sufferings of the Jewish people, in this case the small Jewish population in Bacharach, an "isolated, powerless group" which had been persecuted for centuries. Having settled in Bacharach as early as Roman times, the Jewish community had preserved its individuality in the hostile environment, as is clearly illustrated by the observance of religious ceremonies.

The description of a Passover seder with the details of its ancient ritual is the focus of the first chapter. Heine's personal involvement, an obvious enchantment, lends a special aura to the scene. First the customs are described:

> As soon as night falls the woman lights the lamps, spreads the tablecloth, puts three of the unleavened breads on its center, covers them with a napkin, and on this raised surface she places six little dishes containing symbolic foods, an egg, lettuce, horseradish, the bone of a lamb, and a brown mixture of raisins, cinnamon, and nuts.

In the house of Rabbi Abraham everything has been prepared accordingly:

The men sat in their black cloaks, black broadbrimmed hats, and white collars; the women, in strangely glistening garments of Lombard stuffs, wore gold and pearl ornaments around their necks and in their hair, and the silver Sabbath lamp poured its festive light onto the devoutly joyous faces of young and old. Reclining, as law enjoins, on the purple velvet cushion of a chair raised above the others, Rabbi Abraham read and chanted the Haggadah, and the mixed choir chimed in or responded at the prescribed places.

The event which causes the rabbi and his wife, Sarah, to leave their home and city during the ceremony begins with the entrance of two strangers, who introduce themselves as "men of your faith" on a journey and receive the rabbi's permission to take part in the seder. The reader first becomes aware of a disturbance as it is perceived by Sarah. At first everything continues as before. Then Sarah becomes alarmed upon noticing the distorted, horror-stricken look on her husband's face. As she watches he composes himself almost instantaneously, his features becoming smooth and calm, and he is overcome by a jovial mood Sarah finds out of character. His "exuberant gaiety," expressing itself in a grotesque game with his cap and beard, with the melody of the Haggadah text, and with the ritual itself are deeply disturbing to her, while the other guests relax and enjoy the merry atmosphere. When all are washing their hands before the evening meal, the rabbi nods to his wife and withdraws unnoticed. She follows him, still holding the silver washbasin and unaware of the reason for his behavior. Not until they are some distance up the Rhine—from Heine's geographical description one can imagine that the couple walked about an hour—does the rabbi break the silence after throwing the washbasin, his last possession, into the river. He says that he had seen the bloody corpse of a child under the table, placed there by the strangers in order to accuse him of murder and destroy him. Only through his cunning were they able to escape. The chapter ends with the couple's journey by boat to Frankfurt am Main.

The second chapter tells of the arrival of the two refugees in Frankfurt and of their path through the bustling trading city to the ghetto, where they participate in a synagogue service. Sarah, from whose perspective in the women's court of the synagogue the service is presented, faints when her husband's voice blends in with the sad murmuring of the death prayer and she hears him chant the names of the friends and relatives they left behind in Bacharach.

The third chapter tells of the encounter with Don Isaak Abarbanel, a baptized Spanish Jew whom the rabbi had known from his student days in Toledo. In this character Heine combines two different historical figures who had impressed him during his studies. He also introduces a number of ghetto

Jews in the second and third chapters, more as caricatures than characters. As Lion Feuchtwanger stated, the third chapter is evidence of Heine's "facility with language in his later years." It is "extraordinarily smooth and elegant," particularly in its dialogues.[8]

Heine did not finish the novel. He had begun writing it during his student days in Berlin and Göttingen between 1823 and 1825, but not until 1839–40 when he was in Paris did he complete chapter 2 and write chapter 3. He wanted to publish it at that time because of the pogroms in Damascus. Since he gave no indication as to how the novel would continue, it is pointless to speculate on further plot developments. On careful consideration the fragment seems complete as it is; nothing is missing. Just how the story of Abraham and Sarah might go on would be a banal question.

The exemplariness of the rabbi has often been questioned by literary researchers, and his flight from Bacharach has been interpreted as a lack of responsibility to his community by the critics Lion Feuchtwanger, Erich Loewenthal, and Jeffrey Sammons. However, it would seem important to consider that every emigration means that the refugee leaves others behind to suffer and that their misfortune oppresses him, insofar as he is a responsible person, wherever he goes. The scene in Bacharach illustrates that the rabbi could not have helped anyone if he had stayed behind. Admittedly, he first tells Sarah that the strangers' plot was directed against him alone and that their relatives would survive. Then he murmurs the prayer for the dead for them at the synagogue the next day. Also, his apparent lightheartedness may seem unfitting: upon their arrival in Frankfurt he speaks to his wife "smiling cheerfully" and greets her after the service with a "cheerful expression." But the rabbi's behavior in such instances can be defended psychologically. His conduct is an expression of consideration for his wife, of the composure of a pious man who is grateful for having been saved, and of the inability of the couple to speak of the horror openly. With care and deliberation Heine lets their emotions show through to their outward behavior. Moreover, it cannot be overlooked that the names Abraham and Sarah suggest a mythical prototype. There are many allusions to the biblical Abraham within the novel, and Sarah's beauty is reminiscent of the biblical Sarah (Gen. 12:11). Finally, the word "legend" in the title would not be understandable or justified had Heine not believed that the rabbi should have fled.

Heine's second unfinished novel, *From the Memoirs of Herr von Schnabelewopski* (*Aus den Memoiren des Herrn von Schnabelewopski*, 1834), is narrated quite differently. Here the title character tells his story in the first person in the tradition of the picaresque novel. Events follow each other in simple succession: Schnabelewopski's childhood and youth in Poland, departure from his homeland, half-year stay in Hamburg, sea journey via Cuxhaven to Amsterdam, and experiences as a theology student in Leiden. The reason he originally left home was to study theology in accordance with his parents' wishes. However, the stations on his journey and circumstances of his life in Leiden are more important to him than this ultimate goal. Experiences and knowledge gained from travels to foreign places are the theme of his narration. He tells of the country and people at the different locations, of his love affairs, and of theological as well as personal disputes among the students in Leiden in which Schnabelewopski himself remains a passive participant. His name is probably analogous to Schelmuffsky, the title hero in a novel by Christian Reuter, an author who was popular among and often quoted by the Romanticists.

Charles Sealsfield (Karl Postl, 1793–1864) stands out as an important novelist of the era. His works are characterized by their combination of historical novel, *Zeitroman*, and political literature. They serve as a means of analyzing a political situation on which the author takes a firm stand. Sealsfield's position is that of a citizen of the United States of America. In his novels the political system and conventions of public life in a land which, when he arrived there in 1823, had not yet been independent from England for fifty years serve as a norm. In light of this he can be regarded as a politically engaged author.

Sealsfield grew up in Bohemia, completed his theological studies at the Order-of-the-Cross in Prague, was ordained a priest, and served for a number of years as secretary to the religious order. In 1823 he fled from Austria via Germany and Switzerland to Louisiana in the United States. Powerful patrons, probably Freemasons, helped him to escape from the sphere of influence of the "tyrant-priests" as well as from Austrian police spies.[9] The patrons apparently provided him with money, advised him on the details of his journey, and used their influence on his behalf even in later years. In his biography of Sealsfield, Eduard Castle suggests that the author's exclusive use of the name Charles Sealsfield—his American passport was made out in this name—and concealment of his true identity as the priest Karl Postl might be traced back to a promise made to his patrons. Yet Karl J. R. Arndt's explanation that the author considered his priestly vow to be binding seems just as convincing. Karl Postl represented the "deceased" priest; "reborn . . . in the new world," he began a new life with the name Charles Sealsfield and was careful, because of his religious convictions, that no one recognized him as the priest Karl Postl.[10] This would seem to explain his seclusion and loneliness, particularly in later life, and also his reluctance to appear publicly during his active middle years.

His impressive knowledge of the American landscape and people can be attributed to extensive travels in the years directly following his flight and to studies of journals and scholarly literature, as well as to contact with many people and involvement in various activities. Later he lived between countries and continents, used his knowledge as a basis for his writings and also in diplomatic work, and spent much time in Switzerland, where he finally settled in his old age. He wrote not only novels but also informative works; several combine fiction and nonfiction.

His first important novel, which originally appeared in English under the title *Tokeah; or the White Rose* (1829), was published several years later in German as *Der Legitime und die Republikaner* (*The Legitimate One and the Republicans*, 1833).[11] Sealsfield's German version is an artistic, tasteful, and more insightful reworking and expansion of the English text. It is the version which will be interpreted here.

The main character is the Indian chief Tokeah, whose bitter experiences with the white man illustrate the tragic fate of his entire people during the colonial period in North America. However, the new title—*The Legitimate One and the Republicans*—indicates that the author was not merely concerned with the tragic hero Tokeah, whose defeat was inevitable, but wished to demonstrate a far-reaching problem of human society within a specific historical context. The historical era is underscored on the title page: "A Story from the last Anglo-American War." Roughly the second half of the novel focuses on the defense of New Orleans and ultimate victory by the republicans over the British troops in January 1815. The Indian chief, until now the central figure, almost disappears from the scene. The unquestionable legitimacy of his claim to land in North America seems to justify his profound hatred for the whites, and from an objective standpoint there is no doubt about the white man's injustice. In all three volumes of the novel a quote from Thomas Jefferson, stating that he trembles for his people when he thinks of the guilt they bear for their injustices against the original inhabitants, is printed as a motto on the reverse side of the title page. As the reader might expect, the author supports this motto with considerable evidence throughout the novel. In his preface he also sides with the Indians. But reflections and information accompanying the action, coupled with a secondary plot involving a young Englishman, reveal early the broad context within which the fate of the Indians should be seen. The author demonstrates that the historical events in the novel are much too complex to be viewed from a single perspective. The reader gradually understands that a condemnation of the white settlers in favor of the Indians' cause accomplishes little.

In chapter 41 a judgment is finally spoken from a historical-philosophical viewpoint. The scene resembles a formal trial. Presiding is General Andrew Jackson, victor in many battles against the Indians as well as against the British in the recent Battle of New Orleans. When the German version of the novel first appeared in Zurich, Jackson was president of the United States. He receives Tokeah and his followers in the role of spokesman for those who have proven themselves to be stronger and who now claim to own the land. He also acts as a man of the Enlightenment, a progressive thinker who represents the "better" side and carries out the will of God.

The stand he takes against the Indians is the same as that expressed by President Jackson in his second annual message to Congress on December 6, 1830. Jackson said,

> Philanthropy could not wish to see this continent restored to the condition in which it was found by our forefathers. What good man would prefer a country covered with forests and ranged by a few thousand savages to our extensive Republic, studded with cities, towns, and prosperous farms, embellished with all the improvements which art can devise or industry execute, occupied by more than 12,000,000 happy people, and filled with all the blessings of liberty, civilization, and religion?"[12]

Similarly, in the novel the general says,

> The Great Spirit has made the lands for the white men, and for the red men, that they may live from the fruits that grow on the earth, and dig the soil, and plough the ground: but not for hunting grounds, that some few hundred red men lead a lazy existence in a territory where millions might live and prosper.

In his "Message on Indian Affairs" on February 22, 1831, President Jackson declared, "My opinion remains the same, and I can see no alternative for them [the Indians] but that of their removal to the West or a quiet submission to the State laws."[13] Sealsfield's general explains to the Indians the philosophical justification for this program:

> The fate of the red men . . . is hard in many respects, but it is not inevitable; barbarism must always yield in the battle against enlightenment . . . but you have the means in your hands to join this enlightenment and to enter into our bourgeois life. Yet if you do not want this and prefer to be wild legitimate ones instead of respected citizens, then you must not protest against your fate.[14]

Only after the general has spoken these words does it become apparent that the novel has a political purpose. The conscious effort of the republicans to shape a new world has priority over the legitimate claims of the original owners of the land. At the same time, the oppressed are shown how to overcome their fate: they have the possibility of becoming part of the enlightened society of the republicans. Clearly, Sealsfield does not see the conflict between the Indian and white man as a racial problem but as a question of political systems and social concepts. His view of mankind resembles that presented by Johann Gottfried Herder in his *Outline of a Philosophy of the History of Man (Ideen zur Geschichte der Philosophie der Menschheit*, 1784– 91): man is a homogeneous species whose members are of the same descent. As different as they may seem, they are shades of the same being and are all dedicated to the single goal of humanitarianism. Sealsfield was convinced that, as Herder stated, man "come[s] into the world weak, in order to learn reason" (*Outline*, book IV, chapter 4) and must use his power of intellect to do justice to his destiny, regardless of his continent of birth or nationality. Sealsfield's concept was shaped by the Weltanschauung of the eighteenth century. If one evaluates the Indians' behavior by this standard, they fare badly.

Yet Sealsfield definitely wanted his readers to know that he saw the other side. The novel's preface not only contains arguments against the white set- tlers but even refers directly to the ideas presented in Jackson's speech. The central theme of the preface is that the "remains of this interesting people can only be saved by transplanting them to a suitable territory of virgin forests where they, in direct contact with related tribes, can revive their languished nationality and cultivate their deteriorated customs." The author knew from personal experience how much sorrow this solution brought to the displaced Indians, for he witnessed a group being transported across the Mississippi, an experience which supposedly first aroused his interest in the Indian problem.

The story of Tokeah, the chief of the Oconees, is the story of one such Indian transplanted from Georgia to the territory west of the Mississippi. Rejected by the majority of a tribe that had consorted with the whites, was corrupted by their influence, and had resettled in Alabama, he and a small band of followers migrate to a narrow, relatively inaccessible strip of land between the Sabine and Natchez Rivers. In these surroundings the Indians are able to lead a satisfying, peaceful life, devoted to their customs and crafts. But even here disaster befalls them; their idyll is destroyed when they are raided by the pirate Lafitte during the wedding night of Tokeah's daughter Canondah, who is killed by the enemy. The entire village burns, and many Indians die. Tokeah had once been on friendly terms with the pirate but had broken off the friendship. Because of his imprudence and incorrect assess- ment of the enemy, the Indians neglected to keep careful watch that night. Thus what is suggested in the preface as the only possible solution—the retreat to still primitive lands—proves unsuccessful. When Tokeah is re- ceived by Jackson, he is a failed and ruined man. He expresses no hope, only hatred and despair, when he tells Jackson that he wishes to go to a place "where he will never see white men again."

In the second part of the trial scene, the general turns his attention to the white girl who accompanies Tokeah. Her story began on a stormy December night, the first scene of the novel, when Tokeah, still bloodstained after a massacre, brought her as an infant to the home of a white trader, a "backwoodsman" in Georgia. He demanded that the trader's wife care for the child. The trader, Captain John Copeland, was forced to obey; his attempts to notify the authorities of the incident were unsuccessful, since the chief kept a watch on his every move and threatened to scalp his family. For six years, Tokeah paid for the child's sustenance with furs, until one day he came to take her away to his wigwam. At this time he and his tribe were to resettle west of the Mississippi, and the Americans had begun to advance into Louisiana.

Copeland is one of the settlers who takes possession of the newly acquired land. After Tokeah releases him of the responsibility of caring for the child, the reader temporarily loses sight of him. In chapter 21 he reappears as a country squire in Opelousas, Louisiana, and a major in the war against the British. From now on he is the representative of the republicans, interpreting the freedoms of the land at every opportunity. The narrator tells us that "the seven years during which we did not see him had brought about a positive change" in his character. Sealsfield explains the nature of this change in careful detail. This is important insofar as the author is showing how a person develops under the particular conditions of the new continent. His considerable prosperity and prestige in the community have had a humanizing and cultivating effect on him: "As his affluence increased, the crude selfish being . . . gave way to a humane comfortableness." He represents the free, self-reliant, responsible citizen of a young democracy, who is completely in agreement with its principles and ideals.

As his biographer Eduard Castle substantiates, Madame de Staël's *De l'Allemagne* (1810) and *Corinne ou L'Italie* (1807) were among Sealsfield's literary models. Literary researchers have also long been aware of Sealsfield's indebtedness to Sir Walter Scott. He expressed strong admiration for Scott, "this truly great man" who elevated the novel to that "which it is today, a cultural lever." Scott had a dramatic effect on the "faculties of thought and judgment in his nation and in the world at large" by bringing the story of the past into "the realm of kitchen and hearth" (*Morton*, 1846 edition). In the same sense, Sealsfield wished to do his part so that the historical novel might "have a more beneficial influence on the *Bildung* of the age." He hoped to help make the thousand "silly, harmful, stupid" books which simply follow the fashion (*Moderomane*) less harmful by providing an "antidote."

Sealsfield not only knew de Staël and Scott but was, in general, a well-read man. He was familiar with James Fenimore Cooper and François-René Chateaubriand, both of whom he viewed critically in the introduction to his novel *Morton*. He found fault with Chateaubriand on the grounds that in

Les Natchez (1826) the portrayal of Louisiana and the main river of the United States was "false in every respect." This comment is interesting in light of Sealsfield's own careful and exact descriptions of the countryside. He does not tell us whether he was at all impressed by Chateaubriand's novels *Atala* (1801) and *René* (1802).

Of Cooper, Sealsfield said that his characters were exaggerated and a certain "scholarly niveau" was lacking, but he considered him an excellent author. By the time Sealsfield began his story of Tokeah, many of Cooper's novels had already appeared—*The Spy* (1821), *The Pioneers* (1823), *The Last of the Mohicans* (1826), and *The Prairie* (1827). As early as 1831, Sealsfield dedicated a critical article to Cooper, the substance of which is readily accessible today in the introduction to *Morton*.[15]

The similarities between *The Last of the Mohicans* and *Tokeah* cannot be overlooked; there is no doubt that Sealsfield learned from Cooper. In both novels an international war provides the background. Plot elements, unusual words, and proper names from Cooper's novel reappear in *Tokeah*. In his introduction to *Tokeah* in the recent edition of Sealsfield's complete works, John Krumpelmann lists some of these parallels but emphasizes "that in his conception of the nature and of the circumstances of the American aborigines Sealsfield differs greatly from the ideal concept of the 'noble savage'" as exemplified by the Indian Uncas and Cooper's other characters. Nevertheless Sealsfield's first novel is, like *The Last of the Mohicans*, basically a romantic narrative. On the title page of the English edition Sealsfield quotes Goethe's Mignon song: "Knowest thou the land where the lemon trees bloom?" to which Krumpelmann remarks, "This description fits Sealsfield's Paradise of Louisiana, with its citrus groves and oranges." A comparison of Sealsfield's two versions shows how he made a romantic narration into a political novel, taking only those elements from the first version which he could use within the new context.

A special theme is the story of the "white rose," the delicate child whose frailty is respected by her robust foster mother as well as by the Indians. Her whimpering leads the wild Indian chief, for whom hatred of whites is his life's law, to an act of humanity. This "white rose," who lives as an angelic being among primitives, a poor orphan loved by all, is typologically a figure from world literature. Whether one sees her in connection with Romulus and Remus, who are nourished by a she-wolf and raised by shepherds, with Moses, found by Pharoah's daughter in the bulrushes and adopted as her son, or with Goethe's Mignon, she has the characteristics of "the heavenly child" described by Karl Kerényi and Carl Gustav Jung. Kerényi and Jung speak of "the *loneliness* of the heavenly child" who is "*at home* in a primitive world";[16] both characterizations apply to the child Rosa. The modern Indian problem is united with a mythical act whenever Rosa speaks in defense of the Indians; in the irreconcilable conflict between whites and Indians she represents hope. This is already apparent in the opening scene when Tokeah asks for "milk for a small daughter" and brings forth a "beautiful child, wrapped in valuable furs" from his bloodstained blanket. The white woman's motherly reaction is quite natural as a response to the situation. Nonetheless, mythical elements also play a role. Rosa herself says later, "In the hereafter the white and red men will not murder each other any more, they will rejoice and will be blessed forever." But the Indian girl Canondah, whose function as a protectress also has mythical origins, considers it impossible that the "great spirit" will not have "separate meadows for the white and red men" in eternity.

The surprising reappearance of Rosa's "very noble father" may seem disturbing in a political novel. The father who is suddenly found again and is "very noble" is also an ancient motif. It was employed in the baroque novel as well as in the eighteenth and early nineteenth centuries. Simplicius, Agathon, and Titan suddenly discover that they are sons of "very noble" fathers. Rosa's attempt to depart from Tokeah on friendly terms is reminiscent of Iphigenia's bid for Thoas's "Farewell" (Goethe, *Iphigenia auf Tauris*). The political realities exclude the possibility of Rosa's success, even though both parties have long grown weary of the struggle. Before leaving Georgia, Copeland said, "I long for a quieter place," and Tokeah often said that he was "tired of the whites." This does not suggest, however, that there could be a reconciliation. Both sides desire freedom, but the Indian chief must "search for it where the white man has never set foot." The fact that Rosa cannot follow Tokeah, but instead goes with her father, is motivated emotionally, politically, and mythically; from the mythical standpoint there can be no doubt as to her decision.

Sealsfield's second novel, *The Viceroy and the Aristocrats or Mexico in the Year 1812 (Der Virey und die Aristokraten oder Mexiko im Jahre 1812,* 1834), also deals with contemporary historical events, but, rather than concentrating on an individual's fate, here Sealsfield turns his attention to the struggles among different political groups in Mexico at the beginning of the nineteenth century. Rebellious masses of various races and racial mixtures—Indians and Negroes, mestizos, mulattos, and zambos—living in miserable poverty and without social rights, threaten the capital city with varying degrees of success. They are led by revolutionaries, primarily priests, some of whom are respectable, others unscrupulous. At the head of the government, forcibly held together by Spain, is the Viceroy Venegas, who exploits the country unconscionably for his own personal advantage, while to all appearances he is a generous and kindly father to his people and a model of propriety in his personal life. The small group of Spanish nobility, likewise interested only in maintaining its privileged position at the expense of the common people, regards the Creole aristocracy with arrogance and opposes its participation in the government and the army. Nevertheless, the Creole aristocrats do not feel that they or the state would benefit if they were to join forces with the insurgents.

Sealsfield unfolds the entire picture of Mexican political and social life at that time from the standpoint of a citizen of the United States. For example, he denounces the false, rhetorical language at the Viceroy's court as an instrument of degradation and stultification, claiming that the phrases used there sound "so disgraceful, unmasculine, and even absurd . . . in our masculine, free American language" that it would almost be impossible to reproduce them. It has never been conclusively proven that Sealsfield visited Mexico, but, from his descriptions of Mexico City and its surroundings as well as the Tenochtitlan Valley, it would seem probable that he had spent at least some time there. Whatever the case may be, he was not incapable of portraying lands and people he had never seen with "great power," as in *Scenes in Poland I. 1794.*[17]

Morton or the Great Tour (*Morton oder die grosse Tour*, appeared 1835 as *The Great Tour*, retitled 1846), an unfinished novel, tells of the young American Morton, who is associated with the Philadelphia banker Girard and enters the world of international finance. As in *Tokeah*, the story of an individual again points to a more general theme: the worldwide power of money and the related dangers to human character. "Here money takes the place of love; it covers many, or all, sins." By exposing the financiers and criticizing the international monetary system, Sealsfield displayed his continued support for Andrew Jackson, who as President strongly opposed the idea of a national bank.

Different in design and theme from all his other works written up to that time is Sealsfield's *The Cabin Book* (*Das Kajütenbuch*, 1841). Its complicated structure has given rise to debate as to whether the work is a novel or a novella cycle.[18] The evening discussions among the group of people in the cabin provide the frame for a number of shorter narrations; one of these, *The Prairie at the Jacinto* (*Die Prärie am Jacinto*), has often been acclaimed as an important work of German prose. Both the frame discussions and the short narrations revolve around the problem of the annexation of Texas to the United States of America.

Sealsfield's works were widely read in his time. They were translated into English and French and were very popular in America, England, and France. In the mid-1830s pupils in Zurich secretly read *Tokeah* and *Viceroy* at their school desks. Even though the novels have long been forgotten, they are still interesting texts and are far more exciting and pleasant to read than the novels of the Young Germans. Their advantage over the novels of Laube, Theodor Mundt, Gustav Kühne, and Gutzkow is that they contain enthusiastically advocated, concrete political concepts which are based on the author's direct experience. Thus they captivate the reader.

The novels of the representatives of Young Germany were lacking the very fullness of life which they sought, desired, and propagandized. They suffered from a lack of material. "In a word: one must learn to narrate," Heinrich Laube once said. But what should one narrate? Can one learn to narrate without having something to tell about? Of course, the genuine narrator creates his material; he has it; he finds it everywhere. But the Young Germans could not use just any material. It had to fit their themes, and their themes were politics, the state, freedom, and the struggle against Metternich's system. Yet what was there to say in regard to these topics besides prison experiences and oppression in a narrow world?

Sealsfield could talk endlessly about these very subjects. It was said that in his later years,

> while sitting on the sofa with both hands folded in his lap and an unblinking gaze, he could extemporize for half-hours at a time in such glowing colors and perfect sentence structure that his listeners followed spellbound into an unknown land. North America with its republican institutions was more important to him than anything! American freedom was his ideal.[19]

This did not mean, however, that he never spoke critically of the United States. Sealsfield did not glorify the new political system, but he was indeed fascinated by it. This was what his contemporaries in Germany were missing. They had only negative experiences and possessed no alternative to a situation which they rejected. Therefore, their political concepts had to remain vague. In their own surroundings there was nothing which could have provided them with a vision of what could actually be achieved in political life.

Heinrich Laube's (1806–1884) trilogy *Young Europe* (*Das junge Europa*, 1833–37) testifies to the helplessness of the times. Its parts are *The Poets* (*Die Poeten*, 1833), *The Warriors* (*Die Krieger*, 1837), and *The Citizens* (*Die Bürger*, 1837). Of the three *The Warriors* is considered to be the most significant. It has even been said that in some respects it is "the most successful of all Young German prose works."[20] *The Warriors* is the story of a failed revolution, the Polish revolution of 1830–31. Laube's portrayal of scenes from this struggle is vivid and historically accurate. During the rebellion he lived as a private tutor near the Polish border, where he heard many first-hand reports. Stirred by the events, he studied Polish history and questioned a wounded Polish officer he met in Breslau. Thus he was able to describe specifics with regard to battle scenes and geography and to characterize the leaders as well as the rival groups among the Polish people. In shaping his material into a fictional work, Laube borrowed motifs from Sir Walter Scott. These are easily recognizable; as an example, the "blacksmith of Wavre," a secret leader of the resistance, admired by all, is comparable to Robin Hood in Scott's *Ivanhoe*.

We see the revolution through the experiences of the main character, Valerius. The reader already knows Valerius from the first novel, *The Poets*, in which young friends of differing opinions and character exchange ideas on the issues of the day and discuss their adventures in love. Valerius is particularly respected and trusted in the group and as an exemplary figure is a most suitable witness to the inevitability of the era's bitter experiences. In his last letter from Germany—the first and third novels of the trilogy are traditional epistolary novels—he writes that he will leave the next day for Warsaw "to fight against the tyrants for the holy rights of a people. I am not very fond of the Polish people, but I will bleed and die for their cause." Valerius's experiences in Poland as a volunteer from Germany completely contradict his hopes and expectations. In the end he no longer believes in the purpose or success of the revolution and is drawn into the general defeat. He summarizes the results of his experiences:

> He who foolishly presumes to master and change world history quickly, as we tried to do in the last years as if it were a mere trifle, should not complain when he is destroyed. Take action if you feel the call, but do not venture to determine the outcome in advance; we only know the world one step at a time. I wish to return to my homeland, to build a hut, to continue to look into the distance, but to act only for the present.

Neither Valerius nor the characters in works by Immermann and Gutzkow have the chance to influence their times productively. Action is replaced by good intentions, many deliberations, and proclamations without concrete results. In some cases the eighteenth-century concept of the efficacy of secret societies plays a role. Secluded from the public and bound by rituals and symbols accessible only to the initiated, representatives of small groups make their ideas for change known, ideas which are in effect the author's analysis of the times. This analysis is the substance of the novels, whereby "the times" refers to a particular historical era. The events that evolve during the era are as unique as the characters who represent it. Young German authors were not concerned with the development of a title character to whom other characters are subordinated, as in Goethe's *Apprenticeship* and the other novels in the same tradition, but, instead, all characters have the similar function of expressing the tendencies of the age. They are all equally important and carry the action forward as a group. This does not mean, however, that some do not stand out more than others or play a central role; at times it is still possible to speak of a main character.

In *The Epigones* (*Die Epigonen*, 1836) by Karl Leberecht Immermann (1796–1840), it is not Hermann, the main character, but his friend Wilhelmi who summarizes the author's analysis of the times proclaimed in the title:

> We are, to express the entire misery in *one* word, epigones, and bear the burden generally felt by every generation of heirs. The great spiritual movement undertaken by our fathers from their huts has provided us with many treasures. . . . But borrowed ideas are like borrowed money: he who manages another's property frivolously becomes increasingly poorer.

Earlier Wilhelmi had explained the implications of this situation for his entire generation: "We cannot deny that a dangerous historical era has come upon us. Men have always had misfortune enough; but the curse of our present generation is that it feels miserable even without a particular cause for suffering." He speaks of an "empty swaying to and fro," a "ridiculous mock earnestness," a "groping for something unknown," a "fear of horrors which are all the more uncanny since they have no shape!" It is "as if mankind, tossed about in its little ship on an overwhelming sea, is suffering from moral seasickness with no end in sight."

In his book *Six Essays on the Young German Novel*, Jeffrey Sammons discusses the title *The Epigones*, claiming that "Immermann's single great coup was to give a name to the malaise that beset the bourgeois intelligentsia." As Sammons points out, the title comes from a Greek word meaning "descendents" or "those who come after." This is a case of "a true neologism, insofar as he [Immermann] gave a known word a new meaning." For

> in Greek tradition, the *Epigonoi* were the sons of the Seven against Thebes, who conquered the city before which their fathers had perished. Thus the term had by no means a pejorative connotation, since the sons accomplished that which the fathers had been unable to do. It was Immermann who gave the word the gloomy sense it was to have ever after: it identifies a mediocre generation following on one of great brilliance, condemned to imitation and amorphousness. The word became a concept of intellectual history—one often abused—and found its way, in Immermann's sense, into other languages; in English it has never achieved much currency, although the larger dictionaries carry it.[21]

Hermann functions as a representative of his times; that is, he is a sufferer and prisoner for whom there is no escape. He hopes to find a solution in the end by trying to turn back industrial development in favor of an agricultural economy. Immermann's portrayal of industrialization credits the modern society with positive aspects which cannot be found anywhere else in the literature of his day. The new democratic working conditions are described as having decided advantages over the feudal relationship between master and servant. Yet Immermann's hero also becomes aware of the many disadvantages of industrialization. He feels a "deep aversion to the mathematical calculation of human energy and human diligence" and is shocked by the unhealthy appearance of the workers and their children and by the increase in criminality. When at the end Hermann is named as heir to both nobility and industry, he decides to close the factories and return the earth to farming. "The earth belongs to the plow, to the sunshine and rain, . . . to the simple working hand." As in Laube's *Young Europe*, the idyll is also the only answer here.

The plot of the novel is not uniform. Widely differing types of conventional motifs are all integrated into the story. For example, the motif of characters who search for their identity and are not who they thought they were was used by seventeenth-century German novelists. In addition, *Wilhelm Meister* significantly influenced individual elements as well as the structure as a whole. The schema of Goethe's novel is combined with the idea of the *Zeitroman* of the 1830s. As tasteless as many aspects of the plot may seem to a twentieth-century reader, the analysis of the times is still worthy of attention. Immermann has captured the duplicity and uncertainties in the years before the July Revolution of 1830.

Immermann's second novel, *Münchhausen. A Story in Arabesques* (*Münchhausen. Eine Geschichte in Arabesken,* 1838–39) is far more artistic than *The Epigones*. It is an important work. Although it is also a *Zeitroman* which followed the *The Epigones* closely in time, there are significant differences between the two. Whereas Immermann previously used fiction as a means of analyzing the times, fiction in *Münchhausen* is not only a means of expression but also the theme of the novel for long periods. Immermann plays an ironic game with the relationship between truth and falsehood and by doing so makes a statement about his times. This is apparent from the title. Just as *The Epigones* is a direct statement on how the contemporaries viewed themselves and their fate, the title *Münchhausen. A Story in Arabesques* is indicative of the novel's dizziness, intangibility, and fluctuations.

The German public had been familiar with the "Lügenbaron" (Baron of Lies) Münchhausen since the late eighteenth century. Baron Karl Friedrich Hieronymous von Münchhausen (1720–1797), a historical figure, entertained his friends with extraordinary fabrications in which he liked to expose lies by intentional exaggeration. During his lifetime colorful mendacious stories from the rich and long-standing tradition of the genre had already become associated with his name. One of the several collections of Münch-hausen stories which appeared in the 1780s is Gottfried August Bürger's (1747–1794) *Wonderful Journeys on Land and at Sea. The Campaigns and Humorous Adventures of the Baron von Münchhausen, as He Was Accustomed to Narrating Them with a Flask in a Circle of Friends* (*Wunderbare Reisen zu Wasser und zu Lande, Feldzüge und lustige Abenteuer des Freiherrn von Münchhausen, wie er dieselben bei der Flasche im Zirkel seiner Freunde selbst zu erzählen pflegt,* 1786).

The word "arabesques," as it appears in the title and occasionally within the novel itself, is used by Immermann to refer to a free structuring of novel segments which are not necessarily logically joined but are nonetheless intertwined to form a whole. The concept was derived from Romanticism; Friedrich Schlegel called the arabesque "the oldest and original form of fantasy."[22] The arabesque gives the *Zeitroman* new dimensions. *Münchhausen* cannot be seen in connection with the *Bildungsroman*, as was the case with *The Epigones*, but rather is closer to Laurence Sterne's novel form. Style and structure are determined by a free play of fantasy, wit, and irony. It is evident that only those who understand this game can grasp the spirit of the times as reflected in the foolish activities at the castle Schnick-Schnack-Schnurr.

The adventurous narrator, a guest at Schnick-Schnack-Schnurr, sets the foolishness in motion, but he also brings about the reversal from insanity to reason. He is actually less a fool than simply a deliberate liar. While he narrates his listeners futilely attempt to find their way through the lies. The situation is characterized by the desperate exclamation of the schoolmaster:

> Herr von Münchhausen, you begin to narrate; then other persons begin to narrate within those narrations, and if one doesn't quickly put a stop to this, then we will truly fall into a narrative abyss in which our reason has to fail. . . . Herr von Münchhausen, I consider you to be a great, wonderfully talented man, but I ask a single favor of you, that you narrate more simply and orderly.

Münchhausen replies, "I can assure you that I am in control of my material, and that in my stories as in my mind everything is coherent. . . . Of course for some people some combinations are too difficult." Münchhausen cannot narrate any differently. In the course of the novel it will become apparent why "some" do not understand him.

It is not only the narrator Münchhausen who is pursuing enigmatic goals but the author as well. In arranging his narration, he places what are supposed to be the first ten chapters after the so-called fifteenth chapter, so that the novel seems to begin with chapter eleven. The reason given for this order is that the bookbinder did not approve of the beginning as planned and

took matters into his own hands. In the part entitled "The Editor's Correspondence with his Bookbinder" (between the fifteenth and first chapters),
the bookbinder explains his position to the fictitious author, who introduces
himself as the "editor":

> You started the Münchhausen stories in a plain manner, as is
> your custom: "In the German countryside where the powerful
> principality of Hechelkram lay in former times, a plateau rises,"
> etc. Then you told about the castle and its inhabitants. . . . This
> style may have been good and useful during Cervantes's times,
> when the readers wanted to enter into the story gently and mildly
> as if into an enchanted grotto. . . . But today the magic of such
> a sweetly captivating style is no longer appropriate. . . . Today
> you have to do more than blow the bass trombone, you have to
> beat the tom-tom and shake the rattles. . . . An orderly style is
> outdated. Any author who wants to get somewhere must take up
> a disorderly style, for then suspense is aroused which does not let
> the reader breathe and chases him wildly to the last page. . . . In
> *one* word: Confusion! Confusion! Sir, believe me, without con-
> fusion you cannot accomplish anything these days.

The bookbinder's satire serves as criticism of the times, but it is also
justified criticism of the planned beginning, "In the German countryside."
This introduction would indeed be a poor way to open such a witty book,
just as poor as the reasons given for shifting the same beginning to another
place in the book. Even the fictitious editor soon admits feeling badly about
having to provide certain information he feels he owes to the reader in the
first chapter. "Is it not a misfortune for the poor narrator that he always has
to warm up old stories?" he asks suddenly. "The things I say there already
seemed to have been worn out by novelists fifty years ago!" By this point at
the latest, the reader becomes aware of what the bookbinder did not understand: the introductory chapter is a parody of the historical novel which,
under Scott's influence, had flourished beyond all bounds in Germany.
Whereas Heine could still use the language of Romanticism for historical
events and their geographical settings in *The Rabbi of Bacharach*, fifteen
years later Immermann thought that the "magic of such a sweetly captivating
style" was no longer appropriate. This style was stale, and he could use it
only in parody. It can be compared to the dilapidated castle Schnick-Schnack-
Schnurr, whose strange inhabitants live from the ideas and experiences of
the past and have no relation to their own present time.

Yet the character Münchhausen belongs to his age. He represents it as
the "Zeitgeist in persona" (spirit of the age personified). The fleeting instant
is his element, for that is where wit and lies come alive and then immediately

vanish again. Münchhausen is both admired and persecuted. There are many speculations and opinions about him, and many believe they know him. But no one knows who he really is. The best statements about him come from Münchhausen himself. He talks about himself with the author Immermann, who actually appears in the novel in order to support his hero when he comes into great difficulty at Schnick-Schnack-Schnurr. What has happened is that after a while Münchhausen's audience no longer believes his lies; they are tired of his stories and disappointed that he has not kept his promise to erect a factory for solidifying air (to be used as a building material). The representatives of the conventional world—baron, mayor, policeman— threaten him with arrest. When Immermann tells him he has gone too far with his mischief and is in an impossible situation, Münchhausen responds that he has "made many fools happy, and since the world is made up of fools," he has "made the world happy," wherever his "roaming foot has touched upon it." Moreover, there is nothing else he can now undertake; neither the military nor the state nor the financial market offers tempting possibilities. There is nothing to do but to "lie, make fun of boasters, wander about, change and transform oneself. . . . A liar I was, a liar I am, a liar I shall be!" He will not stand for any criticism from the author.

A discussion about Münchhausen's originality then ensues. The author and Münchhausen disagree as to whether he is the author's creation or an independent character. Whereas the author expresses the opinion that this is a case of the creation rebelling against the creator, Münchhausen declares with quiet dignity that "you are not the man to create a man like me." When the author asks incredulously, "Are you claiming in complete seriousness to be an independent character?" Münchhausen replies, "Of course. I don't know what I should think of you. Just be careful not to look so small next to me that you disappear, be careful not to be seen as my creation. What could *you* have given or loaned me? You are no genius." Later, several other characters who have been puzzled over Münchhausen's identity finally turn to the author for help; "'Who is he really?' 'Gentlemen,' the author replied, 'I don't know.' 'What?' 'Perhaps I know more about his life than you do,' said Immermann, 'but as to who he actually is, I know no more than you.'" The irony of this passage can be seen in connection with the end of Münchhausen's story: he disappears into a crypt with no exit, and the author cannot say how it happened. Thus Immermann's helplessness as the author is underscored once again. With the assistance of several farmers he spends over an hour in a futile attempt to find the crypt's exit.

The novel contains not only Münchhausen's story, but also a number of other stories, themes, and motifs. For a long time it was regarded as a double novel, and part of it was published separately under the title *Oberhof*. These sections tell the story of a Westphalian farm (Oberhof) and its inhabitants. The plot centers on the romance between Count Oswald and the foundling Lisbeth, who, it is later discovered, is Münchhausen's daughter.

Although the rural world depicted in books 2, 5, and 7 is entirely different from the situation at the decaying castle Schnick-Schnack-Schnurr, there is still an overall unity. Actually, the two strands are closely linked, as in E. T. A. Hoffmann's *Kater Murr*, which inspired Immermann to use a similar form for *Münchhausen*. A pedantic division of the novel into two parts would reflect a misunderstanding of its structure and destroy much of the reading pleasure. The *Oberhof* parts are not a peasant novel as has often been assumed, but, like Schnick-Schnack-Schnurr, the Oberhof functions as a gathering place. In both locations Immermann brings together the characters with whom he carries out an experiment to demonstrate his analysis of the times. Through the interplay of all of the parts of the novel Immermann has created a world rather than merely described one; he has given an analysis, not a picture, of the times. The *Zeitroman* of the era reached its highest potential in Immermann's *Münchhausen*, in which fiction and commentary on the times are one.

Karl Gutzkow's (1811–1878) *Zeitromane* brought him little good fortune. Of the three, *Wally the Doubter* (*Wally, die Zweiflerin*, 1835), *The Knights of the Spirit* (*Die Ritter vom Geiste*, 1850–51), and *The Sorcerer of Rome* (*Der Zauberer von Rom*, 1858–61), it was *Wally the Doubter* which prompted the Federal Diet to issue a decree on December 10, 1835, instructing the German governments to prevent the publication and distribution of all works from the "literary school" of Young Germany and to enforce the penal code with maximum severity. On September 24, 1835, only a few weeks after its publication, *Wally* was banned in Prussia as well as in other German states, and a trial had been initiated against both author and publisher. Gutzkow was charged with "blasphemy, derision of the Christian faith and church, and obscenity." These objections are actually more characteristic of the state authorities at that time than of the content of the book. In the final verdict on January 13, 1836, Gutzkow was found guilty only of a contemptuous portrayal of the Christian faith and received a greatly reduced sentence of one month in prison, which he accepted without appeal. As many of his contemporaries realized and Gutzkow himself stressed, the condemnation of the book was founded on a misunderstanding.

As the title indicates, its theme is religious doubt. "I wanted to portray a state of mind which seemed poetic to me. . . . I had a psychological picture before my eyes and painted it with the colors borrowed from reality." These are Gutzkow's own words from "Appeal to Common Sense. Last Word in a Literary Dispute," in which he asks, "What concern was the church to me as a poet?"[23] He concedes, however, that critics might well question the use of motifs which bring out an emotional reaction in the reader. Gutzkow recognized that the "unity of the work is destroyed if the motifs excite us more than the story itself." But he claimed that "wise and just criticism, . . . which appeals to Aristotle and not to the state or armed authority," would realize that he "only wanted to compose and not to instruct."

On the basis of his bitter experience, Gutzkow characterized the problem all authors of *Zeitromane*—indeed, all literary writers—must face. But his words "compose" and "instruct" and the distinction between them are probably not entirely clear to modern readers. Gutzkow meant that when interest in the material itself becomes too strong (he said "motifs" rather than material), the aesthetic effect of a work is endangered and is replaced by a discussion of the contents. In theory, the political author would be very satisfied with such a success and would see his goals attained. But Gutzkow was not satisfied and complained that he had been misunderstood. "I wanted to depict a loss of faith, not as a denial of faith but in order to show a psychological phenomenon." The novel ends with a "triumph of religion in general as something sacred without which one cannot live. What is the crime here? A reasonable person would see poorly chosen material; but not a sacrilege."

Gutzkow did not feel that he was the victim of his convictions, but rather of the "misère of German literature." He could not succeed in the struggle against the authorities because, as he argued, "Talent stands alone, without protection. . . . One is nothing against the official who keeps warm under the wings of the state." What Gutzkow describes here as the "misère of German literature" is the result of the cultural gap between the classes in Germany, a situation which also concerned Immermann. A fictional character in *Münchhausen* states that "unfortunately . . . our upper classes lag behind the people" and speaks of the "barbarity of the first class," the class responsible for politics and culture.

This still does not explain why the writer Wolfgang Menzel attacked Gutzkow so maliciously in his *Morning Paper for the Educated Classes* and continued the assault for many weeks, thereby alerting the government censors. Gutzkow was advised to bring a libel suit against Menzel. He did not do so, nor did he hold the nobility responsible for the poor educational level of state officials in his "Appeal to Common Sense." He merely characterized the existing gap from his own individual, elitist standpoint.

> I do not write for the masses. My style and education distance me from the average intelligence. When writing I have always thought of myself in communication with gifted people. . . . If the future leaves me in a condition to devote my strengths to the revival of our national literature, my writings will attract only a select circle of the insightful and informed. I can deal with these people alone, with well-read men familiar with the spiritual developments of our age, with women who are sufficiently mature for serious views.

The novel *Wally* could in fact only be received by the circles Gutzkow described. Its many dialogues are often clever and witty, but they can be difficult to follow because topics of music, literature, morality, and religion are touched upon and then dropped. The title character Wally, a young woman from well-to-do nobility, is presented from the beginning as an excitable person, particularly sensitive in her reactions to religion. She cries or blushes when references to Christianity are made. In the first part of the novel she enters into a spiritual union with Cäsar, a cynical man who says that neither he nor Wally is "made for illusions." At a ball in the second part, she tells Cäsar that she intends to marry a Sardinian diplomat. Cäsar's farewell request is that she show herself nude to him, as Sigune did for Schionatulander in the medieval work *Titurel.* At first Wally is outraged, but she soon comes to feel that her virtuous indignation is absurd; the "true spirit of poetry," she decides, is irresistible and of greater value than "all laws of morality and custom." She reads the Sigune story, which makes the tenets of her own upbringing seem less compelling, and fulfills Cäsar's wish by allowing him to come during her wedding night and draw back a curtain. The scene is modest: "So stood Sigune a trembling moment; then the Sardinian diplomat embraced her from behind. . . . The curtains closed and Schionatulander stumbled home. The diplomat suspected nothing." After the wedding Wally lives in Paris with her husband and partakes of the pleasures there until she realizes that the diplomat is using her against his own brother Jeronimo. He is taking advantage of Jeronimo's love for Wally in order to swindle him out of his inheritance and destroy him. After Jeronimo shoots himself in front of Wally, she leaves Paris with Cäsar, who has since visited her and enlightened her as to her true situation.

The third part consists essentially of Wally's diary entries. She loses Cäsar, whom she loves completely, to the Jewess Delphine, but this is only part of her anguish. Her suffering stems primarily from her increasing religious doubts. Her main question is: why did God not give man the "capacity to understand Him?" She finally asks Cäsar to send her a letter explaining his own views on Christianity and religion. As the reader might expect, the skeptic's writings give her no comfort; when she reads his "Confessions," she experiences a mental collapse. In despair over the impossibility of finding answers to questions about God, Wally finally commits suicide. In one of the last paragraphs before her death, the narrator says of her, "She the doubter, the uncertain one, the enemy of God, was she not more pious than those who find comfort in a faith they do not understand? She had the deep conviction that man's life is miserable without religion."

Many references to contemporary works can be found in Gutzkow's first novel. There are allusions and unidentified quotations as well as references to specific authors and works. In the first part of the novel, Wally, not yet twenty years old, pronounces literary judgments on authors such as Gustav Schwab and Adalbert von Chamisso, who "take the liberty of being very boring. . . . Heine's prose is more to my liking than Uhland and his entire bardic grove." She is also familiar with the writings of the Young Germans: "Wienbarg is too democratic. . . . Laube does not seem to want to abolish the nobility, but rather to outdo it. . . . Mundt I only half like." Later she criticizes Rahel Varnhagen von Ense and Bettina von Arnim. The character Wally betrays a literary descent from Friedrich Schlegel's *Lucinde* as well as from George Sand's *Lélia*, with whom Gutzkow compares her in detail in his preface to the second edition. Furthermore, Wally's story bears resemblance to the then famous case of Charlotte Stieglitz, who also committed suicide.

Many of Wally's statements allude to the situation of girls and women in the nineteenth century, such as when she speaks of "this plant-like unconsciousness in which women vegetate" and complains that "nothing is expected of us." The Sigune scene, which caused a great sensation, can be seen in relation to these statements and to the overall situation of women at that time. The crux of this scene is that Wally is marrying a man who means nothing to her and that she does not make an inner commitment, either to the marriage or to her love for Cäsar. Her realization that the poetic spirit takes preference over morality and custom is the author's way out of an unresolved situation. This is what makes the scene so awkward.

An evaluation of the Sigune scene as well as of the novel as a whole is not dependent on questions which courts or officials could decide, but on questions of taste. In this regard *Wally the Doubter* is not pleasant reading. It is of interest today because it attempts to grasp contemporary life from a psychological standpoint and because a book such as this could arouse so much public attention.

In his novel *The Knights of the Spirit*, Gutzkow's objectives were quite different. The work is valuable principally as an experiment in form. Gutzkow wanted to create the *Roman des Nebeneinander* (cross-sectional novel), which seemed to him at that time to be the appropriate form for a *Zeitroman*. He explained that one could understand his idea if one

> visualizes the cross-sectional drawings of a mine, a warship, or a factory in a picture book. Just as hundreds of rooms . . . exist next to each other, with no knowledge of the other but nevertheless part of a comprehensive whole, the cross-sectional novel will provide a glimpse into hundreds of existences which hardly touch each other and yet are all moved by a single great pulsebeat of life.

By showing that "one existence is unconsciously the shell or core of another and each joy is adjacent to a pain," Gutzkow wanted to make the novel even more a "mirror of life" than it had been previously. He had a "social novel" in mind and believed that in such a work, life would be "a concert in which the author plays or directs . . . all the voices and instruments at the same time."[24]

Gutzkow knew well that his goal could only be carried out chronologically. In certain parts of the novel he did succeed in creating a cross-sectional impression with regard to some, even if only a few, segments of contemporary life. Even though simultaneous events are narrated in sequence (because it cannot be done any other way), the reader is made aware that the scenes in question are all taking place at the same hour. They are connected by a plot which is in part a detective story. In one house people rack their brains trying to figure out where a certain picture could have disappeared to, while people in another house are contentedly looking at the lost picture. Above all, Gutzkow was concerned with portraying social contrasts. The plot winds through the different social layers, showing how occurrences in one sphere have an effect on the others. For this purpose an enormous gallery of characters was necessary, including aristocrats and burghers, the homeless, servants, and the proletariat in tenement houses.

Notwithstanding the work's value as an experiment, it must be regarded as a failure. Gutzkow wrote it under the influence of the great feuilleton novel, *Les Mystères de Paris* (1842–43) by Eugène Sue (1804–1857), which is still popular today; it had appeared in the *Journal des Débats* and was a singular, extraordinary success. Gutzkow undoubtedly intended to write a German equivalent, a work which would conform to German life and conditions. But he failed to achieve this goal. In today's print his "Novel in Nine Books" comprises more than four thousand pages. He possessed neither the imagination nor the power of expression, neither the narrative talent nor the artistic language necessary to hold the reader's attention for so long a time. Nor did he understand how to combine the ideas he propagated with the novel's plot in a meaningful and convincing fashion.

The main plot, a family affair, begins when Dankmar Wildungen finds documents proving that lands in the city's possession legally belong to him and to his brother. When the documents mysteriously disappear, the search for them brings people from all social levels into the picture. This was Gutzkow's real purpose. The actual plot seems artificial since it has little to do with the social panorama or with the endeavors for social reform by the order called the Knights of the Spirit. This society, modeled after the Freemasons, considers itself a revival of the Order of Knights Templar. Its members erect a place of consecration, the "Tempelstein." Their "weapon is the spirit," and their goal is to improve the human condition. Although long chapters are devoted to the founding of the society, its effect is never seen. At the end of the novel, its members come together in great numbers at the "Tempelstein." They take an oath which amounts to a rejection of practical action; they aim to "affect the times by their teaching." One has the impression that the novel is really just beginning here.

In the nineteenth century the work was quite well received by the general public as well as by respected authors. Theodor Storm, Friedrich Hebbel, and Keller praised it. After having been long forgotten, it has become a subject of interest again in recent years. Contemporary writer Arno Schmidt in particular recommended it to young authors and wanted to see it regain popularity (*The Knights of the Spirit, of Forgotten Colleagues*, 1965).

Gutzkow's *Sorcerer of Rome* (1858–61), also a nine-volume work, is concerned with the reform of the Roman Catholic church. The author's ideas are propagated by means of a widely branching plot which is interspersed with sensational effects and makes use of adventure and banality.

The plot of the *Zeitroman* was becoming increasingly problematic. To the same extent that a variety of characters could represent the times rather than a single main character, a main plot could also be replaced by a number of plots which are united by the all-encompassing element of time. In his two later *Zeitromane* Gutzkow did not want to do without plots altogether, but he put little effort into them. They are too flat and too weak to draw the reader into the world of the novel. What is missing is that very element Gutzkow emphasized himself: the "single great pulsebeat of life."

Willibald Alexis's (born Wilhelm Häring, 1798–1871) *Peace Is the First Civic Duty* (*Ruhe ist die erste Bürgerpflicht*, 1852) illustrates how closely the historical novel and the *Zeitroman* were related in the nineteenth century. It is set primarily in Berlin between the summer of 1804 and the days after the Prussian defeat at Jena and Auerstedt in October 1806. From the standpoint of its publication date, it is a historical novel, but it has the effect of a *Zeitroman* since the Berlin readers could identify all too readily with the conditions portrayed. This is underscored by the author's own frequent comparisons of the two different times within the novel. In addition, many passages which refer to the historical past could easily be applied to the present as well. The two time periods are even linked by the title of the book, which is a quote from a proclamation issued in placard form by the Prussian minister Count von der Schulenburg after the battle against Napoleon at Jena and Auerstedt had been lost: "The king has lost a battle. Now peace is the first civic duty" (October 17, 1806).

This order to keep the peace was symptomatic of the paralysis that had long predominated in Prussia's political life. Paralysis is also characteristic of the situation after the unsuccessful midcentury revolution. As G. Wallis Field summarizes, Alexis "gave vent to his indignation at reactionary conditions in Prussia under Frederick William IV by re-evoking a similar picture of Prussian enfeeblement half a century earlier when Frederick William III capitulated to Napoleon."[25] Along the same lines, a letter which Gustav Freytag wrote in the spirit of the day in 1854 could also have applied to the situation in 1806: "We had hoped that the day had come when activity and interest in their own fate could again flare up in the Prussian people. This hope was premature" (letter to Salomon Hirzel, April 15, 1854). The readers of Alexis's novel saw their own affairs and problems portrayed and could read this historical novel like a *Zeitroman*. The society it presents is in decay: on the one hand corruption, adultery, and murder, and on the other thoughtlessness, irresponsibility, and stupidity. Dedication to ideals was a rare exception. The events of the novel, as Alexis describes them, show that Prussia's defeat was the inevitable result of the deplorable state of the government and society.

In his article "Willibald Alexis" (1872), the German novelist Theodor Fontane declared *Peace Is the First Civic Duty* to be Alexis's best novel, for it is the "most true-to-life, gripping, and meaningful" of all his works.[26] Fontane's involvement with Alexis's work is of great importance, for Alexis (along with Scott) was one of Fontane's models. At the time when Fontane wrote his article on Alexis, he had already started working on his first great historical novel, *Before the Storm* (1878).

Alexis began writing in the 1820s. He first translated one of Scott's novels, *The Lady of the Lake* (*Jungfrau vom See*, 1822), and then wrote two amusing parodies on Scott (*Walladmor*, 1823; *Schloss Avalon*, 1827). Later he transferred what he had learned from Scott to Brandenburg-Prussian history and published a series called *Patriotic Novels* (*Vaterländische Romane*), which includes *Peace Is the First Civic Duty*. Other novels in the series are *Cabanis* (1832), set at the time of the Seven Years' War, *Roland of Berlin* (*Der Roland von Berlin*, 1840), set in the midfifteenth century, and *The Wrong Woldemar* (*Der falsche Woldemar*, 1842), set one hundred years earlier. The best-known and most widely read work of the series is *The Pants of Herr von Bredow* (*Die Hosen des Herrn von Bredow*, 1846), a light treatment of a sixteenth-century story.

In the first decade after the July Revolution, the Swiss pastor Jeremias Gotthelf (Albert Bitzius, 1797–1854) was already gaining recognition as a prominent author. An active personality, committed to achieving practical results, he had enthusiastically embraced the revolution, expecting that it would bring essential reforms to his native land. Encountering imposing opposition to his ideas, he found himself unable to play more than a limited role in the great changes the revolution did indeed effect. This is the reason for his emergence as an author; the events of his age caused him to become a novelist.

Gotthelf's novels won him acclaim far beyond the Swiss borders. They are original works, created almost independently of literary models. The author may have been favorably impressed by Johann Heinrich Pestalozzi's *Leonard and Gertrud* (1781–87) as well as other Swiss works, but Goethe's novels did not influence him. Gotthelf's creativity was related to his pedagogical activity as a pastor and promoter of general education. He obtained the material for his rich narratives from his professional experiences. His themes are farm and family life, caring for domestics and laborers, the relationship between families and within the community, and the dangers which threaten youth and rural existence. These dangers can come from the outside or from within, that is, from the growth of new attitudes in the outside environment or from the emergence of dark forces within the characters themselves. The author's themes reveal practical as well as mythical aspects. The style in which he brings them to life is entirely his own and is tied to his political ideas and world view. His picture of the centuries-old farms and of their inhabitants seems to stem from archaic times, and his challenge to present generations to master the dangers awakened by the new times also seems to come from this distant past. His novels display a deep understanding of human behavior; he traces the development of inner crises and shows how they can be resolved.

In his early writings Gotthelf did not display the style which characterizes him today. His first epic work was intended as social criticism and appeared under a pseudonym which was quickly exposed and is now commonly used as the author's name: *Life Story of Jeremias Gotthelf, as He Tells It* (*Der Bauernspiegel oder Lebensgeschichte des Jeremias Gotthelf, Von ihm selbst beschrieben*, 1837). The harshness of the author's criticism in this work is an expression of his passionate striving to bring about educational reform in his country. He considered it absolutely imperative that the population be elevated by education so that each individual could live up to the demands of the greatly advanced political democratization in Switzerland. Gotthelf believed in fighting against illiteracy and general ignorance by means of modern primary schools and adult education, and he also wanted to spread and strengthen moral concepts by an intensification of the Christian spirit. The *Life Story of Jeremias Gotthelf* is a didactic story which shows the abuses Gotthelf felt were in need of remedy.

His second novel, *Joys and Sorrows of a Schoolmaster* (*Leiden und Freuden eines Schulmeisters*, 1838–39), also prepared the way for his later writings. The two-volume story of the schoolmaster Peter Käser, narrated in the first person, again tends toward social criticism. Actual educational matters of relevance in the canton of Berne at that time are treated in the novel. The background for the first chapter is an educational decree introduced in Berne in 1836 stating that all teachers must take an examination and would receive a salary of at least one hundred fifty francs if they passed it. On July 31, 1836, the day on which the novel begins, Peter Käser learns that he has not passed the exam. He and his wife and five children must therefore remain victims of poverty on his salary of eighty francs. The novel ends on March 1, 1837, the day on which Peter Käser learns that he will receive the one hundred fifty francs nonetheless. The reasons why Käser, a teacher of the old school, did not pass the test emerge from his life story.

Peter Käser is the son of a very poor weaver who had eight children. The misery of his youth is described by Gotthelf in a naturalistic fashion with many details. His father exploited the boy as an unpaid laborer and cursed him when he left home to become a teacher. Peter never had a proper education, but as a pupil he could memorize and recite quickly and therefore was ahead of his class. His own teacher, a good-natured drinker, suggested that he become a schoolmaster. This seemed to Peter, as to many of his peers, to be a worthy profession, yet the stages in his life show how much poverty, helplessness, and humiliation it brings him. In his simplicity he is unable to comprehend his situation or to appreciate advancements in educational methods. But his good will and loyalty are unshakeable.

In the town of Gytiwyl, Peter Käser befriends the pastor, who is a self-portrait of the author Gotthelf. This friendship attests to Gotthelf's belief in the necessity of joining church and school, a view contrary to the modern ideas of his contemporaries. Whereas they advocated the liberation of schools from the supervision and influence of the church, Gotthelf wanted schools to retain their religious basis. He believed that the two institutions should work together, assuming that the church would undergo major reforms.

The novel *How Uli the Farmhand Becomes Happy. Written for Servants and Masters* (*Wie Uli der Knecht glücklich wird. Eine Gabe für Dienstboten und Meisterleute*, 1841), which appeared not long after the story of Peter Käser, is no longer built on accusation as in the two previous works. In the great form of the peasant novel (*Bauernroman*), Gotthelf's unique, personal style first achieved its full expression. At the same time he was able to integrate the social ideas and experiences which remained his constant concern.

In Uli's novel he gives a picture of a perfect world as a contrast to the unsettling abuses of the day. He creates conditions as they should be. Within this context Uli the farmhand becomes happy. The novel has the form of a *Bildungsroman*, but it is not comparable to Goethe's *Wilhelm Meister*. In Gotthelf's fictional world the peasant environment contains the educative forces which influence Uli, and the instruction is successful because Uli is willing and able to learn. Because his abilities and insight into his own situation are compatible with the demands made of him, the poor, aimless servant is able to become an independent, responsible farmer.

Uli's story begins when he comes home drunk in the early morning.

The farmer's wife, who hears him, wakens her husband so that he will take care of the animals himself. She also tells him that he must speak to Uli, lest he think that he has a right to act that way: "We have to take a certain responsibility; masters are masters, and you can say what you please about the new ways, that what the servants do outside of work is no one's concern: but masters are masters in their home, and what they allow in their home and permit their servants to do is their responsibility to God and man." Thus the thrust of the novel is already recognizable on the first page. Following the short conversation between the farm couple, the narrator explains their behavior. In families whose property had been handed down for so many generations that one can speak of a "peasant nobility" which respected "family custom" and "family honor," every argument or incident which could attract attention was avoided. "The house stands in proud tranquility amidst green trees; its inhabitants move in and around it with quiet, restrained propriety, and above the trees resounds at most the neighing of horses, but not the human voice. Scolding is neither frequent nor loud." If the farmer is dissatisfied with someone, he calls him into the "little room . . . as unnoticeably as possible" and reads him "a chapter in private . . . which the farmer had usually prepared quite well." He doesn't hide his criticism, but he remains fair. "These chapters generally have a good effect because of the fatherly tone, the peacefulness with which they are read, the consideration shown for the other. One can hardly imagine the self-control and restraint in such houses."

A comparison of the beginning of *Uli the Farmhand* with the beginnings of the two earlier novels shows that Gotthelf is now more a poet than a writer, that he is creating a myth rather than telling a story. The style of reporting has yielded to a style of conjuration. This is readily apparent from the first few sentences. The *Life Story of Jeremias Gotthelf* begins, "I was born in the district Imprudence in a year not counted after Christ. My father was the oldest son of a farmer who owned a rather large holding and had four more sons and three daughters." *Joys and Sorrows of a Schoolmaster* begins, "Peter Käser is my name, I am a schoolmaster, and I lay dejectedly in bed on July 31, 1836." *Uli the Farmhand* begins,

A dark night lay over the earth; darker still was the place from which a low voice called "Johannes!" again and again. It was a little room in a large farmhouse; the voice came from the huge bed which almost filled the entire background. In it lay the farmer's wife with her husband, and she called "Johannes!" until he finally began to mumble and asked at last, "What do you want, what's the matter?" "You have to get up and feed the animals. It's already struck half-past four."

The first sentences of the two earlier works reveal a talented author. The reader is immediately willing to go on. If Gotthelf had continued in this fashion his name definitely would have been included among the most noteworthy novelists of the nineteenth century. The beginning of *Uli the Farmhand* shows that he was more than this, that he was a highly original novelist. Naturally he was dependent on his times for material, but his form and imagination are incomparable.

The tone of the novel is already set in the first paragraphs. For the rest of the narrative the decisive question is: how will the farmer deal with his slovenly farmhand? In their first conversation he does not manage to reach an understanding with Uli. Uli becomes angry and is ready to quit his job. The farmer gives him a grace period to think it over and then takes advantage of the convivial atmosphere of a warm night in order to speak to Uli again. While the two are sitting by a stall waiting for a cow to calve, a long pedagogical discussion ensues. At times it becomes a heated debate, since Uli approaches the social issue from the standpoint of class differences, and the farmer is just as lively in defending the opposite position. The central point is that Uli feels perfectly justified in "loitering" and spending time with a wanton girl; these are his only pleasures.

> "Yes, you're one to talk," says Uli, "you have the most beautiful farm far and wide, . . . a full barn, a good wife, . . . beautiful children; you can be satisfied because you have things to enjoy; if I had them I wouldn't be interested in loitering either, or in Anne Lisi. But what do I have? I'm a poor fellow, with no one in the world who cares about me. . . . Mine is a bad lot in the world. . . . Oh, why don't they just beat people like me to death when we come into the world!" And with that big strong Uli began to cry bitterly.

Of course the farmer's position is identical with the conservative point of view. He explains to Uli that he can overcome his poverty within the existing social structure. This is possible by taking the proper attitude toward service. A long sermon follows, one the farmer says he heard from his pastor years ago, which characterizes the relationship between the farmer and his servant: service is not slavery, and the master is not the enemy, but service should be seen as an apprenticeship and the master as "a blessing from God." He who devotes himself fully to work will have joy as well, joy in work itself, and will be able to make a name for himself so that he will be respected by his fellow man.

In his subtitle, *Written for Servants and Masters*, the author lets it be known from the outset that his work is directed toward a particular group of readers. In light of this, debate on its political slant, didactic tone, and enlightened wisdom becomes superfluous. As the title page indicates, *Uli the Farmhand* is meant for those who find themselves in the same situation as the characters in the novel; this is part of the work's fiction and must be considered in its interpretation. Therefore it cannot be judged by modern political concepts, but only according to its own objectives.

One of these objectives was that the farmer's sermon be successful.

> In Uli something new had been awakened . . . without his really knowing it yet. He had to reflect on his master's speech somewhat longer, . . . and more and more it seemed to him that his master was right to a certain degree. It made him feel good to think that he was not created to remain a poor, despised fellow, but could still become a man.

To be sure, Uli cannot understand how he can live on his salary and still be able to save. But again the farmer has a solution; it is not a question of Uli going out less than before and smoking less tobacco. He has to give both up completely, which will allow him to save a large amount from his pay. Also, by resting on Sunday he will be fresher at work.

The farmer advises his servant in the same way on many other occasions. He helps him when he gets into trouble and also shows him how to do more skilled work. In the fall he let Uli "sow the field while he harrowed it, let him plough while he did the servant's work. He had told Uli that he must also learn this if he wanted to become a foreman, . . . for there is nothing sadder than a poor little farmhand who doesn't understand half the work." Uli receives the attention Jeremias's father did not get in the *Life Story of Jeremias Gotthelf*. It is characteristic of the novel's style that the points to be made are stated outright. For example, the reader is told that the master "let Uli work the plow, which hundreds of fathers do not allow their own sons to do. . . . They never trust them with plowing or sowing for fear that a handful too much corn might be used or some other mistake might be made."

By means of an ideal character like the farmer Johannes, Gotthelf was able to make his pedagogical ideas clear to a large audience. Everything the farmer does is exemplary. He not only educates Uli to be a model servant but also helps him on his way to becoming an independent farmer. This demonstrates Gotthelf's belief that the poor do not have to remain poor and degraded if they are given a proper education and infused with the self-confidence that each of God's creatures must possess. As Gotthelf explained in his essay on the plight of the poor (*Die Armennot*, 1840), man receives strength through God's grace, and just as man believes in God, he must also believe in his own strengths and have faith "that they will be able to carry him through life." The farmer helps Uli develop exactly those qualities which Gotthelf spoke about in his essay: "The strength and will to work, to become independent in the world." When the time is ripe, the farmer Johannes recommends to a relative, the farmer Joggeli, that he hire Uli as a foreman. The second part of the novel shows Uli on the new farm, where he is no longer associated with an exemplary farmer. Joggeli is obstinate, greedy, underhanded, and distrustful. The farm is poorly kept. Uli has to muster all of his strength to make his way in this difficult environment. The servants, negligent and rebellious, oppose him brutally. Joggeli gives him no support, undermines his efforts, injures his pride, but always gives in when it looks as if he might lose Uli. The good spirit in the house is Vreneli, a poor, illegitimate relative who grew up on the farm and directs the household with as much competence and discretion as Uli manages the farm. Uli's natural ally from the beginning, she is deeply hurt by his relationship with the farmer's daughter Elisi, a vain and silly girl.

The last part brings a satisfying solution devised and carried out by Joggeli's wife. Uli obtains the farm on lease, the farmer Johannes vouches for him financially, and Vreneli forgives Uli and marries him. The interplay of characters in this last part is cheerful and relaxed. Even Joggeli's obstinacy is no longer oppressive, but seems rather to be harmless eccentricity. In the end he too contributes to the solution, for actually he has long since recognized Uli's worth.

All of Gotthelf's novels after *Uli the Farmhand* are bound stylistically and thematically to conditions in Switzerland, but they treat different problems within this framework. The importance of the Christian spirit, which must pervade the farmer's life if property is not to bring him unhappiness, is the theme of *Wealth and Welfare* (*Geld und Geist*, 1843–44), and the danger of superstition and quackery is demonstrated in *Anne Bäbi Jowäger* (1843–44). In *Katie the Grandmother* (*Käthi die Grossmutter*, 1847) Gotthelf again places a woman in the center. She is a woman of limited capabilities like Anne Bäbi, but this time the emphasis lies on her piety and goodness and on a glorification of poverty. In the same year that *Katie the Grandmother* appeared, Gotthelf also published *Uli the Tenant Farmer* (*Uli der Pächter*, 1847), a continuation of *Uli the Farmhand* which shows the difficulties Uli must overcome as an independent tenant farmer until he finally becomes owner of the farmstead.

Two novels, *The Cheese Dairy* (*Die Käserei in der Vehfreude*, 1850) and *Spirit of the Times and Spirit of Berne* (*Zeitgeist und Berner Geist*, 1852), are reactions to the political events of 1848. They no longer focus on the situation of individuals or single families as in Gotthelf's previous novels but on the stories of entire groups. In *The Cheese Dairy* the whole village is used as a metaphor. Gotthelf's deep disappointment with the political developments in his country is expressed by his description of the democratic manner in which the cheese dairy is founded. Although the author's choice of cheese preparation is a cheerful way of speaking about his society, the bitterness of his criticism is always present. The book is comparable to Wieland's *Abderites*, and the richness of its allusions makes it stimulating reading. *Spirit of the Times and Spirit of Berne* is even more closely tied to contemporary events. It is basically a polemical work in which Gotthelf takes a stand on the questions of his day.

New Experiences with Human Nature

The history of the German novel after 1830 was not limited to the *Zeitroman*. On the one hand, authors were devoting their efforts to describing the times, but simultaneously there were intensive efforts to develop a new image of man in the novel. Once eighteenth-century authors had discovered the novel as a means of depicting man's inner story, novelists continued to be involved with the inner story in the nineteenth and twentieth centuries as well. Regardless of whether Goethe and Wieland were admired or rejected, whether they were known or remained unread, the tradition they had begun was carried on. Of course the forms were not the same as in the 1700s: they were changed, refined, and adapted to modern thought and themes. As for the subject matter itself, the inner story was particularly engaging to authors and readers who were becoming increasingly receptive to psychological questions and research.

The new picture of man which emerged from the novels of the period reflected the individual's disharmony and uncertainty when confronted with life's demands and showed how infrequently society gave him help or support. His behavior with other people, in love, professionally, and in equivocal situations revealed the inconstancy and helplessness of human nature. The attempt to give literary expression to new experiences with human nature gave rise to important works which have a special place in the history of German literature. Their authors—Eduard Mörike, Ludwig Tieck, Gottfried Keller, Adalbert Stifter, and Wilhelm Raabe—followed naturally in the tradition of the Age of Goethe. They not only adopted individual aspects of Classicism and Romanticism but were imbued with the spirit of that age. At the same time their style tended more towards objectivity and concreteness. These authors' works are characterized by their intensity and subtlety with regard to both the visible world and the inner life of man.

Eduard Mörike (1804–1875) had difficulty expressing his experiences with human nature in the prose of a novel. His *Nolten the Artist* (*Maler Nolten*, 1832) often finds disfavor with critics and readers alike. The story begins quite awkwardly, and at first the reader does not understand what is happening. Eventually the plot line becomes clear: the artist Theobald Nolten has distanced himself from his fiancée, the forester's daughter Agnes, in part because of rumors that she has abandoned him for another, but also because he is fascinated by Countess Konstanze. But Nolten's friend, the actor Larkens, convinced that the relationship between the engaged couple should be saved, writes letters to Agnes in Nolten's handwriting and, in addition, arranges for evidence of Nolten's relationship with Agnes to fall into the countess's hands. When the countess subsequently rejects Nolten, he returns to Agnes. Their love suffers, however, from an inner flaw which Agnes senses.

This tension has to do with a third woman, the gypsy Elisabeth, who had waylaid Agnes and told her she and Nolten were not meant for each other. Elisabeth is the daughter of Nolten's uncle and a gypsy woman whose portrait, painted by the uncle, Nolten had seen years ago in the attic of his parents' home. The reader learns of the bond between Elisabeth and Nolten in an insertion titled "A Day from Nolten's Youth." Larkens claims he wrote it according to what Nolten told him. We learn that as a young man, Nolten was on an outing with his sister when he came across the gypsy woman Elisabeth in the forest. He recognized in her the features which had so excited him when he saw the portrait in the attic. It seemed to him that the mystery of life was in her eyes, and a secret bond was formed between them at this meeting. He does not see Elisabeth again; thus he is all the more attached to the portrait. Nolten had always liked to draw and paint, but after the fleeting encounter with Elisabeth, the drive became "irresistible, and his vocation as an artist was decided."

Just as the background of Nolten's emotional life is related here in a separate prose section, similarly Larken's confession to Nolten, written before he disappears from the city, is set off from the narrative flow as a separate text, a letter with the heading "Larkens to Nolten." In it Larkens admits that there is no specific reason for his disappearance; "let it suffice to say that I feel uncomfortable in my own skin. I am trying to convince myself that I can shed it." All that matters to him is Nolten's reconciliation with Agnes. He reveals to Nolten what he did for him during the months in which Nolten was occupied with Konstanze. From the papers Larkens left him, Nolten realizes that the countess knows of his relationship with Agnes and that Elisabeth approached Agnes and caused her to doubt the relationship.

The lyric poems Mörike inserted throughout the novel are of great importance to its theme and structure. Even more intensely than the prose insertions, which set off what is personal, confessional, and enigmatic, the poems bring to light hidden realms of inner life which affect and determine the course of events. In his preparations for a revision of the novel, which was not published until after his death (1877), Mörike concentrated even more on lyrical insertions. In this version Agnes quotes a poem in a letter to Nolten: "Can one person belong to another on earth / As completely as one desires / In a long night I reflected upon it and had to answer no!" The characters' inadequacies in love are expressed here even before they become apparent from the plot. The poem, not composed by the author until later, contains the central theme of the novel. In a poem in the original version,[27] shortly after Nolten's return Agnes expresses her feeling that despite their reconciliation and the gay mood, misfortune awaits her:

> Rose season! how rapidly,
> Rapidly,
> You have gone away!
> If my love had just been true,
> Just been true,
> I would not be afraid.

The song she sings for Nolten says more about her than the plot itself and functions not only as a foreshadowing but, more importantly, is evidence of an accurate perception of the events.

The misfortune foreshadowed in the poems comes to pass on a journey during a stay at a country estate. Shortly beforehand Larkens committed suicide. Among his papers Nolten finds the Peregrina poems—these are some of Mörike's best-known poems today—and realizes that a fantasy about his relationship with Elisabeth is described in the lyric cycle. Driven by a "strange anguish," he suddenly tells Agnes of his vagaries, leaving nothing unsaid except mention of Elisabeth. Agnes, deeply disturbed by his confession, withdraws from him. After once again speaking with Elisabeth, who surprisingly appears at the estate the next day, she becomes hopelessly insane. In a dramatic scene Elisabeth, who is also unmistakably mad, insists on her right to Nolten in front of everyone at the estate. Nolten rejects her but cannot prevent her from declaring her love all the more passionately and accusing him of disloyalty to her as well as to Agnes. Agnes subsequently finds her death in a well that had played a role in a legend of faithful lovers. Nolten, consumed with grief, dies the night before her burial. Elisabeth had died a few days before him, and Konstanze survives him by only a few months.

Lyrical insertions also have an important function in the last part of the novel. Again they express knowledge that goes far beyond the external events. They actually contain a second plot which is concerned with the characters' inner stories and is separated from the events narrated in prose by means of the lyric form. All the poems in this part belong to Agnes. They deal with the novel's central theme: man's failure in love. Moreover, they allude to the certainty of God's love and to man's expectation of salvation.

In the period preceding her death, Agnes seems to those around her to be in a state of terrible distress and frightful mental disturbance. However, her songs display utmost clarity and masterful form. The character who is thought to have lost her mind provides with her songs the link between specific events and the overall situation; she relates man's failure in particular circumstances to human failure in general. Whereas Nolten and Konstanze must inquire into their own guilt, Agnes knows that the nature of human love is manifested in the inconstancy of the lovers. Following a long prose insertion about the Christian legend of the two exemplary lovers Alexis and Belsore, who remain loyal to each other through all trials, Agnes sings the song of the wind, in which the restlessness of the wind is a metaphor for the homelessness of love. This motif had already been evoked in the famous poem, "Here I lie on the hill of spring."

> O tell me my only love,
> Where you stay, that I may stay with you!
> But you and the winds have no home.

In the same sense the winds are asked at the end of the novel: "Tell me where love's homeland is / Its beginning, its end!" And the answer follows that love is like the wind, eternal and unceasing, but not always constant. The spiritual songs Agnes sings on the day before her death are compatible with the ideas expressed in these poems; an awareness of man's fragility and need for redemption prevails. Although *Nolten the Artist* has all the characteristics of a tragic novel, with the gloominess and inevitability becoming more and more disquieting towards the end, the songs nevertheless create an atmosphere of conquest and liberation.

The fact that Mörike's novel advances into realms of psychology which were not yet explored at the time has been little recognized or appreciated. The author's insight into psychology is particularly evident in his treatment of the main character's artistry. The description of Nolten's paintings at the beginning of the novel later proves to be compositionally justified in view of his mental state. That Mörike chose to make his main character a painter should not be interpreted as a concession to public taste; *Nolten the Artist* is not just another of the many *Künstlerromane* (novels about artists) written in that day. Nolten's artistry is closely bound to his story, for as a painter he exposes the demonic roots of his misfortune even before the misfortune is recognizable as such. Before anything has actually happened, he indicates the direction all events will take. Elisabeth alone is true to love, whereas love entangles all the others in disloyalty and guilt. This gives the novel its uniform structure and is crucial to an understanding of Mörike's psychological insights.

Mörike himself was rather perplexed about his novel from the outset. The question of genre was never decided. On the title page he designated the work a "Novella in Two Parts." The word novel was not used until the second version appeared after his death. Mörike originally used both denotations in his letters, but later he preferred the term novel. His irresolution may be due in part to the fact that at the time the two forms were not seen as distinctly separate; therefore, the terms were not unequivocally defined. Other prose works from the nineteenth century which are regarded as novels today, such as Heinrich Laube's *Young Europe*, Ludwig Tieck's *Vittoria Accorombona*, and Conrad Ferdinand Meyer's *Jürg Jenatsch*, were called novellas by their authors. After using the word "novel" in his review of *Nolten the Artist*, Friedrich Theodor Vischer specifically added in parentheses, "or novella, we don't want to argue here about nomenclature, I prefer to call the book a novel."[28] This remark shows that up to a certain point it was left to individual discretion whether to view a work as a novella or a novel, but that one did differentiate between the two, even if primarily on the basis of feeling. Mörike did this himself.

In *Nolten the Artist* many traditional motifs are recognizable. Researchers have been concerned for years with whether Elisabeth is closer to Ophelia or to Mignon and whether autobiographical or literary influence is greater. The dispute is futile since, whatever their origins, the elements have been fused in such a way as to take on a new character. Friedrich Gundolf insightfully declares that Mörike is "in body and soul deeply related to the so-called decadents, not only a Swabian and German descendant of Schiller and Hölderlin, but a European compatriot of Baudelaire and Poe."[29] A comparison with the modern European *Gesellschaftsroman* (novel of manners or society) proves to be totally unproductive. Mörike does use characters long known to German literature: baron, countess, painter, actor, innocent girl, president, forester, pastor, the homeless, craftsmen, servants. But even though many classes are represented and all the representatives have individual characteristics, the societal life in the novel is completely lacking in dynamics. Mörike's only concern is the inner story of his main characters, who are frail, torn people. With the exception of Elisabeth, who lives outside of society, they are all unstable. Their guilt comes from within themselves, not because of outside pressures, and most definitely not because of society. Within the framework of his conservative view of society, Mörike presents, even before Georg Büchner, an image of man which did not become generally recognized until the twentieth century.

Society is full of conflict and uncertainty in Ludwig Tieck's two historical novels, *The Rebellion in the Cévennes* (*Der Aufruhr in den Cevennen*,

1826) and *Vittoria Accorombona* (1840). The first work remained unfinished, but a continuation of the plot, as Tieck had planned, seems unnecessary, since the part we have serves to exhaust the theme. Tieck's portrayal of the religious war of 1702 renders the turbulence of the times convincingly: "Where is certainty or security today such as existed in previous times? Everything is turmoil and battle cries, and the strangest misfortunes drive men to and fro. . . . And fear becomes ever greater and suspicion ever stronger."

A tumultuous era is also portrayed in *Vittoria Accorombona*, the story of a poet. Tieck states in the preface that he originally found the material for the novel in John Webster's tragedy *The White Devil* (1612). He deliberately set the novel at a time somewhat later than in Webster's play so that events occur during a period of crisis and decline in the Italian states. The historically documented date of Vittoria's second marriage, for example, has been changed to 1585, about twenty-five years later than in *The White Devil*. The dissolution of the states, the helplessness of the individual against merciless enemies, and the complete lack of freedom in making personal decisions are all essential plot elements that characterize the age. Whether the work should be termed a historical novel rather than emphasizing its other aspects has been the subject of literary research. Wolfgang F. Taraba called it a *Bildungsroman*, family novel, and *Zeitroman*,[30] thereby indicating that none of these designations alone is completely accurate.

In addition to giving a picture of the times, Tieck says in his preface that he was equally interested in providing a "soul-painting." He portrays an exceptional, impressive woman in a brutal age. His intent was to show how a cultivated woman could live in such a time. It is a historical fact that Vittoria Accorombona was murdered; Tieck also ascertained that other prominent women were murdered during the same time period. In his introduction he mentions Eleonore von Toledo, who was killed by her husband, Julius Pietro of the Medici family, in a country manor on a July night in 1576, and Isabella, the wife of the Duke of Bracciano, who died mysteriously in her husband's isolated castle a few days later. These two women serve as contrasting figures to Vittoria Accorombona. As a cultured poet she was a particularly suitable subject for Tieck's "soul-painting," since it is natural and credible that such a character would have a great command of language and that she would freely express her thoughts and feelings. For his "soul-painting" Tieck primarily uses Vittoria's own language in poems and narrations, discussions of art and politics, debates on vital questions, and her self-interpretations.

The reader is first introduced to Vittoria's family: her mother Julia, also an impressive character, and her three brothers. A very dangerous circle around Vittoria is formed by men who menace her. In addition a number of neutral characters appear in her mother's salon. The seventeen-year-old Vittoria's unconcerned partiality for "friendly little Camillo" leads to a discussion between mother and daughter that touches on the central questions of the novel. Julia recommends that she marry "an excellent and eminent man" who is worthy of her. But Vittoria totally rejects marriage and confesses that she has a "horror of all men" when she thinks of "belonging to them" and "sacrificing" herself to them. "Just look at them, even the best ones we know, even the most distinguished; how inadequate, poor, incompetent, and vain they all are. . . . Oh woe! If I am to retain my cheerfulness in their company, then I must shroud myself in a dream of levity and lull my observations to sleep." It seems unthinkable to her that she should devote herself to "these heartless, bored, greedy" men.

With this confession the first of the two focal points of the novel's inner story is revealed. The second is Vittoria's capacity for love, which does not emerge until long after her mother has wed her to Peretti, nephew of the Cardinal Montalto. He is a very weak man completely undeserving of her. The marriage must be seen within a political context; Julia and Vittoria were drawn into the political arena when Marcello, Vittoria's brother, was captured with his leader and their entire band. At that time armed bands were openly at war with the government troops. The marriage to Peretti seemed to offer a solution to political and personal difficulties. In submitting to the arrangement, Vittoria has no illusions: "I am harnessed like a plough horse to the yoke of daily habitude and will draw the furrows of straight and conventional monotony like other people. . . . I have been cast aside, destroyed, it had to happen, I am experiencing my so-called destiny, which in my language is: worthlessness."

In the third book Vittoria meets Duke Bracciano. After his first visit, she says, "Now I have seen a real, genuine man. . . . Every word that comes from his lips is important." A conversation the next morning makes it apparent that she already comprehends the full implications of her situation, even though she does not yet know who the stranger is. She realizes that her feelings for the unknown guest and her commitment to Peretti are on different levels and explains that her promise to Peretti cannot obligate her to repress her feelings. No one has ever received a declaration of love from her, for she says she does not know "what the word means." The special nature of her reaction is underscored by her assertion that, no matter if the stranger is a traitor, a murderer, a judge of the high court, or a beggar, her soul is "chained to his forever." This language indicates that Vittoria's love is an outburst of feeling which cancels nature's laws, disregards moral concepts, and annuls the rules of society.

During the same time that Bracciano socializes in her home, Vittoria's marriage goes to ruin. Though Peretti abandons himself to frivolities in disreputable society, she refuses to give herself to Bracciano. Her resistance stems from an unwillingness to break her word to Cardinal Montalto and her mother.

This is the other side of the argument that her promise to Peretti does not mean she must restrain her feelings. Not until after Peretti's murder and the reigning Pope's death does Bracciano succeed in marrying Vittoria. Shortly afterward, Montalto is elected Pope and introduces brutal measures to restore order in Rome. Bracciano and Vittoria leave the city and spend happy months at Lake Garda from spring to autumn. Then Bracciano is poisoned by his enemies, and Vittoria retreats to his palace in Padua, where she too is murdered. The novel ends with the downfall of the entire family.

The problem of human development within the limits of given conditions also exists for Heinrich Lee, the main character in Gottfried Keller's (1819–1890) *Green Henry* (*Der grüne Heinrich*, 1854–55). At an early age Heinrich is trapped by circumstances he cannot master and to which he eventually succumbs. The novel ends—at least in an early version—with his death. Keller explained why the book ends "tragically" to his publisher Eduard Vieweg and to the literary historian Hermann Hettner. Hettner wrote to Keller that at first he thought things had gone too far "when the hero pays for his confused educational ambitions with his life," but gradually he was able to realize that in this way "the seriousness of the *Bildungstragödie* [tragedy of *Bildung*] becomes all the more convincing" (June 11, 1855). Keller's response reveals the importance of the novel's second main character: Heinrich's mother. The feeling that he is to blame for her death makes life unbearable for Heinrich. Returning home after an absence of seven years, he arrives just in time for her burial. Impoverished because of her son and with no hope of his return, she has lost the will to live. After the mother dies under these circumstances, "noble and untroubled happiness in life or marriage," Keller wrote, "would well be unthinkable for Heinrich" (June 25, 1855, letter to Hermann Hettner). In a later version of the novel (1879–80) Heinrich lives on, but he is subdued and withdrawn, without hope or vitality. He dedicates himself to a government position. Not until years later does he recover from the death of his mother, but even then he is absorbed with memories and lives in the past.

When Hermann Hettner speaks of a *Bildungstragödie* and the author cannot imagine any happiness for his hero after what has happened, the question arises as to how all this gloominess came about, especially after Heinrich had set out like a "true king into the bright world" to become a painter, with "a heart full of hope and blossoming confidence in his breast." The question is all the more subtle since young Heinrich Lee did not find himself in political conflict with his country. It is neither the Germany of the Restoration period under which Laube and Gutzkow suffered, nor Austria from which Sealsfield fled, but Switzerland, at peace with itself, pleasant and sunny, which the hero decides to leave. In the first chapters, which tell of the twenty-year-old's departure from home and journey across Switzerland to Germany, the reader can feel how much the author loves his country. It is apparent that Keller approves of his country's institutions and is convinced that its social conditions in combination with the inviolability of the laws guarantee each individual personal freedom and allow him to shape his fate according to his own will. When Heinrich arrives in Germany, he can speak so sensibly and enthusiastically about his homeland that at first it is hard to imagine where the great misfortune, the *Bildungstragödie*, has its roots.

For an understanding of this, one must look to Heinrich's "Story of Youth," which is told in the first person and comprises over half the book (the earlier version will be discussed here). Personal destiny and individual inclination are the basis for the difficult path on which the young boy finds himself. He loses his father early, grows up in a large city dwelling as the only child of a devoted mother, and fails to make connection with the bourgeois world of practical life. Keller wrote to Hettner, "My purpose was twofold: on the one hand to show how few guarantees of a proper education are offered even today in an enlightened and free state like Zurich, if these guarantees are not already provided by the family or individual circumstances, and on the other to show the psychic process in a rich mind" (March 4, 1851). The fact that school cannot do justice to the needs of the dreamy little boy is demonstrated by many small incidents from the first day on, until finally the fourteen-year-old is expelled because of a minor, somewhat unclear offense and is on his own. Actually he finds the situation quite agreeable, for he is glad to learn as an autodidact, reflecting, groping, and surrendering himself to his inner life.

As Heinrich reports in his "Story of Youth," from his earliest childhood he gave shape to the visible world according to his inner pictures, ideas, wishes, and dreams, abandoning himself to creative deceptions. For example, when he observed the snowcapped mountains and the clouds from the windows of his mother's house, he did not want to distinguish between them as their appearance changed with the weather; rather, he delighted in the way they flowed together and considered the mountains to be something alive like the clouds. His mother could explain that they were mountains, but her words were "empty sounds." Heinrich "also used to give life to other things" by calling them cloud or mountain if they filled him with "respect and curiosity." A young girl he liked who wore a white dress received the name "the white cloud" and a long, high church roof was "the mountain." The golden, gleaming rooster on a bell tower, which was the last thing to be seen before dark, seemed to him one evening to be God himself, and another time God was the colored tiger in his picture book.

In Heinrich's words, the pictures in his mind became "interwoven with real life such that I could hardly tell them apart." This is what happens when the seven-year-old makes up a grand story one day about how some older pupils persuaded him to take a walk and on the way forced him to repeat indecent words. While telling the story he actually believes it himself. When the pupils are punished he does not regret it, but is actually pleased that "poetic justice rounded off my tale so beautifully and visibly."

Heinrich's unfortunate expulsion from school is also the result of his blending of fantasy and reality. He unwillingly lets himself be drawn into a student demonstration which originally did not attract him at all but sweeps him along once he begins to participate. The thought of people's movements and revolutionary scenes intoxicates him and suddenly he finds himself at the head of the demonstration, making suggestions as to how to organize it more effectively. Later his comrades claim that he was the main culprit. Keller emphasizes that a school which "expels even the most good-for-nothing pupil" deserves a "certificate of spiritual poverty"; the state is responsible for the education of its children. But even those who think of themselves as "educators par excellence" are guilty of "moral laziness . . . , sluggishness, and indolence."

The expulsion from school of the good-natured boy—the lack of appropriate guidance from understanding educators—seems to be one of the roots of the *Bildungstragödie*. On Keller's part this is severe social criticism. It is particularly significant that Switzerland is the land of Pestalozzi (1746–1827), and one might naively expect that the story of a Swiss boy in the decades after Pestalozzi's death would tell of exemplary public schooling.

A comparison of Heinrich's boyhood with the story of Anton Reiser is revealing. Despite his poor social position, Reiser often finds personalities who show understanding for him. Nevertheless, he runs away from school to become an artist, a goal at which he, like Heinrich, does not succeed. Both Karl Philipp Moritz and Gottfried Keller incorporated autobiographical material into the stories of their young heroes. Gottfried Keller was expelled from school in 1834, and the sharpness of his criticism of the schools is founded on personal experiences.

After leaving school Heinrich is exposed to a rich and beautiful world in the village where his parents were born. His uncle always receives him warmly for unlimited vacations in the country. A large circle of relatives is friendly to him, and he has the time and energy to devote to his first experiences in love. No school could have offered him the bright pictures his active imagination encounters in the fullness of country life or the warmth and comfort he experiences by living among people who are at peace with themselves.

The story of Heinrich's double love for Anna and Judith is unique in the history of the German novel. Pierre Daniel Huet, the first European theoretician of the novel, had already established in the seventeenth century that novels are "des fictions d'aventures amoureuses."[31] His first translator,

Eberhard Werner Happel, used the word *Liebesgeschichten* (love stories). In general this was quite true of German novels, regardless of the subgenre and whether or not the love story was the main theme or accompanied another theme. But neither before nor since the first version of *Green Henry* has a love story of such richness, which evolves so completely as a prototype and yet is undeniably bound to a specific present time, been written in the German language. Alexander Durst shows that the epic representation of *Green Henry* was preceded by a lyrical phase.[32] Unlike Mörike's *Nolten the Artist*, however, in which the lyric poem is a separate entity which is interspersed in the prose and outshines it, in *Green Henry* the lyric passages have been completely absorbed into the prose so that the radiance comes from the prose alone. The poems themselves are not a part of the novel (there are only a few verses in *Green Henry*), nor do they equal the artistic niveau of Keller's narrative style.

Heinrich's relationship with Anna and Judith lasts for five years. As he grows to manhood he learns to love and discovers his own capacity for love. When he finds love again many years later, he is able to think of it in relation to the fine education in love received from Anna and Judith. He is released from their love when Anna dies, for he then takes leave of Judith in order to be true to Anna. For part of the five years of his double love he lives in the city with his mother and devotes himself to his training as a landscape painter. He also spends time, particularly in the beautiful season of the year, as the welcome guest of his relatives in the country. He visits Anna at the home of her father near the village; in turn, Anna, a friend of Heinrich's cousins, often comes to his uncle's house. Heinrich's love for her evolves under the eyes of the sociable relatives. As a serious, restrained love between two very young people, it is respected by society.

By contrast, Heinrich's relationship with the older woman Judith is concealed and secretive from the start, though at first he visits her in her small house during the day. Later their nocturnal meetings bring the decisive fulfillment of their relationship. Both Heinrich and Judith are always aware of their age difference. Judith's behavior is mature and responsible, while Heinrich abandons himself to her. He describes his visits to her at an early stage in the relationship:

> Through our contact I had come to feel at home with her, and since young Anna was always in my thoughts, I was glad to stay with beautiful Judith. In that unconscious time I took one woman for the other and did not consider myself guilty of disloyalty in the least when, in view of the developed, full woman, I was more comfortable thinking of the absent, tender bud than anywhere else, even than in her presence.

In the fourth year his happiness with Anna grows, followed by an intensification of his love for Judith. After a passionate scene between Anna and Heinrich on the day of their participation in a performance of *William Tell,* Heinrich spends the night with Judith and confesses at her request—she has long known of Heinrich's feelings for Anna—what has occurred between Anna and himself. The love dialogue which ensues analyzes his feelings and ends in a way corresponding to the scene with Anna that afternoon. After he leaves Judith's, he is overcome with despair. Contrite, in tears, amid self-accusations, he wanders at dawn: "I felt myself split in two and would have liked to hide from Anna with Judith and from Judith with Anna." Although he resolves not to go to Judith any more, he remains attached to her and visits her while Anna is lying on her deathbed.

During this period of time, Heinrich's last summer of love in Switzerland, a scene of special significance occurs. On a nightly walk with Judith he suddenly loses sight of her and shortly afterward sees her clothes on stones near the water; then he sees her bathing. Before his eyes she comes closer, climbs out of the water, and puts on her clothes. Keller cut out this scene in the later version, which, as Werner Günther correctly remarks, "betrays in an almost appalling way what lack of understanding and what bourgeois prudery the elder Keller showed for his early creation."[33] It is certainly not a question of "nudities," the word Keller uses in a letter to Emil Kuh (September 10, 1871), for the scene is not portrayed in that way. Furthermore, it would seem that this incident is indeed part of Heinrich's development. Shortly after the scene, Anna's death is reported. The narrator lingers as Heinrich's deathwatch, the casket preparations, and the funeral march are described. On the day after Anna's burial, Heinrich takes leave of Judith and swears that he will never see her again. Soon afterward Judith emigrates to America.

During the same period in which Heinrich's experiences with love take place, he attempts with some success to learn landscape painting in his native city in Switzerland. He makes significant progress under the temporary direction of a capable and educated, but very unhappy, teacher, who emphasizes careful imitation of nature. But he does not improve sufficiently during his years in Germany and finally gives up painting altogether. The pitfall Heinrich faces in art is, as the narrator explains when he takes up the story again after the section "Story of Youth," his tendency to speculate and invent. Heinrich himself speaks of the "sheer cliff between fantasy and reality" with regard to his love affairs. This theme is of continual fascination to both the author and the reader throughout the entire "Story of Youth," and in every case the author succeeds in bridging the "sheer cliff" and maintaining a lively tension between fantasy and reality.

Keller's talent with prose did not, however, carry over to painting—the author himself attempted unsuccessfully to become a landscape painter—

and his hero Heinrich Lee was no more gifted than he. Heinrich is unable to express himself on canvas, even though he fills his portfolio with new sketches and adds to his knowledge in many areas. Since he started out with little money, he is soon in dire financial need, incurs debts, and must ask his mother for money. But he incurs new debts and needs help from her again. He is hungry and gradually sells everything he owns, including his paintings, to a secondhand dealer who gives him the chance to earn a little money at odd jobs. At last he heads for home.

In the later version, in which Heinrich arrives home in time to see his mother only shortly before her death, Judith returns home from America several years later because she has heard of Heinrich's misfortune. Although now a respected and prosperous government official, Heinrich is still heavily burdened by the suffering and death of his mother. Not until he tells Judith everything that has happened does his anguish begin to subside; he feels "redeemed" by her. Judith remains with him until her death. The mild ending is the main difference between the two versions. Keller also added several episodes and characters in the later version, and passages which were previously spontaneous and critical of the times became more detached and measured. The narrator's reflections were deleted, shortened, or rewritten, and the structure as a whole is different in that in the later version Keller uses the first person throughout and begins with Heinrich's background and childhood rather than with his departure from Switzerland.

Unlike Gottfried Keller, Adalbert Stifter (1806–1868) was not concerned with the development of his youthful narrator Heinrich Drendorf in *Indian Summer* (*Der Nachsommer*, 1857), but rather with the development of an exemplary world. A utopian existence unfolds before the reader. Heinrich's parental home and the environment he later enters are both ideal realms whose eternal order he effortlessly adopts. He experiences no conflict or tension because by nature he is at harmony with these ideal realms. They exist outside of and offer a contrast to the society at large. At all times Heinrich's parents provide him with everything he needs. He is allowed to pursue his studies according to his inclinations; he is not only given the opportunity to expand his knowledge, but is actually encouraged to do so when the time comes. He is provided with money and taught how to manage it. His living quarters are always arranged to meet his wishes and needs. Conversations are geared specifically to his interests, and themes he is not yet receptive to are evaded.

Throughout the novel the utopia of a secure human existence is portrayed through the objects the characters possess and the things among which they live. When the narrator speaks more about the places where his characters appear than about the characters themselves, his intent is to depict spiritual life and to develop characters whose essence is expressed in their external surroundings. At the same time, the reader is constantly made aware that the characters themselves have created and continue to create their environments. One learns how every object was acquired; in every room and every house the process of consciously arranging the living quarters to suit specific purposes is related. The narrator begins with a description of the apartment where he spent his childhood and proceeds to the house outside the city which his father later acquired. He lingers for a long time on the description of the estate, the Asperhof, with its "rose house," where he is a frequent guest. Later he includes the nearby Sternenhof and ends with his father's purchase of the Gusterhof, which lies between the Asperhof and the Sternenhof and will be furnished in the future.

Significantly, Heinrich does not learn the name of his host at the rose house until late in the story. Throughout the entire region he is known as "the Asperherr" or "the Aspermeier," because it is common practice to "call the owner of an estate after the estate, not after his family." This was also the case with the previous owner of the Asperhof. It is equally noteworthy that the Asperherr's title of nobility, like his property, was not inherited at birth but was awarded to him for his services to the state. "Surely you know that I am the Baron von Risach," is how he introduces himself to Heinrich near the end of the book after Heinrich's story is completed.

Risach is actually the novel's main character. The reader only gradually becomes aware of this, since the narrator begins with his own story. He was raised in an exemplary burgher home where the same spirit prevailed as in Risach's surroundings. His father's views on Heinrich's education and career are important to the work's thematic unity. Unlike Wilhelm Meister's father, Heinrich's father, a successful businessman and collector of beautiful objects, believed his son should follow the "desires" of his "heart" in choosing his course of study. Whereas the others maintained that Heinrich must dedicate himself to a profession useful to society, his father took the view that "man is not there primarily for society, but for himself. And if each person is there for himself in the best way, then he is also there for human society. . . . And those men who develop their inner qualities the furthest are most often the helpers and saviors of their fatherland in times of danger." This utopian idea is often associated with Heinrich's path, and Risach elaborates on it in reference to his own past at the end of the novel. Heinrich's story ends when he marries and begins a family. He leaves the question of how he will be "of use" open: "I will manage my property, will otherwise be of use, and each endeavor, even in science, now has simplicity, substance, and importance." With this the novel ends. There is no need to discuss the ending further, since Heinrich's story is only the framework and foundation for Risach's characterization; Heinrich's meeting with Risach is the fictional motivation for presenting the novel's central character.

The layout of the large country estate, where Heinrich seeks shelter from a threatening storm, and the rich decoration of the rose house, where he frequently stays as a guest, reveal the personality of the owner. Risach's way of life is likewise shown in his behavior toward colleagues, employees, acquaintances, and friends. Of particular importance to him are Mathilde and her two children, Natalie and Gustav. Gustav is raised and taught by Risach at the Asperhof. Mathilde and Natalie, who live on Mathilde's property, the Sternenhof, often stay with Risach, particularly during rose blossom time. This is how Natalie and Heinrich meet. Their love, restrained and left unspoken for a long time, leads to an engagement and marriage approved of by the older generation.

Just before the marriage Heinrich learns the painful story behind the current harmony at the Asperhof and Sternenhof. Risach tells it in different sections. First he speaks of his attitude towards public service, then of his childhood and youth in modest surroundings, of his career path, and finally he tells the story of his love for Mathilde. The first part of his narration is self-interpretation. He explains why he was not suited for civil service, which he pursued so successfully for so many years.

> First of all I wanted to be master of my actions. I liked to sketch my own picture of what I should do and carry it out solely with my energies. . . . A second characteristic of mine was that I wanted very much to see the results of my actions. . . . Action taken merely to fulfill an instruction . . . could cause me pain. . . . You can see I was lacking two main things to be a state servant, the ability to obey, which is a basic requirement, . . . and the ability to actively subjugate oneself to the whole. . . . I always wanted to make basic changes and improve the foundation instead of proceeding . . . within given limits. I wanted to determine the goals myself and to do each thing as it should best be done, without regard for the entirety and without considering that my actions might rip a hole somewhere else which could do more harm than my success does good.

Risach explains that he entered his career at a very young age, before he understood it or himself. He then continued with it to the best of his ability, for once he had begun he would have been ashamed of not doing his duty. If he accomplished some good, then it was because he demanded the most of himself and also because contemporary events brought him up against problems he could solve in his own way. "But how deeply I suffered when I was involved in forms of action which were opposed to my nature, I can hardly describe to you. . . . At that time I always and invariably used to think of the adage about something having fins that must fly and something having wings that must swim. Therefore at a certain age I resigned my post."

With these statements Risach discloses that the beautiful world he created at Asperhof is the counterpart to a troubled career, and the property he now enjoys was acquired only with difficulty. The same is true of his late companionship with Mathilde. The fulfillment of their love in earlier years was denied by Mathilde's parents. When Risach suggested separation to Mathilde in compliance with her mother's request, Mathilde interpreted it as disloyalty. It was rose blossom time, and in her unhappy passion Mathilde called to the roses to witness her love and his unfaithfulness. While she was crying desperately into the rose blossoms, Risach pressed the thorns into his hand until it bled. In memory of this, he later planted many roses at the wall of his house at the Asperhof and cultivated them with extraordinary care. One day he found Mathilde and her son standing before the roses. She confessed to having long since realized how unjust she had been to him in her passion. An "Indian summer without a preceding summer" united them in their later years. The roses were the sign of their separation and reunion.

The narrator's speaking tone is that of a neutral scientist. He reports his observations as they occur to him, generally without assigning priorities. Thus many banalities are described which the reader would rather not hear about in such detail. The exemplariness of all the characters is manifested in social habits which are reported again and again; the frequent expressions of thanks, for example, become somewhat tiresome. At the same time the steady, serious tone makes for a restrained style in moments of emotional agitation. There are scenes in which passionate emotions run their course without a word being spoken. For example, when Heinrich first experiences Mathilde's arrival at the beginning of the rose blossom season, he says,

> We walked out past the green lattice and walked to the sandy spot in front of the house. The people in the house must have been told that we were coming, for two of them brought out a large armchair and placed it at a certain distance with its front side facing the roses. The woman sat down in the chair, put her hands in her lap and looked at the roses. We stood around her. Natalie stood to her left, Gustav next to Natalie, my host stood behind the chair and I went, in order not to be too close to Natalie, to the right side and somewhat further back. After the woman had sat for some time she stood up silently and we left the place.

The affection between Heinrich and Natalie is reported in the same way. Their reserve is a contrast to the unrestrained emotion displayed by Mathilde and Risach in their younger years. The serene atmosphere of Indian summer is the unifying force which, upheld and sustained by Risach's mature generation, affects all of the other characters.

Almost at the same time as Stifter's *Indian Summer*, Wilhelm Raabe's (1831–1910) *Chronicle of Sperling Street* (*Die Chronik der Sperlingsgasse*, 1857, published under the pseudonym Corvinus) appeared. It was the first of many successful novels in a literary career that extended over decades. Raabe was long misunderstood by researchers and readers alike. Regarded as a good-natured, friendly narrator of idyllic life, he was appreciated for his humor and moral strength and thus was forgiven for the presumed disorderliness of his presentation. Modern researchers judge Raabe differently and reject previous interpretations of his work as "incorrect."[34] The familiarity with new novelistic forms of the twentieth century has facilitated an understanding of his structural composition, particularly in his later works. Raabe independently assimilated the entire novel tradition of the eighteenth and nineteenth centuries in his writings. The novels of Goethe, Sterne, and Jean Paul, of Thackeray and Dickens, the ideas of the Young Germans and the *Zeitroman* of his own time, Immermann's *Münchhausen* and Freytag's *Debit and Credit* are all recognizable in his works. His ingenious use of quotations from many areas of literature is a special quality of his style. At the same time he created novels which were significant indications of what was to come.

In the *Chronicle of Sperling Street*, the twenty-three-year-old author already understood the refined technique of mixing different time periods through the fictitious medium of a reminiscent old man who functions as narrator. To be sure, the work has a continuous plot—the story of a young pair, Elise and Gustav, who grow up on Sperling Street and are married in the end— but the narration is not restricted to this plot strand alone. Contemporary and past occurrences, placed next to each other in a chain of episodes, are fused in the memory and experiences of the chronicler who uses many forms: exposition, letter, dream, and reports of third parties. Raabe was fully aware of the unique nature of his procedure and even refers to it within the work. The narrator explains that he is not writing a novel. As he says, the "contents will not be very cohesive. I linger a moment and then jump years ahead; I paint pictures and give no plot." The artistic unity of the narration is provided by the setting: the "dream book and picture book of Sperling Street," an "invaluable stage of all the world, where war and peace, misery and happiness, hunger and excess, all of life's antinomies are reflected." The artistic method is expressly described as a series, comparable to "those old, naive notes . . . which narrate events from the past, present, and future in colorful succession." This corresponds to dream pictures passing by: "One picture after the other passes me by like in a laterna magica, disappearing if I try to hold on to it. . . . Every second brings something new." Such a style precludes a monumental ending. That in the end the young pair is "happy in beautiful Italy" is a cheerful parody on an old schema. Throughout the story, the time during which the chronicle is being written plays an important role. The narrator begins to write "on the 15th of November" and ends "on the 1st of May. Evening." It is a known fact that Raabe began writing his novel in Berlin on the fifteenth of November, 1854, and completed it in the summer of 1855. At the time he was living on Spree Street (*Spreegasse*), which was renamed Sperling Street (*Sperlingsgasse*) in 1931 on the occasion of his hundredth birthday. In allusion to political events and social conditions of the times—the Crimean War (1853–56) and the misery of those who emigrated to America for example—the book begins with a comment on the times: "These are truly bad times! Laughter has become costly in the world, frowns and sighs cheap. In the distance lie bloody dark the thunderclouds of war, and nearby sickness, hunger, and want have laid down their sinister veil;—these are bad times!" The sentence about bad times is repeated twice again in the same paragraph.

From here the transition is easily made to the personal situation of the narrator, a lonely old man who says of himself, "I am old and tired; it is the time when memories take the place of hope." The narrator's demeanor is an artistic technique as well as a reaction to the times; they cannot be separated. It would not be out of place to characterize the *Chronicle* as a *Zeitroman*, but this does not define the work. Despite its weaknesses, primarily its sentimentality, it anticipates much of Raabe's later artistry.

The works of Raabe's middle period in Stuttgart (1862–70) are of interest today only as the early works of a prominent author. They show how Raabe was searching for material, themes, and techniques. Noteworthy is *Three Quillpens* (*Drei Federn*, 1865) because Raabe split the first person narrator into three separate narrators, as indicated in the title. Three of the novels in particular—the so-called "Stuttgart trilogy"—were very popular at one time but are now less highly regarded: *The Hunger Pastor* (*Der Hungerpastor*, 1864); *Abu Telfan or the Return from the Mountains of the Moon* (*Abu Telfan oder Die Heimkehr vom Mondgebirge*, 1867); and *The Burial Cart* (*Der Schüdderrump*, 1870). The term "Stuttgart trilogy," first used by Wilhelm Jensen, comes from Raabe's own view of these novels as a unit.[35] He speaks of this at the end of *The Burial Cart*. However, the plots of the three are not related.

The three most remarkable novels from Raabe's later period, *Old Nests* (*Alte Nester*, 1880), *Stopfkuchen* (1891), and *The Documents from Vogelsang* (*Die Akten des Vogelsangs*, 1896), are designated the "Brunswick trilogy," probably in analogy to the Stuttgart trilogy. They are so closely related in style and theme that the term trilogy is indeed accurate. With these works Raabe's literary achievement reached its peak. At the same time, the endeavors of nineteenth-century novelists to express new experiences with human nature which went beyond those of the Age of Goethe came to an end.

The three novels all have a narrator who reminisces in the first person. Each belongs to the world of average men and tells the story of an exceptional character who intrigues him. In all three cases, the relationship between narrator and hero begins as a boyhood friendship. With the narrator's fascination for a contrasting figure, the ordinary world opens itself up to the unusual. To what extent the narrator is to be regarded as a mediator between the two extremes of the ordinary and the unusual remains undecided.

In the first of the three novels, the realm of the "old nests," where the narrator Fritz Langreuter and the hero Just Everstein grew up, exists in the mind of the narrator as an invulnerable realm set apart from the "evil, stormy world." Nevertheless, the old nests are eventually destroyed, in this case by speculators. The castle itself, Schloss Werden, is completely devastated, and at the spot where the young companions once sat in the misshapen walnut trees—these were the "nests"—there is later a road. But Just Everstein's farm, the Steinhof, which at first is also lost, is recovered and prospers even more than before. In the narrator's consciousness, however, the two belong together: the nests in the walnut trees of Schloss Werden and Just Everstein with his Steinhof. The reason the castle is not rebuilt is historical; in Raabe's opinion the nobility no longer represented a viable way of life, as was already shown in *The Burial Cart*.

Whether or not Just Everstein has rightfully been characterized as an eccentric depends on one's interpretation of the novel as a whole.[36] Similarly, it is questionable to regard his story as a *Bildungsroman*, as has often been done. In *Old Nests* Raabe pursued a number of objectives and interwove several plots, resulting in a novel composition which does not fit into any specific category. In any case, the work as a whole is a confrontation with and parody of Immermann's *Münchhausen*. Not only can the structurally important settings of Schnick-Schnack-Schnurr and Schloss Werden, Oberhof and Steinhof, be compared, but Raabe even refers to Immermann within the novel itself.

As interesting as the narrative structure of the novels of the Brunswick trilogy is, there is still some doubt regarding Raabe's rank as a novelist. Even the novel *Stopfkuchen. A Tale of the Sea and Murder* (*Stopfkuchen. Eine See- und Mordgeschichte*, 1891), does not help to decide the question conclusively, although experts speak of it as Raabe's masterpiece[37] and call it "one of the most important German novels of the nineteenth century."[38] It was primarily this novel which led modern researchers to reevaluate Raabe's writings.[39] The author himself considered it to be his best work. To the present day it still receives more attention from critics than any of Raabe's other novels; its sophisticated form and ambiguous statement entice scholars and allow for a wide range of interpretations.

While journeying back to his family and property in South Africa, the narrator Eduard writes down what he experienced during a short visit home to Germany. The visit forces him to realize that he has no advantage over those who stayed at home and that he has always been entangled in all of their affairs. Shortly before his arrival home, the mail carrier Störzer, whom the young boy Eduard had often accompanied on his rounds, dies. It was Störzer who told Eduard stories from Le Vaillant's *Voyage dans l'intérieur de l'Afrique* and awakened in the school-weary boy the desire to travel there.

Just as the young Eduard was attracted by faraway places, his friend Heinrich Schaumann, called *Stopfkuchen* (cake eater) because of his appetite, dreamed of becoming master of Rote Schanze, a farmstead situated on a former fortress from which the city was fired upon in the Seven Years' War. There the farmer Quakatz, suspected of having murdered the livestock dealer Kienbaum, lived as an outcast with his little daughter Valentine. He was sent to prison several times, but there was no proof of his guilt, and he always had to be released. Nonetheless the community considered him guilty. Young boys took delight in mocking him, tormenting his daughter, and throwing stones at them and their property. During one such attack on Rote Schanze, Stopfkuchen, resting under the hedge, came to Valentine's defense. He won her friendship and soon thereafter the farmer's confidence. This was all the more important to him because he felt just as rejected by his own peers as Quakatz did on Rote Schanze. He was always somewhat lazy and slow, had "weak feet," a large body circumference, and little success in school. When Eduard visits him after Störzer's death—many years have passed since their boyhood friendship—he is in fact the proprietor of Rote Schanze. Eduard notices at once that the place is completely transformed. It makes a peaceful, friendly impression, and Stopfkuchen, harmoniously married to Valentine, is leading an idyllic life. On the day of their reunion he gives Eduard a detailed account of how this all came about.

This account culminates in the solving of the mystery of Kienbaum's death. Stopfkuchen leads up to the disclosure slowly and takes a long time before even indicating that he knows the truth. Not until evening, when he accompanies Eduard into the city, does he finish the story in the inn so that the waitress can overhear it and then spread the tale. One learns that it was the mail carrier Störzer who killed Kienbaum. Störzer committed the deed by accident and never had the courage to confess to the authorities. Kienbaum had always tormented him, called him names, and made fun of his long mail routes. On that particular evening, Kienbaum was in a mischievous or bad mood and hit him with a whip. Störzer grabbed a stone with his hurt hand and threw it, not with the intention of killing Kienbaum but as a defensive reaction to the whip lash. Kienbaum's horses bolted, and hours later they were found at their stall with the dead man. Stopfkuchen found out the truth after the death of his father-in-law but did not want to reveal it while Störzer was still alive. Eduard's visit seems to him to provide the proper occasion.

The stories told here are at once banal and grisly, whether they center on the livestock dealer Kienbaum, the mail carrier Störzer, or the farmer Quakatz. Karl Hoppe draws attention to two newspaper notices found in Raabe's papers after his death, both of which "were undoubtedly of importance in the conception of *Stopfkuchen*." The first, from the *Braunschweiger Tageblatt*, "supplied Raabe with the basic elements for his *tale of murder*"; the other, from the *Münchener Neuesten Nachrichten*, "may possibly have inspired him to create the character of the rural mail carrier Störzer."[40] The horror stories have been skillfully worked into the total composition. But the problem of crime which concerned Hermann Broch and Robert Musil forty years later does not yet emerge here, which is why the banal story of the mail carrier as such is not sufficient to be emotionally upsetting. It "was only an accident," as Störzer asserts most convincingly. But all the same, as he tells Stopfkuchen, it burdened him with "his [Kienbaum's] and my fate, and the sorrowful fate of the father-in-law, too." The structure of the novel is determined by the fact that all the fates and stories coincide and in that way become significant.

They are not significant in their own right. Nor is Stopfkuchen the hero at Rote Schanze that he sees himself to be. Claude David justifiably labels him an "arch-philistine" and points to his "arrogant self-satisfaction," complete identification with the role he has assumed, and sterile way of life.[41] Raabe emphasized the autobiographical significance of the novel, which indicates that he considered Heinrich Schaumann to be a success and saw his secluded life, led undisturbed and to his own liking, as the result of a life struggle which turned out well.

This view is the opposite of what Goethe had bequeathed to future generations approximately sixty years earlier in the *Travels*. Neither the ethos of utility, nor the great social problems of the time, nor the role of the renunciants in solving them, nor the visionary element is of consequence here. Stopfkuchen's outlook is contrary to all of the values in Goethe's world; nor are Goethe's values represented by the narrator Eduard. Quite the contrary, Eduard exposes the utopian character of Lenardo's words, "The time has passed when one ran adventurously into the wide world." Because as a boy Eduard yearned for "Le Vaillant's Africa, his Hottentots, giraffes, lions, and elephants," and because adventure enticed him, he went out into the world and built his existence without regard for usefulness or practicalities. His reaction to Stopfkuchen shows that despite his long absence he remains attached to his home and actually has never totally left it. What happened at home did not occur in a past he had long forgotten. They are not old stories that no longer concern him or belong to lost times. Instead, they are his own affairs. What happens at home is of the greatest importance to him. Whereas the narrator in *Old Nests* was fascinated by his hero at all times but remained personally neutral, in *Stopfkuchen* the narrator is drawn out of his original neutrality and self-assurance. He goes through changes in his thinking and is deeply affected in the end. Overwhelmed by the hero of the narration, who himself functions as narrator for long stretches, he wins a new understanding of himself. Stopfkuchen's effect on Eduard is an expression of Raabe's support for Stopfkuchen within the novel. It is a statement of commitment to a view of man which once and for all supplanted the spirit of the Age of Goethe. Something new had begun which could not yet be defined. Raabe's finesse in the narrative form masks the emptiness of his characters' daily lives.

Similar to *Stopfkuchen* in its structure and ambivalent theme is *The Documents from Vogelsang*. The title calls to mind Raabe's first work, and here again a street is the setting and artistic focus. The narrator and his counterpart grew up in the Vogelsang, a small street outside the city. They left the Vogelsang and went their separate ways. When the story opens, the narrator Dr. Karl Krumhardt has had a splendid legal career and is living in fine surroundings corresponding to his prestigious position. His friend Velten Andres died alone in a bare room in Berlin. The story of the highly gifted, congenial Andres, "who was equipped for all forms and conditions of life," is the great subject of Karl Krumhardt's narration.

> He, my friend, was everything in his short life: scholar, businessman, airman, soldier, sailor, newspaper writer—but by bourgeois standards he did not amount to anything, nor can I bring forth anything in these documents to show that he ever went to any real trouble for anything but that little girl from the Vogelsang, who is now the widow Mungo from Chicago.

This girl, Helene Trotzendorff, is one of the group of young people who grew up carefree in the Vogelsang, just like the youths in the environment of Schloss Werden. Later she joined her father in New York and married a millionaire. Velten followed her to New York prior to her engagement but could not win her and later returned to Germany. He was not able to gain a footing anywhere. Krumhardt cannot ascertain the deeper reasons for his friend's unsuccessful life: "I have not remained in the dark about anything in his life except—about the man himself." Helene knows more about him. After Velten's death, she admits to Krumhardt that he was always attached to her and that they met in many parts of the world. But her statements do not result in a comprehensive picture; the reader learns only fragments of Velten's story.

The inner story of man, which was the great theme of the newly developing eighteenth-century novel, is not what is described by Karl Krumhardt and Helene Trotzendorff. Nor was this Raabe's intention. On the contrary, he wanted to show his hero's mysteriousness and inexplicability, the uncertain element in his character, exactly that which makes the depiction of his inner story impossible. Whereas Agathon and Werther continuously express themselves and thereby create the stucture of their own inner stories, Velten Andres obscures important facts and leads others astray. He is not a rounded, independent character whose inner life corresponds to his visible behavior but is only understandable as a counterpart to Karl Krumhardt. He can even be regarded as Krumhardt's other self.

Krumhardt, the representative of the average and normal, defines his relationship to the unusual man who lives outside society with Lessing's words: "I sent him into the world because I did not want to live alone with him under one roof anymore" (*Der Ungenannte*). Krumhardt interprets this quote in a way significant for the entire epoch.

> My whole life long I have had to live with this Velten Andres under one roof, and in heart and soul he was not always a house companion of the most comfortable kind—a roommate who made demands not always easily reconcilable with the other's habits, a companion with expectations which often disarranged the entire spiritual household of the solid citizen such that no thing seemed to be in its right place anymore.

Krumhardt had tried to become free of him, but did not succeed, and now that Velten is "gone forever," he wants to hold his domestic authority more firmly than ever: but *I can no longer live with him under one roof*. So I am writing on."

Krumhardt's statements imply that *The Documents from Vogelsang* is not the story of Velten Andres or of the reasons for his failure, but of inner events related to the "spiritual household of the solid citizen." The novel is concerned with the narrator Krumhardt, with his inner, ungratified possibilities, with the parts of his being which are not actualized in his bourgeois form of life. It is his second nature which does not give him peace. He tries to free himself of it by writing about its homelessness and restlessness. One can speak of a special form of the doppelgänger or of a complementary figure in the sense of the Romanticists and Goethe; this would not be a mistake in light of Raabe's erudition.

But it may be even more important to look to later authors for an understanding of Raabe's concept of man. Krumhardt's statement that he does not think Velten "ever went to any real trouble for anything but the little girl from the Vogelsang" is thought provoking. In the 1890s, while Raabe was working on his last novels, Sigmund Freud achieved his fundamental insights on sexuality and recognized that his patients' neurotic disturbances were not a result of brain damage or a hereditary condition but were related to their "reminiscences," to their memories of certain experiences. Raabe and Freud followed different paths and used very different means to arrive at similar conclusions. As early as 1879, Wilhelm Jensen said, "Raabe is undoubtedly one of the deepest thinkers of our time. The area of his research is human life, and he has thought about everything, knows everything that has ever affected it and affects it today."[42]

As in *Stopfkuchen*, Raabe's formal achievement, his artistry in *The Documents from Vogelsang* is impressive. Again he has integrated additional plots into the composition. The changes brought about by the advance of modern life are the primary reason for the dissolution of the Vogelsang, where the most different types of people still lived together as good neighbors. These changes are demonstrated by a number of events and characters, all of which are closely interwoven in the main plot. Historical and contemporary time always play a role in Raabe's writings; the "old nests" have their place in man's consciousness as well as in a geographical location. Man's ability to remember the past is the prerequisite for narration and for the immediacy of history. Just as the interflow of time levels in Raabe's novels is unthinkable without the historical sense of the nineteenth century, which first separated the time levels, the complicated narrative in Raabe's late novels is unimaginable without a knowledge of man's ability to remember and an understanding of his consciousness, which effortlessly combines different time levels, creating new relationships independent of time. Raabe apparently knew all of this as is also evidenced by his two later historical novels, *The Odfeld* (1889) and *Hastenbeck* (1898). Through the intricacy of the narrative process in all the novels of the Brunswick trilogy, he gave shape to experiences with human nature which were still unspoken at that time.

Raabe's loose, light style may be the reason that the depth of his narrative form was not recognized for decades and that even today his novels, with all respect for his achievement, still have the effect of literary entertainment (*Unterhaltungsliteratur*). Of course it is always an advantage when a novel is entertaining, but in general Raabe's style does not seem quite compact enough to the modern reader. It may be that by means of this style he wished to make his works appealing to a wide audience.

Gesellschaftsroman—*Theodor Fontane*

It is no longer appropriate to apply the term "Realism" to German novels written in the latter half of the nineteenth century. This literary designation, often used in theoretical discussions at the time and still popular today—even in the most recent studies one often finds the period from approximately 1850 to 1890 referred to as the Age of Realism—has proven to be too vague and ambiguous for further use in the language of modern research. What has become widely accepted as a literary truth is in effect a misrepresentation, for the novels of these years cannot be characterized by the term. The difficulties scholars face when using it in the twentieth century are illuminated by Claude David: "If one agrees with Erich Auerbach . . . that Realism is the 'serious presentation of the contemporary, daily, social reality at the base of continuous historical development,' then without a doubt this genre is scarcely represented in nineteenth-century Germany."[43]

In the 1860s the way was prepared for a new wave of historical novels. This wave reached its peak in the 1870s, then quickly ebbed by the end of the following decade but did not disappear completely until the midtwentieth century. An important forerunner of the revived historical novel was Viktor von Scheffel's (1826–1886) *Ekkehard, a Tale of the Tenth Century* (*Ekkehard, Eine Geschichte aus dem zehnten Jahrhundert*, 1855). It tells the story of Ekkehard, a monk of the St. Gall Abbey, who is chosen by the young, widowed Duchess of Swabia to reside in her castle in Hohentwiel and tutor her in Latin. The duchess, hurt by Ekkehard's aloofness, rejects him when he finally admits his affection for her. After fleeing, he writes the Latin heroic epic "Waltharius," which he wraps around an arrow and shoots into the Duchess's castle before leaving the country. Scheffel's own translation of "Waltharius" into German comprises chapter 24 of *Ekkehard*, and his formidable appendix to the novel contains comprehensive scholarly notes. The fact that he combined the monks Ekkehard I (d. 973) and Ekkehard II (d. 990) into one literary figure and that other historical data are not entirely correct does not detract from the book. It was widely read in the nineteenth century and well into the twentieth century. *Ekkehard* has an atmosphere all its own, "a poetic work through and through," as Theodor Fontane wrote. He considered it one of the best books he had read, adding that it was "reminiscent of Sir Walter Scott's finest works."[44]

Of the historical novels which followed, only a few are of significance.

The "majority of historical novels are simply a horror," Fontane said in 1875 in a review he wrote of *Our Forefathers*.[45] In the 1860s Heinrich Laube published another trilogy, *The Great War* (*Der grosse Krieg*, 1865–66), in which he attempted to give a complete picture of the Thirty Years' War from its beginning to the death of Bernhard von Weimar in 1639. Laube's literary career was consistent with the times in that he began with the *Zeitroman* of the Young Germans and later turned to the historical novel of the 1860s and 1870s. Karl Gutzkow's later novels, *Hohenschwangau* (1867–68) and *Fritz Ellrodt* (1871), are not impressive. Adalbert Stifter's (1806–1868) *Witiko* (1865–67) is an important work, however. The action takes place in thirteenth-century Bohemia and centers on the battles between the Duke of Bohemia and the princes who elected him. The preservation of ideals at all times, even in conflicts, is the basis of the utopian content. But instead of the private sphere, as in *Indian Summer*, now the state is the realm in which one strives to attain humanitarian goals. Whereas in *Indian Summer* the threatening counterforce is the passion of love, in *Witiko* it is political passion: lust for power and violent rebellion against justice and order.

In the 1870s a group of novels called *Professorenromane* (professor novels) was highly regarded. In every case these novels were the product of industrious research. Displaying a vast knowledge of the subject matter, the authors wrote fluently and with a careful eye to the current times. In his eight-volume work *Our Forefathers* (*Die Ahnen*, 1872–81), Gustav Freytag (1816–1895) narrates episodes from the history of a German family dating from the great migrations in the fourth century to 1848, combining events in the personal lives of his heroes with the course of German history. Although not a masterful work, *Our Forefathers* is skillfully written, and it appeared at an opportune time with regard to national political thought. Freytag satisfied the public's wish to glorify the present by describing the illustrious past.

In the same category, Felix Dahn's (1834–1912) *A Struggle for Rome* (*Ein Kampf um Rom*, 1876) was extremely popular. Adults and youths alike were fascinated by the glory and decline of the Ostrogoth empire in Italy and eagerly read about the last Ostrogoth kings and their enemies. Dahn knew how to endow all the different characters with individual traits. A reading public in search of a political identity found role models in the heroic Gothic tribe. In the following decades Dahn, a professor of legal history, continued to publish historical novels, including the thirteen-volume *Short Novels from the Age of the Great Migrations* (*Kleine Romane aus der Völkerwanderungszeit*, 1882–1901), the three-volume *Julian the Apostate* (*Julian der Abtrünnige*, 1894), and the twelve-volume *The Germanic Kings* (*Die Könige der Germanen*, 1866–1911). His primary concern was the subject matter itself, for which the form of the novel seemed best suited at the time.

The Egyptologist Georg Ebers (1837–1898) used his material even more forcefully than Freytag and Dahn to refer to problems of his own day. His most famous novel is *An Egyptian King's Daughter* (*Eine ägyptische Königstochter*, 1864). In *Uarda* (1877), also set in ancient Egypt, Ebers alludes to the contemporary struggle between the German state and the Roman Catholic church by means of the historical struggle between Egyptian priests and kings. Ebers later used material from other areas, such as Greek and Spanish/ Dutch history, but he also returned to Egypt. During his lifetime, a complete edition of his works appeared in thirty-two volumes (1893–97). A fashionable, successful author, he had a wide circle of readers.

In the 1870s and 1880s, Conrad Ferdinand Meyer (1825–1898) was also occupied with historical topics. By literary standards Meyer is far superior to the authors of the *Professorenromane*. Unlike his contemporaries, who were inclined to write works of great length, he preferred the novella. In a single event or episode he symbolically pointed to basic life patterns. Meyer was a complicated, nervous person. History provided him with a way of expressing his personal experiences; he needed the historical distance in order to give shape to his view of man and existence. The title character in *Jürg Jenatsch. A Story of the Grisons* (*Jürg Jenatsch. Eine Bündnergeschichte*, 1876) is an inscrutable figure whose story takes place during the Thirty Years' War. Originally a reformed pastor and later exclusively a general and politician, Jenatsch changes sides several times while fighting for the independence of the Grisons and finally even changes his religious faith. During a celebration at which he is honored by the canton as its liberator, he is suddenly attacked and overpowered by his enemies.

Along with the historical novel, the *Zeitroman* was still a popular genre. Gustav Freytag's *Debit and Credit* (*Soll und Haben*, 1855) was an enormous success; it went through hundreds of printings. Freytag was strongly influenced by Dickens and Thackeray. His popularity in Germany had to do with the fact that his characters radiate a quality captured from the English authors. Also, the reader's self-image was elevated by Freytag's portrayal of the burgher class, which is shown to be a solid, respectable, patriarchal order that is superior to the less dependable aristocracy. The hero Anton Wohlfahrt makes his way, as in the *Bildungsroman*, through burgher and aristocratic circles. Nonetheless, his social rise can take place only within the burgher class. In the end he does not marry an aristocratic woman, as the reader might assume, but marries the sister of the man who owns the firm where Anton began as an apprentice, thereby becoming a partner. Thus he fulfills the ideals of the burgher class Freytag extols. The fast-moving plot with its surprising turning points is designed to hold the reader's attention until the end. Freytag's second novel, *The Lost Manuscript* (*Die verlorene Hand-*

schrift, 1864), was less successful. It is an awkward narration about a professor who, while looking for an ancient Tacitus manuscript, finds his wife.

Friedrich Spielhagen (1829–1911) and Paul Heyse (1830–1914) also published a number of *Zeitromane.* Spielhagen achieved widespread fame after the publication of his first novel, *Problematic Natures (Problematische Naturen,* 1861), which once again treats the theme of torn, frail characters. Fontane praised its structure, but admitted that it had greatly vexed him: "We are genuinely glad that they [the problematic natures] are finally dead and that the world is free of these annoying characters who constantly appeal to our interest and are thoroughly incapable of awakening it." Today Spielhagen is known more for his theory of the novel than for his novels, which are no longer readable. Spielhagen rejected the idea that the narrator can step forward and assert himself as in Goethe's *Elective Affinities.* The author, he claimed, does not have the right to "interrupt the hero's role" and "destroy the reader's illusion."[46] He demanded objective narration and believed that the narrator's inserted reflections were unpoetic. Of Spielhagen's theory of the novel, Fontane said, "that the narrator is not allowed to speak . . . seems to me to be pure nonsense. In fact, the very best, most famous, most delightful narrators, particularly among the English, have *always* done so" (January 14, 1879, letter to Wilhelm Hertz).

Heyse's *Children of the World (Kinder der Welt,* 1873) and his second *Zeitroman, In Paradise (Im Paradiese,* 1876), take place in Berlin and Munich respectively. These two cities were also chosen as settings by other novelists of the period, which meant a loosening of nineteenth-century provincialism, at least to some degree. The so-called "Berlin novel" was created, and, besides Fontane, its main representative was Max Kretzer (1854–1941). Kretzer's best-known novel, *Master Timpe (Meister Timpe,* 1888), depicts the downfall of a craftsman unable to cope with the battle against machine and capital.

Wilhelm von Polenz's (1861–1903) *Farmer Büttner (Der Büttnerbauer,* 1895) is concerned with the same theme transferred to a rural environment. The work is the second novel of a trilogy; *The Pastor of Breitendorf (Der Pfarrer von Breitendorf,* 1893) is the first part, and *Grabenhäger (Der Grabenhäger,* 1897) is the conclusion. What all three works have in common is their criticism of the times, focusing on the Protestant church, the state, and, above all, capitalism. Lenin called *Farmer Büttner* one of his favorite books. Tolstoy wrote an introduction to the Russian edition in 1902 and praised the book as a genuine work of art. Its historical value lies in the objective presentation of the changing agricultural conditions of the day. The power of the usurer, that is, "the cold hand of capital" to which the farmer loses his land, is likened to the subordination of farmers in times past. In fact, compared to this new "yoke," the labor under which Farmer Büttner's forefathers suffered was "featherlight." Whereas Farmer Büttner does not understand the reason for his unhappiness and only has a "dim feeling" that a "great injustice" is being done to him, his son Gustav gradually turns to new ideas, rejects conservative thinking, and becomes a Social Democrat.

Among the many other authors of Berlin novels, the name Paul Lindau (1839–1919) should be mentioned, not so much for his two novels, *The Train to the West* (*Der Zug nach dem Westen,* 1886) and *Poor Girls* (*Arme Mädchen,* 1887), but because of an interesting review of *The Train to the West* written by Fontane. In a modified version of the review, Fontane makes the point that "we still have no great Berlin novel which depicts our life in its entirety in the way that Thackeray portrayed life in London, encompassing all classes, in his best novel *Vanity Fair.*"

The novels by Michael Georg Conrad (1846–1927) take place in Munich. Conrad was an enthusiastic follower of Emile Zola (1840–1902) and planned a ten-volume series to be modeled after *Les Rougon-Macquart* (1871–93). Only three volumes appeared, however, all under the title of the first volume, *What the Isar Whispers* (*Was die Isar rauscht,* 1887). There is a decisive difference between *What the Isar Whispers* and Zola's novels, such as *L'Assommoir* (1877), *Nana* (1879–80), and *Germinal* (1885). These belong to the great French tradition of Balzac and Flaubert, were written by a man who was equally involved in art and politics, and—no matter how one feels about Zola's idea of hereditary and environmental determinism—they are powerful reading. None of the aforementioned German works is comparable to Zola's novels.

Gottfried Keller's later *Zeitroman, Martin Salander* (1886), shows the virtuous man in battle with unscrupulous persons. Even though he survives the battle and his son shows promising talents, the picture of the times which evolves is gloomy. Keller was skeptical and troubled about the future. It is difficult to determine whether that was the reason he could no longer create an inviting novel form. In any case, the narration is colorless and uninspiring.

Theodor Fontane (1819–1898), however, was able to create convincing novels. He was the first to break away from the descriptive style characteristic of the majority of German novels in past decades. Recognizing his contribution, Thomas Mann spoke of an "evaporation of the contents" in Fontane's novels ("The Old Fontane," 1910).[47] With this evaporation, Fontane's style led into the twentieth century even more decisively than Raabe's. Fontane's novels were a transition and a preparation for modern forms and already contained much of what Thomas Mann, Hermann Broch, and Robert Musil were to express later from a different perspective.

Fontane was already fifty-nine years old when his first novel, *Before the*

Storm (*Vor dem Sturm*, 1878), appeared. Although he had never written a novel before, he had read extensively and had studied the genre for decades, as evidenced by his many essays and letters. In particular, he was interested in the relationship between the historical novel and the *Zeitroman* and wrote significant essays on Sir Walter Scott and Willibald Alexis. He summarized the fruits of his deliberations in question and answer form in his review of Gustav Freytag's *Our Forefathers*, "What is the purpose of the *modern* novel? What *material* should it choose? Is the range of its material unlimited? And if *not*, within what limits of time and space does it have the best chance of proving itself and satisfying the hearts of its readers?" His answer is as follows: "The novel should be a picture of the times in which we live, at least the reflection of a time at whose border we ourselves have stood or of which our parents have spoken." He believed it "characteristic" that even Sir Walter Scott did not begin with *Ivanhoe* (set in 1196), but with *Waverley* (set in 1745), to which he "expressly added the second title '*Tis Sixty Years Since.*" Scott was quite correct in feeling that "two generations is approximately the limit which, as a general rule, it is *not* recommendable to exceed." Not until he was successful as a novelist did Scott feel secure enough to delve into the past.

What is striking about Fontane's statements is not his call for the *Zeitro-man*, for this was not new at all. Nor was it a new idea that "all narrative literature which has survived over the last 150 years" essentially fulfilled the requirements which Fontane had outlined. He accurately observed that the "great English humorists of this and the former century depicted *their* times; the French novel, in spite of the elder Dumas, is a . . . *Gesellschaftsroman* [novel of manners or society]; Jean Paul, Goethe, yes even Freytag (in *Debit and Credit*) wrote about *their* world and *their* times." All of this is not of consequence for the history of the German novel, however. Much more striking is the fact that the narrative material of significant novels from the first half of the twentieth century is also rooted in the time period which Fontane defined, a period which the authors had experienced themselves or about which their "parents had spoken." This is the case in *Buddenbrooks* (1901) and *The Magic Mountain* (1924) by Thomas Mann, *The Sleepwalkers* (1931) by Hermann Broch, and *The Man without Qualities* (1932) by Robert Musil. Moreover, it is astonishing that as early as 1875 Fontane set the temporal limits which a novel, insofar as it is a *Zeitroman*, may not exceed even today if it is to have the best chance of "proving itself and satisfying the hearts of its readers." One need only think of the success of Günter Grass's first two novels, *The Tin Drum* (1959) and *Dog Years* (1963), and of other novels after the Second World War which were faced with the task of coming to terms with the events of the preceding decades. The productive results of combining the historical novel and the *Zeitroman*—two forms which were long

thought of as separate—became evident in the twentieth century when authors chose as their setting that period on the border of the present which is
already historical but is nonetheless part of the reader's personal experience.

If one considers that Fontane had *Before the Storm* in mind for well over
a decade before publishing it, then the time setting of the work conforms
with his own rule and only seems to have been overstepped a bit due to its
delayed completion. *Before the Storm* is a historical novel which tends towards a *Gesellschaftsroman*. It bears the subtitle *Novel from the Winter of
1812–13*. This is the same period Leo Tolstoy dealt with in *War and Peace*
(1868–69). *Before the Storm* cannot compare to Tolstoy's great work; the
strong wind of history that sweeps through the Russian novel is hardly de-
tectable even as a light breeze in Fontane's *Before the Storm*. Nonetheless,
the historical atmosphere directly preceding the Wars of Liberation affects all
the characters and determines their lives.

Many scenes in *Before the Storm* take place in Berlin, but the primary
setting is the Prussian countryside west of the Oder River between Küstrin
and Frankfurt, where the ancestral seat of the family Vitzewitz, Schloss Hohen-Vietz, is located. Noblemen, farmers, and citizens of Brandenburg and,
to a lesser extent, Berlin, make up the circle of characters. They are Fontane's primary concern. In an early stage of his work on the novel, he said
that "amiable characters" should "entertain the reader, perhaps eventually
win his love, but without turmoil and éclat. Stimulating, cheerful, and if
possible, witty conversation" was most important to him. Such a statement
of purpose was new to the nineteenth century. Indeed, Fontane accomplished his goal, for the book is pleasant reading. Although its plot is not
terribly significant, there is a great deal of action. The reader glides from one
episode to another, always warmed and impressed by truly amiable characters
who demonstrate that they are members of fine society by their self-assured,
correct, appropriate conduct in all situations. It is a society which comprises
all ages and classes and also gives a place to outsiders.

Two young Polish immigrants, Kathinka von Ladalinski and her brother
Tubal, create unrest at Hohen-Vietz. To the older generation they seem to
be the right marriage partners for the young members of the Vitzewitz family,
Lewin and Renate, and for a while Lewin and Renate agree. They both feel
an honest, deep affection for their prospective partners and are willing to wait
for their feelings to be reciprocated. Yet their aunt, the Countess Pudalga,
describes the true situation in a letter.

> Mais les choses ne se font pas d'après nos volontés. I am sure of
> the young people from Hohen-Vietz, but not of those from the
> house of Ladalinski. Kathinka accepts Lewin's homage, but oth-
> erwise she is just playing with him; Tubal has some feeling for

Renate, qui ne l'aurait pas? But it is nothing more than the admiration evoked by youth and beauty everywhere. So there are difficulties which, I believe, lie in Kathinka's indifference and in Tubal's superficiality of emotion. Et l'un est aussi mauvais que l'autre.[48]

The countess's elegant letter handles the delicate topic with sophistication and is characteristic of Fontane's artistry. In a letter written to Mete Fontane, the author said of his *Gesellschaftsromane*, "My entire attention is focused on allowing the characters to speak as they do in real life. Wittiness (which sounds a bit arrogant) flows most easily from my pen. I am, betraying my French heritage once again, a causeur in speaking and writing; but because I am above all an artist, I know where witty causerie belongs and where it does not" (August 24, 1882). Already in his first novel Fontane lets each person speak in an individual manner. This is the reason he does not need a forceful plot. Conversation replaces the plot and is the substance of the novel. The society and its problems take shape in and from the conversations. Therefore, both historical novel and *Zeitroman* become a *Gesellschaftsroman* which comes to life through the speech, and occasionally the eloquent silence, of its characters.

There are many characters in *Before the Storm*. Researchers like to use Fontane's terms "portrait gallery" and "panoptic" to describe the work. The overwhelming fullness of human life, which captivates the reader, is reminiscent of Balzac, Tolstoy, Dickens, and Thackeray. However, it cannot be said that Fontane was directly influenced by them or that he imitated them. He greatly admired William Makepeace Thackeray (1811–1863) and for years preferred him to Dickens; *Vanity Fair* (1847–48) was one of his favorite books. But *Before the Storm* is fundamentally different from *Vanity Fair*. Fontane was not trying to depict *vanitas vanitatum*, but simply wished to present "amiable characters." He believed that art has the responsibility to glorify and transfigure and was convinced that literature has "different laws of truth from history."[49] A novel should "first be judged according to aesthetic principles." He did not want to give ugliness too much space.[50] Though some might feel that Fontane contradicts himself, he personally saw no inconsistency in claiming that the "modern novel should be a picture of the times." As he explained in his review of Freytag's *Our Forefathers*, "*What is the purpose of a novel?* It should, while avoiding all exaggeration and ugliness, tell a story we *believe*."

Fontane talked about the unique structure of *Before the Storm* in response to criticism from Paul Heyse. He wrote to Heyse that *Before the Storm* is a *Vielheitsroman* (pluralistic novel). In addition to "novels such as *Copperfield*, in which we see a man's life from its beginning," those which "closely examine a multifarious time period instead of an individual" are also legitimate (December 9, 1878). As is so often the case with Fontane's theoretical statements, it seems at first as if this were nothing fundamentally new. But a comparison with Robert Musil's reflections on modern narration in the first volume of his novel *The Man without Qualities* (1930) shows the importance of Fontane's comments; Fontane was already working with concepts similar to Musil's. Fontane knew that readers, as Musil later said, prefer a simple narrative sequence, but unlike Musil he thought that the narrative thread depended on the fact that the novel just has one hero and relates his story alone. Therefore for Fontane narrative problems first emerged when the attempt was made to present a multifarious time period. He conceded to Heyse that "narrations 'with *one* hero' " would always possess greater dramatic interest, but stressed that "the *Vielheitsroman* with all its breadth and retardations, with its masses of portraits and episodes," could nevertheless equal the *Einheitsroman* (unitary novel), if not in its "effect," then in its "artistry." Against the charge that *Before the Storm* was weak in composition, he argued that, quite to the contrary, herein lay its strength. One would hesitate to take issue with this proud defense, for in fact Fontane's *Vielheitsroman*—the term is quite useful—was the most modern nineteenth-century novel to have appeared. The author was right about his book. Other historical novels of the day all fell short of *Before the Storm*; the only work of equal originality was Immermann's *Münchhausen.*

Fontane did not publish another work like it, but instead concentrated on the *Gesellschaftsroman*, a genre that did not yet exist in Germany. *Before the Storm* had already tended in this direction. In the works that followed, Fontane wrote of high society and of good people from the lower classes. In these circles one has a sense for what is, as Goethe would say, "proper" (*das Gehörige*): one behaves with decorum, and there are always a few people, particularly among the lower classes, who are good-hearted. In *Before the Storm* this was taken for granted, for otherwise the characters would not have been amiable. In the series of novels beginning with *L'Adultera* (1882), it is no longer taken for granted but is something special and exceptional. This gives the novels a pointedness, concentration, and emphasis not yet found in *Before the Storm*. With the exception of *Stechlin* (1898), in which many elements from *Before the Storm* recur, they all show a slice of a world that as a whole remains unilluminated. For this reason the form of most of these novels borders on the novella.

The majority of Fontane's *Gesellschaftsromane* are *Eheromane* (novels of marriage). As the basis for his plots he often used actual incidents that he had heard of locally. When reproducing them in novel form, he stressed the underlying social conventions and revealed the social structure within which the marriage partners were confined. The code of honor, general patterns of behavior, and individual reactions provided a plot system which could be varied from case to case by a shift in emphasis. There is no doubt that conditions during the last two decades of the nineteenth century supplied Fontane with rich material, both with respect to actual events as well as to the customs and attitudes which came to prevail as the profile of the young *Kaiserreich* emerged. Of equal importance was Fontane's confrontation with Goethe's *Elective Affinities*. Jürgen Kolbe provided important insights into this relationship and spoke of Fontane's "renewal" of *Elective Affinities*.[51] An evaluation of Fontane's *Eheromane* cannot be based upon the problems of the late nineteenth century alone; his place within the tradition of Goethe's influential novel must also be taken into account.

The artistic merit of *L'Adultera* (1882) is controversial, as is the case with most of Fontane's *Eheromane*. Scholars are almost evenly divided between admiration and limited criticism. The simple triangle story is not a piquant story of adultery, nor can this be said of Fontane's other *Eheromane*. If many of his contemporaries saw moral laxity in the work and were scandalized, this only shows how accurately Fontane described his society and how little the critics understood his moral views. The plot is uncomplicated, almost banal. Melanie de Caparoux, well-bred and appealing, the "spoiled child of a rich and fashionable home," was without means after the death of her father and at seventeen married the financier, van der Straaten, a man twenty-five years her senior. Ten years later, when a compatible partner for Melanie appears, a widely traveled, elegant young businessman's son from Frankfurt am Main, she leaves her husband to marry him. Society condemns her and her own children turn away from her, but the pair endures the ostracism. When they come into financial difficulties, Melanie handles herself most impressively; she reduces household expenses and earns money by giving lessons.

This plot, which contains a number of elements later found in *Effi Briest* (1895), is the motivation for what is actually important: the conversations. They develop, as is customary in a *Gesellschaftsroman*, at breakfast, in the drawing room, at formal dinners, on excursions into the country. Peter Demetz speaks of the "follow-up discussions, which (like in Jane Austen's novels) make the just completed social event and its conversations the topic of renewed conversation."[52] Like the plot, the conversations revolve primarily around the main characters, van der Straaten and Melanie, whose manner of speaking—an ironical, impersonal dialogue without warmth—is the cause of their separation. Van der Straaten, "accustomed since his youth to saying and doing whatever he liked," makes use of ambiguous speech to express what society forbids; most of all he enjoys saying things the others consider improper. His provocative behavior is demonstrated to the reader early in the book on the occasion of an evening gathering and is interpreted by the guests in a "follow-up" conversation. Some of the guests feel sorry for Melanie, but others think that van der Straaten is so rich that he can say what he wants. In addition, his wife receives enough from him that she ought to be able to tolerate him. What Melanie herself feels is revealed by the narrator, who tells us how glad she is to spend the summer outside the city. Van der Straaten only visits her there every third day and "in the days between she enjoyed the happiness of her freedom. . . . She had peace from his expressions of love and unabashedness." Her constant self-control is evident even in her first dialogues with van der Straaten. Later she characterizes the tone of the house as "a little biting, a little ambiguous, and always improper," and says of her husband, "he knows so wonderfully how to say things that injure and expose and humiliate." Her separation from him is a direct result of this. Before leaving she tells him, "I am tired of this despicable lie. . . . I'm not leaving out of guilt, but out of pride" and "in order to restore my self-respect. . . . I want to be able to see clearly and hold my head up again." Van der Straaten's manner of speaking oppresses her, and she frees herself from it. The fact that honest affection for another man brings her to take this step and that she leaves one marriage for another is not forgotten for a moment: the plot is structured around it. Van der Straaten has long been expecting adultery.

L'Adultera differs from Fontane's later Eheromane in that the main characters' actions are sure and straightforward, the adulterous woman is genuinely committed to another man, and the ending is friendly. Fontane anticipated criticism of the moral issue and hence incorporated his contemporaries' indignation into the novel. Melanie knows she will face gossip and self-righteous condemnation, and Fontane shows how she is ostracized when she begins her new marriage. At the same time he takes her side. Perhaps this is the reason why he elaborated on the story, giving Melanie strength and insight when her second husband has financial problems.

All of Fontane's later Eheromane can be viewed under the aspect of the "tragic novel" in the sense of Goethe's Elective Affinities. They are similar to Goethe's novel insofar as one partner is always destroyed by the conflicts that arise; they differ in that passions seldom play a role. Fontane's Eheroman is a Gesellschaftsroman, not a novel of love. Marital problems are treated as societal problems and are deadly serious. Feelings may be dealt with, but they may also be disregarded; since they are related to marriage, they affect the person's position in society. If duels and suicides occur again and again, this shows that the individual sees no escape from the expectations of society.

Fontane worked with this theme in A Man of Honor (Schach von Wuthenow, 1882), a historical narrative set in Berlin in 1806. Schach, a cavalry captain in an elite Prussian regiment, shoots himself immediately after his marriage to Victoire von Carayon. She is an amiable woman of fine character who was once known as a beauty but has been disfigured by pockmarks. Schach frequented her mother's drawing room, courted both mother and daughter, seduced the daughter, and then withdrew. He was afraid that society would ridicule him if he married an unattractive woman. When the king insisted upon the marriage, he acquiesced, but then found escape by taking his own life. In a letter at the end of the novel, von Bülow, a former staff officer and a critic of his times, interprets Schach's behavior as an example of a false concept of honor, as dependence on that which is "more wavering and arbitrary" than anything else and is "based on quicksand": the "opinions of society." He says that the "holiest commandments, the most beautiful and natural emotions" are sacrificed to society, this "false god." Schach fell victim to this "worship of a false honor, which is nothing but vanity and eccentricity."

Victoire, who is less absolute in her judgment, has the last word, again presented in the form of a letter. In her opinion, it is not certain that Schach really did not have the strength to defy ridicule; in any case, he knew that "all the world's ridicule finally weakens and dies." More important was her feeling that he had belonged to those men "who are *not* made for marriage." Caring primarily about appearances and "*external* things," he could not imagine a life together with her. Her answer to the question, "How are the mysteries to be solved?" is: "They can't be. A vestige of darkness and inexplicability remains, and we cannot peer into the final and most secret motives of others or even of ourselves." These two opinions, placed next to each other in letter form at the end of the novel without further commentary, show the wide range of possible interpretations of the tragic events.

Yet the problems of the *Gesellschaftsroman* are even more complicated. Not only did Schach have the mockery of society to fear; he was also subject to its demands, represented by Frau von Carayon. Without once taking the couple's feelings into consideration, she makes it clear to Schach that even if Victoire is willing to make the sacrifice and release him from his obligation, she has no intention of complying with her daughter's wishes. As she explains, "I belong to a society by whose code I abide and whose laws I obey; that is how I have been brought up, and I have no desire to sacrifice my social position for the sake of my beloved daughter's magnanimous notions. . . . Therefore I must insist that what has happened be duly legitimized." A greater contrast between this loyalty to society on the one hand and von Bülow's condemnation of it as a "false god" on the other can hardly be possible. Nonetheless, the two positions belong together; both contribute to a discussion of the same theme. If one also includes Victoire's comment that "society reigns supreme. What it sanctions is valid, what it condemns is reprehensible," then one has in a minimum of space a complete lesson in social paradoxes. How to live with these contradictions is the question raised anew in each of Fontane's *Gesellschaftsromane*. Fontane's artistic style does not allow for solutions, but only for conversations which approach the question from different sides.

In *Count Petöfy* (*Graf Petöfy*, 1884), *Cécile* (1887), and *Beyond Recall* (*Unwiederbringlich*, 1892), the main characters also all commit suicide. The problems of love between members of different classes are treated in *Trials and Tribulations* (*Irrungen Wirrungen*, 1888) and *Stine* (1890). These novels take the reader into the milieu of the Berlin lower classes (as does the posthumous novel fragment *Mathilde Möhring*, 1914). *Stine*, artistically inferior to *Trials and Tribulations*, again ends with a suicide.

The cycle of *Eheromane* culminates in Fontane's most famous and widely read work, *Effi Briest* (1895). At the age of seventeen, Effi Briest is wed to her mother's former admirer, Baron von Innstetten, and is taken from the warm atmosphere of her parents' home and her circle of young friends into a gloomy, somewhat eerie governor's residence. Her husband's conduct is proper but insensitive. The young wife is left alone much of the time and must learn to hide her distress from her husband. Her liaison with Major Crampas, more a diversion than a strong emotional attachment, provides her with a brief escape and at the same time causes her great anxiety. She is relieved to end the affair when Innstetten is transferred to Berlin. Seven years later Innstetten discovers letters from Crampas, insists on a duel in which he kills the major, and then abandons Effi. Scorned by society and condemned by her parents, Effi lives with a good-hearted servant in a small Berlin apartment until an elderly doctor persuades her parents to let their sickly daughter return home. She dies there in peaceful contentment.

Effi's story is bound to its times. Both decisive plot elements—Effi's early marriage and Innstetten's reaction to the letters—stem from customs of the day which (here the narrator leaves no doubt) do not make for a sensible ordering of human affairs. Effi's marriage is questionable from the very beginning. The dialogues between mother and daughter before the wedding and between the parents afterward touch on all the delicate points. As soon as Effi is informed by her mother that Baron Innstetten has "asked for her hand," the reader knows that there will be problems. Effi's reaction is, "Asked for my hand? Truly?" Although Frau von Briest emphasizes that it is "not a matter to joke about," the question of the seriousness of the courtship would persist if this were not a *Gesellschaftsroman*. Only within the context of this genre can the almost unbelievable courtship be taken seriously. Like a matchmaker, Frau von Briest reminds her daughter that "if you don't say 'no,' which I can hardly imagine from my smart Effi, then by the time you're twenty you'll already have what others have at forty. You'll surpass your mother by far." Effi has neither the time nor the opportunity to consider her mother's recommendation, nor is she given any further explanation of the situation awaiting her. She is merely consulted one month before the wedding about her wishes for the dowry and ceremony. On this occasion she is also asked whether she loves Innstetten. Effi's answers regarding Innstetten are somewhat unsettling to her parents, or at least this is what they say in their discussion after the wedding. They point out that their daughter is pleasure-loving and ambitious. Since Innstetten is career minded, she should be satisfied. But Frau von Briest suddenly expresses the opinion that this is "only half." Effi's "penchant for play and adventure" will hardly be nourished and Innstetten will not particularly amuse her, nor will he try to help her alleviate boredom. When Effi realizes this, "she will be insulted. And then I don't know what will happen. For as gentle and compliant as she is, she can also be rabid." This is an accurate prophesy of Effi's life with Innstetten. What will happen is already interpreted here by her mother. In addition, Effi had answered the question whether she loved Innstetten very naively. Her father brings this up in the discussion with his wife and says that if Effi doesn't really love him, that "would be bad. For with all his good qualities, he is not the man to easily win her love." This is also an important foreshadowing of later events. Frau von Briest confirms her husband's feelings and admits that she also has her doubts. Upon observing Effi's cool reaction to a letter from Innstetten, her mother felt "her heart sink."

It is characteristic of the novel's style that these questions are discussed in such detail after the wedding, whereas they did not seem to be of importance beforehand when the decision was made. Then it was only a question of finding a good match. Of course, after the fact the Briests would have been very pleased to learn that Effi was content in her marriage. Not until after the wedding has taken place do they admit to the importance of her feelings and suddenly see all the potential dangers.

A comparison of the parents' dialogue after the wedding with the conversation between mother and daughter beforehand shows that Frau von Briest does not accurately repeat what her daughter tells her. Moreover, she conceals an important objection to Innstetten raised by Effi as well as her confession that she is afraid of him. After praising Innstetten, Effi admits, "And I could almost say I am entirely in favor of him, if he only . . . yes, if he were only a little different." According to the pastor, Innstetten is "a man of principles," while Effi says, "and I . . . I have none. You see, Mama, that is something that torments and worries me. He is so kind and good to me and so considerate, but . . . I'm afraid of him." Effi's clairvoyant fear is all too well founded. After her confession, the conversation breaks off; Frau von Briest does not reply. In both dialogues love is respected but fear ignored.

When Effi begins her married life, the story unfolds as has been anticipated in the conversations. It is now only a question of how it will happen. Major Crampas and the "ghost" in the house in Kessin as well as Innstetten's attitude towards the ghost all weave the net in which Effi is caught. She is extremely uncomfortable in her new home; since the first night, when she hears the sound of long curtains being swept across the floor by the wind in the room above her bedroom, she cannot free herself of the feeling that there is something strange all around her. After that night she suggests to her husband that the curtains be shortened or at least the windows closed. Later, when she realizes that she will often be left alone in the house, she requests that they move, for she feels particularly threatened by the ghost of a "Chinaman" who is buried in Kessin and, as Innstetten tells her, lived for a time in the house as a servant and friend of the former owner. In neither case does Innstetten comply with her wishes. His own attitude towards the ghost of the Chinaman remains ambiguous. As opposed to Effi, he does not want to be rid of it or get away from it. Effi's fear does not seem important to him. Later Effi learns from Crampas, who knew Innstetten from his military days, that Innstetten had thought the same way when in the regiment and enjoyed telling ghost stories. Aside from the fact that Innstetten's haunted house is something out of the ordinary which could help him in his career, Crampas believes that he uses it as a way of educating his young wife. Effi calls this "a calculated apparatus of fear" and says, "All warmheartedness was lacking and it almost bordered on cruelty."

Effi's relationship to the major is never described in detail. It is as if the narrator is reporting from a perspective which allows only Effi's reaction to her new experiences to be seen and not the experiences themselves. It is this reaction which is decisive to the narrator. The enchanting and transforming power of the secret liaison changes not only Effi's facial features but her entire person. Innstetten is slow to notice the change: "And how well you look! . . . You used to have something of the spoiled child and now all at once you look like a woman." After the interlude with Crampas has long faded into the past, it comes to light, and Innstetten acts as the "man of principles" Effi had feared when she hardly knew him. Like Botho von Rienäcker in *Trials and Tribulations*, he makes a decision contrary to his own wishes to satisfy society. Yet Innstetten conforms more consciously and resolutely than Botho, who simply sees no other choice and is pressured by the circumstances and his family to abandon the young girl he loves. Innstetten is not pressured by anyone; he renounces Effi merely on principle. He knows that he has a genuine alternative which is actually the only decent course of action: to forgive Effi. But his respect for the concept of society means more to him than his wife whom he still claims to love. Ingrid Mittenzwei sees Innstetten as a failure: "It was not Effi's responsibility to destroy the letters, but Innstetten's—as her husband, not as the baron. He fails because he puts the nobleman above the married man."[53] This is an accurate judgment from a humanitarian standpoint, regardless of whatever else one might say about the social system as a whole. Effi's statement at the end that Innstetten "was right in all he did" can be explained as the forgiveness of a dying woman and as the author's wish to glorify her. Nonetheless, the sharpest comment which can be directed against Innstetten in an *Eheroman* comes from Effi and is her last word on him: "as noble as anyone can be who has no real love."

Effi Briest has been compared with the great novels of passion—Gustave Flaubert's (1821–1880) *Madame Bovary* (1857) and Leo Tolstoy's (1828–1910) *Anna Karenina* (1873–76)—and has been criticized for its lack of passion. A comparison with Goethe's *Elective Affinities* could also result in the same criticism. Yet the degree of passion is certainly not a viable criterion for judging a work's quality, but merely serves to characterize it. *Effi Briest* is a genuine *Gesellschaftsroman*, insofar as the views of the society in which it is set are also its primary concern. Society is not the background for the novel's action but the theme itself. Here it is not passion but fear which is the main character's strongest emotion.

Before writing *Effi Briest*, the author had already moved beyond the genre of the *Eheroman* in its narrow sense with *Jenny Treibel* (*Frau Jenny Treibel*, 1893). Here he expressed his dislike for the bourgeoisie by showing the hypocrisy of a woman who constantly refers to her ideals, but actually is motivated only by greed and family pride. The reader is struck by the severity of Fontane's attack on her. The characters in Frau Treibel's circle are also depicted with scorn. Some are insignificant and weak, some ridiculous and silly, displaying pretentious and dishonest behavior. On the whole the work has more of a plot than Fontane's other novels.

Fontane structured his last two novels, *The Poggenpuhl Family* (*Poggenpuhls*, 1896) and *Stechlin* (1898), differently from his previous works. Of *The Poggenpuhl Family* the author said, "The book is not a novel and has no contents. The 'how' must take the place of the 'what'" (January 14, 1897, letter to Siegmund Schott). *The Poggenpuhl Family* is a delicate composition which presents a subtle world. A humanitarian atmosphere pervades all the relationships, in particular between servant and master. In *Stechlin* this atmosphere is largely attributable to the title character, Dubslav von Stechlin, of whom it is stated at the outset, "His finest quality was a deep humanitarianism that came straight from his heart." Everything Dubslav says and does throughout the book can be seen in this light. It is he who gives the work its inner cohesiveness, which has always been poorly understood by critics. Dubslav is not the main character with regard to the plot, nor is he the most active character. Yet from the very beginning he sets the tone by which everything is decided and judged. When Dubslav's son Woldemar describes his fiancée Armgard's family, he speaks of the similarities between his future father-in-law, Count Barby in Berlin, and his own father Dubslav: "the same Bismarck head, the same humane traits, the same friendliness, the same good spirits." They are most similar in "the entire atmosphere of their homes, the liberality." Woldemar says he knows no other man who is "inwardly as free" as his father and has "no trace of selfishness. And this beautiful trait (ah, so rare), the old count has it too."

A character of particular importance is Count Barby's older daughter Melusine. Beautiful and charming, she brings the lightness and joy of her personality to the drawing room conversations. Dubslav is very impressed by her. When her sister Armgard mentions this to her father after the two sisters have visited Dubslav, Count Barby considers it to be a good sign:

> There are so many people who have a natural hatred for every-
> thing charming, because they are so lacking in charm them-
> selves. All narrow and arrogantly stiff individuals . . . all phari-
> sees and would-be greats, all the self-righteous and vain feel injured
> and hurt by people like Melusine, and if old Stechlin has fallen
> in love with Melusine, then I already love him for it, because
> that means he is a good man.

Melusine provides the Barby home with a counterbalance to Dubslav's circle. The fact that the young pair, Armgard and Woldemar, and the other characters do not play a more prominent role has been faulted by critics and scholars. But this is entirely in keeping with the structure of a novel which is not concerned with single characters but with affinities that lie beneath the surface.

Fontane knew that in *Stechlin* he had deviated greatly from the traditional novel form. "In the end an old man dies and two young people marry; that is about all that happens in five hundred pages. There are no entanglements and solutions, no conflicts of the heart or conflicts at all, no tensions or surprises." Various persons "meet and discuss God and the world. Nothing but talk, dialogue . . . Naturally I think this is not only the correct, but indeed the only way to write a *Zeitroman*, yet at the same time I know only too well that the general public thinks otherwise" (letter draft to Adolf Hoffmann, Berlin, 1897). As with *Before the Storm* twenty years ago, Fontane again characterizes the distinctive quality of his work quite accurately. At that time he spoke of the *Vielheitsroman* (pluralistic novel) and defended it in a letter to Paul Heyse; now he describes the structure of his last novel in much the same way, declaring his procedure to be not only correct but also mandatory in light of his intentions. From his statements it is easy to see how similar the two novels are. It is not surprising that now as before he has no illusions about the limited appeal of his work.

Discerning readers have always appreciated *Stechlin*. In 1920 Thomas Mann said that upon rereading Fontane's late work he was "delighted . . .

enchanted!" One word was "constantly on my lips: 'sublime.' "[54] Ten years earlier he had written to Maximilian Harden, *"Effi Briest is in my judgment still the best German novel since Elective Affinities.* What else was and is there?" (August 30, 1910). Weighing the quality of one against the other, he explained to Conrad Wandrey, "And there it stands: If *Effi Briest* extends furthest beyond Fontane's epoch in a social-ethical sense, then *Stechlin* does so artistically."

Thomas Mann's Buddenbrooks *and Its Time*

Three years after *Stechlin,* Thomas Mann's (1875–1955) *Buddenbrooks, Decline of a Family (Buddenbrooks, Verfall einer Familie,* 1901) appeared. It was the first novel of an author who was to be productive all his life and accorded international acclaim. Since *Buddenbrooks* is close to Fontane's last novels in time and similar in style and content, a comparison is unavoidable. In many respects, the novel creates the impression that Fontane's artistry has been continued, that its author is a younger, more energetic brother of the now tired representative of the late nineteenth-century novel. Young Tony Buddenbrook's marriage can certainly be seen as a variation of the *Effi Briest* theme, and the death of the aged Dubslav Stechlin as a prelude to the many deaths in the Buddenbrook family. If one considers 1901, the year of publication of *Buddenbrooks,* to be a turning point—in historical research this is a widely accepted practice—then one must ask the question: to which of the two centuries does the work belong? (When the advance copy of Fontane's *Stechlin* appeared, October–December 1897, Thomas Mann had already begun planning *Buddenbrooks.*) Those who include it in the nineteenth century, and there are many who do so, have to admit that the nineteenth century then stretches far into the twentieth, for the style of *Buddenbrooks* can still be heard in Thomas Mann's last works. Of course centuries, insofar as they are regarded as spiritual epochs, cannot be defined by exact dates. Not only are the boundaries fluid, but many phenomena remain alive for long periods of time. Why shouldn't the nineteenth-century style continue until the midtwentieth century, especially in the case of the elderly Thomas Mann? However, it is not that simple. *Buddenbrooks* not only contains elements passed down to its author, but it anticipates much of what is to come. It represents an entire epoch which did not end in 1901; rather, 1901 is more its middle point. The modernity of *Buddenbrooks*'s theme and style can only be recognized when one considers the novels written in the decade immediately following it.

The contrast between the works of Thomas Mann and those of his brother, Heinrich Mann (1871–1950), is great. Heinrich Mann's satirical distortion of the Wilhelmine Age in novels such as *In the Land of Cockaigne* (*Im Schlaraffenland*, 1900), *Small Town Tyrant* (*Professor Unrat*, 1905), and *Man of Straw* (*Der Untertan*, 1918) was quite foreign to his brother. The differences in style can be demonstrated by comparing Heinrich Mann's *Small Town Tyrant* with the chapter on Hanno's school day in *Buddenbrooks*. Heinrich Mann's destructive criticism destroys not only the teacher but the entire theme as well. Professor Raat's tyrannical attitude towards his students is grotesque and condemns itself. His personality is unique. Therefore readers might enjoy his story and become involved with the other characters as well, but this interest comes to an end when they finish the book. By contrast, the school chapter in *Buddenbrooks* is more universal and expresses in classic form a theme of great importance to the twentieth century. Heinrich Mann's other *Gesellschaftsromane*, such as the earlier work *The Hunt for Love* (*Die Jagd nach Liebe*, 1903) and his later novels, *The Poor* (*Die Armen*, 1917) and *The Head* (*Der Kopf*, 1925) all exhaust themselves in destructive criticism of their times. *The Little Town* (*Die kleine Stadt*, 1909) is a more balanced composition which attempts to present an alternative to the Wilhelmine society in an Italian milieu. Also written in reference to contemporary happenings was the historical novel *Henri Quatre*, published by Mann in two volumes while in exile: *Young Henry of Navarre* (*Die Jugend des Königs Henri Quatre*, 1935) and *Henry, King of France* (*Die Vollendung des Königs Henri Quatre*, 1938). *Henri Quatre* is Heinrich Mann's most important work, yet it shows the author's limited relationship to literary tradition. Whereas Fontane's historical novel was an artistic experiment, the product of a long confrontation with Scott, Alexis, and Freytag, Heinrich Mann was concerned above all with subject matter. That is what separates him from Thomas Mann, who was an artist of language and had a gift for working productively with traditional forms.

Ricarda Huch (1864–1947) was also sensitive to tradition. Eight years before *Buddenbrooks* she had already published a novel about the decline of a bourgeois family, *The Recollections of Ludolf Ursleu the Younger* (*Erinnerungen von Ludolf Ursleu dem Jüngeren*, 1893). In *Vita somnium breve* (1903), later retitled *Michael Unger* (1913), she again takes up the theme of her first novel, but this time the plot does not lead to a downfall. The "life sketches" of the poor and outcast in *From Triumph Alley* (*Aus der Triumphgasse*, 1902) deal with the longing for beauty and love. *Of Kings and the Crown* (*Von den Königen und der Krone*, 1904) as well as the Garibaldi stories, including *The Defense of Rome* (*Die Verteidigung Roms*, 1906) and *Garibaldi and the New Italy* (*Der Kampf um Rom*, 1908), are characterized by a turn to history and loosening of the plot structure. *The Life of Count Federigo Confalonieri* (*Das Leben des Grafen Federigo Confalonieri*, 1910), which leads the reader into Italian history in the first half of the nineteenth century, has a stricter epic form. Artistically, Huch's most important work is *The Thirty Years' War* (*Der grosse Krieg in Deutschland*, 1912–14). A history of this war, it could well be termed a *Vielheitsroman*. Ricarda Huch was one of the first German women to study at a university, and she was awarded a doctorate in history from Zurich. She began her career as a lyricist. At the turn of the century she pursued scholarly research on the history of Romanticism and became one of the leading representatives of the Neo-Romantic movement. Her books *The Golden Age of Romanticism* (*Blütezeit der Romantik*, 1899) and *Growth and Decline of Romanticism* (*Ausbreitung und Verfall der Romantik*, 1902) were long considered standard works.

The novels of Friedrich Huch (1873–1913) express another possibility of the epoch. *Peter Michel* (1901), which appeared in the same year as *Buddenbrooks*, is evidence of the author's originality. It is the story of a simple, affable man who extricates himself from a modest, yet difficult environment but is ultimately engulfed by such a world again. The next four novels followed in rapid succession: *The Siblings* (*Die Geschwister*, 1903), *Changes* (*Wandlungen*, 1905), *Mao* (1907), and *Enzio* (1910). Remote from the everyday world, the characters in these novels are preoccupied with themselves and their feelings and at the mercy of their finely tuned sensitivities. Problems of music and art hold captive those who are susceptible. All the characters are attracted to death, which seems to be the fulfillment of a tired life. Whereas Felicitas in *The Siblings* dies of illness, the sensitive boy, Thomas, in *Mao* ends his own life after everything that meant home and security to him has been taken away. Enzio, a talented musician, beautiful and loved, also takes his own life.

Pitt and Fox (1909) is Friedrich Huch's most substantial work. The two brothers, Pitt and Fox Sintrup, represent different possibilities of human behavior. They grow up in an affluent manufacturer's family. Fox, the younger of the two, begins early to conform to the shallow morality of his environment. An opportunist, he realizes that in a society in which everyone practices deceit, participating oneself is the quickest way to success. Pitt on the other hand lives as a stranger among strangers and withdraws even as a child. He is a difficult man, without plans or goals, a restless searcher filled with a fear of bourgeois ties. Two women characters whose progressive views are particularly interesting are Pitt's friends, the artist Herta and the musician Elfriede.

Robert Walser (1878–1956) also focuses on the restless, driven young man. His style resembles that of Friedrich Huch, but language as such is a much more decisive element than in Huch's works and takes priority over any particular theme. Regardless of the situation, the searching youth reveals himself in his manner of speech. In the first novel, *The Siblings Tanner* (*Geschwister Tanner*, 1907), the main character, Simon, speaks so convincingly that one feels compelled to listen even though what he says has little substance and is really only talk. On the first page of the novel, after only a few introductory sentences from the narrator, Simon plunges into one of his speeches. He outlines his credentials to the owner of a bookstore: "I'm a born salesman: gallant, alert, polite, fast, blunt, decisive, mathematical, attentive, and honest—but not as stupidly honest as I might look." After going on like this for awhile, he is hired. Just one week later he quits the job, again with a hearty speech. He doesn't like his desk and paperwork is not really for him. "You have disappointed me," he tells the proprietor. "Don't have such an astonished look on your face; it can't be helped. I'm leaving your business today and ask that you pay me my wages." Simon's continuing search for jobs and his temporary employment in various professions afford the opportunity for aggressive speech, and the reader learns, "I haven't the time to stay in one and the same profession . . . and it would never occur to me to rest, like so many others, on one type of career as if on a featherbed." All the situations in which Simon finds himself evoke commentary and monologues.

Like Simon in Walser's first novel, both Joseph in *The Assistant* (*Der Gehülfe*, 1908) and Jakob in *Jakob von Gunten. A Diary* (*Jakob von Gunten. Ein Tagebuch*, 1909) enter voluntarily, yet nonetheless pressured by their situation of homelessness, into a dependent relationship which causes them internal conflict. While the *Siblings Tanner* presents a series of episodes that all follow the same course—subjugation and liberation—the two other novels focus on a single struggle. *The Assistant* begins with Joseph Marti's appearance at the home office of the industrialist Tobler, to whom he had been referred by an employment agency. With his new job, Joseph is also accepted into the family. He not only has to maintain a proper relationship with his employer, a somewhat coarse, but good-natured, jovial man, but must also get along with his employer's wife and somehow do justice to the demands of a business heading for collapse. Tobler designs fantastic, useless objects, and since he is not able to raise the necessary funds for their manufacture, he falls deeper and deeper into debt. Joseph Marti's activity is gradually reduced to the single task of turning away creditors, while all the time living well and enjoying excellent food and plenty of cigars. As the work in the office decreases he takes on responsibilities in the house and garden, which in no way burden him. The generous and luxurious life style of the Tobler home is preserved to the end. What troubles Joseph is his work situation: he constantly sways between self-confidence and subjugation. He feels protected and supported by his position and membership in the Tobler home. But he is afraid of Tobler, whose "presence always made Joseph fear a scene. Yes, this man had a look about him as if something were being held back. . . . It was as if it might break out any minute." Joseph is in conflict with himself over his situation until the very end. He rebels and then always gives in again. Frau Tobler, who at first seemed arrogant to him, becomes his confidante. He feels that the house is his home and knows at the same time that he "belonged to a house that was slowly ceasing to exist." After Tobler has a fit of rage on New Year's Day, Joseph packs his belongings and leaves.

The Berlin educational institution of Herr Benjamenta in *Jakob von Gunten* is also farcical and near collapse. Jakob, the first person narrator, requested to be admitted there after having run away from his father. The book, written in the form of a diary, begins, "One learns very little here. There are not enough teachers, and we boys from the Institute Benjamenta will never amount to anything, that is, we will all be something very small and subordinate in later life. The instruction we receive consists mainly of indoctrinating us with the virtues of patience and obedience, two traits which promise little or no success." Jakob confesses that he wishes for quite the opposite; he would like "to be rich, travel in droshkies and waste money." Yet the pupils are all alike in one regard, "in their complete poverty and dependence." In the course of the diary one gets to know individual pupils, learns something about the customs in the school, about Jakob's trips to the city, and, above all, about his thoughts. A model pupil is the young Kraus, who is particularly talented in obedience and plans to become a servant. The headmaster favors Jakob, assures him of his affection, and yet makes it clear to him that he is completely in his control. Early in the novel we learn that "Herr Benjamenta is a giant, and we pupils are dwarfs by comparison." The institution heads for collapse and the teacher, Fräulein Lisa, with whom Jakob was also personally involved, dies. In the end Jakob agrees to stay with the headmaster and go into the desert with him.

Franz Kafka thought highly of Robert Walser and called *Jakob von Gunten* "a good book" (letter to Eisner, 1909?). Walter Benjamin, who devoted an essay to Walser, says that Walser's characters come "from insanity. . . . They are characters whose insanity is behind them. . . . They are all cured."[55] Since Robert Walser himself spent many years in a sanatorium, such an interpretation seems obvious. Yet it does not entirely explain the novel's events. The ease and freedom with which the young boys move and speak is their dominant trait. Still the question remains: to what extent does this enable them to assert themselves against their superiors and to defeat the system. After all, in the last two novels the power structure collapses on its own rather than as a result of protest or rebellion on the part of the young boys. Besides, the power structure is often accommodating and friendly; by no means is it absolutely evil, but rather an unpleasant nuisance.

Robert Walser's novels are excellent examples of originality in portraying a certain type of adolescent. As such, they are important to an understanding of the history of the German novel in the first decade of the twentieth century, in particular with respect to the classification of *Buddenbrooks*. Works equal in quality with a similar theme are Friedrich Huch's *Mao* and Robert Musil's important narrative, *Young Törless (Die Verwirrungen des Zöglings Törless*, 1906). Whereas in *Törless* and Walser's *Jakob von Gunten* the theme of adolescent psychology is illuminated by concentrating on the problem of boarding school education, *Mao* focuses on the sensitive individual. It is a known fact that for Robert Musil and Rainer Maria Rilke the boarding school years meant a great deal of suffering and had lasting repercussions. Musil's own experiences are the basis for his treatment of the theme in fiction.

This is also true of Hermann Hesse (1877–1962). His flight at fourteen from the seminary at Maulbronn is reflected in his novel *Beneath the Wheel* (*Unterm Rad*, 1906). Here insensitive teachers and parents drive a good-natured boy to suicide, while another boy breaks out in search of his own direction in life. An earlier work, *Peter Camenzind* (1904), is a story of *Bildung* reminiscent of Gottfried Keller's *Green Henry*. It begins in the idyll and returns to it. Emil Sinclair in *Demian. The Story of a Youth by Emil Sinclair* (*Demian. Die Geschichte einer Jugend von Emil Sinclair*, 1919) is also a youthful searcher. Hesse returned to the same theme again and again, making use of romantic and oriental elements as well as vague symbols derived from his long psychiatric treatment. In ingratiating language and conven-, tional images, he deals with general questions of human development whose fictional treatment had been appreciated by wide circles of German readers since the last third of the eighteenth century and found an international audience in the twentieth century. Hesse's later novels, *Steppenwolf* (*Der Steppenwolf*, 1927), *Narcissus and Goldmund* (*Narziss und Goldmund*, 1930), and *The Glass Bead Game* (*Das Glasperlenspiel*, 1943), once more deal with the same theme, inherited from the age of Classicism and Romanticism, of discovering one's identity. Hesse heightened the theme by incorporating modern psychological and anthropological insights, and at the same time he made it conform to the level of understanding of a broad audience.

In Thomas Mann's own words, when he wrote *Buddenbrooks* he was really only interested in the "story of the sensitive latecomer Hanno and possibly that of Thomas Buddenbrook." The theme of the sensitive boy was timely and continued to capture the imagination of authors for years to come. It was a theme of the new century, even though Conrad Ferdinand Meyer had presented it earlier in his novella, *The Sufferings of a Boy* (*Das Leiden eines Knaben*, 1883). In the new century, reform movements were begun in schools with the purpose of easing the hard life of young boys. Thomas Mann's criticism of the school in which Hanno Buddenbrook spends dreadful hours corresponded to the convictions of leading twentieth-century pedagogues. The chapter which relates a day in the life of little Johann demonstrates why this type of school, which places primary emphasis on learning by memorization, is destructive, not only for boys of Hanno's temperament but for all young people. It is even harmful for the versatile Kai von Mölln, who observes the goings-on with a knowing smile. This type of school, which forced teachers and pupils into a system of domination and subjugation, is a complete distortion of pedagogical ideals. Thomas Mann's description of the Latin class shows how for many boys cheating becomes the only way out of a threatening situation. Hanno's own dishonest behavior makes him physically ill, and the deleterious effect on the others' development is obvious. By describing Hanno's entire day and not just the school hours, Thomas Mann shows the split in the boy's life and illustrates the relationship between the general theme of inhumanity in school with the seemingly more specific theme of spiritualization. In Hanno's case, spiritualization is connected with a natural musicality which his mother has always encouraged. The fact that spiritualization was actually not a theme peculiar to this one case but rather a "part of the intellectual history of the European bourgeoisie" later surprised Thomas Mann greatly. In a speech delivered in his home town of Lübeck, Thomas Mann said: "One gives what is most personal and is surprised to have hit on something national. One gives what is most national—and look, one has hit on the general and human."[56]

In the same chapter one is reminded that schools were not always like the one Hanno attends. When Hanno's father and uncle were pupils, they had a "jovial and kind old gentleman" as director, and classical education was an end in itself, pursued with "ease, leisure, and cheerful idealism." In a letter written in 1930 to Walther Rehm, Thomas Mann expressed thanks for a book, saying, "The spirit of humanism emanating from it flatters my deepest instincts; it is as if I am touching native soil. This is where I am still at home, that is, in the nineteenth century, although it was already in decline when I was born." The background story of Hanno's short life has to tell of those times in which the author believed he was still at home. The native soil which was lost had to be reevoked in order to show what is meant by the "decline." That the background story took on its own "very independent, self-sufficient life" can be attributed to the author's sense of history.

Judging strictly from content, one could falsely conclude that the work is a historical novel and a novel of "fine society" as well. Indeed, it spans the years between 1835 and 1877, hence conforming to the subtitle of Scott's *Waverley, 'Tis Sixty Years Since*, and meeting Fontane's requirement: "The novel should be a picture of the times in which we live, at least the reflection of a time at whose border we ourselves have stood or of which our parents have spoken." It can hardly be assumed that Thomas Mann was familiar with Fontane's article on Gustav Freytag, from which this quotation was taken, or was influenced by Fontane or Sir Walter Scott in any other way in his choice of time setting. His decision was most likely determined by his sense of being existentially bound to the time upon whose border he himself stood, to the life of which his parents had spoken. After all, his intention was to describe the background of his own inner life. *Buddenbrooks* is not a historical novel but rather is concerned with modern consciousness.

For his theme of decline and spiritualization Thomas Mann needed to call up from history the picture of a content, well-to-do burgher family living in a free, imperial city. The social gathering with which the novel opens introduces three generations of such a family with their circle of friends. The occasion is a housewarming celebration in the stately home on Meng Street. In reproducing the dinner table conversation, the author takes the opportunity to present, at an early stage, the problem of family downfall. The topic of conversation is the previous owners of the Buddenbrooks' home, the Ratenkamps, who had lived there since 1682. They experienced a brilliant rise to success, but over the last twenty years all were witness to the sad decline of their firm. "The conversation came to a silence that lasted for a half minute. Each person looked at his plate and thought of this once so illustrious family which had built and lived in the house, but had come so far down in the world and had moved out in poverty." Debate follows on whether the reasons for the failure are to be seen simply in the choice of a bad business partner or if the opposite was true, that is, that the poor choice was a result of the decline already in process.

While the first part of the novel serves as a prelude in which many of the work's motifs are touched upon, the actual story begins with the deaths of the elder Buddenbrook and his wife in the second part. The flourishing business passes into the hands of the second son, Consul Jean Buddenbrook. It is his four children, Thomas, Christian, Tony, and Clara, on whom the greater part of the novel focuses. They grow up before the reader's eyes and are the generation leading into the family's decline. Tony marries and divorces twice, bringing great misfortune upon herself and the family. Clara, considerably younger than the others, marries a pastor and dies at an early age of cerebral tuberculosis. Christian shows neurotic signs even as a young boy. He is unable to find footing in a profession, spends years abroad in England and South America, and upon his return attempts halfheartedly to work in the Buddenbrooks' firm. He socializes in bachelors' clubs and leads a life outside the bourgeois society, but marries a bourgeois woman who ultimately has him committed to a mental institution.

After Jean Buddenbrook's death, Thomas becomes head of the firm. As the oldest son, he was groomed for the firm from an early age and fulfills his duties superbly. His reputation is excellent, and he becomes the first member of the family to be elected to the senate. However, a nervousness and frail health unknown to the older generation begin to show themselves early. His pungent Russian cigarettes, exaggerated concern about his wardrobe, and a certain haste in later years when carrying out projects such as the building of a new house are all interpreted by the narrator as indications of an easily weakened nature. It becomes apparent that the danger to him and the Buddenbrook family comes from a sphere which lies outside the business world and did not exist for the earlier generations. Thomas's wife, Gerda Arnoldsen from Amsterdam, is a representative of this sphere. Her unusual and elegant appearance is expressed in leitmotivs. When she approaches her mother-in-law for the first time in the Meng Street home, the narrator states,

> Gerda, who walked across the bright carpet with free and proud grace, was tall and sensual. With her heavy, dark red hair, her closely set brown eyes beset by bluish shadows, the wide, shimmering teeth which she showed in a smile, her straight, strong nose and her wonderful, nobly shaped mouth, this twenty-seven-year-old girl possessed an elegant, strange, haunting beauty.

Thomas is well aware that he has taken an unconventional step in his choice of a bride. It is a telling sign that in their first dinner conversation he and Gerda soon leave "the realm of old anecdotes" and turn "to more serious and captivating matters," to music, Dutch painting, and literature.

Thomas becomes aware of his own downfall at a time when, as seen from the outside, he has just reached the pinnacle of his success. Within just a few years what he knows can no longer be hidden: "that Thomas Buddenbrook, at age forty-two, was an exhausted man." Already sympathetic to death, he reads Schopenhauer's chapter "On Death and its Relation to Our Personal Immortality." In his testament he arranges for the dissolution of the firm and dies a few months later when he collapses on the street following an unsuccessful treatment of a bad tooth.

Thomas Mann attached great importance to the statement that "Thomas Buddenbrook's life . . . is the life of a modern hero" (August 31, 1910, letter to Julius Bab). The "exhausted Thomas Buddenbrook's determination to keep up a dignified appearance" shows a "great deal of heroism" (March 28, 1906, letter to Kurt Martens). This idea preoccupied Thomas Mann for years and found expression again, but in a different form, in *Death in Venice* (1912). Here Thomas Mann said that it is the sufferer alone who has the possibility of a heroic demeanor; it is

> questionable whether there is any heroism other than that of weakness. In any case which heroism is more timely than this one? Gustav Aschenbach was the poet of all those who work at the verge of exhaustion, the overburdened, already worn out, still holding themselves upright, all these moralists of achievement who, slight of figure and scarce of means . . . win at least for a time the effects of greatness.

Whereas Thomas Buddenbrook only gradually, over the course of years, comes to experience the suffering which makes him a modern hero, his son Hanno suffers from earliest childhood. Plagued by sickness, troubled by his relationship to his father, and out of place at school, Hanno comes alive only in his music. But music cannot counteract the unhappiness in his life, and at the age of sixteen he dies of typhoid fever.

The narrator's seemingly objective description of the typhoid disease and his silence about Hanno's death are actually signs of extreme emotion. The reader learns that in a certain stage of the disease the doctor cannot say if it has been caused by an infection, whether it can be combated by the resources of medical science, "or if it is quite simply a form of dissolution, the attire of death itself, which could just as well appear in another mask." Similarly, at the beginning of the novel it was impossible to decide whether the bad management on the part of the Ratenkamps' partner was the cause or effect of the family's ruin.

PART TWO

THE
TWENTIETH-CENTURY
GERMAN NOVEL

4 / New Forms of the Novel

The Notebooks of Malte Laurids Brigge (Die Aufzeichnungen des Malte Laurids Brigge, 1910) by Rainer Maria Rilke (1875–1926) is the first German novel to give shape to the new artistic will of the twentieth century. It is concerned with the attempt of the "sensitive latecomer," Malte Laurids Brigge, to survive and find a new beginning in a world of sickness and death. This theme is reminiscent of that of Thomas Mann's Buddenbrooks, as is the narrative material that Rilke used to develop his theme. Not only does the reader get to know Malte, the fictitious author of the Notebooks, but also a large circle of his relatives from two previous generations and their mode of life. However, Mann and Rilke introduce the two families in completely different ways. Unlike Mann, Rilke does not show the generations in succession, nor does he give a comprehensive summary of Malte's origins. Malte's parents, grandparents, aunts, uncles, and children appear in his memories as people who played a role in his childhood and made an impression on him for various reasons; in some cases he knew them only from what he had heard from others. Their place in the Notebooks is determined by their meaning and function within the total composition. Since the work disregards temporal succession, the age and generation of the characters do not affect their placement in the narrative. Similarly, Malte's attempt to find a new beginning is not told as a story using conventional techniques. There is no chronological progression which can be brought to a conclusion with definable results. The reader is directly involved in Malte's endeavors, but often he does not have enough information to understand them; he must draw his own conclusions and sense the relationships himself. Nor is he told in the end whether Malte's attempt is successful or not. The reader has no way of knowing what eventually becomes of Malte, but, as far as the novel itself is concerned, the question is not important. This, too, is further evidence of the newness of its form. In Rilke's letters one does find the suggestion that Malte went to ruin, though the relevant passages leave some room for doubt. From the novel itself, it would seem that this is not the case, since it is Malte himself who speaks until the very end of the Notebooks. In later parts he merely withdraws from an active role in the narrative and writes about other characters instead of speaking directly about himself. In this way he can clarify his ideas in an attempt to define his existence.

The personal life of the narrator, like everything else, is not presented to the reader cohesively; it must be pieced together from occasional remarks. The twenty-eight-year-old Dane, Malte Laurids Brigge, descended from respected nobility on both sides of the family, lives alone in Paris under oppressive conditions. His room is poorly heated and shabbily furnished. He wanders for hours through the city, reads for long periods in the library, visits museums, and takes his meals in the most inexpensive small restaurants. He usually feels faint and is often ill, at times going to a doctor or just lying in bed with a fever. With regard to his past, we learn that Schloss Ulsgaard, the Brigge's property where Malte spent his childhood, and Schloss Urnekloster, where at age twelve or thirteen he spent a few weeks with his maternal grandfather, Count Brahe, have both passed into new hands.

The *Notebooks* is written in the form of a diary in which Malte enters his thoughts as they occur to him. In a much-quoted letter Rilke said, "It is as if one found disordered papers in a drawer and, finding no more at the moment, had to be satisfied. From an artistic point of view, this is poor unity, but in human terms it is possible, and what emerges is nonetheless a sketch of life and the shadow network of forces astir" (April 11, 1910, to Countess Manon zu Solms-Laubach).[1] Short and medium-length prose sections, which in most cases do not seem logically joined, follow one another. They contain Malte's present experiences in Paris, childhood memories, personal observations on history, literature, and art, and his reflections. He begins one theme, then drops it. Then he begins a second and a third. Suddenly the second theme and perhaps the first are continued again. In the first of the two parts into which the *Notebooks* is divided, there are dates which suggest—within the fictional context—that the entries are being presented in the order they were written. The first section is headed by the date September 11, and we have the impression it was written after Malte's first walk through the city. In the fourth section we learn that Malte has been in Paris for three weeks. Mention is made in the eleventh section of an autumn morning and of carnival time in the sixteenth and eighteenth sections. Such references, which are no longer found in the later sections, do not, however, contribute to establishing a time frame. Malte only mentions them in passing as he attempts to come to terms with himself.

With the help of his experiences in Paris, Malte frees himself from traditional ideas and struggles for a new life. After three weeks in the city, he realizes that he is "learning to see" in a new way; everything affects him more deeply than before. "I have an inner self of which I was unaware. Everything goes there now. What happens there I do not know." His reports of what he sees on the streets come from this inner self: "I recognize everything here, and therefore it enters my heart so easily; it is at home in me." As he observes the outcast and dying on the streets of Paris, what he sees occurs not only in the city but in his mind. He can perceive and recognize the visible happenings because they already exist within him; a division between his inner and outer worlds does not exist. Thus it does not seem appropriate to speak of Malte's "subjective world";[2] the terms "objective" and "subjective" no longer apply to this novel. Instead, *Malte Laurids Brigge* shows how the relationship between consciousness and reality has changed in modern literature.

The speaker and his subject flow together throughout the entire novel. There is no distinction made between the two. Malte's memories affect him in the same way as his immediate experiences on the street. When he tries to explain what he remembers of Schloss Urnekloster, he says, "It is not a building, it is all divided up inside me; here a room, there a room . . . everything dispersed within me. . . . That room alone . . . is completely preserved in my heart." For Malte places as different as Urnekloster and Paris are connected, and people far apart in time and space also exist side by side. His grandfather, Count Brahe, had experienced people of different ages and generations similarly: "Time sequence was of no importance to him whatsoever." Furthermore, in the same way that people from Malte's past are joined with his present, so are historical figures from chronicles, such as Charles VI of France, Charles the Bold of Burgundy, the czar-pretender Grishka Otrepioff, and many others.[3] Malte relates to them in much the same way as he does to Baudelaire's poem "Une Charogne," the tapestries of the Dame à la Licorne in the museum at Cluny, Bettine, and the legend of the prodigal son.

The *Notebooks* ends with the familiar story of the prodigal son, which Malte introduces as follows: "It would be difficult to convince me that the story of the prodigal son is not the legend of one who did not want to be loved." In retelling the story, Malte modifies it to conform to his own personal situation. Whereas the significance of the biblical story lies in God's grace which makes it possible for the prodigal son to return home at any time, Malte emphasizes the necessity of the son's departure and justifies it as a spiritual process. Malte's own spiritual process also demands solitude. The changes he undergoes in Paris, which, he observes, have already started three weeks after his arrival, are only possible "at the cost of being alone." He speaks of a "completely different view of all things," of "a changed world, a new life full of new meaning." In the beginning, these changes are related to Malte's experience with the wretched and poor of Paris. For him, the significance of this experience lies in the opportunity to see the essence in this "terribleness and seemingly total repulsiveness." He thinks of his Paris experience as part of the general horror surrounding humanity. "The existence of atrociousness in every particle of the air, . . . all the misery and terror there has been in places of execution, torture chambers, madhouses, operating rooms, under bridge arches in late autumn: all this is of a tenacious immortality." Malte believes that in his childhood his mother shielded him from this horror by the mere power of her existence.

The protective and at the same time restrictive role that family and house have in the legend is also alluded to in the sections of the *Notebooks* which unfold the world of Malte's childhood following the appearance of his mother. The way in which the mother is introduced is characteristic of Rilke's entire style. When the silence of the night evokes an atmosphere of horror, Malte says,

> O silence in the staircase, silence from the adjoining rooms, silence high up on the ceiling. O mother, O you alone who removed all this silence, long ago in my childhood. She who takes the silence upon herself says, don't be frightened, I am here. . . . You strike a light and already the sound is you. . . . You are the light around the familiar, intimate things.

His mother, a very delicate woman, was not equal to this atmosphere of fear in later years and died young. She never appears as a clearly profiled person, as do Thomas Mann's characters. Many of her traits are revealed to the reader, yet she remains shadowy, which makes her credible as a figure from Malte's memory. Rilke was careful to portray all of Malte's other relatives in the same way, a type of characterization that marks the beginning of a new literary style.

The legend of the prodigal son, a chronological story composed by Malte, should not be used to construct an analogous story for Malte himself. The external facts alone indicate that this would be out of place. Malte's situation in Paris is not identical to the departure of the son in the legend. Malte's relatives die. Their homes do not offer him the possibility of return, a fact which he often mentions with regret in the first parts of the novel. In addition, Malte's experiences do not constitute a story, as was emphasized at the beginning of this chapter. He finds himself in Paris, notices very soon that he is changing under the effect of the city, and, upon realizing this, begins to write. In conventional terms, the plot develops when he begins to write. "I have done something about my fear. I sat the whole night and wrote," he says after just a few weeks. After writing continuously and drawing from many realms of life, he finally ends the *Notebooks* with the legend, a variation of his own case, and in doing so shows acceptance of his situation. In retrospect, he interprets this situation as necessary and appropriate because he sees solitude—which for him means lonely endurance in the face of horror—as the only way to gain new insights.

In the case of the character created by Malte, horror is only one stage on a long path which ends with the attempt to return. Malte says of his character, whom he simply calls "he," that as a young boy "he" felt his family forced him through their love to be something that he was not. He "stood under the suggestive power of their love day and night, between their hopes and suspicions, before their censure or praise." When wandering about alone

one day, the "secret of his life that never yet had been" was revealed to him, and he was afraid to return home because they were waiting for him in order to force him to be a certain person again. Malte as narrator asks the question: "Will he stay and live out the lie they ascribe to him . . . ? Will he divide himself between the delicate truthfulness of his will and the coarse deceit that spoils it for him?" The answer is: "No, he will go away. . . . Go away forever." This means that he can now be open to all the changes he might undergo. The endless expanses he traverses are the expanses of his mind which he recognizes in the visible world. Only his childhood still seems unconquered in the end. This is the reason "the estranged son returned home." The fact that his leaving is forgiven shows that he is still not understood. Malte says, "It must have been indescribably liberating for him that everyone misunderstood him. . . . From day to day he became more aware that the love of which they were so vain . . . did not apply to him." The outcome of his return justifies his departure.

In the *Notebooks*, the counterpart to the prodigal son is the woman in love. This is evident from the individual sections devoted to her as well as from her place within the work's structure. Rilke was occupied for years with historical figures of great women in love. He speaks of them in long letters and also in the *Duino Elegies (Duineser Elegien)*. From their example he came to understand how they grow beyond the beloved who has abandoned them and how the entire strength of their love radiates from them when they endure what has happened as lonely women, busy with some occupation or other. For Malte, the woman who loves and is alone becomes a present reality in the desolation of Paris when he reminisces about Abelone, his mother's youngest sister, a woman important to him in his youth. Abelone is the last in a series of relatives presented in the first part of the *Notebooks*, and a special section is devoted to her. A figure corresponding to her appears in the tapestries described by Malte: "There are tapestries here, Abelone, wall tapestries. I imagine that you are here, there are six tapestries, come, let us walk past slowly." In each of the tapestries there is an "oval blue island," on which there is "always a figure, a woman in different dress, but always the same woman. Sometimes there is a smaller figure next to her, a maid servant; and the heraldic animals are always there, large, also on the island, part of the scene." The heraldic animals are a lion and a unicorn. The woman is always occupied with something: "She feeds the falcon. . . . She weaves a garland." She plays the organ; she takes a necklace from a chest. "She holds the banner herself." In the last tapestry she shows the unicorn its reflection in a mirror. The section ends, "Do you understand, Abelone? I think you must understand."

It becomes clear here that Rilke has very consciously ordered the "disordered papers"; he describes the woman in the tapestries in the last section of the first part of the novel and tells the story of the prodigal son in the last section of the second part. The wall tapestries are the bridge between the two parts as well as the center of the *Notebooks*, for not only do they end the first part, but they begin the second. The new section opens by pointing out that the tapestries of the Dame à la Licorne no longer hang in the old castle for which they were designed and woven, but in a museum: "The time has arrived when everything is coming out of the old houses. They can no longer keep anything." The tapestries bring Malte to the topic of the modern girls who linger before them: "In the museums there are a great many young girls who have left homes somewhere that no longer keep anything." These modern girls begin to sketch before the tapestries, for that is why they "left home one day, rather violently." Nevertheless, they sometimes wonder "whether it would not have been possible to stay after all," but decide that it is better to sketch: "Now that so much is changing, they want to change, too." After centuries of woman's dedication to love, they have grown weary, Malte says, and are no longer willing to lead the kind of life shown on the tapestries. Departure, then, is the overall theme with which the second part of the *Notebooks* begins. The two thematic motifs—the women in love and the prodigal son—are overlapping and interwoven in that the departure of the girls foreshadows the prodigal son's departure. Malte himself asks whether men could not also begin "to learn the labor of love." Throughout the entire second part both motifs recur again and again, illustrated by new characters. Other motifs obscure them for a time and then allow them to become visible again.

Malte speaks directly to and about his age. It can be established that everything in the novel takes place in the same present time; moreover, this present time is a concrete era which is readily recognizable. The artistic girls in Paris who left their families are figures from the early twentieth century. At the time he wrote *Malte*, Rilke knew about the life of independent women from personal experience. He was married to the sculptress Clara Westhoff (1878–1954), was a friend of the painter Paula Becker-Modersohn (1876–1907) until her death, and had a close relationship with the author Lou Andreas-Salomé (1861–1937) for decades. In her two novels, *Ruth* (1895) and *Ma* (1901), Lou Andreas-Salomé's subtle characterizations illustrate the situation of the woman who wanted to achieve independence at that time. Rilke owes much in insight and style to these novels, just as the contact with Andreas-Salomé, who was fourteen years his senior, may have prepared him for his companionship with the two women artists of his own generation. He renewed contact with the writer after marrying Clara Westhoff and called this a "return at last to the one woman living in maturity and serenity" whose "in some way prodigal son" he thought himself to be (November 9, 1903, letter to Lou Andreas-Salomé). Rilke still remained attached to Clara Westhoff and their daughter Ruth after their common household failed because of financial reasons.

These biographical facts are not directly reflected in the *Notebooks*—the style alone would preclude this—nor did Rilke want to be identified with Malte. Yet his restless, homeless life and his many different types of relationships with women created the experiential basis for the *Notebooks* insofar as an unusual work demands an unusual life for its author.

This novel represents the breakthrough to modern German literature of the twentieth century. Its new form is so inextricably tied to its contents that the meaning or theme as such cannot be abstracted. Rilke himself tried to do so often. Several years after completing the *Notebooks*, he finally found phrases which not only give a general explanation of his intentions in this work but go far beyond this to give an indication of other productive authors' intentions in the decades to come. The author says that *Malte Laurids Brigge* is concerned with one thing alone: "How is it possible to live when the elements of this life are completely incomprehensible to us?" He asks the question, "If we are continually inadequate in love, uncertain in decisions, and incapable in the face of death, how is it possible to live?" A confession follows:

> I did not succeed, in this book written with the deepest inner commitment, in expressing the full extent of my amazement at the fact that for millenia men have dealt with life (not to mention God) and yet still face these first, most immediate and, strictly speaking, sole responsibilities . . . as such helpless novices, between fright and excuses, oh so pitifully (November 8, 1915, letter to Lotte Hepner).

These statements of Rainer Maria Rilke can also be directly applied to Franz Kafka's (1883–1924) posthumous novels—*America* (*Amerika*, 1927), *The Trial* (*Der Prozess*, 1925), and *The Castle* (*Das Schloss*, 1926). Franz Kafka's request that after his death his friend and executor Max Brod destroy the novels together with the rest of his unpublished writings can be explained in part by the fact that they were unfinished. Yet it is important to understand that they did not remain unfinished because Kafka died while working on them, but rather because he had stopped writing them. Whereas in each of his short stories he was able to take one specific case to its conclusion, in the novels, whose form demanded a comprehensive statement, he must have felt, like Rilke, that he "did not succeed." He spoke of the false hope "that a unified whole will be constructed from these little pieces" and wondered about the "purpose of keeping works that have 'even' failed artistically" (December 1917, letter to Max Brod). Nevertheless, Max Brod believed that the three novels were "the most precious part of the bequest. . . . These works alone will show that the real importance of Franz Kafka, who with some justification could previously be considered a specialist, a master of short prose, lies in the great epic form." This conviction led Brod to assume responsibility for publishing Kafka's novels posthumously. He justified his action with the explanation, "Almost everything that Kafka published I took from him by means of cunning and the power of persuasion" (Afterword to *The Trial*, 1925). Kafka's relationship to his own works was curiously ambiguous. It was left to his friend Max Brod to protect and save the texts. But Kafka researchers have not subscribed to Brod's interpretations. An unequivocal interpretation of Kafka's work does not seem possible, at least not in our age.

Kafka wrote his first novel, published under the title *America*, in 1912, primarily during the months of October and November. Sometimes he called the work "Der Verschollene" (The one who disappeared) or "the American novel," but usually simply "the novel." The first chapter, "The Stoker" ("Der Heizer"), appeared separately in 1913. During the period of work on the novel, Kafka also wrote the short narrative *The Judgment* (*Das Urteil*), created during the night of September 22–23, 1912, and *The Metamorphosis* (*Die Verwandlung*), written from mid-November to the beginning of December. In a letter to his publisher Kurt Wolff he wrote that "The Stoker," *The Metamorphosis*, and *The Judgment* belonged "together inwardly and outwardly." He said he would not like to forego showing their relationship in a "book entitled, perhaps, *The Sons*" (April 11, 1913). This book was never written. But the comment proves that as early as the spring of 1913 Kafka had other plans for "The Stoker" and thus had abandoned the novel as originally conceived. He discontinued work on it and left it unpublished, although he had already written part of a final chapter, "The Nature Theater of Oklahoma." According to Brod, he especially loved the beginning of this chapter and read it aloud in a heartwarming fashion.

Karl Rossmann, the main character of the novel, is a likeable boy from Prague who is sent to America by his poor parents at the age of sixteen because a servant girl had seduced him and had his child. As his ship enters New York harbor in the opening scene, he falls into conversation with a stoker, whom he then tries to help when the stoker complains to the captain about unfair treatment from his superior, Schubal. In this Karl is opposed by his uncle, a wealthy senator who comes to meet his ship. In America Karl enters a remarkable world. The view from his room onto a New York street, the American desk with a hundred compartments, the shower, horseback riding, English lessons, the fantastic shipping company founded by his uncle— all this adds up to an ironical, absurd view of America, an America in which anything is possible. After two and one-half months Karl's uncle turns him out on the street; Karl had displeased him by accepting an invitation to spend an evening with Pollunder, one of his uncle's business associates, in a country house near New York. It is a confusing house of huge proportions which is being renovated. Pollunder's daughter, who, Karl learns, is engaged to an acquaintance of his, provokes Karl by nearly pushing him out the window, and, when Karl resists, she beats him by her superior wrestling techniques. Finally he has to play the piano for her, while her fiancé, unbeknownst to Karl, listens with amusement. When Karl tries to leave the house in order to return to his uncle as quickly as possible, Green, another of his uncle's friends who is also visiting Pollunder, hands him a farewell letter from his uncle along with his suitcase.

Thus led astray and punished for the second time, he is left alone in a world which must be as incomprehensible to him as the country house with its dark halls. "Two scoundrels," Delamarche and Robinson, whom he meets in a cheap hotel immediately after having left the elegant country house, take advantage of him and have designs on the small amount of money he has. He joins them in order to find a job with their help but leaves them the next day when Grete Mitzelbach, the head cook in the Hotel Occidental, finds her young Austrian compatriot a job in the hotel as an elevator boy. Karl would have been well provided for had not Robinson, urged on by Delamarche, made trouble for him two months later, resulting in his dismissal. The two unpleasant companions force him to work as a servant for the aging singer Brunelda. In the meantime, Delamarche has become her lover, and the three live with her in a room filled with used furniture. From the balcony Karl observes the public life below with astonishment. Late one night, a young man on a neighboring balcony who studies at night, works during the day in a warehouse, and continuously drinks black coffee instead of sleeping, explains the election campaign Karl saw in the street: the candidate is well-qualified for the judicial post, but no one really thinks he can be elected; he will end up just wasting money. The neighbor also advises Karl to stay with Delamarche since positions such as Karl seeks are hard to find; it is easier to become a "district judge here than a doorman" in a warehouse. Personally, he says, he is only studying "on principle," for studies give him neither satisfaction nor future prospects. "What prospects could I possibly have? America is full of fraudulent doctors." After this conversation Karl temporarily puts aside his doubts about the servant's job and lies down to sleep. "As he closed his eyes, he was comforted by the thought that he was still young and that Delamarche would surely release him one day; this household really did not look as if it were made for eternity." The novel could almost have ended here. However, two further fragments tell of lengthier service with Brunelda.

Karl Rossmann behaves properly in all situations. He is always composed, sensible, and morally irreproachable. The clarity and conciseness of his speech and thought provide a permanent counterbalance to the confusing situation at hand. Up to the Brunelda sections, the entire narration shows how Karl Rossmann psychologically masters his life's adventure. Success and failure are less important than his personal reactions.

In the stoker scene, for example, Karl does not meet with success, but nonetheless he supports the stoker against Schubal. When his uncle interjects that enough has been said about the stoker, claiming that all the other men present are certainly of the same opinion, Karl replies, "But that's not the point in a matter of justice." These words have no effect; but the sentiment has been spoken. It is the uncle's affair to smooth things over, and Karl no longer protests when he has to follow his uncle and leave the stoker to fend for himself. But this does not mean that he dismisses the matter from his mind. While the captain has a boat lowered so that the uncle and nephew can reach land as quickly as possible, Karl reevaluates the situation:

> "Time is pressing," Karl said to himself, "but without insulting everyone, there is nothing I can do. I can't leave my uncle now that he has just found me. The captain is polite but that's it. His politeness ends where discipline begins. Anyway, I'm sure he feels the same way as my uncle. I don't want to speak with Schubal, and I'm even sorry that I shook his hand. And all the others here are no good."

Karl simply approaches the stoker once more to tell him what must be said: he has to "stand up for himself, say yes and no, or else the others will have no idea of the truth." When Karl begins to cry, his uncle smooths that over, too.

Just as Karl's behavior in this scene reflects an exact understanding of how to keep within the limits placed on him, in later situations he always knows how far he can go and when he must give up. He does not resist when he is cast out by his uncle or dismissed from the Hotel Occidental. But each time his judgment can be heard. In the country house near New York he tells Green the facts, undaunted by his catastrophic situation and well aware that he can no longer do anything to change it: "You went . . . too far." He still would have been able to return to his uncle before the deadline had not Green delayed him: "And you are the one to blame that I missed it." In this sentence guilt and negligence are conclusively established. The author stands behind Karl Rossmann, for the entire chapter leads up to this statement. All the details as well as the plot line substantiate it; by any standard, the evening was unpleasant and confusing. Whatever the reasons for his lateness may be, Karl knows that he was not at fault. He expresses his opinion firmly and decisively: "It was ultimately your responsibility to bring me back to my uncle in your automobile, . . . especially since I so urgently asked to go back." Green has to listen to this accusation and literally pushes Karl away; he "shoved him . . . out through a small door, which he flung open in front of him. Astonished, Karl found himself in the open air. Before him a stairway without railings . . . led downward."

It is characteristic of the novel's style that neither these events nor the dismissal from the Hotel Occidental is followed by emotional, impulsive reactions on Karl's part: no self-accusations, no desperation at his misfortune, no great display of outrage. The chapter "A Country House Near New York" briefly reports how Karl finds his way out of the garden without being molested by the dogs which were turned loose. Unable to tell the direction to New York, he says to himself—and with this the chapter ends—"that he didn't necessarily have to go to New York, where no one was expecting him and one person in particular was definitely not expecting him. So he chose an arbitrary direction and set out on his way." The next chapter, "The Road to Ramses," begins: "In the small inn where Karl arrived after a short walk, . . . Karl asked for the cheapest bed, . . . for he thought he must begin to save immediately." The only thing that occupies his mind before he falls asleep in the chair is the photograph of his parents, which he has come across among his belongings. He is deeply absorbed in thoughts of both parents. When the picture is missing the next evening, he is ready to give up the entire contents of his suitcase for it. "It was more important to me than everything else I have in my suitcase," he says, adding, "It is irreplaceable, I cannot get another," and, "It was the only picture I had of my parents." His parents alone evoke a warm emotional reaction in Karl. When fired from the Hotel Occidental he is again reserved and untouched, although here once more, as in the break with his uncle, a human relationship is destroyed, the one between Karl and the motherly head cook, Grete Mitzelbach.

In the events preceding Karl's dismissal, the author again carefully establishes "guilt" and "negligence." This time Karl's negligence is indisputable, but it cannot be said that he is guilty. He is unable to refute the accusations made against him, however, because no one is willing to listen to his arguments. " 'It is impossible to defend oneself if there is no goodwill,' Karl said to himself and did not answer the headwaiter anymore." He is experienced in enduring injustices and also reacts here with detachment and insight. His own "goodwill" remains inexhaustible throughout. This is particularly evident at the end of the seventh chapter, when, after the conversation with the student, he lies down to sleep on the foul-smelling sofa, filled with good intentions for the future.

Part of the book is missing between the seventh and the last chapters. The reader learns that after serving Brunelda, Karl Rossmann held several other jobs, finally worked in a questionable office, and did not use his own name for a long time. When he is supposed to give his name at the Nature Theater of Oklahoma, the only thing he can think of is the name he was called on his last few jobs: "Negro." Karl's attention is attracted to the Nature Theater by a poster announcing plans to hire people that very day. "Whoever thinks of his future belongs with us! Everyone is welcome! Whoever wants to become an artist, come forward!" The theater can use everyone, "each person in his place!" Wages are not mentioned. Karl Rossmann is most impressed by the sentence: "Everyone is welcome." From the public nature of the announcement he concludes that it can not be dishonorable work and that he, too, will be accepted. "He asked for nothing better, he hoped to find the beginning of a respectable career at last and perhaps it was here." Among the hundreds of women dressed in angel's gowns who are playing the trumpet on high platforms when Karl approaches the recruitment area, one woman surprisingly addresses him by his real name, Karl, and he happily recognizes his old friend Fanny. She lets him come up to her platform and play a song on her trumpet. After a short conversation with one of the men, he is accepted by the office for "European Intermediate School Pupils" as "Negro, technical worker"; he had stated that at one time he had wanted to become an engineer. At the common meal for those accepted he meets Giacomo, whom he had known at the Occidental and who had lost his job as elevator boy when Karl was hired. Karl quickly allies himself with Giacomo, and together they enjoy a trip lasting two days and two nights that is supposed to lead to Oklahoma. The novel breaks off during their journey.

Max Brod reported that the final chapter "was to end harmoniously. In mysterious words Kafka smilingly suggested that in this 'almost limitless' theater his young hero would find a career, freedom, support, yes even his home and parents again as if through paradisiacal magic." Kafka knew and often stressed in conversations that this novel was "more hopeful and 'brighter' . . . than anything else" he had written. Brod also emphasized "that Franz Kafka liked to read travel literature and memoirs very much, that Franklin's biography, from which he liked to read aloud, was one of his favorite books, and that a longing for freedom and distant lands was always alive in him. But he never traveled further than to France and Northern Italy, and it is the dawn of fantasy which gives this book of adventure its particular color" (Afterword to *America*, 1925).

In a diary entry dated September 30, 1915, Kafka compared Karl Rossmann with the main character of *The Trial*, which he was then writing. "Rossmann and K., the guiltless and the guilty, both indiscriminately killed as punishment in the end, the guiltless one with a lighter hand, more pushed aside than beaten down." Wilhelm Emrich has already pointed out that there is not necessarily a contradiction between the diary entry and Brod's statement about the novel's ending.[4] Rossmann is in fact unable to find a place

in the career world of the unfamiliar continent; he is pushed aside everywhere, "killed as punishment," sinks deeper and deeper, even gives up his
name, and after the seventh chapter is a *Verschollener* (one who has disappeared), about whom even the reader learns nothing more. Fanny's call to
him with his correct name "Karl" may have a special meaning, as may the
meeting with Giacomo, now a friend in this new world, although a compet-
itor at the Hotel Occidental. The fact that Rossmann can again establish
relationships with people on his own terms may mean that his survival has
begun. In any case, the tone of the last chapter is hopeful.

It should not be forgotten that Kafka's remark about "Rossmann and K."
was made from a later perspective than the novel *America*. Furthermore, the
significance of a diary entry is different from that of a novel's text, particularly
when the novel is of as great artistic merit as *America*. A diary entry can be
a momentary, passing remark made in a particular mood. At that moment
the author may not have his novel completely in mind, for creative writers
often forget their own productions quickly and are amazed when they later
reread them. On the other hand, such an entry can be a profound, illuminating explanation.

Kafka's personal situation in 1915 was fundamentally different from his
situation during the writing of *America*. The serious consequences of his
unhappy relationship with Felice Bauer had already begun. Kafka met Felice
in August 1912, proposed to her for the first time in June 1913, and then
proposed again in January 1914. She accepted the proposal in April 1914,
and they became officially engaged on May 30, 1914. Kafka broke the engagement on July 12, 1914, but was not able to forget her. He began to see
her again in January 1915, and in early July 1917 they became engaged for
a second time. But the engagement was broken in late December 1917 after
Kafka's tuberculosis had been diagnosed on September 4 of that year. Kafka's
curious tie to Felice Bauer, his wish to establish a family on the one hand
and reluctance to marry on the other, meant intense suffering for him. In
early August 1914, approximately three weeks after the first engagement was
broken, Kafka began work on his novel *The Trial*, and he continued writing
it the following year.

This novel also remained unfinished. According to Max Brod, the main
gap comes before the final chapter, that is, in the same place as in *America*.
Brod, who took the manuscript in 1920 and "at that time immediately put it
in order," had to decide how to arrange Kafka's chapters, which already had
titles but were in no particular order. In making his decisions Brod says he
had to rely on his intuition. The order he chose has been challenged by
literary scholars but has never been disproven. In his afterword, Brod spoke
of the novel's fragmentary nature: "Since . . . according to the author's verbal
statements the trial was never supposed to reach the highest court, the novel

was in a sense impossible to complete; that is, it could be continued ad infinitum." Max Brod called the trial itself mysterious, an accurate characterization. Because literary criticism has not been content to accept this quality of mystery, countless interpretations have been proposed and these in turn challenged and replaced by newer interpretations.

The novel begins with Josef K.'s arrest and ends with his execution. The arrest itself is most certainly mysterious and the execution simply its ultimate consequence. After receiving the apparently official notification that he has been arrested, Josef K. can continue to go to work. He is a respected bank official and on the day of his arrest has just turned thirty years old. From the first moment, Josef K. does not know what to think of the apparent arrest. He tells the man called the "inspector" that the matter could not be very important: "I come to that conclusion because I have been accused but do not know of the slightest offense that might be charged against me. But even that is secondary, the main question is, who has accused me? What authority is conducting the proceedings?" Here Josef K. has posed the key questions which concern him to the end and are never answered: the question of his guilt and the question of the identity of the judicial authority. The inspector does not respond to the questions and firmly resists giving any information beyond the fact that K. is under arrest. It is very important to note that he refuses to confirm K.'s assumption that he has been accused: "By no means can I tell you that you have been accused. Actually, I don't even know whether you are or not. You are under arrest, that is correct—but I don't know any more than that." In the course of the novel the judicial authorities are discussed often and at length, procedural options are described, and the possible courses the trial can take are enumerated. Josef K. rushes from place to place and tries his best to understand and settle the matter, but he accomplishes nothing and cannot clarify the aforementioned key questions, even though everyone is anxious to advise him. This advising begins on the first morning with the guards, who admit that they are minor officials but nevertheless think themselves capable of understanding the proceedings of their institution. "Our institution . . . is not looking for guilt among the population, but is, as the law states, drawn to guilt and must therefore send out its guards. That is the law." Josef K., who is baffled, replies, "I don't know that law," and then has to listen to the guard Franz remark, "See, Willem, he admits that he doesn't know the law and at the same time claims to be innocent."

This remark shows the absurdity of the situation in which Josef K. and all the other characters involved with him find themselves. The entire course of events is marked by this absurdity. On the evening of the arrest, K. has a long conversation with his neighbor, Fräulein Bürstner, who says that if she is to act as advisor, then she has to know "what it is all about." K. can only reply, "That's just the trouble, . . . I don't know myself." Nevertheless, on the Sunday morning of the first inquiry, to which K. has been summoned by telephone, he speaks in detail about the proceedings, making the point right from the outset that "it is only a trial if I recognize it as such." There is no doubt, he continues, that a "large organization" is behind all the actions of this court. It not only employs "bribable guards" and "foolish overseers and magistrates," but supports a "high level judiciary . . . with a large, indispensable body of servants, clerks, gendarmes, and other assistants, perhaps even executioners." In answer to his own question about the meaning of this great organization, he says, "It lies in arresting innocent persons and initiating senseless and generally, as in my case, ineffectual proceedings against them." He adds that in view of the senselessness of it all, corruption among the officials can hardly be prevented. At the end of the inquiry, Josef K. has the impression that the spectators at the hearing are also a corrupt group belonging to the court. K.'s negative opinion of the court, formed during his arrest as well as at the first inquiry, is confirmed when he visits the court offices in the attic, where he becomes physically ill.

Just as the arrest is not an actual arrest, the first inquiry is not a real inquiry. The reader wonders why K. talks constantly throughout it, and it almost seems understandable that, as he leaves the room, the magistrate points out that he has just deprived himself of "the advantage . . . that a hearing affords the arrested in every case." One is struck by the fact that in the next chapter (chapter 3), Josef K. is already called the "accused" and also considers himself to be accused. Why and at what point he became an accused man remains unknown. It was explicitly stated that the arrest does not mean that an accusation has been made. It is possible that a part of the novel is missing here; the fragmentary nature of *The Trial* could be the reason for the sudden and unusual use of the term "accused." Even the examining magistrate spoke of the "arrested" at the end of the second chapter, and in the third chapter K. still says to the court usher's wife, "supposedly I was arrested—that is, I am arrested." K. does not protest, however, when, in the next scene of the same chapter, the usher says to him, "Aha, so you are the accused K.," and later even confirms the usher's statement, "You are accused," with "Yes." In the corridor of the court offices—still in the third chapter—he refers to the others who have been accused as his colleagues and says to one of them, "I, for example, am also accused," and then, "You don't believe that I am accused?" The reader in any case has not heard anything about the accusation and must be surprised that K. not only accepts it as a fact, but, in addition, almost seems proud of it.

It seems unlikely, however, that a part of the novel is missing here. Instead, the transitionless change from arrested to accused within the same chapter is a manifestation of Kafka's new style. What has occurred is illogical, as is the entire process of the trial. For example, when on that first

Sunday morning K. is looking for the hearing room in the house described to him, he sees not only the stairs he wants to use, but three additional flights of stairs, and he has the feeling that there is yet another passageway to a second courtyard. He stands still, not knowing which way to go. Finally he goes up the first set of stairs, "remembering the guard Willem's statement that the court is drawn to guilt, which would actually mean that the hearing room had to be up those stairs which K. chose by chance." Continuing his search in the huge building with many tenants, he is reluctant to ask the location of the court of inquiry and therefore asks for a carpenter named Lanz, whom he invents in order to have the chance to look into the rooms. Directed about by helpful people, he searches through the different floors of the building in vain until finally he "knocked on the first door on the fifth floor. . . . 'Does a carpenter named Lanz live here?' he asked. 'This way please,' a young woman said . . . and pointed with her wet hand to the open door of the adjoining room." It really is the right room. "K., who found the air too stifling, stepped out again and said to the young woman, who must have misunderstood him, 'I asked for a carpenter, a certain Lanz?' 'Yes,' said the woman, 'go in, please.' K. probably would not have followed her had she not approached him, grasped the door handle and said, 'I must close it behind you, no one else may go in.'" K.'s appearance before the court magistrate at the appointed time, even if he is a little late, proves that he already finds himself in agreement with those who are conducting the trial. He has understood—recalling the guard's words—that he can use any stairs, and thus has accepted at least the possibility of his own guilt. For their part the employees of the court understand what he wants, even if he invents a fictitious person; they understand him better than he understands himself and fulfill his unspoken wish. The woman even directs him to the correct door a second time and makes it clear to him that it is the right one, completely unperturbed by his repeated request to be directed elsewhere. No words are lost in discussing how the woman can know that K. is not looking for the carpenter Lanz, who doesn't even exist, but rather for the hearing room, and it is taken for granted that she gives the right information to the wrong question with an indifferent, polite phrase and a self-assured pointing gesture. The effect is humorous, insofar as the reader is expecting a traditional logical sequence.

Not only the style, but also the subject matter and type of plot differ from that of the eighteenth- and nineteenth-century novel. *The Trial* tells how Josef K. lets himself be drawn into a dubious judicial process, or, expressed somewhat differently, how he draws the judicial process toward himself from the very moment that he acknowledges it, for the proceedings can only exist if he recognizes them as valid. He acknowledges them by allowing himself to be summoned by telephone and setting out on that Sunday morning to appear at the inquiry. After this, the course of the trial is virtually decided. He finds the courtroom, or one could say, the courtroom finds him. No matter which stairs he takes, he will still approach the court. If we view the events as the convergence of K. and the court and their gradually becoming one, then the woman's response to K.'s question about the carpenter is no longer surprising. Its interpretation is immaterial. What is important is that it shows that K.'s intentions are in agreement with those of the court.

The same agreement is recognizable when, a week later, K. goes from being "the arrested" to being "the accused" for no apparent reason. This change takes place on both sides at the same time. The usher merely says aloud what K. does not dispute. K. had protested the arrest with emotion, but now he just accepts the new status. In the next chapter he finds the two court guards being thrashed in a storage closet of his bank. This invasion of his place of work shows how far the trial has now penetrated into his life. His attempt to free the guards through bribery indicates that he sees himself as part of the institution. The court is now closing in on him from all sides. Soon his relatives have learned about his trial. His uncle takes him to an attorney named Huld, whose assistance K. accepts, again an acknowledgment of the proceedings. The lawyer, though a complete stranger to K., has also already heard about his trial, which, he explains, is a consequence of his contact with legal circles. A chief clerk emerges from a dark section of the lawyer's room as proof of the lawyer's close relationship with the court. While the two men talk, K. goes off with Leni, the lawyer's private nurse, who becomes K.'s lover. But even this does not mean escape, for Leni also knows about his trial and advises him to confess; only then would it be possible to slip away. From the lawyer K. learns that the indictment will not be made available to the accused or his attorney; the defense must rely on conjecture and deduce the charges and evidence from the hearings. The lawyer also says that personal relationships to court officials can influence the progress of the trial in its later stages. This information has a crushing effect on K.: "The thought of the trial never left him again." He realizes that he can no longer escape from the trial. "His previous contempt for the trial no longer mattered. . . . He was now in the midst of it and had to defend himself," to reject unconditionally "any thought of possible guilt." There was "no guilt. The trial was nothing but a big business."

K. indulges in such deliberations during office hours and decides to dismiss the lawyer and prepare his own defense. One difficulty he sees here is that due to his ignorance of the accusation, his brief will have to contain his entire life story in detail. Also, the preparations will require all his energy and be detrimental to his profession; he will have to place himself completely at the disposal of the court. Actually, all of these thoughts show that he has long since fallen under the power of the court. He is no longer proficient in dealing with the bank's customers, who must wait for him and even then are not received. When he hears about a painter named Titorelli who does portraits of judges and is said to be willing to give information about the court, he leaves the bank immediately during office hours to call on him. The court is in complete possession of him although he resists it with all his strength.

The painter with his information, the final consultation with the lawyer, and the conversation with the clergyman in the cathedral are of no help to K. Nor is the story "Before the Law," which the clergyman tells him, a source of concrete advice. The clergyman describes K.'s trial and its outcome with the sentence: "The judgment does not come all at once, the trial gradually becomes a judgment." K. has known for a long time that this is so and that his trial is not going well. The clergyman articulates what K. is thinking: "I am afraid it will end badly. You are thought to be guilty." Of course K. protests, "But I am not guilty." Nonetheless he is emotionally prepared as he is led to his execution on the eve of his thirty-first birthday. Again the legal institution and K. are in agreement. It is only in the last moment that K.'s strength fails him; he is unable to "grasp the knife" and "stab himself."

One might ask why K. is ready when he is led to execution. If indeed he is relying on the clergyman's statements, then it should be noted that these are formulated so carefully that a continuance of his struggle will not seem hopeless: "You are thought to be guilty . . . at least for the time being." The question of guilt is never decided, just as an accusation is never precisely defined. Nor does K. ever confess to anything; he always emphatically denies any guilt. Regardless of how we may judge K.'s behavior during the trial, whether we approve of his search for helpers or not, his actions do not seem all that incomprehensible. But even if some readers disagree with this, the question of K.'s guilt has to be taken separately. The fact remains that any crime K. may have committed had to have occurred before his arrest. But of this the reader learns nothing. Information is even given in the novel's opening sentence which suggests his innocence: "Someone must have slandered Josef K., for he was arrested one morning without having done anything wrong."

Here it is important to consider Kafka's narrative style. In all three novels, the narrative perspective is limited almost entirely to that of the main character. Whatever we find out that goes beyond his experiences, thoughts, and opinions is restricted to what others tell him. Huld's and Titorelli's long expositions on the nature of the court as well as many other bits of information K. receives—from the guards, the inspector, the court usher and his wife, Leni, Block, and others—are dependent on the narrative style. In the same way, what we do or do not learn is also a result of the style, since there is no one available who can provide the information. The possibilities for expression which Kafka created for himself with this style were immeasurable. The narrator determines the appearance of the characters who give K. information, and these characters relate only what they can know from their own narrative perspective. At least this is the impression they give. They can deceive, lie, or conceal something, but again there is no informant present who can correct or supplement what they say. No one knows—neither the reader nor K.—if the guard who arrests K. is telling the truth when he claims the authorities are, "as the law states, drawn to guilt." The inspector categorically denies knowing more than that K. is arrested. "Perhaps the guards said something else," he conceded to K., "but then it was just idle talk." For K. it is of the greatest importance to know whether an accusation or any type of charge is behind the arrest and whether the authorities are really drawn to his guilt. The reader would also like to know more about this. The danger of deception which exists for K. exists for the reader as well, who is most likely to be deceived by K., because the narrator uses K.'s perspective. An additional point is Kafka's particular use of *style indirect libre*. He integrates it so smoothly into the objective narration that the reader often hardly notices the transition. But he still reveals nothing about the innermost thoughts of his characters. K. may even be hiding an offense of which only he is aware.

In any case K. seems, at least temporarily, to understand that guilt does not always have to be something clear-cut. He realizes that it is necessary to reject any thought of possible guilt from the very beginning if anything is going to be accomplished; one should "not play with thoughts about some kind of guilt, but hold as firmly as possible to the thought of one's own advantage." K. knows that one is weakened in battle by guilt feelings, and he tries to resist because he wants to survive.

K.'s readiness for execution is not an admission of guilt, but a consequence of defeat in the trial. Even if we assume that the clergyman was deceiving neither himself nor K.—which is not proven—K. does not necessarily have to pay attention to what he says. The clergyman tells him explicitly, "The court wants nothing from you. It takes you in when you come and lets you go when you leave." K. could leave, as could the man in the story the clergyman tells, "Before the Law," but he does not. Just as his thoughts become more and more consumed by the trial and he gradually begins to accept it, so is he ultimately absorbed by it, and, when "the trial . . . becomes the judgment," he accepts that, too, and even believes that he is obligated to destroy himself. It is said that "K. now definitely knew that it was his obligation to grasp . . . the knife." He is killed "like a dog" in a quarry somewhere outside the city. It is actually not a contradiction that K. subjugates himself to the court by accepting his execution and yet still asks, "Where was the judge he had never seen? Where was the high court to which he had never come?"

Kafka's last novel, *The Castle*, is also concerned with integration, subordination, and respect. He worked on it during 1921 and 1922. As in *America* and *The Trial*, no background information is given; the novel opens in the midst of the main action, which here is distributed over seven days. K.— not the same character as Josef K., but one who has a similar function within the novel—arrives at a village late one evening, is given a straw mattress in an inn, and soon after falling asleep is awakened because he needs a "permit from the count" in order to stay the night; as is explained, the village is the "property of the castle." Very adroit in his replies, K. says he is the land surveyor and has come at the behest of the count; his assistants will be arriving in a vehicle with the equipment the next day. A telephone inquiry to the castle seems to prove K. a liar: "Land surveyor? Impossible. He's a common, lying vagabond, or probably worse." But a moment later a call comes from the castle to retract the first response: "It was the office boss himself on the telephone." Now K. is referred to as "Herr Land Surveyor." The next morning a revealing conversation takes place between K. and the innkeeper in which each tries to sound out the other and in doing so reveals important information. K. says that he has traveled far from his wife and child. Afterwards he walks through the village and tries to reach the castle, but he cannot find a path that leads directly to it. Fleeting conversations with several villagers indicate that their relations with the castle are curiously strained. While they do in fact accept K. as the land surveyor, they treat him with reserve. When he returns to his inn, the Brückenhof, two strange fellows introduce themselves as his assistants. Shortly afterward the castle's messenger, Barnabas, brings him a letter from a key castle official named Klamm—one of the most important characters in the novel—informing him that he has been accepted into the service of the castle and that the mayor is his immediate supervisor. K. spends the night in a different inn, the Herrenhof, where he is denied access beyond the bar, since this is the hotel in which the castle officials stay when they come to the village. K. wins the barmaid Frieda, who until then was Klamm's lover, and they spend the night together on the floor in puddles of beer in front of Klamm's door. They leave the Herrenhof the next morning and spend the day and the following night in K.'s room in the Brückenhof.

On the fourth day of his stay in the village, K. learns from the mayor that no land surveyor is needed. He is then appointed school custodian. That evening he receives a second letter from Klamm, this time expressing satisfaction with K.'s surveying. K. spends the night (the fourth) with Frieda and his assistants in a school classroom. The next morning he dismisses the assistants. He and Frieda realize that their relationship has already become less intense. K. performs his duties in the school and later lingers in Barnabas's house, waiting for a message from the castle. Barnabas's sister, Olga, tells him the story of their family's ostracism and downfall, which reveals much about the castle officials and life in the village. Meanwhile, Frieda leaves him and returns to the Herrenhof. Summoned there for a discussion with a castle official, Erlanger, K. sees Frieda again in the corridor, but she rejects him and claims he has brought great disgrace upon her by his visit to the Barnabas family. By this time she already has one of the assistants in her room. In his search for Erlanger, K. accidently enters the office of a clerk who seems to be able to help him, but K. falls asleep. Early the next morning—after K.'s fifth night in the village—Erlanger tells him that, out of consideration for Klamm, K. must set Frieda free so she can return to the bar. K. then watches as files are distributed in the corridor to castle officials who are waiting for them in their rooms. K.'s presence causes great confusion among the officials; they are not permitted to leave their rooms while he is there. Exhausted, he sleeps an entire day and night on a barrel in the Herrenhof bar and then has a long conversation with Pepi, Frieda's successor. They talk mostly about Frieda, to whom Pepi must give back her job. The novel breaks off after a talk between K. and the innkeeper's wife.

Kafka did not write a final chapter to the novel, but in his afterword to *The Castle* Max Brod reports what Kafka told him about the planned ending. "The presumed land surveyor" was to die of exhaustion. As the community gathers around his deathbed, the decision would arrive from the castle that K. actually has no legitimate claim to live in the village, but "in consideration of certain extenuating circumstances he will be allowed to live and work here." It is important to note that Brod speaks of the presumed land surveyor and that the castle's decision is similar to the result of the telephone inquiries on the first evening in the village. On that evening the castle had given two different answers in immediate succession. We never learn what the second answer is based on or why K. is tolerated in the village and accepted as land surveyor. Apparently the castle has reasons for not driving him away immediately. Even K. assumes this when the second call from the castle cancels the first. He believes that "in the castle one knows everything necessary about him, has weighed the relative strength of both sides and smilingly accepted the battle." The reader cannot know what is meant here. Nor did Brod learn from Kafka what the "consideration of certain extenuating circumstances" refers to. Thus the most important questions remain unanswered: what should one think of K.'s assertion that he is the land surveyor summoned by the count? How can it be explained that he announces that his assistants will come in a vehicle with the equipment when such a vehicle never arrives? How can he talk to the innkeeper about his wife and child the first morning, then move into the inn on the second morning with Frieda as his fiancée, and discuss his wedding in detail with the innkeeper's wife? As in *The Trial*, one might ask whether the discrepancies can be explained by the fragmentary nature of the novel or whether they are intentional. But again, there can be no doubt that discrepancies are part of Kafka's unique style.

The attitude of the officials toward K. is just as contradictory as his statements about himself. The men in the castle tolerate his activity but keep him at a distance. Just as he cannot find a way to the castle on the first day, although he comes close to it, on the following days he finds no opportunity to speak to Klamm, even though he is staying in his immediate vicinity. All his personal efforts fail, and everyone assures him that there is absolutely no way to enter the castle or to speak to Klamm. "No foreigner may enter the castle without permission," one of the assistants tells him. When K. tries to obtain such permission on the telephone, the answer from the castle is: "Neither tomorrow nor any other time." A second attempt ends with the curt answer: "Never." The innkeeper at the Herrenhof, who does not want to let K. stay the night, explains that the men from the castle are "extremely sensitive; I am convinced they are unable, or at least unprepared, to endure the sight of a stranger." Later K. is told that "Herr Klamm is a man from the castle, which in itself means . . . a very high rank. But what are you . . . ! You are not from the castle, you are not from the village, you are nothing. Yet, unfortunately, you are something after all: a stranger, one who is superfluous and always in the way, who is constantly causing trouble."

K. for his part is consumed by thoughts of the tension between freedom and subjugation brought about by his work situation. These two concepts play a role in his relations to Klamm and the castle from the very beginning. When the innkeeper asks him the first morning if he would like to live in the castle, K. not only answers that it would depend on his work—if his work were in the village, he would also want to live there—but continues, "Also, I am afraid that life up there in the castle would not suit me. I always want to be free." Thus from the outset K. rejects being integrated into the castle, even though he does not yet know anything about life there. All he knows is what he heard the previous evening—that this village is the "property of the castle." Also, from the reaction of the people in the inn to the two telephone conversations, the castle's dominance over the village is apparent. K.'s statement that he "always wants to be free" means that he has no desire to belong to the ruling class. Rather than sharing in its power as a functionary, he wants to face it as a free person. The stand he takes at this early stage is formulated and explained more clearly when he analyzes Klamm's first letter. "Only as a village worker," he says, "withdrawn as far as possible from the men in the castle," would he be "in a position to accomplish something in the castle." He does foresee one "danger" to his freedom, a danger expressed in Klamm's letter: "It was work. Service, superiors, labor, wage regulations, accountability, workers, the letter was full of this, and even if other, more personal things were said, they, too, came from this same point of view." K.'s efforts to speak to Klamm are, regardless of the reasons he gives, aimed at overcoming this danger. He admits to the innkeeper's wife the possibility that he may not be able to endure the sight of Klamm without a door between them. "But if I succeed in standing firm, then it is not necessary that he speak to me, it will be enough to see the impression my words make on him, and if they make none at all or if he doesn't hear them, then I will still have the satisfaction of having spoken freely before a powerful man."

Many elements of the novel indicate that the character Klamm cannot be explained rationally. It is particularly striking that Klamm seems closely connected to the facts underlying the inconsistencies in K.'s statements. For example, although the vehicle with the assistants and equipment does not arrive, two assistants do come to the inn the day after K.'s arrival. To K.'s incredulous question whether they are the "old assistants" he had sent for, they answer affirmatively. He asks about the equipment and is told they have none. He asks about land surveying and is told that they know nothing about it. "But if you are my old assistants, then you must know about it," K. says, pointing out the obvious discrepancy. K. did not fail to notice that the assistants "came from the direction of the castle." Their presence is so unreal and intangible that it is difficult to say anything specific about them. Characteristically, K. cannot tell them apart and therefore refuses to regard them as separate individuals. He is also quite unfriendly to them, primarily because of his uncertainty about what to think of them. After he has forbidden them to speak to anyone without his permission, he explains to them, "I am a stranger here, and if you are my old assistants then you are also strangers. Therefore we three strangers have to stick together." He demands that they shake hands on this, expecting that the challenge will bring out the truth, but the assistants extend their hands "all too willingly." The narrator's words are a sign of the assistants' dishonesty. K. then refuses to shake hands. In a subsequent telephone conversation with the castle authorities, the question whether they are the old or new assistants again arises. After the castle authorities mention the names Artur and Jeremias, K. says, "Those are the new assistants," but the reply comes, "No, those are the old ones." Finally, in Klamm's second letter K. is not only praised for his own surveying work but for the "work of the assistants," whom he has successfully kept at their jobs. Klamm addressed the letter, "To the Herr Land Surveyor at the Brückenhof," although K. had accepted the position as school custodian that same day.

Those who think it important to stress that K. is an impostor who passes himself off as a land surveyor hired by the castle must also take into consideration the fact that Klamm addresses him as the land surveyor and does so in the same mysterious, unsubstantiated way in which K. had made his assertion. The assistants also seem to fit into this mysterious pattern; Frieda's statement that they are "Klamm's messengers" puts them in a different perspective. "Their eyes, these simple and yet sparkling eyes," Frieda says, "remind me somehow of Klamm's eyes. . . . It is Klamm's glance that sometimes meets me in their eyes."

Klamm, the secretive, seemingly inaccessible man of power, is not quite as mysterious in his relationships with women as in his administrative affairs. He has possessed many women and continues to fascinate them for years. Their unforgettable experiences with him outshine their marriages without, however, hurting their husbands. It is well in keeping with life in the village that K.'s relationship to Klamm is not only determined by K.'s professional position but that Klamm's influence even extends into K.'s intimate affairs. K. is an exceptional case, since Frieda returns to Klamm. In the village K. met many women who had relationships with castle officials, in particular with Klamm.

The novel is not only about K. and the castle officials but also about women, who are allowed to speak at great length. They are women of very different types and situations who tell their stories and give their opinions. By listening to them, K. learns about their lives, and by responding to them he has the chance to define more precisely his own views and intentions. The most important female character is Frieda, who is frequently talked about by others but seldom speaks herself, although in several scenes she does have her turn to speak. However, the scenes in which the innkeeper's wife, Olga, and Pepi speak are more illuminating. Frieda is most impressive in her first scene in the bar; thereafter, she is more important for what she does for K. than for what she says. Her importance as a character is established through K.'s interpretations.

Max Brod believed that the relationship between K. and Frieda reflected "in a pejorative way" Kafka's love for the writer Milena Jesenska-Polak. In Herr Klamm, Brod saw "an exaggerated and demonized picture" of Milena's husband, the Austrian intellectual Ernst Polak, from whom Milena "could not free herself inwardly."[5] Like Klamm, Polak was undoubtedly an imposing personality who exercised great power over women.

Elements from Kafka's biography can also be linked to Kafka's choice of setting. Kafka's father was born in Vossok, a village one hundred kilometers south of Prague. As Klaus Wagenbach discovered, this area provides a setting comparable to the village and castle in *The Castle*.[6] This would suggest that Kafka integrated childhood memories into the novel. Neither Brod nor Wagenbach wished to overemphasize autobiographical aspects but merely wanted to call attention to certain parallels. There is no doubt that Kafka, like any other author, incorporated memories and personal experiences into his work. But the novel contains far more than this. The question whether K. has a right to live in the village—whether his claims are merely based on presumption or perhaps should indeed be given consideration—is an expression of Kafka's own existential problem. As early as 1913 he wrote in his diary of "the terrible uncertainty of my inner existence." In the meantime he had become terminally ill, had lived in different localities, and had come to the realization that there was no longer any place for him.

As all interpreters have recognized, Kafka's novels must be read differently from the way one reads an eighteenth- or nineteenth-century novel. Kafka is not telling the inner story of a character, and he is not presenting an inner state, which is Blanckenburg's main requirement for the modern novel of his time. The emphasis lies neither on the internal nor on the external, nor on the interplay between the two. Many of the discrepancies and inconsistencies arise because internal and external events are intermeshed and difficult to distinguish from each other. The incomprehensibility of the world into which Kafka's heroes are placed is related to this loss of a distinction between inner and outer worlds. Since each of these was already regarded as infinite in itself, it is understandable that the effect of fusing the two must be disturbing, confusing, and contradictory.

As opposed to Malte Laurids Brigge, Kafka's heroes no longer have any possibility of emotional ties to history, to literature and art, or to childhood experiences. Instead, they hold fast to the illusion that they will finally be able to come to terms with their environment, although the way in which their conflicts began was absurd enough to preclude any such hope. Kafka demonstrates that there can be no resolution of the conflicts by presenting the corruptness of bureaucratic systems that feign an order they do not possess. A contrast to the confusing world Kafka presents is the clear flow of speech. It forces the reader to continue following even though he is led through labyrinths and into inexplicable adventures, even though no meaning lies waiting to be found by interpretation. Nothing more is meant than what occurs. That the characters may be destroyed seems just as plausible as that they remain entangled forever.

Kafka's contemporaries did not regard him as a singular and unique author to the same extent that later generations did. Musil recognized early how close Kafka was to Robert Walser; in a review of *Observation* (*Betrachtung*, 1913), Kafka's first book, Musil said that it seemed like a "special case of the Walser-type" of novel (*Literarische Chronik*, 1914). Just as Kafka was familiar with Walser's *Jakob von Gunten*, he may have also read *The Other Side* (*Die andere Seite*, 1909), Alfred Kubin's (1877–1959) only novel. He was in personal contact with Kubin and admired his art. *The Other Side* is a "fantastic" novel in which the narrator is invited, on behalf of his former school friend Patera, to a dreamland in Asia. At first all his wishes seem to be fulfilled there, but soon disquieting, then confusing, and finally startling events develop. The narrator's fruitless efforts to be admitted to see his friend Patera, the grotesque forms of rejection, arousal of new hopes, and subsequent withdrawal of what has already been granted call to mind K.'s endeavors and experiences in *The Castle* and *The Trial*. Kubin probably also had an influence on Gustav Meyrink's (1868–1932) novel *The Golem* (*Der Golem*, 1915). Although the basic composition of *The Golem* is quite different from that of Kafka's works, both authors associate the city of Prague with anxiety.

No matter how one sees Kafka in relation to the literature of his time, he stands out boldly because of his epic style. Precisely at the time he was writing, in the second decade of the twentieth century, a literary style known as Expressionism developed, which was not favorable to the novel. Klaus Günther Just speaks of the "dilemma of expressionistic narrators" and emphasizes that they lacked "the epic in the sense of narrative calmness."[7] Klabund (pseudonym of Alfred Henschke, 1890–1928) wrote a number of short novels in his own personal style of expressionistic prose, which consisted of short sentences strung together to create simple stories. The novels in turn could be joined with other short novels to form a larger unit. His *Moreau the Soldier* (*Moreau. Roman eines Soldaten*, 1916) deals with the life of the French general Jean Victor Moreau. It is written in the form of a brief sketch, containing only what is characteristic and decisive, without psychological and narrative filler. Three additional biographical novels in the same style form a group with Moreau: *Mohammed the Prophet* (*Mohammed. Roman eines Propheten*, 1917), *Peter the Czar* (*Pjotr. Roman eines Zaren*, 1923), and *Rasputin the Demon* (*Rasputin. Roman eines Dämons*, 1929). His historical novels include: *Brackie the Fool* (*Bracke. Ein Eulenspiegelroman*, 1918) and *The Incredible Borgia* (*Borgia. Roman einer Familie*, 1928). Kasimir Edschmid (pseudonym of Eduard Schmid, 1890–1966), who drew up the theoretic program for the Expressionists, also tried to write novels employing expressionistic techniques. His novel *The Agate Balls* (*Die achatnen Kugeln*, 1920) shows, however, that these techniques are not suitable for the novel.

Despite his praiseworthy efforts on Kafka's behalf, Max Brod (1884–1968) did not create an original form in his own numerous *Zeitromane* and historical novels. Brod used the medium of the novel to depict human problems. He was a master at his craft. Contemporary themes are treated in works such as *Schloss Nornepygge* (1908), *A Czech Servant Girl* (*Ein tschechisches Dienstmädchen*, 1909), *Jewesses* (*Jüdinnen*, 1911), *Arnold Beer* (1912), and *The Great Venture* (*Das grosse Wagnis*, 1918). The best known of his historical novels is *The Redemption of Tycho Brahe* (*Tycho Brahes Weg zu Gott*, 1916), in which Tycho and Kepler, representatives of two different world views, confront each other intellectually and personally. Novels like *Franzi, or a Second-Class Love* (*Franzi, oder eine Liebe Zweiten Ranges*, 1922) and *Three Loves* (*Die Frau, nach der man sich sehnt*, 1927) were, as the titles indicate, written for a different audience. Later in life Brod again turned to religious themes in *The Master* (*Der Meister*, 1952), a novel of Jesus, and *Poor Cicero* (*Armer Cicero*, 1955). The wide variety of topics and problems suited Brod's inclinations. He did not search for an original form but used existing techniques to serve his diverse purposes.

This has often been the case since the 1920s. In that decade the body of novel literature began to grow, and the novel came to be used more and more for ideological purposes. The great experiments in form of Hermann Broch and Robert Musil, as well as the mythical novel, evolved against this background.

Whereas Rilke and Kafka expressed a new artistic will almost exclusively through their works and only occasionally made personal statements about their objectives in letters, diary entries, and reflections, Hermann Broch (1886–1951) and Robert Musil (1880–1942) developed theories of the novel and narration which they were careful to set down in writing. Yet neither author wrote a comprehensive summary of all aspects of his theory. The reason for this lies in the medium itself, for the novel is an art form which is constantly in flux.

From an early age Hermann Broch was inclined towards philosophy and mathematics, but in compliance with his father's wishes he was trained as a textile engineer and became director of his father's textile factory at age twenty-two. Although he was successful in this career and invented a cotton combine soon after earning his diploma, in 1909 he began studying philosophy, psychology, and physics at the University of Vienna in addition to working at the factory. He was "dismayed and disappointed" upon realizing that within the academic framework he had no right to ask "even one of the many metaphysical questions" he had come there burdened with and "that there was no hope of any type of answer." What the university offered him—"scientific positivism" and the "search for a method of thought"—was not enough. It disturbed him that at that time "an agreement between apriorism and empiricism was no longer possible," and he was troubled by the conclusion he drew, namely that "the truth and thus ethics have become a pragmatic function of practical life." He believed this development was the source of "all the tension and strife" which eventually erupted into World War I; "national, economic, state, and social interests overlapped and were in mutual conflict everywhere, each demanding acceptance of its values alone," and a means of subordinating this "relativity of values" to a higher order was nowhere to be found.[8] Such thoughts gave rise to Broch's fundamental concept of the loss of the absolute in man's consciousness since the late Middle Ages and the related decline of values (*Verfall der Werte*).

These ideas are central to Broch's first great novel, a trilogy entitled *The Sleepwalkers* (*Die Schlafwandler*, 1931–32), written after he sold his father's factories in 1927. The individual novels are: *1888. Pasenow or Romanticism* (*1888. Pasenow oder die Romantik*); *1903. Esch or Anarchy* (*1903. Esch oder die Anarchie*); *1918. Huguenau or Realism* (*1918. Huguenau oder die Sachlichkeit*). The author introduced the term "polyhistorical novel" (*polyhistorischer Roman*) to describe his work's originality. According to Broch, a novel of this type should reflect and interpret its times, revealing its totality in a scholarly way. To this end Broch believed that the author's main task was to blend scholarship and poetry. He explained that polyhistorism was not achieved by including " 'scholarly' discourses in the book" or by choosing scholars as novel heroes, as leading authors of his time had done. "Though Gide, Musil, *The Magic Mountain*, and, in the final analysis, Huxley, are symptomatic of the coming polyhistorical novel, you will find the dreadful contrivance of 'scholarly' discourse in all of them" (August 5, 1931, letter to Daniel Brody). These novelists, Broch said in another letter, had no real idea of scholarship; they tried to bring "elements of *Bildung*" into the novel. To them "scholarship is like a block of crystal from which they break off one piece or another in order to garnish their narrative, usually in an inappropriate place, or to outfit a fictional scholar with it." His own ambition, which he definitely regarded as a risk, was to bring "live scholarship" to the novel. This should occur in two ways, "on the one hand, by making it intrinsic to a plot and to characters who have nothing more to do with 'Bildung' and thus do not engage in those dreadful scholarly conversations, and, on the other hand, by expressing it nakedly and directly and not as conversation filler" (August 3, 1931, letter to Frau Daniel Brody).

The latter method of bringing scholarship to the novel refers to the essays on the decline of values in the third part of *The Sleepwalkers*. They are not written by a character in the novel. Instead, Broch expresses his opinion as the author "nakedly and directly"; that is, he steps out of the fictional framework. Broch said in this regard, "Artistically it is just as legitimate for an author to step forward as to hide, provided that this, like all techniques, is subordinated to the architectonic" (June 24, 1930, letter to the Rhein-Verlag). However one might feel about the contents of the inserted essays, they in fact could not be removed from the work without destroying its "architectonic," a concept Broch preferred to structure to underscore how deliberately the polyhistorical novel is constructed. This structuring distinguishes it from representative works of the nineteenth century as well as from conventional twentieth-century novels.[9]

The Sleepwalkers is concerned with the problem of crime, or, more specifically, with the nature of the criminal. In the third volume the murderer Huguenau is introduced, a "value-free" man who cannot be judged by the society in which he commits his deeds because his contemporaries neither understand him nor are they equal to him. Broch lays the groundwork for a confrontation with Huguenau by exposing him as a representative of a type and thus demonstrating the ethical problem involved in condemning him. The exposure is not psychological, for, as Broch explains, his objective was not the psychological but the epistemological novel (*erkenntnistheoretischer Roman*). He emphasized that here he takes a different direction from James Joyce. The epistemological novel goes beyond psychological motivation to "epistemological principles and to the actual logic and plausibility of values" (July 16, 1930, letter to Frau Daniel Brody). For Broch, the character Huguenau stands at the "null-point of value atomization" in the "transition from one value system to a new one." The transition must

pass through a generation devoid of any relation to the old or new value systems, a generation whose very lack of any ties, whose near insane indifference to the suffering of others, whose most radical stripping away of values provides the ethical and therefore historical legitimization for the cruel disregard to which everything human is subjected in times of revolution.

Just as the value-free man appears at a certain time in history, the people he meets are also dependent upon history. In the first two parts of the trilogy, Broch focuses on the officer Joachim von Pasenow and the bookkeeper August Esch, showing how the core of their existence is romanticism and anarchy, as stated in the novels' titles. Both characters have been decisively influenced by their professions and see the world as an ordered system in which everything must have its place.

It is significant that as a boy Pasenow was sent to cadet school by his family, although he was "not in the least glad" to go. Later he was hardly much happier when he was expected to quit the military service and take over the family estate after his brother's death in a duel. Before the duel, his brother had written to him, "I hope that you have found more value in your life than I found in mine," and warned him about giving up his military career. As an officer, Joachim definitely did not find values which would have given him an advantage over his brother. Nor did he come to identify completely with his profession, but, after years of routine, "the uniform had come to symbolize many things." He felt "protected and secluded" in uniform and did not like to wear civilian clothes.

The uniform has a different meaning for Eduard von Bertrand, a character who constantly emerges in Joachim's consciousness and plays an important role in the plot. Broch referred to him as the "passive main character of the entire novel" (April 10, 1930, letter to G. H. Meyer, Rhein-Verlag). Bertrand went through military school two years ahead of Joachim von Pasenow, but later he left military service and became an independent businessman. In the first part of the novel he is, as a civilian and clear thinker, the contrasting figure to Joachim, the uniformed "romantic." The entire plot is accompanied by his judgments, which are expressed directly, indirectly in Pasenow's thoughts, or by the narrator. It is from Bertrand's standpoint that statements crucial to the interpretation of the novel as a whole are made about the concept of romanticism: "And because it is always romanticism when worldly things are elevated to an absolute, the real and strict romanticism of this age is that of the uniform." This defines Joachim's relationship to his world as well as to his uniform. It is the "true function of the uniform to display and establish order in the world and abolish the blurriness and flux of life." By laying aside the uniform Bertrand faces life and its uncertainties and leaves romanticism behind. Joachim's basic mistrust of Bertrand and his deep-seated irritation at Bertrand's speech and behavior result from his own insecurity. In all situations Bertrand is superior and noble, and his judgment is on a high intellectual niveau. Pasenow is incapable of recognizing this and merely detects, like a "sleepwalker," that with Bertrand another world begins that is beyond his grasp.

Esch's relationship to order is similar to Pasenow's. As a bookkeeper—a "perfect bookkeeper" and later head bookkeeper—he is master of a painstakingly achieved, complicated, and never-failing order. Every uncertainty is tracked down and wiped out. Whoever violates this order, whoever makes a mistake that results in the incorrectness of the whole, is soon recognized as guilty, punished, and possibly excluded from the realm of responsible order. Esch's conflict with the world, his fight for justice, and his feeling of obligation to report dishonesty to the police stem from his need to see the same accuracy and certainty in the world as in his office ledgers, for "we must have order." Yet he must admit to himself that the world is not in perfect order, for again and again he finds that there is something wrong, an "inexplicable accounting error." Resentful and restless, he shuttles among people and institutions, driven to find solutions which, however, he is too limited to comprehend. Gradually he believes he has found a just means of opposing the "accounting errors . . . that slip into the world so insidiously"; he is seized by the idea of sacrifice, which will bring about a "deliverance unto justice." He feels compelled to go to the highest authority he knows, Bertrand, who is president of the Central Rhine Shipping Company where he works. He admires Bertrand and yet at the same time feels he must judge—and therefore sacrifice—him. His visit with Bertrand in Badenweiler is experienced as a mystical act. Though Esch threatens to file a complaint with the police— he knows of Bertrand's homosexual relations and also blames him for the imprisonment of a Social Democratic functionary—Bertrand receives his guest with kindness and offers no resistance. He invites Esch to share a meal with him and takes leave of him cordially. Nonetheless, Esch reports him to the police the next day. By this time Bertrand has committed suicide. In the same way that Pasenow never fully grasps his own situation, Esch never progresses beyond a vague, dreamlike comprehension.

The main setting of the third part of the novel is a small town in a valley adjoining the Mosel. The majority of primary characters in the different tapestrylike plots come together here. Pasenow is now the town commandant, the highest military authority in the area, and Esch is owner and publisher of the *Kurtrier Message*, a local newspaper. Wilhelm Huguenau, a young Alsatian businessman from Colmar, had deserted his regiment on the Belgian front in early spring 1918 and had wandered to the little town in the Mosel region. By fraudulent manipulations he is able to gain control of Esch's newspaper, managing to win support from Pasenow. Esch and Pasenow have a common base in their sectarian religiosity, and both feel instinctively that Huguenau is their enemy. They are unable to see through him, however. When Pasenow finally has the proof in his hands that Huguenau is a deserter, he does not possess the strength to expose him; Huguenau's effrontery and threats of extortion catch him unaware. The deserter goes free, and Pasenow is left a broken man. After the outbreak of the revolution in the fall of 1918, Huguenau murders Esch in the general confusion and then leaves the city. After returning home, he again devotes himself to the world of business "in the spirit of his ancestors, solidly and for profit."

Whereas one could explain Huguenau's hostility towards Pasenow as self-defense, the same cannot be said in the case of Esch's murder. In the last section of *Huguenau*, titled *Epilogue*, Broch examines this murder closely, asking how it is to be understood and evaluated and how Huguenau himself might have justified it. "He didn't need to give it any thought, and in fact he didn't," Broch states. "But if he had done so, then he would only have said that this behavior was reasonable" and correct at the time, "that in less warlike or revolutionary times he would have refrained from the deed, which however would have been a pity." Here Broch leaves no doubt as to the unscrupulous nature of a man who feels neither shame nor regret at the thought of the murder. Broch speaks of the "breakthrough of irrationality," made possible "since no value system hindered him and contained the irrational." In the "absolute freedom of values of an individual who has become autonomous and isolated," Huguenau committed a "type of holiday act." Not only did the general circumstances allow for it, but he committed the deed at a time when his business ethics were also suspended.

Broch expressed his theme in the third part of *The Sleepwalkers* in a special way through the form. He himself called it a "novum of the novel form" (June 22, 1931, letter to Daniel Brody) and described his new technique in one of his self-commentaries: "The book consists of a series of stories which are all variations on the same theme, namely man's banishment back into loneliness—a banishment due to the decline of values—and his new productive strengths which arise from the loneliness." The individual stories are woven together like a tapestry, each rendering a "different state of consciousness," ranging from the totally irrational ("Story of the Salvation Army Girl") to completely theoretical rationality ("Decline of Values"). "The other stories take place on staggered intermediate levels of rationality between these two poles" (July 23, 1931, letter to Frau Daniel Brody).

Of the numerous insertions, the "Story of the Salvation Army Girl" deserves particular mention because of its narrator, Dr. Bertrand Müller. In the sections by Dr. Bertrand Müller, the many allusions to ideas and images that were associated with Eduard von Bertrand in the first two novels of the trilogy led Karl Robert Mandelkow to make the assumption that the two persons are identical. Furthermore, Mandelkow claims that this person is the author of the essays on the decline of values.[10] Other Broch scholars have not concurred but have merely confirmed a similarity and affinity between the characters. That Mandelkow's evidence and line of argument are impressive is indisputable, but they should not be regarded in a positivistic sense. In the modern novel, characters overlap, intertwine, and can no longer be separated as "characters" as in the nineteenth century. The closeness of the two Bertrands, the uncertainty concerning their relationship, the suspicious name repetition, and the recurrence of ideas and images are of course intentional on the part of the author and are not a mere question of "physical identity: yes or no?" The uncertainties make for a particular fascination in the third part of the novel which also has a retroactive effect on both previous parts. However, the question of the authorship of the essays must be seen somewhat differently. In light of Broch's statements on the polyhistorical novel, it is not possible that Eduard von Bertrand / Bertrand Müller is the author of the essays on the decline of values. It was exactly this sort of "scholarly" discourse by fictional characters that Broch wanted to avoid, preferring instead to present scholarship "nakedly and directly."

Broch's relationship to his contemporaries is not a question of literary dependency—even in the case of James Joyce—but of lively confrontation with others who had similar objectives. "Superficial observers believe that I am emulating Joyce because I have studied him," Broch wrote in a letter seven weeks before his death. He felt he need "not expressly assert" that this could not be further from his thoughts (April 11, 1951, to Karl August Horst). Twenty years earlier he had specifically singled out Joyce from all the other modern authors mentioned in connection with the polyhistorical novel: "Joyce has nothing to do with the *Bildung* disorder of the others, but neither his method nor his superior virtuosity can be imitated, quite simply because they are unique" (August 5, 1931, letter to Daniel Brody). The manner and extent to which this method brought scholarship to the novel is detailed by

Broch in a section of his Joyce essay that is of fundamental importance to the history of the novel. In this section it becomes clear how narration since Albert Einstein differs from previous forms of narration, which of course does not mean that modern narration is dependent on the natural sciences. It is more a case of parallel phenomena whose deep-seated relationship is beyond doubt.

Broch's reasoning is as follows: whereas classical physics was satisfied with "observing and measuring the phenomena under investigation" and took the "medium of observation, the act of seeing," into consideration only insofar as it could result in errors—whether "through the defectiveness of the human senses" or "of man's measuring instruments"—the theory of relativity has "discovered that there is a fundamental source of error beyond this, namely the act of seeing itself. . . . Therefore, in order to avoid this source of error, the observer and his act of seeing . . . must be included in the field of observation," thus creating the "theoretical unity of physical object and physical subject." As a parallel to this Broch explains that the

> classical novel was satisfied with observing real and psychic conditions of life and with describing these in language. . . . What Joyce does is considerably more complicated. With him the realization is always there that one cannot simply place the object within the field of observation and describe it, but that the subject—that is the narrator and no less the language with which he describes the object—is also part of the field of observation.

What Joyce aspired to was the "unity of depicted object and means of depiction in the broadest sense."

Much of what Broch says about Joyce applies to his own writing as well. In reading *Ulysses* (1922), he may have become particularly aware of his own artistic direction. About 1930 he read *Ulysses* in German translation (1927) while working on *The Sleepwalkers*. It is, however, beyond question that he designed and also executed the trilogy in his own poetic style, a style comprising his entire world of thoughts, feelings, and desires. Broch clearly differentiated between *The Sleepwalkers* and Joyce when he spoke of the epistemological novel. The unity of depicted object and means of depiction which he described in the case of Joyce was undoubtedly an artistic necessity for Broch as well. The narrative upsurges, transitions into lyrical prose, dreamlike haziness of events (Esch's trip to Badenweiler), and "near symphonic fullness" (January 28, 1932, letter to Daniel Brody) of the ending of *The Sleepwalkers* prove that for Broch, who was primarily concerned with the "breakthrough of irrationality," the unity between subject and object came from within as an expression of his own creative personality.

There are many similarities between Broch's novel and *The Man without Qualities* (*Der Mann ohne Eigenschaften*, 1930–1942) by Robert Musil. Manfred Durzak quotes from an article by David Marani in which Broch and Musil are compared to each other, perhaps for the first time: "Both are looking for new approaches, both find rational reality insufficient, both advance into the irrationality of the possible toward a vision, both reveal the darkest areas of the soul, both know irony and satire, both dare theoretical-philosophical digressions within the novel."[11] These characteristics apply not only to the novels of Broch and Musil, but are tendencies which can be traced through the entire epoch; they found shape in Expressionism and were the precondition for the mythical novel.

That Musil's novel remained unfinished is most certainly related to its composition as a whole. There is no plot to be brought to a conclusion. What is decisive is neither plot nor conclusion but the narrative development of themes and problems which expand infinitely. Musil's primary concern in presenting them was the "unity of depicted object and means of depiction" of which Broch spoke. Musil says in this regard that the problem of "how I come to narrate is both my stylistic problem and the existential problem of the main character, and of course the solution is not simple."[12] The relationship between the author's narrative problem and the "existential problem of the main character" can be seen throughout the work in every chapter, and, near the end of the first volume (1930), Musil explains the direct connection between the two. The main character, Ulrich, realizes that the law "of narrative order" corresponds to wishful thinking. Man, "overburdened and dreaming of simplicity," longs for the law "of that simple order" which "consists of being able to say: 'When that had happened, then this came to pass!' " Because the "simple succession" is comforting, he reduces the "overwhelming multiplicity of life" to one dimension. He feels better if he can "string everything that has happened in time and place onto one thread, that famous 'narrative thread' which also makes up the thread of life." People "love the orderly succession of facts because it looks like an inevitability, and they feel protected somehow in the chaos by the impression that life has a 'course.' " The novel has "made artificial use" of this. The reader feels comfortable even when "the wanderer . . . rides on the country road in pouring rain or crunches with his feet through the snow in 30 degree below zero weather," if only the events are told in chronological order. Ulrich realizes that this "would be hard to comprehend if this eternal epic artifice with which the nannies calm their little ones . . . were not already a part of life itself." This insight helps Ulrich to understand his own situation, for he notices that he has personally "lost this primitive epic which private life still holds onto, even though publicly everything has already become unnarratable, no longer following a single 'thread,' but spreading out in an endlessly woven surface."

Musil's personal opinion was that "seemingly chronological narration is primarily a problem of ordering, ordering the events in a way which imitates the passing of time, but never claims to be identical with it."[13] This standpoint does not mean that the novel or narration as such is in a crisis, as has sometimes been maintained, but merely allows for the possibility that narration does not necessarily have to be chronological, or—insofar as one insists that the concept of narration implies a chronological sequence—that a novel does not necessarily have to consist of narration. Of course, there will always be chronological narrations because people enjoy them. On the other hand, reflection, dialogue, and many other forms had long been part of the novel.[14] Musil's problem was not whether there would continue to be novels—he never questioned that—but only "how I come to narrate" (he even uses the word narrate); because the means and the object of narration are a unity, his narrative problem is also the existential problem of the main character.

This existential problem is evident as early as the fourth chapter of the first part. The chapter is entitled: "If there is a sense of reality, there must also be a sense of possibility." The fact that Ulrich is the man without qualities has to do with his sense of possibility. He who possesses a sense of possibility "does not say, for example: Here this or that has happened, will happen, must happen; instead, he invents: Here this could, should, or might happen. And if one explains to him that something simply is the way it is, then he thinks: Well it could probably be different though." The sense of possibility is a creative predisposition. It can be defined as the ability "to imagine everything which could 'just as easily' be, and not to take what is more seriously than what is not." Whoever wishes to express his rejection of the man of possibilities calls him a fool, a know-it-all, a faultfinder. Whoever wishes to praise him calls him an idealist, but this description only applies to the "weak variety," those who are inadequate in the face of reality and for whom "it is really a deficiency" that they have no sense of reality. "The realm of the possible, however, includes not only the dreams of unstable persons, but also the yet unawakened intentions of God." Possible experiences and possible truths are not to be equated with real experiences and truths that are simply missing the quality "real." Instead, "they have, at least in the view of their followers, something very godly about them—a fire, a flight, a will to build and a conscious utopianism that does not shy away from reality but treats it as a challenge and invention." A comparison between the sense of reality and the sense of possibility reveals the essence of creativity. The possibilities contained in a thousand deutsche marks, it is argued, "are no doubt there whether one possesses them or not. . . . But a fool puts them into a stocking, says the realist, and an industrious person does something with them. . . . It is reality that awakens the possibilities, and nothing could be more absurd than to deny that." But this can be denied, bringing a further thought into the picture: in reality there are always the same possibilities, even in the thousand marks. The possibilities are repeated "until a man comes along for whom a real thing means no more than an imagined one. It is he who gives the new possibilities meaning and direction, and he who awakens them."

Part of Ulrich's existential problem—and thus part of the author's narrative problem—is that the sense of possibility has certain effects on its possessor: "Such a man is . . . by no means uncomplicated." His ideas are "nothing but realities yet unborn." Naturally he also has a sense of reality, "but it is a sense for possible realities," and this sense "reaches its goal much more slowly than the sense most people have for their real possibilities." As an "unpractical man," which he not only seems to be, but actually is, he remains "unreliable and unpredictable in his dealings with people," for his actions mean something different to him than to them. It is especially significant that his relationship to himself is also different from theirs, for he does not possess a sense of reality with respect to his own person either. This is the reason for the designation "man without qualities." It is not a judgment from the standpoint of those around him, but rather an ironical formulation of his existential problem. The chapter ends with the sentence: "And since the possession of qualities presupposes a certain joy in their reality, it is understandable that someone who cannot even produce a sense of reality with regard to himself can suddenly discover that one day he sees himself as a man without qualities."

Ulrich's sense of possibility is not only the reason for his lack of "qualities" and hence his passivity but also for the predominance of the utopian idea within the novel. Musil's utopia is never clearly defined. "Utopias mean approximately the same as possibilities." They are the countermovement against present conditions, against given realities; they point towards everything that is not but could be. The narrator tells us that Ulrich tried three professions in his desire to "become a man of importance"—he was an officer, an engineer and, with considerable success, a mathematician. He abandoned all three, though, since they did not suit his intentions. "But what intention did he actually have?" the narrator asks and after some deliberation answers ironically that "he could only say that he felt further from what he had really wanted to be than he had felt in his youth, that is, assuming that it had not remained unknown to him altogether." With yet sharper irony the narrator continues, "He saw . . . within himself all the abilities and qualities favored by the times in which he lived—with the exception of making money, which he did not need to do—but he had lost the possibility of applying them." Therefore Ulrich decides "to take a year off from his life in order to search for an appropriate application of his abilities." Utopianism and irony are fused in an explanation which seems to account for Ulrich's crucial decision, but actually defies logical reasoning, as indicated by the way the narrator plays with the words "qualities" and "possibilities."

The story begins at this point in Ulrich's life, in August 1913. The date is given at the end of the first paragraph, which is a parody on a meteorological report. The indication of place is also treated mockingly. Vienna is named, yet it is subsequently stressed that no particular importance should be attached to the name of the city. It is not always necessary to know exactly in what city one is staying; "that draws attention from more important things." Just as the author specifies time and place, but at the same time does not take them very seriously, he similarly creates uncertainty in the first chapter about the characters. He speaks of two people on a busy street whose demeanor gives evidence of their social background—"obviously" members of a "privileged social class." They also "knew . . . who they were and that they belonged in the capital city and imperial residence." But who are they? "Assuming they were named Arnheim and Ermelinda Tuzzi, which is however not the case, for in August Frau Tuzzi was in the company of her husband in Bad Aussee and Dr. Arnheim was still in Constantinople, then one is still faced with the puzzle of who they are." The puzzle described here shows that the author approached the problem of identity in a manner corresponding to the work's composition as a whole and to the "existential problem of the main character." Before Ulrich's sense of possibility has ever been mentioned, an example of the method it implies is given. The narrator proceeds from the possibility that the two people on the street are Arnheim and Ermelinda Tuzzi, characters who appear later in the novel, proves that it cannot be them, and then returns to the presumed possibility—which is now an unreal possibility, a mere supposition—and from there he constructs the puzzle of their identity. This demands concentration and careful thought from an educated reader, who must follow the sentence construction without first being informed that an identity problem exists; familiarity with the problem as such is presupposed. This is not a philosophy textbook, but a fictitious narration which offers inexhaustible entertainment because the questions are all left unsettled and because they are commented upon by an ingenious narrator.

The most important plot element in the first book is the "parallel action," a "great patriotic action" to which Ulrich is appointed secretary. The undertaking involves preparation for celebrating the seventieth jubilee of the rule of Kaiser Franz Joseph I in 1918, which is to be a "parallel action" to the thirtieth jubilee of the reign of Wilhelm II. Since both monarchies fell at the end of World War I, the irony of the "patriotic action" is evident to the reader from the outset. Through his connection with the parallel action, Ulrich comes into contact with a number of characters. They all embody his own possibilities and potentialities. At the same time, they are also related to each other as variations of certain traits and aspirations. Their function in the novel is to reflect and contrast. The events in which they take part are only the motivation for this and have no importance in and of themselves. Similarly, the characters from Ulrich's personal circle do not function in their own separate plots, but only in relationship to each other and to Ulrich.

His antagonist is decidedly the sex murderer, Moosbrugger, with whose case Ulrich is intensely involved. He is present at the last trial session when Moosbrugger hears his death sentence read aloud and responds by saying that he is satisfied, adding, however, that an insane man has been condemned. It is stated:

> That was an inconsistency; but Ulrich sat there breathlessly. That was clearly insanity and, just as clearly, no more than a distortion of our own elements of being. It was mangled and darkened; but somehow it occurred to Ulrich that if mankind could dream collectively, then Moosbrugger had to come into existence.

The knowledge that Moosbrugger concerns him directly can bring Ulrich into an emotional turmoil which affects his entire existence. Yet his personal involvement is not on the level of observable reality, but rather within the realm of images and dreams. He does not see Moosbrugger as the embodiment of drives which others merely repress, nor is he concerned with helping Moosbrugger escape; he rejects his friends' suggestions aimed at freeing Moosbrugger. In connection with a conversation about Moosbrugger he has the idea: "It is really true that one man . . . does not mean much more to the other than a series of metaphors." In great agitation he finally realizes that "there is nothing more foreign in the image of a murderer than in any other image. . . . Half begins to make sense, while the other half redissolves into nonsense. An escaped image of order: that is what Moosbrugger meant to him!"

Ulrich achieves this insight into the meaning of the murderer as an extreme image of the world when he is in a state of trance. He is not only a mathematician but is capable of experiencing mystical ecstasy. In the "other state" (*der andere Zustand*) divisions are dissolved and relationships become clear, allowing the true nature of things, which ordinarily is distorted, to emerge. Beginning in the second book (1933), Ulrich's tendency toward mystical experiences is actualized in his relationship to his sister Agathe, whom he meets again directly after his father's death. To their surprise, in the reunion scene they are both wearing almost identical Pierrot-like pajamas, and they immediately find themselves in relaxed conversation. Ulrich is attracted to his sister and regards her without irony. Soon the thought occurs to him that she is "a dreamlike repetition and variation of himself."

He loves himself in his sister and his sister in himself. Agathe leaves her husband, which she had already resolved to do, and joins Ulrich. Their conversations revolve around their unusual relationship as twins. Ulrich points out that the "longing for a double of the opposite sex" is age-old. One wishes for "the love of a being who should be fully like us yet also different from us." Through his contact with Agathe, Ulrich's relationship to himself and to everything around him changes. Since to him she embodies the self and self-love as well as the other and love for the other—resulting in the identity of the two—he also experiences the identity of self and world. The "other state," in which the love between brother and sister creates the magic of new life, is shaped by constantly changing scenery, moods, conversations, and undertakings, all leading towards incest as an accompanying subliminal process. The feeling between brother and sister can be "perverted and it can be a mythos," Musil said in his diary. "The Journey to Paradise," as an early version of the section containing the journey of love was titled, does not of course allow the "other state" to become permanent. As is to be expected, Musil had no solution or conclusion for a process which, insofar as it is actualized in chronological sequence, must lead to an ending but, nonetheless, retains its utopian quality in the mythical realm.

As praiseworthy as it was for the scholar Adolf Frisé to print (in the 1952 edition) Musil's drafts for the continuation of single plot strands, it was inappropriate to use these drafts as a basis for constructing the novel's ending. The drafts lack exact dates; early ones are placed next to later ones, and occasionally Frisé took parts of different drafts to make one chapter. To the literary interpreter many of the sketches seem to be superseded by the parts Musil completed and are only valuable as early experiments.

The last part published by the author himself is his second book, which appeared in 1933 and bears the subtitle *Third Part—into the Millenium*. Here the characters from the first book reappear and the questions raised there—in particular the case of Moosbrugger—are discussed again, but they no longer form the main substance. Instead, Ulrich's relation to Agathe is in the foreground. In this connection the problem of crime recurs, for Agathe alters her father's testament in Ulrich's presence in order to disinherit her husband. Whereas Moosbrugger's crime was totally repulsive, here it is specifically stated that Agathe presented a "beautiful sight" during her crime, and Ulrich, "completely bewildered," has to realize that the line between good and evil does not exist here. Again, an evaluation of the moral question is tied in with his own existential problem. A conclusive decision is made neither here nor in the case of any of the other questions discussed; such a decision would have contradicted the intellectual style of the novel.

Although Musil worked on the novel almost without interruption until his death in 1942, he did not succeed in creating a final, completed version.

His miserable living conditions—after 1939 he lived in exile in Switzerland, and even before that had struggled with financial difficulties and sickness—may have hampered his work. However, this is certainly not the decisive reason that the novel remained a fragment. The reason lies much more in the work itself, in its design and narrative style, which are connected to the existential problem of the main character. In his last years Musil knew that his approach to problems exceeded his intellectual strength. Since his concern was not for the historical period of 1913 but for his own present time, he could not find an answer to the question of how his main character should live in that epoch. Recent research has proven that he gave contemporary thought, including the insights of renowned psychologists and philosophers, considerable attention in Ulrich's reflections.[15] Yet Musil was too much of an artist to make his book a compendium of solutions. His undertaking was "an intellectual adventure," a "research journey" whose end he could not foresee.[16]

5 / Tendency toward Myth

Robert Musil is no exception to his time when he has Ulrich regard his love for Agathe mythically. A turning towards myth, a fascination with and acknowledgement of archetypal patterns, is also found in other contemporary novels. Whether one can actually ascribe to Thomas Mann "something like mythical intuition," as Kerényi has done, is justifiably seen by Hans Wysling as doubtful, but it is beyond question that Thomas Mann's involvement with myth was deep-seated.[1] It was less a matter of the "return of the European spirit to the highest, the mythical realities," than of unforgettable impressions from childhood and youth. The importance of these first became fully apparent to Mann in later years, when he recognized the aesthetic possibilities they contained.[2] He had lived with fairy tales and mythology since he was a child; they were a world imparted to him through stories and readings at home and in school. He tells how he assimilated them into his games and daydreams:

> At an early age I was as much at home outside Troy and on Ithaca and Olympus as the other children were in the land of Leatherstocking. And what I had absorbed so zealously, I acted out in play. I hopped through the rooms as Hermes with winged shoes made of paper; as Helios I balanced a brilliant gold halo on my ambrosial head; as Achilles I mercilessly dragged my sister, who played Hector for better or worse, three times around the walls of Troy. But as Zeus I stood on a small, red-lacquered table, which served as the mountain of the gods.[3]

While working on the *Joseph* tetralogy, he reported that its conception had "long and deep roots" in his spiritual life; as a boy he already had had a "pronounced interest in ancient Oriental, particularly ancient Egyptian life and read relevant books on the subject" (May 23, 1935, letter to Louise Servicen). That the importance of the mythical world then diminished for the adolescent boy corresponds to the natural development of the modern intellectual, but that it was not lost or forgotten links Thomas Mann with many other representatives of his time whose relationship to the mythical realm may well have come about in a similar way.

Royal Highness (*Königliche Hoheit*, 1909), the first novel Thomas Mann published after *Buddenbrooks*, is a fairy-tale-like story. Klaus Heinrich, the second-born prince in a very small Grand Duchy in Wilhelmine Germany, was born with a malformed left hand. His distressed father, fearing that his son could later be hindered in performing his official duties, cannot become reconciled to a "prince with one hand." The minister of state reminds him of a Gypsy woman's hundred-year-old prophecy that a prince with one hand would "give more . . . to the country than others would with two"; he would bring "the greatest good fortune." The fulfillment of this prophecy forms the basis of the novel's plot. At first the reader learns that the principality is in a state of neglect and impoverishment; the Old Castle is dilapidated as are all the other nearby castles belonging to the ducal family. Young Klaus Heinrich, who is always urged to hold his stunted hand in such a way as to conceal it, is leading a monotonous and lonely life. After the Grand Duke's death, Klaus Heinrich's older brother does not feel capable of fulfilling his duties. Therefore, he appoints Klaus Heinrich his permanent representative, conferring on him the title of Royal Highness and leaving practically all ceremonial duties to him. For Klaus Heinrich this means an empty life, full of weariness and exertion. As popular as he is among the people, he remains a representative with no relationship to the substance of what he represents. The festivity with which the public surrounds his appearances prevents him from seeing the reality of their living conditions. The turning point comes through Imma Spoelmann, the attractive, unconventional daughter of an American multimillionaire who buys and settles in one of the ducal castles. Klaus Heinrich breaks out of his narrow existence by approaching Imma, though without really knowing where his contact with her will lead. Imma allows him to associate with her, but she rejects his way of life—all appearance and show—and mistrusts his feelings for her. While they are engaged in a struggle with each other, the entire population takes an interest in the pair; to the people Imma is the "child of a king or fairy from a land of fable, a princess in the rarest sense of the word." The court takes advantage of the situation; it informs Klaus Heinrich that the state's finances have been dissipated and declares its willingness to support the personal wishes of the prince, provided that he keep the welfare of all in mind. In other words, every concession will be made to Imma regarding her nonaristocratic descent if her father agrees to replenish the state's coffers. Klaus Heinrich immediately begins reading economics books and finally wins Imma's confidence through his dedicated "studies for the common welfare." With their engagement her elevation in rank begins, which should lead from countess to princess to queen. Imma's father, however, is not impressed. In his dealings with the representatives of the court, he constantly refers to the prince as "the young man" and says, "If he had only learned something and had a respectable occupation!" But he finances the state, and the land flourishes.

The novel is, in Thomas Mann's words, an "instructive fairy tale" and not a "realistic picture of court life in the early twentieth century." He did use a "mass of documentary evidence" for his depiction of life at court and observed much with his own eyes, but what was actually important was that he narrated from his own life; he says he never really worked with any other "material." The novel analyzes princely life as formal and irrelevant, as a life "of performance," and shows the "redemption of His Majesty through love."[4]

In 1905 Thomas Mann married Katja Pringsheim. Before their engagement he felt himself to be like the prince fighting for Imma Spoelmann. Imma

> did not prevent him from calling once or twice a week, did not prevent him from speaking to her, pleading and entreating, and now and again holding her hands between his. But she was only being tolerant, she remained unmoved, her fear of making a decision, her reluctance to leave her aloof and mocking realm and avow her loyalty to him, seemed unconquerable.

In Thomas Mann's letters from the year 1904, there are formulations which recur in *Royal Highness*. For example, on July 14 he wrote, "A neurologist and good psychologist . . . confirmed to me (as I had long suspected) that this fear of making a decision is a notorious sickness." Similarly, he mentions a certain "awkwardness or something like it," which Katja Pringsheim felt in the beginning of their relationship and which she interpreted as a reaction to his behavior (June 1904). In the novel Imma reproaches the prince: "No, it is not confidence you inspire in a person, but coldness and self-consciousness, and even if I were to make an effort to get closer to you, this sort of awkwardness would prevent me from doing so." Just as the prince, taking up Imma's words, implores, "Yes, make somewhat of an effort and don't ever become confused again by that sort of awkwardness, or whatever it is," and just as he calls her the "happiness" which he could no longer do without, Thomas Mann wrote in 1904 to Katja that to be healed of the artificiality in his life, of the "lack of innocent faith" in himself, is only possible through the happiness Katja can bring him: "Be . . . my salvation . . . and never be confused by that 'awkwardness or something like it'!"

It is noteworthy that the novel is written on so many different levels. Both a fairy tale and a comedy, it objectively depicts life at court and also reflects the author's personal experiences. Furthermore, the difficulties presented by the prince's purely representative existence illustrate Thomas Mann's feelings about the difficulties of an artistic life. "You know," he wrote to Katja, "what a cold, impoverished, purely depictive, purely representative life I led for years. You know that for years, *important* years, I thought nothing of myself as a person and only wanted to be an artist" (June 1904). This self-interpretation helps explain the inclusion of the idea of redemption ("Be . . . my salvation"), a mythical motif which is not merely an element of the fairy tale but also an expression of man's highest expectations.

A transparency of style and multiplicity of levels characterize all of Thomas Mann's subsequent novels. The worldwide appeal of *The Magic Mountain* (*Der Zauberberg*, 1924) is due in part to a style which allows it to be read in completely different ways. The autobiographical motivation for the novel was the author's three-week visit in 1912 to an Alpine sanatorium in the Swiss town of Davos, where his wife spent six months recovering from a mild case of tuberculosis. Mann intended to use the "strange impressions" he had of the patients' and doctors' conduct and to write a "humorous companion-piece" to *Death in Venice*, "a sort of satire" in which "the fascination of the death idea" would now be "humorously treated." But the material soon revealed unexpected dimensions. The First World War intervened, bringing new experiences. Other work was pressing. In the end, the sanatorium material became a long novel which appeared in two volumes. Its autobiographical motivation seemed to lie much further in the past than the number of elapsed years would indicate. Although the entire epoch that comes to life in Mann's portrayal of Davos in 1912 was now a part of history, the novel caused a great sensation upon publication. It was discussed and criticized in medical circles. Many people saw it, then and even later, as "a satire on life in a lung sanatorium. . . . But the critique of sanatorium therapeutic methods is only the foreground of the novel. Its actuality lies in the quality of its backgrounds."[5]

Hans Castorp, the main character, is part of all the novel's levels, its foreground as well as its background. After his engineering exams, the twenty-three-year-old from Hamburg travels to Davos on his doctor's recommendation. He is to stay three weeks to recuperate and visit his tubercular cousin, Joachim Ziemssen, in the Berghof sanatorium. The three weeks become seven years. When Hans Castorp undergoes an examination in the third week on account of a cold and fever, Dr. Behrens, the head physician at the Berghof, finds a "moist spot" on his lung and advises him to stay. Not until the outbreak of the First World War does Hans Castorp leave Davos. The last one hears of him is that he took part in the war as a volunteer; the narrator cannot say whether or not he survived.

As stated in the foreword to the novel, Hans Castorp's story took place a long time ago. Stories must "be in the past, . . . the more in the past, the better for them in their capacity as stories and for their narrator, the murmuring conjurer of the imperfect tense." Yet this has nothing to do with the passage of time, but rather with the fact that the story takes place before a turning point, "in the old days, in the world before the Great War." Just as the story's time frame seems fairy-tale-like by reason of its proximity to that turning point, which is actually not so remote from the narrator, it "could . . . be," the narrator says, that the story "also has this or that . . . to do with the fairy tale otherwise." The fairy tale is mentioned here with caution. Even though the title and the recurrence of the number seven (seven tables, seven years, seven months, seven minutes) would seem to require no further explanation, they alone do not reveal what type of mythical elements are present in Hans Castorp's story, nor is it even certain that such elements are present at all. It is only from the entirety of the novel that one can see how Hans Castorp's story is held together by a multilayered fabric of mythical concepts. The narrator and the individual characters contribute to it, each in his own way, throughout the work.

The narrator himself is very active. He gives hints from the beginning, and from chapter to chapter he points out—unobtrusively and reservedly, yet audibly for the alert reader—that there is something special about a story which is, as he says in the first sentence, "highly worth telling." On the last page, at the end of the seventh book, he explains that "it was a hermetic story." The word "hermetic" had been discussed by the Jesuit, Naphta, and the Italian humanist, Settembrini, in two different conversations in the last part of book 6, and Hans Castorp, present both times, made an important contribution to the first discussion.

Naphta uses the word in connection with the alchemic and magical conceptions of the Freemasons. He defines it as *tightly closed*, including the atmospheric effect of self-containment as part of his definition. A "symbol of alchemist transmutation . . . was above all the tomb . . . the place of decomposition. It is the quintessence of all hermetics, nothing more than the container, the well-preserved crystal retort in which matter is pressed to its final transformation and purification." Hans Castorp at first lingers on the word itself, rolling it around on his tongue and losing himself in its aura: "'Hermetics' is well said, Herr Naphta. 'Hermetic'—I always liked that word. It's truly a magical word with vast, indefinite associations." He thinks of canning jars,

> hermetically closed jars with fruit and meat. . . . They stand for days and years and when one is opened . . . the contents are completely fresh and untouched. . . . Of course that is not alchemy and purification, it is just preserving, and thus the name preserves. But the magic of it is that what was preserved was withdrawn from time, hermetically sealed off from it, time passed it by.

Time—one of the central themes of the novel—is thus connected with hermetics.

However, the meanings of the word "hermetic" and their function within the novel have not yet been exhausted. By elucidating the mystical and occult rites of certain lodges when novices are initiated and tested, Naphta leads directly into the events of the novel. His exposition can serve as a model of a hermetic story. According to the narrator, Naphta did not mean for it to be Hans Castorp's story. Nonetheless, Castorp's story may be measured against Naphta's model. Naphta's summary is as follows: "The path of mysteries and purification was beset with dangers, it led through fear of death, through the realm of decomposition, and the learner, the neophyte, is youth eager for the wonders of life, desirous of an awakening to demonic experiences, led by masked ones who are only shadows of the secret." At this point towards the end of the sixth book, the reader is in a position to compare Hans Castorp's situation on the Magic Mountain with the neophyte's situation described by Naphta. For example, the doctors who always wear smocks, one white, the other black, are comparable to the "masked ones." Castorp's answer, which sounds so simple, is ironical and ambiguous: "Thank you so much, Professor Naphta. Excellent. So that is hermetic pedagogy. It can't hurt that I learn something about that, too."

Since the word "hermetic" is derived from Hermes, it can also be directly applied to the god himself. Thomas Mann once called him his "favorite deity."[6] In the second conversation on hermetics, Hermes' two forms are described. Settembrini argues for Hermes Trismegistus, who is identical with the Egyptian god Thoth, the "inventor of writing, protector of libraries, and stimulator of all intellectual activity." He gave man the literary word and agonistic rhetoric. Naphta meanwhile refers to the "guide of departed souls" who was "an ape, moon, and soul deity, a baboon with a crescent moon on his head . . . a god of death and the dead . . . father of hermetic alchemy."

The entire novel is marked by the concepts tied to the word "hermetic" in the two conversations of the sixth book. Hans Castorp's journey from Hamburg to Davos is a journey into a hermetic realm. It is expressly stated that it is a long journey. The last part of the trip, "the actual adventurous part," is "a rapid and difficult ascent . . . on a wild, rocky route . . . into the high mountains." The narrator emphasizes the frightening and unusual aspects of the journey. Naphta's model can already be applied here, on the first page of the first chapter, for the path of the neophyte is "beset with dangers." Hans Castorp becomes excited; "being lifted up" into foreign realms, "swaying" between the habitual world "fathoms deep" below him and the unknown world up above, the young traveler feels dizzy and ill shortly before his arrival. The feeling of familiarity upon seeing his cousin, Joachim Ziemssen, who meets him at the train station, cannot alter the strange effect this world has on him. "One's ideas change here," Joachim says, after they have climbed into the coach on their way to the sanatorium.

When, two and one-half weeks after his arrival, Hans Castorp stays in bed on Dr. Behrens's orders and agrees to remain as a patient in the sanatorium for an indefinite time, he has not only changed his ideas but has also undergone changes of a psychic and physical nature. Directly after entering the sanatorium he notices that his cheeks are hot. Whether the Davos air really brought out a "latent illness," as Behrens claims, whether Hans Castorp would have remained healthy if he had not come to Davos, whether his "moist spot" would have healed by itself like the other "old spots" Behrens found, "one cannot know," as the narrator has the incorruptible Joachim Ziemssen say while withholding his own opinion. Thomas Mann reported in his Princeton lecture that about ten days after his arrival in Davos he, like Hans Castorp, came down with a cold. The doctor there found a "moist spot" on his lung and advised him to undergo treatment in the sanatorium for a half year: "If I had followed his advice, who knows, I might still be there! I wrote *The Magic Mountain* instead." Three weeks in the sanatorium were sufficient to give him an idea of "the dangers of such a milieu for young people—and tuberculosis is a disease of the young." He speaks of the "charmed circle of isolation and invalidism" on the mountain.[7] A comparison of the autobiographical statements with the corresponding passages in the novel illustrates how myth and irony determine and complement each other in the fictitious narrative. The juxtaposition and interaction of these different artistic treatments of the material contribute to the multileveled nature of the novel, and their seamless tie makes Thomas Mann's style unique. What Hans Castorp's "moist spot" really is remains unanswered, an example of the novel's irony.

What is certain, however, is that Hans Castorp obeys the doctor's orders. He was "bedridden . . . because Hofrat Behrens, the highest authority in the world . . . had ordered it." The fact that the directionless young man feels a need for authority is stated several times in the chapter preceding the medical examination. Moreover, the doctor's instructions coincide with his own innermost desires. The hermetic atmosphere has not only caused his "burning cheeks," but beginning on the first day, in addition to the fact that his customary cigar has lost its taste, Hans Castorp feels a strange heartbeat. That evening an unusual chill comes over him; he feels miserable, "feverish and shivering." His uneasiness concerning Madame Chauchat begins on this day as well. She always comes to the dinner table a bit too late and lets the glass door slam behind her. Hans Castorp, annoyed because he despises door slamming, does not realize until the third time that the sound is caused by a woman, who goes with a "peculiar slink" to the "Good Russian Table." She has broad cheekbones and narrow eyes and reminds him "of something or someone." That evening he sees her twice again in the social room and each time tries to recollect of what or of whom she reminds him. That night, his second in Davos, he dreams that Madame Chauchat gave him a pencil in the courtyard of his school.

Hans Castorp becomes aware of his dream's "prototype" on the last day of the first week (thus on the *seventh* day) when he is suddenly overcome by weakness during an outing and enters into a trancelike state. He has gone out alone to escape from the sanatorium bustle for awhile, for it seems to him that the irregularities in his physical health have more to do with the sanatorium than with the "process of acclimatization." During the trance he relives a schoolyard scene which actually took place when he was thirteen years old. At that age he observed a boy named Pribislav Hippe, called "Kirghiz" by his classmates because of his Slavic features, with "extraordinary involvement," but without trying to define his feelings. His excitement and tension, disappointment and fulfillment, finally culminated in the schoolyard scene. A year later the relationship was over; nothing special had happened in the meantime. Hans Castorp had boldly precipitated the schoolyard scene by approaching Pribislav Hippe, to whom he had never spoken, before a drawing class and asking, "Excuse me, can you lend me a pencil?" Only a few words were exchanged. Hippe asked him to return the pencil, explained its mechanism, and warned him not to break it. Hans Castorp "was never happier in his life than in this drawing class because he could draw with Pribislav Hippe's pencil. . . . He took the liberty of sharpening the pencil and kept three or four of the red-lacquered shavings in an inner drawer of his desk for almost a year." He returned the pencil to Hippe quickly and matter-of-factly.

The reliving of the schoolyard scene shows the inevitability of Hans Castorp's preoccupation with Madame Chauchat. When he comes to himself again after his trance, he comprehends the link between the past and the present: "What a remarkable likeness to her—to her up here! Is that why I am so interested in her? Or, perhaps: is that why I was so interested in *him?*" Each further encounter with her convinces him anew of the identity of Chauchat and Hippe. It is not a question of mere resemblance; "they were the same eyes. . . . Everything was exactly like Pribislav." This is an overpowering realization. Moreover, Madame Chauchat's physical appearance and conduct provide him with an insight into the nature of sickness. He realizes that her door slamming, lax posture, and inconsiderate glances are manifestations of the illness that gives her a certain degree of freedom and licentiousness.

Through Hans Castorp's enchantment with Madame Chauchat, the hermetic realm reveals characteristics of the Venusberg, the legendary mountain which does not let its visitors go free. Enthusiastic and at the same time fearful, he is confined "in a small space." This applies both to his concrete situation in the Berghof and to his state of mind. "That the long-forgotten Pribislav met him again up here as Madame Chauchat and looked at him with Kirghiz eyes was like a confinement within the inevitable and inescapable—inescapable in a comforting, but also uneasy sense. It was promising and at the same time uncanny, even threatening." With regard to Hans Castorp's motive for staying, the narrator conjectures that he "would not have prolonged his stay by even this much [it is October, two months after his arrival] if any reasonably satisfying explanation of the meaning and purpose of life had reached his uncomplicated soul from the depths of his time." This shows how a novel tending toward the mythical can also take on aspects critical of the times. It must be pointed out that Joachim Ziemssen's decision is the opposite of Hans Castorp's; he does not let himself be ensnared on the Venusberg, although he is exposed to the same enticements as Hans Castorp. For Joachim there is no uncertainty about the meaning and purpose of life. His willful departure against the doctor's advice after eighteen months in Davos demonstrates that Hans Castorp's decision to stay was not the only choice available to him.

Hans Castorp gives the mythical dimension of his emotional bond an individual imprint on Walpurgis Night, seven months after his arrival, when he repeats the Pribislav Hippe schoolyard scene with Clawdia Chauchat. Until that point he had not spoken to her. Using the German "du" form of address permitted during the festival of *Fasching*, he asks her, "Do *you* happen to have a pencil?" The scene, modified to fit the situation, is played through carefully. Hans Castorp is in utmost agitation and deathly pale, while Clawdia, smiling, is untouched by his passion. She rummages through her leather purse, takes out a small silver pencil and warns him, "Prenez garde, il est un peu fragile";[8] and she explains the simple mechanism to him "with their heads bent over it," just as in the scene which is the prototype of this repetition. During the love dialogue which follows, he holds her pencil in his hand and reveals—mostly in French—his inner world to her. The scene ends with her warning upon leaving the room, "N'oubliez pas de me rendre mon crayon."[9]

Much of what Thomas Mann said about the relationship between myth and epic in his speech "Freud and the Future" was already realized in *Magic Mountain*. This is evident in the scene Hans Castorp so consciously celebrates. The legitimization of his love lies in the fact of its repetition, physically represented by the pencil in his hand. Hans Castorp possesses insight into his individual myth. His feeling of certainty towards the woman who regards him with a smile of amusement derives from a consciousness of the inescapability of what has already happened once before. After Clawdia has left the sanatorium, he must wait there for her return.

Making use of the special situation at *Fasching*—such as the "du" form of address, the festive dress, and the general informality—Hans Castorp celebrates several things at the same time. He experiences as an individual what Thomas Mann later describes to be a general phenomenon: "The festival is the negation of time, an event, a solemn act that takes place according to a prototype. What happens is not happening for the first time, but ceremoniously and according to pattern; it is of the present and it recurs, just as festivals recur in time."[10]

As Thomas Mann emphasized at Princeton, one of the basic themes of the novel is that of heightening, which "is always referred to as alchemistic." The heightening of Hans Castorp's personality is seen not only in his behavior at the festival but also in the clarity with which he explains his emotions to Clawdia Chauchat and in the certainty of his judgment concerning problems she mentions so casually. On the one hand, the hermetic realm as such plays a part in the heightening of his ability to think, to feel, and to judge. Hans Castorp's alertness, his willingness to expand his knowledge in all fields of science and culture, the thoroughness of his readings during the rest cure, and his constant reflection on the readings all contribute, as Naphta says in the sixth chapter, to "transsubstantiation to something higher. Thus a heightening . . . magical pedagogy."

On the other hand, a stimulating and catalyzing element is Herr Settembrini, to whom Hans Castorp directs a speech of thanks on *Fasching* before he turns his attention to Madame Chauchat. He thanks him for taking such a friendly interest in him over the past seven months. Hans Castorp conversed with the Italian humanist on his first morning in Davos and immediately received from him a mythical interpretation of the world of the Magic Mountain and a warning about its dangers. Settembrini called the two doctors, Behrens and Krowkowski, by the names Minos and Rhadamanthus, the judges of the dead. When he heard that Hans Castorp was healthy and only there for a visit, he compared him to "Odysseus in the land of the shades," and spoke of his "boldness in descending to the depths where the dead reside so futilely and meaninglessly." Hans Castorp's objection to the term "depths"—after all, he had "climbed up about five thousand feet"—did not deter Settembrini: "It only seemed that way to you! Upon my honor, that was a deception. . . . We have sunk very low, indeed." During this conversation Settembrini strikes a familiar pose, "with feet crossed, leaning on his walking stick." In *Death in Venice*, Aschenbach observes the foreign wanderer in the same pose. According to the German author Lessing, this was the way death must have been portrayed in classical antiquity.[11]

Thomas Mann himself emphasized that the characters in the novel were "nothing but exponents, representatives, emissaries" from spiritual worlds, but, he hoped, not "mere shadow figures and walking parables." Actually, many readers had reassured him that they found these characters to be "very real people indeed."[12] One character Thomas Mann mentions specifically in this regard is Settembrini, to whom Hans Castorp says at the *Fasching* celebration, "You are not just any person with a name, you are a representative, Herr Settembrini." What Settembrini represents is Hermes in his different forms, the "guide of departed souls" in Hades, the "god of death and the dead" of whom Naphta speaks, and also the Trismegistus whom Settembrini himself reveres—the "humanistic Hermes," responsible for culture, writing, speech, and intellectual endeavors. Furthermore, Settembrini is the representative of a specific Weltanschauung; liberal and progressive, he opposes Naphta's extremism in their verbal duels. The subjects debated between Settembrini and the Jesuit Naphta, who appears in the eleventh month of Castorp's stay on the mountain, are philosophical and political questions current during the period of the novel's conception. By participating in these confrontations, Hans Castorp expands his knowledge and learns to take a position in battles of opinion.

When the novel appeared, many readers followed the discussions between Settembrini and Naphta with particular suspense, since the topics were relevant at that time; today their value is primarily historical. It is characteristic of the *Zeitroman* that the conditions criticized and the ideas discussed generally become history after only two decades. *The Magic Mountain* is a *Zeitroman* "in a double sense," Thomas Mann stated, "first in a historical sense, in that it seeks to present the inner significance of an epoch, the prewar period of European history. And secondly, because time is one of its themes . . ."[13]

What is meant by "pure time" is discussed in conversations and reflections throughout the novel and is expressed through its structure. Hans Castorp was told early in his stay that the concept of time in the Berghof is different from that in the flatlands. "Our smallest unit of time is the month. We compute in a grand style—that's a privilege of shades," Settembrini informs him at their first meeting, thus proving that he does not completely belong to the Berghof society, for here one does not compute time. "It doesn't pass at all. . . . there is no time," Joachim had said the previous evening, admitting the next morning that it was a pleasure to take his temperature for then one could tell what a minute "really" was. Hans Castorp recognizes the problem very quickly; with time "there is no 'really' at all," he corrects Joachim. It is as long or as short as it seems to a person, "but how long or how short it is in reality, no one knows." In the chapter "Excursus on the Sense of Time," the narrator says that

emptiness and monotony . . . do in fact stretch the moment and the hour . . . , but they shorten and dissipate the larger and largest time periods, even down to nothing. Conversely, a rich and interesting substance is capable of shortening the hour and even the day and lending them wings. On a large scale, however, it gives time breadth, weight, and solidity so that eventful years pass much more slowly than those poor, empty light ones which are blown away by the wind and vanish.

Therefore, the longer Hans Castorp is on the Magic Mountain and the more dominated by habit his days become, the shorter time becomes for him. His first day is the longest, and the narrator requires more narrative time for it than he uses later for months and years; adapting to Hans Castorp's way of experiencing time, he can cover longer and longer time periods in less narrative time. Hans Castorp finally loses all sense of time and no longer even knows how old he is. His hermetic enchantment into timelessness has transpired, made possible "by virtue of the lack of a time organ within us" and by "our absolute inability to determine the passing of time, given no indication from the external world, to any degree of accuracy at all."

While Hans Castorp experiences time as a cyclical movement which is almost the same as stasis, the narrator relates happenings which provide points of reference for the reader. Among these are Joachim's departure for the flatlands in the sixth chapter, his return, and his death. During his absence, Hans Castorp's ski excursion (during his second winter in Davos) is reported in the chapter "Snow," a chapter which, like the book's ending, is free of irony. A vision during a perilous snowstorm brings Hans Castorp insight into life and death based on the realization that, "for the sake of goodness and love," man should not allow "death to rule . . . his thoughts." This knowledge is, however, soon lost to him; on the same evening he doesn't really understand it anymore. Not until the end of the novel does the narrator refer to it again, but it is merely mentioned in a final flourish. The main event in the seventh chapter is the appearance and death of Mynheer Peeperkorn, the traveling companion with whom Clawdia Chauchat returns to the Berghof.

Thomas Mann tells how "in narrative need" he looked for a character who "had long been anticipated in the composition" and who suddenly stood before him in the person of Gerhart Hauptmann. The two authors were together in Bolzano at the time. Exclaiming "He's the one!" he recognized in Hauptmann the model for Mynheer Peeperkorn, a character who "dwarfs the intellectual chatterers and pedagogues, the dialectical squabblers of the Bildungsroman."[14] The colonial Dutchman from Java, a coffee planter, distinguishes himself from the entire circle of patients at the Berghof by "the mask-like magnificence of his appearance"; when one saw him, one knew what it meant to be a "personality." Irony and admiration are evenly balanced, particularly in the complicated relationship which develops between Peeperkorn and Hans Castorp. In addition to the epic luster he imparts to the seventh chapter, the function of the Dutchman is to dissolve Hans Castorp's emotional tie to Clawdia Chauchat. At the bedside of the deceased Peeperkorn, Castorp addresses her with the formal "Sie" for the first time. This is the end of his story, or at least we can say that whatever might happen to him from now on is no longer part of *this* story.

In 1926, not long after the completion of *The Magic Mountain*, Thomas

Mann began writing the tetralogy *Joseph and His Brothers* (three-volume complete edition, 1948), which appeared in separate, successive volumes: *Joseph and His Brothers* (*Die Geschichten Jaakobs*, 1933), *Young Joseph* (*Der junge Joseph*, 1934), *Joseph in Egypt* (*Joseph in Ägypten*, 1936), and *Joseph the Provider* (*Joseph der Ernährer*, 1943). Many themes and ideas from *The Magic Mountain* are continued and expanded in the Joseph novels. Whereas in the earlier novel Thomas Mann blended myth with the material of a *Zeitroman*, allowing mythical concepts to penetrate and illuminate the material, here myth itself constitutes the substance of the novel. Thomas Mann used the biblical tale of Joseph from Genesis, in particular chapters 27–50, and consulted an immense body of literature on the history of religion and civilization. He studied the legends, tales, and myths of biblical Palestine and the oriental world associated with it, from the Egyptian to the Assyrian-Babylonian realms, including ancient Greece and Phoenicia.

In his speech "Joseph and His Brothers" (1942), Mann referred to a comment Goethe had made on the biblical story of Joseph: "This natural story is most delightful, but it seems too short and one is tempted to elaborate on it."[15] Mann said that this remark could serve "as a motto" for his novel. At the same time he admits that in "filling in the details of the brief story," he played an artistic game by feigning exactness and reality and by exposing "something very vague and distant" to a sharp focus. It is all an "artistic pretense." Of course not everything happened the way he described it, "for it didn't happen at all"; the scholarly and historical material was a means of "simulating reality." Mann claimed that, despite its seriousness, "the soul of the novel is its humor."

The reader of the *Joseph* novels must be aware of how to approach the work. Although investigations oriented towards the history of religion have contributed much to its interpretation, the work itself is not religious history, but fiction. Its purpose is not to provide information, and those unfamiliar with the historical background can nonetheless read it with great pleasure. Regretting the public's lack of understanding, Thomas Mann wrote soon after the appearance of the first volume, "I always have to think of Goethe's lament: 'One could amuse the people, if only they were amusable!'" and continued, "Not a novel? Well, then, it isn't one, but rather a book of readings and stories about man" (November 1, 1933, letter to Rudolf Kayser). One should in fact read the work as such, abandoning oneself to the narrator and to his game with myth. As the author explained many times, his interest in the history of myth and religion grew over the years as his tastes turned "away from the bourgeois-individual towards the typical, general, and human" (February 20, 1934, letter to Karl Kerényi).[16] He considered the mythical to be identical with the typical and said, while working on the third volume, that "one of the sources" of his "desire to narrate at length" was a "feeling of *humanity*," an "interest in man's fate in general, his origins, his position in the cosmos, and his future . . . a new *human interest*," which had likewise been awakened in his contemporaries through the emotional experiences of the last decades (May 23, 1935, letter to Louise Servicen).

The novel begins with a prelude entitled "Journey to Hell." A "fantastical essay," it introduces the mythical novel as an adventurous journey into the "underworld of the past" and into "dizzying underworld abysses of the past." Nevertheless, the journey leads to "people like us." The first volume, *Joseph and His Brothers*, tells of Jacob's deception to receive the blessing intended for Esau, his flight and sojourn with Laban, his years of service for Rachel, the discovery that he has been wed to Leah, the birth of his sons, his return home, and Joseph's early years. Jacob's story is told in a fascinating manner, as indeed are all the stories related throughout the four books.

Thomas Mann's essayistic game with the relationship between character and mythical role is also remarkable. For example, it is difficult to distinguish between Eliezer, who is Jacob's head servant and Joseph's teacher, and the first Eliezer, Abraham's servant, who, according to Thomas Mann, lived six hundred years earlier and wooed Rebecca in the name of Abraham's son, Jizchak (Isaac). Eliezer tells young Joseph the famous story in the first person, and it does not detract from Joseph's delight "that the 'I' of the old man proved itself not to be tightly closed, but rather seemed open in the back, overflowing into what existed earlier, beyond his own individuality." Eliezer "actually" should have told the story in the third person. "But then what does 'actually' mean here," the narrator asks, "and, after all, is man's 'I' a concrete, self-contained thing strictly confined within its temporal fleshly borders?" He asks this as a man of the twentieth century and continues his game with time intervals and with the intermeshing of characters as a game with myth. He speaks of a "philosophy of life, . . . which sees the purpose of individual existence in filling a given form or mythical pattern . . . with present time." This thought is illustrated by a story told about Jizchak which relates an experience his father had, so that one can ponder whether Jizchak had the same experience or whether he simply made it his own "because he differentiated less sharply between 'I' and 'Not-I' than we . . . are used to doing, or were used to doing before beginning this narration." Again the reader is made aware that the theme of the character with fluid contours is something that concerns him directly, and by now he must also understand—particularly since "the soul of the novel is its humor"—to what extent he, too, is implicated when the narrator asserts, "We do not deceive ourselves as to the difficulty of talking about people who do not really know who they are."

The explanation for this "wavering state of consciousness" is quite simple: the characters of the novel do not take expanses of time into consideration.

They telescope into a short period the sequence of generations which actually extends over centuries. There must have been many generations between Jacob, Joseph's father—of whom the novel tells—and the patriarch Abraham. However, since the same names are used again and again, the situations and events are the same or similar, and the individuals, unaware of precise differentiations in time, cannot distinguish "as clearly as daylight" between their "present and a previous present" or between the "borders" of their "individuality" and those of ancestors, one can never be certain just which Abraham and which Eliezer are being discussed at any given moment. Moreover, Jacob can also be Abraham if the situation calls for it. When Jacob wishes to settle outside Shechem, a very high price is demanded from him in the expectation of "hard bargaining. . . . But Jacob did not bargain. His soul was moved and elevated by imitation, return, recurrence. He was Abraham who came from the East" and who did "not quarrel about the price" outside Hebron. "The centuries did not exist. What had been, was again." This event illustrates Thomas Mann's concept of "life in myth," of which he spoke many times.

In the three-volume edition of the *Joseph* novels, the first part of Joseph's story is printed in volume 1 following the tales of Jacob. It describes the conflict between Joseph and his brothers, which arises because Joseph displays special talents and is favored by his father. The jealous brothers abandon him in a pit. Traveling Ishmaelites free him two days later, buy him from the brothers, who claim he is a nameless slave, and take him to Egypt. The second volume, *Joseph in Egypt*, tells of his journey there and his stay in the house of Potiphar, the Pharoah's chief officer. Compared to the patriarchal, pastoral society where Joseph was raised, Egypt—as Thomas Mann presents it—is a modern, civilized world with a decadent culture. Joseph is promoted to chief steward, becomes Potiphar's reader, personal servant, and confidant, acquires Egyptian habits and ways of thinking, and gets into trouble as a result of the unhappy passion of Mut-em-enet, who is living in a formal marriage with the eunuch Potiphar. The volume ends when Joseph is judged by Potiphar and condemned to prison; once again he must go into the "pit." The last volume, *Joseph the Provider*, tells of his time in prison, where he is immediately appointed overseer. As in the well-known biblical story, he becomes the pharoah's favorite by interpreting his dream of the fat and lean cows and the full and thin ears of corn. Granted the highest powers of authority, Joseph takes over the administration of grain in the entire land, managing his resources so well that in time of famine neighboring peoples buy grain in Egypt. Joseph's brothers also come to Egypt for this purpose. At their reunion the story from Genesis of Benjamin and the silver cup is retold, and finally all the brothers emigrate to Egypt with Jacob. The work ends with Jacob's death.

The principle which determines the substance and artistry of the novel is enunciated in a key sentence from Thomas Mann's lecture on "Freud and the Future": "Character is a mythical role."[17] At the end of the third volume it is again stressed that roles are being enacted. Joseph tells his brothers, who fear he will take revenge on them after their father's death, "When he blessed me, did you not hear our father say that my life was only a game and a reminiscence?" He explains further that before his death Jacob intentionally remained silent about what had "been played out" between Joseph and his brothers, for Jacob "too was in the game, God's game. . . . But if it is a question of forgiveness among men, then I am the one who must ask you for it, for you had to play the villains so that it would all turn out this way." When Jacob called Joseph's life a game, an allusion, he added that it was a "favored" life, "suggestive of holiness," yet not entirely serious. He predicted that songs will one day be sung "about this game of life, . . . for it was a holy game after all." The novel must be understood in this sense. Myth is not limited to borrowings from the Bible and other sources but is the very principle which penetrates and orders the entire tetralogy.

Thomas Mann's *Joseph* novels should not be associated with the large number of novels with religious themes which appeared at that time. These works stood more or less in the service of religious confessions and goals. They were part of the ideologically engaged literature that played an important role on the book market after the First World War but is almost totally forgotten today. Owing to their conventional style, they are also of little significance for the history of the novel. Even Gerhart Hauptmann's (1862–1946) novel *The Fool in Christo, Emanuel Quint* (*Der Narr in Christo Emanuel Quint*, 1910), while highly regarded in its time, deserves mention today solely because of its famous author. The work is characteristic of an epoch in which, amidst a great deal of polemicizing against the established churches, the attempt to define a personal attitude towards the fundamental tenets of the different religions was decisive for many people. A broad audience was receptive to the theme of the God-seeker who must find his own way because his personal yearnings and impulses ensure him more religious substance than the dogma debated by the theologians.

Erwin Guido Kolbenheyer (1878–1962) dealt with this theme repeatedly in novels such as *The God-Intoxicated Man (Spinoza)* (*Amor Dei*, 1908); *A Winter Chronicle* (*Meister Joachim Pausewang*, 1910); the *Paracelsus* trilogy: *The Childhood of Paracelsus* (*Die Kindheit des Paracelsus*, 1917), *The Star of Paracelsus* (*Das Gestirn des Paracelsus*, 1921), and *The Third Reich of Paracelsus* (*Das dritte Reich des Paracelsus*, 1925); and *The Blessed Heart* (*Das gottgelobte Herz*, 1938). In the *Paracelsus* trilogy, particularly in the introductions to the novels, ambiguous notions of Christianity and Teutonism make for a dilettantish, pseudophilosophical conglomeration. The novel ends with the words "Ecce ingenium teutonicum" ("Behold the German spirit"). Kolbenheyer wanted to create a mythical work, but he obstructed his own path by mystifications and contributed to the confusion of an age which found its political expression in 1933. Hermann Stehr (1864–1940) also wanted to convey a religious message in his novels, the most famous of which, *The Farmstead of the Saintly* (*Der Heiligenhof,* 1918), was highly regarded outside Germany. Other authors of the time also found a large audience for their religious themes. The novels of Franz Werfel (1890–1945), Werner Bergengruen (1892–1964), Gertrud von le Fort (1876–1971), Ina Seidel (1885–1974), Elisabeth Langgässer (1889–1950), Jochen Klepper (1903–1942), and Edzard Schaper (1908–1984) were widely read.

In addition to Thomas Mann, the authors Hans Henny Jahnn (1894–1959) and Hermann Broch in particular possessed an insight into myth as archetypical images transcending specific religious doctrines. Both failed, however, in their attempt to create a novel determined by myth. Jahnn's *Perrudja* (1929) and Broch's *Mountain Novel* (*Bergroman,* 1936) are works designed on a grand scale which demonstrate that their authors are important novelists. They are attempts to show man confronted by pressures from many sides; bound by the forces of nature and at the mercy of social ties, he suffers from his inadequacy. The landscape is of major significance in both novels. The setting of Jahnn's work is the Norwegian mountains. In legendary isolation, Perrudja abandons himself to dreams, trances, and visions and experiences his inner world, what he sees and what he reads, as a unity. In the concrete world he is closely associated with animals, particularly horses, but his love relationships—both with men and women—are failures. As the preface emphasizes, Perrudja is not a hero; his story is that "of a man more weak than strong." He is driven and uncontrolled, yet he has inexhaustible wealth at his disposal. In the latter part of the novel it is revealed that, as the owner of an international concern, he is the richest man in the world, a fact which even he did not know. He decides to fight for a better world, which, freed of the sickness of civilization, would be upheld by the young. But Jahnn's utopian ideas are not convincing. The work remained unfinished. The theme of a weak man who is not a hero is, within a different context, again central to Jahnn's great work *River without Banks.*

Hermann Broch's *Mountain Novel* is also set in the mountains, in the villages of Upper and Lower Kuppron. Broch planned a trilogy, but did not progress beyond the first stages of the first part. Therefore, little can be said about the function of myth within the total composition, especially since a comparison of the three existing versions of the first part shows a fluctuation in his intentions. The only thing that is certain is that he was concerned with myth. In the beginning stages of his work on the project he often spoke of his "religious novel." Later, titles like *Demeter* and *Demeter or the Enchant-*

ment appear. Hans Albert Maier believes that Broch definitely planned to title the final work *Demeter*,[18] and, judging from the contents, this assumption seems justified. As early as 1936, Broch spoke of an "earth and mother cult" in reference to the first volume (January 16, 1936, letter to Daniel Brody). The main character, Mother Gisson, has been interpreted as a Demeter-Kybele figure.[19] Mother Gisson is set apart from the entire population by her extensive knowledge and superior insight. She knows the mountain and its buried tunnels in which gold was once mined; she knows when and where certain herbs can be found, how to heal the sick, and she possesses the gift of prophecy. Her antagonist is the immigrant Marius Ratti, a demagogue who confuses and dominates the villagers with his verbose speeches and promises. He preaches chastity and advocates a community of men, condemning the machine and the cities and promising to find gold in the mountain with a divining rod. During the dedication of a mountain church, he induces the village community to carry out the ritual murder of a young girl, Irmgard, who has long been subservient to Marius and willingly lets herself be slaughtered. The narrator, an elderly doctor, tells how even he was caught up in the general frenzy and did not offer opposition. Mother Gisson's behavior during the murder scene, included only in the first version, remains unclear; it is true that she speaks imploring words, but she does not actively intervene. In a later plot summary entitled "The Enchantment (Novel)," which was probably written shortly after Broch's arrival in America (1938), Mother Gisson herself falls victim to the frenzy. In the earlier version she dies a natural death at the end.

Whether or not the critics interpret Irmgard's slaughter as an analogy to Hades' abduction of Persephone and regard Mother Gisson as the Great Mother—Demeter or Kybele—it still cannot be overlooked that the novel as a whole is a failure. Irmgard's murder, presented as a twentieth-century occurrence in a civilized country, can only be seen as a terrible aberration of a group gone mad. The duel of words between Mother Gisson and Marius before the butcher commits the deed is supposed to reveal the mythical aspects of the situation, but as such it seems entirely inappropriate. Broch knew this himself and was unable to continue this problematic work. In "The Enchantment (Novel)," he wrote of the role mass psychology plays in the *Mountain Novel.* "Men of great sobriety and self-criticism," he said, can be "won for the most fantastic undertakings" under the influence of mass psychology; "archaic tendencies" break out, and the individual becomes the prey of "incomprehensible forces." According to the essay, the reasons for this lie in the "individual's constant readiness to turn to nature and myth" in a time of the decline of religion. What remains to be discovered is "how readily the mythological tendencies in the soul can break out."[20] The extent to which the political experiences of the 1930s are incorporated here is self-evident.

Broch expanded these ideas in his essay, "The Mythical Heritage of Poetry."[21] Here he sees myth as the origin of and presupposition for every form of narration, indeed for all human communication. In developing his argument, he refers specifically to Jung's conception of the archetype. Whereas in his earlier essay on James Joyce, Broch saw poetry's mission and its right to exist in the totality of cognition, now, from a new standpoint influenced by the concept of myth, he regards the novel as "aimed not only at the totality of the intellect, but also at a totality of life," and thus meant to illuminate the hero's entire being, including his hidden dimensions.

Broch's essay "The Mythical Heritage of Poetry" appeared in the same year as *The Death of Virgil* (*Der Tod des Vergil*, 1945) and is useful in its interpretation. The novel presents the last eighteen hours of the dying poet Virgil's life, from his entrance and landing in the harbor of Brindisi to his death in the palace of Augustus. The book was a great success when it first appeared and was considered by Erich Kahler and others to be Broch's most important work. Thomas Mann counted it "among the greatest achievements in German literature." Albert Einstein was, as he wrote to Broch, "fascinated."[22] The reaction of Broch's contemporaries has to do with the particular linguistic style of the book. Broch himself believed that he had "tried something completely new." He called the work—although presented in the third person—an interior monologue and said that accordingly it was "to be seen as a lyrical work." This suited his purposes, since the lyrical expresses "the deepest realities of the soul." As in his essay, in which he states that the interplay of mythos and logos is "man's essence," he says in his "Comments on *The Death of Virgil*" that this book uncovers "the incessant interplay between the rational and irrational" in "every moment of the hero's life, as in every sentence of the book."[23] The book could be called "a lyrical self-commentary." As the author explains, this lyrical self-commentary possesses musical qualities and allows for endless motif variations. Moreover, it can solve "one of the most difficult problems of the novel, that of simultaneity," in a new way. For Broch, the problem of simultaneity lies in how to depict the multitude of situations and associations of a single moment in a time sequence without sacrificing the impression that all the happenings, regardless of which part or level of life they belong to, are joined and enveloped by this moment. He believed that as "even the longest symphony" must give the listener "an experience of unity"—for it was constructed precisely in order to "negate time"—the novel could also convey an impression of simultaneity. Through "lyrical commentary" Broch succeeded in making "the unity of all life, including the past and even the future," evident "in a single point in the present."

The first part of the book, entitled "Water—the Arrival," begins with Virgil's entrance into the harbor with the fleet returning from Greece. Here we see how Broch's theory of art is confirmed in practice. The totality of the world is captured in a single moment: the sea, sky, wind, and coast, the emperor's fleet with its seven ships, all serving different purposes, Augustus's tent on the middle ship, and on the ship behind it, the poet Virgil, deathly ill. The author lingers to present Virgil's sickness, his conflicting, ever-changing perceptions of his body and himself, his rethinking why he gave in to Augustus and left Athens, his dwindling hope of completing the *Aeneid* and of living on afterwards, the inevitability of his fate, a glance back at the course of his experiences and at his origins. An infinitude appears on two pages while simultaneity is unremittingly maintained, and no end to the "experience of unity" and the "negation of time" can be foreseen. The interior monologue captures the concrete world around the poet Virgil as well as the world surging inside him, both of which oppress him at the same time. In unfolding these realms, what is expressed at the end is always present at the beginning, and the beginning continues to be heard throughout. Although it is only possible to write in a sequence, this lyrical motion is not a progression, but rather a form of simultaneity with no beginning or end. What Broch said about his lyrical prose is correct; it gives us the "totality of a moment."[24] The following passage is a good example:

> He was a peasant by birth, one who loved the peace of earthly life, whom a simple and stable life in the rural community would have befitted, who would have been destined by birth to be allowed to stay, to be forced to stay, and who, in accordance with a higher fate, was not set free from his home and yet not detained there; he was driven out, out of the community, out into the most naked, evil, and wild loneliness of the human throng; he was chased away from the simplicity of his origins, chased out into the world towards ever-increasing diversity; and if anything had become larger or farther in this way, then it was only the distance from real life, for truly, this alone had grown: he had walked only on the edge of his fields, he had lived only on the edge of his life; he had become restless, fleeing death, seeking death, seeking his work, fleeing his work, one who loves and yet is pursued, erring through the passions within and without, a guest of his life.

The artistic procedure is as follows: a theme is introduced with "He was a peasant by birth, one who loved the peace of earthly life." In this seemingly clear opening statement everything resounds which Virgil will say about the restlessness and torment of his life away from home, until the sentence ends with "pursued, erring through the passions within and without, a guest of his life." Without the resonance of the complete passage—all of its parts joined together by the rhythm of speech up until the last "a guest of his life"—the beginning would merely be a statement of fact. Such a factual declaration may of course introduce a narration, but it would be meaningless in Virgil's lyrical self-commentary. The "incessant interplay between the rational and irrational" precludes an unequivocal narrative introduction and a simple succession of narrative events. At each moment Virgil is aware of the contradictory and inexplicable nature of his experiences, and he reacts with feeling and emotion, with logic and insight to the ever-present realization that, as Einstein wrote in his letter to Broch, cognition cannot be fully explained by means of logic, for "the essence remains mysterious." [25] That Virgil "was not set free from his home and yet not detained there" cannot be accounted for logically, although the situation itself is not without logic. The same is true of his departure from Greece. He is not able to answer the questions: "But why had he ever given in to Augustus's pressure? Why had he ever left Athens?" The two events—the departure from Greece and from his home—belong together; they are analogous events, each elucidating the other. Virgil did not leave Greece voluntarily; "No! it had been like a command from the inevitable powers of life and fate." Similarly, a "higher fate" is spoken of in connection with his conflicting feelings about his home.

The presentation of Virgil's personal suffering does not end with this emotional section. His sufferings in his present situation must be added to those of the past. The narrative flow becomes somewhat quieter, but the contents reveal a renewed intensification. The poet, prepared for death, must admit to himself that he will not enjoy the privilege of dying in peace: "And now, almost at the end of his strength, at the end of his flight, at the end of his search, when he had fought his way through and was ready to make his farewell, fought his way to readiness and was prepared to take upon himself the final solitude, . . . at this point the powers of fate had seized him again," forcing him towards "the diversity outside, . . . towards the evil which had overshadowed his entire life." Here a shift takes place: the interior monologue turns to the concrete world, which is unsettling and disturbing to the poet, stimulating his senses and thoughts at a time when he would like to surrender himself to his "inner return" to "final solitude." The various sounds of the ship and water and the noise of gluttonous eating on deck are a burden to his mind and senses. He is compelled to think of the oarsmen chained in the ship's hull and of the greed of the passengers with their insatiable appetites. His eyes roam and his body senses the preparations for landing while his thoughts sway to and fro, mixed with longings and presentiments, until the sound of a slave musician attracts his attention, and it grows dark.

With the shift of the interior monologue toward the concrete world, a new theme is introduced which proves to be central in Virgil's life: the poet's relationship to his fellow man. He believes that human nature is manifested in the sounds reaching his ear from the activity on deck: "Since early morning the sounds of eating rang out from there." To the suffering poet the main characteristic of the travelers is their animal greed.

> The entire ship flared with voracity. Oh, they deserved to be portrayed accurately just once! A song of greed must be dedicated to them! But what purpose would that serve?! The poet can do nothing; he can redress no evil; he is heard only when he celebrates the world. . . . And was it imaginable that the *Aeneid* should be granted a better, a different fate? . . . He knew this public only too well, a public which accords the difficult, knowledge-burdened, and actual labor of the poet just as little recognition as it does the bitterness-filled, bitterly difficult work of the oarsmen.

Of course there are also worthy people among the travelers, "but during the inactivity of the journey they had shed most of what they otherwise were with downright epicurean self-denudation." To the sick poet they seem unmasked under these conditions. "He had nothing in common with them, although fate had brought him into their midst; they disgusted him."

Aroused by the behavior of his fellow travelers, Virgil comes to recognize that he is alone in the society in which he lives, and later, at the sight of the masses on the shore of Brindisi, he realizes how questionable the entire rule of Augustus is. He sees the people "whose spirit and honor" he had praised in the *Aeneid* exemplified in the mob that, after awaiting the emperor with a dull brooding, breaks out in roaring exultation on his arrival, "worshipping itself in the worship of one man." This multitude seems unfathomable and menacing, an "urban rabble," cruel, shallow, and rootless. Overcome by disgust at the thought of his public abandoning itself to greed, Virgil "made sure that the case with the manuscript of the *Aeneid* was untouched next to him." Upon landing, the case with the manuscript again serves as the endangered counterbalance to the alienating stir of the masses: "Amidst the tramping of many rushing feet he lay still, his hand tightly clasping the handle of the leather manuscript case so that it would not be snatched from him."

After landing, a group of bearers comes at the emperor's order to carry Virgil, who, following the events with particular alertness, sees that his cloak is left behind and then picked up and carried after him by a "quite childish-looking boy with dark curls." To Virgil, the manuscript case, "whose two carriers he had curtly ordered next to the stretcher," is more important than the cloak. Nonetheless, he does not let the cloak out of his sight and is preoccupied with the boy.

He wondered where the boy, who seemed so astonishingly familiar, could have appeared from, since he had not noticed him on
the entire voyage. He was a somewhat plain, awkwardly peasant-
like boy, certainly not a slave, certainly not one of the attendants,
very youthful, with light eyes in a brownish face, and, as he stood
at the railing, waiting, because there were crowds everywhere, he
threw a secret glance up to the stretcher from time to time, looking away gently and amusedly and shyly whenever he felt himself
observed.

In the same certain, nonchalant way in which he grasped the cloak, the boy
takes the lead in the bustle of the city and brings the small train accompanied
by an imperial servant through the overcrowded squares and narrow alleys to
the palace of Augustus. There he refuses to be sent away by the imperial
servants or by Virgil, with whom he stays until the end. His name is Lysanias.

Using traditional mythology, Broch created a mythical figure in this boy.
An article by Curt von Faber du Faur which discusses the mythology Broch
integrated into his writing compares the ancient god Telesphorus to Broch's
Lysanias.[26] If Faber du Faur is right, which seems to be the case, then the
writings of Kerényi (in particular "The Heavenly Child,"[27] which first appeared in 1940, and "Hermes the Guide of Departed Souls,"[28] which first
appeared in 1942) had a decisive influence on Broch. An illustration in "The
Heavenly Child" must have provided the stimulus for the physical appearance of Lysanias. Furthermore, a marble statue in the Louvre depicting Telesphorus with a writing tablet and two scrolls may have been especially
important to Broch. In both cases the boy is wearing a cloak. Faber du Faur
considers the statue in the Louvre to be the "very image of Broch's Lysanias."
Broch himself only conditionally confirmed Faber du Faur's assertions. In a
letter dated April 11, 1951, he wrote, "Here at Yale I learned . . . from my
colleague, Faber du Faur, that . . . Lysanias has all the attributes, down to
the smallest detail, of the boy-god Telesphorus . . . a god completely unknown to me up to that point. Such things can only be seen as proof that it
had to be so." Broch had already explained to Hermann Weigand on February 12, 1946, that he had radically eliminated "everything 'learned'"; there
had been "no use of '*Bildungsmaterial.*'" That "nevertheless the most varied
death symbols from ancient religions appeared from my subconscious was an
almost pleasant surprise." Such statements can be considered characteristic
of Broch; it was not unusual for him to forget what he had read.

Lysanias is both Telesphorus and Broch's poetic creation in one. He is
the soul's guide and "endbringer," the messenger of death and the reincar-

nation of the young Virgil, servant and lover, corporeal figure and spirit. With his appearance the novel's main event begins: the death of Virgil.

Though Virgil notices the boy immediately, he does not recognize him or know how to interpret his furtive glances. "A game of glances? A love game? Should he, a sick man, once again be drawn into the painful game of foolish sweet life, he who is lying down once more be drawn into the game of those who are standing up?" He watches in amazement as the boy clears a way through the mob for him, "the cloak thrown over his shoulder." Lysanias keeps a vigilant eye on the manuscript case, glances up at Virgil from time to time, swings a torch, and shouts merrily, "Make way for Virgil! . . . Make way for your poet!"

The way finally leads—which the young boy apparently knew from the beginning—up a wretched alley that fills Virgil with horror. Worse than the dirt and smell and the shadowlike swarm of children and goats molesting the bearers are the nasty insults from women leaning out of the windows. On his stretcher carried high above the activity in the alley, Virgil is defenseless. The women taunt and threaten him, neither respecting the sickness in his feverish eyes nor taking anything else into consideration which might explain his privileged position. Virgil feels the disgrace and covers his face. In the torrent of abuse he detects a warning and the truth, "insanity heightened to truth." Every insult "tore a bit of superiority from his soul until it was naked, as naked as an infant's." This experience of ascending to Augustus's palace through the slum alley contributes to his decision to destroy the *Aeneid*.

In the second part of the novel, entitled "Fire—the Descent," Virgil decides to burn his major work; it is his last night in the quiet guestroom of the palace high above the city. After the boy has gone to the feast of Augustus, Virgil remains alone and abandons himself to the images, thoughts, dreams, and visions, which—heightened by the fever—illuminate the process of dying; "he listened for death." In the transition between life and death, the poet believes that he has not fulfilled man's moral obligation to help others. He condemns his entire writing as the awakening of "a false belief in helping others." Against his better judgment, he had hoped that "the power of beauty, the magical power of song . . . would exalt him, the poet, to the rank of bearer of knowledge in a reestablished community of man. . . . Such a punishable overestimation of poetry!" While he reflects on the misuse of beauty, he is overcome by the memory of Plotia, the woman he failed in love. .

The destruction of the *Aeneid* is the central theme of the conversation between Octavian and Virgil the next day. It takes place in the third part of the work, "Earth—the Expectation." When Octavian comes into the room he has already been informed of Virgil's intention. In the conversation, which takes up more than a hundred pages—it is later said that it lasted "far more than an hour"—Octavian's aim from the beginning is to save the *Aeneid*. Virgil admits to himself very early that Octavian's glance is drawn to the manuscript case. His struggle to keep control over it is hopeless, no matter how he belittles it or explains the necessity of its sacrifice. When Octavian leaves the deathbed, the bearers follow him with the case; the emperor takes the poet's manuscript. No other outcome was to be expected, for through all the arguments and differences of opinion shimmered the love of two men which could not be damaged by such a monstrous deed as the burning of the *Aeneid*. Well aware of how the game will end, the emperor shows understanding, resorts to anger, and then gently reminds the poet of their common bond: "Do you remember, Virgil?" His patience with his dying friend and the recurrent melody of verses from the *Aeneid*, which will most certainly not be destroyed, create an atmosphere of humanity that lends the work its harmony.

Lysanias, who disappeared for a time, is present at the end of the scene, and from his hand Octavian takes the *Aeneid*. Lysanias also accompanies Virgil at the end in "Ether—the Homecoming," the fourth and final part. The boy is sitting on the bow of the ship of death.

6 / The Novel during the Weimar Republic

Independent of the new century's great experiments in novelistic form a body of literature evolved during the Weimar Republic which was produced by many talented authors and was rich in thematic and topical variations. The authors were committed to social criticism and ideological goals and saw that their needs were best met by the traditional, chronologically structured narrative. Just as Goethe's novels continued to have an effect throughout the nineteenth century—although contemporary modes of thought had long since prevailed—twentieth-century novelists could choose between the experiments of their own age and the traditional forms from the previous century: the *Zeitroman*, the historical novel, and the *Gesellschaftsroman*. Even today a wide circle of German-speaking readers does not consider these obsolete and may even prefer them to the more complex modern forms. It stands to reason that a traditional, easily understood method of narration is particularly well-suited to didactic aims. The novel can serve to propagate ideologies only if it is straightforward and uncomplicated. Therefore, the author with social, political, and ideological commitments is bound by limits which he may not exceed without injuring his goals, that is, without sacrificing a wide audience. Most authors in this group kept basically to the same path all their lives, tending not to vary their styles or themes greatly. What does vary is the quality and subject matter of novels written at different times in an author's career. Alfred Döblin, who was inclined towards experimentation and created original forms, occupies a special place among these authors.

This literary trend reached its climax in a series of impressive novels which appeared between 1925 and 1932. Some of them achieved worldwide success, were printed in large editions, and were translated into many languages. Yet today only a few are still known to the German-speaking public. As values, literary tastes, and political realities changed over a half century, many of the once famous works underwent a radical devaluation, and others still remain controversial. A listing of the most famous titles will not entirely reveal the diversity and breadth of this literature which encompasses social, nationalistic, and religious themes as well as statements of political engagement, confessions of faith, and analyses of the times. Nevertheless the names of representative novels will serve to define boundaries and provide points of reference: *Jew Süss* (Lion Feuchtwanger), *The Devil* (Alfred Neumann), A

Nation without Space (Hans Grimm), *The Case of Sergeant Grischa* (Arnold Zweig), *The Veil of Veronica* (Gertrud von le Fort), *Class Reunion* (Franz Werfel), *The Maurizius Case* (Jakob Wassermann), *Revolt of the Fishermen of Santa Barbara* (Anna Seghers), *Berlin Alexanderplatz* (Alfred Döblin), *All Quiet on the Western Front* (Erich Maria Remarque), *Success* (Lion Feuchtwanger), *The Wish Child* (Ina Seidel), *Little Man—What Now?* (Hans Fallada), and *Radetzky March* (Joseph Roth). The list could easily be lengthened since these authors were prolific writers whose activity spanned several decades.

These authors' involvement with current events stems from the emotional experience of the First World War and its aftermath. In the nineteenth century, attempts to develop the *Zeitroman* were seldom successful; authors found little inspiration in their own times, and, burdened by the oppressive weight of a great tradition, they felt dependent upon its themes and motifs. Their relation to their own times was founded more on theoretical considerations than on strong feelings rooted in contemporary events. By contrast, the First World War, the Revolution of 1918, and the postwar chaos had made the transforming effect of historical events on people and society so obvious that authors could not resist giving literary form to such overwhelming occurrences. A neutral, distanced manner of presentation was out of the question; the author's personal involvement determined his view of the epoch.

The books that deal with the experience of war demonstrate this with particular clarity. As unassumingly as Erich Maria Remarque (pseudonym of Erich Paul Remark, 1898–1970) narrates *All Quiet on the Western Front* (*Im Westen Nichts Neues*, 1929), he nonetheless shows emphatically how man is changed by war. It is a twofold process: on the one hand, human nature is laid bare, and on the other, the soldiers accept the realities honestly and openly. The willingness to acknowledge facts that were previously concealed or denied is characteristic of the new man, for whom social conventions have become obsolete. Shocking situations, such as in the opening scene, exemplify this: after half the company has fallen at the front, the rest of the unit is glad to receive double rations of bean soup and tobacco. The young soldiers display their unabashed delight over the large portions. As survivors they have no option but to view their physical needs objectively and without shame and to help their comrades as long as they can still be helped. Only the present hour is important to them; the world of parents and educators had slipped away during the first barrage. Warfare contradicts the ideals with which they grew up, and they have no idea how they will ever be able to return to a life so totally disrupted by war.

Like the majority of war novels of its day, *All Quiet on the Western Front* has no particular plot. In diarylike, chronologically ordered sketches, Remarque presents incidents from the war experiences of a group of young soldiers who went to school together and volunteered for the army under pressure from a teacher. The book alternates between periods at the front and peaceful interludes, horrifying battles and scenes of young comrades passing time together, episodes in the field hospital and at home on furlough. When the soldiers occasionally discuss the problem of war, they do so with few words and without intellectual pretension; they are its victims and see no sense in it. They realize that their enemies, the French and the Russians, are, like themselves, entangled in something utterly foreign to them and are also suffering. In their eyes the real enemy is Himmelstoss, the drill sergeant who bullies the recruits. The company commander, Bertinck, is regarded as a magnificent front-line officer. The novel's main character is the forty-year-old reservist, Katczinsky, an experienced and unselfish man who stands by the others. After his death all that remains to be reported is the death of the narrator. The last of seven in his class, he falls on a day so uneventful that the military report simply states: "All quiet on the western front." The narrator functions as the spokesman for the youths who, as a group, represent an army of millions of simple soldiers. As characters they do not differ substantially from each other, nor is the narrator particularly distinguished from the rest. It is a generation which, according to the author's preface, was destroyed by the war, including those who managed to escape its shells. The narrator argues along the same lines, claiming that on the front soldiers become "human animals." But these assertions are contradicted by the altogether humane behavior of the soldiers in all situations, which would seem to suggest hope for the future. The book was a worldwide success, sold millions of copies (probably six to eight million), and was translated into approximately thirty languages. Remarque was influenced by Henri Barbusse's (1873–1935) *Le Feu–Journal d'une escouade* (1916), a war novel published while the war was still being fought.

Man's transformation in war is also depicted in Ernst Jünger's (b. 1895) *Storms of Steel (In Stahlgewittern*, 1920), but the work is written from a standpoint quite unlike that of *All Quiet on the Western Front*. For Jünger, war provided the possibility for an intensified existence. As a young man he ran away to join the Foreign Legion and escape the narrowness of the bourgeois world. His "longing for the unusual" led him to seek adventure in the trenches on the western front. The basis for his novel was the diary he kept during almost four years of service. The novel itself underwent three revisions between 1920 and 1934 as Jünger endeavored to make it less personal and more objective. Nonetheless there is no doubt in the reader's mind that Ernst Jünger displayed unusual bravery as a shock troop commander. He was wounded fourteen times and awarded the *Pour le mérite* (Medal of Honor) in September 1918. His highest ideal was the preservation of individuality in battle. In his novel the main character wages a life and death struggle to master existence through adventure. The story begins with the recruit's arrival at the scene of battle and ends with the telegraphic message stating that he has been awarded the *Pour le mérite*. In between lie the countless experiences of a young man who is comfortable in his situation. He sees himself not only as a soldier but also, justifiably, as a combat specialist. As a shock trooper operating between immovable fronts, he finds the method of fighting at which he excels and which brings him personal glory. Though he shows great presence of mind and initiative in actual combat, his real talents lie in special operations—reconnoitering, stealing up to the enemy line, observing the enemy position from close range, appearing and disappearing instantly. His attitude towards the adversary is determined not by hate, but by "sportsmanlike respect," and his own self-confidence comes not from a feeling of national superiority but from a faith in his own personal fate. War is a profession. During breaks in action, he is relaxed and at ease. The dugout is comfortable; he leisurely drinks tea, smokes, and reads. In his diary, the narrator records the number of dead and matter-of-factly notes who was wounded and whether he was maimed, or how he died. The most horrible injuries are juxtaposed with cheerful scenes. The world Jünger unfolds is so logical and perfect that we could easily think that it has to be so, that there is no other world, and that our own behavior would not substantially differ from that of the young narrator. The many characters around him all seem to be subject to the same law as he; most are destined for a death which they approach in delirium, the very delirium in which the narrator survives his adventure.

   Storms of Steel is a very singular war novel. One might well ask to what extent it may be compared to other war novels of its time, for the sense of purpose it imparts is purely individual and inseparable from the personality of the author. Towards the end, even he can no longer entirely believe in what he is doing. Familiarity with war has begun to subdue his fascination and to give rise to the feeling that "the purpose with which one set out had consumed itself and was no longer sufficient."

   The attitude towards war is also intensely personal in Hans Carossa's (1878–1956) *Romanian Diary* (*Rumänisches Tagebuch*, 1924, later titled *Tagebuch im Kriege*). It too is based on diary entries which the author later worked into a carefully composed book designed to reach a final climax. Its fictional time setting spans about two and one-half months near the end of 1916. As Carossa once was himself, the first person narrator is a military doctor who pays little attention to combat activity as such. Instead, he is preoccupied with other experiences that are either stimulated by the war or arise despite it. In his dreams, feelings, and thoughts he assimilates these experiences in the sense of the book's motto: "Steal the light from the jaws of the viper!" The narrator knows that the context within which he performs his medical service is evil; however, he does not consider his responsibility to be protest or accusation, but rather the cautious preservation of spiritual strength.

By contrast, decided opposition to war is expressed in Georg von der Vring's (1889–1968) *Private Suhren* (*Soldat Suhren,* 1927) and Ludwig Renn's (pseudonym of Arnold Friedrich von Golssenau, 1889–1979) *War* (*Krieg,* 1928). In its time *Private Suhren,* the first German antiwar novel, was considered by literary experts to possess great artistic merit and was translated into other languages. In a refined style and with impressive scenes, the author presents the desperate situation of a young painter drafted into the army. Alienated by barracks drills and demoralized by military life, he can survive only in dreamlike memories of past experiences. While the meaninglessness and cruelty of the military possess him day and night, his own poems come to life within him and provide a sustaining contrast to the insufferable realities of the present.

As opposed to von der Vring's book, Ludwig Renn's war novel is deliberately inartistic. The monotonous language and matter-of-fact tone in which events are narrated correspond to the gray sameness which leaves its mark on the soldiers and threatens their individual existence. The narrator and main character is Ludwig Renn, an enlisted man whose name the author took as his own after the book was published. Unlike the character in his novel, the author was a highly decorated career officer. With his choice of main character and adoption of the fictitious name, he sided with the average man and took a stand against his peers. The novel tells of Renn's years of tireless active duty. He serves with complete loyalty and dedication and has but one wish: "If only the war would end!"

The simple man who does not want war but nonetheless serves loyally is also honored in Arnold Zweig's (1887–1968) famous book, *The Case of Sergeant Grischa* (*Der Streit um den Sergeanten Grischa,* 1927). Unlike the other war novels discussed here, it has a distinct plot and a narrator who never appears or participates in the events but who is able to place Grischa's story within a historical and ideological context. The plot is based on an actual case: a Russian prisoner of war who escaped from a German camp was captured again by the Germans and shot as a spy. Zweig heard of the case in the fall of 1917 and soon afterward used it as the basis for a play (*Spiel vom Sergeanten Grischa,* 1921), but the play attracted no attention. Zweig's great success first came when he worked the "shocking event" ("*unerhörte Begebenheit*") into the traditional novel form.

To understand the novel's composition, one must see how Zweig develops Grischa's story within the political context of the times. In March 1917 Grischa flees from the prisoner of war camp in Lithuania after having heard about the revolutionary activities in Russia: the abdication of the Czar, red flags in the cities, no further exchange of fire on the front, deserters searching for their families in the German-occupied territory. In order to reach home Grischa must find a way through the battle lines in the opposite direction, for he comes from Vologda in northeast Russia, where he has a wife and a child whom he has never seen. The reasons behind his decision to escape—the Revolution, the hope that the war will end, and his inner restlessness—contribute to his ill fate, for it is precisely this type of reaction which the German High Command fears. To prevent the Russian mood of collapse and disbandment from spreading to the German armies, Schieffenzahn, the commander-in-chief of the occupied eastern territories, issues a decree that all Russian deserters who do not surrender to the Germans within three days are to be tried by a military court and shot as spies within twenty-four hours. Since Grischa is not a deserter, the law would definitely not have affected him had he not, after being recaptured, claimed to be a deserter. He makes this claim at the instigation of Babka, a young Russian partisan whom he had met during flight and whose lover he had become. Since she could not dissuade him from returning home and was convinced that he would be recaptured by the Germans, she gave him the identification tag of a dead deserter named Bjuschew, informed him about Bjuschew's personal data, and advised him to use this identity if captured. After Grischa has been informed of the death sentence, he proclaims his real identity and the dispute over Sergeant Grischa begins. It is in his favor that all of his statements from this point on are found to be true. The commanding general himself, General von Lychow, as well as a large group of other people well-disposed to Grischa take up his case. But the dossier comes into Schieffenzahn's hands; he regards Grischa's case as a "political matter" and decides that the legal side of the case must clearly "yield to the military-political side." From the point of view of military discipline, the appeal lodged in Grischa's behalf must be rejected as "unfounded and injurious to the common good" and the death sentence carried out in accordance with the law. Schieffenzahn does not concur that Grischa's identity has been successfully proven, even if it has been made "probable to a certain degree."

One of the most important themes of the book is Grischa's transformation between the pronouncement of his death sentence on May 4, 1917, and his execution on November 2, 1917. After fleeing from the prison camp and leaving Babka, he is in high spirits. Feeling a strong will to live, he believes that he has made the right decisions, is "happy . . . to have leapt into the wild and random adventure of flight," laughs loudly over his resemblance to the lynx in the woods, drives it away with his laughter, and cooks his rabbit stew over a large fire although he can not afford to draw attention to himself. Even after his arrest he is as "happy-go-lucky and unsuspecting as a fish." He cleans a rifle "with enthusiasm" and is taking part in a rollicking bayonet duel with the guards at the precise moment that his sentence is being read aloud in ceremonial fashion. What happens to him now and how his thinking changes is reported in detail, step by step. According to reports by the guards and the medic, he becomes a changed person after the sentencing. Previously

> willing, alert, in very good spirits and always active, he now preferred, if left undisturbed, to spend his days on the plank bed in his cell. . . . To lie on the plank bed meant more than just lying on the plank bed. It meant: to think. . . . That he had been dealt a death sentence amidst the lightest and merriest thoughts, first he had to recover from that.

Indeed, his mood soon improves and his living conditions are tolerable, but nonetheless he now sees the world with different eyes. Just as a "man, once wounded, never again goes into battle with the same unsuspecting bravado of his first weeks, for Grischa all things, all sights and occurrences seeped down into a deeper level of his soul." He "moved slowly from the active side of the world to the side where one keeps silent; without leaving the one, he also came to feel at home in the other." This explains his refusal to flee again when Babka, who was able to find him, makes the necessary preparations for escape and then a second time when the general's adjutant attempts to rescue him from prison on the evening before execution. Grischa explains his new attitude very simply: "Because I have had enough . . . I don't want to go on." There are several reasons for his resignation. On the one hand, it expresses his psychological fatigue combined with the belief that flight has little chance of success and would only lead to imprisonment again. "He did not want to go to a new prison." In addition, he begins to interpret his situation according to the theological concepts of the Jewish carpenter Täwje, from whose biblical analogies he concludes: "I am lost." On the next to the last evening of his life, he sends away Babka, who is carrying his child, and lies down to sleep, "slept away his life, lived his dreams. In him death was at work. . . . He made his peace with those he had killed." The next day he calmly goes to Täwje to choose his coffin—one he had made himself—and on the morning of his last day he digs his own grave before distributing his modest possessions.

    A change in mental attitude similar to Grischa's transformation is also to be found in novels by Feuchtwanger and Döblin. Feuchtwanger later said that the title character in his novel *Jew Süss* (1925) impressed him by the way he let himself fall (*Sichfallenlassen*). Jew Süss himself, Feuchtwanger explains, was not particularly important to him, but he saw "the way from Europe to Asia," the image of the "east-western man" in Süss, in his "vigorous grasping and convinced surrender, in his wild action and serenely strong inaction."[1] Of course at the time that Arnold Zweig was writing *Grischa*, he could not yet have known of this particular statement by Feuchtwanger made in 1929, but he was familiar with *Jew Süss* and was friends with Feuchtwanger. There is no reason to doubt that the central occurrence in *Jew Süss*—the surprising *Sichfallenlassen* of the once active financier—served as a model for Zweig, and that he adapted it to the character of the Russian sergeant who had moved "from the active side of the world" to the contemplative side.

Ten years before the appearance of *Jew Süss*, Döblin had already treated the theme of inaction and nonresistance in his novel set in China, *The Three Leaps of Wang-lun* (*Die drei Sprünge des Wang-lun*, 1915). Here experienced men know that the attempt "to conquer the world by action must fail," and Wang-lun says that one can hear from elders everywhere that "only one thing helps against fate: nonresistance." Both during and after the First World War, many people in Germany were receptive to the wisdom of the East; poets, scholars, and educated men alike professed Eastern religions. Arnold Zweig himself had a special relation to Eastern Judaism, and his character Täwje speaks as its representative with the great authority of a believer.

A further theme which the *Grischa* novel shares with other works of the same period is that of the trial. Zweig presents the case in such a way that doubts are not cast on the court of law itself; the outcome cannot be attributed to a miscarriage of justice or to corruption on the part of the judge. Rather, this is a case in which the judicial institution is forced to defer to a decision based on political considerations. Zweig does not delve further into the concept of justice itself.

Grischa's case is unsettling to everyone, as is underscored by the many debates about it. That no way can be found to free him shows the extent to which all the others, from the general to the simple soldier, are also trapped by the circumstances. Just as General Lychow, who is enraged at the interference with his judicial authority, finally capitulates, so does Corporal Sacht, who swore on the day of the sentencing that he would never shoot Grischa. Later Grischa was placed under his guard and a friendly relationship developed between the two. When the young adjutant tries to rescue Grischa from prison on the eve of execution, Sacht foils the attempt because he is afraid of serious consequences for himself, even though the officer is willing to assume complete responsibility. All of these characters are imprisoned; hence, the question of liberation applies to them all.

How the problem might be solved—albeit in the future—is alluded to in the last chapter. The critical scene, set in November 1917, is introduced when Sacht, who has fallen ill after Grischa's execution and is on his way home for convalescence, misses his train by two minutes. This means he will lose almost a full day of his leave and that his children will wait in vain at the Berlin station. Then a miracle occurs: the fireman sees the latecomer and the train stops, which is against regulations. "We ought to be able to manage that at least. . . . I'd laugh if we couldn't," says the engineer. According to Zweig's political views, the workers must bring about liberation; an officer on the train accentuates this point when he says angrily, "The rabble is beginning to feel its strength," and a doctor, also traveling on the train, thinks, "The people have their finger on the valve of war. They don't realize it yet. . . . But when they do . . ." This brings the author to his main theme: the rejection of militarism, the wish of the masses for peace. It is an integral part of the plot from beginning to end. In the final chapter Zweig summarizes it again and illustrates positive action by the common man, whereas up to that point one saw only his impotence, inability to act, and helplessness.

The structure of Zweig's *Grischa* parallels that of Lion Feuchtwanger's (1884–1958) early historical novels, *The Ugly Duchess Margarete Maultasch* (*Die hässliche Herzogin Margarete Maultasch*, 1923) and *Jew Süss* (*Jud Süss*, 1925); in all three works a clearly profiled main character is able to assert himself for a time, but is finally defeated in the struggle of political forces. The individual traits and situations of the main characters are also similar, despite the fact that their stories are set in completely different times and places: *The Ugly Duchess* in fourteenth-century Tyrol, *Jew Süss* in eighteenth-century Württemberg, and *Grischa* during the First World War. The Duchess Margarete Maultasch is a striking personality of great talents and great weaknesses, as is Jew Süss. As a woman, Margarete must constantly defend herself against oppression, despite her royal heritage, her intelligence and strength, and her political achievements. Likewise, the Jewish financier is never fully accepted socially despite brilliant success and great wealth; he is ostracized and frequently insulted in public. Zweig's Grischa does not have any embarrassing, negative qualities like Feuchtwanger's two figures, but like them he is a character of strength who suffers. He is a hero decorated with the Cross of St. George and at the same time a despised prisoner of war who is led to execution with his hands tied behind his back. His submission to an overpowering situation links him to both Jew Süss and Margarete Maultasch.

The duchess is a widow entirely dependent upon herself and, after the death of her three children, she is left without blood relations to succeed her. She is completely encircled by her opponents and finally abdicates voluntarily to Rudolf von Hapsburg. In the climactic scene between Rudolf and Margarete a brief exchange of words ends with a gesture expressing nonresistance and inactivity: "She rose and with a quiet, strangely lifeless motion held her powdered hands out, palms upwards, and then let them fall. Slip and fall. Then everything fell from her, the Tyrol, the cities, her work and the work of her forefathers, of Albert, of Meinhard the strong and violent,

Heinrich's work and her own. Now she was destitute and bare." Rudolf, who is portrayed as a rational man "not in the least given to sentimental or pathetic gestures," is "profoundly and strangely" moved by the "ugly woman standing before him, naked, humble, weary of sovereignty and fate. He knelt on one knee, said that he regarded the country as a trust from her hands; he would remember that he was nothing but her governor."

Jew Süss also surrenders voluntarily. For years he pursues his financial interests without restraint and enjoys power and luxury, but he always feels uneasy when two representatives of the Jewish community, Rabbi Gabriel and Isaac Landauer, let him know that they do not approve of his extravagant life style. In their remarks they touch on ideas concerning the entire situation of Judaism which are developed in passages introducing the third and fifth books of the novel. These are the same concepts which eventually prevail when Süss resigns, which are at work earlier in his dreams, and which play a part in his decision to plot against the Duke of Württemberg to whose power his own is wed. They are deep-rooted concepts which, as is explained in book 3, are shared by Jews all over the world.

Only a few could have expressed it, some would have resisted recognizing it clearly. But it pulsed in the blood of all, it was in their innermost soul: the deep, hidden, certain awareness of the senselessness, the inconstancy, the worthlessness of power. . . . They knew that to exercise and to endure power is not what is real or important. Had not the colossi of power all been destroyed, one after the other? But they, the powerless, had left their mark on the world.

In book 5 the author traces the origin of this common knowledge to the land of Canaan, "where the Orient and the Occident meet," where the "thirst for life and personality, the will for action, pleasure, and power" of the West coexists with the wisdom of the East: "nonresistance, surrender to nothingness, renunciation . . . the bliss of nondesire." The sons of the small Jewish tribe "went out into the world and live according to the doctrine of the West." Nonetheless they "are not quite comfortable with action, they are at home on the bridge between action and renunciation." And they always "look back to Zion . . . where the ways of the West meet the ways of the East." Against this broad background must be seen Jew Süss's surprising behavior at the end of the fourth book, when he calls upon the duke's followers to arrest him after the duke's death. Because his enemies wish it, his trial leads to the gallows despite the fact that he is not found guilty of any crime and, according to prevailing law, cannot be convicted. During his imprisonment he becomes more and more apathetic, increasingly distances himself from the proceedings, and takes no advantage of the possibilities for escape. The German Jews who hope to buy his freedom for 500,000 guilders, a huge sum at that time, are not successful, but they are at least able to bury him according to their religious beliefs.

Both of Feuchtwanger's novels resemble Alfred Neumann's (1895–1952) historical novel, *The Devil (Der Teufel*, 1926), in structure as well as in a number of motifs and plot elements. Neumann's work is set in fifteenth-century France and revolves around Louis XI's struggles to preserve the unity and power of his state against hostile nobles. But the main focus of the novel is the psychologically complex character Oliver Necker, a barber from Ghent. Familiar with many types of crime at an early age and already called the "devil" as a child, Necker becomes the king's adviser and closest friend. An affinity extending beyond rational explanation draws the two together from the first day they meet, and they often discuss and interpret their bond within the novel. Imbued with the belief in the magic of their brotherhood and convinced that they must transgress the limits of traditional moral values, they pursue their political goals with the greatest brutality and insidiousness imaginable. After the king's death, Necker surrenders to his enemies and submits to a trial and death on the gallows in an attempt to maintain the dignity and prestige of the kingdom. He sacrifices himself for the kingdom just as he had previously sacrificed his personal life, his marriage, and his reputation for the king. The incomprehensibility of his motives goes hand in hand with his puzzling and demonic personality. Although Oliver Necker and the king are committed to a "higher" goal—the idea of the kingdom— from a humanitarian standpoint both are clearly negative figures for whose murderous deeds there is no justification. Neumann's novel was well-received and widely read by his contemporaries, captivating readers by its emphasis on psychology, its intensive scrutiny of political behavior, and its colorful historical backdrop.

The revival of the historical novel in the 1920s, as exemplified by Feuchtwanger's two novels, Neumann's *The Devil*, and somewhat earlier, Döblin's *Wallenstein* (1920), is a striking fact. This renewed interest in the genre cannot be attributed to any direct influence by the nineteenth-century historical novel. To be sure, works by Felix Dahn and Gustav Freytag still captivated school-age readers, but the literary impact of Sir Walter Scott's historical fiction had come to an end. Its tradition had ebbed like the wave of historical novels during the Wilhelmine Age. In the 1930s, when debate on the historical novel arose among emigrant authors, Feuchtwanger and Döblin expressed viewpoints of fundamental importance, from which one can see the role they assigned to the historical novel and what they thought it could mean to the emigrants.

Feuchtwanger countered criticism of the genre in his essay, "On the

Sense and Nonsense of the Historical Novel": "For my part I confess that I passionately love the historical novel."[2] He claimed that the use of historical material was an effective means of developing a theme, a means whose importance had been recognized by authors of every age. Homer, the authors of ancient tragedy, and the writers of the Old Testament had used historical material in order to present and illustrate ideas to which they were committed and which they wished to see realized. Feuchtwanger said that it had never occurred to him to "depict history for its own sake," but that for him the "costume, . . . the historical dress" was strictly "a stylistic tool, a means of creating the illusion of reality in the easiest possible way." He could not imagine that a "serious novelist working with historical material could regard the historical material as anything but a means of achieving distance, a metaphor which enables him to reproduce himself, his own feelings, his own time, and his view of the world as faithfully as possible." In his own novels Feuchtwanger was concerned first and foremost with a theme for which he then had to find the appropriate material. He claimed that he was more successful when the material he used was historical rather than contemporary. Wanting to deal with the theme of a man on the path "from action . . . to inaction, from deeds to observation," he first attempted to use the contemporary figure Walter Rathenau but "failed. Then I went two hundred years into the past and tried to describe the career of the Jew, Süss Oppenheimer: I came closer to my goal." Similarly, a theme which long preoccupied him— "the conflict between nationalism and internationalism in the heart of a man"—could be best demonstrated by writing of the Jewish historian Flavius Josephus, because in a contemporary treatment there is always the danger that "personal resentments" might "obscure and taint" the portrayal. Feuchtwanger's *The Jewish War* (1932) is indeed a convincing novel in which contemporary issues appear within a larger context through the use of historical material.

Alfred Döblin's (1878–1957) views on the genre in "The Historical Novel and Us" seem at first glance to come from his experiences as an émigré in the 1930s. He argues that the primary responsibility of the author in exile, who is attempting to "find his historical parallels, to localize himself historically, and to justify himself," must lie in achieving "distance" from "the sphere of violence, inhumanity, and cruelty."[3] But it cannot be overlooked that Döblin's *Wallenstein* (1920), which appeared much earlier, was also written from this same position. An important work, it captivates the reader on any page to which one might turn. Döblin said, "If a novel cannot be cut into ten pieces like an earthworm and each piece continue to move by itself, then it is worthless."[4] He recommends as models great literary figures like Homer and Cervantes, Dante and Dostoevski, who showed that "each moment justifies itself, just as each instant of our lives is a total reality, round, fulfilled.

'Here I stand, here I die,' says every page." Corresponding to this notion, the structure of *Wallenstein* consists of a chain of pictures, scenes complete in themselves. As Döblin stated in 1913, "one doesn't narrate, one builds."[5] Four years later he elaborated on this idea: "The novel has nothing to do with plot. . . . In a novel one stacks, piles, rolls, shoves. . . . 'Forward' is never the watchword of the novel."[6] This theory fits in with Döblin's statements on the conception of *Wallenstein*. He admits that he was not interested in the Thirty Years' War as such, which he knew only from hazy school-day memories as "a dismal, desolate affair with many battles, many adversaries." Rather, he was fascinated with the visual images which emerged from the material and used these visions to "build" his novel.

What evolved was neither a novel about Wallenstein nor about the Thirty Years' War. The center stage belongs to Kaiser Ferdinand II; the work is concerned "with his soul."[7] It begins and ends with him. The title, *Wallenstein*, refers to the "time and conditions" into which Ferdinand was born. Wallenstein, a "man of realities," a "scene shifter of history,"[8] knows how to manipulate the world in which Ferdinand, beleaguered and groping for solutions, must strive to find a place for himself. The Kaiser loves pleasure, is capable of mystical entrancement, and is influenced by dreams, but he must make decisions concerning power and property. He can never know if these decisions are right or wrong, only that they will have grave consequences. His father confessor asks, "How can you reconcile your standing there, looking so powerful that one must indeed call you emperor, with your being so incapable of doing what you wish?" Long tormented by the predominance of others and by nature unable to defend himself against them, he finally gains self-confidence through the strength instilled in him by Wallenstein, who is his exact opposite. A transformation takes place within him when he realizes that "he could turn to any side and it would be the right one. It was in his power to choose, and nothing could possibly go wrong." This feeling of independence brings with it a new attitude toward his office and his duties. He is no longer a helpless victim; the events now seem to take place at a distance, and political pressures do not affect him. Without emotion or fanfare he eventually vanishes from the court and lives unrecognized, for a time among vagabonds, for a time alone in the woods, and temporarily in prison, where he is tortured. In the end he is killed by a savage forest dweller, a creature that is goblin, ape, and man all in one. While wandering through the land, he encounters Wallenstein's meager funeral procession. At one point he says of his own life: he "had occupied a high office, but had given it up because there is little purpose to ruling. Everything runs by itself. . . . They might do with him what they wished, it would not hurt him."

Döblin's demand that authors reject the sphere of "violence, inhumanity, and cruelty," as set forth in "The Historical Novel and Us," is already met in Ferdinand's story. Döblin wrote it under the impact of the First World War. Military heroism had been exposed in his eyes, and the militarists in *Wallenstein* are treated with bitter sarcasm. They all pursue their own ends and use ideals as camouflage, as hypocritical attempts to rationalize their actions. The pope is portrayed as the most dangerous of all; the clergy is also criticized, and even Gustavus Adolphus is not spared, although he is treated more mildly than the others.

While the transformation Ferdinand undergoes is not the same as that of Jew Süss, Grischa, and Oliver Necker, it is nonetheless comparable. Unlike the others, the Kaiser stands outside the world of active men, the "scene shifters" of history, from the very beginning. A sufferer who is never able to rule effectively, he uses the power Wallenstein procures for him only temporarily in order to act. Of decisive importance is his altered consciousness, which liberates him so totally that he can abandon (*von sich abtun*) everything. In this abandonment he reacts to the earthly condition in a manner true to his own nature. The abandonment characterizes both the Kaiser himself and the conditions around him. It also corresponds to the *Sichfallenlassen* of Jew Süss.

The main character also undergoes a change in consciousness in Döblin's most famous novel, *Berlin Alexanderplatz. The Story of Franz Biberkopf* (*Berlin Alexanderplatz. Die Geschichte von Franz Biberkopf*, 1929). It is the story of a weak man inclined toward violence, who becomes entangled in crime, earns his living for a time through robbery and procurement, loses his right arm, spends several years in prison, and gratifies his baser instincts in relationships with prostitutes and the criminal Reinhold.

The novel owes its reputation to its style, which has been designated naturalistic by some, expressionistic by others, but in fact should not be considered in traditional terms. Döblin created an original form through the combination of various narrative techniques. Allegories and parallel narrations complement the main plot; subplots are intertwined with the events reported. Variations on the Old Testament stories of Job and Abraham's sacrifice of Isaac as well as quotes from the third chapter of Ecclesiastes are also blended into the text. Rhymes, rhythms, and allusions connect related elements, lend weight to statements, and enliven the narrative flow. Verses appear surprisingly within the prose to provide hints of myth and of future events. Quotes from all realms imaginable—the telephone book, prison regulations, children's rhymes, folk songs and popular hits, population statistics, advertisements—are arranged in the montage to add to the impression of overflowing life. The use of the Berlin dialect creates a special atmosphere all its own. Thus a complex artistic pattern evolves picturing a world in which everything seems to be connected and each detail is part of a meaningful whole.

One has the impression that the main story, embedded within this cosmos, cannot be anything but meaningful, especially since the narrator claims that it is "exemplary." But careful studies have revealed that no general conclusions can be drawn from Franz Biberkopf's story. Even Döblin became entangled in contradictions when interpreting it, and Döblin scholars emphasize that *Berlin Alexanderplatz* has been misinterpreted again and again[9] and that the great success of the novel is based on "errors," on "numerous misunderstandings."[10] Since those who sought to interpret the novel were well-known Germanists and respected critics, one can assume that, without seeming to place too much trust in scholarship or criticism, the vulnerability of their interpretations can be attributed to the special nature, or, more sharply formulated, to the incomprehensibility of the work.

What has not been sufficiently stressed in previous interpretations of the work is the significance of the contemporary political situation on the eve of the National Socialist rise to power. The many obscurities in the characters' behavior, their inner uncertainty and inappropriate behavior must be interpreted in light of the problems of the times. Helpless in the face of the confusion of 1928, Franz Biberkopf is unable to understand the political developments and is swept along by external events. This helplessness is not unique to Franz but characterizes the general situation at that time. Furthermore, as an uneducated man Franz is not in a position to analyze and solve his problems. The narrator contends that Biberkopf's "eyes are opened. He is made completely aware of where the fault for everything lies. . . . It lies within himself." But this takes neither the social nor the psychological situation of Biberkopf and his partners into account. Indeed, the novel as a whole serves to disprove the narrator's oversimplification.

Berlin Alexanderplatz shows how traditional concepts of morality, guilt, and responsibility become questionable within a specific environment and must be reassessed. This loss of validity of the traditional values is the central theme of the great experimental novels of that epoch; it was the reason Rilke, Kafka, Musil, and Broch felt compelled to find new forms. Yet the search for a new image of man was not restricted to this small group. All authors were confronted with the problem of whether the old values should be defended, and under what circumstances, or whether they should be abandoned altogether. The questions were far-reaching, urgent, and could not be answered with a simple yes or no. That the trial motif achieved such importance in twentieth-century literature and was treated in so many different ways is due to the lack of a judicial authority.[11] In its place arguments had to be tested, different viewpoints considered, and criteria for decisions established. Whereas Döblin restricted the plot of his novel to a specific milieu in which the moral standards of bourgeois society clearly were not valid, other authors chose more diversified settings in which different concepts and viewpoints met and overlapped.

One such author is Lion Feuchtwanger, who insightfully presents a theme of contemporary history within the context of the legal and moral thought of the age in his novel *Success. Three Years in the History of a Province* (*Erfolg. Drei Jahre Geschichte einer Provinz*, 1930). "The true main character," he said, is "the state of Bavaria." Set primarily in Munich during the years 1921 to 1924, the novel focuses on Hitler's putsch in November 1923 and the perjury trial of Dr. Martin Krüger. The two events hold the expansive plot together for its almost one thousand pages and define the novel's two levels. The story of Dr. Krüger, whose trial takes place in the first of the novel's five books and who dies in prison at the end of the fourth book, is of central importance until the end. An art historian and author of well-known books, Dr. Krüger had procured paintings for the state art gallery in Munich. These displeased the conservatives in Bavaria and irritated Flaucher, the philistine minister of education. Brought to trial on a false perjury charge, Krüger is convicted and imprisoned. His delicate heart condition is ignored by the prison doctor, and, when help finally comes from America through the mediation of the Swiss author Jacques Tüverlin, it is too late. Krüger's story illustrates the politicization of justice and the resultant injustice to the individual. It also brings to light the characteristics of the state of Bavaria and sets the scene for the incipient Hitler movement in Munich. The leader of the movement appears for the first time in the second book under the name Rupert Kutzner and founds a new party, "The True Germans" (chapter 13). The growth of his influence in connection with the overall situation in Germany—inflation and the occupation of the Ruhr by the French—is dealt with in the third and fourth books. The last chapter of the novel presents Kutzner's defeat at the *Feldherrnhalle* and his trial. The two trials, one in the first book and one in the last, are related by virtue of the questions they raise about judicial institutions and the contemporary history that they reveal. The novel ends with the determined fight against injustice undertaken by two of the main characters—Johanna Krain, who married Krüger in prison, and Jacques Tüverlin—after Krüger's death.

The work can be designated a *roman à clef*, since a number of contemporary figures can be recognized among the characters. They are not, of course, entirely identical, but there are unmistakable similarities between Kutzner and Hitler, General Vesemann and Ludendorff, Flaucher and von Kahr, Balthasar Hierl and Karl Valentin, Kaspar Pröckl and Bert Brecht, and many others. Feuchtwanger incorporated his own traits in the character of Jacques Tüverlin, and—whether as a self-portrait or an ideal—used him to illustrate his view of the author's importance and responsibility. At the end of the novel, Tüverlin is writing a book entitled *The Book of Bavaria or The Carnival of Justice*.

From the outset, Feuchtwanger indicated that Krüger's story was not an isolated case. The first book includes an overview of legal conditions around the world, which begins: "In the years following the Great War, justice was more politicized than usual all over the world." Similarly, toward the end of the novel we read that "during that epoch one spoke everywhere on the planet of a crisis of law. The concept of justice had become uncertain, threadbare. . . . It is possible that in Bavaria justice was administered with particular malice and inflexibility, though things were not much different anywhere else." Tüverlin, who can be trusted as an objective witness since he is a foreigner and a Swiss citizen, views the situation for a long time with reserved skepticism. But even he is finally enraged by "Bavarian injustice," and his indignation makes him creative. Johanna, who assists him with the last part of his book, is convinced that it "will help to make things better in their country."

This is precisely what Feuchtwanger and the other novelists discussed in this chapter saw as the function of the writer. Their novels were meant to serve social and ideological goals so that things might become "better in their country." By placing such importance on the concept of justice, Feuchtwanger met the wishes and demands of broad circles of readers during that decade; his success is undoubtedly due to the fact that he knew how to write what the public wanted to read.

Whereas the authors of *Sergeant Grischa* and *Success* denounced the politicization of justice, Jakob Wassermann (1873–1934) demonstrates in *The Maurizius Case* (*Der Fall Maurizius*, 1928) that, even though legal institutions are not perfect, the concept of justice is worth defending. The unjust conviction of Leonhart Maurizius raises doubts about the validity of the legal system as a whole. Circumstantial evidence presented by Baron von Andergast, the public prosecutor, and perjury on the part of Waremme, the primary witness, send the accused to prison for murdering his wife. Released after eighteen years, but not "pardoned" (*"rehabilitiert"*), he sees no way to begin a new life and throws himself from a moving train. He is indisputably a victim of the law, but the public prosecutor also becomes a victim of the case. After renewed study of the records and several long visits with Maurizius in prison, he realizes that the verdict, of which he had once been so proud, was wrong. A pedantic person bound to the letter of the law, he would never have given the case his attention again had not his sixteen-year-old son Etzel taken it upon himself to find out the truth. Father and son are both occupied with resolving the case at the same time and come to the same conclusion: the son by finding Waremme in Berlin, winning his confidence, and obtaining a confession of perjury from him, and the father because he finally finds the strength to accept the truth. For the father this means a complete mental breakdown. After Etzel's return home and angry protest against Maurizius's release without "pardon," the baron must be taken to a sanitarium, a "broken, guilty man."

In their struggle against each other, father and son represent two different positions towards justice. Etzel is filled with an active belief in justice, a belief which he says he was born with. "I can . . . hardly describe how I feel when injustice is done, whether to me or to others, it makes no difference." He gives enthusiastic expression to his convictions: "Justice is like birth. Injustice is death." Justice is the "heartbeat of the world," the "most important thing in the world," the "only flag we can still look up to."

The young man's unconditional demands cannot be reconciled with the prosecutor's conception of justice. It is not that the father takes justice less seriously, but, unlike Etzel, he feels a sense of responsibility towards the apparatus of the law. Justice and law are not one and the same, he tries to explain to Etzel. He does not want the institution's reputation to be damaged irresponsibly; a reopening of the case, he believes, would not benefit Maurizius but only damage the prestige of the judiciary. In Etzel's opinion, such views are "withered. Dead tradition. Law without soul." Wassermann is on Etzel's side. He shows that Baron von Andergast represents a bloodless, rigid judicial system without heart or regard for the people it is called upon to judge. Wassermann's direct involvement with the events of his day, his wish to bring about change, to abolish old systems, and to create something new, unites him with other progressive authors of the Weimar Republic.

The same critical attitude can be found among Austrian writers of the period. In *Class Reunion* (*Der Abituriententag*, 1928), Franz Werfel (1890–1945) tells the story of a judge who, on the day of his class reunion, recognizes a defendant as a former school companion whom he had once treated very badly. His memories of events lying far in the past and confrontation with his feelings of guilt comprise the body of the novel. When in the end it turns out that the accused man was not his school companion and is not even the wanted suspect, Sebastian declares in great agitation that a "substitute for justice" has been "sent" to him. Here as in the novella *Not the Murderer, the Murdered Is Guilty* (*Nicht der Mörder, der Ermordete ist schuldig*, 1919), which first brought him recognition as a prose writer, Werfel expresses his conviction that in the difficult relationship between accused and accuser the roles can be exchanged at any time.

During the same period of time, Wassermann and Werfel each produced a number of widely read novels. Wassermann began writing during the last decade of the nineteenth century. His most famous novels prior to *The Maurizius Case* are *Caspar Hauser* (1908), *The Goose Man* (*Das Gänsemännchen*, 1915), and *The World's Illusion* (*Christian Wahnschaffe*, 1919).

Two later works, *Etzel Andergast* (1931) and *Kerkhoven's Third Existence* (*Joseph Kerkhovens dritte Existenz*, 1934), were supposed to form a cycle with *The Maurizius Case*, but they are actually closer to *The World's Illusion* in theme, structure, and style.

Werfel began his literary career as a dramatist and poet. His first great novel was *Verdi. A Novel of the Opera* (*Verdi. Roman der Oper*, 1924). A year after *Class Reunion*, his novel *The Pure in Heart* (*Barbara oder die Frömmigkeit*, 1929) appeared. In *The Pascarella Family* (*Die Geschwister von Neapel*, 1931) the dominance of the father, and with it the legitimacy of the old order, is overcome. Werfel began writing his great historical novel, *The Forty Days of Musa Dagh* (*Die vierzig Tage des Musa Dagh*, 1933), in the summer of 1932. It tells of the Armenians' heroic struggle against the Turks in 1915, and parallels were soon drawn between the situation of the persecuted Armenians and that of the Jews.

In contrast to the novels of social criticism, the small number of nationalistic works written during the Weimar Republic are limited in vision. A *Nation without Space* (*Volk ohne Raum*, 1926) by Hans Grimm (1875–1958), a *Zeitroman* of huge proportions once widely read and much discussed, is noteworthy today only as an example of the propaganda which misled an entire generation. Hans Zöberlein's (1895–1942) *Faith in Germany* (*Der Glaube an Deutschland*, 1931), with a preface written by Adolf Hitler, is a war novel full of naive national pride. With regard to literary quality and content, there is no doubt that Grimm's book is superior to Zöberlein's.

Meanwhile, the conservative author Ina Seidel (1885–1974) was able to create a unified, balanced composition with her historical novel *The Wish Child* (*Das Wunschkind*, 1930). It tells of a woman's sorrowful experiences in a time dominated by wars (1793–1813). As a person secure within herself, she survives the loss of her husband and sons. Historical tensions between Catholicism and Protestantism, southern Germany and Prussia, and the burgher class and the aristocracy give the plot its impetus and provide material for an unbroken chain of impressively designed scenes. Christian concepts and ethical values lend harmony to the work. Gertrud von le Fort's (1876–1971) style and language are more emotional. *The Veil of Veronica* (*Das Schweisstuch der Veronika*, 1928) expresses her commitment to Catholicism, to which she, like her heroine, converted in Rome. Both Seidel and le Fort found an appreciative audience in circles receptive to their ideas, and a large readership remained loyal to them for years.

The novels of Joseph Roth (1894–1939) have a broader appeal and still provide stimulating reading today. Roth's distinction as a novelist can be attributed to his genuine narrative ability combined with an extraordinary gift for social analysis and a sense for myth. His Galician homeland imparted to him the traditions of Eastern Judaism as well as a belief in the Hapsburg monarchy's humanitarian mission of multiethnic unity. The destruction of his birthplace, Brody, and of the world of his childhood during the Russian invasion at the beginning of World War I as well as the fall of the Hapsburg Empire had a lasting effect on him. The problem of homecoming, which for him was unsolvable, is the central theme of his early novels and is found throughout his works. It determined his attitude toward himself and his world until his death in Parisian exile.

In *The Spider Web* (*Das Spinnennetz*, 1923), Roth's first novel, characters of very different origins and disposition illustrate the theme of the homecomer for whom home no longer exists. Conceived while Roth was working as a journalist in Berlin and published in serial form in a Viennese workers' newspaper (*Arbeiterzeitung*) from October 7–November 6, 1923, it is a work of utmost political relevance. With his characteristic keen observation and stylistic certainty, Roth laid bare, as early as 1923, the roots of the development of National Socialist rule by portraying his main character, Theodor Lohse, as the type of man who—fostered by the dangerous conditions in Germany after the First World War—was represented in many variations among Hitler's followers. In his afterword to a 1970 edition of the novel, Peter W. Jansen says, "Nothing prevents us from seeing in Theodor Lohse the later Heinrich Himmler or from casting the horoscope for figures like Heydrich or Höss."[12] Though he lives in Berlin-Moabit near his relatives, Theodor Lohse is a homeless person like all of Roth's representative characters. But, unlike the others, his horizon is narrow and he has no humanitarian impulses. Ambitious and unscrupulous, and at the same time cowardly and mentally limited, he can be misused for any purpose and shrinks from no deed which will bring him money, prestige, and power.

A contrasting figure is Benjamin Lenz, an Eastern Jew from Lodz in Galicia, who reappears in many variations in Roth's later novels. This alert, intelligent, widely traveled man acts as a spy for several different sides. He allies himself with Lohse and betrays him at the same time. His inconsistent behavior derives from his innate rejection of Western Europe, where he must live and support himself, but which is foreign, even despicable, to him. As opposed to the assimilated Jews who cooperate with anti-Semitic organizations, he rejects conformity and integration. He feels that the end of the European world is near and has no doubt that he will outlive it. Most of what he earns through his diverse espionage activities he gives to his family, financing his brother's chemistry studies, helping his aged father, and providing a dowry for his two sisters. But for Lenz himself, a return "home" does not seem possible. At the end of the war he "came to Germany with the defeated army," and where he will go from there remains an open question. All that is certain is that he rejects the sham solutions of Theodor Lohse and his accomplices.

That there is no return home and that security cannot be found any-where are ideas not restricted to Roth's novels which deal with a return from war, such as *Hotel Savoy* (1924), *The Rebellion* (*Die Rebellion*, 1924), *Flight without End* (*Flucht ohne Ende*, 1927), *Zipper and His Father* (*Zipper und sein Vater*, 1928), and *Right and Left* (*Rechts und Links*, 1929). In *The Silent Prophet* (*Der stumme Prophet*, ca. 1929), an unpublished fragment (first printed 1964) which Roth occasionally called a "Trotsky novel," the homelessness of the main character is again the overriding theme. Friedrich Kagran avoids military service in anticipation of the revolution, only to have his hopes dashed. In the newly forming Soviet Union there is no permanent place for him, and his revolutionary endeavors are not appreciated by those in power. Since the West also offers no refuge, he voluntarily follows an exiled friend, Berzejew, to Siberia, where he was once a prisoner in the time of the czar.

During the years of work on these novels Roth traveled widely as a jour-nalist for the *Frankfurter Zeitung* and spent four months in Russia in the fall of 1926. *Flight without End* was written as a direct result of this journey and contains Roth's thoughts on the East-West alternative. With the story of the Austrian first lieutenant Tunda, a prisoner in Russia who takes part in the revolution on the side of the Bolsheviks and later flees to the West but is not able to find a footing in Austria, Germany, or France, Roth gives shape to his own experiences and deliberations. He presents them again from a differ-ent perspective in *The Silent Prophet*. For Roth personally, there was no acceptable place to live in the Communist states or in the western democra-cies. Whereas he, like his character Tunda, was forced to stay in Western Europe because there was, in effect, no other choice, in his novels he was able to offer an alternative to civilized Europe by depicting life in Siberia. "For people like us, Siberia is the only place to live!" Berzejew writes to Kagran when he tells him of his banishment.

Again and again Roth portrays fictional characters who, like Benjamin Lenz and the Siberian outsiders, do not ally themselves permanently with any of the groups in power. Instead, they cut across different lines, maintain contacts on all sides, and are masters of many situations. Their most pro-nounced representative is Nikolai Brandeis in *Right and Left*. Though Bran-deis is only a subordinate figure in the plot, Roth was so intensely involved with him that he eclipses the novel's main characters. Deeply troubled by the revolutionary events, almost to the point of insanity, Brandeis leaves Rus-sia and is, when the reader is introduced to him, very successful in the bus-iness world in Berlin. He is portrayed as a respectable, insightful, obliging man who has money and is able to make a profit whenever the opportunity arises. The reader immediately sees that he is a "striking man" whose special qualities often alienate him from society. His sudden departure at the end of the novel is surprising: after taking advantage of the inflation to accumulate great wealth and achieve considerable power, he abandons everything and disappears. "He did not yet know where he would go. The earth seemed to him to be the same everywhere. . . . Without me, Brandeis thought, the world will continue its eternal, monotonous course." The novel ends as he boards the train to leave.

Roth strikes a new tone in *Job. The Story of a Simple Man (Hiob. Roman eines einfachen Mannes*, 1930). From the first sentence, through rhythm and choice of words, the language is suggestive of myth. As a Job figure of the twentieth century, Mendel Singer, a pious Jewish teacher in Volhynia, is subjected to extreme suffering which he cannot understand. For many years he tries to overcome this suffering through faith and prayer, to regard it as a trial, as a test imposed by God, until one day his tolerance is exhausted and he turns away from God. In the end an apparent miracle comes to pass; his youngest son Menuchim, a feebleminded epileptic whom Mendel had left behind in Russia when he emigrated to America, appears before him as a healed man. He has also become a famous composer and conductor. The comparison between Mendel and Job is drawn within the novel itself by Mendel's Jewish friends in New York. An important aspect of this comparison is the question of guilt, which is linked with Roth's personal problem, his wife's mental illness. This biographical element is reflected in the novel by the sudden insanity of Mendel's beautiful daughter Miriam, which gives Mendel the last push towards religious rebellion. Illness is more directly associated with guilt in the case of Menuchim. Mendel's friends point out to him that perhaps he is not completely guiltless in the eyes of God: "You were given a sick son and you acted as if he were a bad son." Just as Mendel Singer attempts to justify himself to his friends, Roth also tried to free himself from self-accusations concerning his wife's sickness, but without complete success.[13]

With the inclusion of the question of guilt, the novel diverges from the biblical story of Job in which guilt plays no role. God said of his "servant Job," when he delivered him to Satan, that he "escheweth evil" (Job 1:8); his trials are strictly a test of faith. Further comparison between Roth's character and the biblical model reveals that Mendel Singer, as is stated in the novel's subtitle, is not a great man like Job of the Old Testament. An "ordinary Jew" in all respects, it is his excess of suffering alone which singles him out. Jehovah's cruelty and grace transcend his powers of comprehension, and he is denied the genuine struggle with the Supreme Being which distinguishes Job and honors Jacob. Discerning readers have found the ending particularly unsatisfactory, and Roth acknowledged their objections.[14] Just as Roth's "homecomers" cannot return home, Mendel Singer is not granted the metaphysical security which one would expect from the title.

In *Radetzky March* (*Radetzkymarsch*, 1932), Roth's most famous novel, the Hapsburg empire has a function comparable to that of the world of Judaism in *Job*. *Radetzky March* is a historical novel which takes place between 1859 and 1916. It laments the collapse of the Austrian monarchy as the loss of a world which could no longer be saved and which left all those belonging to it hopelessly abandoned in an emptiness they had started to feel much earlier. By tracing three sons in three successive generations of the Trotta family, Roth demonstrates the decline of the monarchy. At Solferino (1859), the infantry lieutenant Trotta saved Kaiser Franz Joseph's life by throwing him to the ground in a dangerous situation; he himself was wounded by the bullet intended for the Kaiser. After the battle he is ennobled, promoted, decorated with the highest honor, and granted in the Kaiser's favor. Years later, when he learns from his son's school reader that his deed has been portrayed as a bold act of heroism, he is outraged by the exaggeration. Protests to the authorities and finally to the Kaiser have no effect, and he resigns his commission. His son, Franz, whom he forbids to enter the military, becomes a district governor in a small town. He is a model of the conservative, conscientious official, infused with a sense of Austria's importance, a dignified representative of the power of the Hapsburg dynasty. Franz sends his son, Carl Joseph, to the military academy for the cavalry. Every Sunday the military band plays the Radetzky March in front of his house, and for young Carl Joseph it becomes the melody of his holidays at home, music linking his family past and his expectations for the future to a belief that his life has a purpose. But his military service in dismal garrisons soon causes him to doubt the system as a whole. He realizes that the traditions according to which he has been raised have long since become outdated, preserved only out of habit and mental sluggishness. A helpless victim of monotony, he becomes entangled in personal problems, falls prey to alcohol, and is burdened by debts. His father is able to solve some of these problems by personally asking the Kaiser to pardon his son and by taking care of his debts, but he cannot fully comprehend Carl Joseph's suffering, although he gradually comes to recognize and respect it.

The most subtle portrayal in all of Roth's works is the change undergone by Franz, the district governor, as his world collapses around him. Of the three Trottas in the nobility, he was the most secure in his world, at one with himself and his responsibilities. The hero of Solferino had to adjust to the nobility and took his leave prematurely, just as Carl Joseph eventually takes his leave. But Franz stays in his office until the end; he can only die in it like his Kaiser. That one should no longer serve the fatherland, as Count Chojnicki tells him, because "the fatherland is no longer there," is incomprehensible to him. What brings him insight into the situation is the pain he feels over his son's alcoholism. He senses in Carl Joseph's detachment and withdrawal a deeper suffering which he cannot help to alleviate; at this point he also feels his own security slipping away. As he becomes aware of the general downfall, his attitude towards Carl Joseph also changes. He understands that for his son he can no longer be the authority he always assumed himself to be and feels only the responsibility to try to help him. Yet he believes he has no more advice to give. Carl Joseph's feelings match those of his father: "He was homesick for his father but at the same time he knew that his father was no longer his home." When he later departs, his father does not interfere, and Carl Joseph assumes responsibility for his own decision. After a brief stay in the country, he dons his uniform again at the outbreak of the war and is killed soon afterwards. Franz dies in 1916 on the same day on which the Kaiser is buried.

Common to all of the Trottas is an inability to establish human contact or to enjoy life. This immobilization and enervation of its representatives characterize the downfall of the Austrian monarchy. Judging the work as a whole, one is tempted to speak of an interplay and interrelationship between personalities and political and social disintegration, but the narrator gives no credence to the idea that any reason for the disintegration is to be found within the characters themselves. He shows no way in which they could defend themselves or retard the decline of the monarchy. Not only the Trottas but everyone knows sooner or later that the collapse of the Hapsburg rule is inevitable. What the collapse will mean in practical terms remains unclear to them; they only sense impending, immeasurable misfortune, and their uneasiness determines their behavior. Therefore they seem paralyzed and weary of life.

The narrator reports the events from a point in time when the downfall of the Danube monarchy has long since become a historical fact. Assuming a retrospective air, he projects himself into the position of his characters and tries to estimate how much they recognized of the imminent downfall and how much of the future remained obscure to them. Both the narrator and the fictional characters look back and use the word "then" mournfully. They helplessly confront the present and have no expectations for the future.

The same is true of the author. Soon after finishing the novel he left Germany. Although he had felt as if he were in exile since his return from the war, the emigration of 1933 was an exile he could not endure. In the last years of his life he continued writing stories and novels, but as his dependency on alcohol increased, he lost his power of artistic expression and his compact style.

At the same time that Roth was inventing characters who searched in vain for a way to return home, Anna Seghers (pseudonym of Netty Reiling, 1900–1983) was concerned with the character of the revolutionary. With the publication of *Revolt of the Fishermen of Santa Barbara* (*Aufstand der Fi-*

scher von St. Barbara, 1928), Seghers emerged as a prominent novelist. It is the story of an unsuccessful labor strike whose temporal and geographic settings are not specified. As employees of an impersonal fishing company, the fishermen see themselves as unable to influence their own living conditions and are totally inexperienced in defending their rights. With the arrival in the village of a stranger, Hull, the story of the revolt begins. A revolutionary familiar with the tactics of resistance and wanted by the authorities, Hull is immediately respected by the fishermen as a man who understands their affairs. After the rebellion fails, he does not flee to safety, which he could easily do, but instead remains loyal to Santa Barbara, the site of his efforts, and submits to arrest there. He does not represent the functionary with a specific assignment found in Seghers's later works—professionals who, when their mission fails, are simply sent elsewhere—but is a lonely, driven man, filled with a hunger for life and a fear of death, who acts solely upon his own initiative.

His relationship with the parentless fisher boy, Andreas, anticipates the relationship Seghers later depicts between experienced proletarian fighters and youthful beginners. Andreas, likeable and proud, longing for fulfillment and joy, becomes convinced through his contact with Hull and the fisherman Kedennek, who is killed during the strike, that the fishermen's struggle must not be allowed to be ended by strikebreakers. The young boy takes it upon himself to prevent them from going out to sea by performing an act of sabotage: "All that was needed was a screwdriver and a saw. It was quite easy." From the beginning Andreas assumes that the deed will cost him his life. After surviving the shipwreck, he does not try to escape from Santa Barbara. The police pursue him, and he dies on the cliffs where he has been hiding. His destruction has the effect of a transfiguring sacrificial death. However it illuminates only the place in which it occurs. That his act of sabotage might go beyond Santa Barbara to have a meaning within the context of world revolution cannot have influenced Andreas, who knew nothing of the international unity of uprising workers or of their backing in the Soviet Union, the theme of Seghers's novel *The Comrades*. Accordingly, the possibility of flight lay outside his realm of thought. He lived and died in Santa Barbara, where he felt a close bond with the people.

These facts, so important to the plot, are also crucial to Seghers's style. Since she knows of the broader framework in which the strike and its failure take place—that is, since she knows more than her characters—she sees them against a wider horizon of which they remain unaware. This gives her language, images, and statements a double meaning. The rebellion is a mythical occurrence in which the participants remain unenlightened as to the nature and consequences of their endeavor. They act spontaneously, in response to the situation at hand, and accept the ensuing suffering as their fate.

In 1928, the same year in which the *Revolt of the Fishermen of Santa Barbara* was published, Anna Seghers joined the Communist party. Apart from its personal significance to the author, the year was also of great importance for the further development of German literature as the charter date of the *Association of Proletarian Revolutionary Writers* (*Bund proletarisch-revolutionärer Schriftsteller*, BPRS). The establishment of this group marked the first formal organization in Germany of a literary movement committed to class struggle. Its representatives, after being forced into exile by Hitler, lived to experience the founding of a new state, the German Democratic Republic, in which they believed their objectives could be fulfilled. They viewed a separation from the bourgeois left as a political necessity. Literature, they maintained, must serve as a weapon for class struggle, as a means of propaganda, as a party-oriented tool whose purpose is to mold political opinion. The formation of the association in 1928 was preceded by the growth of a German-language proletarian literature. German authors had already participated in the "First International Conference of Proletarian and Revolutionary Authors" in Moscow in 1927.

Among the earliest works belonging to the body of proletarian revolutionary literature are *Third-Class Passengers* (1927) by Kurt Kläber (pseudonym for Kurt Held, 1897–1959); *Burning Ruhr. Novel from the Kapp Putsch* (1928) by Karl Grünberg (1891–1972); *The Kaiser's Coolies* (1929) by Theodor Plievier (1892–1955); *A Proletarian Narrates. The Life of a German Worker* (1930) by Ludwig Turek (1898–1975); *Storm over the Ruhr* (1930) and *Rolling-Mill. Novel from the Duisburg-Hamborn Industrial Region* (1932) by Hans Marchwitza (1890–1965); *Machine Factory N & K* (1931) and *Rosenhof Street. Novel of a Hamburg Working-Class Street* (1931) by Willi Bredel (1901–1964).[15] The novels are of documentary value today, lying on the border between fiction and historical presentation. Bound to a naturalistic style, the authors sought to reproduce conditions which they rejected in the name of those deprived of their rights.

Although Kläber was one of the founders of the BPRS, he was not able to achieve a militant, future-oriented narrative tone in his novel. The third-class passengers on a ship from New York to Europe have no idea how they can change their oppressive situation. By contrast, Plievier expressed his political engagement masterfully in an intense presentation of maritime war from the viewpoint of the simple seaman or "coolie." The uprising of 1917 as well as the Revolution of 1918, with which the book ends, shows that despite defeat, the coolies have come to understand the importance of resistance.

In *Burning Ruhr,* Grünberg presents the unsuccessful battle of revolutionary workers as a first step towards the future success of world revolution with much more force than Plievier. Like Turek's *A Proletarian Narrates* and the works of Marchwitza and Bredel, *Burning Ruhr* is representative of the writings of proletarian revolutionary authors. These novels were constructed according to a specific schema. They have a straightforward plot with main elements which are historically verifiable and events which are based on the author's own experiences and set during the Weimar Republic. Exemplary working-class figures clarify and prove the value of their ideas concerning the struggle of their class for more just conditions. Tireless and persistent in large and small matters, they seek ways to survive through setbacks and losses against a background of labor agitation and strikes, miserable working conditions, and proletarian poverty. Negative characters illustrate the erroneousness of the nationalistic alternative as well as the lack of élan and ideological clarity among Social Democrats. The hostility of employers and the brutality of the military towards workers in connection with the uprising following the Kapp Putsch are denounced. The putsch itself, which also functions as a significant event in novels by Turek and Marchwitza, spurs the workers on to heroic action. Those dedicated to the struggle realize that it will go on for years, but they do not doubt that the workers will triumph. Even when the ending brings defeat, the authors' orientation toward the future and their belief that their cause is just and is not lost keep the plot moving suspensefully towards a goal that lies beyond the novel itself.

Bredel and Marchwitza remained active novelists in the last years of their lives and found new material with which to illustrate their political goals. Their novels occupy a secure place in the official literary history of the German Democratic Republic. They are not of aesthetic value, but that was not their purpose. Moreover, since they are not meant for readers who expect entertainment from a novel and want to be spellbound by a plot, their audience is limited. This is true of the entire body of proletarian revolutionary literature, a literature which nonetheless deserves recognition as a historical phenomenon

Another novel which, on the basis of literary quality, hardly deserves mention is *Little Man—What Now?* (*Kleiner Mann—was nun?,* 1932) by Hans Fallada (pseudonym of Rudolf Ditzen, 1893–1947). Yet it achieved worldwide success. In a chain of amusing scenes, a world is constructed which reflects the situation of millions of people in the early 1930s. What may have been particularly engaging to readers is the tender tone and warmth of feeling which distinguish the private sphere—as an island of love and strength—from the dangerous world of merciless career struggles. The friendly young couple whose story constitutes the novel's plot is sorely oppressed by the economic misery of the common man and the hardships of unemployment. "Things will change," the young wife says to her husband. "Keep a stiff upper lip. Things will get better." Anyone who speaks in such a manner is surely convinced that he can have no influence on how "things" will improve. This was the opinion of many on the eve of Hitler's electoral victory in 1933.

In summary, the ideological literature of the Weimar Republic may serve as a model example of a literature which had practically no effect despite the authors' best intentions to change their society. The novels found many readers, but they had little influence on the political development of the country from which their material, ideas, themes, and inspiration were derived. The ideologies advocated by and in the novels either could not be implemented at all, or, if they were implemented, then it was by men who most certainly did not develop their views from novels. The authors' opposition to war, their pleas for social justice, and their analyses of historical or contemporary events cannot be shown to have influenced public opinion. On the contrary, the ideas which came to prevail found few proponents among novelists during the Weimar Republic. Therefore, after the collapse of the Republic, the majority of known and respected German novelists were forced into emigration.

7 / Traditional Forms and the Totalitarian State

The German and Austrian novelists who left their countries after Adolf Hitler came to power continued to regard the novel as their means of expression. Whether they found refuge in Los Angeles, Moscow, or Haifa, in Switzerland or France, in Mexico or Scandinavia, they worked to complete novels begun earlier and to carry out new plans. Thomas Mann finished the *Joseph* novels and wrote *Lotte in Weimar* (1939) and *Doctor Faustus* (1947). Robert Musil struggled until his death to complete *The Man without Qualities*. Hermann Broch worked on his *Mountain Novel* and created his great work, *The Death of Virgil*. Joseph Roth was occupied with ideas for new novels until his death in exile in 1939. Heinrich Mann published the important two-part work *Henri Quatre*. Lion Feuchtwanger and Franz Werfel remained productive and were highly successful. Alfred Neumann stayed with the historical novel. Anna Seghers wrote a host of novels, including her famed *The Seventh Cross* (1942). The working-class authors Bredel and Marchwitza conceived their best-known works. Arnold Zweig continued writing his cycle *The Great War of the White Men* (*Der grosse Kreig der weissen Männer*). Klaus Mann (1906–1949), the eldest son of Thomas Mann, and Oskar Maria Graf (1894–1967) wrote antifascist novels. Bert Brecht turned to the novel for the first time. These examples illustrate that the tradition of the German novel was kept alive in exile.

Not surprisingly, the expulsion of the country's most renowned authors resulted in literary impoverishment within Germany itself. Significant novels simply did not appear. Among the works widely read were *The Baroness* (*Die Majorin*, 1934) and *The Simple Life* (*Das einfache Leben*, 1939) by Ernst Wiechert (1887–1950), *Secrets of the Mature Life* (*Geheimnisse des reifen Lebens*, 1936) and *The Year of Sweet Deceptions* (*Das Jahr der schönen Täuschungen*, 1941) by Hans Carossa, and *Lennacker* (1938) by Ina Seidel. These three authors were already known before 1933 and now proved themselves capable of filling the existing gap for many readers, particularly with their newer works. They chose to present psychological rather than concrete events and knew, while occupying themselves with their characters' inner lives, how to give subtle hints which could be applied to contemptible occurrences in public life. The ambiguity possible in literature was often used effectively in those years by authors of the "inner emigration." This term refers to writers dissenting from National Socialism who remained in Germany and expressed their criticism of the regime in a disguised, indirect manner. Noteworthy examples are Jochen Klepper, who wrote about the Prussian king, Friedrich Wilhelm I, in his historical novel *The Father* (*Der Vater*, 1937) and Ernst Jünger, whose *On the Marble Cliffs* (*Auf den Marmorklippen*, 1939) could be read as a *roman à clef*. In Werner Bergengruen's *A Matter of Conscience* (*Der Grosstyrann und Das Gericht*, 1935), the game of deception is taken so far that it is not at all clear which side the author is on.

Though dramatically affecting authors' lives and careers, the critical events of 1933 did not result in new novelistic forms. While subject to the anxiety of their new living conditions, authors in exile nonetheless continued to write as they always had. Some found their capacity diminished and others reached their highest level of achievement. The decline of important authors such as Roth and Döblin was due to personal circumstances. In essence, the novel tradition remained unaffected by fluctuations in a single author's productivity.

Significantly, the course of the novel as an art form did not take a new turn within Germany, either. What did change, however, in direct connection with the Hitler period were themes and content. These changes did not begin in 1933. Long before the National Socialists came to power, authors had called attention to the significance of this movement in their novels. In Joseph Roth's *Spider Web* and Lion Feuchtwanger's *Success*, the movement and the reactionary circles which lend it support play a decisive role in the plot. The authors of working-class novels, in particular Grünberg, saw the nationalistic groups as a counterforce to their own aspirations. They prepared the way for the antifascist novel. But the new themes proved to be much more far-reaching. To sense their implications, one need only look at three important novels written before 1933: *The Blinding* (*Die Blendung*, 1935; written 1930–31) by Elias Canetti, *The Comrades* (*Die Gefährten*, 1932) by Anna Seghers, and *The Jewish War* (*Der jüdische Krieg*, 1932) by Lion Feuchtwanger.

Elias Canetti (b. 1905) wrote *The Blinding*, his only novel, at the age of twenty-five. It is an important work. The main character, Dr. Peter Kien—resident of a large city (one thinks of Vienna), reclusive scholar, and highly qualified sinologist with a large library—spends his days absorbed in absurd habits, constantly misjudging himself and his world. As his insanity increases, he engages in the most senseless enterprises and finally sets fire to himself and his books. The novel's central motif is contained in its title. Just as the word "blinding" has many meanings, there are equally as many interpretations of the motif. Throughout the work it is used in various ways and linked to a number of characters, but it is associated primarily with Peter Kien. Another motif that recurs again and again is that of fire. From the beginning fire is associated with the idea of the burning of a library. There is also a close relationship in Canetti's world between fire and the masses. Like

290 Twentieth-Century German Novel

the motif of blinding, the phenomenon of the masses is at work in the novel in many different ways.

Peter Kien views the masses differently from his brother Georges, the director of a psychiatric clinic in Paris. Peter detests them. On the street he tries not to notice people, looking past them or at the ground. He makes a distinction between the fickleness of the masses and his own pertinacity, between the cultured person and the uneducated masses: "Sometimes the mud of the illiterate swamp engulfs scholars and their books. No country in the world is protected from natural catastrophes." In a grand speech to his books, he excuses himself to them for having married his uneducated housekeeper, Therese, in the belief that she would take good care of his library: "I forgot myself because I forgot our great master Mong who says, 'They act and do not know what they do; they have habits and do not know why; they walk their entire lives, yet they don't know their way: that is how they are, the people of the masses.'" Peter Kien concludes that one must "always and without exception . . . beware of the people of the masses. . . . They are dangerous because they have no culture, and therefore no power of reason." By secluding himself from them, Peter Kien believes that he can determine his own position. He considers himself to be one of the few who do not belong to the masses.

Georges, however, speaks of the "masses in us," of man's "urge to be absorbed into a higher animal species, the masses." Sometimes, he says, "the masses come over us, a roaring storm, a single raging ocean in which every drop is alive and has the same will." Georges calls culture the individual's "ring of fortresses . . . against the masses within himself."

Much of what is said here will seem familiar to the informed reader. It is obvious that Canetti read and incorporated Nietzsche and Le Bon into his novel. It is, however, not the originality of his ideas which is at issue here, but the parallel between their function in the novel and their historical relevance. While Canetti was working on *The Blinding*, Adolf Hitler was addressing huge rallies, appealing to man's "urge" to become part of a mass, to be integrated into the masses. Canetti has Georges recognize that "countless people go crazy because the masses in them are particularly strong and find no satisfaction." The main plot line, Peter Kien's story, shows how a man who feels nothing but contempt for the masses cannot master them, either within himself or in the outside world. This is due partly to his blinding, but blinding alone does not bring about his downfall. What happens to Peter Kien must be seen in connection with all the characters and all the motifs. Skillfully using his narrative techniques, Canetti shows how all the characters live in a state of constant deception about the others. Dreams, *style indirect libre,* and interior monologues keep the reader informed of their thoughts and ideas. They are all blinded; each misinterprets the behavior of the others and draws a picture of the intentions and wishes of the others based on his own preconceptions. The dialogues, such as those between Kien and his feebleminded wife, Therese, in the first part and between Kien and the eccentric dwarf Fischerle, who is his servant for a time, in the second part, show the total gap between the two sides of argument. The poles are so far apart that the conversants do not realize how inappropriate their replies are. Each is pleased with his own quick repartee and believes he is outshining the other. In these verbal duels the word is disengaged from the subject at hand, becoming an autonomous weapon which heightens the excitement of battle.

The conversation between the brothers Peter and Georges Kien in the third part of the novel shows that the blinding is absolutely insurmountable. Whereas Peter Kien was dealing up to that point with inferiors whose mentality he could never understand and who in turn lacked the capacity to judge his behavior, now the one sitting across from him is his own brother, who has known him since childhood and is an educated, successful psychiatrist. The appearance of the psychiatrist in the last phase of Peter Kien's story would seem heavy-handed if it were not the ultimate demonstration of the utter entrapment of the characters. Though the signs are obvious, Georges does not realize that his brother is mentally ill and close to suicide. He is incapable of analyzing this extreme case and believes that Peter will live on out of love for his books provided that Therese and the caretaker are sent away, the apartment with its library is put in order, and Peter is led back to his interrupted work.

But Georges is wrong. Peter Kien cannot return to his previous existence; his delusions now separate him from it. He has long since lost the ability to differentiate between what has really happened and the fantasies of his imagination. He believes, for example, that he has murdered his wife and has been brought to trial; this fantasy is as real to him as an actual humiliating experience with the police when he is interrogated, treated like a thief, and stripped down to his shirt. Left alone in his apartment after Georges's departure and suffering from his delusions, he himself sets the fire that preoccupied and troubled him, both waking and sleeping, throughout the novel. "Do you know what that is, a library fire?" he asks at one point. "A library fire . . . just try to imagine it! Tens of thousands of volumes— that's millions of pages—billions of letters—each single one burning— pleading, screaming, roaring for help—it tears apart one's eardrums; it tears at one's heart." He refers to the burning of the library in Alexandria in the third chapter of the first part and later to the great book burning in China: "I admit that the smell of burning . . . still stings my nostrils." Fire is never far from the thoughts of the intellectual loners Peter and Georges, and it also occupies the minds of the masses, as is shown in an impressive mob scene.

Admittedly, many readers may be surprised that Peter Kien himself commits arson after he has taken such elaborate precautions to protect his library. But the astonishment of readers who were not sufficiently attentive has been anticipated by the author in Georges's false diagnosis. That Peter's conduct goes beyond conventional psychology is evident from the conversation between the brothers.

The many references to fire and book burning make vivid Canetti's concept of the masses which pervades the novel. In a later work, *Crowds and Power* (*Masse und Macht*, 1960), a "passion to destroy" is characteristic of the masses, who are symbolized "most powerfully" by fire, the "most impressive of all means of destruction." Even without these quotations from *Crowds and Power*, there can be no doubt in the reader's mind that in the novel fire is associated with a corresponding substance within the characters themselves, a substance which unites them and which Georges refers to as "the masses within us."

Just how powerless Peter Kien is against the masses within himself is illustrated by his dream in the third chapter of the first part of the novel and by the accompanying plot events. In the dream, the "most horrible one he could remember," burning books are four times transformed into burning people and the people back into books. Kien does not grasp the connection between his books and his daily, domestic life, but it is made apparent to the reader through the decisive change in his personal situation. On the day before the dream, Kien for the first time offers Therese, his housekeeper for eight years, a book to read. Her acceptance makes Kien uneasy. The dream directly follows this scene. The next morning Kien has to keep his promise and gives Therese the book. With great surprise he sees how carefully she treats it and asks her, "What would you do if a fire were to break out?" Her shocked answer is, "For heaven's sake, save the books!" Kien decides to marry her in the belief that she will take care of his library: "In case of fire I can depend on her."

Therese and the dream of the burning books are closely interrelated. She provokes the dream; to Peter Kien she represents the threat to his library. The thought that she might use his library unleashes his innermost fears, as is demonstrated by the dream. After he has dismissed the dream from his conscious mind with a superficial interpretation, he decides that Therese is the "best means" of defense against the threat. He accuses himself of having misjudged her, thereby taking a step to rectify his prejudice against uneducated people, and sees marriage to her as a way of saving his library. He realizes that he is mistaken immediately after the wedding when Therese unfeelingly sweeps a number of books off the divan. Little by little, she takes over the four large, book-filled rooms in which Kien had previously lived alone. To the same extent that she advances within the library, the subconscious realm expressed in Kien's dream also gains strength, controlling him in the daytime as well as at night, overpowering his reason, and finally taking complete possession of him, resulting in his setting his library on fire.

The scholar's self-destruction allows for various interpretations. Peter Kien's behavior—his loud laughter when the flames finally reach him, his mistaken belief that he murdered his wife, his appearance before the police undressed—points to a concept of man which goes far beyond a satire on scholars and has only gradually come to be understood in the twentieth century. Canetti's novel can be seen in relation to *Doctor Faustus* by Thomas Mann and *The Tin Drum* by Günter Grass, for it already contains, like a prophecy, a model of the bitter experiences which had just begun to become realities in Europe when the novel was being written: brutality and inhumanity, the power of feeblemindedness, and the eruption of a senselessness which is deeply rooted in man and proves to be more powerful than any type of rationality. The scholar of extraordinary intelligence is not only a victim of all this, but in his own way he is also a participant. He is unfit for resistance against the forces of destruction; indeed, he promotes them and in doing so loses control of himself, so that in the end he actively destroys. Just as important as Peter Kien are the characters associated with him, who all contribute to the final ruin.

It is superfluous to draw specific parallels between the Hitler period and Canetti's novel, especially since there is no possibility of influence or stimulation. Suffice it to say that this work contains a theme unknown to the novel of the 1920s.

The same is also true of Anna Seghers's *The Comrades* (1932). Long before the author herself went into exile, she wrote a novel about the exiled and those who fight illegally in their own countries. The "comrades" are Communists from Hungary, Poland, Bulgaria, Italy, and China who, in the period following the First World War, are persecuted for their political convictions. They knowingly risk their lives and must either leave their countries or face long prison sentences. They dedicate their lives to the goals undertaken, whether they are living in exile or actively participating in the resistance in their own countries as Communist party functionaries. The novel's structure corresponds to its content: independent plot strands run side by side; the comrades all follow their own paths and in general know nothing about each other. They are united by the ideas of the Communist movement and see their mainstay in the Soviet Union. The international character of their struggle is demonstrated by the shifts in scene from one country to another. In each case, plot tension is created by the question of how the survivors will conduct themselves after failure and defeat. Anna Seghers develops her theme by showing the solidarity of workers and farmers and the lack of direction among the majority of intellectuals.

The material and inspiration for the novel came from Seghers's contacts as a student in Heidelberg with immigrants from Hungary and other Eastern European countries. In her choice of form, she may have been inspired by the American writer John Dos Passos. In a letter to Georg Lukács (June 28, 1938) she defends Dos Passos, citing *Manhattan Transfer* (1925).[1] The political position and substance of her novel can be interpreted as her answer to the world created by Dos Passos. There is a marked contrast between the isolation in the overwhelming city of New York, as expressed by Dos Passos through the juxtaposition of separate plot lines, and the solidarity of comrades joined by Communist ideals. As opposed to the hopelessness of the homeless in the huge chaotic city, Seghers describes the hope and striving of the comrades in their own countries as they try to fulfill the goals which they believe have already been achieved in the Soviet Union. Seghers's different plot strands evolve naturally from the many different settings, which are meant to prove how comprehensive the international movement is. Though the fighters may have no contact with each other, they are all part of one common effort.

Just as *The Comrades* anticipates many of the problems of those who emigrated from Germany after 1933, Lion Feuchtwanger's historical novel, *The Jewish War* (1932), presents a subject that is directly related to the catastrophe of the German Jews and of the German people as a whole, incipient at the time of its publication. The book is the first and most impressive part of the *Josephus* trilogy, which Feuchtwanger completed in emigration with the volumes *The Jew of Rome* (*Die Söhne*, 1935) and *Josephus and the Emperor* (*Der Tag wird kommen*, 1942). He had already touched on questions of Judaism, depicted clearly profiled Jewish characters, and given vivid expression to the religious customs and sufferings of those living in the Diaspora in *Jew Süss* and *The Ugly Duchess*.

As his theoretical writings show, he recognized early the danger threatening German Judaism from the increasingly influential National Socialist party.[2] Of particular importance to an understanding of the trilogy is his essay "Nationalism and Judaism" (1935), the first major work Feuchtwanger wrote after expatriation. What characterizes "Jewish nationalism," Feuchtwanger contends here, is solely the "commitment to a spiritual principle." Evidence of this is the fact that "the Holy of Holies of the Jewish temple contained nothing, absolutely nothing, an invisible God whose name the Jews did not even dare to pronounce, whom their high priests could call by name only once a year." But in literature, in the written word, Feuchtwanger continues, the "immaterial" could "in a certain sense become material," and therefore "next to the Chinese, the Jews are the most literary people in the world." Feuchtwanger had already argued along these lines in an article written in 1930, explaining that "one of the earliest insights" of the Jewish "group" was that "literature is the memory of mankind." In "Nationalism and Judaism," he states that "this knowing reverence for literature is one of the characteristic features of the Jewish disposition and thus of Jewish nationalism." Against this conceptual background, it is of decisive importance that the main character of the trilogy is the historian Flavius Josephus, the author of the famous work, *History of the Jewish War* (written between A.D. 75 and 79), which presents the emotional story of the destruction of Jerusalem by Titus in A.D. 70. Josephus took part in the war—first as a Jewish commander in Galilee, later in Titus's ranks—and was an eyewitness to the conquest of Jerusalem and the destruction of the temple.

In his portrayal of Jewish nationalism, both in the novel and essay, Feuchtwanger shows its dubious aspects. He calls the tolerance of the Romans "a tolerance that is unimaginable today," explaining that "it was—strangely enough—the Jews who, at the beginning of our era, introduced nationalism into what was then a fully cosmopolitan world." Feuchtwanger makes it clear that in doing so the Jews brought about their own destruction. "What the majority of white men first learned from the World War or perhaps will be forced to learn from a second world war—namely the senselessness of regional-political nationalism—was hammered into us, the Jews, eighteen hundred years ago in a very bitter, unforgettable way." As these statements show, Feuchtwanger does not blindly side with the Jews.

His endeavor to view all sides with justice and tolerance lends the novel a high degree of political sophistication and makes it captivating reading, assuming the reader is receptive to the material: the late Roman period, the details of Jewish and Roman life styles, the wide range of settings (Rome, Jerusalem, Galilee, Egypt), and the interesting personality of Josephus. The intellectual's entanglement in events of world history, his inability to influence them, and his passionate will to be equal to their demands are special themes which give the novel the quality of a twentieth-century *Zeitroman* rather than a historical novel. Just as Feuchtwanger avoids black and white depictions in the area of politics, his character portrayal is also subtle and not bound to fixed moral categories. In the eyes of those defending Jerusalem, Josephus is a traitor when he appears on Titus's behalf before the walls of the city in order to negotiate and save the temple. The paradox of his situation is obvious to the reader. The momentous burning of the temple, which is described in detail and is the culmination of all the plot strands in the trilogy's first volume, and Canetti's library fire are comparable events, notwithstanding the differences of the two works with respect to genre and artistry.

As Feuchtwanger's *The Jewish War* and other historical novels of the Weimar Republic prove, the historical novel was revived in the twentieth century even before the emigration of authors from the totalitarian state began. When the authors emigrated, they already possessed in the historical novel a newly tested instrument, adapted to the sociological and psychological methods of their time, an instrument which, as the many examples of the 1930s show, they knew how to use with great skill. What Elke Nyssen contends, namely that the "formation of a specific historical consciousness and the new orientation of the emigrants in their historical situation" were decisive for the "evolution of the historical novel," is misleading. The facts prove that the historical novel did not, as Nyssen believes, evolve from the "situation of emigration." Nor did a "specific historical consciousness" develop among the emigrants which could have provided the impulse for a new artistic form; one simply cannot speak of a common consciousness or of the emigrants' "new orientation" (in the sense of acquiring new concepts as a result of their common plight as exiles).[3]

The exiles, scattered throughout the world, cannot be seen as a unified group. They were divided by opposing world views, backgrounds, artistic and life styles, reasons for emigration, material and personal conditions in exile, and differing degrees of success in their work. In addition, they were burdened by the resentments and irritations which, even without the strain of emigration, often tend to disturb the atmosphere among highly individualistic, sensitive personalities. After all, being individualistic was essential to their artistic existence. As can be seen from examining the different literary careers in their entirety, a writer's productivity in exile was tied to the potential he displayed earlier. Those like Thomas Mann, who were able to further expand their artistry, or like Hermann Broch, to advance into new realms, were exceptional cases, but in their own way they too were subject to the difficulties of exile. Most of the emigrant authors suffered from the fact that they were uprooted from a historical tradition which, at least at first, nothing could replace. Of course, sooner or later the authors came to see the questionableness of the nineteenth-century nationalist view of history; but a new picture of history to fit their most recent experiences was lacking and perplexity prevailed. In such a situation, the modern form of the historical novel gave support and help to many; it was a convention whose demands they knew how to meet. Material could be taken from books by methods which the authors had learned and practiced since school days and this material arranged according to points of view which the contents themselves suggested. Some application to the present could always be found, regardless of the segment of world history presented. For the course of world history—as was already recognized in the 1920s and as historical studies proved—had been determined everywhere by force and the obsession for power; everywhere certain individuals had rebelled, refusing to give up their ideals despite the egocentric behavior of the rulers and their often demonic acts of cruelty. Bruno Frank (1887–1945) offered a model with his A *Man Called Cervantes* (*Cervantes*, 1934).

Alfred Neumann continued his work on the historical novel, using material from nineteenth-century French history as the basis for a trilogy, *Another Caesar* (*Neuer Cäsar*, 1934), *Gaudy Empire* (*Kaiserreich*, 1936), and *Friends of the People* (*Volksfreunde*, 1941). The setting for *The Pact* (*Der Pakt*, 1950), the "most important novel of his exile period," is America shortly before the Civil War. It is, in Neumann's words, the "extraordinary story of an American pre-Hitler," the intellectual William Walker from Tennessee, whose "quite obscure" biography Neumann had discovered soon after his arrival in America in February 1941.[4]

A Hitler figure is also the focus of Lion Feuchtwanger's *The Pretender* (*Der falsche Nero*, 1936), a novel from the time of the Roman emperors. Today Feuchtwanger's *The Oppermanns* (*Die Geschwister Oppenheim*, 1933) and *Paris Gazette* (*Exil*, 1940), which, together with *Success* (*Erfolg*, 1930), form the *Waiting Room Trilogy* (*Wartesaal-Trilogie*), read like nineteenth-century historical novels, although they describe events of the Hitler era. In his later years, Feuchtwanger remained active as a historical novelist, giving particular attention to the period of the French Revolution. The titles of his later novels are *Proud Destiny* (*Waffen für Amerika*, 1947–48), *This Is the Hour. A Novel about Goya* (*Goya oder Der arge Weg der Erkenntnis*, 1951), and *'Tis Folly to Be Wise* (*Narrenweisheit oder Tod und Verklärung des Jean-Jacques Rousseau*, 1952). In these works he abandoned the idea of resignation, of *Sichfallenlassen*, which had preoccupied many authors in the 1920s, to stress the moral responsibility of resistance. Like his characters, Feuchtwanger himself underwent a change in attitude as a result of his experiences in the Hitler period.

In contrast, Joseph Roth did not change his outlook. In *The Ballad of the Hundred Days* (*Die hundert Tage*, 1936), he was concerned—in the same spirit as his works from the 1920s—with the humiliated Napoleon, forced to abdicate, who "felt . . . that one could see clearer and further with eyes that were tired and unhappy rather than fresh and sharp."

In his two-volume work *Henri Quatre*, which includes *Young Henry of Navarre* (*Die Jugend des Königs Henri Quatre*, 1935) and *Henry, King of France* (*Die Vollendung des Königs Henri Quatre*, 1938), Heinrich Mann placed the results of his extensive research in the service of political aims. He wanted to give the resistance against Hitler a sense of eventual success through the instrument of historical material. Like Feuchtwanger, Heinrich Mann believed in progress, in the power of reason, and in the significance of world history. He had planned to write the life story of Henri Quatre as early as 1925 and began work on it in 1932. The changed political conditions under which he completed the biography intensified his commitment to the French king, whom he portrays as a man who believes that virtue will prevail over force and that nothing is as deeply rooted in the common people as goodness. The ideas which the king represents in the novel correspond to

Mann's own views at a time when he was an active participant in the efforts of the popular front in Paris, the movement between 1935 and 1939 in which Communists, socialists, and bourgeois democrats tried to join forces. Yet it soon became apparent that the effort to reach an understanding among the proponents of different ideologies in the antifascist emigrant movement was doomed to failure and that the very ideas which Heinrich Mann advocated in *Henri Quatre* had nothing in common with socialism in its Stalinist form.

Bertolt Brecht (1898–1956) rejected the idea of unity among the different emigrant groups from the beginning. This rejection followed from his theory of fascism. Brecht held that fascism is a "historical phase" of capitalism which occurs of necessity when the capitalist system finds itself in danger. Beneficiaries of this system see fascism as a means of defending by force the existing distribution of wealth. Therefore, when the development has reached a certain point, brutality becomes unavoidable and no one can stand up against the criminality which is now part of the system. At the Paris writers' convention (1935), Brecht "deliberately antagonized the bourgeois democratic writers" with this analysis.[5] He thought it his responsibility to motivate them to change their views.

Brecht intended to demonstrate the obvious link between capitalism and crime in the *Threepenny Novel (Der Dreigroschenroman,* 1934). He wrote it soon after his flight from Germany into exile in Denmark, presenting in it his conclusions about the most recent political events as well as ideas derived from years of sociological study under the influence of Karl Korsch and Korsch's interpretation of Marxism. The novel is not simply a prose version of *Threepenny Opera* (1928) but is based on a new underlying concept. Brecht also invented new techniques to match his new ideas, and he gave the novel a straightforward plot: the rise of the gangster Macheath to the position of influential industrialist. In the beginning, Macheath owns a number of shops which he keeps supplied with wares through his gang's burglaries. In the end he controls two banks, his own shops, and the chain stores that were previously owned by his two competitors. In order to function within this plot, the characters taken from the opera had to be changed and new ones introduced. The plot was moved back to the turn of the century to show that the development of new practices in the business world was a result of changes in general conditions occurring at that time. Macheath himself repeatedly speaks of the difference between now and then.

> It is strange. . . . These shops don't want to stay the way they are. It used to be that one started a business, let's say a hardware store, and it stayed a hardware store. Today it always wants to become something else. Whatever you do: it can't stay as it is. A hosiery shop has to become a factory or it goes out of business. The fac-

tory . . . when it can't pay its rent anymore, wants to open chains.
In big business it's no different. . . . That's not progress, it's escape. . . . How can one build character like that?

This passage, like many others, is separated from the rest of the text by italics,
a device Brecht used to accentuate his ideas. The italicized passages have the
same function as the reflections in the novels of Broch, Musil, and Thomas
Mann; they express, on a separate level, the narrative's intellectual content.
Furthermore, they possess a fascinating life of their own, exhibiting literary
mastery and brilliant perceptiveness. "What is written here is said for the first
time," Walter Benjamin wrote,[6] thus characterizing Brecht's successful artistic transformation of the ideology he had absorbed and of his own theory of
fascism.

As the italicized passages—in which the characters often interpret their
own behavior—and the plot reveal, the characters' most important trait is
their ability to adapt to new situations. Closely related to this trait is the fear
of losing one's footing, of sinking into the bottomlessness of life in uncertain
times. These fears manifest themselves in insecurity and mistrust, unscru-
pulousness and malice. All the male characters in the *Threepenny Novel* fit
more or less into this mold. The most pronounced case is Peachum, who
plays a major role here as in the opera. Peachum's fear—"of ending up under
the bridge arches, . . . having been deceived by someone more clever, unscrupulous, or energetic"—is an important factor in his criminality and a
primary motivating force in the society Brecht constructs in the novel. Fear
also lurks behind Macheath's industriousness. It is not as naked and elemen-
tary as Peachum's, but Macheath is well aware of it. In his last speech (in
italics), held before a group gathered to celebrate his success, he discusses his
rise from a different milieu, pointing out that in general one attributes a
man's success to "his ambition or to a grand, complicated plan," but in his
case it was something else: "To be honest, I didn't have a grand plan. It's just
that I always wanted to stay out of the poorhouse." Just before this he admitted, "I make no secret of it, I come from the lower classes." The world of
misery he came from loomed as a constant threat as he made his way in the
business world.

Macheath's speeches—often parodies, full of clichés, banalities, and
distortions—show the former street robber's endeavor to bring his existence
into conformity with the times and to master life by using his head. For
example, he explains to the robber Grooch that as a "little craftsman" Grooch
is a member of a dying class: "What is a skeleton key compared to stock?
What is a bank robbery compared to founding a bank? What, my dear Grooch,
is the murder of a man compared to hiring a man? . . . You have to work
within the law. It's just as good a sport!" Nonetheless it sometimes seems to

him that his earlier life had more dignity. "Repulsed" by the bank representatives, he says to himself, "This haggling really disgusts me, a former street bandit! Here I sit and squabble over percentages. . . . Why not just say: The money, or I'll shoot? How undignified to take shelter behind judges and bailiffs! That demeans me in my own eyes." The parabolic character of the novel is evident in such reflections. The former street robber considers himself superior to the representatives of a sphere into which he has been able to advance. An open robbery was more respectable than the seemingly civilized practices in the capitalistic system.

Brecht's fragment, *The Business Affairs of Mr. Julius Caesar (Die Geschäfte des Herrn Julius Caesar)*, written in 1938 and 1939 and published for the first time in 1957, a year after his death, is similar in design to the *Threepenny Novel*. Twenty years after Caesar's death, a Roman lawyer, who is also the narrator of the novel, would like to follow his book on Solon with a biography of Caesar and tries to collect material. The information he receives does not conform to his expectations. His ideas about Caesar are refuted by the facts, which, indeed, seem plausible, as well as by the statements of witnesses who are obviously well-informed. The report breaks off at a point when it has become certain that Caesar will be elected consul. As in the *Threepenny Novel*, the plot describes the rise of the main character to an influential position of power. But the novel's tension has nothing to do with this plot. Instead, it is due to the fact that from the material which the narrator unfolds before the reader, ostensibly in the same order in which he himself acquires it, a picture of Caesar evolves which contradicts everything written in fiction and nonfiction of the Hitler period about great men, leaders, and politicians in world history. It is the antithesis of the idealized concept of the leader.

The picture the narrator presents of Caesar derives in large part from the information he receives from the financier, Mummlius Spicer, who originally met Caesar in his capacity as a bailiff. Spicer gained more and more control over Caesar's finances, enabling him to wield political influence and to become a rich man himself. His portrait of Caesar, based on a materialistic view of history, is greeted with little enthusiasm by the biographer. He expresses his annoyance at Spicer: "The little he [Spicer] could say about the founder of the Imperium, one of the greatest men in world history, would show him quite clearly to be a particularly depraved offspring of an old family." What Spicer says about Caesar's early career can be compared to Macheath's comments on his own rise to success. The politician was not motivated by ambition or a grand plan but was always in need of money, living deeply in debt. Candidacy for office in Rome cost a fortune. When everything was spent, one still had to finance the next candidature. "No wonder that he . . . grasped at every suggestion, political or nonpolitical, which could help him keep his head above water"; he did not even own the chair he sat on. Spicer emphasizes that Caesar was not greedy and that it was not his intention to change "yours" into "mine." In fact, he saw no difference between "mine" and "yours." This is important for an understanding of the overall theme. Caesar's "business affairs" are not motivated by covetousness or avarice; it is simply that he must survive in a capitalist system and thus has no other course of action open to him.

Throughout the novel Brecht obviously saw the evaluation of Caesar in relation to the problem of evaluating Hitler. Important in this regard is another of the biographer's sources, the fictitious diary of Rarus, who was Caesar's slave, secretary, and to a certain extent confidant. Occasionally Rarus expresses admiration for his master's great abilities, but he also stresses that Caesar was "never a politician of great stature" and "never will be." What "Rome needs more than ever, the strong man who goes his way unswervingly and forces his will upon the world, realizing a great idea, that is not Caesar. . . . He is in politics because he has no other choice. But he is not a born leader." The concept of the strong man as described by Rarus corresponded to the expectations of large segments of the German population who were not looking for a politician but for a savior. The "great idea" they wanted him to realize derived from vague mystical notions and from self-interest. Rarus's evaluation of Caesar is based on similar expectations.

This novel fragment is the most important of the historical novels written by emigrants during the 1930s. It is a demanding, ingenious book which, for the most part, makes fascinating reading.

A second novel fragment, the *Tui Novel* (*Tui-Roman*) was written between 1934 and 1943. The Tuis occupied Brecht even before the completion of the *Threepenny Novel* and long after finishing *Caesar*. He defines the Tuis within the novel: "The TUI is the intellectual in this day of markets and wares. The one who rents out intelligence." He explains the word itself: "In Chima, Tuis were named by abbreviating the word for those members of the caste of tellect-ual-ins, those who worked with their heads." Chima or the Chinese Republic is the Weimar Republic. The drafts, plans, and stories belonging to the *Tui Novel* show that Brecht wanted to denounce "Tui thinking" and to demonstrate the Tuis' guilt in the decline and fall of the republic. These same concepts determined his behavior at the Paris convention of 1935.

That a novel's wide appeal is due in large extent to its plot is proven by the extraordinary success of Anna Seghers's *The Seventh Cross* (*Das siebte Kreuz*, 1942). From an artistic standpoint, her novel *Transit* (1948) is superior. Moreover, it stands out as an exceptional work among all of the prose written by emigrants dealing with the theme of exile itself. Bruno Frank's *Lost Heritage* (*Der Reisepass*, 1937), Klaus Mann's *The Volcano* (*Der Vul-*

kan, 1939), Lion Feuchtwanger's *Paris Gazette* (*Exil*, 1940), Erich Maria Remarque's *Arc de Triomphe* (1946), and Walter Hasenclever's *The Outlawed* (*Die Rechtlosen*, 1940; published 1963) can only serve as a foil to Seghers's novel. She alone succeeded in capturing and expressing the unique situation of refugees. Yet, in spite of this, *Transit* never had the impact, never found as many readers as *The Seventh Cross*, and it seems to be more a work for scholars. This may have to do with the sobriety of its plot or the fact that the German-speaking public could not relate to the experience of exile but could easily become involved with Georg Heisler's story in *The Seventh Cross*, which is set in Germany.

In many ways the two books belong together and are the best of Anna Seghers's writings during her years in exile. Her earlier post-1933 novels, including *A Price on His Head* (*Der Kopflohn*, 1933), *The Way through February* (*Der Weg durch den Februar*, 1935), and *Rescue* (*Die Rettung*, 1937), were more limited in scope and did not yet have the élan of the two later works. The style of these later novels reflects the sense of personal liberation Anna Seghers achieved during the intensive debates on literature held within the context of the popular front movement. Her turning to myths and fairy tales during this period (*Sagen vom Räuber Woynok*, 1936) and her determined defense of her own artistry in letters to Georg Lukács show her taking a personal direction. "They had managed to remove all the magic from the world," she says of certain writer colleagues who "believed" themselves to be in "complete possession of the method of realism," but had, in Seghers's opinion, sacrificed the ability to experience life directly; the "primary reaction," as she calls it, had been "completely buried."[7] Here we see unmistakably that Anna Seghers is opposing the theorizing of her friends in the party with the immediacy of her own experiences and creativity.

The theme of the two novels can only be understood in light of this immediacy. Both are concerned with the survival of the individual in situations of utmost danger and insecurity. *The Seventh Cross* tells of the successful escape of the Communist George Heisler from a concentration camp. It shows the strength of the individual under pressure and the dependability of sympathizers who never doubt the seriousness of their responsibility. The political conviction which unites them is rarely discussed, although it is obviously the underlying reason for their solidarity and thus for their willingness to assist a fugitive. Heisler serves an important function as an example of endurance, both in the prison camp before flight, when he does not betray the others despite extreme pressure, and in the days of his lonely wandering, when he eludes capture and must, at each moment, be equal to the demands of being pursued. His flight also serves to bring new life to the fragmented and weary circles of former comrades in battle. Previously they could only hide; now they feel called upon to act.

Seghers shows how slim Heisler's chance for survival is by having the other six prisoners fail in their attempt to escape. As portrayed in the novel, the situation in Germany in autumn 1937 would almost seem to rule out the possibility of success, especially since uncertainty about the activity of spies and informers is so great that one must always be prepared for betrayal at the hands of those who fear for their own security. In addition, Heisler has no personal relationships he can depend on; he had left his wife and disappointed his close friends. His mother is kept from helping him by a family which will definitely not endanger itself. A lover to whom he goes for help is long since committed to the side of the opponents. All these facts, skillfully woven into the plot, provide elements of suspense. For example, Heisler's wife, who knows all the people who might help him, does not reveal any names under questioning despite severe threats. A former suitor of Heisler's wife learns of the manhunt through the newspapers and, laying aside his resentments, thinks only of his responsibility toward the fugitive. A friend whom Heisler had neglected immediately declares his willingness to help and provides invaluable assistance. Thus the seemingly inactive apparatus of secret resistance comes to life, and before long Heisler has a passport, money, and passage on a Rhine tugboat destined for Holland. Without these efforts on the part of others, he could not have survived.

The German people, seen both individually and in groups as they come into contact with the fugitives, play an important role. Anna Seghers obtained information from refugees and emigrants about the situation in the country which Hitler and his supporters were terrorizing. It seems almost as if Seghers, by depicting the differences in behavior of the Germans, is carrying out an experiment with people she has known for a long time. Her impressionistic style permitted her to sketch and characterize each individual case. Why do some reveal information which will harm others? Why do others remain silent although one might expect them to speak out? These questions are touched upon time and again as the narration proceeds, and often several answers are given. Not only are there as many different explanations as there are people, but for each person there may be more than one explanation. Who can understand why the old farmer denounces the Jewish doctor who treated Heisler's wounded hand? This results in the doctor's deportation to a concentration camp and could cost Heisler his life. But a member of the Hitler youth throws Heisler's pursuers off the track, and Heisler is able to move on. The boy had understood something fundamental. "In his young heart something had stirred, a warning or a doubt, something which some people claim is inborn, others say is not inborn but develops little by little, and still others claim does not exist at all."

This quote is characteristic of the novel. The question is not answered in terms of ideology; in fact, no answer is given and a certain mystery remains. One cannot explain just what caused the Hitler youth's reaction. Seghers also works with the irrational at other points in the book, as in the last sentence: "We all felt how deeply and terribly external powers could strike to the core of man, but we also felt that at the core there was something unassailable and inviolable."[8] What is being referred to here? The novel's introduction points in the same direction when it is reported that seven plane trees were felled and made into crosses for the fugitives who would be captured. The prisoners' triumph—the novel's ending is already revealed in the introduction—is the seventh cross, which remains empty because Heisler does not return. The prisoners' own power, which they suddenly feel in this triumph, has long been underestimated, although it is the "only force" which can "suddenly grow immeasurably and incalculably." The style is such that much more is meant than is actually said. It probably was not possible for Anna Seghers to say certain things. She believed resolutely in the strength to survive and in the ultimate victory of the revolutionary ideals to which she subscribed. It is characteristic that she so often uses the verb "to feel."

In *Transit* there is also an invulnerability which cannot be motivated logically, but here it has nothing to do with specific political beliefs. The young German mechanic who is the main character and narrator is not a member of a political party. The feeling of his "own impregnability"—it was "just a feeling"—emerges in him as he confronts the chaotic situation of fugitives and refugees in France after German troops entered the country in the spring of 1940. Thousands see their only chance of evading capture in departure by ship from yet unoccupied Marseilles. Departure hinges on the possession of many papers which are desperately sought in foreign consulates, French passport offices, and travel agencies. What is needed are a ship ticket, departure and entrance visas, a residence permit for a foreign country, character references, a work permit, and—particularly difficult to obtain—a transit pass for the countries through which one must travel. In addition, each person must obtain a residence permit for Marseilles in order to prepare for departure. The dates on all the papers must agree, and a ship must be found that will leave at the right time. In the meantime, people in the overcrowded city sit in waiting rooms, stand in long lines on the streets, and pass time in cafés and hotels with nothing to do but wait.

Anna Seghers found herself in this situation before she and her family could finally leave Marseilles in March 1941. The novel was written while she waited in the city and during the ocean journey, and completed in Mexico. Much of what it describes are her own experiences, presented from the perspective of a young German mechanic who never really intends to leave Europe and, in the end, remains in France. According to his own report in the first person narrative, he fled from a German concentration camp, was interned in France, and escaped again. In Paris the papers of a German writer named Weidel, who had committed suicide, fell into his hands, including proof that Weidel was invited to live in Mexico and would receive an entrance visa and travel money. French friends took him with them to a yet unoccupied part of France; there he was given money and valid papers under the name Seidler and was referred to a cousin in Marseilles, where he was to stay until he could be accommodated on a peach farm near the Mediterranean.

In Marseilles, the dizzying experience aptly described by the word "transit" begins. The nameless German, now known as Seidler, becomes caught up in a confusing struggle for his own identity. At first he does not understand the information he receives, as when he is told that people "only leave you in peace here . . . if you can prove that you intend to leave." Again and again it is stressed that the most important thing is transit. When he asks what transit means, he is told that it is "permission to travel through a country when it is certain that there is no intention to stay." The words "visa," "transit," "stay," "depart," "traverse," "arrive" all take on a meaning beyond the normal usage. By virtue of the atmosphere in which they are used, they come to refer to man's existential situation.

Despite his intention to stay, the young man sees himself forced to play the role of a person in transit. He must act as if he were the writer Weidel who wants to go to Mexico. This deception temporarily solves the problem of being allowed to stay in Marseilles. He receives permission to remain in the city, is able to extend the expiration date with the help of the Mexican consulate, receives the transit permit and authorization to depart, and eventually even has a ship ticket. In other words, he tries to obtain everything he does not want, and is successful, in order to be able to do what he wants: to stay in Marseilles over the winter until he can go to the peach farm. Like everyone else, he has to wait for appointments and papers. But, unlike the others, he cannot reveal his true objectives, nor would anyone believe him if he did. "For fugitives must continue their flight, they cannot suddenly grow peaches." The narrator had already described the fugitives' emotional state: "Everything was in flight, everything was temporary, but we didn't know yet if this state would last until tomorrow or for another few weeks or years or even for the rest of our lives."

Just as transit means more than the authorization needed to travel through a country, the peach farm in southern France is more than simply a place to work. Like the Rhine-Main landscape with its apple trees and flocks of sheep in *The Seventh Cross*, it functions as an unchanging rural world where men have lived for thousands of years. It has proven itself to be indestructible, regardless of how many wars passed over it or how many peoples took possession of it. On the last pages of *Transit*, as on the first pages of *The Seventh Cross*, man and land are united in a special way. The young German is interested not only in cultivating grapes and peaches in southern France, but is prepared to take up arms on the side of France to defend the land in the belief that he would not die "without leaving something behind. . . . When one bleeds on familiar land, then something of oneself grows there like something of the shrubs and trees one tries to clear."

The ideas expressed by Anna Seghers likewise played a role in conservative circles living in "inner emigration." It is important to emphasize that this way of thinking was related to fundamental concepts of European humanism and had nothing to do with the perversion of these same ideas to the ideology which, in National Socialist jargon, was called *"Blut und Boden"* (blood and soil). Opponents of fascist thought could recognize each other by their common fascination with the enduring effect that antiquity and Christianity had had on the rural landscape of the Rhine and Main regions. The fondness for France, which gradually began to prevail after the First World War, is connected with these ideas. They are given a mythical quality by Ernst Jünger in *On the Marble Cliffs* (*Auf den Marmorklippen*, 1939).

The book tells of the destruction of an old cultural landscape, called the Marina, by a negative force embodied in the head forester. Jünger later said that this was a character from his dreams and that one should not interpret the work as an allegory. He did not write it as a *roman à clef* and rejected the idea that characters in the novel could be equated with persons in public life at that time. The head forester was not to be seen as a portrait of Hitler, Stalin, or Göring; from the work's style it is evident that Jünger is not describing specific historical events and persons. His use of a symbolistic style must be taken into consideration when interpreting the work.

The symbolistic style did not create problems for Jünger's readers; what is alienating today was familiar to readers then. To them it was evident that the book surpassed everything written in Germany during those years. They found the language and imagery clear and beautiful, unique and elevating. What was surprising was the content, which had to be understood as a political statement; no other interpretation was possible. Of course many may not have understood it as such, but discerning readers knew that to write and publish this book within Germany meant resistance. That the government allowed its publication caused much speculation. In view of Ernst Jünger's reputation, he could not easily be liquidated. He had received the *Pour le mérite* and, when the book appeared soon after the outbreak of the Second World War, was serving in the military as a reactivated officer. In a court of law one would not have been able to prove that the novel was defamatory, and this again was related to its style. It was perfectly suited both for revealing and concealing its message. For years to come readers spoke of the head forester, of Braquemart and Biedenhorn, and of Köppelsbleek and the Rue-hermitage, realizing that these referred to typical phenomena rather than to something specific.

When interpreting the work, it is also important to keep in mind that the novel begins at a time when the Marina had already gone up in flames. The story of its destruction is told in retrospect, and the novel resembles an elegy, related by a first-person narrator who has been deeply affected by the events. He has lived with his brother Otho on the perimeter of the Marina for many peaceful years, senses danger approaching, and is able to escape with Otho from the final catastrophe. Well informed and yet emotionally involved, he imparts to his narration a combination of exactness and feeling.

What is meant by the destruction—the novel's main theme—is revealed in a description of one of the novel's primary figures, the

> old man who lurked deep in his woods. . . . He, who hated the plow, the grain, the vine, and the tame animals and was repulsed by bright villages and man's open nature, was not interested in ruling over such abundance. He only rejoiced when moss and ivy grew on the rubble of cities and when bats flapped their wings in the moonlight amidst the ruptured cross vaultings of cathedrals.

A reader in the 1940s could relate this description to his own situation. The "old man who lurked deep in his woods" is often referred to in previous chapters as the head forester. Much has been said about his influence, raising the question as to what type of a person he is. This question is now answered through reference to his negative attitude toward plow, grain, vine, and domestic animals and to his unwillingness to rule over "such abundance." Destruction is his element. He can only rejoice when cities and cathedrals lie in rubble. At the end we read,

> Now the extent of the ruin became evident in the high flames, and the old and beautiful cities on the edge of the Marina shone far into the distance as they burned. They sparkled in the fire like a chain of rubies. . . . Even the remote villages and hamlets in the country burned, and fire raged in the proud castles and cloisters in the valley.

Such passages do not lend themselves to the question whether the head forester is Hitler or Stalin. The novel can only show how these tyrants should be classified and how it was possible for them to gain such influence. From the imagery statements emerge which can be applied to the conditions of the times.

The novel's passages on fear can serve as another example. The narrator emphasizes that the head forester's power to destroy did not come to him accidentally and that it was only partially contingent on the number and type of his followers from the forests. Following a war, the "old order in the Marina" was no longer the same, even though this was not immediately recognizable. To the same "extent that the debilitation increased," the head forester began to draw closer. Wherever he went, a "cloud of fear" went ahead of him. "He was wrapped in fear, and I am convinced that the source of his power lay therein much more than within himself. He could only have an effect when things had become unsteady on their own. Then, however, his forests were favorably situated for an attack on the land." Readers who can relate to Jünger's imagery and who experienced the rise of the totalitarian states will understand immediately what is meant by "then, however, his forests were favorably situated." The theme of fear is taken up again later. At a time when the decline has already proceeded quite far, it sometimes appears as if the advance of the enemy forces has subsided and as if "everything" is like it "was before." "Precisely therein lay a masterful tactic of the head forester: he administered fear in small dosages which he gradually increased toward the goal of crippling all resistance."

While occupied with studies of botany and philology, the two brothers in the Rue-hermitage (named after the rue plants in the area) observe events from the marble cliffs, cultivate friendly relationships with Father Lampros and the wild shepherd Belovar, and weigh the possibilities of resistance. They realize the terrifying nature of the impending catastrophe when on a forest outing they come upon the "torture-hut" Köppelsbleek. A skull is hanging on the gable, the gable frieze is made up of human hands fastened with nails, and skulls grin from the surrounding trees. When the final battle is imminent, Braquemart and young Prince Sunmyra visit the brothers to obtain information. The character Braquemart in particular, to whom Jünger devotes powerful passages, stimulated much debate among contemporaries. Joseph Goebbels, Adolf Hitler's minister of propaganda, felt that he had been portrayed in him.[9] To the present day the character type "Braquemart" can be recognized in many variations in public and professional life. When Braquemart and Prince Sunmyra visit the brothers, they are on their way into the forests to launch an attack on the head forester's innermost realm. Of course they are repulsed. The narrator tells us that "they were like halfmen—Braquemart, a pure technician of power who saw only small parts but never the roots of things; and Prince Sunmyra, a noble spirit who knew justice but resembled a child who dared to enter the woods where wolves howled." Summoned by Father Lampros, the narrator follows them and is witness to a murderous battle between the dogs in which the head forester's bloodhounds kill Belovar and his dogs. The narrator tries to kill Chiffon

Rouge, the "head forester's favorite dog," but is at first not able to shoot and then is distracted. The bloodhounds pursue him back to the Rue-hermitage, where Chiffon Rouge is fatally bitten by a large poisonous snake which is one of the domestic animals on the premises. From the marble cliffs one can see the entire Marina in flames. After setting fire to the Rue-hermitage, which means the loss of years of research, the brothers flee by ship to Alta Plana, where they are warmly received by a young friend.

The novel tells of downfall and survival, thus reflecting the expectations of the author as well as of many other Germans. Numerous allusions to contemporary events are identifiable and testify to Jünger's perception and foresight. For example, the narrator suspects that Braquemart took a poison capsule at the "right time," just as Hermann Göring later made use of such a capsule. As Hansjörg Schelle has stressed, the parallels between the novel and reality are limited to details, whereas with regard to the whole there is a striking discrepancy: "In the book one has the impression that the head forester is victorious, but in reality the counterforces prevail."[10] As correct as this may be, it cannot be forgotten that destruction and murder in real life were atrocious, and that no counterforce could prevent it. Moreover, who can claim that the head forester and his followers are not still advancing today, today as always, while others live in the Rue-hermitage or the Marina?

The relevance of the novel is not limited to 1939, its publication year; its statement applies both to past and future. *On the Marble Cliffs* cannot be designated a *Zeitroman*, the genre characteristic of so many nineteenth-century novels. Actually, the applicability of its content beyond the literary frame to a specific time and place is dependent upon the reader.

Just as Ernst Jünger's novel was not a conventional *Zeitroman*, Thomas Mann's *Lotte in Weimar* (1939), which appeared in the same year as *On the Marble Cliffs*, was not a conventional historical novel. The book was written between the last two volumes of the *Joseph* tetralogy (*Joseph in Egypt*, 1936; *Joseph the Provider*, 1943) and is closely related to them in its ironic treatment of an extraordinarily intricate subject which can be understood on many levels. Goethe's involvement with Charlotte Kestner (née Buff) as a young man became public property in 1774 with the publication of *Werther*. But few readers knew that the widowed Charlotte paid a visit to Goethe in Weimar decades later. The facts documenting this visit in September 1816 were sparse, but this was precisely what allowed the artist's imagination such freedom. In shaping the little noticed event of Lotte's visit into a novel, Thomas Mann drew upon his years of intensive study of Goethe to realize an "old dream" by having "Goethe himself walk" in the pages of a novel (December 28, 1937, letter to Alfred Neumann).

The realization of this dream had little in common with the historical novels written at that time by other emigrants, as comparison of just a few pages from the novels of Alfred Neumann, Lion Feuchtwanger, or Heinrich Mann with a sample passage from *Lotte in Weimar* would reveal. The difference lies in the artists themselves. While the others retold, rearranged, and supplemented the material with their own inventions, Thomas Mann designed the material anew. He invented everything, using outside information only to stimulate his creative impulses. Mann was reflecting on his own creativity as well as Goethe's when he had Goethe's secretary, Riemer, ponder the enigma of Goethe's genius in the third book of the novel and find the key in "an all-embracing irony." But what is the irony which is the secret of creativity? Riemer quotes Goethe in this regard: "'Irony,' he said, 'is the grain of salt which makes what is served palatable.'" This definition raises new questions rather than providing an answer, and the search for an answer occupies the fictional characters throughout the work.

The entire work revolves around Goethe. His personality is revealed through the eyes of others until, in the seventh of nine books, the reader is confronted with the overwhelming inner world of the artist in his morning reveries. His interior monologue, continued until about noon and interrupted three times by conversations, forms the first part of Mann's direct portrayal of Goethe. The second part takes the form of a luncheon mentioned in Goethe's diary to which Charlotte Kestner was invited several days after her arrival in Weimar. It gives Mann the opportunity to present Goethe in society.

The "all-embracing irony" behind Mann's conception of Lotte's journey is alive throughout, in every scene and every detail. It shapes the arrival scene and Lotte's ensuing daydream as well as the episodes between Lotte and her visitors on the first morning. This parade of callers begins with an English artist who collects celebrities in her sketchbook and persuades Lotte to sit for a portrait. The artist is still in the room when Dr. Riemer arrives. Before he has gone, Adele Schopenhauer appears. She is relieved in turn by August von Goethe. He has come to deliver his father's invitation to a luncheon in three days, an invitation prompted by Lotte's short letter to Goethe announcing her arrival in Weimar and expressing her desire to see him. In the course of the morning, Lotte gains insight into her own situation. Dealing with Goethe, she realizes, is a "tormenting enigma" not only for her, but for everyone around him. Her particular problem is that, when she set off on the journey to Weimar, time played no role in her mind. What had happened forty-four years ago was still fully alive for her, and moreover, she had relived the scenes with Goethe again and again in her mind.

For Goethe, however, the repetitions took place with different women. Even Lotte herself was a repetition, and now he was experiencing repetition in Marianne. To "relive what he had once lived" with "heightened spirituality" meant "intense rejuvenation" for him. Here, too, irony dominates. Reflecting on the news of Lotte's arrival, Goethe thinks to himself, "When present and past become one, which was always a tendency in my life, the present can easily assume a spectral character."

As she converses with her visitors, Lotte herself comprehends the spectral quality of her return. It is fully demonstrated to her during the reunion at Goethe's house. Her meeting with the ceremoniously formal genius, who purposely keeps her at a distance, seems to her to be "a new acquaintance with an old man." Nonetheless, a reconciliation does take place. Allowing his imagination free rein, Thomas Mann brings Goethe and Lotte together a second time. After an evening theater performance, which Lotte views alone from Goethe's box, he rides with her in his coach to the hotel. According to Thomas Mann this was "the only truly unreal scene" in the novel (March 3, 1940, letter to Heinrich Mann).

Two years before its publication, Thomas Mann wrote that the book would be "something ingenious as well as very German" (November 14, 1937, letter to Gottfried Bermann Fischer). This remark is surprising insofar as Mann often has Goethe speak with irritation about the Germans. As Mann portrays it, Goethe himself sees his isolation and his problematical relationships with others as a result of his feeling foreign among his German countrymen. In Goethe's statements about the Germans, Thomas Mann's own situation and his feelings as an emigrant can be heard in all their intensity. "They believe that they are Germany, but I am Germany, and if it were to be destroyed with all its roots and branches, it would live on in me." It is in this sense that Thomas Mann understood *Lotte in Weimar* to be something "very German." Many of Goethe's remarks on the Germans are simply a reflection of the times during which Thomas Mann wrote the novel. As early as 1946 he admitted to an "impudent anachronism" which he had "allowed himself," adding, "Of course one can't call the reference to the late Adolf anything but that. Today I could forego it, but then he was not yet the late Adolf, and so I couldn't (October 4, 1946, letter to Victor Mann). He is referring to the passage in which Goethe reproaches the Germans "for gullibly surrendering themselves to every rapturous scoundrel who addresses their lowest impulses." Thomas Mann's irritability in his interpretation of Germany derives from the distress he felt over the knot of questions and problems which at that time, and for years after the Second World War, were called the "German problem." Though the discussion has since died down, the problem as such persists.

This problem also underlies his great later work *Doctor Faustus. The Life of the German Composer Adrian Leverkühn. As Told by a Friend (Doktor Faustus. Das Leben des deutschen Tonsetzers Adrian Leverkühn. Erzählt von einem Freunde*, 1947). He had already begun writing the book during the war in the spring of 1943. It is the story of a purely imaginary character, the highly gifted composer Adrian Leverkühn, who lived from 1885 to 1940 and in later life was stricken with a grave illness. The narrator, who tells Leverkühn's story in reports written from May 1943 to May 1945 is Serenus Zeitblom, a classical scholar and prematurely retired teacher. Opposite in character from Adrian Leverkühn, Zeitblom was his boyhood friend and remained attached to him all his life, showing him great admiration and reverence. As he presents Leverkühn's life story, he also comments from the perspective of an "inner emigrant" upon the events of the escalating German catastrophe; Zeitblom's agitation over the situation corresponds to the exiled Mann's own despairing concern. Through contextual and structural parallels, Leverkühn's story and the defeat of Germany are intertwined and mutually illuminating. By his own admission Adrian Leverkühn is in collusion with the devil over a period of years, like the historical Dr. Faust. Through the pact with the devil he achieves a refinement of his art but also delivers himself over to inevitable destruction. In terms of the plot, this means that he knowingly risks infection from a diseased prostitute, whom he incorporates into his music as Hetaera Esmeralda, the name of a species of butterfly in his father's collection of illustrations. As his paralysis gradually progresses, Leverkühn creates a series of significant, original works and spends the last ten years of his life in mental derangement.

From the information in the novel no conclusive decision can be made on the question of personal guilt. Not only are Leverkühn's background and education shown as determining factors in shaping his thinking, but his passionate attraction to Esmeralda is a demonic involvement to which the term guilt cannot be unconditionally applied. It is true that four years after Leverkühn has contracted the disease, the devil appears to promise him artistic creativity and brilliance for an allotted amount of time. But Leverkühn's surrender to Esmeralda in Bratislava was not a calculated effort to improve his musical ability. After all, when he undertook the long journey to find her again a year after their first meeting, he was not aware that she was ill. His two attempts to be treated medically also prove that he did not intend to gain artistic advantage through illness. Why he does not continue to seek medical help after the strange incapacitation of both his doctors—one dies and the other is arrested—remains open. Not until his conversation with the devil establishes the incurable nature of the sickness does the afflicted Leverkühn accept it and recognize it as a part of himself.

In his lecture, "Germany and the Germans," held in Washington in May 1945, Thomas Mann used the metaphoric language of his novel to emphasize, in opposition to other emigrants such as Brecht and Feuchtwanger, that there were "not two Germanys, a good one and a bad one, but only one, whose best turned into evil through devilish cunning."[11] While the "devilish cunning" is presented with utmost subtlety within the fictional framework and is recognizable in man's gradual descent towards ruin, the concept is unsatisfactory in political terms. Mann's lecture is indicative of his own intellectual heritage—that part of himself which he calls German— and of his penetrating uneasiness at the thought of his own entanglement in guilt.

The altered conditions in Germany after the defeat in 1945 had as little direct effect on the history of the German novel as the events of 1933. Authors again reacted to the situation with the means they had at hand. It would be many years before a new novelistic style would emerge. Until that time and well beyond it, traditional forms prevailed, enriched and permeated by themes that had arisen since the early 1930s.[12]

That the chapter on the German novel in the totalitarian state also continues beyond the end of the war is a result of the political situation. With the founding of the German Democratic Republic (GDR) on October 7, 1949, a nation was again established on German soil which claimed, and still claims today, to have the right to exercise complete control over literature by setting its guidelines and prohibiting the appearance of statements or portrayals it finds unacceptable. Everything published within its sphere of influence must receive official sanction; novels, regardless of their type, can only be published if the functionaries of the state's cultural organ consider them of value as "socialistic German national literature."[13] The basis for such a literature was created by the leftist authors who, with few exceptions, chose to live in the Soviet zone of occupation after the war and were soon being published in large editions. Heinrich Mann's *Man of Straw* (*Der Untertan*, 1918), Arnold Zweig's *The Case of Sergeant Grischa* (1928), Johannes R. Becher's (1891–1958) *Farewell* (*Abschied*, 1940), and Anna Seghers's *The Seventh Cross* (1942) reached a large public and became required reading in schools. Other works that became well known were Hans Marchwitza's *Kumiak* trilogy (1934, 1952, 1959), Ehm Welk's (1884–1966) *Kummerow* novels (1937, 1943), and Willi Bredel's trilogy, *Relatives and Acquaintances* (*Verwandte und Bekannte*, 1941, 1949, 1953). An author of considerable natural talent was Erwin Strittmatter (b. 1912) with his folkloristic novels: *The Oxcart Driver* (*Ochsenkutscher*, 1952), *Tinko* (1953), and *The Miracle Worker I and II* (*Der Wundertäter I und II*, 1957, 1973). Stefan Heym, (b. 1913), who achieved great success with *The Crusaders* (*Kreuzfahrer von heute*, 1950), tended towards the historical novel in which he denounced occurrences in the communist world. Some of his novels, such as *The Papers of Andreas Lenz* (*Die Papiere des Andreas Lenz*, 1963) and *The King David Report* (*Der König David Bericht*, 1972), are available in the GDR, but others, including *Lassalle* (1969), *Libel or the Queen against Defoe* (*Die Schmähschrift oder Königin gegen Defoe*, 1970), and *Five Days in June* (*Fünf Tage im Juni*, 1977), are banned.

Soon after the war, representatives of the East German Communist party, the SED (*Sozialistische Einheitspartei*), expressed their dissatisfaction with the fact that authors, regardless of whether they had returned from exile or remained in Germany, still tended to select themes derived from their previous experiences: antifascism, exile, democratization, confrontation with their own bourgeois background, problems and motifs from the history of the working class. Beginning in 1948, the SED required that authors participate productively in building the new state and depicting its development. Endless debates between dogmatists and artists characterized the cultural-political scene in East Germany from then on. In the first years after the founding of the nation, so-called "formalism"—the particular form of literary modernity represented by the works of Joyce and Kafka—was explicitly condemned. Moreover, any rejection of art's political function (*Parteilichkeit*) was condemned with crude vehemence. Thus the boundaries were delineated beyond which artists cannot venture even today. Further restrictions followed in the next decade when it was determined that content must conform to a socialist consciousness and to socialist daily life.

Of vital importance to the discussions which took place in East Germany in the 1950s was the Soviet program of Socialist Realism. This is not the definition or description of a literary phenomenon which was seen as a variation of nineteenth-century Realism ((*bürgerlicher Realismus*), but rather is a plan for using literature as an instrument of the totalitarian state. The theoretical concept of Socialist Realism was formulated in talks which Stalin held with Maxim Gorky and other writers in Gorky's villa in October 1932, at which time Stalin spoke of authors as "engineers of the human soul." Socialist Realism was developed and propagandized by the Soviet cultural functionary Shdanov and by Gorky himself, whose ideas of revolutionary romanticism and heroism came to be regarded as the pillars of this concept. Shdanov believed that every author must include "revolutionary romanticism as an integrating part" of his literary creation, for the "entire life of our party, the entire life of the working class and its struggle consists of combining the hardest, most sober practical work with the highest heroism and with grandiose perspectives."[14] Gorky called revolutionary romanticism a "pseudonym for Socialist Realism."[15]

In his last years, Maxim Gorky (1868–1936) still created significant works exhibiting an impressively mature style. Most well known is the second version of his drama *Vassa Zheleznova* (1935). However, the writings of this period do not correspond to the theory of Socialist Realism which he advocated. Nor did the Communist party choose this drama or any of his other later works as exemplary fiction. Instead, they declared his novel *The Mother*, from the year 1907, to be a classic work of Socialist Realism, and a drama which also originated at that time, *The Enemies* (1906), was performed in 1935 in Moscow at Stalin's personal request. The two early works, which express Gorky's direct involvement in the Revolution of 1905, can be considered models of the standards established by the Communist party in the 1930s. They are also Gorky's only works which focus on industrial workers.

The Mother is one of the most remarkable books of the twentieth century, and a familiarity with it is essential to an understanding of the development of the novel in East Germany in the 1950s. It is a work of great logic and clarity in design, in individual motifs, in character development, and in the revolutionary principles expressed in conjunction with plot events. Gorky based his plot on the historically documented workers' struggles in Nizhni-Novgorod and Sormovo (1901–2). In a series of carefully linked scenes, he presents a progressive action whose dynamic energy derives from the conflict between revolutionaries forging ahead in pursuit of their goals and the counteraction of the opposition. Both the revolutionaries and their opponents are made up of widely differing types of characters, in part from different social classes. The revolutionaries include class-conscious factory workers striving for knowledge and a new order, a small group of farmers, a few intellectuals, and isolated members of the propertied classes and the nobility. They are all individually profiled, positive characters. The opposition is portrayed much less vividly and endowed solely with negative characteristics. It includes the factory owner, the wholesale merchant, the landlord, police officers, gendarmes, spies, and judges who represent czarist rule. The revolutionaries are defeated and punished with imprisonment or exile to Siberia, but those conquered in the present will clearly be the victors of the future. As they challenge their opponents and seek new opportunities for battle, they become exemplary fighters. In confrontations with the enemy, even when humiliation or annihilation result, they prove themselves to be heroes. The title character, whose son is the workers' leader, develops from a fearful, beaten, despondent worker's widow into a dependable, cunning fighter imbued with the ideals of victory. At first simply impressed by her son's attitude and by the humanity of his friends, by the intensity of their meetings and the seriousness of their endeavors, she is soon enthralled by their revolutionary ideals. She follows her son in the crucial hours of battle and participates in the revolutionary activities after he has been arrested. When the mother herself is arrested—the book ends here—she has come to embody the positive hero whom the Socialist Realists later wished to see portrayed in every novel and whose very traits they undoubtedly took, in large part, from her character.

The novel is written in a naturalistic style and is comparable to Zola's *Germinal* (1885). The romanticization and glorification of the revolutionaries and the naturalistic means by which this is achieved are not incongruous; they seem to belong together and are compatible with the book's design and underlying concept. Nevertheless, the characters' perfection is embarrassing to a reader who does not find himself inspired by revolutionary romanticism. He can only regard their ideal behavior as a manifestation of naive optimism and is surprised by the simplicity and lack of depth of Gorky's image of man, which is bewildering in the case of such a gifted author. While writing *The Mother* he apparently forgot—or wanted to forget—much of what he otherwise knew. That he possessed insight into life's demonic forces and had no illusions about the unpredictability and emotionalism of the Russian character is proven by his other works, whether written before or after *The Mother.*

The scheme according to which he constructed the novel is very simple, as simple as the sentiments of the title heroine: the battle between rich and poor is between good and evil. It is only a question of joining together and courageously defending the good without regard for personal consequences. The good will then eventually emerge victorious and the evil will be overcome. The system of values according to which the positive characters are modeled is equally as simple. The mother learns these values from her son, who always behaves correctly and acquires the insight and knowledge necessary for battle through diligent study.

An examination of the East German novels written to conform with the rules of Socialist Realism reveals that their basic characteristics are already to be found in Gorky's novel. Under pressure from the party, East German authors adapted the theoretical and practical model he supplied to the conditions of their newly created state. The historical realities of this nation and the unique situation of its divided loyalties between East and West provided new perspectives, so that plot structures were richer and more complex than in Gorky's novel. Yet what he had established as the central theme was preserved: the new relationship of man to work. "We must make work the new hero of our books, that is, the man who has been organized by the processes of work," Gorky stated in 1934. He explained to what extent the changes in the distribution of wealth would transform the motivation to work since the working masses would come to understand that they "are only working for themselves."[16]

The official literary critics in East Germany considered Anna Seghers's novel *The Decision (Die Entscheidung,* 1959) a masterpiece of Socialist Realism and awarded it the *Nationalpreis erster Klasse,* the highest national prize. The title refers to the political stance which Seghers uses as a criterion for judging her characters: their decision in favor of Walter Ulbricht's new nation. The novel is set between 1947 and 1951. Its plot is supposed to illustrate how new socialist working conditions develop in Kossin, the fictitious setting of a state-owned steel mill, while at the same time disturbances from the West, instigated by the former owners of the nationalized works, are set in motion to thwart that development. Western agents, active as spies, blackmailers, and propagandists, induce workers and several leading engineers to flee to the West. Since, however, the workers in Kossin make the right decision by increasing their competitive productivity, the enemy's plots are foiled. The advocates of socialism often programmatically contrast the old and new, there and here, then and now. The new relationship to work, in Gorky's sense, is the novel's central concern and is predicated on the ownership of the steelworks by the people. The enemies of the new order cannot be painted black enough. For example, young Otto Bentheim, who is to take over his family's factory in the West, is shot by a worker at a carnival ball for a misdeed committed as an SS criminal during the war.

It is unbelievable how flatly the work is narrated! Anna Seghers completely subjugated herself to the demands of the party. *The Decision* and its sequel *Trust* (*Das Vertrauen*, 1968) must be seen purely as commissioned work. The one-dimensional image of man which corresponds to the dogmatism of vulgar Marxist politics and is inadequate in every domain of life prevents the development of a smooth narrative flow. Like all of her writer colleagues who wanted to comply with the state's wishes, Anna Seghers found herself in a hopeless situation.

The authors of the younger generation did not fare much better. Although the hard line was eased somewhat beginning in the early 1960s, this only meant a lengthening of the leash on which authors were held; the gain was deceptive. More readable novels did begin to appear, but only because at that particular moment their publication was allowed. Still it became apparent that despite years of state control, talent could not be buried.

The novels of Johannes Bobrowski (1917–1965), *Levin's Mill* (*Levins Mühle*, 1964) and *Lithuanian Pianos* (*Litauische Klaviere*, 1966), are skillfully narrated and appealing in language and theme. Both are concerned with the question of different ethnic and national groups living together. In the first novel they are Germans, Poles, Jews, and Gypsies living in West Prussia after the founding of the German Empire in 1871, and the second novel tells of Germans and Lithuanians in the German-Lithuanian border territory in the year 1936. The intricate structure of the second novel, with its distribution of the events on several levels and its interweaving of these levels, shows how receptive the author was to new means of expression.

In the 1960s Christa Wolf (b. 1929) and Hermann Kant (b. 1926) also made use of modern narrative techniques which had evolved in other German-speaking countries ten years earlier. For both authors, as for Anna Seghers, the division of Germany, the independence of East Germany, and the responsibility of its inhabitants to recognize the state were of primary thematic importance. As in Seghers's *The Decision*, the act of "defection," of leaving the country without the government's permission, provides a basic element of drama, both in Wolf's *Divided Heaven* (*Der geteilte Himmel*, 1963) and in Kant's *The Auditorium* (*Die Aula*, 1965).

In *Divided Heaven*, the story begins in late August 1961 when the main character, Rita Seidel, a student of education, regains consciousness after an accident in the railroad-car factory where she was working. Her sustained illness leads the doctor to believe that she is suffering from a deeper emotional disturbance. As the reader learns from the retrospective narration which then begins, Rita was engaged to the "defector" Manfred Herrfurth, a chemist. Having visited him in West Berlin shortly before her accident and just prior to the building of the Berlin wall, she decided not to accompany him to West Germany. Their relationship began as a tender love story and was just as important to Manfred as it was to the "pretty and sensitive girl." Almost imperceptibly, they began to move in separate directions, partly because their experiences were different and partly because they reacted differently to these experiences. While Manfred pursued his career in the cool atmosphere of a chemical institute, Rita was impressed by working conditions in the factory. Here as in the pedagogical institute she came into contact with people whom she found enriching and supportive; thus she felt capable of handling whatever difficulties might arise, whereas Manfred felt himself to be alone with his problems. One day he left and sent Rita a letter from West Berlin asking her to follow him there.

Descriptions of Rita's situation in the sanitarium in the fall of 1961 are blended into the narration of events from her memory. Occasionally scenes revolving around the same theme shift back and forth between the present and the past, and the style also changes from *style indirect libre* to a seemingly more informative, objective tone. Yet the atmosphere surrounding the main character is maintained throughout, a certain spiritual climate which becomes particularly poignant when feelings of love are concerned. Even when problems from the realm of politics and industry are discussed, such as work norms, competition, and production levels, they are colored by Rita's emotions. This emphasis on moods and emotions inhibits an objective analysis of the central questions—why Manfred left East Germany and Rita stayed. Christa Wolf does not offer a genuine discussion of this question, and her characters are unable to broach it. As the situation is portrayed within the novel, Manfred really has no compelling reason for leaving the country. True, a project of his has been rejected for no valid reason, but that could happen anywhere. And Rita has no reason not to follow him. Asked about her love for Manfred after the visit to Berlin, she explains that West Berlin "remained foreign" to her, while "here everything is warm and close." In Rita Seidel, Christa Wolf has created a character who speaks in emotional terms. For a genuine answer one would need a character with more substance and greater verbal facility. Moreover, one day spent in West Berlin is hardly enough to give Rita an insight into a world which is, quite naturally, "foreign" to her. Rita makes an emotional decision, giving as little thought to the questionable situation to which she is returning as Christa Wolf herself did. Both author and fictional character are also related in their stereotypical view of life in West Berlin.

In Christa Wolf's second novel, *The Quest for Christa T.* (*Nachdenken über Christa T.*, 1969), the contours are as blurred as in *Divided Heaven*. The narrator touches upon many questions and themes while retracing the life of a friend (Christa T.) who died of leukemia. But her "quest" for her friend does not lead to any conclusions. Christa T.'s "attempt to be herself" and her "difficulty in saying I" are themes which have been competently engaged by German authors for two hundred years. In a totalitarian state, it may be of service to call attention to human individuality; in western democracies, however, this must appear banal. Strangely enough, Christa Wolf's novel does not even link the difficulties in asserting one's individuality to the given political system. Who prevented Christa T. from finding herself and achieving self-actualization? As the life of the deceased is presented, everything seems as favorable as it could possibly be for human development. A literary undertaking such as this can only be successful if it is written with utter honesty and integrity.

Of Hermann Kant's two novels, *The Auditorium* and *The Imprint* (*Das Impressum*, 1972), the former was particularly successful. As in Christa Wolf's novels, the plot takes place on two time levels. From the standpoint of his present time in 1962, the narrator Robert Iswall, a journalist, looks back on his student days in Greifswald from 1949 to 1952, a significant period because an opportunity was then provided for workers and farmers to earn an academic degree. Their concerns, not the usual concerns of adolescents but of goal-oriented young adults, bring to light problems existing in the new East German state. The narrator presents his former comrades as profiled personalities and shows how they conduct themselves later in important positions. His tone, predominantly cheerful and light, allows for much critical comment on persons and conditions in the country. These comments can pass as products of playful high spirits or keen insight and do not weigh heavily. They detract in no way from the author's deep commitment to the GDR and its governing party.

8 / Fiction as a Statement

There have been many attempts over the past few decades to characterize post-1945 German literature. Countless articles have appeared on individual authors as well as on particular themes in their works. The widely divergent viewpoints and directions of scholarship reveal just how different the possible approaches to contemporary literature are. What picture will eventually emerge from the profusion of articles and essays is not yet certain. But one constant seems to be that "a wide aesthetic distance" exists between the general reading public and professional literary criticism, so that "literary critics are writing over the heads of the general public, and this by no means applies to the uneducated public alone. The attitudes of the two groups are so disparate that the concept of literature itself has different meanings for them."[1] In short, there is disagreement among critics and a gap between them and the reading public. Just how literary texts are "actualized" by "the receptive reader, the reflective critic, and the creative author" in the "process of aesthetic reception and production," which, according to Hans Robert Jauss, makes for the history of literature, is very difficult to determine with regard to post-1945 literature.[2] In order to utilize the wealth of individual insights presently available in books, journals, and dissertations, institutes for literature with large staffs would first have to be created to collect information and statistics on readers' reactions, as publishing houses now do, and attack the problem of reducing the distance between the general reading public and professional literary criticism. Until such measures have been taken we can only continue to work with the methods we already have.

As was indicated in the previous chapter, the year 1945 did not mark the beginning of a new epoch in the history of the novel. Just as the authors of the political left in East Germany at first continued to write as they had been accustomed, one can see from the dominant names in the other German-speaking countries that the tradition also remained uninterrupted there. Regardless of whether the authors of the 1950s fell back on Christian heritage, myth, Asiatic philosophy, or other religious and ethical concepts, they always attempted to interpret the world according to spiritual principles and to assign man a place within a larger order. That these traditional methods of interpretation were no longer appropriate to the experiences of the twentieth century and that the Weltanschauungen as such had become questionable was first expressed in the novels published by Uwe Johnson, Günter Grass, and Martin Walser around 1960. An author like Wolfgang Koeppen, who had already departed from the conventional path in the early 1950s, could not be appreciated until later.

In the novels published directly after the end of the war, a tendency toward spiritualization prevails. The common theme that man can survive catastrophe and personal suffering by his spiritual strength alone was welcomed by many German readers (in the Soviet zone of occupation as well) in the period immediately following Hitler's death. Franz Werfel's *Star of the Unborn* (*Stern der Ungeborenen*, 1946), Ernst Barlach's (1870–1938) *The Stolen Moon* (*Der gestohlene Mond*, 1948), and Elisabeth Langgässer's *The Quest* (*Märkische Argonautenfahrt*, 1950) appeared posthumously; Langgässer's *The Indelible Seal* (*Das unauslöschliche Siegel*, 1946) had been published during her lifetime. Hermann Kasack's (1896–1966) *The City beyond the River* (*Die Stadt hinter dem Strom*, 1947) and Edzard Schaper's *The Freedom of the Prisoner* (*Die Freiheit des Gefangenen*, 1950) belong to the same group. Thomas Mann's *Doctor Faustus* (1947) has already been discussed in chapter 7.

The problem of guilt and repentance was treated by Hermann Broch in *The Guiltless* (*Die Schuldlosen*, 1950) as well as by Thomas Mann in *The Holy Sinner* (*Der Erwählte*, 1951). Both works have a place in literary history commensurate with their artistic originality. Thematically they are rooted in the discussion of German guilt which dominated thought at the time they were conceived, but they transcend this specific theme to encompass much wider horizons. *The Guiltless* was Broch's last novel. Thomas Mann later published *Confessions of Felix Krull, Confidence Man* (*Bekenntnisse des Hochstaplers Felix Krull*, 1954), a fragment he had been working on, despite many interruptions, since 1910.

The later novels of the Austrian Heimito von Doderer (1896–1966), *The Strudlhof Stairway* (*Die Strudlhofstiege*, 1951) and *The Demons* (*Die Dämonen*, 1956), fall within the same period of time. These large-scale novels incorporate the narrative tradition of the *Gesellschaftsroman*. They show how wide the panorama of possibilities in fiction was at that time. By contrast, Hans Henny Jahnn's trilogy *River without Banks* (*Fluss ohne Ufer*, 1949–61) is related to the "new forms in the twentieth century" and can be compared in particular to Musil's *The Man without Qualities* and Thomas Mann's *Doctor Faustus*. The immeasurability of human existence, which was the aging author's concern, is expressed by the title of the trilogy. The characters themselves are, as Jahnn said in a letter, the "scene of events, . . . or, expressed musically, of themes, stanzas, motifs, chords, rhythms" (April 29, 1946, to Werner Helwig). The plot, insofar as it can be grasped at all, serves only to motivate events which occur within the characters. Such events are visible in the lonely individual's attempt to break out of his isolation and to achieve reality in relationships with others, primarily with other men. Like mythical occurrences, the events seem to be marked by a repetition which is inescapable. The impressive prose often captivates the reader.

While the established authors in the first years after the Second World War were still committed to the past and to general topics, the authors Böll, Nossack, and Koeppen, who were just beginning their literary careers, turned to the contemporary situation. The most famous of the three is Heinrich Böll (b. 1917). His first novel, *Adam Where Are Thou?* (*Wo warst du, Adam?*, 1951), another story of homecoming, shows the plight of the individual lost in wartime confusion. Böll's next two novels, *And Never Said a Word* (*Und sagte kein einziges Wort*, 1953) and *The Unguarded House* (*Haus ohne Hüter*, 1954) followed suit as criticism of the social conditions in postwar Germany. Again the individual is the helpless victim of circumstances. Just as Böll's pacifism was not bound to any specific doctrine but was an expression of his humanitarianism, his concern for the less fortunate in the newly developing affluent society derives solely from his compassion for others' suffering. In *And Never Said a Word* the separated couple, Käte and Fred Bogner, relate, alternating from chapter to chapter, their experiences during their most recent weekend together. The confining and depressing situation in the one room in which they were living with their three children had finally led Fred to leave his family two months earlier. He roams about the city, sleeping in one place or another, never having enough money from his job, and trying to keep his marriage intact by occasionally spending time with his wife. *The Unguarded House* is narrated from the changing perspectives of five characters. In two families the men were killed in the war, and the widows must lead their lives and raise their children alone. Their two sons are confronted much too early with the problems of adulthood and must cope with the concerns of puberty and with feelings of shame and moral uncertainty on their own.

Böll's novels are flatly superficial and are narrated with no marked talent. However, they brought him immediate success and were soon known outside of Germany, particularly in the countries under Soviet influence and in Scandinavia. Their rapid success can be attributed to their themes as well as to their easily understandable, artless prose. Readers appreciated the uncomplicated narrative structure of these novels and the fact that a world with their own cares and worries was portrayed. It was also a relief for the Germans that guilt was not a central theme. The simple man who wore a uniform in the war is counted among the sufferers but not among the guilty. All those who did not feel adequate to the frightening postwar conditions felt themselves understood here. Böll's tendency to sentimentalize, his wish to educate and promote change, and his emphasis on love and religion, especially on the combination of the two in brotherly love, also suited the tastes of many readers.

Notwithstanding the many experiments of the sixties and seventies which were to give the novel a new direction and make it the most interesting genre of the time, Heinrich Böll, who was awarded the Nobel Prize in 1972, continued undisturbed on his accustomed path. Admittedly, his later novels—*Billiards at Half Past Nine* (*Billiard um halbzehn*, 1959), *The Clown* (*Ansichten eines Clowns*, 1963), and *Group Portrait with Lady* (*Gruppenbild mit Dame*, 1971)—are more deliberately constructed than his previous works, but the aim and style are basically the same: Böll is still striving to present characters in a world which can be comprehended by traditional means. What concerns him is man's moral failure as well as his moral potentialities. His social criticism is directed less toward fundamental changes in the system than toward changes in man himself. As in his earlier works, the emphasis is placed on the *humanum*. Böll can thus be classified with that group of authors from the 1920s who wrote novels in the service of social criticism and pursued didactic goals.

Hans Erich Nossack (1901–1978), who was in his fifties when he achieved recognition as a novelist, belongs to a different generation. He was highly regarded in France, where Jean Paul Sartre promoted his works. His central literary theme is also the fundamental problem of his own existence: voluntary isolation, withdrawal from an environment that is experienced as foreign, the emergence of new meaning on the brink of despair. Nossack was close to Kasack and felt inspired by Barlach and Jahnn. From *Nekyia* (1947), the story of a man's homecoming, to *The Stolen Melody* (*Die gestohlene Melodie*, 1972), his characters move in a world similar to the ones created by those authors. They are outsiders, as in his works *The Impossible Proof* (*Unmögliche Beweisaufnahme*)—which is the third section of *Spiral. Novel of a Sleepless Night* (*Spirale. Roman einer schlaflosen Nacht*, 1956)—*The Younger Brother* (*Der jüngere Bruder*, 1958), and *The D'Arthez Case* (*Der Fall D'Arthez*, 1968). As with Böll, Nossack's success in the 1950s may have to do with the fact that his novels read well and contain no significant innovations in language or composition.

Wolfgang Koeppen's (b. 1906) three novels—*Pigeons in the Grass* (*Tauben im Gras*, 1951), *The Greenhouse* (*Das Treibhaus*, 1953), and *Death in Rome* (*Der Tod in Rom*, 1954)—are of significant literary value and are again receiving attention today. In these novels Koeppen approached the contemporary, postwar situation from different angles, employing the modern narrative techniques and structural forms developed by Joyce, Dos Passos, and Döblin. The novels he had written in the 1930s, *An Unhappy Love* (*Eine unglückliche Liebe*, 1934) and *The Wall Sways* (*Die Mauer schwankt*, 1935; retitled *Die Pflicht*, 1939), either do not deal with the social and political situation at the time or do so in a veiled and indirect way.

Pigeons in the Grass is set at the time the novel was written in a metropolitan city occupied by the Americans, easily identifiable as Munich. By presenting a number of simultaneous events, Koeppen gives a picture of the course of a single day. The events affect various people—Anglo-Saxons, black Americans, and Germans—and progress in separate scenes which alternate from person to person. The majority of characters have nothing to do with each other; nor do they know each other in the beginning, but in the course of the day they meet and become important to each other even though no relationships develop. The quote from Gertrude Stein placed at the beginning of the novel—"Pigeons in the grass, alas"—sheds light on the title and underscores the novel's theme. The title metaphor recurs often within the novel, as when one of the American teachers touring the city sees birds "squatting in the grass" and thinks:

> We don't understand any more than the birds. . . . The birds are here by chance, we are here by chance, and perhaps the Nazis were here only by chance, Hitler was an accident, his politics were a cruel and stupid accident, perhaps the world is a cruel and stupid accident of God, no one knows why we are here, the birds will fly off again and we will move on.

Later the popular author, Edwin, gives a well-attended lecture in the Amerika-Haus on the occidental spirit and occidental freedom in which he refers to Gertrude Stein, whom he does not regard highly and whose ideas he rejects:

> Like pigeons in the grass, Edwin said, quoting Stein, . . . certain overcivilized minds regarded people as pigeons in the grass by attempting to expose the senselessness and seeming randomness of human existence, picturing man as free from God and then letting him flutter freely in the void, senseless, worthless, . . . at the butcher's mercy . . . while we know, Edwin said, that every pigeon has its cote and every bird is in God's hand.

The intertwining, sometimes colliding paths of the fictional characters resemble the directionless to and fro of pigeons pattering along in the grass. Not all of the characters introduced survive the day. The old servant Josef, for example, is killed quite senselessly by the Negro soldier, Odysseus Cotton. Throughout the many scenes of the novel, violence and racism prevail, innocent people are killed, children are unwittingly entangled in the disputes of adults who themselves do not know why they are quarreling and do not even want to quarrel. What all the characters have in common is that they do not find a way to themselves or to others.

In this novel there is no larger order which can unite people and enable them to be at peace with themselves. Koeppen emphasizes that the appeal to spiritual values found in the works of other postwar authors is ineffectual in the world of his novel. In great detail he describes how the conservative author Edwin calls upon his audience, who are for the most part unresponsive and somnolent, to recognize the power of the spirit, insisting that "we live only in the spirit" and evoking "the great names of Homer, Virgil, Dante, Goethe." The German author Philipp, sitting in the audience, realizes that the lecture is an exercise in futility. Edwin's image of pigeons fittingly describes the situation of those in the audience, who are also the novel's characters. Theirs is a ruined world falling deeper into ruin and devoid of harmony. Following the example of Dos Passos, Koeppen juxtaposes otherwise unconnected scenes and brings together radically disparate spheres to create an impression of diffusion, of a world with no comprehensive and binding system of reference.

As opposed to *Pigeons in the Grass*, Koeppen's *The Greenhouse* is narrated linearly and presents a main character who stands out in relief against his surroundings. Compressed into two days, it is the story of Keetenheuve, a representative in the Bonn *Bundestag* who comes home from his wife's funeral on a spring morning in 1952 and takes his life on the evening of the following day by jumping from a bridge into the Rhine. As the reader learns from flashbacks, particularly in the first two chapters, Keetenheuve spent the Hitler years in exile and hoped to make a positive contribution to the reconstruction of Germany after returning home at the end of the war. He was elected to the *Bundestag* and married a very young girl, the spoiled daughter of a Nazi *Gauleiter* (regional leader) and *Statthalter* (governor) who had been abandoned when her father poisoned himself and his wife in 1945. In both the personal and public realms, reality fell short of Keetenheuve's expectations. His marriage failed when his insecure wife fell victim to alcohol and lesbian procurers, and he failed in the political arena as well, being forced to admit that he was chasing after "phantoms" and was misunderstood by the other members of his own party, the Social Democrats.

> Politics and love, they both came to him too late. Elke loved him, but he was chasing . . . after phantoms, the phantom of freedom which people feared, . . . and the phantom of human rights which only became important when one suffered injustice oneself. The problems were endlessly difficult and one could easily lose heart.

Koeppen did not want his book to be read as a *roman à clef*, insisting that it has its "own poetic truth." Nonetheless, several leading politicians are easily recognizable (Adenauer, Schumacher, Heuss), and the *Bundestag* debate in the fifth chapter, in which Keetenheuve represents the opposition, revolves around the concrete question of rearmament in Germany, which is decided by vote in the chancellor's favor (Adenauer), as was the case in history. These actual historical events characterize the political stage on which the fictional character Keetenheuve acts as a loner. In his opposition speech, his thought-provoking arguments are not as important as the fact that he himself is not sure if he is right: "Those who are listening to me . . . know that I have no better prescription than they do for curing the patient at once, and so they continue to believe in their own therapy." The decisive reason for his weariness has already been given: "He didn't enjoy his eternal stance of opposition any more, for he asked himself: Can I change it, can I do it better, do I know a way?" Because he no longer believes in the politics he is representing, life as a politician becomes a burden to him. Things have developed far beyond his powers of comprehension and he asks, "What is good and what is bad in this field which extends far into the future, far into a dark realm?" From interior monologues it becomes apparent that as Keetenheuve becomes increasingly disillusioned with politics, he also becomes uncertain of his identity. His loss of personality manifests itself in his increasing discomfort in the atmosphere of the "greenhouse." The warm Bonn climate, often called a greenhouse climate, refers symbolically to Germany as a whole: "a large public greenhouse, Keetenheuve saw strange flora, greedy, carnivorous plants, giant phalli like chimneys full of smoldering smoke, blue-green, red-yellow, poisonous, but it was an opulence without marrow or youth, everything was overripe." The novel's "own poetic truth," of which Koeppen spoke, is expressed in Keetenheuve's mounting distress and goes far beyond criticism of contemporary society.

Despite the many actual experiences from the author's present time contained in Koeppen's *Death in Rome*, the novel can only be seen as a vision or an experiment. Otherwise it would be a preposterous and highly contrived story. The members of a German family (the Judejahns and Pfaffraths) and a German couple they once knew (the Kürenbergs) meet in Rome. Some of the family members had arranged to meet there, while others appear by chance. Those who planned to meet are Gottlieb Judejahn and Friedrich Wilhelm Pfaffrath, who is accompanied by his wife, Anna, her sister Eva (she is Judejahn's wife), and his son Dietrich. Judejahn is a former SS general who escaped from Germany, was condemned to death in absentia at the Nuremberg trials, and is currently a military instructor in an Arab country; Pfaffrath was formerly an *Oberpräsident* (highest civil official of a province) under Hitler and is now a mayor. They are meeting to discuss the possibilities for Judejahn's return to Germany; Pfaffrath hopes to use his influence to help him. They have no doubt that after Germany has regained its sovereignty the Nuremberg verdicts will be annulled, and it even seems possible that Judejahn could be credited with years of service and entitled to a pension. Those who are in Rome by chance are Judejahn's son Adolf, who is a Catholic clergyman, and Siegfried Pfaffrath, the mayor's other son, who has broken with his family and is in Rome for a music convention at which a symphony he has written is to be performed. It is to be conducted by Kürenberg, who has come to Rome with his Jewish wife for that reason. Formerly the general music director of the city where the Pfaffraths lived, Kürenberg had once appealed unsuccessfully to *Oberpräsident* Pfaffrath to save the life of his father-in-law. Ilse Kürenberg's father was murdered, his possessions destroyed, and she emigrated with her husband.

The plot takes place within a span of two-and-one-half days and is narrated in part chronologically, in part simultaneously. The author uses his narrative options freely according to his purposes. His characters come together in different groupings and at different places, and at one point they finally all meet (except for Eva Judejahn, who has already left the city) at the same time and place. There are two narrators, an anonymous third-person narrator and a first-person narrator. The first-person narrator is Siegfried Pfaffrath, who describes his own situation in Rome, characterizes, like the third-person narrator, those around him, and reflects on himself and the others. Flashbacks are an essential part of the narration and are used by both narrators. They underlie and lead into the experiment carried out when the characters are brought together.

The negative main character is Judejahn, a murderer who still represents unchanged the ideas of the Hitler period: primitive and brutal, egotistical and power hungry in every situation. The Pfaffraths are conformists and followers, completely aware of all of Judejahn's criminal acts; both the father and his son Dietrich are, as always, intent on holding influential positions. The antithesis of Judejahn and the Pfaffraths is Siegfried. In interior monologues and conversations with Adolf Judejahn, he outlines his own position. On the one hand is his revulsion at the conditions which marked his youth— attendance at an elite Nazi boarding school, fear of his dangerous uncle, war, and imprisonment behind barbed wire—and on the other hand, his joy over the freedom achieved, over the visit to Rome, and a desire to assert his independence. Siegfried has little hope for the future, but at the same time he does not intend to offer opposition or influence people positively for "they can't be changed." His relatives, who are present at the performance of his symphony, cannot understand his music, but nonetheless join in the applause (with the exception of Adolf) and appear backstage afterwards. This musical evening, which brings the main characters together, is comparable to Edwin's evening lecture in *Pigeons in the Grass* and the *Bundestag* session in *The Greenhouse*. In all three cases the purpose of the scene is to show the gap between the performer or speaker and his public.

The scene backstage after the concert is ghostly; it is like a bad dream which could well have provided the stimulus for the entire novel. Siegfried reports how he notices a terrible rejection on Ilse Kürenberg's face when she congratulates him; following her glance, he looks behind him, recognizes his parents and Dietrich approaching him, "and standing behind them paralyzing me was the nightmare of my youth, Uncle Judejahn returned from the dead, grinning at me as if to say that he had risen again and now I have to settle with him, that the old power was there again." Siegfried admits that he is ashamed of his family, a "Pfaffrath-Judejahn family reunion." Ilse Kürenberg knows instinctively "who . . . the man in the background" is, the man who is "undressing her with his eyes." When Judejahn learns who she is, he feels sorry that she "had escaped from him" and is disturbed at the "thought of the unsuccessful final solution to the Jewish problem." The next morning he shoots Ilse Kürenberg from his hotel room while she is standing at the window of an opposite room. He also dies shortly thereafter.

The reason for Koeppen not writing any more novels after *Death in Rome* may have to do with the hideousness of the vision underlying this novel. Siegfried's fears were most likely also those of the author. The possibility of again being delivered over to the monstrous criminality which burdened his youth is what secretly motivates Siegfried: "In dreams day and night I see the Brown Shirts and national stupidity marching. And therefore I want to live my life for as long as the nationalistic god is debilitated and cannot stop me. It is my only chance." In answer to Adolf's question as to why he does not fight against the symptoms of disaster, he admits to knowing no way. His helplessness is the novel's central theme. Fear and despair, which are reflected in his music, result from this helplessness. No doubt the author found himself in the same emotional state as Siegfried when he posed the hypothetical question: what would happen if Judejahn were to return? In response he gave the horrifying picture of his new deeds.

It is therefore not sufficient to interpret *Death in Rome* as a social-critical analysis of the German situation, especially since, as such, it would not be accurate; the Germans did not consist only of Judejahns, Pfaffraths, and occasionally a respectable emigrant. What the novel, with its characters Siegfried and Adolf, depicts is the situation of sons from National Socialist families. Earlier Keetenheuve had recognized that "of course" people "stayed the same" after 1945. The parents did not change, but they did not live forever. What is still a stimulating theme after thirty years is that of the "faithless sons" who, in their parents' opinion, "broke away from the clan" and live "with the enemy." How well Koeppen himself was able to distinguish between the special situation of these sons and the general situation of people at that time is not entirely clear from his novel and can probably only be answered by examining his works as a whole.

In the same year that Koeppen's last novel appeared, Max Frisch (b. 1911) published *Stiller* (1954). The book marks the beginning of a new period in the history of the German novel, a period which began to flourish just a few years later. It was not Frisch's first novel. He had already written *J'adore ce qui me brûle* or *The Difficult Ones* (*J'adore ce qui me brûle oder Die Schwierigen*, 1943), which was an expanded, revised version of his first novelistic attempt, *Jürg Reinhart* (1934). These early works are still conventional. Despite a subtle treatment of plot and a thematic resemblance to Frisch's later novels, they do not yet possess the intensity and distinct profile of *Stiller*, *Homo Faber* (1957), and *Call Me Gantenbein* (*Mein Name sei Gantenbein*, 1964).

In *Stiller* Frisch found his great, unmistakable novelistic style. The game with different narrators and methods of narration, which was set into motion by Koeppen after the Second World War and is still very much alive today, is played masterfully. It is not a question of technique or skilled craftsmanship, but of a narrative style which is inseparable from the work's composition as a whole, so that the poetic substance of the novel is realized in the style and forms a unity with it.

Frisch's rapid ascent to world success in the second half of the 1950s had to do with the understanding he achieved as a neighbor to a defeated nation whose people were struggling with the problem of their own identity and of a guilt which weighed on all. It is very much to the credit of the two Swiss authors, Max Frisch and Friedrich Dürrenmatt, that they recognized in the German problem a general human problem, and it was no coincidence that Dürrenmatt's play *The Visit* (*Besuch der alten Dame*, 1956), also brought its author a breakthrough to world success. Like *Stiller*, Dürrenmatt's *The Visit* demonstrates in breathtaking fashion possibilities of human behavior which previously were not recognized. It should not be overlooked that in the year *Stiller* was published, Frisch had to admit to the failure of his first marriage. Of course, a whole complex of experiences underlies such a novel; it is not the moral crisis of a neighboring people alone but also concerns of a personal nature which are given expression in the novel's first and most important sentence: "I'm not Stiller!"

The man who begins his diary with these words is in prison. It is an actual prison; he measures his cell in shoe lengths. He also describes his arrest as an actual event for which there is a concrete reason. He was traveling to Switzerland with a passport made out to James Larkins White. But a fellow traveler on the train recognized him from a picture in a magazine as Anatol Ludwig Stiller from Zurich, who had been missing for over six years. In the trial which follows, the authorities undertake to prove that he really is the missing person who must bear the name Stiller and reassume all the responsibilities it carries.

For the prisoner much more than this is at stake. He had hoped to replace Stiller with James White, a new, different person, and registers everything he is told about Stiller from the standpoint of this fictitious person. As if it were information about a stranger, he records what he learns in a notebook which his defense attorney has given him with the advice that he should write down the truth about his life. This is how "Stiller's notes in prison," a diary, comes to be. It contains the experiences and reflections of the prisoner during imprisonment; information others give him about his past as Stiller, which he is presumably only recording; stories and accounts from Mr. White's experiences in California, Mexico, Texas, and New York; and finally, allegories, such as the story of Isidor and the tale of Rip van Winkle. The fictitious James White is a talented narrator. Those who have an ear for his narrative style no longer ask the question whether everything is true, whether everything really is the way he tells it. What is certain is that it is all relevant to the issue. The public defender Bohnenblust does not understand this and accuses his client of lying. When Stiller roars, "I'm not Stiller!" he roars back, "Then who are you?" This is, indeed, the question. The diary writer has already answered it for himself in the loneliness of his prison cell.

> I am not their Stiller. What do they want from me? I am an unhappy, worthless, unimportant person who has no life behind him, none at all. Why do I tell fibs? Just so they will leave me my emptiness, my nothingness, my reality, for escape is not possible, and what they are offering me is escape, not freedom, escape into a role. Why don't they just give up?

If he were to admit that he is Stiller, he would have to accept the role they have prepared for him and would have to be "their Stiller." Somewhat later he admits to himself that the thought of repetition distresses him, the thought of "making his life . . . repetition by recognizing: That is me!" He realizes that it frightens him to remember: "everything in me is in flight, flight without hope of getting anywhere, simply out of fear of repetition."

At the root of his fear of repetition is the fear of repeating failure. Years prior to his imprisonment, Stiller had singled out what he called his "defeat in Spain" as the core of his experience with himself and as proof that he is a failure. The story allows for many interpretations. Stiller, a volunteer in the Spanish Civil War, was ordered to guard a small ferryboat at the Tagus River. When after three quiet days a group of four Franco loyalists came across the river, he refrained from shooting them. They disarmed and bound him, and he spent two days lying in the brush before he was found by his comrades. Under questioning, he later claimed that his Russian weapon had not fired. The fact that Max Frisch chose this ambiguous story as the key in Stiller's mind to his flight from himself and from repetition is connected with Frisch's idea that sooner or later every person "invents a story which he, often under great sacrifices, accepts as his life." The many interpretations of the events at the Tagus throughout the novel allow Frisch to illustrate the view he later expressed many times that "every I which speaks is a role," that "every I, even the I which we live and die, is an invention."[3] When the story of the Tagus is told for the first time, Stiller gives it an interpretation which in no way points to failure. Asked at a large social gathering why he did not shoot, Stiller's explanation is that he

> hated the fascists, otherwise he would not have gone to fight in the Spanish Civil War as a volunteer; but at the break of day at the Tagus . . . he perceived the four fascists simply as people, and it was impossible for him to shoot at people, he just couldn't. And that's that!

An admiring friend calls it a "victory of humanity, a victory of concrete experience over everything ideological." What a grand role Stiller can fabricate from his inability to shoot at the Tagus! Many times Stiller comes away "from his Spanish anecdote with honor," and Julika, his wife, has to listen to this version for years. But suddenly, when they meet for the last time before his disappearance, he speaks of a "defeat in Spain," which was the "beginning of all ills." Seven months earlier he had told his lover, Sibylle, that he had not shot at the Tagus because he was a coward. For years he has "still dreamt of it: I would like to shoot, but it won't shoot. . . . It's the typical dream of impotence." Toward the end of his notebook Stiller writes, "I know that I am not the missing Stiller. And I never was. I swear it, even if I don't know who else I could be. Perhaps I am no one." How should he know what happened at the Tagus?

In order to force the man who has broken out of the role "Stiller" back into his place, the authorities bring forth many witnesses and arrange for on the spot investigations. They want to prove to the man who denies his past that he is wrong. In his notes he remains true to the fiction that the people who appear are unknown to him and were known only to the man who disappeared; they are his friends, his brother, his wife, and his former lover. The most important are the two women, Julika and Sibylle. Sibylle, whose relationship with Stiller took place before his flight, is by coincidence the wife of the public prosecutor, Rolf, who relates to Stiller from the beginning as an understanding friend and is in many ways his foil. Sibylle had abandoned Rolf after the affair with Stiller ended; she then lived alone in New York for over two years before returning to Rolf. Rolf is Max Frisch's great attempt to show that a man whose marriage is threatened by another man can behave in such a way as to restore the marriage. Rolf himself draws a parallel with the situation of the betrayed husbands in *Anna Karenina* and

Effi Briest, and as a positive character he has a decisive impact on the novel. He possesses ethical values and sets standards of behavior. Therefore, the author gives him the "Afterword" (one-eighth of the book's length). After Stiller is judged by the court to be Stiller, he writes no more. Rolf gives a short report on Stiller's life with Julika, first in a pension at Lake Geneva and then in Glion above the lake. He judges Stiller's case and tries, insofar as possible, to fit it into a framework of conventional values, the same values that apply when he stands by Stiller in the last night before Julika's death.

The appearance of the people who can testify to Stiller's past serves to interweave the events from the time period which Stiller rejects with those of the present to form a unified plot. This plot reveals itself as a great novel of love in which the roles are played by two engaging women and two amiable men. For a time Stiller is loved by both women, but he disappoints both and, in the end, lives alone. Rolf loses Sibylle, but wins her again; they represent the couple which comes together at the end. Both display composure and deliberation in their actions. Sibylle frees herself, achieves independence as a woman, and possesses in Rolf a partner who is her equal. Sibylle had come to understand Stiller very quickly: "A comical, but secretly very depressed man, one who had invisible banderillas in his neck and bled." She also knows what to think of his interpretation of the Tagus anecdote. After seven months of their affair she rejects him and aborts his child.

Julika, meanwhile, is at Stiller's mercy and never understands many things about him, although she genuinely loves him. At his side she becomes deathly ill twice. As "beautiful Julika,'" she lends the novel its radiance. Every scene in which she appears belongs entirely to her. But Stiller struggles in vain to be close to her. Like an elfin being, she remains far from him; he feels like "an oily, sweaty, stinking fisherman with a crystal water nymph." Her career as a dancer preoccupied her completely for many years; she continued to pursue it while married and during Stiller's absence directed a ballet school in Paris, which she gave up in order to live with him again. The picture the reader receives of her, the impression of her irresistibility, is created by Stiller himself as one who loves her and confirmed in essence by Rolf as an objective observer. When Rolf sees her on her deathbed, he quotes Stiller's description of her outward appearance in the "Notes," confessing that he suddenly had the "horrible feeling that Stiller had never seen her as anything but a dead woman." For the first time, he "came to the deep, absolute realization, which human words could no longer change," of Stiller's sin. This is Rolf's judgment; whether the reader wants to accept it or not is left up to him.

The questions posed about man's nature are not answered by Max Frisch from a fixed perspective, but are illuminated by means of modern narrative techniques. The breadth of the novel's structure—the round dance of characters who enter and then leave the scene, the graphic descriptions of the past with Julika at the center, and then Sibylle—is aimed not at a solution, but at increased insight, at the development of a theme. Frisch presents his questions about man by approaching them from many angles. In a novel as comprehensive as this, a single narrator is generally no longer sufficient, except in the case of a first-person narrator whose limited perspective is made known from the beginning and whose particular perspective is the theme of the novel, as in Frisch's *Homo Faber.*

Homo Faber. A Report (*Homo Faber, Ein Bericht,* 1957), Frisch's second, widely read novel, only seems at first glance to be simpler than *Stiller* in structure and theme. Its sole narrator is characterized by the title. He often interprets his perspective in the following spirit: "I am a technologist and used to seeing things the way they are." In the same breath with such assertions, however, he refers to previous events which he failed to see the way they were. These events form the novel's plot.

The fifty-year-old engineer Faber travels with his daughter Elisabeth, whom he calls Sabeth, across Italy to Greece as her lover, not knowing that they are related. Sabeth meets with a fatal accident between Corinth and Athens when she is bitten by a snake and falls from a small embankment. In an Athens hospital she is treated only for the snake bite; the skull fracture of which she dies on the day after her admittance to the hospital is not diagnosed. Her mother, who is living in Athens, turns out to be the art historian Hanna Landsberg, whom Faber had loved during his student days in Zurich. He knew that she had been pregnant with his child, but thought that she had had an abortion. To be sure, he had noticed early that Sabeth resembled Hanna, but by using incorrect dates he had dismissed the possibility that she could be his daughter. On seeing Hanna again in Athens, his old feelings for her are revived, and he again becomes attached to her.

His report has two parts. The first part, written in Caracas, was begun two and one-half weeks after Faber left Athens. He later returns to Athens and writes the second part in an Athens hospital before his death. It contains reflections, travel impressions from the period following his first stay in Athens, and his last confrontations with himself under Hanna's influence.

Faber accompanies his account of the events in the first part of his report with musings in which he tries to clarify his position on them in his own mind. As he does so, the narrowness of his perspective as Homo Faber becomes evident. He is clearly wrestling with ideas which he thinks are Hanna's. In this process of self-interpretation, he uses her perspective as a contradiction to his own, trying to disprove it and articulate his own views. The first of his theoretical expositions begins, "I don't believe in fate or providence; as a technologist I am used to calculating with the formulas of probability. What has providence to do with it?" He admits that many things came together, "more than a coincidence, an entire chain of coincidences," and continues, "But why providence? I don't need any mystical explanation for the occurrence of the improbable; mathematics is enough for me." A few remarks later, he says again, "And if at some time it does occur, the improbable, then for us there is no cause for amazement, shock, or mystification." Here, early in his report, Faber for the first time touches on a theme which will continue to disturb him—the significance of statistics. They play a major role in his conversations with Hanna after Sabeth's doctor says that the mortality rate from snake bites is three to ten percent. While Faber is "soothed" by the thought of the conclusiveness of statistics, Hanna stresses that she has "only one child" and not a hundred daughters of whom she would only lose three to ten if they were "all bitten by a viper." Faber says,

> Regarding statistics: Hanna didn't want to hear about them be-
> cause she believed in fate, I could see that immediately, though
> Hanna never said so explicitly. . . . She spoke of myth like one
> of us would speak of the law of thermodynamics. . . . Without
> astonishment. Oedipus and the Sphinx, . . . Athena, the Eri-
> nyes, or rather Eumenides, and whatever else they are all called,
> they are facts for her.

There is no passage in the text to prove that Hanna ever professed a belief in fate or spoke of providence. Because she is not impressed by Faber's calculations of probability, he concludes that there is some type of "mystification." He knows of no other alternative to his own limited world of ideas and does not realize that his calculations are irrelevant anyway after Sabeth dies of the undiagnosed skull fracture rather than the snake bite.

Though Homo Faber does not understand Hanna's way of thinking, he was so impressed by her personality during their reunion in Athens that thoughts about her and memories of their time together in Zurich crop up again and again in his report. Conversations between them then revolved around the same differences of opinion as they do in Athens. From a four-page passage dedicated to Hanna's situation in 1936, we learn: "I called her a dreamer and an art lover. And she called me: Homo Faber." Hanna had, he says, a "propensity toward mysticism, if not hysteria. I happen to be the type who has both feet on the ground. Nonetheless we were very happy together, it seems to me, and actually I have no idea why we didn't marry then." Hanna knows very well why. "That would have been a mistake," she tells him twenty years later. After all, she was the one who recognized how limited he was as a technologist and gave him his name.

What disturbs Faber and does not allow him to lay aside his search for an explanation of the events is the problem of his guilt. No matter how one chooses to judge his knowledge or lack of it from the author's skillfully arranged presentation, the theme of incest was treated so masterfully by Thomas Mann in *The Holy Sinner* (1951) that it was hard to imagine how another contemporary work could surpass it. Max Frisch did succeed in creating a new variation. Where Thomas Mann is ironical, Frisch lets his Homo Faber slip into sentimentality, which also has its amusing side. The reader senses that what Thomas Mann's Sibylle confesses to the pope also applies to Homo Faber.

> On the surface the soul makes a pretence of having been diabolically deceived, but deep down, where the truth lives quietly, there was no deception at all, the oneness was apparent to her at first glance. . . . She would have been unworthy of the papal ear if she were not to confess the ruses of her soul without guile.

Homo Faber cannot speak like that; he has to continue to insist that he knew nothing, although he is accustomed to "seeing things the way they are." Since irony is not at his command, he can only escape into sentimentality: "What difference does it make that I prove my innocence, the impossibility that I knew anything. I have destroyed my child's life and I cannot make that good again." Frisch's variation lies on the one hand in his speaking tone, while on the other he varies the "oneness." It is the resemblance of mother and daughter, even though "Hanna was dark, Sabeth blond, or more precisely reddish," and they are built differently. But Sabeth has a "Hanna-girl-face." There are, in addition, many small, unmistakable indications of a resemblance, and what cannot be ignored is their love of art. Homo Faber says of his enjoyable visit to Italy, "The only thing that bothered me was her need for art, her mania to see everything. No sooner were we in Italy than there wasn't a single place where I didn't have to stop. . . . I'm not used to traveling like that." The mother is an "art-lover" and has a predisposition "toward mysticism, if not hysteria"; the daughter has "a mania to see everything." "I thought of marriage as never before" is his attitude toward all this. In Athens he is immediately captivated by Hanna, to the extent that she must repeatedly turn him away. He now knows "that Hanna, who is sitting before me, is her mother, the mother of my lover and also my lover." After Sabeth's death he is determined to marry Hanna.

Homo Faber is searching for something in Hanna which he lacks in himself. Therefore he feels drawn toward her, even in the last hours before his death. During his trips he often makes mention in his diary of stomach pains. In the Athens hospital he at first believes the statistics again, assumes the operation will go well, and tries to convince Hanna of this too; he finds it difficult to accept the fact that he is going to die. But his relationship to the world, his style of reporting, and his attitude toward Hanna have changed. He is now open to the phenomena of life and also open to Hanna's concept of these phenomena. He no longer speaks of mystification. He simply records, without protest, Hanna's interpretation of his attitude and her opposing position, admitting to whatever points he does not understand. He writes,

> My mistake: that we technologists try to live without death. In her words: You don't look at life as a whole, but merely as addition. . . . My mistake with Sabeth: repetition, I behaved as though age did not exist, therefore contrary to nature. We cannot do away with age by continuing to add, by marrying our own children.

This statement achieves its weight in that it stands alone without commentary.

As in the first part of the novel, Faber again includes the second opinion in his self-interpretation, but now as valid statement rather than as opinion contradictory to his own. Hanna takes on a function comparable to that of the public prosecutor in *Stiller*. Both are bound up with the story of the main character and at the same time possess the authority of an institution. But Rolf is able to reestablish his relationship with Sibylle, whereas Hanna's entire existence collapses as a result of her relationship with Faber, and she has to admit to her own guilt. She had concealed the child from him in order to have it for herself alone. Nonetheless, Faber takes the main burden upon himself without looking for a further explanation or excuse. In the end, he is simply a man who loves his partner and overlooks her guilt. His report closes with the words, "Hanna always knew that her child would leave her one day, but even Hanna could not have suspected that on this journey Sabeth would meet none other than her father, who would destroy everything." Just one month earlier, he had claimed to see things the way they are, a claim which dissolved under the power of events and the certainty of love.

As opposed to *Stiller* and *Homo Faber*, the novel *Call Me Gantenbein* (*Mein Name sei Gantenbein*, 1964) does not have a progressive plot in the traditional sense. Even without an epic course of events, the narrator's standpoint can be determined, for there is a fictitious "I" who speaks from beginning to end. He seems to be in a position very close to that of the author. In any case, he represents the author's ideas and has control over his experiences. A sentence which could serve as the work's motto is: "A man has had an experience and now he is searching for the matching story—it is not possible to live with an experience which remains without a story." Since, in Frisch's opinion, the "I" itself is an invention and "every I which speaks is a role," the fictitious "I" of the novel can imagine several different lives to go along with his experiences. He decides in favor of Gantenbein, as the title indicates, but he also tries Enderlein and Svoboda. The search for a story which expresses one's experiences is compared to buying clothes. "I try stories on like clothes," the main character says at one point, and "you can't go through the world naked; so I force myself, turn around in front of the adjustable mirror in order to test the cut."

The experience for which the stories must be invented has to do with a deserted apartment in which the former owner is sitting "in his coat and cap . . . on the arm of a stuffed chair," playing with a corkscrew. This is the place where his marriage failed. The question remains as to exactly what happened. The utensils left behind provide no clues: "I can't imagine how we lived here, . . . although her blue robe is still hanging in the bathroom." The realities as such cannot be reconstructed, but with the help of imaginary circumstances, models can be created which provide insights into the past occurrences. The invented stories have the function of such models.

Let us take the following imaginary circumstances: following an accident, a man must lie in the hospital for a long time with bandaged eyes. When the bandages are removed, he can see, but he keeps this fact secret and plays the role of a blind man from that point on. Behind his dark glasses he observes people who behave more freely towards him than they normally would. He is careful to react as if he were blind, and they do not notice his game. In his marriage with the actress Lila—at times his female partner also has other professions (the fictitious "I" is experimenting)—he can overlook many things because he supposedly does not see them. He has no profession and can cater completely to the wishes of his wife without her realizing it. When he notices that she is lying to him, he gives no sign of his feelings.

The novel's charm lies in Gantenbein's superior deceptive maneuvers and in the others' surprising lack of awareness. Gantenbein plays chess, prepares the dinner meal for guests, and empties the ashtrays at the right time. He cleans the apartment for Lila and picks her up from the airport after each of her many professional trips. His jealousy finally destroys the marriage. Upon arrival at the airport, Lila is always accompanied by a man, the same man, who carries her luggage and leaves her shortly before she is to meet Gantenbein. In the apartment there are flowers she does not mention; he knows about letters she says nothing about. The problem is formulated:

> Hopefully I will never slip out of my role. What does it help me to see! It may be that Gantenbein, not adequate to the greatness of his love, occasionally tears the dark glasses from his face—only to immediately put his hand before his eyes, as if they hurt. . . . If Lila knew that I can see, she would doubt my love, and it would be hell, a man and a woman, but not a pair; it is the secret

a man and a woman keep from each other which makes them a pair.

Another time he says, "What I see and what I do not see is a question of tact. Perhaps marriage itself is only a question of tact."

When *Call Me Gantenbein* appeared in 1964, the literary scene was quite different from when *Stiller* was published less than ten years earlier. In the meantime, Günter Grass (b. 1927), Uwe Johnson (1934–1984), and Martin Walser (b. 1927) had established reputations as novelists. This younger generation had given the course of the novel in Germany a new direction, impressing readers and critics alike. In 1959 Grass's *The Tin Drum* and Johnson's *Speculations about Jacob* appeared, in 1960 Walser's *Half Time*. In the years following, Grass wrote *Dog Years* (1963), *Local Anesthetic* (1969), and *From the Diary of a Snail* (1972); Johnson published *The Third Book about Achim* (1961), *Two Views* (1965), and *Anniversaries I, II, III* (1970, 1971, 1973); and Walser produced *The Unicorn* (1966) and *The Fall* (1973).

The beginning of a new era in the history of the German novel and the wide attention the novels immediately received is a very special phenomenon. Everything which had been achieved up to that point within the realm of twentieth-century fiction was incorporated into the novels of the three authors who, at the time of their first great successes, were still quite young. They were familiar with the literature of Germany as well as that of foreign countries, at least with the major representatives. It would be pointless to search for influences, since there is no doubt that the cultural and literary background which this well-read generation acquired as a matter of course had an effect upon their writings; it is easily recognizable. What is illuminating is to investigate the authors' partialities and predilections, for this is what characterizes their writings. In their sensational achievements of 1959–60, each of the three authors showed a pronounced and unmistakable individuality. They each emerged as original artists by using modern means of expression for their own purposes as if these were long-standing traditions. After all, the works of the avant-garde from the first third of the twentieth century, which many today still call the "modern novel," were, from the standpoint of the year 1960, long since part of the literary tradition. The achievement of the generation of Grass, Walser, and Johnson lies not in inventing or discovering new forms but in using them with a particular sensitivity to the unity of narrative form and content.

In shaping their novels, the three authors incorporated very different experiences. Günter Grass was driven from his home in Danzig and came to West Germany; Uwe Johnson grew up in East Germany, where his first novel was written but could not be published; and Martin Walser has always lived in his home in southwest Germany. As dissimilar as their experiences are, the ways in which the authors transformed them into fiction are closely related. They expressed their experiences in large-scale *Zeitromane* whose structures reflect a common world view. This world view could only be given literary form by employing the means of expression which were developed subsequent to Einstein's formulation of the theory of relativity and which conformed to Heisenberg's insight that the conventional dichotomy between the individual and the world, between subject and object, is no longer valid and that time and place are not fixed, independent categories. In 1928, Döblin had already stressed that "art forms are connected with a certain way of thinking and a general milieu," and he denounced authors in all countries—they make up "the solid majority"—who still construct their novels naively, as an "isolated sequence," who "reel and rattle off. . . stories" with "an actual beginning and an actual end, as if such things existed,"[4] and give the matter no further thought.

Twenty-five years later, despite Broch, Musil, and Thomas Mann, the situation had hardly changed. Even Grass, Walser, and Johnson were notable exceptions in their understanding of the relationship between art form, way of thinking, and world view. Their novels are related in that their structures do not allow for an "actual" beginning or ending; they do not offer an "isolated sequence," but each gives us, in its own way and on the basis of its own material, a comprehensive, multidimensional complex that has no beginning and no end. How the narrator approaches this complex, from what angle, whether he uses one point of reference or several—these are questions of artistic procedure. The author also decides what time frame to use. Since life runs its course in time and can only be related chronologically, a sequence of events, marked by dates, can be found in these novels. But though the chronology helps in orientation and in defining a time interval, it does not give the novel its structure. In 1931, Musil said that "seemingly chronological narration is primarily a problem of ordering, ordering the events in a way which imitates the passing of time, but never claims to be identical with it." We know that Grass made meter-long "chapter plans and timetables" for his novel's chronology, and he provides the reader with exact references to time. Johnson and Walser also carefully indicate dates, thus helping the reader to follow the narration. The coherence of the epic world, however—the connection between its parts—is not determined by the time sequence but is a function of the author's narrative consciousness.

In *The Tin Drum* (*Die Blechtrommel*, 1959), Günter Grass brings the reader into the world of the novel by the mediation of the lonely narrator Oskar Matzerath, who is lying in bed in a mental hospital. As is revealed later in the novel, for reasons of boredom Oskar has become involved in a court case in which he is convicted and declared insane, which is why he is sent to the sanitarium. His trial, the "ring-finger trial," has to do with a ringed woman's finger which was retrieved by a dog he was walking. At Oskar's request, the possession of this ring finger is used by his friend Gottfried as grounds for a murder charge. In order to lend credibility to the charge, Oskar flees to Paris and allows himself to be arrested there. His situation in the room at the sanitarium suggests comparison with Stiller's situation in prison. What strikes the reader is that Oskar so decidedly applauds his seclusion: "my bed is the goal I have finally reached." Thus on the first page the reader is provided with a glimpse into Oskar's entire story. That is, it has no "real beginning" in Döblin's sense, but is immediately there in its entirety, which, incidentally, is likewise true of Frisch's *Stiller*. The decisive difference between the two novels, a difference affecting theme, main characters, and structure, is that Oskar, notwithstanding his alternating between first and third person, has no identity problem and is completely comfortable with his actions and decisions. This ties in with his views on human nature—a basic recognition of each person's individuality—and with his independent standpoint in questions of novel technique, on which he elaborates in the first chapter.

Just as the narrator reaches out on the first page to reveal the entire novel, he develops as his first character a literary figure who appears at the beginning not only by reason of chronology but because she eclipses all the other characters even at the end: the grandmother, Anna Bronski. From the role she plays throughout the novel we see that she is not included merely as part of the family history. Of course it is important for the reader to know that Anna Bronski and Josef Koljaiczek are the grandparents of the tin-drummer Oskar, for many things in his nature can perhaps be traced back to them and thus be better understood. Moreover, the grandmother belongs to the world of Oskar's childhood. But the reader is deceiving himself if he thinks that here Grass is simply beginning with background material. The grandparents never leave the scene entirely. In Oskar's mind they are not bound to a certain time or to an early stage of his life. They do not belong to the past, but are actually more a part of the future. Many times Oskar toys with the fantasy that Grandfather Koljaiczek has become a rich lumber merchant in Buffalo. Even in the last part of the book, both during flight and on his birthday, he reflects on the possibility of going for a time to his grandfather in America. His grandfather is actually closer to him than his father. The uncertainty as to whether Koljaiczek, who was fleeing from the authorities, drowned in the Gulf of Danzig or managed to escape stimulates his grandson's imagination.

Within the novel it is never explicitly said that Grandmother Anna Bronski has died. In Oskar's mind she lives on. Grass indicates her function with the title of the first chapter, "The Wide Skirt." Just as in the beginning, when she sits granting protection "in her skirts at the edge of a potato field" and lets the arsonist Koljaiczek hide under them, it seems to Oskar in the last chapter

that "flight in the direction of grandmother's skirts is the only promising possibility." Since the "political realities, the so-called Iron Curtain," obstruct his
way, he must "cross out" as a flight destination the "four skirts" of his "grandmother Anna Koljaiczek, which to this day still billow protectively in the
Kashoubian potato fields." Now fear can take hold of him. The "Black Witch,"
the image which represents fear to Oskar, is the antithesis of the grandmother
and appears to him in many shapes after he has intentionally surrendered to
fear in order to escape the emptiness. On the escalator in Paris, as he moves
toward his arrest, he would have liked to see "in place of the criminal officers
the opposite of the terrible Black Witch: my grandmother Anna Koljaiczek
standing there like a mountain, ready to receive me and those following me,
after a joyful ascent, under her skirts, into the mountain." In this way the
novel's beginning and ending are joined. The white bed in the sanitarium, a
hiding place where Oskar feels safe and protected from the confusion of life
outside the institution, corresponds to grandmother's skirts. The flight which
could not lead to grandmother leads instead to the bed in which Oskar is still
to be found when he finishes writing his memoirs. The narration only appears to be progressing in a forward direction; actually it "no longer follows a
single 'thread,' but spreads out in an endlessly woven surface."

The Tin Drum has been interpreted as a picaresque novel[5] and labeled
"anti-Meister"; certain elements of the work would seem to indicate that the
literary experts who make such claims are in the right. But it is more important to realize that all this describes the novel only in part. The life story of
the tin drummer which seems to emerge is for the artist Grass only a means
to an end, that of expressing what is unnarratable in narrative form. This is
already evident in the novel's first chapters, in which the reader is told in no
uncertain terms that he must set aside all of his expectations. True, one could
draw a parallel with Wilhelm Meister when Oskar decides immediately after
his birth to "flatly reject" his "father's suggestion, that means everything connected with the grocery business"; Wilhelm Meister also refuses to comply
with his father's career wishes for him. Again one could draw a comparison
when Oskar, as a three-year-old, decides not to grow any more, but simply
to be the one who is "superior . . . to the adults, . . . who was completely
finished inside and outside, while they had to chatter about development
until their old age." There are indeed points of comparison here, but they
can only lead to the conclusion that the two works are not comparable; Grass
is speaking of something totally different from Goethe. Grass himself states
this unmistakably, for example in Oskar's explanation, "I may as well come
right out with it: I am one of those infants who hears everything, whose
mental development is already complete at birth and from then on needs
only to be confirmed."

By having his narrator Oskar use the perspective of the three-year-old

Oskar for long stretches while in the sanitarium, Grass indulges in a game
with perspectives, for the adult Oskar often reverts to his present standpoint,
mixing and linking it with that of the supposed child. He portrays his grandparents from his adult perspective and does the same with his parents until
the scene of his birth. Then, with the startling inclusion of the infant's perspective in the description of his own birth, the artful game begins, only to
be dropped again in the chapter, "The Photograph Album." This chapter
culminates in an interpretation of a photograph of the three-year-old: "There
I have it, the drum. It's hanging right in front of my tummy, brand new with
red and white markings. . . . At that time I succeeded in finding a position
which I had no reason to give up." The reader must accept the fictional
premise that this narrator, in possession of the highest degree of intelligence
and great powers of observation from birth, decides to stay the size of a three-
year-old until his twenty-first year. He thereby finds himself in an advantageous situation as an observer: he sees the goings-on of adults and of his era
from the best possible perspective, from below, while those around him take
little notice of him because of his physical retardation.

Although the novel is carefully divided into three parts, the epic world
which unfolds before the reader consists of a tapestry of episodes. What gives
them their unique quality is the encounter between the author's inexhaustible material and the three-year-old who seems to miss nothing. Hidden
under the table, in the clothes closet, in the house entrance, under the
grandstand, he does his mischief; always alone and independent, he becomes
an artist on the drums and breaks glass by singing when it serves his purposes.
As the gravity of the political situation increases, he is the medium through
which the reader participates in the events. In the *Kristallnacht* of 1938,
Matzerath goes into the city with his son in order to be present at the burning
of the synagogue. While he is "warming his fingers and his feelings over the
public fire," Oskar runs to the toy store where he always gets his drums and
whose Jewish owner revered Oskar's deceased mother, is witness to the liq-
uidation of the store, and sees the dead merchant sitting before the water
glass from which he took his last sip. Just as Oskar is concerned about his
drums here, the same is the case at the outbreak of war in 1939. Whereas he
was still a neutral observer in the fall of 1938, now he is entangled in the
events in an ambiguous way. His uncle, Jan Bronski, who was his mother's
lover, is shot as an insurgent subsequent to the defense of the Danzig Post
Office. Since Bronski left the post office on the evening before the fighting
began, but then went back again with Oskar (Oskar wanted the janitor at the
post office to repair his drum), Oskar acknowledges that he is guilty of Bronski's death. All of this takes on an added significance since Oskar sees Bronski
as his "presumed father," a description he also uses in reference to his legal

father Matzerath, who was killed in 1945 when the Russian troops entered Germany, at which time Oskar was again caught up in the events.

Oskar's childishness, maintained until his twenty-first year, is linked to a high degree of wickedness. Of relevance here is that *The Tin Drum* is, along with many other things, a satire. Above all, it is the narrator's self-satire; he does not charge anyone with more guilt than himself and uses his own case to demonstrate the process of becoming involved in guilt. He shows how the seemingly childish Oskar is drawn into the events, does not resist, and finally—whether intentionally or unintentionally remains open—commits deeds which harm others. Characteristically, the narrator often reports the same events in different ways on different occasions. Different versions are possible both for the death of his presumed fathers and of his mother. Concerning the death of her daughter, Anna Bronski says, "My Agnes, she died because she couldn't stand the drumming any more." This is a judgment which, in light of Anna Bronski's mythical role, cannot be refuted, even though the plot allows for other reasons. Later, Oskar confesses to guilt in all the cases, specifying exactly what he did wrong, but he often exaggerates so much that what he says could easily be contested.

The question of guilt cannot be decided on the basis of the events described; in fact, they are depicted in such a way that the question does not even have to be posed. Jan Bronski's return to the Polish post office on the eve of September 1, 1939, has to do with his conflicting feelings about a political situation which demands from him a patriotic decision quite foreign to his nature. Oskar's request to have his tin drum repaired becomes a catalyzing factor. In the description of the streetcar ride into the city, the game with perspectives is especially impressive. Is it the near thirty-year-old narrator who interprets Jan Bronski's behavior or does the fifteen-year-old Oskar already understand what the ride means? It is again typical of the novel's style that it cannot be determined from which perspective Oskar is narrating here or what type of guilt is meant. But it is absolutely certain that Oskar, taking shelter behind his age during the arrests in the Polish post office, realizes that the "Judas theatrics" by means of which he saves his drum cause Jan Bronski's destruction. His confession follows soon afterwards:

> On the first of September '39—. . . that is the date of my second great guilt. Even when I am feeling most sorry for myself, I cannot deny it: my drum, no, I myself, the drummer Oskar, brought first my poor mama, then Jan Bronski, my uncle and father, to their graves.

When *The Tin Drum* appeared, the third part, set in West Germany, was thought to be less impressive than the first two parts. Yet it cannot be said that this judgment is final. It in no way detracts from the poetic luster of the scenes set in Danzig to claim that the third part, Oskar's tenancy in the former bathroom of Zeidler's Düsseldorf apartment, reproduces in an unsurpassable way the vacuum which prevailed in Germany after the collapse in 1945. Zeidler, the "bottom half of his face hidden beneath fluffy soap suds," receives Oskar at the apartment door, saying, "If you don't like the room, say so immediately. I'm shaving and then I have to wash my feet." Oskar takes a look at the room.

> I couldn't possibly like it because it was an inoperative bathroom, a good half of it covered with turquoise-green tiles and the rest with a busy wallpaper. Nevertheless, I did not say that it was impossible to like it. . . . I declared my willingness to rent the room with bathtub for forty marks a month.

From this point on, Oskar begins his path into a world which has to be rebuilt after the loss of his homeland. His new life begins, as he sees it, with the question of who lives behind the doors of the other rooms opening into the narrow corridor of Zeidler's rooming house. Oskar's bizarre love for the nurse Dorothea, whom he never sees, is kindled by the milk-glass door of her small room and intensified by her footsteps in the morning when she comes back from the night shift and in the evening when she returns from the day shift.

> Oskar did not always remain seated in his chair when he heard the nurse in the corridor. Often enough he played with the doorknob. For who can resist it? Who doesn't look up when something goes by which might be going by for him? Who stays in his chair when every nearby sound seems to serve the sole purpose of making him jump up?

Excitement is created by the nurse's mail, which Oskar regularly examines; one day he even steams open a letter. The culminating points of the relationship are Oskar's visit to her room in her absence and his contact with her in the dark, a grotesque situation which begins in the w.c., takes its fruitless course on the coconut-fiber matting of the corridor, and causes the nurse to move out of her room that night. Although Oskar the drummer becomes rich from his great concert tours and recordings, he keeps his bathroom at Zeidler's, not only because he has found a friend in another room, the flutist Klepp, but also because he feels attached to the nurse's room, which he has also rented. In front of huge audiences, Oskar drums children's songs and scenes from childhood, while the listeners, in general more advanced in age, lose their inhibitions to the point of infantility. Feeling lonely by virtue of this activity which isolates him from Klepp, he experiences Dorothea's abandoned room as a special place of escape.

> [I] wandered from the bathtub of my room down the coconut runner of the corridor into Dorothea's room, stared into the empty clothes closet, let myself be mocked by the mirror over the commode, despaired over the heavy, unmade bed, took refuge in the corridor, fled from the coconut fiber into my room and couldn't stand it there either.

With the occurrences in Zeidler's apartment and Oskar's mass performances, Grass gives shape to emptiness. His creative talent—the ability to portray vividly and concretely—is at least as powerfully at work here as in the parts dedicated to the three-year-old. By means of Oskar's experiences, Grass shows what befell the population crowded together in a reduced postwar Germany. At the same time, the problems of intellectually and artistically active circles looking for new options are raised, for with the defeat of the National Socialist ideology, the resistance against it naturally came to an end as well. Many years were to pass before new beginnings could be found. To conquer the emptiness, to resist the paralysis was the first priority. A scene which says much about the times is the one in which Oskar responds to Klepp's question about his competency in "questions of music" by beating the drum again for the first time since Matzerath's funeral. After several hours of playing together, he has given Klepp, who spends many hours in bed, a "reason for getting up," and that same day Klepp suggests that they start a jazz band together.

When Oskar submits to the ring-finger trial and stages his flight to Paris, he is looking for an escape from boredom and loneliness. He has not yet found it on his thirtieth birthday in the sanitarium. For this reason he looks back to the skirts of his grandmother. Günter Grass, however, did find a new direction with his novel, It led not back into the past but rather directly into the present. *The Tin Drum* was a worldwide success and was translated into many languages. In France (*Le Tambour*) and in the United States, it was a bestseller. The German public also realized, somewhat slower than elsewhere, that Günter Grass was to be respected as an author of unique talents and that his work was not to be judged by conventional criteria.

With *Dog Years* (*Hundejahre*, 1963), Grass continued in the same direction. The novel is even subtler and more complex than *The Tin Drum* and has three narrators. The plot begins in the Danzig region in 1926, leads to West Germany at the war's end, and concludes in 1957. The two main characters, Eddi Amsel and Walter Matern, narrators of the first and third books, are on opposite ends of the turbulent occurrences. They have been blood brothers since the age of eight. From his childhood Amsel, intuitively following his inspirations, constructed impressively ghastly scarecrows, and in Matern he had someone to help him in the sale of the scarecrows as well as protect him. Amsel's father was a Jew. The friendship ends during the Hitler period. Matern, first a Communist and then a member of the storm troopers, leads a brutal assault on Amsel—who is now making movable scarecrows in storm trooper uniforms—with eight accomplices; they knock out his teeth and roll his bleeding body up in the snow. Amsel survives, has thirty-two gold teeth made, becomes a ballet master in Berlin under the name Haseloff (he is also called Goldmouth), and in this way makes it through the Hitler years.

As in *The Tin Drum*, the third part of the novel is particularly important as a picture of the postwar period, but the analysis offered here far surpasses that in *The Tin Drum* in its multidimensionality, its denunciation and parody, its vision of the future. Matern is the narrator. He tells how he travels around West Germany to take revenge on former superiors and comrades from the Hitler era by harming them in various ways, particularly by seducing their wives and daughters; he has come to "judge." He is not aware of his own guilt; it only becomes clear to him gradually. The human phenomenon he represents is described in his own words: "An empty closet full of uniforms of every conviction. I was red, wore brown, put on black, changed colors: red. Spit at me." During this time Matern is accompanied by Pluto, a dog which belonged to Adolf Hitler, ran away from him to the West at the war's end, and chose Matern as his master.

In the long run, Matern cannot help being encircled by the past. In order to escape the increasing pressure, he decides to flee to East Germany, first leaving the dog at the Travelers' Aid in the Cologne station. As he descends from the train for a short stop at the Berlin station Bahnhof Zoo, Goldmouth comes toward him with the dog. The two spend an evening and a night together in Berlin bars. They tell stories from the past, and the old tensions surface again. Amsel's cleverness, insightfulness, and superiority provoke Matern as in earlier years, and Matern falls back into old patterns of behavior. After losing control and uttering a racial slur, Matern "sinks to the ground." He is at Amsel's mercy and says, "Do whatever you want with me!" Amsel takes him to Hanover and shows him his huge underground factory, the firm of Brauxel and Co. (Amsel also bears the name Brauxel, which he uses as narrator of the novel's first part). The factory, located in a former potash mine, mass produces and exports scarecrows of different types. Matern is horrified by the underground spectacle and calls it a hell, referring to hellish laughter, hellish torture, hellish shame. But Brauxel informs him that the miners, "who have been working in the mountain for twenty years, are prepared to find hell everywhere above ground, but below ground no hell could be confirmed." After the tour Brauxel chains the dog to the entrance of the main shaft, explaining, "He shall be a guardian here and nonetheless not be named Cerberus. Orcus is up above!"

One might ask the question whether the reunion of the former friends at the end of the novel is to be interpreted as a vision or as an actual occurrence. In *The Tin Drum* Grass had already accustomed his reader to the idea that in the realm of fiction more happens than was previously the case. The end of *Dog Years* should be understood in the sense of this expansion of fictional possibilities. It is true that from a psychological point of view, one could interpret the meeting at Berlin's Bahnhof Zoo as Matern's hallucination, and their evening and night together as well as the visit to Brauxel's factory could then also be seen as products of Matern's imagination. But such a rational interpretation does not aid in understanding the novel. It can only mislead, for it is not Matern's old guilt and his relationship towards it which are at issue at this point in the novel; these were already sufficiently treated. Instead, the critical issue is what is happening at the present time and will recur again and again. When Matern tries to flee, Amsel is already standing in his way. For structural reasons Amsel would have had to reappear in the novel at some time anyway. In a style characterized by its creative imagery, Grass turns his attention to both characters at the same time at the end of the novel. Their unbridgeable differences emerge once again, sharply outlined, in the dreamlike scenes of the last part. Their individuality could not be changed or destroyed by the experiences of the era; they survived their devastated homeland as well as their own defeats and perform their old deeds anew.

In his third novel, *Local Anesthetic (Örtlich betäubt*, 1969), Grass experimented to achieve a different means of expression. He no longer attempted to express himself in pictures and episodes, but through the alternation of differently structured scenes. One group of scenes demonstrates how the narrator's different levels of consciousness overlap, which means that different subject areas are intermeshed. The other group of scenes presents chronological events in a conventional manner. Much dialogue is included. The temporal reference point is the author's present time while writing the novel in early 1967. The past is included in the form of bits of memories as well as short, chronological summaries. The narrator Starusch, a forty-year-old teacher in West Berlin, often speaks of the fact that he was the leader of the "Duster Gang" (also mentioned in *The Tin Drum*) in Danzig, and on different occasions he relates incidents from his youth. Unlike Grass's first two novels, here this period of time is not presented as a cohesive world; only bits and pieces are brought to light. Many scenes take place at the dentist's office; the extensive dental treatment which the teacher must undergo provides the novel's backdrop. In order to distract the patient's attention from his pain, the dentist places a television in front of the chair. The running program, the patient's simultaneous reflections and memories, his discussions with the dentist, and details from the dental treatment are woven together in the scenes which probe into Starusch's consciousness. Since these scenes are often fatiguing for the reader, the chronologically constructed scenes and narrations offer him relief. The same is true of the sections dedicated to the younger generation from Starusch's professional circle. The likeable student Scherbaum, who plans to burn his dog in public in protest against the use of napalm in Vietnam and then refrains from doing it in the end, functions as an antitype to Starusch's memory-burdened generation.

The novel's importance lies in its intensive endeavor to present specific contemporary problems in novelistic form. The author draws upon current themes such as the treatment of pain in modern dentistry, the incipient youth and student rebellions, the attempt to come to terms with the past in Germany, and personal relationships between all types of partners. Grass wanted these themes to be recognized as modern concerns. This can be seen in the partnerships which rarely existed as such previously, if they existed at all. They are partnerships between dentist and patient, teacher and student, parents and son, and an engaged couple. In the youth rebellion Grass seized upon a complex social phenomenon which had already assumed extreme and violent forms. Technically complicated dental treatments, which were only recently developed, are parodied in the dentist's lectures and explanations and in his references to the significance and progress of modern research. By presenting all these themes in the novel—not as ornamentation but as the main substance—Grass took on a task which had relatively little to do with his previous work.

He further developed this new form in *From the Diary of a Snail* (*Aus dem Tagebuch einer Schnecke*, 1972). The book presents itself as a diary written during Grass's travels in 1969 as a political campaign speaker for the Social Democratic Party (SPD). It begins with the election of Gustav Heinemann to the presidency of the Federal Republic of Germany on March 5, 1969. With this election, which was a victory for the SPD, the snail makes its "entrance." In a conversation with his children, the author explains what the snail means. Before he gives the answer though, he describes the snail's character in the form of a riddle:

> Its victories are brief and seldom. It crawls, crawls off to hide, crawls on further with its muscular foot and leaves its quickly drying traces in the historical landscape, across documents and boundaries, amid construction sites and ruins, through drafty systems of thought . . . past thwarted revolutions.

And then the dialogue: "And what do you mean by snail?" "The snail, that's progress." "And what's that, progress?" "To be a little faster than the snail."

The countertheme, melancholia, as depicted on Dürer's engraving, is also discussed with the children. That it is mentioned many times throughout the book can be explained by the fact that during his political travels the author was gathering materials for a lecture he was to give in 1971, the Dürer year, in Nuremberg. The lecture was titled "On Standstill and Progress" and is printed verbatim at the end of the book. Amidst his remarks on progress and standstill, his references to politicians, and several portraits, Grass tells the children the story of an imaginary person, Dr. Hermann Ott, called Doubt. The action-filled story is structured chronologically and has the function of satisfying the children's wish for a suspenseful story. Of course, its content is also important. Doubt experiences the expulsion of the Jews from Danzig and survives the war in a cellar.

Despite the fact that Martin Walser has never achieved the international reputation of Günter Grass, he has remained a respected literary figure in Germany for over two decades. His best novel to date is still *Half Time* (*Halbzeit*, 1960), although the two other novels with which it forms a trilogy, *The Unicorn* (*Das Einhorn*, 1966) and *The Fall* (*Der Sturz*, 1973), are also important statements on the times. *Half Time* attests to the turning point in Walser's literary development which took place immediately following his first novel, *Marriage in Philippsburg* (*Ehen in Philippsburg*, 1957), a conventional book in comparison with *Half Time*. As Walser himself emphasized, the turning point came about as a result of his involvement with Marcel Proust (1871–1922), whose novel *A la recherche du temps perdu* (1913–27) he intensively studied in the German translation. What he found particularly impressive was, in his own words, the "exactness of the Proustian exploration into man's consciousness." For Walser, a differentiation between "important-unimportant" was no longer possible; Proust's narration deals with those things "in all their importance" which one "had not even noticed until then." The narrative style of *Half Time* must be understood in this connection. Walser tried to actualize what he admired in Proust. But Proust's great theme, the supposed recovery of times past, did not impress him. He believed that "the search ends with a quite un-Proustian result,"[6] that neither celebrations of memory nor art can bring back what is lost. "There Proust was wrong. Nothing can be saved. Not even through art."[7] Instead he was convinced that Proust's influence will "dawn on us in our daily lives . . . when we conquer our indifference for a few moments and satiate our awakened interest" in the things around us.[8]

In *Half Time* Walser was able to develop a style which, though influenced by Proust, was distinctly his own by choosing as his narrator Anselm

Kristlein, who is also the main character. As the first-person narrator, Anselm functions as the novel's medium. The material Walser wishes to discuss is entirely contingent upon Anselm's unique way of receiving impressions. The character Anselm can be judged only according to this function as a medium. Nothing about Anselm—neither his profession as a traveling salesman nor his uncompleted university studies, neither his family, marriage, extramarital affairs, and friends nor his unusual verbal ability, humor, or powers of observation—is used by the author to serve a plot or to present a personality. Walser was concerned only with telling, in the Proustian way he had so admired, of those things "in all their importance" which were "not even noticed until then."

Walser, who was also familiar with Joyce, achieved his purpose by first having Anselm narrate for a whole day, from morning to night, and almost into the next morning (375 pages). The opening sentences immediately reveal that the author is proceeding in a manner previously unknown in the German language: "As difficult as it was for me to wake up, it was equally difficult for me to fall asleep. I was not yet finished with the day when the night took over. I was not yet finished with the night when the day broke. Actually the sun was harassing me." Anselm's entire existence, extended by means of flashbacks into the world of his grandfather, becomes "important" in his narration. In the sections following the first full day, some events are spread out over weeks and months, while others only fill up single days and are then reported again in great detail.

Anselm's professional life takes up a large part of the narration. In the first chapter, entitled "Mimicry," he speaks about his experiences as a traveling salesman over the past ten years. He is only able to survive by deception since there is no need for the products he has to offer. The most important thing he learns is that sales success does not depend on the quality and usefulness of the product. The conclusion drawn from his experiences becomes a Weltanschauung: "I learned that optimism and pessimism are equally ridiculous in view of the terrible disorder that keeps the world alive." Anselm expresses this world view in a metaphor which recurs regularly throughout the novel, "the gray cat who plays with our terrestrial globe." The metaphor is on his mind when he awakens. It points to the novel's metaphysical dimension, which is already touched upon in the title.

Walser was directly influenced by Proust in his depiction of parties and social gatherings, which comprise entire sections of the novel. They demonstrate the difficulties people have living together; the "embarrassments, insults, and injuries" which occur during the social events are reminiscent of Proust.[9] Genuine festivities in which the people experience an intensification of life and are relieved from their daily routine are not possible under the circumstances presented in *Half Time*. Nevertheless, there are always people who are anxious to participate in the social events, and Anselm insists to his wife, Alissa, that he take part in all the goings-on outside of their home. Before going to Josef-Heinrich's "eleventh engagement" on the evening of the novel's first day, he realizes why he must participate. In his mind he accuses Alissa of wanting to "seal the family bunker more and more hermetically." Alissa

> is satisfied if I find her beautiful. . . . But when I, alone with her in the room, say something which is, so to speak, nice, . . . I have the feeling that I am alone in a gigantic theater, and on the no less gigantic stage up above, Alissa is constantly bowing to my applause. . . . We are marionettes which, in the absence of the actors and the audience, make a helpless attempt to clap their joints. Alissa doesn't notice it.

Anselm says that he "yearns" not only for women: "I need noise, talk, gossip, that's what nourishes me, you understand, and if I'm not nourished, then I can't nourish Alissa." In the case of the "eleventh engagement," the invitations, whose sender is unknown, are an indication of the embarrassment to come. But the evening exceeds all expectations and turns out to be an unbroken chain of mental cruelties. Walser later speaks of man's "habit of wounding"[10] and says on another occasion, "The question asked is the same everywhere: how can one live at all, let alone with others."[11]

The novel's structure is not simply a linear progression. The narration begins on June 18, 1957, and ends on March 21, 1958. Between these dates Anselm advances in his career to the position of advertising expert, is sent for several weeks to the agency's main office in New York for a special course, and is supposed to become the "first mass consumption specialist" in the German branch. Admittedly, he is successful professionally and is able to master any difficulties quickly, but in other areas he is faced with unsolvable problems; they result in recurring stomach ailments that can only be cured by operating. The narration begins and ends during the morning hours in the bedroom, that is, in Alissa's realm. Both at the beginning and at the end, Anselm has slept at home for the first time after an extended stay in the hospital; he has returned home to Alissa. His relationship with his wife is the large arch which encompasses everything narrated. This relationship expresses itself in concrete ways throughout the novel. Even when Anselm is talking about their past, one sees that his relationship with Alissa is something concrete. This is not the case with the other women with whom he is involved.

In addition to a number of primarily sexual relationships, which are only of passing interest to Anselm, two women play a particularly important role in his life: Melitta, a barber's daughter who ran away from her father, and Susanne, a beautiful and widely traveled Jewess. Melitta represents the prototype of feminine seduction. She takes no notice of Anselm; he does not even know if she sees him. Meanwhile Alissa builds her entire existence upon the marriage to Anselm. But he constantly gravitates away from her, and again and again finds himself drawn towards Melitta. According to his own confession, his entire narration serves the purpose of finding the way to her, but he never succeeds.

The relationship which is the shortest, yet at the same time has the strongest effect on Anselm, is the one with Susanne. For a period of time she represents to him the "horizon," the hope that he needs: "man needs a horizon, so to speak, where else can he look during the process of collective bargaining with fate." In the first two and one-half months of their relationship, Anselm's behavior is characterized by searching and waiting. "A door through which Susanne had once come was, in a sense, hope." When she, as is her custom, appears late for engagements or does not come at all, he enjoys the expectation and her charms are enhanced in his thoughts. Anselm's feelings for Susanne during this period are not unrelated to the fact that she is engaged to another man. For her own sake, Anselm must hope that she marry the other man; he cannot presume to win her himself. Just as Melitta's presence endangers and finally destroys the mythos Anselm has built around her, Susanne also loses her exalted position as she comes closer to him. After it has become apparent that her engagement will not last, Susanne becomes Anselm's lover on the autumnal equinox, September 22. This date is tied in with the vernal equinox, after which the novel ends. The dates of the two equinoxes are suggestive of a metaphor which Anselm uses to characterize his relationship with Alissa: the ellipse, not the circle. A simple circular rotation offers too little variation. The circle is "the most unnatural shape . . . deadly perfect, empty, deceptive movement, because there are no differences in weight, no gravitational changes. . . . Alissa is not that stupid. Alissa allows the ellipse," Anselm says after being with Susanne. On October 18, he travels to New York, and after returning in early December, he learns that Susanne has left the city on her own initiative during his absence; no one knows where she went.

Whereas in Martin Walser's *Half Time* there is only one main speaker, in *Speculations about Jakob* (*Mutmassungen über Jakob*, 1959), Uwe Johnson distributed the narrative voice among a number of speakers. Their differing standpoints and judgments make the novel as a whole into the very thing which it is about: speculations about Jakob. In addition to his narrator's report, Johnson uses dialogues and interior monologues. In neither case, however, does he specify who is speaking. The dialogues or dialogue fragments could be spoken by the characters who function in the plot and are known to the reader, by other characters unknown to the reader, or by anonymous speakers whose views represent general opinion. By bringing out opposing opinions and speculations in the dialogues, Johnson has found a way to incorporate various interpretations of the novel's events into the novel itself. The interior monologues are spoken by three of the main characters, Gesine, Rohlfs, and Jonas Blach. They are not attached to their monologues by name but are nonetheless easily identifiable from the content. They tell what they have experienced, explain how they see things from their perspective, give their opinions on the others, and reconstruct events at which they were not present according to what they imagine might have happened. The monologues are set apart from the rest of the text by italics, a stylistic means comparable to the italicized passages in Bert Brecht's *Threepenny Novel* and in Faulkner's works.

The novel opens with its central question: was the railroad man Jakob Abs, who was run over by a train, the victim of an accident, did he take his own life, or was he murdered by the state. "But Jakob Abs always cut across the tracks," is the first sentence of the novel. "And that is really the beginning of the story," Johnson said in response to an interviewer's question regarding the form of the novel, i.e., the "threefold division into narration, dialogue, monologue." Johnson said he realized that the first sentence was the "beginning of a conversation, a protesting beginning which did not want to believe the story."[12]

Most of the story takes place in East Germany, and all the motifs underlying the plot are taken from Johnson's situation there while writing the novel. A main theme is defection, which immediately brings to mind Anna Seghers's *The Decision* and Christa Wolf's *Divided Heaven*. But a comparison with these novels as well as with the program of Socialist Realism and its prototype, *The Mother*, by Gorky shows that, in spite of similarities in specific instances, the differences predominate. The Hungarian uprising in the fall of 1956, for example, does provide the historical backdrop for Johnson's story, but it cannot assume the same function as the workers' struggles in Nizhni-Novgorod and Sormovo in Gorky's novel. As a conscientious railway dispatcher, Jakob even refuses to take part in sabotaging the transfer of Russian troops to Hungary; he considers the opposition to be senseless and is guided solely by the demands of his work. Nor are he and his mother proletarians like the title heroine and her son in Gorky's novel. Like millions of others, Jakob and his mother experienced much hardship at the end of the war, but after fleeing from Pomerania, they arrived in Jerichow with a horse and cart and made a successful adjustment. Jakob's father, who was killed in the war, was an agriculturalist and held the post of farm inspector. That Jakob himself advanced from switchman to inspector may speak for his diligence, but otherwise says nothing. The plot affords no opportunity to point to the achievements of the working class. The topic of propaganda is only presented in one of two ways: either parodied by an anonymous speaker in a dialogue or meant as a serious statement by Rohlfs, a captain in the state security agency and one of the novel's main characters. He fits the description of a functionary in the Communist party as found in the works of Socialist Realism: convinced of Marxist doctrine, intelligent, enormously active, and at pains to make a friendly impression. It is he who sets the plot in motion. With Rohlfs's failure to carry out his assignment, Johnson delivers a concrete example of his opposition to the functionary ideology. "You're not a good loser," the English philologist Dr. Blach says to Rohlfs at the end of the novel when Rohlfs has him arrested in order to have some result to show after the failure of his extravagant mission.

This elaborate mission resembles a detective story. The reader gains insight into it through Rohlfs's interior monologues and the narrator's reports. The character around whom everything revolves is Gesine Cresspahl, who fled from East Germany and is employed as an interpreter at NATO headquarters in West Germany. She is the only daughter of the sixty-eight-year-old, widowed cabinetmaker Cresspahl, who lives in the fictitious Baltic Sea town of Jerichow. Rohlfs's aim is to enlist Gesine for espionage. He begins by approaching Frau Abs and her son Jakob, who had both been housed by Cresspahl after their flight from Pomerania and stayed on permanently in the Cresspahl home. Frau Abs worked as a cook in a hospital and cared for young Gesine. Gesine looked upon Jakob as an older brother and remained in contact with him even after she left home for Leipzig to study English and he went to work for the railroad in a town on the Elbe. As Rohlfs's investigation reveals, the relationship between the two also remained intact after Gesine's defection. When Rohlfs questions Frau Abs about Gesine, however, she denies any relationship and flees the next day via Berlin to West Germany. This is Rohlfs's first setback. Things take a favorable turn when Gesine suddenly appears in the town on the Elbe and Jakob then takes her to visit her father in Jerichow. Rohlfs is able to meet with Gesine, afterward allowing her to leave East Germany unmolested on the condition that she agree to meet with him again in West Berlin. By the time this second meeting comes to pass, Jakob is no longer alive; he had visited Gesine in West Germany and was run over by a locomotive on the morning of his return home. In his second conversation with Gesine, Rohlfs is forced to admit that his judgment of Jakob has always been incorrect and that despite detailed research he has misconstrued Jakob's motives. His mission has failed in every respect.

That the speculations about Jakob lead nowhere has to do not only with the novel's form but also with Jakob's character, the political situation in which he has become entangled, and the human condition in general. In a time of mistrust, secrecy, and suspicion, when people must conceal their motives and loyalties, it becomes almost impossible to rely on one's assessment of a person or situation. As early as the first conversation between Rohlfs and Jakob, after it has become clear that Jakob is totally opposed to working with the state security agency, the narrator says, "The times . . . were . . . such that an individual had little control over his own life and had to answer for things he hadn't started." Shortly after Jakob has signed an agreement to keep silent and has consented to another meeting—in these matters he has no choice—he talks with his old friend, the locomotive engineer Jöche, and the narrator speaks of a "change" that had affected Jakob. Jakob can no longer be completely honest with Jöche but must allow him to continue believing a rumor that Jakob knows is not true. At this point Jakob realizes it is not "as if things really were the way they look." For Jakob the "change" means that at every step, even in the smallest details, he must control and modify his behavior.

The idea of possibly leaving East Germany to escape the pressure from Rohlfs is quite alien to Jakob's thoughts. He is so much at one with his life and his work that he does not even consider starting over again in a new environment. This is noteworthy insofar as flight is an ever-present alternative, as proven by Frau Abs's sudden decision to leave. For precisely this reason Rohlfs asks Jakob at the beginning of their second talk why he has not left; he has given Jakob enough reason. A dialogue (Gesine and Blach) inserted at this point provides an opportunity for further discussion. One side (Gesine) claims that Jakob was astonished at how one could even ask such a question. If he were simply not to go to work one day, without serving notice, then his superior would be left "standing there" and would "not know where to find a substitute in the next one and one-half minutes; he doesn't deserve that kind of treatment from me, that would be unfriendly of me." On the other hand, he could hardly give notice, "since in that case he would have to work for three more weeks, and that wouldn't help him." Gesine knows that Jakob "finishes what he begins and leaves everything in order. . . . Polite accommodating dependable and so on and so on." He is not the type to leave. Gesine's comments to Rohlfs in West Berlin amount to the same thing. From what she says, one can see how difficult it was to deal with Jakob during his visit in West Berlin. His uneasiness from the first day on was a consequence of his prior decision not to stay there. It was impossible for him to participate openly in discussions; he represented the views he had learned in East Germany. With these "he came visiting," Gesine says, "and he did not understand the citizens of the Occident, because they had never heard anything" about such ideas.

Gesine's attitude towards Jakob in her dialogue with Blach and in her West Berlin dialogue with Rohlfs seems rather distanced. The general picture she gives of Jakob's behavior in West Germany reflects her helplessness during his visit. At this time she no longer saw him as her "older brother"; not long beforehand she had admitted to Jonas Blach, "It is my soul that loves Jakob." Now she admits to Rohlfs that she has "settled here. I don't even need the expeditions to Jerichow anymore." She has to accept the fact that Jakob left her before his death, that their paths had divided once and for all, and that he, as a dutiful employee, had felt obliged to serve a state to which she did not wish to return. The division of Germany could not be overcome by individuals.

Due to her detachment from Jakob, Gesine is more independent toward Rohlfs in West Berlin than she was in their first discussion. Jakob's death may also be a factor in her openness; now no one and nothing can hurt him. As for Rohlfs, once there is no more reason to conceal the irreconcilability of their positions, his friendly behavior is fully exposed for what it is. His kindness applies only within his system, within the measured space of his own perspective. In his eyes Jakob was, and this comes as a surprise to Rohlfs himself, guilty of crimes against the state: "I don't see why I should call it anything else." That Rohlfs has, as Gesine tells him, always "deserved mistrust" and that Jakob would have "deceived him to the end, if it had been possible," about Gesine's visit to East Germany seem to be no more clear to him than the fact that Jakob could not have legally obtained the money for his hotel in West Germany or the ticket to travel to his mother. Rohlfs does not understand how he is "impoverishing reality" by remaining unenlightened, for what Gesine explains to him does not fit into his categories. At the very beginning of their conversation she had said to him, "You considered Jakob to be a man of justice; but it was not your justice." Meanwhile, Rohlfs can only accept one system of reference and holds the view that "reality is not unreasonable."

The story of the functionary told by Johnson is paralleled by Friedrich Dürrenmatt's (b. 1921) novel *The Pledge* (*Das Versprechen*, 1958). Rohlfs's belief that reality is reasonable corresponds to the structural principle of the detective story, whose falseness Dürrenmatt wishes to expose. The work, subtitled *Requiem for the Detective Story*, presents the brilliant detective Matthäi, who experiences a complete mental breakdown after seeing that his accurate calculation of a crime has not proven true in reality. The perpetrator, whose patterns of movement Matthäi could predict beyond a doubt, is killed in an automobile accident on the day he is to be captured. This does not come to light until many years later. Dürrenmatt's narrator, a retired police captain, claims that the flaw in detective stories is that their plots are constructed logically. Reality, however, "can be grasped only partially through logic." On the one hand, one "never" knows "all the necessary factors," and moreover the "coincidental, incalculable, incommensurable" play "too large a role." The detective cannot expect that "his calculation should also be correct in reality." Banalities as well as absurdities must be taken into account. "Our reason only illuminates the world dimly. Everything paradoxical settles in the shadowy area of reason's borders." Matthäi fails because he denies reality, because he attempts to "enforce a flawless framework of reason."

At almost the same time, both Dürrenmatt and Johnson develop characters who proceed from the illusion that they can calculate life's events. Matthäi and Rohlfs are excellent calculators, which makes the stories about them suspenseful and entertaining. Their failure provides the substance of the novels, in Johnson's case with a political dimension.

Johnson used the theme of a divided Germany twice again in his novels. *The Third Book about Achim* (*Das dritte Buch über Achim*, 1961) and *Two Views* (*Zwei Ansichten*, 1965) revolve around characters from East and West Germany and vary the means of expression used in his first novel. Less experimental than *Speculations about Jakob*, they are works from a period of transition and incubation, before the author could see his experiences in a new context.

In his great work, *Anniversaries. From the Life of Gesine Cresspahl* (*Jahrestage. Aus dem Leben von Gesine Cresspahl*, 1970, 1971, 1973, 1983),[13] Johnson places the problems of Germany's past within the framework of world history. He tells of the experiences of Gesine Cresspahl and her ten-year-old daughter Marie in New York between August 1967 and June 1968. The fictional premise is that Gesine, who works in a bank, tells her daughter the story of their family. Gesine's own childhood (she was born in 1933) as well as her recent family history are unfolded to Marie in connection with the political events of that time. The entire epoch of the Third Reich is called up before the reader. Gesine can illustrate its effect on the lives of individuals by relating the experiences of her parents, Heinrich and Lisbeth Cresspahl. The insights to be gained here are in turn tied in with contemporary political events (the war in Vietnam, the assassinations of Robert Kennedy and Martin Luther King, the student revolution), which Gesine reads about in the *New York Times*, and with the practical experiences of mother and daughter in daily life in the American metropolis.

Johnson again uses narration, dialogue, and monologue in *Anniversaries*. But the narrator's standpoint has now changed in that Gesine herself is the narrator and the "entire story supposedly comes from" her perspective. For Uwe Johnson, Gesine is a living person.[14] At the same time she functions within the novel as a model of an intelligent person who attempts to come to terms with a segment of the contemporary world. Gesine assimilates her experiences in three ways: she narrates, converses with her daughter intensively, and confronts her experiences in italicized monologues by inventing, reconstructing the past, speaking with the dead, and expressing her own opinions. The narrative forms which are distributed among different speakers in *Speculations about Jakob* are all concentrated on Gesine in *Anniversaries*. This is appropriate to the novel's content, for Gesine is its speculative, deliberating subject.

The results of her contemplations are expressed in the novel's title. Gesine experiences "anniversaries" in New York; the same things are repeated in new variations.[15] In a different place, a different time, and under different circumstances Gesine again becomes a witness to war, racial strife, murder, and robbery. She finds it just as impossible to disengage herself from the disturbing realities of the times—the reports of violence and injustice in all the countries of the world—as to escape from the terrible memories of her childhood. Moreover, it weighs on her conscience that her child is living in such a jungle of prejudices and delusions and that, like her mother, she will one day have to live with troubling childhood memories. Gesine becomes very ill when she tells of her mother's death. Lisbeth Papenbrock was the victim of many prejudices, had a sensitive conscience, and died a gruesome death. While Gesine tries futilely to free herself from the threatening image of her mother, she is confronted with the unsettling reports of terrifying deaths in New York. Past and present are united in a picture of a dreadful world in which she knows she is a victim without seeing any possibility of resistance.

A work which belongs to the group of highly subtle and original writings by Grass, Walser, and Johnson is Ingeborg Bachmann's (1926–1973) significant novel *Malina* (1971). With this novel the acclaimed lyricist created a new and independent novel style, founded in the congruence of world view and characterization. The male title figure Malina is not only the lifelong companion of the female narrator but a part of her own personality as well.[16] These two characters—the unnamed first-person narrator, who is only identified as "I," and Malina, who is introduced at the beginning of the novel as a high official in the Army Museum—are blended into one, although they can also confront each other as independent characters. At times Malina withdraws and is ignored by "I"; while she is preoccupied with her love for another, for Ivan, he does not disturb her. As the relationship with Ivan begins to weaken, Malina steps forward forcefully, and when the relationship is over he alone dominates. "I" disappears "into the wall"; "It was murder," is the last sentence of the novel. The events are only comprehensible if one realizes that here the internal and external worlds are one. Moreover, the traditional concept of time is no longer valid, as Bachmann indicates within the novel and discusses at length in her *Frankfurt Lectures* (1959–60).[17] By incorporating into her novel the insight that time and space are no longer independent, absolute categories, Ingeborg Bachmann expanded the possibilities of fictional expression, as Günter Grass also did in his own way. Because the narrator's reality is not determined by conventional ideas, she must use new means of narration to make herself understood. Her struggle to become free of an oppressive tradition finds expression in her dreams, which Malina helps her to interpret. Whether he is her masculine partner or represents the masculine side of her personality, whether the differentiation between masculine and feminine still has validity at all, does not have to be conclusively decided. That this question remains unanswered conforms to the statement of the novel, a novel which represents the search for a new feminine identity.

The innovative writer Arno Schmidt (1914–1979) went to extremes in search for his own personal style. Of all the post-1945 authors who attempted to find new means of expression, he was the most consistent in following a course leading to prose that recreates the process of consciousness. *The Stone Heart* (*Das steinere Herz*, 1956), *The Egghead Republic* (*Das Gelehrten-republik*, 1957), and *The Godforsaken Village or Mare Crisium* (*Kaff auch Mare Crisium*, 1960) are experimental novels which set into practice the ideas Schmidt presents in his theoretical writings. He wanted to construct prose works according to principles which would be compatible with mental processes. His monumental book *Zettel's Dream* (*Zettels Traum*, 1970), a continuation, summary, and intensification of everything he had achieved in his earlier works, was a sensation. Published as a facsimile of the typescript, it comprised 1330 pages and was printed in several columns on oversized paper. The unique orthography, the distribution of the text over several columns, and the author's habit of making frequent unexplained references demand from the reader an adjustment to the peculiarities of this novel. In his language and all other means of expression, Arno Schmidt had always deviated from traditional practices, thereby making things difficult for the reader. Heinrich Vormweg, who has given us a thorough evaluation of Arno Schmidt's works as well as remarkably insightful aids to their interpretation, calls his writing "the great challenge in German prose since 1945."[18] The question remains whether it is really impossible for as talented and versatile an author as Arno Schmidt to become part of the literary mainstream and reach a large circle of readers.

In chapter 6 the fact that the general public often prefers a conventional style was mentioned in connection with the limitations faced by authors who wished to effect political and social change. One has the impression that even today few readers are willing to acknowledge experimental novels as attempts to express themes which are intended to be more serious and closer to the human condition than those in traditional works. Almost without exception, the authors who have come into prominence since the 1950s have incorporated traditional elements into their novels: as Mister White, Stiller is a fascinating narrator; Grass's first two novels leave much room for episodic narrations; Uwe Johnson is favorably disposed towards storytelling; and in *Half Time*, Martin Walser makes use of the legend and short narratives and is always conscious of inventing something new to hold the reader's attention. The public was willing to follow these authors, although their novels made great demands upon them and were structured very differently from traditional forms. Readers may not have understood everything, but evidently there was enough offered which was comprehensible. The authors reached, at least to a certain extent, an agreement with their public about content; the contemporary themes of their novels concerned everyone, but were presented as pure fiction: "one cannot live with an experience that remains without a story" (Max Frisch, *Call Me Gantenbein*). The authors without whom contemporary German literature could not have achieved its current international stature created stories to fit the experiences of the times and used fiction to make their statements.

Notes

Chapter 1. Two Beginnings

1. Rehm's history consists of two small volumes (Göschen), the first of which
is simply a revised version of an older *History of the Novel in the Nineteenth Century* (*Romangeschichte des 19. Jahrhunderts*) by Hellmuth Mielke.
Other attempts to write a history of the German novel remained fragmentary. In 1926, Hans Heinrich Borcherdt published the first volume of a
History of the Novel and the Novella in Germany (*Geschichte des Romans
und der Novelle in Deutschland*), but he did not continue in the same
fashion; the only subsequent volume was *The Novel of the Age of Goethe*
(*Der Roman der Goethezeit*, 1949). Heinrich Spiero's posthumously published *History of the German Novel* (*Geschichte des deutschen Romans*,
1950) is a collection of a great deal of material, but it is not a scholarly
history. Since Spiero's publication in 1950 only two longer articles have
appeared. Günther Weydt and Rudolf Majut presented a summary of the
history of the German novel in *Deutsche Philologie im Aufriss* (vol. 2,
1954) and Hildegard Emmel wrote the article "Roman" in the *Encyclope-
dia of German Literary History* (*Reallexikon der deutschen Literaturgeschichte*) in 1972.
2. Chretien de Troyes's Arthurian romance *Yvain or Le Chevalier au Lion*
was the source for Hartmann von Aue's popular medieval epic *Iwein* (c.
1200).
3. "Der Roman des Barock," in *Formkräfte der deutschen Dichtung*, ed. Hans
Steffen, 2d. ed. (Göttingen, 1967), 21.

Chapter 2. Goethe and His Contemporaries

1. Karl Robert Mandelkow, "Der deutsche Briefroman. Zum Problem der
Polyperspektive im Epischen," *Neophilologus* (1960–61): 44–45.
2. *Frauenromane* depict the particular fate of women, their sufferings, and
the problems of their self-realization. They are written by women and,
generally speaking, are also read by women.
3. Alfred Anger, *Literarisches Rokoko* (Stuttgart, 1962), 39.
4. See Friedrich Sengle, *Wieland* (Stuttgart, 1949), 180.
5. *Goethes Werke* (Weimar, 1887), 1:413.
6. See Hildegard Emmel, *Weltklage und Bild der Welt in der Dichtung Goethes*
(Weimar, 1957).
7. Herbert Schöffler, "Die Leiden des jungen Werther. Ihr geistesgeschicht-
licher Hintergrund," in *Deutscher Geist im 18. Jahrhundert* (Göttingen,
1956), 167.
8. Peter Michelsen, *Laurence Sterne und der deutsche Roman des 18. Jahrhunderts* (Göttingen, 1962), 91.

9. See Hildegard Emmel, *Was Goethe vom Roman der Zeitgenossen nahm* (Berne, 1975).

10. For a discussion of this concept see Goethe's review "Gabriele von Johanna Schopenhauer," in *Johann Wolfgang Goethe. Gedenkausgabe der Werke, Briefe und Gespräche* (Zurich, 1950), 14:319–22. Here Goethe associates the tragic novel with absolute passion.

11. Quotation from Fritz Martini, "Der Bildungsroman. Zur Geschichte des Wortes und der Theorie," *Deutsche Vierteljahrsschrift* 35 (1961): 44–65.

12. Eduard Berend, "Einleitung zur hist. krit. Gesamtausgabe," in *Jean Pauls Sämtliche Werke, 1. Abt. 10. Bd. Flegeljahre* (Weimar, 1934), 7.

13. "Über Goethe," in *Novalis. Schriften* (Stuttgart, 1960), 2:640–48.

14. On January 25, 1827, Goethe wrote to Eckermann, "What is a novella other than a shocking event?"

Chapter 3. From Heinrich Heine to Thomas Mann

1. Heinrich Heine, "Französische Maler. Gemäldeausstellung in Paris 1831," in *Heinrich Heine. Sämtliche Schriften* (Munich, 1971), 3:72.

2. Hermann Broch, "James Joyce und die Gegenwart" (1936), in *Hermann Broch. Gesammelte Werke. Dichten und Erkennen* (Zurich, 1955), 6:206.

3. Alexander Jung, *Göthe's Wanderjahre und die wichtigsten Fragen des 19. Jahrhunderts* (Mainz, 1854), 1.

4. Karl Rosenkranz, *Studien* (Halle, 1839), 340.

5. The term Young Germany *(Junges Deutschland)* was first used by Ludolf Wienbarg in a series of lectures published in 1834 as *Ästhetische Feldzüge*. It denotes a trend towards liberality at a time of repression under Metternich. Ironically, it was the federal government which gave coherence to the unstable group of Young German writers when the Federal Diet *(Bundestag)* issued a warning on December 10, 1835, to all the German governments to use the full force of the law against authors, publishers, and promoters of writings from the "Young German school." The five writers named in the original decree were Heinrich Heine, Karl Gutzkow, Heinrich Laube, Ludolf Wienbarg, and Theodor Mundt.

6. Ludolf Wienbarg, *Wanderungen durch den Thierkreis* (Hamburg, 1935), 256.

7. The subtitle of *Waverley* is 'Tis Sixty Years Since.

8. Lion Feuchtwanger, *Heinrich Heines Fragment "Der Rabbi von Bacherach"* (Munich, 1907), 41.

9. Eduard Castle, *Der grosse Unbekannte. Das Leben von Charles Sealsfield (Karl Postl)* (Vienna, 1952), 98.

10. Introduction to the first volume of the new edition of Charles Sealsfield's works: *Charles Sealsfield (Karl Postl 1793–1864) Sämtliche Werke* (Hildesheim, 1972).

11. The first American edition (Philadelphia) was entitled *Tokeah; or The White Rose*; the London edition of the same year bore the title *The Indian Chief; or, Tokeah and the White Rose. A Tale of the Indians and the Whites.*

12. Frances Newton Thorpe, *The Statesmanship of Andrew Jackson as Told in His Writings and Speeches* (New York, 1909), 112.

13. Ibid., 132.

14. This juxtaposition of passages from the general's speech in Sealsfield's novel with the texts of actual speeches held by President Andrew Jackson is found in Hildegard Emmel's article "Recht oder Unrecht in der neuen Welt. Zu Charles Sealsfields Roman *Der Legitime und die Republikaner*," in *Amerika in der deutschen Literatur* (Stuttgart, 1975), 75–80.
15. See Karl J. R. Arndt, "The Cooper-Sealsfield Exchange of Criticism," *American Literature* 15, no. 1 (March 1943): 16–24.
16. C. G. Jung and K. Kerényi, "Das göttliche Kind," *Albae Vigilae* 6/7 (Amsterdam, 1940): 25.
17. Castle, *Der grosse Unbekannte*, 297ff.
18. For a thorough discussion of the structure see Walter Weiss, "Der Zusammenhang zwischen Amerika-Thematik und Erzählkunst bei Charles Sealsfield (Karl Postl), *Literaturwissenschaftliches Jahrbuch* 8 (1967): 95–117.
19. Castle, *Der Grosse Unbekannte*, 585.
20. Jeffrey L. Sammons, *Six Essays on the Young German Novel* (Chapel Hill, 1972), 109.
21. Ibid., 127–28.
22. Friedrich Schlegel, "Gespräch über die Poesie," in *Kritische Ausgabe*, ed. Hans Eichner (Munich, 1967), 2:319.
23. "Appellation an den gesunden Menschenverstand. Letztes Wort in einer literarischen Streitfrage," dated 1835 and printed in the second edition of *Wally die Zweiflerin* in 1852.
24. "Noch einmal über den Roman des Nebeneinander," in *Vom deutschen Parnass* (1854), 111–12.
25. G. Wallis Field, *A Literary History of Germany. The Nineteenth Century, 1830–1890* (New York, 1975), 41.
26. "Willibald Alexis," in *Theodor Fontane. Sämtliche Werke*, part 3, vol. 1 (Munich, 1969), 407–62.
27. This interpretation is based on the first version, as is common practice today.
28. This review is found in *Eduard Mörike, Werke und Briefe* 5 (Stuttgart, 1971).
29. Friedrich Gundolf, *Romantiker. Neue Folge* (Berlin-Wilmersdorf, 1931), 224.
30. Wolfgang F. Taraba, "Tieck. Vittoria Accorombona," in *Der deutsche Roman*, ed. Benno von Wiese (Düsseldorf, 1965), 1:329–52.
31. *Traité de l'Origine des Romans* (Paris, 1670).
32. Alexander Durst, *Die lyrischen Vorstufen des "Grünen Heinrich"* (Berne, 1955).
33. Werner Günther, *Dichter der neueren Schweiz* (Berne, 1968), 2:34.
34. Hermann Helmers, ed., *Raabe in neuer Sicht* (Stuttgart, 1968), 9.
35. Hermann Helmers, *Wilhelm Raabe* (Stuttgart, 1968), 37.
36. Herman Meyer, *Der Sonderling in der deutschen Dichtung*, 2d. ed. (Munich, 1963), 272.
37. Roy Pascal, "Die Erinnerungstechnik bei Raabe" (1954) in Helmers, *Raabe in neuer Sicht*, 134.
38. Hubert Ohl, "Eduards Heimkehr oder Le Vaillant und das Riesenfaultier. Zu Wilhelm Raabes *Stopfkuchen*" (1964), in Helmers, *Raabe in neuer Sicht*, 275.

39. Romano Guardini, "Über Wilhelm Raabes *Stopfkuchen*" (1932), in Helmers, *Raabe in neuer Sicht*, 12–43.
40. Wilhelm Raabe, *Sämtliche Werke* (Göttingen, 1963), 18:421f.
41. Claude David, "Über Wilhelm Raabes *Stopfkuchen*," *Lebendige Form. Festschrift für Heinrich Henel* (Munich, 1970), 267.
42. Quotation from Hans Oppermann, *Wilhelm Raabe in Selbstzeugnissen und Bilddokumenten* (Hamburg, 1970), 142.
43. Claude David, *Geschichte der deutschen Literatur. Zwischen Romantik und Symbolismus. 1820–1855* (Gütersloh, 1966), 49.
44. In Hans-Heinrich Reuter, *Fontane* (Darmstadt, 1970), 963.
45. "Die Ahnen," in *Theodor Fontane. Sämtliche Werke*, 308–25.
46. Friedrich Spielhagen, *Beiträge zur Theorie und Technik des Romans* (Leipzig, 1883), 208.
47. "Der alte Fontane," in *Thomas Mann. Gesammelte Werke* (Oldenburg, 1960), 9:9–35. English translation by H. T. Lowe-Porter in *Essays of Three Decades* (New York, 1947), 287–306.
48. "But things don't work out the way we wish. . . . Tubal has some feeling for Renate, who wouldn't? . . . superficiality of emotion. And the one is just as bad as the other."
49. "Der Zug nach dem Westen," in *Theodor Fontane. Sämtliche Werke*, 568–70.
50. "Willibald Alexis," in *Theodor Fontane. Sämtliche Werke*, 407–62.
51. *Goethes "Wahlverwandtschaften" und der Roman des 19. Jahrhunderts* (Stuttgart, 1968), 156–95.
52. Peter Demetz, *Formen des Realismus: Theodor Fontane* (Munich, 1964), 143.
53. Ingrid Mittenzwei, *Die Sprache als Thema. Untersuchungen zu Fontanes Gesellschaftsroman* (Bad Homburg, 1970), 144.
54. Thomas Mann, *Rede und Antwort. Gesammelte Abhandlungen und kleine Aufsätze* (Berlin, 1922), 99–112.
55. "Robert Walser," in *Walter Benjamin. Gesammelte Schriften* (Frankfurt, 1977), 2:324–28.
56. "Lübeck als geistige Lebensform" (1926), in *Altes und Neues* (Frankfurt, 1953), 290–314.

Chapter 4. New Forms of the Novel

1. In translating Rilke, I have borrowed a few phrases from M. D. Herter Norton's *The Notebooks of Malte Laurids Brigge* (New York: 1964).
2. Judith Ryan, "'Hypothetisches Erzählen': Zur Funktion von Phantasie und Einbildung in Rilkes *Malte Laurids Brigge*," in *Jahrbuch der deutschen Schillergesellschaft* 15 (1971): 341–74.
3. William Small, "Karl VI.—Aas und Heiliger: zu Rilkes Malteroman," in *Rilke heute. Beziehungen und Wirkungen*, ed. Ingeborg Solbrig (Frankfurt, 1975), 93–103.
4. Wilhelm Emrich, *Franz Kafka* (Bonn, 1958), 246.
5. Max Brod, *Franz Kafka* (Berlin, 1954), 269f.
6. Klaus Wagenbach, "Wo liegt Kafkas Schloss?," in *Kafka-Symposion* (Berlin, 1965), 161–80.

7. Klaus Günther Just, *Von der Gründerzeit bis zur Gegenwart: Geschichte der deutschen Literatur seit 1871* (Berne, 1973), 342f.
8. "Autobiographie als Arbeitsprogramm," in *Hermann Broch. Massenpsychologie. Schriften aus dem Nachlass* (Zurich, 1959), 35–237.
9. Hartmut Steinecke, *Hermann Broch und der polyhistorische Roman* (Bonn, 1968), 85.
10. Karl Robert Mandelkow, *Hermann Brochs Romantrilogie "Die Schlafwandler"* (Heidelberg, 1962), 151f.
11. Manfred Durzak, *Hermann Broch. Der Dichter und seine Zeit* (Stuttgart, 1968), 115.
12. "Aus Brief an G. 26. I. 31," in *Robert Musil. Gesammelte Werke in Einzelausgaben. Prosa, Dramen, Späte Briefe* (Hamburg, 1957), 726.
13. Ibid., 727.
14. Friedrich Schlegel, "Brief über den Roman," in *Friedrich Schlegel. Kritische Schriften*, ed. Wolfdietrich Rasch (Munich, 1956), 325f.
15. Renate von Heydebrand, *Die Reflexion Ulrichs in Robert Musils Roman "Der Mann ohne Eigenschaften". Ihr Zusammenhang mit dem zeitgenössischen Denken* (Münster, 1966).
16. Robert Musil, "Vermächtnis (Notizen)," in *Gesammelte Werke in Einzelausgaben. Der Mann ohne Eigenschaften* (Hamburg, 1952), 1646.

Chapter 5. Tendency toward Myth

1. Hans Wysling, *'Mythos und Psychologie' bei Thomas Mann* (Zurich, 1969), 6.
2. Karl Kerényi, *Romandichtung und Mythologie. Ein Briefwechsel mit Thomas Mann* (Zurich, 1945), 17.
3. "Kinderspiele" (1920), in *Thomas Mann. Gesammelte Werke* (Oldenburg, 1960), 11:327–29.
4. Thomas Mann, "Über 'Königliche Hoheit'" (1910), in *Rede und Antwort, Gesammelte Abhandlungen und kleine Aufsätze* (Berlin, 1922), 342–47.
5. "The Making of *The Magic Mountain*," in *The Magic Mountain* (New York: Random House, 1952), 717–27.
6. Kerényi, *Romandichtung*, 32.
7. "The Making of *The Magic Mountain*," 719.
8. "Be careful, it's a bit fragile."
9. "Don't forget to return my pencil."
10. "Freud und die Zukunft" (1936), in *Thomas Mann. Gesammelte Werke* 9:478–502. English translation by H. T. Lowe-Porter in *Essays of Three Decades* (New York, 1947), 411–28.
11. "Wie die Alten den Tod gebildet," in *Gotthold Ephraim Lessing. Gesammelte Werke* (Gütersloh, 1966), 2:120–71.
12. "The Making of *The Magic Mountain*," 724.
13. Ibid., 723.
14. "Gerhart Hauptmann" (1952), in *Thomas Mann. Gesammelte Werke* 9:804–16.
15. "Joseph und seine Brüder—Ein Vortrag" (1942), in *Thomas Mann. Gesammelte Werke* 11:654–69.

16. Kerényi, *Romandichtung*, 19.
17. "Freud und die Zukunft," 494.
18. Hans Albert Maier, "Einleitung zur kritischen Ausgabe des Bergromans," in *Hermann Broch. Bergroman* (Frankfurt, 1969), 4:17.
19. Beate Loos, *Mythos Zeit und Tod* (Frankfurt, 1971), 103–31.
20. Hermann Broch, "Die Verzauberung (Roman)," in *Hermann Broch. Bergroman* 4:257–61.
21. "Die mythische Erbschaft der Dichtung" (1945), in *Hermann Broch. Gesammelte Werke. Dichten und Erkennen* 6:239–49.
22. Quotation from *Hermann Broch. Gesammelte Werke. Briefe* (Zurich, 1957), 8:227.
23. "Bemerkungen zum *Tod des Vergil*," in *Hermann Broch. Gesammelte Werke. Dichten und Erkennen* 6:265–77.
24. "Die mythische Erbschaft der Dichtung," 241.
25. Quotation from *Hermann Broch. Gesammelte Werke. Briefe* 8:227.
26. *Wächter und Hüter. Festschrift für Hermann J. Weigand zum 17. November 1957* (New Haven, 1957), 147–61. Reprinted in *Hermann Broch. Perspektiven der Forschung*, ed. Manfred Durzak (Munich, 1972), 177–92.
27. C. G. Jung and K. Kerényi, "Das göttliche Kind," *Albae Vigilae* 6/7, Amsterdam (1940).
28. "Hermes der Seelenführer," *Eranos-Jahrbuch* (1942).

Chapter 6. The Novel during the Weimar Republic

1. Lion Feuchtwanger, "Über 'Jud Süss' " (1929), in *Centum Opuscula. Eine Auswahl* (Rudolstadt, 1956), 390.
2. Lion Feuchtwanger, "Vom Sinn und Unsinn des historischen Romans" (1935), in *Centum Opuscula*, 508–15.
3. Alfred Döblin, "Der historische Roman und Wir" (1936), in *Aufsätze zur Literatur* (Olten, 1963), 163–86.
4. Alfred Döblin, "Bemerkungen zum Roman" (1917), in *Aufsätze zur Literatur*, 19–23.
5. Alfred Döblin, "An Romanautoren und ihre Kritiker, Berliner Programm" (1913), in *Aufsätze zur Literatur*, 15–19.
6. Alfred Döblin, "Bemerkungen zum Roman," 19–20.
7. Alfred Döblin, "Der Epiker" (1921), in *Aufsätze zur Literatur*, 335–45.
8. Alfred Döblin, "Epilog" (1948), in *Aufsätze zur Literatur*, 383–99.
9. Klaus Müller-Salget, *Alfred Döblin. Werk und Entwicklung* (Bonn, 1972), 294f.
10. Fritz Martini, *Das Wagnis der Sprache. Interpretationen deutscher Sprache von Nietzsche bis Benn* (Stuttgart, 1954), 339.
11. See Hildegard Emmel, *Das Gericht in der deutschen Literatur des 20. Jahrhunderts* (Berne, 1963).
12. *Das Spinnennetz* (Frankfurt: Fischer Bücherei, 1970), 127.
13. See David Bronsen, *Joseph Roth: Eine Biographie* (Cologne, 1974), 382f.
14. Ibid., 386f.
15. The German titles are: *Passagiere der III. Klasse; Brennende Ruhr. Roman aus dem Kapp-Putsch; Des Kaisers Kulis; Ein Prolet erzählt. Lebensschilderung eines deutschen Arbeiters; Sturm auf Essen. Die Kämpfe der Ruhr-*

*arbeiter gegen Kapp, Wetter, Severing; Walzwerk. Roman aus dem Duis-
burg-Hamborner Industriegebiet; Maschinenfabrik N & K; Rosenhofstrasse.
Roman einer Hamburger Arbeiterstrasse.*

Chapter 7. Traditional Forms and the Totalitarian State

1. Anna Seghers, "Briefwechsel mit Georg Lukács," in *Über Kunstwerk und Wirklichkeit. I. Die Tendenz in der reinen Kunst* (Berlin, 1970), 173–85.
2. Lion Feuchtwanger, "Über jüdische Belange," in *Centum Opuscula. Eine Auswahl* (Rudolstadt, 1956), 439–99.
3. Elke Nyssen, *Geschichtsbewusstsein und Emigration* (Munich, 1974), 31.
4. Guy Stern, "Alfred Neumann," in *Deutsche Exilliteratur seit 1933. Band I, Kalifornien* (Berne, 1976), 542–70. The Neumann quotation is found on p. 558 of this article.
5. Klaus-Detlef Müller, *Die Funktion der Geschichte im Werk Bertolt Brechts* (Tübingen, 1967), 72.
6. Walter Benjamin, "Acht Jahre," in *Bertold Brechts Dreigroschenbuch*, ed. Siegfried Unseld (Frankfurt am Main, 1960), 187–93.
7. Anna Seghers, "Briefwechsel mit Georg Lukács," 175.
8. In translating this passage, I have used part of James A. Galston's translation (*The Seventh Cross*, [New York: 1968], 286).
9. Ernst Jünger, *Werke. Tagebücher* (Stuttgart, 1960), 3:451.
10. Hansjörg Schelle, *Ernst Jüngers 'Marmor Klippen.' Eine Interpretation* (Leiden, 1970), 37.
11. *Thomas Mann's Addresses. Delivered at the Library of Congress 1942–1949* (Washington: 1963), 45–67.
12. See Guy Stern's insightful article "Über das Fortleben des Exilromans in den sechziger Jahren," in *Revolte und Experiment. Die Literatur der sechziger Jahre in Ost und West. Fünftes Amherster Kolloquium zur modernen deutschen Literatur*, ed. Wolfgang Paulsen (Heidelberg, 1972), 165–85.
13. Quotation from Hans-Dieter Sander, *Geschichte der Schönen Literatur in der DDR* (Freiburg, 1972), 9.
14. Andrei A. Shdanov, "Rede auf dem I. Unionskongress der Sowjetschriftsteller (1934)," in *Marxismus und Literatur. Eine Dokumentation in drei Bänden*, ed. Fritz J. Raddatz (Reinbeck bei Hamburg, 1969), 1:352.
15. Quotation from Jürgen Rühle, *Das gefesselte Theater. Vom Revolutionstheater zum Sozialistischen Realismus* (Cologne, 1957), 40.
16. Maxim Gorky, "Rede auf dem I. Unionskongress der Sowjetschriftsteller (1934)," in *Marxismus und Literatur*, 339.

Chapter 8. Fiction as a Statement

1. Peter U. Hohendahl, "Das Ende einer Institution?—Der Streit über die Funktion der Literaturkritik," *Revolte und Experiment. Die Literatur der sechziger Jahre in Ost und West. Fünftes Amherster Kolloquium zur modernen deutschen Literatur*, ed. Wolfgang Paulsen (Heidelberg, 1972), 42.
2. Hans Robert Jauss, *Literaturgeschichte als Provokation* (Frankfurt am Main, 1970), 172.

3. Horst Bienek, *Werkstattgespräche mit Schriftstellern* (Munich, 1962), 24f.
4. Alfred Döblin, " 'Ulysses' von Joyce" (1928), *Aufsätze zur Literatur* (Olten, 1963), 287.
5. See Wilfried van der Will, *Pikaro heute. Metamorphosen des Schelms bei Thomas Mann, Döblin, Brecht, Grass* (Stuttgart, 1967). Also Heiko Büscher, "Günter Grass," in *Deutsche Literatur seit 1945*, 2d. ed., ed. Dietrich Weber (Stuttgart, 1970), 516f.
6. Martin Walser, "Leseerfahrungen mit Marcel Proust" (1958), in *Erfahrungen und Leseerfahrungen* (Frankfurt, 1965), 141f.
7. Martin Walser, "Freiübungen" (1963), in *Erfahrungen und Leseerfahrungen*, 103.
8. Martin Walser, "Leseerfahrungen mit Marcel Proust," 142f.
9. Stephen Petro, "Die Bedeutung Prousts für Martin Walsers Roman *Halbzeit*. Nachgewiesen an den gesellschaftlichen Zusammenkünften," (Ph.D. diss., University of Connecticut, 1976), 60.
10. Ibid., 78.
11. Martin Walser, "Imitation oder Realismus" (1964), in *Erfahrungen und Leseerfahrungen*, 93.
12. Horst Bienek, *Werkstattgespräche mit Schriftstellern*, 94f.
13. Because volume four did not appear until late 1983 when this book was already in press, it is not reviewed here.
14. Ree Post-Adams, "Antworten von Uwe Johnson. Ein Gespräch mit dem Autor," *The German Quarterly* 50, no. 3, (May 1977): 243f.
15. See Roberta Tracy Hye, *Uwe Johnsons 'Jahrestage': Die Gegenwart als variierende Wiederholung der Vergangenheit* (Berne, 1978).
16. See Ellen Summerfield, *Ingeborg Bachmann. Die Auflösung der Figur in ihrem Roman 'Malina'* (Bonn, 1976).
17. Ingeborg Bachmann, *Gedichte Erzählungen Hörspiel Essays* (Munich, 1964), 302.
18. Heinrich Vormweg, "Prosa in der Bundesrepublik seit 1945," in *Die Literatur der Bundesrepublik Deutschland*, ed. Dieter Lattmann (Munich, 1973), 279.

German Novels in English Translation

This bibliography is restricted to works discussed or cited and makes no claim to overall comprehensiveness. For additional editions the reader should consult the standard bibliographies (Bayard Quincy Morgan, Richard Mönnig, Patrick O'Neill). For reasons of space only one edition of each translation is listed, usually the most recent American edition. Only in the case of older translations that may be difficult to locate did it seem necessary to give more than one edition and provide publishers' names.

BERGENGRUEN, WERNER. A *Matter of Conscience* (*Der Grosstyrann und das Gericht*). Translated by Norman Cameron. London: 1952.

BOBROWSKI, JOHANNES. *Levin's Mill*. Translated by Janet Cropper. London: 1970.

BÖLL, HEINRICH. *Acquainted with the Night* (*Und sagte kein einziges Wort*). Translated by Richard Graves. New York: 1954.
  And Never Said a Word. Translated by Leila Vennewitz. New York: 1978.
———. *Adam Where Are Thou?* Translated by Mervyn Savill. New York: 1955.
  And Where Were You, Adam? Translated by Leila Vennewitz. Harmondsworth: 1978.
———. *Billiards at Half Past Nine*. Translated by Patrick Bowles. London: 1965.
  Billiards at Half Past Nine. Translated by Leila Vennewitz. New York: 1975.
———. *The Clown*. Translated by Leila Vennewitz. London: 1972.
———. *Group Portrait with Lady*. Translated by Leila Vennewitz. New York: 1973.
———. *Tomorrow and Yesterday* (*Haus ohne Hüter*). New York: 1957.
  The Unguarded House. Translated by Mervyn Savill. New York: 1957.

BONAVENTURA. *The Night Watches of Bonaventura*. Edited and translated by Gerald Gillespie. Austin, Texas: 1977.

BRÄKER, ULRICH. *The Life Story and Real Adventures of the Poor Man of Toggenburg*. Translated by Derek Bowman. Edinburgh: 1970.

BRECHT, BERTOLT. *Threepenny Novel*. Translated by Desmond I. Vesey and Christopher Isherwood. Harmondsworth: 1962.

BROCH, HERMANN. *The Death of Virgil*. Translated by Jean Starr Untermeyer. London: 1977.
———. *The Guiltless*. Translated by Ralph Manheim. Boston: 1974.
———. *The Sleepwalkers*. Translated by Edwin and Willa Muir. New York: 1964.

BROD, MAX. *The Master*. Translated by Heinz Norden. New York: 1951.

———. *The Redemption of Tycho Brahe.* Translated by Felix Warren Crosse. New York: 1928.

———. *Three Loves (Die Frau nach der man sich sehnt).* Translated by Jacob Wittmer Hartmann. New York: 1929.

CANETTI, ELIAS. *Auto-da-fé (Die Blendung).* Translated by C. V. Wedgwood. New York: 1979.

CAROSSA, HANS. *Roumanian Diary.* Translated by Agnes Neill Scott. New York: 1930.

———. *The Year of Sweet Illusions (Das Jahr der schönen Täuschungen).* Translated by Robert Kee. New York: 1951.

DAHN, FELIX. *A Struggle for Rome.* Translated by L. Wolffsohn. London: 1878.

DÖBLIN, ALFRED. *Berlin Alexanderplatz. The Story of Franz Biberkopf.* Translated by Eugene Jolas. London: 1974.

DODERER, HEIMITO VON. *The Demons.* 2 vols. Translated by Richard and Clara Winston. New York: 1961.

DÜRRENMATT, FRIEDRICH. *The Pledge.* Translated by Richard and Clara Winston. Harmondsworth: 1964.

———. *The English Faust-Book of 1592.* Edited by H. Logeman. Ghent: 1900.
   The History of Doctor Johann Faustus. Translated by Harry Gerard Haile. Illinois: 1965.
   The History of the Damnable Life and Deserved Death of Doctor John Faustus. Edited by William Rose. New York: 1969.

FALLADA, HANS [DITZEN, RUDOLF]. *Little Man, What Now?* Translated by Eric Sutton. London: 1969.

FEUCHTWANGER, LION. *The Jew of Rome. A Historical Romance (Die Söhne).* Vol. 2 of *Josephus* trilogy. Translated by Edwin and Willa Muir. Bath: 1968.

———. *Josephus (Der jüdische Krieg).* Vol. 1 of *Josephus* trilogy. Translated by Willa and Edwin Muir. New York: 1972.

———. *Josephus and the Emperor (Der Tag wird kommen).* Vol. 3 of *Josephus* trilogy. Translated by Caroline Oram. New York: 1942.

———. *The Oppermanns (Die Geschwister Oppenheim).* Vol. 2 of *Wartesaal* trilogy. Translated by James Cleugh. New York: 1964.

———. *Paris Gazette (Exil).* Vol. 3 of *Wartesaal* trilogy. Translated by Willa and Edwin Muir. New York: 1940.

———. *Power (Jew Süss).* Translated by Willa and Edwin Muir. New York: 1967.

———. *The Pretender (Der falsche Nero).* Translated by Willa and Edwin Muir. New York: 1937.

———. *Proud Destiny (Waffen für Amerika).* Translated by Moray Firth. London: 1952.

———. *Success (Erfolg).* Vol. 1 of *Wartesaal* trilogy. Translated by Willa and Edwin Muir. New York: 1930.

———. *This Is the Hour. A Novel about Goya.* Translated by Helen Tracy Lowe-Porter and Frances Fawcett. New York: 1964.

———. *'Tis Folly to Be Wise (Narrenweisheit)*. Translated by Frances Fawcett. London: 1955.

———. *The Ugly Duchess*. Translated by Willa and Edwin Muir. London: 1972.

FONTANE, THEODOR. *Beyond Recall*. Translated by Douglas Parmée. London: 1964.

———. *Effi Briest* (abridged). In *The German Classics of the Nineteenth and Twentieth Centuries*, Vol. 12, edited by Kuno Francke, translated by William A. Cooper. Albany: 1913.

 Effi Briest. Translated by Douglas Parmée. Harmondsworth: 1976.

 Effi Briest. Translated by Walter Wallich. London: 1962.

———. *Grete Minde*. London: 1955.

———. *Jenny Treibel*. Translated by Ulf Zimmerman. New York: 1976.

———. *A Man of Honor (Schach von Wuthenow)*. Translated by E. M. Valk. New York: 1975.

———. *Stine*. In *Twelve German Novellas*, edited and translated by Harry Steinhauer. Berkeley: 1977.

———. *A Suitable Match (Irrungen, Wirrungen)*. Translated by Sandra Morris. London: 1968.

 Trials and Tribulations. In *Harvard Classics, Shelf of Fiction*, Vol. 15, translated by K. Royce. New York: 1917.

———. *The Woman Taken in Adultery and The Poggenpuhl Family*. Translated by Gabriele Annan. Chicago: 1979.

FRANK, BRUNO. *Lost Heritage (Der Reisepass)*. Translated by Cyrus Brooks. New York: 1937.

———. *A Man Called Cervantes*. Translated by Helen Tracy Lowe-Porter. New York: 1935.

FREYTAG, GUSTAV. *Debit and Credit*. Translated by L. C. Cummings. New York: Abbott, 1909.

 Debit and Credit. Translated by Mrs. Georgiana Malcolm. London: Bentley, 1858; New York: 1882.

 Debtor and Creditor: A Romance. Translated by N. J. Stewart. London: Blackwood, 1857.

———. *Ingo*. Translated by Wolf von Schierbrand. New York: P. F. Collier, n.d.

 Ingo, the first novel of a series entitled Our Forefathers. Translated by Mrs. Malcolm. New York: Holt, 1873.

———. *Ingraban, the second novel of a series entitled Our Forefathers*. Translated by Mrs. Malcolm. New York: Holt, 1873.

———. *The Lost Manuscript*. Translated by Mrs. Malcolm. London: Chapman & Hall, 1865.

FRISCH, MAX. *Homo Faber. A Report*. Translated by Michael Bullock. Harmondsworth: 1974.

———. *I'm Not Stiller*. Translated by Michael Bullock. New York: 1962.

———. *A Wilderness of Mirrors (Mein Name sei Gantenbein)*. Translated by Michael Bullock. London, 1967.

GELLERT, CHRISTIAN FÜRCHTEGOTT. *History of the Swedish Countess of Guildenstern*. London: Scott, 1757.

The Life of the Swedish Countess de G. Translated by Rev. Mr. N. London: 1776.

GOETHE, JOHANN WOLFGANG VON. *Elective Affinities.* Translated by Robert Dillon Boylan and James Anthony Froude. New York: 1963.
    Elective Affinities. In *The Works of J. W. von Goethe,* Vol. 5, edited by N. H. Dole, translated by Thomas Carlyle. New York: 1902.
    Elective Affinities. Translated by R. J. Hollingdale. Harmondsworth: 1971.
    Elective Affinities. Translated by Elizabeth Mayer and Louise Bogan. Westport, Conn.: 1976.
    Kindred by Choice. Translated by H. M. Waidson. London: 1966.
———. *The Sorrows of Young Werther.* Translated by R. D. Boylan. London: 1949.
    The Sorrows of Young Werther. In *The Works of J. W. von Goethe,* Vol. 5, edited by N. H. Dole, translated by Thomas Carlyle. New York: 1902.
    The Sorrows of Young Werther. In *Great German Short Stories and Novels,* edited by V. Lange, translated by William Rose. New York: 1952.
    The Sorrows of Young Werther and *Faust.* In *The World's Great Classics,* translated by James Stuart Blackie. New York: 1969.
    Sorrows of Young Werther and Novella. Translated by Elizabeth Mayer et al. New York: 1973.
    The Sorrows of Young Werther, and Selected Writings. Translated by Catherine Hutter. New York: 1962.
    The Sufferings of Young Werther. Translated by Bayard Quincy Morgan. New York: 1957.
    The Sufferings of Young Werther. Translated by Harry Steinhauer. New York: 1970.
———. *Wilhelm Meister: Apprenticeship and Travels.* Translated by R. O. Moon. London: 1947.
    Wilhelm Meister's Apprenticeship and Travels. Translated by Thomas Carlyle. New York: 1962.
———. *Wilhelm Meister's Apprenticeship.* Translated by R. Dillon Boylan. London: 1867.
    Wilhelm Meister's Years of Apprenticeship. Translated by H. M. Waidson. London: 1977.
———. *Wilhelm Meister's Theatrical Mission.* Translated by G. A. Page. London: 1913.

GOTTHELF, JEREMIAS [BITZIUS, ALFRED]. *The Joys and Sorrows of a Schoolmaster.* 1864.
———. *Story of an Alpine Valley, or Katie the Grandmother.* Translated by L. G. Smith. London: Gibbings, 1896.
———. *Uli the Farmhand* (abridged). In *The German Classics of the Nineteenth and Twentieth Centuries,* Vol. 8, edited by Kuno Francke, translated by B. Q. Morgan. Albany: 1913.
    Ulrich the Farm Servant. Translated by Julia Firth. New York: 1907.
———. *Wealth and Welfare.* New York: 1976.

GRASS, GÜNTER. *Dog Years.* Translated by Ralph Manheim. Harmondsworth: 1969.
———. *From the Diary of a Snail.* Translated by Ralph Manheim. Harmondsworth: 1976.

———. *Local Anaesthetic*. Translated by Ralph Manheim. Harmondsworth: 1973.

———. *The Tin Drum*. Translated by Ralph Manheim. New York: 1971.

GRIMMELSHAUSEN, HANS JAKOB CHRISTOFFEL VON. *The Adventures of a Simpleton*. Translated by Walter Wallich. New York: 1963.

> *The Adventurous Simplicissimus*. Translated by A. T. S. Goodrick. Lincoln, Nebraska: 1969.

> *Simplicius Simplicissimus*. Translated by G. Schulz-Behrend. Indianapolis: 1965.

> *Simplicius Simplicissimus*. Translated by Hellmuth Weissenborn and Lesley Macdonald. London: 1964.

———. *Courage, the Adventuress and The False Messiah* (*Die Landstörzerin Courasche und Das wunderbare Vogelsnest*). Translated by Hans Speier. Princeton, New Jersey: 1964.

> *Mother Courage*. Translated by Walter Wallich. London: 1965.

> *The Runagate Courage*. Translated by Robert L. Hiller and John C. Osborne. Lincoln, Nebraska: 1965.

———. *The Singular Life Story of Heedless Hopalong* (*Der seltsame Springinsfeld*). Translated by Robert L. Hiller and John C. Osborne. Detroit: 1981.

GUTZKOW, KARL. *Wally the Skeptic*. Translated by Ruth-Ellen Boetcher-Joeres. Berne: 1974.

HAUPTMANN, GERHART. *The Fool in Christ, Emanuel Quint*. Translated by Thomas Seltzer. New York: 1976.

HEINE, HEINRICH. *From the Memoirs of Herr von Schnabelewopski*. In *The Sword and the Flame: Selections from Heinrich Heine's Prose*, edited by Alfred Warner, translated by Charles Godfrey Leland. London: 1960.

> *Memoirs of Herr von Schnabelewopski. A Fragment*. In *Great German Short Stories*, edited by R. Hargreaves and L. Melville, translated by S. L. Fleishman. London: 1929.

———. *The Rabbi of Bacharach*. In *The Sword and the Flame: Selections from Heinrich Heine's Prose*, edited by Alfred Warner, translated by Charles Godfrey Leland. London: 1960.

> *The Rabbi of Bacharach, A Fragment*. Translated by E. B. Ashton. New York: 1947.

HESSE, HERMANN. *Beneath the Wheel*. Translated by Michael Roloff. New York: 1970.

> *The Prodigy* (*Unterm Rad*). Translated by W. J. Strachen. Harmondsworth: 1973.

———. *Demian*. Translated by N. H. Priday. New York: 1948.

> *Demian*. Translated by Michael Roloff and Michael Lebeck. New York: 1970.

> *Demian*. Translated by H. Rosner. New York: 1948.

> *Demian*. Translated by Walter J. Strachan. London: 1969.

———. *Goldmund*. Translated by Geoffrey Dunlop. London: 1968 (originally published as *Death and the Lover*).

> *Narcissus and Goldmund*. Translated by Ursule Molinaro. New York: 1971.

————. *Magister Ludi.* Translated by Mervyn Savill. New York: 1965.
    Magister Ludi: The Glass Bead Game. Translated by Richard and Clara
    Winston. New York: 1973.
————. *Peter Camenzind.* Translated by Michael Roloff. New York: 1973.
    Peter Camenzind. Translated by Walter J. Strachan. Harmondsworth: 1973.
————. *Steppenwolf.* Translated by Basil Creighton. London: 1974.

HEYM, STEFAN. *The Crusaders.* London: 1950.

HEYSE, PAUL. *Children of the World.* New York: Holt, 1894.
————. *In Paradise.* New York: Appleton, 1878.
History of Fortunatus. London: 1816.
    *History of Fortunatus. To Which are Added the Lives and Adventures of
    Ampedo and Andolocia, His Two Sons.* Edinburgh: 1820.

HOFFMANN, E. T. A. *The Devil's Elixir.* Edinburgh: Blackwood, 1824.
    The Devil's Elixirs. Translated by Ronald Taylor. London: 1966.
————. *The Life and Opinions of Kater Murr.* In *Selected Writings of E. T. A.
    Hoffmann*, Vol. 2, translated and edited by Leonard J. Kent and Elizabeth C.
    Knight. Chicago: 1969.

HÖLDERLIN, FRIEDRICH. *Hyperion or the Hermit in Greece.* Translated by Willard R.
    Trask. New York: 1965.
    Hyperion. Thalia Fragment, 1794. Translated by Karl Maurer. Winnepeg:
    1968.

HUCH, RICARDA. *Eros Invincible (Die Erinnerungen von Ludolf Ursleu).* Translated
    by William Drake. New York: 1931.
    The Recollections of Ludolf Ursleu the Younger (abridged). In *The German
    Classics of the Nineteenth and Twentieth Centuries*, Vol. 18, edited by Kuno
    Francke, translated by Muriel Almon and B. Q. Morgan. Albany: 1913.
————. *Garibaldi and the New Italy (Die Geschichten von Garibaldi I and II).*
    Translated by Catherine Alison Phillips. New York: 1928–29.

IMMERMANN, KARL LEBERECHT. *The Oberhof.* In *The German Classics of the Nine-
    teenth and Twentieth Centuries*, Vol. 7, edited by Kuno Francke, translated by
    Paul Bernard Thomas. Albany: 1913.

JAHNN, HANS HENNY. *The Ship.* Vol. 1 of *River without Banks* trilogy. Translated by
    Catherine Hutter. New York: 1961.

JOHNSON, UWE. *Anniversaries: From the Life of Gesine Cresspahl*, Vols. 1 and 2.
    Translated by Leila Vennewitz. New York: 1975.
————. *Speculations about Jakob.* Translated by Ursule Molinaro. New York: 1972.
————. *The Third Book about Achim.* Translated by Ursule Molinaro. London:
    1968.
    The Third Book about Achim. Translated by Helen and Kurt Wolff. New
    York: 1967.
————. *Two Views.* Translated by Richard and Clara Winston. Harmondsworth:
    1971.

JÜNGER, ERNST. *On the Marble Cliffs.* Translated by Stuart Hood. Harmondsworth: 1970.

————. *Storm of Steel. From the Diary of a German Storm-Trooper on the Western Front.* Translated by Basil Creighton. New York: 1975.

JUNG-STILLING, JOHANN HEINRICH. *The Autobiography of Heinrich Stilling.* Translated by S. Jackson. New York: Harper and Brothers, 1844.

KAFKA, FRANZ. *America.* Translated by Willa and Edwin Muir. London: 1973.

————. *The Castle.* Translated by Willa and Edwin Muir. New York: 1974.

————. *The Trial.* Translated by Willa and Edwin Muir. Harmondsworth: 1974.
The Trial. Translated by Douglas Scott and Chris Walker. London: 1977.

KASACK, HERMANN. *The City beyond the River.* Translated by Peter de Mendelssohn. London: 1953.

KELLER, GOTTFRIED. *Green Henry.* Translated by A. M. Holt. New York: 1960.

————. *Martin Salander.* Translated by Kenneth Halwas. London: 1964.

KLABUND [HENSCHKE, ALFRED]. *Brackie, the Fool.* Translated by H. G. Scheffauer. New York: 1927.

————. *The Incredible Borgia.* Translated by Louise Brink. New York: 1929.

————. *Peter the Czar.* Translated by Hermann George Scheffauer. London: 1925.

KOEPPEN, WOLFGANG. *Death in Rome.* Translated by Mervyn Savill. New York: 1961.

KOLBENHEYER, ERWIN GUIDO. *The God-Intoxicated Man (Spinoza) (Amor Dei).* Translated by John Linton. London: 1933.

————. *A Winter Chronicle (Meister Joachim Pausewang).* Translated by H. A. Phillips and K. W. Maurer. London: 1938.

KUBIN, ALFRED. *The Other Side. A Fantastic Novel.* Translated by Denver Lindley. Harmondsworth: 1973.

LANGGÄSSER, ELISABETH. *The Quest (Märkische Argonautenfahrt).* Translated by Jane Bannard Greene. New York: 1953.

LE FORT, GERTRUD VON. *The Veil of Veronica.* Translated by Conrad Bonacina. New York: 1970.

MANN, HEINRICH. *Henry, King of France (Die Vollendung des Königs Henri Quatre),* Vol. 2 of *Henri Quatre.* Translated by Eric Sutton. New York: 1939.

————. *In the Land of Cockaigne (Im Schlaraffenland).* Translated by Axton D. B. Clark. New York: 1929.

————. *The Little Town.* Translated by Winifred Ray. New York: 1962.

————. *Man of Straw (Der Untertan).* London: 1972.
Little Superman. Translated by Ernest Boyd. New York: 1945.

————. *Small Town Tyrant (Professor Unrat).* New York: 1944.

————. *Young Henry of Navarre (Die Jugend des Königs Henri Quatre),* Vol. 1 of *Henri Quatre.* Translated by Eric Sutton. New York: 1937.

MANN, THOMAS. *Buddenbrooks.* Translated by Helen Tracy Lowe-Porter. Harmondsworth: 1975.

Buddenbrooks, with Lübeck as a Way of Life and Thought. Translated by Clara and Richard Winston. New York: 1964.

——. Confessions of Felix Krull, Confidence Man. The Early Years. Translated by Denver Lindley. London: 1977.

Felix Krull. In Stories of Three Decades, translated by Helen Tracy Lowe-Porter. New York: 1961.

——. Doctor Faustus. The Life of the German Composer Adrian Leverkühn as Told by a Friend. Translated by Helen Tracy Lowe-Porter. New York: 1971.

——. The Holy Sinner (Der Erwählte). Translated by Helen Tracy Lowe-Porter. Harmondsworth: 1972.

——. Joseph and His Brothers. Vol. 1, Joseph and His Brothers. Vol. 2, Young Joseph. Vol. 3, Joseph in Egypt. Vol. 4, Joseph the Provider. Translated by Helen Tracy Lowe-Porter. New York: 1948.

——. Lotte in Weimar. Translated by Helen Tracy Lowe-Porter. Harmondsworth: 1976 (originally published as The Beloved Returns).

——. The Magic Mountain. Translated by Helen Tracy Lowe-Porter. New York: 1969.

——. Royal Highness. Translated by A. Cecil Curtis. Harmondsworth: 1979.

MARCHWITZA, HANS. Storm over the Ruhr. New York: 1932.

The Marvelous Adventures and Rare Conceits of Master Tyll Owlglass. Translated by Kenneth R. H. Mackenzie. London: 1923.

Master Till's Amazing Pranks; The Story of Till Eulenspiegel. Retold by Lisbeth Gombrich and Clara Hemsted. New York: 1948.

A Pleasant Vintage of Till Eulenspiegel, Born in the Country of Brunswick; How He Spent His Life, 95 of His Tales. Translated by Paul Oppenheimer. Middletown, Connecticut: 1972.

MEYER, CONRAD FERDINAND. A Boy Suffers. In The Complete Narrative Prose of Conrad Ferdinand Meyer, Vol. 2, translated by George F. Folkers, David B. Dickens, Marion W. Sonnenfeld. Lewisburg: Bucknell University Press, 1976.

The Sufferings of a Boy. In Twelve German Novellas, edited and translated by Harry Steinhauer. Berkeley: 1977.

——. Jürg Jenatsch. In The Complete Narrative Prose of Conrad Ferdinand Meyer, Vol. 1, translated by George F. Folkers, David B. Dickens, Marion W. Sonnenfeld. Lewisburg: Bucknell University Press, 1976.

MEYRINK, GUSTAV AND BUSSON, PAUL. The Golem. Translated by Madge Pemberton. Prague: 1972.

The Golem and The Man Who Was Born Again. Two German Supernatural Novels. Translated by Thomas Moult. Dover: 1976.

MUSIL, ROBERT. The Man without Qualities. Translated by Eithne Wilkins and Ernst Kaiser. London: 1979.

——. Young Törless. Translated by Eithne Wilkins and Ernst Kaiser. London: 1979.

NEUMANN, ALFRED. Another Caesar. Translated by Eden and Cedar Paul. New York: 1935.

——. *The Devil.* Translated by Huntley Paterson. New York: 1928.

——. *Friends of the People (Volksfreunde).* Translated by Countess Nora Wydenbruch and the author. New York: 1942.

——. *Gaudy Empire (Kaiserreich).* Translated by Eden and Cedar Paul. New York: 1937.

NICOLAI, FRIEDRICH. *The Life and Opinions of Sebaldus Nothanker.* Translated by T. Dutton. London: 1798.

NOSSACK, HANS ERICH. *The D'Arthez Case.* Translated by Michael Lebeck. New York: 1971.

——. *The Impossible Proof.* Translated by Michael Lebeck. London: 1969.

NOVALIS [FRIEDRICH VON HARDENBERG]. *Henry of Ofterdingen.* Cambridge, Mass.: Owen, 1842; New York: Moore, 1853.
    Henry von Ofterdingen. Translated by Palmer Hiltry. New York: 1964.
    Heinrich von Ofterdingen. In *Novalis, His Life, Thoughts, and Works,* translated and edited by M. J. Hope. Chicago: McClurg, 1891.

PESTALOZZI, JOHANN HEINRICH. *Leonard and Gertrude.* Philadelphia, London: 1801.
    Pestalozzi's Leonard and Gertrude (abridged). Translated by Eva Channing. Boston: D. C. Heath, 1903.

POLENZ, WILHELM VON. *Farmer Büttner* (abridged). In *German Classics of the Nineteenth and Twentieth Centuries,* Vol. 17, edited by Kuno Francke, translated by Edmund von Mach. Albany: 1913.

RAABE, WILHELM. *Abu Telfan, or The Return from the Mountains of the Moon.* Translated by Sofie Delffs. London: Chapman & Hall, 1881.

——. *The Hunger Pastor.* Translated by Arnold. London: Chapman & Hall, 1855.
    The Hunger Pastor (abridged). In *The German Classics of the Nineteenth and Twentieth Centuries,* Vol. 11, edited by Kuno Francke, translated by Muriel Alman. Albany: 1913.

REMARQUE, ERICH MARIA. *All Quiet on the Western Front.* Translated by A. W. Wheen. New York: 1969.

RENN, LUDWIG. *War.* Translated by Edwin and Willa Muir. New York: 1929.

REUTER, CHRISTIAN. *Schelmuffsky.* Translated by Wayne Wonderley. Chapel Hill: 1962.

RICHTER, JEAN PAUL. *Flower, Fruit, and Thorn Pieces; or, The Married Life, Death, and Wedding of the Advocate of the Poor, Firmian Siebenkäs.* Translated by Edward Henry Noel. Leipzig: Bernard Tauchnitz, 1871.
    Flower, Fruit and Thorn Pieces; or, The Wedded Life, Death and Marriage. Translated by A. Ewing. London: Bohn, 1877.

——. *Hesperus; or, Forty-Five Dog-Post-Days.* Translated by Charles T. Brooks. Boston: Ticknor & Fields, 1864.

——. *The Invisible Lodge.* Translated by C. T. Brooks. New York: Holt, 1883.

——. *Titan: A Romance.* Translated by C. T. Brooks. London: Trubner, 1862.
    Walt and Vult; or, The Twins. Translated by Mrs. Eliza B. Lee. Boston: Monroe, 1846.

RILKE, RAINER MARIA. *The Notebooks of Malte Laurids Brigge*. Translated by M. D. Herter Norton. New York: 1964.
> *The Notebooks of Malte Laurids Brigge*. Translated by Stephen Mitchell. New York: 1983.

ROTH, JOSEPH. *The Ballad of the Hundred Days* (*Die hundert Tage*). Translated by Moray Firth. New York: 1936.
———. *Flight without End*. Translated by David le Vay. New York: 1977.
———. *Job: The Story of a Simple Man*. Translated by Dorothy Thompson. New York: 1931.
———. *Radetzky March*. Translated by Geoffrey Dunlop. New York: 1974.
———. *The Silent Prophet*. Translated by David Le Vay. London: 1979.

SCHEFFEL, JOSEF VIKTOR VON. *Ekkehard*. Translated by Sophie Delffs. New York: 1965.
> *Ekkehard*. Translated by N. H. Dole. New York: 1902.
> *Ekkehard*. Translated by Helena Easson. New York: 1911.

SCHILLER, FRIEDRICH VON. *The Ghost-Seer*. In *The Works of Friedrich Schiller*, Vol. 5, edited by N. H. Dole, translated by H. G. Bohn. New York: 1902.

SCHLEGEL, FRIEDRICH. *Friedrich Schlegel's Lucinde and the Fragments*. Translated by Peter Firchow. Minneapolis: 1971.
> *Lucinda*. In *The German Classics of the Nineteenth and Twentieth Centuries*, Vol. 4, edited by Kuno Francke, translated by P. B. Thomas. Albany: 1913.

SCHMIDT, ARNO. *The Egghead Republic* (*Die Gelehrtenrepublik*). Translated by Michael Horovitz. London: 1979.

SEALSFIELD, CHARLES. *The Cabin Book; or, National Characteristics*. Translated by S. Powell. London: Ingram, Cooke, 1852; New York: St. John & Coffin, 1871.
> *The Cabin Book, or Sketches of Life in Texas*. Translated by C. F. Mersch. New York: Winchester, 1844.
———. *The Indian Chief*. In *Charles Sealsfield: Sämtliche Werke*. Vols. 4–5, edited by Karl Arndt. Hildesheim: 1972.

SEGHERS, ANNA. *Revolt of the Fishermen*. Translated by M. Goldsmith. London: 1929.
> *Revolt of the Fishermen of Santa Barbara and A Price on His Head*. Translated by Jack and Renate Mitchell and Eva Wulff. Edited by Valerie Stone. London: 1961.
———. *The Seventh Cross*. Translated by James A. Galston. New York: 1968.
———. *Transit*. Boston: 1944.

SEIDEL, INA. *The Wish Child*. Translated by G. Dunning Gribble. New York: 1935.

SPIELHAGEN, FRIEDRICH. *Problematic Characters*. Translated by Prof. Schele De Vere. New York: Holt, 1888.

THÜMMEL, MORITZ AUGUST VON. *Journal of Sentimental Travels in the Southern Provinces of France, Shortly before the Revolution* (abridged). London: Ackerman, 1821.

TIECK, LUDWIG. *The Rebellion in the Cevennes. An Historical Novel.* Translated by Mme. Burette. London: Nutt, 1845.

———. *The Roman Matron; or Vittoria Accorombona. A Novel.* London: Bury St. Edmunds, Newby, 1845.

VRING, GEORG VON DER. *Private Suhren; the Story of a German Rifleman.* Translated by Fred Hall. London: 1928.

WACKENRODER, WILHELM HEINRICH AND LUDWIG TIECK. *Outpourings of an Art-Loving Friar.* Translated by Edward Mornin. New York: 1975.

WALSER, MARTIN. *Marriage in Philippsburg.* Adapted by J. Laughlin. Translated by Eva Figes. Norfolk, Conn.: 1961 (originally published as *The Gadarene Club*).

———. *The Unicorn.* Translated by Barrie Ellis-Jones. London: 1971.

WALSER, ROBERT. *Jakob von Gunten.* Translated by Christopher Middleton. Austin, Texas: 1969.

WASSERMANN, JAKOB. *Caspar Hauser, the Enigma of a Century.* Translated by Caroline Newton. New York: 1973.

———. *Doktor Kerkhoven.* Translated by Cyrus Brooks. New York: 1964.
    Kerkhoven's Third Existence. Translated by Eden and Cedar Paul. New York: 1934.

———. *Etzel Andergast.* Translated by Cyrus Brooks. New York: 1929.

———. *The Goose Man.* Translated by Ludwig Lewisohn and Allen W. Porterfield. New York: 1922.

———. *The Maurizius Case.* Translated by Caroline Newton. New York: 1964.

———. *The World's Illusion (Christian Wahnschaffe).* Translated by Ludwig Lewisohn. New York: 1976.

WERFEL, FRANZ. *Class Reunion.* Translated by Whittaker Chambers. New York: 1929.
    Class Reunion. In *Twilight of a World,* translated by Helen Lowe-Porter. New York: 1937.

———. *The Forty Days of Musa Dagh.* Translated by Geoffrey Dunlop. New York: 1967.

———. *The Pascarella Family (Die Geschwister von Neapel).* Translated by Geoffrey Dunlop. New York: 1932.

———. *The Pure in Heart (Barbara oder Die Frömmigkeit).* Translated by Geoffrey Dunlop. New York: 1931.

———. *Star of the Unborn.* Translated by Gustave O. Arlt. New York: 1976.

———. *Verdi. A Novel of the Opera.* Translated by Helen Jessiman. New York: 1947.

WIECHERT, ERNST EMIL. *The Baroness (Die Majorin).* Translated by Phyllis and Trevor Blewitt. New York: 1936.

———. *The Simple Life.* Translated by Marie Heynemann. London: 1954.

WIELAND, CHRISTOPH MARTIN. *The Adventures of Don Sylvio de Rosalva.* Introduction by E. A. Baker. New York: Dutton, 1904.

————. *The History of Agathon*, 4 vols. London: Cadell, 1773.

————. *Private History of Peregrinus Proteus the Philosopher*. London: Johnson, 1796.

    Confessions in Elysium; or, The Adventures of a Platonic Philosopher (abridged). Translated by J. B. Elrington. London: Bell, 1804.

————. *The Republic of Fools, Being the History of the State and People of Abdera, In Thrace*. Translated by H. Christmas. London: Allen, 1861.

WOLF, CHRISTA. *Divided Heaven*. Translated by Joan Becker. New York: 1976.

————. *The Quest for Christa T.* Translated by Christopher Middleton. London: 1971.

ZWEIG, ARNOLD. *The Case of Sergeant Grischa*. Translated by Eric Sutton. Harrisburg, Penn.: 1970.

Index

Note: All titles of works are indexed under their author's name.

381

Hildegard Emmel, a professor emeritus of the University of Connecticut, received her doctorate from the University of Frankfurt am Main. She held professorships at the Universities of Rostock, Greifswald, and Ankara and guest lectureships at the Universities of Yüveskülä and Oslo. After a thirteen-year period of research and writing, Professor Emmel produced the three-volume *Geschichte des deutschen Romans* (1972, 1975, 1978), the only complete history of the German novel in existence. She is the author of two books on medieval literature and is also known for her books and articles on Goethe as well as literature of the twentieth century.

At the specific request of Professor Emmel, Ellen Summerfield undertook the translation and revision of the *Geschichte des deutschen Romans* for the English-speaking reader. Summerfield was a graduate student in German at the University of Connecticut and wrote her doctoral thesis under Emmel's supervision (Ph.D., 1975). She has lived in Germany for five years, most recently as director of the Middlebury College School in Mainz. Summerfield is currently director of international programs and associate professor of German at Linfield College. She is the author of a book in German on Ingeborg Bachmann (Bonn: Bouvier Verlag, 1976) and several journal articles.

The manuscript was edited by Doreen Broder.
The book was designed by Edgar J. Frank.
The typeface for the text is Electra,
based on a design by W. A. Dwiggins in 1935.
The display face is Friz Quadrata.
The text is printed on 60-lb. S. D. Warren's olde style text paper,
and the book is bound in Holliston Mills'
linen finish cloth over binder's boards.

Manufactured in the United States of America.